MICROSOFT CD-ROM YEARBOOK 1989-1990

FOREWORD BY BILL GATES

COMPILED BY SALLEY OBERLIN AND JOYCE COX

Microsoft PRESS

PUBLISHED BY
Microsoft Press
A Division of Microsoft Corporation
16011 NE 36th Way, Box 97017, Redmond, Washington 98073-9717

Copyright © 1989 by Microsoft Press
All rights reserved. No part of the contents of this book may be reproduced or transmitted in any form or by any means without the written permission of the publisher.

ISBN 1-55615-179-9
ISSN 1042-0908

Printed and bound in the United States of America.

1 2 3 4 5 6 7 8 9 FGFG 3 2 1 0 9

Distributed to the book trade in the United States by Harper & Row.

Distributed to the book trade in Canada by General Publishing Company, Ltd.

Distributed to the book trade outside the United States and Canada by Penguin Books Ltd.
Penguin Books Ltd., Harmondsworth, Middlesex, England
Penguin Books Australia Ltd., Ringwood, Victoria, Australia
Penguin Books N.Z. Ltd., 182–190 Wairau Road, Auckland 10, New Zealand

British Cataloging in Publication Data available.

Microsoft Press has not undertaken a comprehensive investigation of the facts and representations of the authors with regard to historical information, technical explanations, or descriptions of systems, products, or processes. Consequently, although it has no knowledge of any inaccuracies in the authors' treatments of particular topics, Microsoft Press makes no warranties or representations regarding their accuracy and disclaims all liability therefor. The views expressed in the articles written by the authors do not necessarily reflect the views or official position of Microsoft Press or Microsoft Corporation.

The views expressed in the articles written by the employees of Apple Computer, Inc. are the personal views of the authors and do not necessarily reflect the views or official position of Apple Computer, Inc.

The following articles are copyrighted by Apple Computer, Inc.:
"Tools for Multimedia Presentations" by C. Joseph Williams
"Designing a CD-ROM Interface" by Linda Stone and Rachel Rutherford
"Making Things Move: Regenerative Animation in Frame-Buffer Display Systems" by Jay Fenton

The following article is copyrighted by John Einberger:
"The Application Development Process" by John Einberger

The following articles are copyrighted by HyperMedia Publishing:
"CD-ROM: The Final Countdown" by Lou Casabianca
"The Potential of Hypermedia" by David Traub

The following article is copyrighted by the Jet Propulsion Laboratory:
"Digital Image Storage on CD-ROM" by Mike Martin

Other copyright acknowledgments and trademarks are located in the back of the book.

CONTENTS

Contributors of New Articles   vii
Foreword by Bill Gates   xi
Acknowledgments   xiii
Introduction by Min S. Yee   xv

SECTION I
CD-ROM Yesterday, Today, and Tomorrow
1

SECTION II
The Optical Media Family
39

SECTION III
Who's Doing What in CD-ROM?
93

SECTION IV
The Making of a CD-ROM
231

SECTION V
CD-ROM and the Law
421

SECTION VI
The CD-ROM Business
459

SECTION VII
Directory Listings
647

Sources 913
Trademarks 922
Index 925

CONTRIBUTORS OF NEW ARTICLES

AIKEN, Calvin
Software Engineer, TMS, Inc.
110 W. 3rd Street
P.O. Box 1358
Stillwater, OK 74076
Phone: (405)377-0880
FAX: (405)372-9288

ARAKAWA, Minoru
President, Nintendo of America
4820 150th Avenue N.E.
Redmond, WA 98052
Phone: (206)882-2040
FAX: (206)882-3585

BANGASSER, Thomas F.
Consultant, Bangasser &
 Associates, Inc.
1162 Twenty-second Avenue East
Seattle, WA 98112
Phone: (206)323-7575

BASTIAENS, Gaston
Director, Consumer Electronics
Interactive Media Systems
Philips International B.V.
Building HWD2
Eindhoven, The Netherlands
Phone: 31-40-791-111
FAX: 31-40-757-043

BENGE, Bruce
Marketing Manager, TMS, Inc.
110 W. 3rd Street
P.O. Box 1358
Stillwater, OK 74076
Phone:(405)377-0880
FAX: (405)372-9288

BOWERS, Richard
Director of Development, Applied
 Information Technology Research
 Center
1880 MacKenzie Drive
Suite 111
Columbus, OH 43220
Phone: (614)442-1955
FAX: (614)442-6522

BOWMAN, Chris
Director of Marketing, KnowledgeSet
 Corporation
888 Villa Street
Suite 500
Mountain View, CA 94041
Phone: (415)968-9888
FAX: (415)968-9962

BREWER, Bryan
President, EarthView Inc.
6514 18th Avenue N.E.
Seattle, WA 98115
Phone: (206)527-3168

BUDDINE, Laura
President, Tiger Media Inc.
10810 Paramount Boulevard
Suite 201
Downey, CA 90241
Phone: (213)862-5591

BURKE, Dennis
Development Manager, ALDE
 Publishing
4830 West 77 Street
P.O. Box 35326
Minneapolis, MN 55435
Phone: (612)835-5240
FAX: (612)835-3401

BUTLER, Matilda
President, Knowledge Access Inc.
2685 Marine Way
Suite 1305
Mountain View, CA 94043
Phone: (415)969-0606
FAX: (415)964-2027

CASABIANCA, Lou
Publisher, HyperMedia Publishing
145 Natoma Street
San Francisco, CA 94105
Phone: (415)243-0775

CINNAMON, Barry
President, Bureau of Electronic
 Publishing
P.O. Box 43131
Upper Montclair, NJ 07043
Phone: (201)746-3031

CORDDRY, Tom
Executive Producer, Fourth Microsoft
 International Conference on
 CD-ROM
14534 Edgewater Lane N.E.
Seattle, WA 98155
Phone: (206)882-8080
FAX: (206)883-8101

COX, Joyce
President, Online Press Inc.
14320 N.E. 21st Street
Suite 18
Bellevue, WA 98007
Phone: (206)641-3434

CULBERTSON, Jim
Director of Product Marketing, OWL
 International
2800 156th Avenue S.E.
Bellevue, WA 98007
Phone: (206)747-3203
FAX: (206)641-9367

DAYNES, Rod
Director of Project Development—
 Telecommunications, WGBH
 Education Foundation
125 Western Avenue
Boston, MA 02134
Phone: (617)492-2777

DILLON, Mark
Senior Vice President of Production,
 American Interactive Media
1111 Santa Monica Boulevard
Suite 1000
Los Angeles, CA 90025
Phone: (213)473-4136
FAX: (213)479-5937

EINBERGER, John
Vice President of Software
 Development, Micro Decision-
 ware, Inc.
2995 Wilderness Place
Boulder, CO 80301
Phone: (303)443-2706
FAX: (303)443-1735

FENTON, Jay
Staff Engineer, Apple Computer, Inc.
292 S. La Cienga Boulevard
Suite 301
Beverly Hills, CA 90211
Phone: (213)657-9261

FISHER, Bob
U.S. Sales Manager, Philips & DuPont Optical
1409 Faulk Road
Suite 200
Wilmington, DE 19803
Phone: (302)479-2500
FAX: (302)479-2512

GAFFNER, Haines
President, LINK Resources Corp.
79 Fifth Avenue
New York, NY 10003
Phone: (212)627-1500
FAX: (212)620-3099

HALL, Bob
Director of CD-ROM Technology, Ellis Enterprises
225 N.W. 13
Oklahoma City, OK 73103
Phone: (405)235-7660

HARRISON, Harvey
Vice President of Business Affairs, Columbia Pictures
3300 Riverside Drive
Suite 322
Burbank, CA 91505
Phone: (818)954-1848

HELGERSON, Linda
President, Diversified Data Resource Inc.
6609 Rosecroft Place
Falls Church, VA 22043-1828
Phone: (703)237-0682
FAX: (703)532-5447

HOLMES, Lyndon S.
President, Aries Systems Corporation
79 Boxford Street
North Andover, MA 01845
Phone: (508)689-9334

ILES, Doug
Applications Support Division, Hewlett Packard
100 Mayfield Avenue
Mountain View, CA 94043
Phone: (415)968-5600

KELLY, Ed
Acquisitions Manager, CD-ROM Group, Microsoft Press
16011 N.E. 36th Way
Redmond, WA 98052
Phone: (206)882-8080
FAX: (206)883-8101

KERNAN, John
President, Educational Services Corp.
6170 Cornerstone Court E.
Suite 300
San Diego, CA 92121
Phone: (619)587-0087
FAX: (619)587-1629

KESTER, Harold
Chairman, Del Mar Group
722 Genevieve
Suite M
Solano Beach, CA 92075
Phone: (619)259-0444

LANGSCHIED, Linda
Coordinator of Online Reference Services, Alexander Library
Rutgers University
College Avenue
New Brunswick, NJ 08903
Phone: (201)932-7014

LUSKIN, Bernard
President, American Interactive Media
1111 Santa Monica Boulevard
Suite 1000
Los Angeles, CA 90025
Phone: (213)473-4136
FAX: (213)479-5937

MARTIN, Mike
Project Engineer for Planetary Data Systems, Jet Propulsion Laboratory
4800 Oak Grove Drive
Pasadena, CA 91109
Phone: (818)354-4321
FAX: (818)354-3437

MATHUR, Ashok
Vice President, TMS, Inc.
110 W. 3rd Street
P.O. Box 1358
Stillwater, OK 74076
Phone: (405)377-0880
FAX: (405)372-9288

MCMANUS, Tim
Director of Marketing, Compact Disc Information Services, Lotus Development Corp.
55 Cambridge Parkway
Cambridge, MA 02142
Phone: (617)577-8500
FAX: (617)225-7058

MEYER, Fred
President, Meridian Data, Inc.
4450 Capitola Road
Suite 101
Capitola, CA 95010
Phone: (408)476-5858
FAX: (408)476-8908

MEYER, Rick
CD-ROM Product Line Manager, Dialog Information Services, Inc.
3460 Hillview Avenue
Palo Alto, CA 94304
Phone: (415)858-4088
FAX: (415)858-3847

MORRIS, Sandra
Application Market Development Group, Princeton Intel Operation
CN 5325
Princeton, NJ 08543
Phone: (609)734-2211
FAX: (609)734-2261

RASKIN, Jef
3530 West Bayshore Road
Palo Alto, CA 94303
Phone: (415)493-2400
FAX: (415)857-1650

RIETDYK, Ron
President, SilverPlatter Information, Inc.
37 Walnut Street
Wellesley, MA 02181
Phone: (617)239-0306
FAX: (617)235-1715

ROPIEQUET, Suzanne
ISV Account Manager, Microsoft Corporation
16011 N.E. 36th Way
Redmond, WA 98052
Phone: (206)882-8080
FAX: (206)883-8101

ROUX, David
Vice President, Information Services Group, Lotus Development Corporation
55 Cambridge Parkway
Cambridge, MA 02142
Phone: (617)577-8500
FAX: (617)225-7058

RUTHERFORD, Rachel
Designer of Demonstration Discs, Apple Computer, Inc.
20525 Mariana
MS 36AG
Cupertino, CA 95014
Phone: (408)974-6370

SCHWERIN, Julie
President, InfoTech
P.O. Box 633
Upper Michigan Road
Pittsfield, VT 05762
Phone: (802)746-8923
FAX: (802)746-8924

SHEAR, Victor
Chairman, Personal Library Software, Inc.
15215 Shady Grove Road
Suite 204
Rockville, MD 20850
Phone: (301)926-1402
FAX: (301)963-9738

SIECK, Steven
Vice President—Electronic Services, LINK Resources Corp.
79 Fifth Avenue
New York, NY 10003
Phone: (212)627-1500
FAX: (212)620-3099

SICKERT, Julie
1301 Amapola
Torrance, CA 90501
Phone: (213)212-6261

STAUFFER, Rick
Marketing Manager, Intel Princeton Operation, DVI Technology
CN 5325
Princeton, NJ 08543
Phone: (609)734-2211

STONE, Linda
Market Development Manager, Business Multimedia Marketing, Apple Computer, Inc.
20525 Mariana
MS 36AG
Cupertino, CA 95014
Phone: (408)974-6370

STRUKHOFF, Roger
Editor-in-Chief, *CD-ROM Review*
80 Elm Street
Peterborough, NH 03458
Phone: (603)924-9471
FAX: (603)924-9384

SUGIYAMA, Takashi
Assistant Manager, Sony Corporation
6-7-35 Kitashinagawa
Shinagawa-ku Tokyo, 141 JAPAN
Phone: 011-03-448-3694
FAX: 81-03-448-3601

TRAUB, David
Associate Producer, HyperMedia Publishing
145 Natoma Street
San Francisco, CA 94105
Phone: (415)243-0775

VONDERHAAR, Mark
Product Development Manager, Congressional Information Services, Inc.
4520 East-West Highway
Suite 800
Bethesda, MD 20814
Phone: (301)654-1550
FAX: (301)654-4033

WILLIAMS, Joe
Senior Instructional Designer, Apple Computer, Inc.
10500 North DeAnza Boulevard
M/S 27AR
Cupertino, CA 95014
Phone: (408)996-6144
FAX: (408)252-6853

ZIMMERMAN, Paula
Application Market Development, Intel Princeton Operation
CN 5325
Princeton, NJ 08543
Phone: (609)734-2211
FAX: (609)734-2261

ZOELLICK, Bill
Vice President, Avalanche Development Company
947 Walnut Street
Boulder, CO 80302
Phone: (303)449-5032
FAX: (303)449-3246

FOREWORD

When CD-ROM was first announced, its potential was more widely appreciated than understood. Today, we have a better understanding of CD-ROM's potential and a greater respect for the magnitude of the task that faces us in fulfilling it. CD-ROM is an inexpensive delivery medium that has been capable all along of supporting a new kind of information product—one that offers tremendous depth and breadth of content, great search and retrieval tools, an easy, intuitive interface, and a rich palette of presentation capabilities, including text, graphics, audio, images, and animation.

For the past four years, we've all been working to create the content, the software tools, and the hardware platforms that will be required to fulfill CD-ROM's potential. This has been a difficult but invigorating process because it has brought together three separate parent industries: publishing, personal computing, and entertainment. To software engineers, content issues and entertainment-value questions are new challenges. To print publishers, computing issues are novel. To participants from the entertainment industry, CD-ROM offers a very different set of capabilities and limitations from other, more familiar media.

Today, in software, print publishing, and entertainment companies large and small around the world, growing numbers of talented people are working hard to develop the great CD-ROM products that will fulfill the immense potential of this medium. To accomplish this, we need to develop a common language, and we need to better understand what each of our points of view has to offer. We need mechanisms for resolving issues, and we need procedures for cooperative ventures. We've made great progress toward these goals since 1984, but we've also raised our expectations of what is possible. For as much as we've accomplished, the need for better understanding of common issues has never been greater.

In an effort to help CD-ROM developers meet this challenge, Microsoft has supported four CD-ROM conferences and the publication of three CD-ROM anthologies. Now, in view of the rapid progress in the many areas of interest to CD-ROM developers, we feel that a yearbook, with its mix of analysis and structured information, is an appropriate next step.

The CD-ROM Yearbook is an effort on our part at Microsoft to broaden the base and accelerate the pace of the CD-ROM industry. We hope it will be a useful tool for all of you who are making pioneering decisions that will lead to great CD-ROM products, who are taking the pioneer's risks and persevering to reap the pioneer's rewards.

I am excited by the quality and vision of the work now underway on CD-ROM products throughout the industry. I believe more than ever that CD-ROM products will be a major force in the expansion of the information industry, extending the benefits of personal computing to a much wider market.

Bill Gates
Chairman
Microsoft Corporation

ACKNOWLEDGMENTS

This book was a team effort if ever there was one. Our thanks to Min Yee, Joan Lambert, JoAnne Woodcock, Dale Callison, Suzanne Ropiequet, Darcie Furlan, Joan Anderson, Bonnie MacKay, Becky Johnson, Jean Trenary, Ron Lamb, Tami Folsom, Steven Crofts, Linda Mitchell, Claudette Moore, Diana Bray, Jeff Hinsch, Dan Newell, Dean Holmes, Natalie Yount, Pat Combs, Steve Lambert, Ted Cox, Pat Kervran, Kirby Jacobson, Susan Lammers, Raleigh Roark, Russ Steele, Norma Benson, Gale Nelson, Roxanna Frost, Greg Child, Sally Brunsman, Kjell Swedin, Julie Dugger, Judy Lowenthal, Amy Cox, Tom Mohr, John Messerly, Charles Mergentime, Doug Hergert, Rich Johnston, Kandis Stenson, Larry Anderson, and Phil Spencer.

Salley Oberlin
Joyce Cox
Online Press Inc.

INTRODUCTION

The idea of publishing an annual review of the CD-ROM industry has been on my mind in one form or another since we held the First International Conference on CD-ROM three years ago. From time to time, I've let the idea drop at various gatherings and taken note of the enthusiastic response. Back at the office, however, more pressing matters always postponed the next step: turning the initial idea into an actual outline for the book. The book business is merciless in this respect: no outline, no book.

Last year, as we were planning the Third International Conference on CD-ROM, it became clear to me that the *Yearbook*'s time had come. Our conference theme that year was "The Industry Emerges." To the surprise of some, in the months after the conference the theme was proven true; the CD-ROM industry was emerging in every respect. More people were getting involved, the products under development were getting more sophisticated, and the number of issues clamoring for resolution seemed to be increasing exponentially. The *Yearbook* idea, which had been content to sit in background mode for two years, took on a life of its own and refused to remain quiet. Before the last phosphors had faded to black on the screens of last year's conference, we decided to proceed with *The CD-ROM Yearbook* project.

You are now holding the result of that decision.

From the outset, I envisioned the *Yearbook* as more than just a directory of products and companies; others have already produced excellent reference works of this sort. Rather, I wanted to provide an overview of the current state of the industry—its technology, philosophy, struggles, and achievements, as well as its participants and products. I wanted the *Yearbook* to offer insights and information both to current players and to those who are considering entering the CD-ROM arena.

Accordingly, we have produced the *Yearbook* in an almanac-like format, with short, readable articles providing a balance between basic and advanced concepts. We combed the CD-ROM literature, selecting existing articles that offer succinct descriptions or analyses of particular aspects of the industry. We took note of forecasts and statistics. We examined the literature of other industries and disciplines, selecting pieces by attorneys, educators, business people, and librarians about the impact of CD-ROM in their areas. We contacted experts and users, commissioning new articles on current issues and concerns. We talked to hundreds of people who had things to sell and services to offer, and compiled listings of titles, hardware, software, conferences, and resources from the mountains of information they sent us.

But we didn't stop there. As CD-ROM technology spreads out into the real world, more and more people are becoming involved in the creation of CD-ROM products. Some people are generating products that simply combine large existing databases with first-generation search engines. Although such products fill basic needs in specific markets, real growth for this industry will be driven by products that offer more. With this in mind, we included information useful to developers of richer CD-ROM products. What can the CD-ROM industry learn from the experts in the information and entertainment industries that are its conceptual if not technological cousins? Which ideas (hypertext, Xanadu, Dynabook—ideas that have been around for a long time) are moving from the realm of theory into the real world, now that they have CD-ROM applications as a vehicle? We looked for articles by professionals in such fields as graphic design, animation, publishing, training, and education, and we commissioned pieces by people who are already exploring ways to integrate the philosophies and techniques of these fields into their CD-ROMs.

It has been immensely gratifying to rediscover in this process that our industry is filled with creative, intelligent, thoughtful, and articulate people. Although the challenges ahead are great, I have absolute faith in the ability of this group to surmount them. Clearly, the CD-ROM industry is thickly populated with visionary workaholics. By drawing together their knowledge and insights, we hope to provide not only information but perspective—perspective on what happened in the CD-ROM industry from its inception through 1988, and perspective on what might happen in 1989. Our goal is to give you food for faster, clearer, and more productive thought. If you find something in the *Yearbook* that helps you create a winning CD-ROM product, we will have succeeded.

Min S. Yee
Publisher
Microsoft Press

SECTION I

CD-ROM YESTERDAY, TODAY, AND TOMORROW

IN THE BEGINNING

THE INDUSTRY EMERGES

THE WAY OF THE FUTURE

IN THE BEGINNING

THE UTILITY VALUE OF INFORMATION
By Thomas F. Bangasser

WHAT IS CD-ROM?
By Roger Strukhoff

The Utility Value of Information

By Thomas F. Bangasser

[As unlikely as it seemed that anyone reading this Yearbook *might be unfamiliar with CD-ROM technology, we thought it best to begin with an overview article that would give newcomers an idea of what all the fuss is about. Here, Thomas Bangasser puts CD-ROM in a nutshell.]*

Ever since Gutenberg invented the printing press, the printed page has served us well. Paper has been the key medium for transmitting information. More paper documents are produced today than ever before. Sales of filing cabinets have never been healthier, and all storage media are experiencing some degree of growth. In fact, microforms and data processing are experiencing unprecedented growth.

Most people agree, however, that we are drowning in information and, more specifically, that the need to handle, store, and distribute information is overwhelming us. It doesn't matter that we can create and disseminate information faster than ever before if our inability to deal with that information makes it unusable.

A key to personal and business success is our ability to make smart, informed decisions. Regardless of culture, users want the right information at the right time, in the right place, in the right format, and at the best price available. These criteria are what we use to judge "the utility value of information."

INFORMATION DELIVERY ON CD-ROM

Recently, the utility value of information has been enhanced by CD-ROM (compact-disc, read-only memory). Accessible at the touch of a finger, CD-ROM is a fast and economical medium, capable of delivering in excess of 600 megabytes of information to an individual's desktop. Furthermore, it is portable, virtually indestructible, relatively inexpensive, and easily replicated, and it is the most cost-effective means of distributing vast amounts of digitized information, whether the nature of that information is text, numerics, graphics, audio, or a combination of them all. No one technology will ever solve all of the problems of getting information into the hands of the people who need it, but the publishing power of CD-ROM transforms the PC into a powerful, value-added information-access device.

Formally introduced in 1985, CD-ROM combines PC power with laser technology and easy-to-use multimedia software. Users search large databases from their local workstations, without high telecommunications costs or problems in connecting with online services. Information can easily be cut and pasted from the CD-ROM format into a word-processing or spreadsheet file, so more punch can be packed into memos and correspondence.

A new publishing industry has developed around CD-ROM. Hardware and software standards are in place and are supported by the major players. Microsoft's release of the MS-DOS CD-ROM Extensions in 1987 allowed the PC environment to overcome the 32-megabyte file-size limitation and provided access to 600 megabytes and more of information. New advancements in data compression will give gigabyte capacity to CD-ROM. Perhaps most important is the acceptance of a worldwide physical and logical file format for CD-ROM. The High Sierra Standard has been formally approved, with

A LASER PRIMER

The word *laser* is actually an acronym; a word made from the first letter of each word of a phrase.... A clear understanding of the phrase *light amplification by stimulated emission of radiation* will help explain how a laser beam is produced.

Light (the "L" in *laser*) is more than the colors we see. Visible light is just a small part of the *electromagnetic spectrum*. It is sandwiched between ultraviolet light and infrared radiation.

The waves of the electromagnetic spectrum can be described using three attributes: frequency, wavelength and energy. If you think of a wave moving through water, an example of *frequency* would be the number of waves passing by you in a minute. *Wavelength* could be measured as the distance either from wave crest to wave crest, or from trough to trough. The more *energy* a storm produces at sea, the higher number of waves created (frequency) and the shorter the distance between the waves (wavelengths).

The electromagnetic spectrum can be categorized from high energy, high frequency, and short wavelength down to low energy, low frequency and long wavelength. Gamma rays, x-rays and ultraviolet light are highly energetic. At the lower end of the scale are visible light, infrared radiation and radio waves.

Visible light can be further differentiated by the colors of a rainbow: red, orange, yellow, green, blue, indigo and violet. These colors range from longer wavelengths (red and orange) to shorter wavelengths (indigo and violet).

Light is said to have a dual nature, as it requires two models to explain its behavior. The behavior of light can be modeled as a wave in some situations, but needs to be thought of as a particle in other settings. For our laser application, we need to look at light as a particle. In light waves, the energy comes in discrete packets called photons. A photon has a specific amount of energy. To **amplify** light (the "A" in *laser*), one photon strikes an excited atom of gas. This atom gives off another identical photon. When these photons are reflected back and forth in the laser, more and more photons are produced, resulting in amplification.

The "S" and "E" of *laser* stand for **stimulated emission.** In a gas laser, electricity passes through atoms causing them to gain energy. The energy will be gained in specific amounts, called *quanta*. The excited atoms will then emit (give off) a photon to release that energy. However, if the photon strikes an atom already in an excited state, an additional photon is produced. When more than half the atoms in the laser tube are excited at any one instant, the energy is high enough for *lasing* to occur.

The "R" of *laser* comes from **radiation.** The radiation referred to here is not nuclear—just different frequencies of electromagnetic energy. The gas that is being excited determines the frequency of energy. For example, nitrogen and krypton fluoride gases lase at higher energies, while carbon dioxide gas emits at very low frequencies....

Now you are part of the select minority that recognizes *laser* as meaning *light amplification by stimulated emission of radiation*.

By Bill Hanshumaker. Reprinted from the 1988 August issue of *OMSI Magazine* by permission of The Oregon Museum of Science and Industry.

minor changes, as ISO 9660 by the International Standards Organization. Most major CD-ROM drive manufacturers have agreed to abide by these standards, thus guaranteeing the information user that all CD-ROM discs, CD-ROM drives, and microcomputers will work together, regardless of make. CD-ROM products have become as physically integrated with PC systems as have such standard peripherals as printers and hard disks.

CD-ROM is positioned primarily in the publishing and database distribution markets, and currently most CD-ROM products are moving into the workplace rather than into homes—especially into information-intensive workplaces. Libraries, law offices, medical research groups, market researchers, and corporate financial research groups are typical buyers. Today, most CD-ROM sales are work-, study-, and research-related, and many publishers believe that on-disc information will become part of a hybrid information-server technology that involves primarily text-oriented online accessing and search capabilities. Other publishers disagree and are gearing up for multimedia applications—the next chapter in the CD-ROM story.

Over 300 CD-ROM titles have been produced, though not all are available in the marketplace. There are references like the catalog of the Library of Congress, *Books in Print, Reader's Guide to Periodical Literature, Ulrich's International Periodical Directory,* the full *Code of Federal Regulations, Business Periodicals Index,* and so forth. And there are encyclopedias, dictionaries, almanacs, style manuals, thesauruses, and more.

Each single-sided CD-ROM is a silver-colored compact disc, 4.72 inches in diameter with the capacity to hold roughly the equivalent of more than 250,000 typed pages (the contents of twenty 4-drawer file cabinets, a 5½-foot-tall stack of 1500 conventional double-sided floppy disks, or the data on 20 30-megabyte hard disks). Although a disk can store images and sound as well as text, the digital format is more economical for text, computer programs, and

THOMAS F. BANGASSER

Home: Seattle, Washington
Job: Consultant
Quote: *"CD-ROM is headed to the desktop of each PC user, and it's only a matter of time."*

databases. For example, if the information in a typical legal library were converted to machine-readable form, one CD-ROM disc would contain approximately 100 fully indexed books. The nine million words and 10,000 pages that constitute the entire 20 volumes of *Grolier's Academic American Encyclopedia* use only one-fifth of a 4.72-inch disc.

CD-ROM PRODUCTION

To make a prerecorded CD-ROM disc, original information is first recorded digitally and then is transcribed to produce a tape that is used to produce a master disc from which copies (replicas) are made. Most of the cost-effectiveness of CD-ROM production is derived from the close relationship between CD-ROM and commercial compact audio technology. Because CD-ROM discs can be mastered and reproduced in the same factories as compact audio discs—and with the same techniques—CD-ROM technology derives all the cost benefits of a consumer-based, mass-production technology.

In the early stages of any new technological market, however, pricing is not nearly as competitive as it will be in the future. With 50,000 or less installed CD drives, economies of scale have not yet had any major impact on pricing strategies. Predictions are that Asian competition will drive hardware costs down through aggressive pricing.

PROS AND CONS

Information users really don't care how or where information is stored or how it gets to them as long as a single, easily performed request gives them what they want. However, CD-ROM advantages are many: high-density storage capacity; readability; user-friendliness; interactivity; low-cost replication for high-volume applications; economy of distribution; local distribution of archival information; ability to free storage space on mainframe computers; inexpensive hardware; virtual indestructibility of discs; substantial space savings; data integrity; ease of database maintenance (though publishing of updates can be time-consuming and costly); subscriber-oriented distribution; and access and local control through a personal computer. In addition, CD-ROM is normally not subject to metering and information can be downloaded at very high rates compared to dial-up lines. Equipment can be moved from one location to another at will and can be used without authorization by many different users. CD-ROM can combine text and images; offers unlimited end user searching; eliminates head crashes; provides powerful search capabilities; enables search terms to be indexed and indexes to be structured and combined in many different ways for faster retrieval; is a powerful stand-alone information system; and has fixed user costs that encourage use. Finally, a most attractive advantage of the system is its increasing simplicity and ease of use.

CD-ROM disadvantages include: lack of currency—most CD-ROM databases are not updated as frequently as online databases; relatively high data preparation costs; lack of reliable data about the archival (shelf) life of optical disc media; and data access that can be slow and inefficient compared to magnetic media and online information retrieval.

Every industry has its infrastructure of major players, communication organs, distribution channels, and industry forums. The CD-ROM market has split into three sectors: business, education, and home consumers. Business is supporting the greatest number of applications and developer opportunities (primarily in narrow vertical segments). Now that CD-ROM standards have firmed up and both hardware and software costs are decreasing, the education and home-consumer markets should show much more market growth.

[Thomas F. Bangasser is a consultant with Bangasser & Associates, Inc., business catalysts and consultants since 1940. The firm has extensive experience in strategic, marketing and operational planning, and specializes in startup ventures and litigation management using micrographics and computer-assisted retrieval systems. Bangasser wishes CD-ROM had been available in the late seventies, when he was President of College and University Press.]

What Is CD-ROM?

By Roger Strukhoff

[In this article, Roger Strukhoff looks at the potential of the young CD-ROM industry and describes some of the ups and downs since its introduction. His vision of CD-ROM is that many fields are coming together in a seamless, multimedia environment.]

Announced in October 1983, CD-ROM received its first major boost at the Microsoft First International Conference on CD-ROM in March 1985. It became established as a serious technology for business by the second CD-ROM Expo in September 1988. Yet the major question remains: "What is CD-ROM?"

CD-ROM is a storage technology. It allows hundreds, even thousands, of computer programs to be stored on a single disc, ready for easy access at the push of a button. CD-ROM can replace as many as 1500 floppy disks.

CD-ROM is a publishing medium. Starting with the Grolier Encyclopedia in 1985, CD-ROM has become the vehicle of choice to deliver book information; chemical databases; research on cancer, drugs, poisons, and hazardous chemicals; biological studies; and NASA's databases from the stars. Micromedex, Silver Platter, H.W. Wilson, R.R. Bowker, and Hoppenstedt are among the many companies that have become CD-ROM publishers. One CD-ROM disc replaces 250,000 pages of paper.

CD-ROM is an information distribution method. Corporations, the FBI, the CIA, and the Navy are all interested in gathering immense amounts of information, replicating it on CD-ROM, and sending the small discs to branch offices. CD-ROM aids bureaucratic inefficiency. CD-ROM competes with online databases. The user interface is friendlier, you don't have to rely on modems and phone lines, and the meter's not running. Dialog, Disclosure, and OCLC have led the way in converting databases from unfriendly, variable-cost online resources to friendly, fixed-cost CD-ROM.

CD-ROM is desktop publishing. Multi-Ad Services and Image Club lead the way in putting presentation graphics on CD-ROM. A new market is born.

ROGER STRUKHOFF

Home: Mount Carroll, Illinois
Job: Editor-in-Chief, *CD-ROM Review* and *Portable Computer Review*
Quote: *"When I can talk to Mom about CD-ROM without her eyes glazing over, then I'll know our little industry has made it."*

CD-ROM is a financial analysis tool. Lotus Development Corporation has been tremendously successful in putting together high-priced, well-crafted tools for financial analysts.

HOW BIG IS IT?

One of the challenges in figuring out CD-ROM is deciding whether it's too powerful or not powerful enough. Take a database of 300 megabytes...let's say 300 megabytes of great literature. That comes to about 60,000 standard book-size pages. If the average length of each of our masterpieces is 750 pages, then we have room for 80 books on this disc.

How long will it take you to read 80 great works of literature? Have you read 80 great works of literature in your life? And if you were to try to publish this disc, how long will it take you to get all the proper approvals from competing publishers, and then get all the great literature in digital format in one place?

The titanic task of putting together multi-hundred-megabyte applications is more of an impediment to creating a CD-ROM market than are hardware prices and availability.

Yet when the subject of images comes up, CD-ROM suddenly becomes a lot smaller. The disc starts to diminish rapidly if you want those images to move. Without compression, a CD-ROM will hold only a few seconds' worth of full-motion video. With compression, its data transfer rate of about 150 kilobytes per second makes it difficult to get that video to look presentable.

In fact, CD-ROM is also tiny when compared to the online databases it is supposed to supersede. Most online databases worth their salt are in the gigabytes, and a CD-ROM application typically presents only a small fraction of the original resource.

CD-ROM can seem to be too small just as often as it can seem to be too big.

HOW BIG WILL IT BE?

The CD-ROM industry today is a much more complex animal than most people imagined three years ago. The "trouble" started at the second Microsoft conference, with the announcement of CD-I. Then there was DVI in 1987. Then CD-ROM XA in 1988. It's clear that plain old CD-ROM (POCDR) is in trouble.

If that weren't enough, we've now seen the emergence of the magneto-optical erasable optical disc. And research continues on increasing the capacity of optical media through shorter-wavelength lasers and tighter data formatting.

Such a new disc would be a constant angular velocity (CAV) disc, with data formatted in concentric circles, and accessible through sectors in 50 milliseconds or less. Contrast that with the constant linear velocity (CLV) style CD-ROM, with data placed in a single continuous groove and allowing maximum storage but slow access times on the order of a half second.

The new CAV disc would not make maximum use of its storage potential because data must be placed at increasing intervals to allow the drive to operate at a single speed. But if data is packed at the stated goal of four times the density of CD-ROM, the CAV format will allow twice the storage of CD-ROM.

In other words, why bother sticking to the CD format as originally developed by Philips and Sony? If a new CD-sized disc evolves with twice the storage and a tenth of the access time, why not move toward that technology?

The challenge to CD-ROM developers and the journalists who cover them is daunting yet delicious. The confusion caused by a continuous stream of new announcements, each of them promising something better than anything that has existed before, is an ally of those who still hold quaint, idealistic notions about twenty-first century education, information delivery, and entertainment.

If CD-ROM had, in fact, been truly standardized in 1985, with no new developments since then, today we would be facing a good news/bad news situation. The good news would be that we would have very little confusion about CD-ROM and a much larger catalog of titles. The bad news is that we would have settled for a least-common-denominator approach and CD-ROM would be realizing its limits today.

What is CD-ROM? Frankly, my dear, I don't give a damn. I'm more interested in what it will be.

[Roger Strukhoff is Editor-in-Chief of CD-ROM Review and CD-ROM Report. He received his B.A. in music from Knox College in 1977, then embarked on a career in technical journalism. His experience includes stints on such publications as UNIX Review, Micro Communications, Portable Computer Review, and Professional Computing.]

AND THEN THERE WAS LIGHT

And God said, "Let there be a laser!"

With that, God created CD audio and it sounded good. Great, in fact. CD audio begat CD-ROM, which begat CD-I, which begat CD-V, which begat DVI.

The compact disc is about to sprout all kinds of computer incarnations which will provide new opportunities for the computer reseller community. One of the first will be CD-V, a format in which a CD is filled with 20 minutes of digital audio and five minutes of video. The first non-music video title we've heard about is "Agatha Christie: The Scoop" (Spinnaker). It's a full motion video interactive movie mystery. Viewers switch tracks on their CD-V players at specified points during the game to uncover clues. There are over 200 paths through the game, so it can be played over and over.

Perhaps even more intriguing than CD-V is CD-I, or Compact Disc-Interactive. This format will combine audio, video, and interactivity to form what is being called "talking books." The Record Group, a Philips subsidiary, has created several titles, the first being an interactive guided tour, "London Any Way You Turn." Another title, called "The Time Machine," will trace the history of civilization from 700 B.C. They are also developing a musical encyclopedia (Look up Bach, read about him, and hear his music), and an interactive fiction movie starring the Firesign Theater. The latter is being produced by Marc Blank, founder of Infocom.

WNET TV in New York City has produced a prototype of a CD-I disc that teaches physics. Spinnaker is developing four CD-I products: a chess game based on their best-selling Sargon III, an SAT tutorial program, and two others which have not yet been disclosed.

The first generation of CD-I players will retail for around $1,500 and software will vary from $19 to $60, according to Emiel Petrone of American Interactive Media. They're scheduled to come out any day now, and they will also be able to play CD-ROMs and CD audio discs, according to several reports.

And God looked upon these exciting new technologies and saw that they were good. After creating the world in seven days, God needed only to work out the marketing, distribution, compatibility, and educating of the public. "These new forms of CD will be available sometime next year," he sayeth.

By Dan Gutman. Reprinted from December 1987 issue of *Computer Dealer* magazine, P.O. Box 1952, Dover, New Jersey 07801.

THE INDUSTRY EMERGES

DATA ON A SILVER PLATTER
By David M. Roth and Kevin Strehlo

THE STATE OF THE CD-ROM INDUSTRY
By Steven K. Sieck and Haines B. Gaffner

Data on a Silver Platter

By David M. Roth and Kevin Strehlo
From *VENTURE* magazine

[In 1987, the authors surveyed the young CD-ROM industry and found a lot of enthusiasm and frenetic activity mixed with some confusion and uncertainty. These descriptions of efforts then underway to build an industry infrastructure bring wry smiles to the faces of some old CD-ROM hands, as they measure how far the industry has come and how far it has yet to go.]

Personal computer makers, like most technology-oriented entrepreneurs, are always on the lookout for smaller, denser, cheaper ways of doing things. Shrinking parts, making them perform better, and selling them for less is the essence of the business.

That's why when computer types saw how much raw data the music industry could pack onto a compact audio disk, they wondered if they could adapt the technology to PCs. Specifically, they wanted to plug CD players into computers, so that PC users could get at mainframe-size data bases without a lot of fuss. They did it.

Now there are rumblings of a new subindustry. It's called CD-ROM, the computer version of CD audio, which translated means compact disk, read-only memory. The technology allows 250,000 pages of information to be packed onto a shiny, palm-size platter. In computers that's 540 megabytes—enough data to fill 1,500 floppy disks. That potential—if you believe CD-ROM's boosters—is destined to do for personal computing what CD audio did for consumer electronics.

"It's like a boatload of real-estate brokers on Plymouth Rock with all of America before them," gushes Frederick Meyer, president of Meridian Data Inc., Capitola, Calif. "There's enough data suitable for publishing on CD-ROM to keep thousands of people busy for a long time." The demand, he insists, will come from major corporations as they convert data from microfiche to CD-ROM, a switch Meyer calls inevitable. Why? "They're not just changing media," he stresses. "They're adding value to information. While microfiche made it more convenient, it didn't add value. CD-ROM lets the computer find data for you."

Some examples: Dial-up data bases now rented by the minute can be "owned" and accessed without time constraints when they're on a CD. Technical documents that consume hundreds of thousands of pages can be transferred to a single disk and updated electronically, at tremendous savings for corporations that do a lot of publishing in-house. In more complex applications, diagnostic systems that employ artificial intelligence techniques promise to take the guesswork out of mechanical repair.

And that's just the beginning. CD-ROM's futurists say the technology will be the basis of interactive classroom instruction and home entertainment programs that allow viewers to alter and interact with what they see on their television screens. That end of the business, known in the industry as CD interactive (CD-I), is still in the prototype stage.

As always the problem is translating technical capabilities into something marketable, no idle concern here. After two years of hype, CD-ROM's growth has been excruciatingly slow: The installed base of CD-ROM players is a minuscule 12,000 to 30,000, and as a result, few companies can claim significant revenues. But that hasn't cooled the enthusiasm of some of the biggest names in computing, broadcasting, and publishing. They have acquired CD-ROM start-ups, spent millions in product development, and resolved technical issues. Now entrepreneurs are beginning to build a manufacturing infrastructure as well as applications that test the technology's promises.

Here's where the entreprenuerial action is:

- Data conversion and support equipment. Manufacturers like Meridian and service bureaus like Reference Technology Inc. (RTI), Boulder, Colo., appear to be on the verge of a boom. Their business is helping corporations convert paper, microfiche, and magnetic tape-based data bases to CD-ROM—a trend that's being driven by ease of use and massive cost savings. It costs $10 to publish a megabyte of information in book form, 2 on CD-ROM.

- Software for data retrieval and indexing. Companies like OWL International Inc., Bellevue, Wash., make huge CD-ROM data bases navigable, thus paving the way for sophisticated new applications. The automated repair system that Hewlett-Packard Co. is building for Ford Motor Co. and the

DISK MEMORY COMPARISON

	CD-ROM	"Laser disk"	Floppy disk	Winchester disk Small	Large
Type	Read-only	Write once	RAM	RAM	RAM
	Optical	Optical	Magnetic	Magnetic	Magnetic
	Removable	Removable	Removable	Fixed	Fixed
Diameter	4.75"	12"	5.25"	8"	13"
Capacity	550Mb	2Gb	360Kb	10Mb	500Mb
Transfer speed	150Kb	150Kb	~22.5Kb	96Kb	300Kb
Rotation speed	200-500 rpm	1800 rpm	300 rpm	3600 rpm	3600 rpm
Track density	16,000 tpi	15,000 tpi	96 tpi	~200 tpi	400 tpi
Bit density	42,000 bpi	<12,000 bpi	2,000 bpi	2,000 bpi	5,000 bpi
Average latency	100 ms	17 ms	100 ms	8 ms	8 ms
Average seek	1000 ms	125 ms	75 ms	100 ms	28 ms

From *CDROM State of the Art Technology Report,* Loecus Informatics Inc.

electronic shopping kiosks that the Del Mar Group, Solana Beach, Calif., built for B. Dalton Bookseller are cases in point.

- Publishing existing data in CD-ROM form. Here dozens of independent entrepreneurs, armed with expertise from previous careers, pursue specialized niche markets. Jonathan Pollard, a former associate producer at ABC News, looked at how much time it took to round up film clips for network documentaries and formed Newsreel Access Systems Inc., a New York company that sells an index of film clips on CD-ROM. Draper Kauffman, former head of technology planning for the Houston city school district, saw how much time people spent fielding phone calls on legal matters. So he committed the state's education-related legal decisions as well as administrative guidelines to a single CD. His company, Quantum Access Inc., now hopes to clone the project for California and 10 other states, while doing a brisk business as a service bureau. In both cases the modus operandi is the same: consolidate dispersed information and make it useful by coupling it to indexing software geared to the needs of a clone market.

Already large, well-established companies have bought their way into most of these markets. Last February Lotus Development Corp. snapped up OS Corp., developer of One Source, a service that puts eight financial data bases, including Compustat, Value Line, and Disclosure II, on a single disk. The product allows users to rule statistics into the popular 1-2-3 spreadsheet for analysis. So far 600 customers have signed up at fees ranging from $11,000 to $27,000 a year, but the revenues aren't likely to do much for Lotus' bottom line. Twenty-five percent to 50% of all revenues from CD-ROM-based information products go back to the original publisher in royalty payments. But for Lotus that's not the issue. One Source is just

> *1987: After two years of hype, CD-ROM's growth has been excruciatingly slow: The installed base of CD-ROM players is a minuscule 12,000 to 30,000, and as a result, few companies can claim significant revenues.*

another bullet in a well-stocked arsenal of add-on products designed to keep current customers hooked on 1-2-3.

...Despite appearances, CD-ROM isn't exclusively a big-company game. Large companies, to be sure, are interested in CD-ROM, but not necessarily as a business. The majority see it as a way to cut the considerable cost of in-house publishing. Consequently, helping corporations convert data bases to CD-ROM is where the bulk of the entrepreneurs—and the dollars—are.

In that part of the business, Meridian Data is king. The seven-year-old company, whose computer system allows users to prepare data for publishing in CD format, has an installed base of 75 units. Meyer, the company's president, expects $5 million in sales for 1987. Most of the big players in CD-ROM—including Microsoft and Lotus—own one of Meridian's machines. Linda Helgerson, president of Diversified Data Resources Inc. and editor of *CD Data Report*, Church Falls, Va., says the majority of all CDs

> *Despite appearances, CD-ROM isn't exclusively a big-company game. Large companies, to be sure, are interested in CD-ROM, but not necessarily as a business. The majority see it as a way to cut the considerable cost of in-house publishing.*

created in-house are done on Meridian's system. "Meyer," she notes, "found a hole through which every single CD-ROM publisher must jump."

Companies that don't bring CD-ROM publishing in-house go to independent service bureaus, which are now beginning to thrive. Reference Technology Inc. (RTI), the granddaddy of the bureaus, may soon strike gold after several years of futile scratching. Launched in 1982 by Binx Selby, founder of NBI Inc., RTI burned through $26 million in venture capital developing a proprietary disk drive that could turn the analog data of video disks into computer-usable bits and bytes. And while the setup handles twice as much information as a CD-ROM at seven times the speed, the cost was prohibitive: $8,000 to $9,000 per drive. RTI still sells the drive, but luckily doesn't have to make a living at it.

Its quick adoption of the $800 CD-ROM player promises to turn things around. Projected 1987 revenues of "under $5 million" should triple in 1988 and produce the company's first operating profit, according to Michael Befeler, vice-president of strategic marketing.

OWL International makes money by selling data retrieval and indexing software to application developers, who in turn pay OWL royalties on the products they sell. The incorporation of OWL's Guide software in the automotive repair system that Hewlett-Packard Co. (HP) is building for Ford Motor Co. illustrates how this works. Ford's 1988 models will feature a new diagnostic system that promises to put a new twist on car repair. By touching a key word or picture of a car part on a computer screen, mechanics get a recommended repair procedure.

...But again, all's not gravy. Even if 95% of Ford's 5,500 U.S. dealers will buy the system, OWL's royalties won't amount to more than $1 million. And that money will be spread out over four years—the rollout schedule for the project. The good news is that other HP-sponsored deals are in the offing, including similar pacts with other manufacturers deemed by HP to be hot prospects for automated diagnostics.

Retailing is the other hotbed of new CD-ROM-inspired applications. The Del Mar Group was founded in 1984 by Harold Kester to build electronic shopping systems. It has 155 systems installed, nine of which are in B. Dalton bookstores. Dalton's systems, $8,500 electronic kiosks known as Bookseller's Assistant, ask customers about favorite authors and genres, then spit out a list of potential titles.

So far Del Mar has absorbed $2.5 million in funding, including a $1.5 million first-round venture capital investment from InterWest Partners, which closed in April [1987]. In fiscal 1986, Del Mar almost broke even on revenues of $700,000. Next year the company expects a profit of 12% on sales of $8 million.

Consumer products on CD, though, are likely to have a tougher time, at least until the $800 price tag of CD-ROM players falls considerably. *Grolier's Encyclopedia,* for example, was recently committed to CD by KnowledgeSet Corp., a Monterey, Calif., startup launched by Gary Kildall, founder of Digital Research Corp., maker of the first mass market PC operating system, CP/M. But sales of the $299 platter have been slow: only 2,000 to 3,000 have moved since it was introduced in January, 1986. Luckily Kildall hasn't pegged his fortunes on the consumer market. For the moment he's counting on the manufacturing end of the CD-ROM business to pay the bills. In March, 1986, he started Publishers Data Service Corp., a separate joint venture with Sony Corp., which functions as a service bureau. Kildall now claims to have hit the breakeven point.

Just how much the CD-ROM business will be worth at the turn of the decade is a matter of spotty conjecture. Today's estimates look only at disk and drive shipments, not at the value of applications, manufacturing services, or soft-

SOLUTIONS IN SEARCH OF PROBLEMS

To understand the uncertainties of CD-ROM's early development (1984–1987), we can examine the common characteristics of this new technology and earlier technologies that emerged from the laboratory rather than the marketplace:

- The telephone in the 1870s. When the telephone was invented, most people lived and worked in small communities. They did not need electricity to talk with their neighbors. Early experiments with telephony in England included music broadcasting to wall-mounted receivers. In other countries, a few voice telephones per community were considered sufficient for the only application that could be foreseen: official communication. Only in the United States, where telephone systems could be added at low cost in the ongoing urban expansion, did telephony begin to play its many contemporary roles. One writer contends that the modern high-rise office building would be infeasible without the telephone, because the elevators would overflow with the business messengers that the telephone displaced. In the U.S. today there are about 550 million daily local calls and an additional 50 million long-distance calls. What began as a solution in search of a problem is now a $60 billion annual business in the U.S. alone.

- The airplane in the 1900s. People were amazed that the airplane flew at all. How could they have imagined that 80 years later airplanes would carry more than 350 million passengers annually? The barnstorming novelty of county fairs is now a $20 billion annual business in the U.S. One-day intercontinental trips are the joy of vacationers and the bane of business travelers.

- Television in the 1930s. Seeing television for the first time at the 1939 World's Fair, a New York Times reporter wrote, "This will never be successful because no one will sit still to look at it." Television is now a $10 billion annual business in the U.S. that has transformed both cultural values and the political process.

- The microprocessor in the 1970s. Used originally in videogames, microprocessors are now the "brains" in scores of devices from microcomputers to cars. Their contribution to the U.S. gross domestic product is evident in the Silicon Valley, Silicon Prairie, or Silicon Forest that every state aspires to have. In countries of the Pacific Rim, microprocessors bring much-needed trade credits to fund the development of other industries.

Like the earlier technologies, CD-ROM leaves the laboratory as a solution in search of problems to solve. It will eventually play a large role in business and society. At first, its role will be to replace other information-dissemination technologies that it outperforms in cost or funtionality. Later, it will perform new functions that in some cases will be unforeseen consequences of its unique characteristics. It is these new functions, more than the replacement functions, that will make CD-ROM as indispensable in our lives as the telephone, the airplane, and television.

By William Paisley and Matilda Butler. From *Microcomputers for Information Management.* Reprinted by permission of Ablex Publishing Corporation.

ware—an omission that no doubt reflects the newness of the market. Another reflection of the market's nascent state is the wide range of those numbers. The projections for the number of installed drives in 1990 roam from a high of 35 million to a low of just under 1 million.

So what's going on? At the moment, experimentation and infrastructure building. Big publishers are working out the economics of CD-ROM, figuring out how to make money without cannibalizing revenues from their on-line services. Small publishers, like NAS and Quantum, are also looking at the economics of CD-ROM publishing, calculating the cost of getting data to disk and appropriate pricing. Service bureaus and hardware makers—the core of the emerging infrastructure—will be the first to see profits from CD-ROM. Ultimately, whatever happens depends on how fast hardware costs drop, the pizzazz of new applications, and, most importantly, whether or not the whizbang entertainment products now envisioned get far enough off the drawing board to attract true mass appeal.

Reprinted from the August 1987 issue of *VENTURE*, For Entrepreneurial Business Owners & Investors, by special permission. Copyright © 1987, Venture Magazine, Inc., 521 Fifth Ave., New York, N.Y. 10175-0028.

The State of the CD-ROM Industry

By Steven K. Sieck and Haines B. Gaffner

[Steve Sieck and Haines Gaffner, spokesmen from LINK Resources, a highly respected market-research company that has been watching CD-ROM technology since its introduction, offer this perspective on the current state of the CD-ROM industry.]

Six years ago, Philips and Sony agreed upon a set of specifications for storing and retrieving computer-readable information on compact discs, defining a system offering computer users with CD-ROM readers direct access to 600 million bytes of information—equivalent in text form to 250,000 pages of text. Today, that capacity no longer seems awesome, and a variety of specialized approaches to encoding and decoding the information (such as CD-I, DVI, and CD-ROM XA) have built upon the original "open" approach.

The first commercial CD-ROM publications emerged only about four years ago. All of them were produced and marketed by small, entrepreneurial information publishers taking on established competitors. Since then, the market has expanded to include the makers and users of more than 300 CD-ROM-based commercial information products, as well as the makers and users of discs that distribute information within organizations or as part of another product or service. The market has expanded almost everywhere that ready, repeated access to large volumes of information is important.

WHAT IT IS TODAY

LINK estimates that in 1988 this multifaceted CD-ROM industry reached more than $200 million in sales of products and services in the U.S. alone. The companies providing the products and services that enable people to use CD-ROMs make up an unusually complex chain of production and distribution roles. Those owning proprietary data published on CD-ROM are reaping the most revenue, followed by software and systems integration vendors, packagers and marketers of information products based on other companies' proprietary data, makers and marketers of CD-ROM drives/readers, vendors of ancillary systems such as authoring systems

STEVEN KURT SIECK

Home: New York, New York
Job: Vice President, Electronic Services, LINK Resources Corp.
Quote: *"More than with any previous publishing medium, the opportunities for using CD-ROM must be understood within the context of a rapidly changing set of competing and complementary information technologies."*

THE APPLICATIONS

As the rest of this *Yearbook* so eloquently testifies, CD-ROM is being used today in business and education, in laboratories and retail stores, on ships and planes, in libraries and repair shops—in just about every area you can think of where information of a certain density is published for use and reuse.

Microcomputer-based publishing systems illustrate how CD-ROM is assuming roles in the delivery of both raw information materials and finished information products. At the *production* level, the little platters provide a reservoir of fonts, images, and tools; at the *publication* level, they are a portable information carrier of remarkable scope and versatility. Now that microcomputers can be used both to publish and to use the same publication, the two different senses of the term electronic publishing—as publishing systems and as electronic information delivery—are beginning to merge.

CD-ROM and its descendant variations may someday become a mass communications medium. But it is clear that in the short run CD-ROM will prove to be less a communications medium than a ubiquitous tool for communicators; not the final message, but part of a "production" step on the way to a final message. Today it is providing image archives for designers and producers, finely sculpted (and sculptable) sounds for musicians, and a variety of information resource tools for writers, marketers, scholars, scientists, programmers, and many others. Tomorrow...

Specialists often prefer information in their fields to be raw and undigested, so that they can find their own meaning, meaning unobstructed by other people's pathways. Outside these specialties, though, something more structured is required. Fortunately, the construction of logical search arguments for CD-ROM databases is becoming less forbidding, and new concepts, such as hypermedia, are being assiduously explored. Still, the key discoveries in the field of

and network servers, and providers of disc mastering and replication services.

Some companies with the potential to make broad use of CD-ROM in delivering information have shown by their lack of public activity that they'd prefer to see CD-ROM go away. But by lowering the barriers to entry into electronic publishing, CD-ROM is leveling the playing field for electronic information providers as much as it is equalizing opportunity for the users. Not only can a small business now use desktop libraries of business information that previously could be used only by specialized researchers in big organizations, but more and more new data publishers will be competing for a share of many existing markets wanting access to high-density information. A fact of life for the established vendors of static, non-proprietary data is that they must help to lead the CD-ROM industry or risk being nibbled to death by it.

knowledge navigation—or, in a few cases, the implementation of those discoveries—still lie ahead.

THE NEXT STEPS

In addition to the eternal quest for better knowledge representation and navigation, three immediate barriers remain to be crossed before CD-ROM's full potential can begin to be tapped. All three barriers are close to falling or are already beginning to fall.

1. Distribution

No matter how good your product, it means nothing if you can't get it in front of customers. And getting CD-ROM products in front of customers today, particularly outside closely defined market niches, remains a tough order. Companies like Datext (now part of Lotus Compact Disc Information Services) have succeeded by building their own direct sales and distribution networks. Others, like the Library Corporation, have leveraged third-party distribution opportunities to the maximum. Building a sales force from scratch is expensive, yet the first vendor to reach a new information market with the appropriate resources usually retains a decisive edge.

The most important channel to watch now is the computer retailer/distributor. (Clark Abt's book store in Harvard Square may be advertising CD-ROM products but, as George Bush likes to point out, Harvard Square is a long way from mainstream America and not many book stores seem to be following Abt's lead.) This year, 1988, has been the year that national retail distribution networks for computers were pried open, enabling CD-ROM products to begin to pour through in 1989.

Ideally, where would *you* prefer to buy your CD-ROM discs? In a book store? A computer store? A record store? From a systems vendor?

> *A fact of life for the established vendors of static, non-proprietary data is that they must help to lead the CD-ROM industry or risk being nibbled to death by it.*

From an automatic dispenser in the lobby of your building? Or by catalog? How about being able to download demonstration excerpts from an online service before deciding to order a disc? The distance we are from answering those questions is the distance the industry still must go to make CD-ROM truly accessible to all the current and potential personal computer owners who can utilize it.

2. Networking

Now that networking of PCs is finally becoming a reality in large organizations (especially in the financial services sector), CD-ROM is emerging as a network resource that is moving toward complete transparency to the user. In networked environments the hardware cost per user shrinks, and convenience (not having to "swap" CDs, for example) increases. Shared information tends to be of more value to a group or an organization, and maintaining commercial data onsite so that it can be merged with internal data on the same network is enabling advanced users of CD-ROMs on networks to create powerful hybrid databases.

The technology of networking, though hardly trivial, is falling into place. The more difficult

HAINES B. GAFFNER

Home: New York, New York
Job: President, LINK Resources Corp.
Quote: *"The CD-ROM industry has been proceeding through the natural evolution of most emerging technologies. CD-ROM is now at the point where the most practical applications are understood and the next three years should see a rapid acceleration in specific defined niches."*

barrier to cross before the industry can reach a golden age of connectivity involves economic and legal issues. How can an information owner ensure that only authorized users can access proprietary information on the network? What will be the impact on revenues from other publishing formats? Who will be responsible for the customer's successful and appropriate use of the information?

Networking would be a complex issue today even if the enabling technology were not evolving so rapidly, and even if information vendors were not prone to exploit closed systems wherever possible to gain strategic advantages that may or may not coincide with customer interests. Despite the tough challenges the industry must address, the benefits of networking are worth the effort. In combination, local networks and CD-ROM servers can rival remote online services in capacity and flexibility, while providing the much faster data rates and more predictable budgeting inherent to CD-ROM publishing.

3. Conversion

It's no accident that Grolier's *Academic American Encyclopedia* was the first print-based encyclopedia to become available through online services and then to become the first and, still, only commercial encyclopedia product available on CD-ROM. It happened because a European parent of the encyclopedia (previous to Grolier) invested millions of dollars in creating a machine-readable encyclopedia suitable for computer searches and more frequent updating.

Aside from databases like Grolier's *Electronic Encyclopedia,* which have previously been digitized for access over online information networks, the creation of new CD-ROM publications has been slow. When you look at the economics of transferring content from non-electronic media to CD-ROM, you can see why: The cost of converting the information to an electronic database is an order of magnitude greater than the cost of creating a CD-ROM application out of the same information; in turn, creating a CD-ROM application costs an order of magnitude more than actually making a disc.

Today the industry is on the threshold of a breakthrough in conversion technologies. Not only is the cost of scanners going down and their intelligence going up, but the next step, unattended ad hoc scanning of multiple-font materials, will trigger a quantum increase in demand for information storage and retrieval—and dramatically lower the cost of producing CD-ROM databases.

CONCLUSION

Despite these barriers and uncertainties, the existing industry is growing at 100 percent-plus annual rates, with internal and "product-associated" discs accounting for a growing share of the market for commercial CD-ROM publications. Perhaps the onset of maturity inevitably brings less excitement. But while the new wave of CD digital media (DVI, CD-I, CD-ROM XA, and so on) explores specific extensions of CD-ROM, the more peaceful sea behind it is filling up with customers saying, "Now I'm ready to buy."

[Steven K. Sieck is Vice President, Electronic Services, LINK Resources Corporation, a leading consulting and research company specializing in the electronic services industry. Sieck is currently responsible for synthesizing LINK research directions, and for directing major proprietary consulting projects for LINK clients.

Haines B. Gaffner is President of LINK Resources Corporation. With over 25 years experience in the information industry, Gaffner specializes in anticipating trends in new technologies and then initiating pathfinding research. Prior to founding LINK, he was Vice President of Business International and of Quantum Services Corporation.]

THE WAY OF THE FUTURE

WHAT'S NEW IN THE AREA OF INTEGRATED SYSTEMS
By Harold M. Kester

CD-ROM: THIS TIME NEXT YEAR
By Linda Helgerson

What's New in the Area of Integrated Systems?

By Harold M. Kester

[For Harold Kester, integrated systems are the way of the future. In this article, he describes three present-day systems that are harbingers of an era when CD-ROM will be a means to an end, not an end in itself.]

Before looking at what is new in integrated systems, I think I should define *integrated systems* in relation to CD-ROM. For this definition, it is helpful to view CD-ROM evolution as a set of four stages, with each stage distinguished from the next by the significant transformation of certain variables that control the functionality of the system. These variables are *data content, search and retrieval methods,* and, most importantly, *the user.*

CD-ROM builds on the stages defined for the computerization of manual systems during the sixties and seventies. Stage 1, manual methods, was the starting point. In preparation for computerization, solving the user's problem involved paper and manual procedures. Data content was generated by people, not computers. Search and retrieval were limited to visual scannings of alphabetically sorted tables of contents, indexes, and glossaries. At Stage 1, the user had to be technically very sophisticated to solve difficult problems.

Stage 2 involved the initial computerization of the manual method. Here, data content consisted of traditional, packaged databases available in an online environment. Search and retrieval depended mainly on the well-developed techniques of "key word in context," Boolean operators, and so on. Although faster and more useful than manual methods, Stage 2 systems still demanded that the user be fairly sophisticated to solve difficult problems.

Stage 3 marked the introduction of CD-ROM. Initially, this stage was merely the repackaging

HAROLD M. KESTER

Home: San Diego, California
Job: Chairman, The Del Mar Group, Inc.
Quote: *"The promise in the marriage between emerging technologies in information science and CD-ROM is to facilitate the user discovering new connections and relationships between disparate data, thus developing new insights about solving today's most challenging problems."*

owner, for example, or a car mechanic, or even an inner-city third-grade student. To provide the required ease of use for these technically less-sophisticated users, the software becomes more complex, particularly in the systems area.

Users in Stage 4 actually represent two extremes. On the one hand, Stage 4 systems designers must shepherd the less sophisticated user; on the other hand, the designers must meet the insatiable appetite of the power user. Stage 2 and Stage 3 software is simply not enough. Stage 4 systems must function in, and integrate with, existing system environments and must meet both a wide range of user needs and new types of data presentation.

Stage 4 data, instead of being a static collection of information, is multifaceted. Of course, traditional text and graphics data are present, but they are enhanced by integration with the outputs of mechanical test instruments or by animation. Some interesting new examples of integrated systems include National Decision Systems' Infomark, Generation III, and Education Systems' World-in-a-Window.

INFOMARK

National Decision Systems (NDS) owns one of the largest demographic databases in the world and has been a major supplier of market-analysis information to retailers, particularly in the area of new-site selection. A portion of this data is known as the Infomark system. In 1985, Infomark was introduced on Reference Technology's 12-inch interactive laser, Classix DataDrive. In 1987, NDS began delivering the product on CD-ROM. The disc contains massive amounts of geographic data and has categorized every U.S. household since the 1980 census.

Infomark breaks down 48 different demographic blocks, or groups of consumers, by geographic region. These demographic types are derived through a set of statistical processes from census reports and other data that NDS has collected. This data, in conjunction with NDS's Vision software and a company's cus-

of existing databases found online and in books. Here, the well-understood search techniques of Stage 2 were transferred to the personal computer and to CD-ROM. Screens were designed to emulate the look and feel of online screens. The user, though computer literate and aware of CD-ROM, still needed some sophistication to solve problems. User knowledge of the technology, however, was still a definite characteristic of Stage 3.

Stage 4 is the integration phase. Here, the variables (data content, search and retrieval techniques, and user sophistication) begin to change rather dramatically. You know you're in Stage 4 when the user says, "CD-WHAT?" Here, the technology is a means to an end, not the end itself.

The Stage 4 user is generally not a researcher or technician familiar with search and retrieval techniques, but rather a person who performs a "noncomputer" function—a retail bookstore tomer database and sales data, aids retailers in site selection, strategic planning, merchandise-mix selection, media planning, and direct marketing.

For example, NDS may determine that a given block is the "suburban gentry" demographic type. All the names and addresses within that block are known. A retailer, knowing the names and addresses of customers, can determine the percentage of "suburban gentry" types that the company sells to and can determine what the average sales are per year. Given this data, the retailer can apply these percentages to other "suburban gentry" blocks to forecast sales. Site-selection analysis is done in a similar fashion. Knowing the demographic types that are geographically close to a proposed site, and knowing the sales efficiency per type, the retailer can predict the most likely effectiveness for the proposed site.

Infomark is an integrated system because simple retrieval of demographic types is not the end result: Forecasting sales or selecting a site is. Yet, the system appeals to nontechnical people. One Infomark user, for example, wasn't sure what I meant when I mentioned CD-ROM. "Oh, that's what the little silver disc is," was the reaction.

GENERATION III

Generation III is another example of an integrated system designed for nontechnical users. Automobiles now contain more electronics than ever before. Many new cars have up to five microprocessors controlling such features as climate, automatic transmission, security, four-wheel steering, and the engine itself. (By 1992, it is predicted that 25 percent of the cost of a car's materials will be for the electronics.) Some garage mechanics embrace this new technology, but others have difficulty reading sophisticated test equipment or are simply uncomfortable with it. These mechanics are finding that they can work on fewer and fewer car models.

> *One Infomark user, for example, wasn't sure what I meant when I mentioned CD-ROM. "Oh, that's what the little silver disc is," was the reaction.*

A variety of products, designed as adjuncts to the less sophisticated in-the-car diagnostic systems, have been developed to assist mechanics. One such product is the General Motors CAMS system, which includes expert-system software and online technical-manual information. These systems, however, are basically Stage 3 systems.

The Generation III system, on the other hand, is intended to help the less technologically skilled mechanic work on electronics-based cars. With Generation III, the mechanic enters the job number and scans a bar code to determine the Vehicle Identification Number (VIN). The job number relates to an electronically recorded work order on which the service writer has described the automotive problem. By means of a menu of pictures, the mechanic can point to the area of the car under evaluation. Using very sophisticated search algorithms, the system retrieves the appropriate parts book, technical manual, technical-service bulletin, labor-time guide, and other related materials for review by the mechanic.

So far, this system, while very useful, still has the characteristics of Stage 3. What makes Generation III a Stage 4 system is the integration of test-equipment outputs with further information retrieval.

> *Emerging information-science technology married to CD-ROM can help us deal better with our increasingly complex world.*

The outputs of the test equipment are a new form of data for CD-ROM systems. For example, the technical-service data on the disc will provide a range of test-limit data for the percent of nitrous oxides that fall within a normal operating range. Gas-analysis peripherals, connected to a personal computer (where the CD-ROM is), provide the current percent of nitrous oxides present at the car's tailpipe. This data is read directly by the computer and compared against the test limits. If the comparison indicates a problem, the system directs the mechanic to the appropriate section of the manual for further tests or probable causes.

In the future, this information will be fed to an expert system that is connected to the car's Engine Control Module (another computer). Here, the diagnostic computer, using information from the CD-ROM, will be able to increase the engine rpm, test the gas output, and, depending on the results, report that the problem is a failed engine sensor.

Generation III is an integrated system for several reasons: The user is technologically unsophisticated when it comes to information retrieval systems; the system incorporates new data types for information retrieval (for example, gas-analysis output); and the goal is not the reading of a technical manual on a CRT, but rather a recommended solution to the problem of fixing the car.

WORLD-IN-A-WINDOW

How many students never realize their potential because their educational experience is a negative one? How many teachers, who hold so much of our future in their hands, are well qualified but unable to provide quality education because they are overloaded and underfunded? These critical issues are being addressed by computerized instruction and automated learning systems.

Education Systems (ESC) is a leader in providing such systems, which have multiple student workstations accessing CD-ROM-based lesson plans through a local area network (LAN). ESC, in conjunction with Encyclopaedia Britannica, Inc., is developing a new CD-ROM product that will integrate with these lesson plans an encyclopedia, a dictionary, an atlas, a notebook, and a word processor. The product is called *World-in-a-Window*.

This automated learning system will "remember" how previously successful students used the system to navigate around the encyclopedia. When a new student has demonstrated certain usage profiles, the system will show the student these previous experiences in a way that will save time and be more seductive, encouraging further exploration.

The system is a true hypermedia system. In addition to presenting textual encyclopedia information, it will incorporate full-color images, animation sequences, audio sequences, and a variety of hot links. The hot links will allow the student to go from one article to another at a click of the mouse. In addition to the suggested hot links (*see also* references already in the encyclopedia), a preprocessor will analyze the text to create new hot links.

If a student does not know the meaning of a word, a click of the mouse on the word will pull up the definition. If a word in the definition isn't understood, another click produces another definition, and so on. Any word found in a "talking" dictionary will produce an audio version of the definition simultaneously with the presentation of a textual definition.

The student will have a variety of ways to access the information in the encyclopedia. The principal method will be directed by the student's lesson plan. For example, an art lesson plan may direct the student to write about a famous painter and suggest several encyclopedia articles to start with—about artists such as Michelangelo, Ching L'ana, Rembrandt, and Degas.

Additional methods of exploring the encyclopedia will include time (through time lines), geography (through a revolving image of a globe with successive zoom capability) and, lastly, curiosity (through a feature called "idea search"). Here, the student will enter a few words about the idea for which information is sought. Using artificial-intelligence techniques, the system will provide a list of encyclopedia articles, ranked in order of relevance, that relate to the idea. If a student's orientation is strongly visual, the system will present only pictures and captions relevant to the idea.

World in a Window is an integrated system because it incorporates new data content (successful student navigation) and because users are not sophisticated (elementary through high-school students).

BEYOND STAGE 4

Today, CD-ROM systems are at Stage 4, the stage of integrated systems, in which information retrieval is not the goal of system usage, but rather a means to other ends.

Of course, development won't end at Stage 4. We can look toward to the future and find even more capable intelligent systems. The most interesting (saleable) products will be those that adapt to and incorporate user behavior—those that somehow "know" the user's way of thinking and using systems. These systems will anticipate and suggest alternatives and provide user-specific "best" answers. Other new technologies are waiting in the wings. Neural network technology, for example, will make these future systems very fast, more accessible through LAN's, and more interesting with hypermedia.

Emerging information-science technology married to CD-ROM can help us deal better with our increasingly complex world. First, the combination will help us sort through a mass of data by providing information and knowledge about the data, instead of limiting its scope to presentation. Secondly, this marriage will help us discover new connections and relationships between disparate pieces of data, thus helping us develop new insights into solving today's most challenging problems. This future is what is truly exciting about integrated systems.

[Harold M. Kester is Chairman and CEO of The Del Mar Group, a leading-edge innovator in integration of expert-system technology, advanced information-retrieval technology, and optical-disc storage techniques. Drawing on experience in product planning and development, as well as CAD/CAM, multitasking operating systems, and high-speed telecommunications, the group specializes in developing application-specific PC-based employee productivity systems.]

CD-ROM: This Time Next Year

By Linda W. Helgerson

[We conclude this section with an upbeat article from Linda Helgerson. Her vision of the CD-ROM industry in 1990 is one of an adolescent technology, past the traumas of childhood but with some growing still to do.]

This is an article about next year: 1990. Do not confuse it with the realities of today, nor with the struggles to publish and install CD-ROM technology now. Also, have faith. What is, is not the same as what will be. CD-ROM is too important, too necessary, for us even to think that things will stay the way they are. There are movements in all sectors that will cause the future to happen as it should.

It's 1990. Five years have passed since the introduction of CD-ROM drives in the U.S. market, and more than 1000 titles are now commercially available worldwide. The average price per disc is between $50 and $200, depending on the subject matter, and a minimum run per master is 500 copies except for prototype discs.

A whole new industry—the electronic publishing industry—is characterized by hundreds of small firms supplying valuable applications to market niches with a growing audience of dedicated personal computer users. A computer purchased by one of these converts contains, as standard equipment, a CD-ROM drive, a high-resolution color monitor with internal graphics processing capabilities, and a 100 megabyte hard disk drive. An optical erasable drive is optional but certainly considered the next step up in rewritable storage devices.

Various vertical markets—library, financial, legal, medical, electronics-design engineering, architectural and construction engineering, the airline manufacturing and transport industry, the automotive and off-road industries, the travel industry, the military, and governments at all levels—have adopted CD-ROM as the means of receiving and using information and, in turn, of disseminating their own information to others.

What is beginning to become standard for each vertical market is the delivery, on CD-ROM, of periodical information pertinent to each market. Known as "periodical libraries," each such disc contains journals, magazines, white papers, conference proceedings, and advertisements devoted exclusively to a particular market segment. Based on findings from market researchers, the subscription rate to any one of these periodicals has increased more than for the corresponding print version, and new subscribers are acquired at a fraction of the marketing costs.

Advertisements residing on these periodical library discs, particularly those linked with online order-entry communications services, result in 50 percent more actual sales than their print counterparts. And, as one would assume, the end users of these electronic periodical libraries feel they learn more, find new information faster, and have more fun in the process than they do with paper. It is rumored that a major airline will announce laptop systems with embedded CD-ROM drives and a selection of periodicals on disc for its first-class passengers within the next 90 days.

Drive manufacturers now realize that, to compete in the delivery of production quantities of CD-ROM drives at a $350 price level, their drives must contain components that are lighter in weight and less expensive than existing models, and that the drives must come with drivers that are interchangeable among models and brands, and come with standard SCSI interfaces—that is, interfaces able to work with all computer peripherals and with all CD-ROM drives.

Previous concerns and issues surrounding the delivery of the logical file-format standard—ISO 9660—have evaporated. The ability to produce CD-ROM titles for any operating system and to read contiguous files flowing over to a second or third disc, as well as the ability to read multiple discs with different search engines, is now solved. Likewise, the delivery of the necessary drivers, previously known as the MS-DOS CD-ROM Extensions, is no problem because of the availability of the requisite public domain software from a number of sources.

Tertiary levels of standards are now begin-

LINDA HELGERSON

Home: Falls Church, Virginia
Job: President, Diversified Data Resources, Inc.
Quote: *"It will take at least ten years before we see all the applications of CD-ROM."*

ning to appear. Some of these file-format standards are specific to an industry, such as the airline and air transport industry, and some are more pertinent to a type of database, such as mapping, planetary data, or technical documentation.

Also this year, we are beginning to see a number of commercially available CD-ROM-based applications that include, as an integral part, audio, overlay graphics, and graphics and color images, as well as full-motion, full-color, full-screen digital video. These applications, targeted initially at the education and merchandising markets, are meeting with instant interest and user satisfaction. Elsewhere, in academia and business, some considerations of the value of multimedia databases are being tested, with results expected during the latter half of 1990.

Finally this year we see the introduction of evaluation units of writable ROMs—disks that conform to the Philips/Sony standard that allow for publish-on-demand capabilities at a premium price for the fast replication of 10 to 50 discs at a rate of six minutes per disc.

The one element differentiating 1990 from previous years of testing and learning is that the

> *Optical technology has lived through the Age of Awareness and is now comfortably sitting, for most personal computer users, in the Age of Understanding.*

barriers to widespread use—some technical and some just plain experience—are now history. Individuals can acquire CD-ROM titles and CD-ROM drives easily and at affordable prices via electronic ordering catalogs and other efficient means. Purchasers can install drives and titles without hassles. End users know what to expect from "basic" retrieval programs, and they use CD-ROM regularly, as a routine part of their professional lives.

What has happened along the way to cause this CD-ROM world of 1990?

INFORMATION HAS INTRINSIC VALUE

People understand the value of information and are willing to pay for it. This attitude is reflected, in part, in the increased number of CD-ROM titles and in the greatly expanded use of CD-ROM in business and education.

Many examples of this new way of delivering and purchasing can be cited. Technical documentation for operating, maintaining, and repairing a piece of equipment, for example, is no longer assumed to be free to purchasers, but rather a necessary element that has a separate value and therefore a price. The real estate industry recognizes that a commission, a realtor's livelihood, requires timely and accurate information and, as a result, real estate agencies and appraisers pay a price for this information, delivered when and as needed, because of the competitive edge it provides. Library patrons no longer assume that information is free and that the only expense involved with acquiring data is their own time. Instead, patrons recognize that, with information stored and available on CD-ROM, it is the speedy access to all relevant information that is important and worth a sum.

As a result of this change in attitude toward the monetary value of information, publishers and users are finding themselves in different economic roles. Historic or static information is priced on the value of the information retrieved. Current, more dynamic data with highly efficient delivery schedules and retrieval capabilities comes with a higher price tag, but again is based on the value of the information retrieved. Therefore, connections from data stored and available locally on CD-ROM has, as an optional component, seamless access to real-time information available from online services or facsimile transfer via courier or voice transfer.

TIMELY AND ACCURATE DELIVERY OF INFORMATION

In essence, the delivery of information itself, with CD-ROM as one essential component, is now integrated vertically and horizontally in many different markets. An individual can view a number of bibliographies with abstracts on a CD-ROM, ask to review the full text of only a portion of the items found, and then print out or download some or all of those considered of value for future reference. Finally, the individual can ask to see if there is any more recent information.

Each one of these requests is a result of a different form of information delivery. CD-ROM stores the bibliographic data. The full text might also be stored on CD-ROM, either alone or in combination with a firm's own database stored on optical write-once disc or optical tape. The command to print out or download automatically logs both the transaction and a debit to the designated account. Updated information from an online or wire service or from the organization's own computing facilities is also logged as a transaction with an appropriate debit.

HARDWARE AND SOFTWARE AS A FUNCTION OF INFORMATION DELIVERY

CD-ROM is both a component of a larger, integrated information delivery system and the cause of such capabilities. Private sector organizations, government entities, and educational institutions now recognize that acquisition of hardware and software *per se* is not the issue and that proprietary impediments to total integration are to be avoided.

This decreased emphasis on certain hardware brands and on specific proprietary systems and software decided upon by technicians is giving way to increased emphasis on the requirements of end users. We are beginning to see each system and the corresponding bank of information and communications services designed specifically for end users. Acquisitions are based on what users require and on the assumption that new directions and increased capabilities will occur. With CD-ROM, many of the costs of operating and maintaining these systems are decreased.

THE USER UNDERSTANDS OPTICAL

Optical technology has lived through the Age of Awareness and is now comfortably sitting, for most personal computer users, in the Age of Understanding. The majority of computer

> *1990: Decreased emphasis on certain hardware brands and on specific proprietary systems and software decided upon by technicians is giving way to increased emphasis on the requirements of end users.*

purchasers and end users understand that read-only, write-once, and erasable optical technologies are all important but for different purposes and applications. This awareness has been difficult to achieve, but only a few remain confused.

MORE HURDLES TO SURMOUNT

All things are not as rosy as they could be for CD-ROM. Drive manufacturers have not yet agreed upon a standard cartridge for CD-ROM discs, so we must still contend with the jewel boxes of yore as the disc protection device, which adds cost to the disc and little more than irritation to those of us who break plastic for a living.

As much as CD-ROM is a central focus to many professions, it is still, unfortunately, affected by the lack of standards throughout the rest of the microcomputer industry. However, there is hope. The marketplace is now deciding what it wants, and there are a number of indications that hardware manufacturers and software publishers will have to reform to survive.

ALL IN ALL, 1990 IS A VERY GOOD YEAR

CD-ROM has passed puberty, and its adolescence should be venturesome, full of the excitement of growing up, and certainly anything but predictable. In anticipation of CD-ROM's wild and crazy years, Microsoft Corporation has announced an annual $10,000 award for the most innovative nonstandard use of a CD-ROM. Rumor has it that a SIGCAT member intends to enter a clock using a disc as the face. Well, I suppose we all have to begin somewhere!

[Linda W. Helgerson is President of Diversified Data Resources, Inc. (DDRI), a consulting firm in northern Virginia that specializes in optical storage technologies and directly related fields. She is also Editor and Publisher of CD-Data Report, *a leading CD-ROM industry newsletter.]*

SECTION II

THE OPTICAL MEDIA FAMILY

CD-ROM
AND
CD-ROM XA

CD-I

DVI

WRITABLE DISCS

CD-ROM AND CD-ROM XA

MS-DOS CD-ROM EXTENSIONS: A STANDARD PC ACCESS METHOD
By Tony Rizzo

THE IMPACT OF CD-ROM XA
By Takashi Sugiyama

MS-DOS CD-ROM Extensions: A Standard PC Access Method

By Tony Rizzo
From *Microsoft Systems Journal*

[The MS-DOS CD-ROM Extensions and the High-Sierra file format, which became ISO 9660, heralded the end of the compatibility problems that plagued early CD-ROM products. Although today's application developers have been freed to concentrate on content and interface issues, Tony Rizzo claims that they can nevertheless benefit from an understanding of how device drivers work.]

Developers of CD-ROM applications need not concern themselves with the details of interfacing CD-ROM drives to the MS-DOS environment. Microsoft, working closely with CD-ROM drive manufacturers, has developed the software necessary to accomplish this. The MS-DOS CD-ROM Extensions, in conjunction with the High Sierra logical disc format, free developers to concentrate solely on their applications and eliminates dependence on any particular manufacturer's drive technology. The MS-DOS CD-ROM Extensions consist of a device driver for a CD-ROM player and a RAM-resident program called MSCDEX.EXE that interfaces with MS-DOS. Together they provide an interesting solution to some rather thorny MS-DOS/CD-ROM interfacing problems.

THE DILEMMA

CD-ROM device drivers are of concern primarily to manufacturers of CD-ROM drives, who write

> *The Microsoft Extensions and High Sierra Group CD-ROM specifications go together like bagels and cream cheese: both are good, but are best together.*
>
> **Alan L. Zeichick**
> **From *CD-ROM Review***

and package them with their products in accordance with Microsoft's "CD-ROM Device Driver Specification." However, an understanding of how these drivers work will benefit CD-ROM application developers.

Unlike conventional hard and floppy disks, CD-ROM discs are read-only, with file structures that can occupy up to 660 MB of data space, part of which might be audio or video information. There is no File Allocation Table (FAT) as there is in a normal MS-DOS file system, and there is no need to dynamically track disc space for allocating data because CD-ROM is a read-only medium. Furthermore, CD-ROM drives cannot be accessed via the standard MS-DOS Interrupt 25h/Interrupt 26h (read/write disk sector) mechanism, and they cannot be looked at by the operating system at a physical level because they are not in MS-DOS file format. Files and directories are not organized as MS-DOS expects them, which is why CHKDSK, FORMAT, and other MS-DOS utilities will not work on CD-ROMs.

MS-DOS interfaces to standard magnetic media through block device drivers that deal with disk drives at the hardware level and transfer blocks of data in multiples of a given sector size. Also, block drivers are able to support multiple devices (for example, two or more hard disks at once), as well as removable media.

MS-DOS makes some assumptions about block device drivers. It assumes there is a FAT, and it attempts to read one when the device driver is initialized. MS-DOS also assumes that it needs to assign drive letters to each unit supported by a particular device driver. Neither of these assumptions is relevant to CD-ROM drives, nor can MS-DOS deal with CD-ROM's 660 MB data space, since MS-DOS versions up to version 3.30 can support a maximum disk space of only 32 MB.

MS-DOS also accepts a character device driver, which deals with information one byte at a time, rather than in blocks. Character device drivers are usually associated with serial I/O devices such as modems, printers, the keyboard, and the video monitor. Character device drivers are assigned a unique name instead of drive letters and do not support multiple units or removable media. Since MS-DOS assumes nothing about them, character device drivers are useful constructs for CD-ROM drivers.

Command Code	Name	Supported CD ROM Command
0	INIT	Yes
1	MEDIA CHECK (block devices)	No
2	BUILD BPB (block devices)	No
3	IOCTL INPUT	Yes
4	INPUT (read)	No
5	NONDESTRUCTIVE INPUT NO WAIT	No
6	INPUT STATUS	No
7	INPUT FLUSH	Yes
8	OUTPUT (write)	No
9	OUTPUT WITH VERIFY	No
10	OUTPUT STATUS	No
11	OUTPUT FLUSH	No
12	IOCTL OUTPUT	Yes
13	DEVICE OPEN	Yes
14	DEVICE CLOSE	Yes
15	REMOVABLE MEDIA	No
16	OUTPUT UNTIL BUSY	No
128	READ LONG	Yes
129	Reserved	
130	READ LONG PREFETCH	Yes
131	SEEK	Yes
132	PLAY	Yes
133	STOP PLAY	Yes

Commands 0, 3, 7, 12, 13, 14, 128, 130, and 131 are the standard codes necessary to write CD ROM device drivers.
Commands 132 and 133 are used to write extended CD ROM device drivers that support audio.
Commands 1, 2, 4, 5, 6, 8, 9, 10, 11, 15, 16, and 129 are not supported CD ROM commands and will return an error code for unknown command.

Figure 2-1. Device driver command codes

What CD-ROM requires is a hybrid device driver closely modeled on character device drivers but supporting, in block driver fashion, multiple units and removable media. In fact, CD-ROM device drivers are character device drivers that have additional fields to support drive letters and multiple units.

The standard MS-DOS character device driver command set consists of commands to control input and output and the device itself, as well as to query the status of the device. The CD-ROM device driver command set consists of a subset of these commands, plus a group of new commands that pertain only to CD-ROM drivers (see Figure 2-1).

CD-ROM DEVICE DRIVERS

Standard device drivers are simply EXE files that do not contain Program Segment Prefixes (PSPs). Because they have no PSPs, they originate at location 0h rather than 100h. A device driver contains a header (see Figure 2-2), which identifies the file as a device driver, defines the device's particular attributes, and provides information that MS-DOS will need when the driver is initialized. There is also a name/unit field that will hold a character device name or, if the device is a block device, the number of units to be supported.

```
DevHdr      DD       -1            ; Ptr to next driver in file
                                   ; or -1 if last driver
            DW       ?             ; Device attributes
            DW       ?             ; Device strategy entry point
            DW       ?             ; Device interrupt entry point
            DB       dup 8 (?)     ; Character device name field
                                   ; or drive letter
```

Figure 2-2. Standard device header format

Commands are passed to standard device drivers from MS-DOS via request headers (see Figure 2-3), which contain system information such as the length of the request header, the command code itself (from Figure 2-1) and any data necessary for the device's operation, as well as a field in which the driver can return a status code. If the device is a block device, there will also be a subunit code to tell the device driver which of its supported units is being requested.

```
ReqHdr      DB       ?             ; Length in bytes of request header
            DB       ?             ; Subunit code for minor devices
            DB       ?             ; Command code field
            DW       ?             ; Status
            DB       dup 8 (?)     ; Reserved
```

Figure 2-3. Request header format

When a CD-ROM device driver is first initialized by MS-DOS, some interesting things happen to maintain its character device driver disguise while it is operating as a block device driver. This makes it necessary for CD-ROM device headers to have three additional fields that are not found in standard character or block device headers (see Figure 2-4).

```
DevHdr      DD       -1            ; Ptr to next driver in file
                                   ; or -1 if last driver
            DW       ?             ; Device attributes
            DW       ?             ; Device strategy entry point
            DW       ?             ; Device interrupt entry point
            DB       dup 8 (?)     ; 8-byte character device name
                                   ; field or drive letter
            DW       0             ; Reserved
            DB       0             ; Drive Letter
            DB       ?             ; Number of Units
```

Figure 2-4. CD-ROM device header format

When MS-DOS installs device drivers, it gets its information from the DEVICE=xxx entries in the CONFIG.SYS field. A typical line in a CD-ROM device entry in CONFIG.SYS might be:

DEVICE=C:\DEV\HITACHI.SYS/D:MSCD001 /N:3

When MS-DOS reads this line, it loads the device driver HITACHI.SYS from subdirectory C:\DEV and issues an INIT command, via a request header to the device driver. The device driver obtains its unique device name, in this case MSCD001, and any other device specific parameters from the command line and completes its initialization. As part of its initialization process, the CD-ROM device driver may determine from the CONFIG.SYS command line what interrupt, port address, DMA channel, or memory address the CD-ROM controller may be using. Another parameter may be the number of units connected (3 in this particular case) that the device driver will use to fill the Number of Units field in its device header, which MS-DOS knows nothing about.

As part of CD-ROM device driver initialization, the driver is responsible for filling out any uninitialized device driver header fields and some return fields in the INIT Request Header before returning. In the driver header, it copies the unique driver name from the command line into the 8-byte character device name field, supplies the strategy and interrupt routine offsets, and sets the device attributes field appropriately (see Figure 2-5). In the INIT Request Header, it records a 0 in the Number of Units field for character device driver compatibility even if the driver supports more than one unit and returns the ending address of the device driver so MS-DOS knows how much space the driver requires. The CD-ROM device driver then returns a status code (see Figure 2-6). Because the device driver is a character driver, MS-DOS will not read the FAT or try to assign a drive letter for the driver before the CD-ROM Extensions are loaded.

Next, the driver returns control to MS-DOS, which goes on to read whatever else might be in CONFIG.SYS and then executes the commands in AUTOEXEC.BAT, if it exists.

Bits	15	14	13	12	11	10	9	8	7	6	5	4	3	2	1	0
	ERR	Reserved					BUSY	DONE	Error Code (if bit 15 on)							

The status word is zero on entry.

Bit 15	Error bit	Set by the device driver if an error is detected or if an invalid request is made to the driver. The low 8 bits indicate the error code.
Bits 14–10	Reserved	
Bit 9	Busy bit	Set by the device driver when the device is in play mode. All requests of the physical device when this bit is set will fail unless play mode is interrupted (using the STOP PLAY function) and a request is then made. Monitoring this bit will tell when play mode is complete.
Bit 8	Done bit	Set by the device when an operation is complete.
Bits 7-0	Error code	0 - Write-protect violation 1 - Unknown unit 2 - Device not ready 3 - Unknown command 4 - CRC error 5 - Bad drive request structure length 6 - Seek error 7 - Unknown media 8 - Sector not found 9 - Printer out of paper A - Write fault B - Read fault C - General failure D - Reserved E - Reserved F - Invalid disk change

Figure 2-6. Status word

At this point, the CD-ROM device driver has been successfully installed and because MS-DOS thinks it's a character device driver, it will ignore the CD-ROM device driver. Once the driver is initialized, MS-DOS itself will never again deal directly with the CD-ROM driver.

MSCDEX.EXE

Along with the CD-ROM drive itself, drive manufacturers are planning to include the CD-ROM device driver and MSCDEX.EXE, a special terminate-and-stay-resident (TSR) program that is really the key to the CD-ROM interfacing. MSCDEX.EXE is typically loaded from AUTOEXEC.BAT with a command line such as:

C:\BIN\MSCDEX.EXE /D:MSCD001 /D:MSCD002 /M:10 /V /L:P

The command line must contain the name that was given to any CD-ROM device driver that was listed in CONFIG.SYS. MSCDEX.EXE goes through the following procedure for each of the identified device drivers:

```
DevHdr   DD   -1          ; Ptr to next driver in file
                          ; or -1 if last driver
         DW   0c800h      ; Device attributes
         DW   STRATEGY    ; Device strategy entry point
         DW   DEVINT      ; Device interrupt entry point
         DB   'HSG-CD1'   ; 8-byte character device
                          ; name field
         DW   0           ; Reserved (must be zero)
         DB   0           ; Drive Letter (must be zero)
         DB   1           ; Number of Units (one or more)
```

Device Attributes

For CD ROM device drivers, the device attributes field is 0c800h.

Bit 15	1	Character Device
Bit 14	1	IOCTL supported
Bit 13	0	Output until busy
Bit 12	0	Reserved
Bit 11	1	OPEN/CLOSE/RM supported
Bits 10–4	0	Reserved
Bit 3	0	Dev is CLOCK
Bit 2	0	Dev is NUL
Bit 1	0	Dev is STO (standard out)
Bit 0	0	Dev is STI (standard in)

Figure 2-5. Sample device driver including attributes field definitions

- Issues a DEVICE OPEN call to MS-DOS using the device driver's name and receives from MS-DOS a handle for the device driver.

- Executes a DOS IOCTL call to obtain the device header address of the CD-ROM device driver.

- Determines the number of subunits that are to be supported by the driver and assigns legal drive letters for each subunit.

- After completing this process for every listed driver and finishing the remainder of its installation, MSCDEX.EXE terminates but remains resident in background mode waiting for requests for the CD-ROM.

The MSCDEX.EXE command line shown above also contains a number of other switches. /M:Value tells MSCDEX.EXE how many sector buffers it should allocate for its own use (the default value is four sectors per drive). MSCDEX.EXE uses the sector buffers to cache sectors from the Path Table, directory sectors, and file data sectors. Allowing it to cache more directory information reduces its need to reread directories from the disc and speeds things up. /V (for Verbose) provides some memory configuration information. Finally, there is an /L switch that allows manual specification of CD-ROM drive letter assignment (drive P: in this case).

THE CD-ROM INTERFACE

At this point, the CD-ROM drivers and drives are set up, but we still have another problem. MS-DOS no longer knows anything about them, so how is it able to access them? Again, MSCDEX.EXE fools the operating system, this time using several components of MS-DOS in a unique way. MS-DOS (Version 3.1 and later versions) has a number of built-in networking features: when MS-DOS sees a request for network drives, it sends the request to the network redirector, which processes the file request and sends the request on to the networking server.

MSCDEX.EXE designates the drive letters it assigns to its CD-ROM drives as network drives. Whenever MS-DOS receives a CD-ROM drive request, it thinks it's a request for a network drive and forwards the request to the redirector. MSCDEX.EXE remains active in the background intercepting these requests, processing those that are really requests for a CD-ROM drive, and passing on the legitimate network requests to the redirector.

MS-DOS issues requests to the network at a virtual file level. MSCDEX.EXE converts these virtual file level requests into physical sector requests that can be understood by the CD-ROM device driver. For example, a virtual file level CD-ROM request going to the network from MS-DOS might read:

OPEN \ DIRECT1\ SUBDIR2\ FILEA
READ x bytes from FILEA at offset y

MSCDEX.EXE intercepts the request, analyzes it, determines that it's a CD-ROM request, translates it to

READ sector z

and sends the appropriate command codes to the CD-ROM driver. Operating at a file level rather than a physical level allows MSCDEX.EXE to circumvent some limitations of MS-DOS such as the 32 MB file limit. Figure 2-7 illustrates the entire process.

The end result: MS-DOS thinks that it has available to it a very large network drive, which it can easily deal with. The MS-DOS CD-ROM Extensions (MSCDEX.EXE plus the CD-ROM device drivers) thus enable a developer to create a CD-ROM based application that will run on any CD-ROM drive attached to any PC.

THE COMMANDS

Now let's take a look at several of the commands supported by CD-ROM device drivers

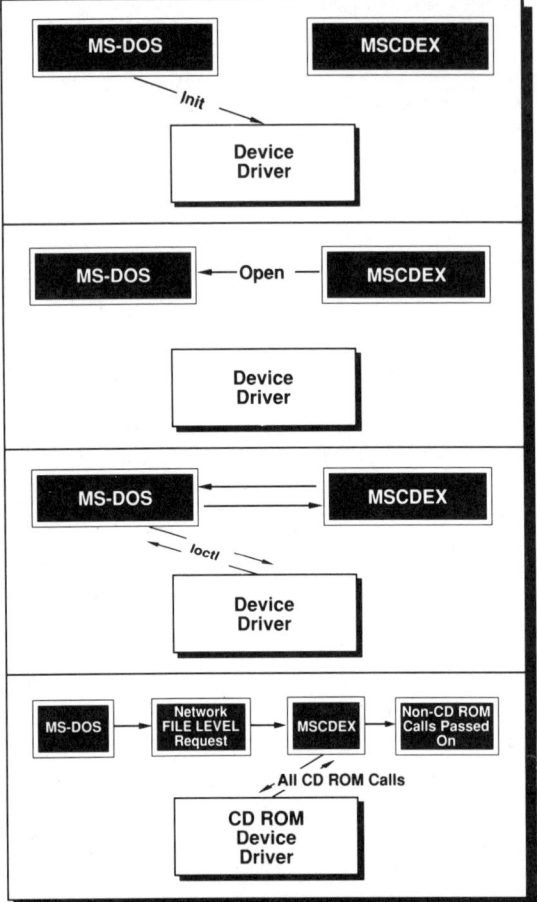

Figure 2-7. Summary of CD-ROM MSCDEX.EXE initialization events

and see how they compare to various standard device driver commands.

Figure 2-8 shows the standard READ/WRITE command control block. Note that this particular control block is used for command codes 3, 4, 8, 9, 12, and 16 (refer to Figure 2-1). For CD-ROM, only command codes 3 and 12 (IOCTL INPUT and IOCTL OUTPUT) are valid.

IOCTL calls will permit MSCDEX.EXE and application programs to send control strings to the device driver that consist of CD-ROM specific commands or requests for information about the status of the device drivers and the CD-ROM drive. Figure 2-9 lists the CD-ROM IOCTL codes for command codes 3 and 12. The transfer address for an IOCTL call points to a control block that is used for communication with the driver. The first byte of the control block serves as the command code for the IOCTL call. IOCTL INPUT calls request and receive information from the device driver about the device. IOCTL OUTPUT calls instruct the device driver to open or close the device door, eject a disc, and so on; in this case, the device responds to the instruction but returns no information.

Figure 2-10 shows the CD-ROM READ LONG command (command code 128). This differs in a number of ways from the standard READ command control block (see Figure 2-8). First, the media descriptor byte, which is set to 0 for IOCTL calls and ignored, becomes the addressing mode byte. This byte will almost always be set to 0, or High Sierra Group (HSG) addressing mode, that is, long address values are read as logical block numbers, as per the HSG format. All CD-ROM drives will support HSG addressing mode, which can be considered the standard or default mode of operation. Interleaving is not yet supported, though it may play a role in file design in later releases of the software.

The standard READ command pointer to a requested volume ID is replaced with a data read mode byte in the READ LONG command. This will usually be set to 0, for cooked mode, in which 2048 bytes are read and verified using error detection and correction. Using raw mode, the entire 2352 bytes are read, including the error detection and correction code. Applications can use this mode if the drive and driver support raw mode by setting this byte to 1.

Perhaps the major difference between READ and READ LONG is that the byte/sector count

```
Read or Write
Command code = 3, 4, 8, 9, 12, 16
CmdName      DB      (dup 13 0)  ; Request Header
             DB      ?           ; Media descriptor byte from BPB
             DD      ?           ; Transfer address
             DW      ?           ; Byte/Sector Count
             DW      ?           ; Starting sector number
                                 ; (ignored on character devices)
             DD      ?           ; ptr to requested volume ID if
                                 ; error 0Fh
```

Figure 2-8. Standard read/write command format

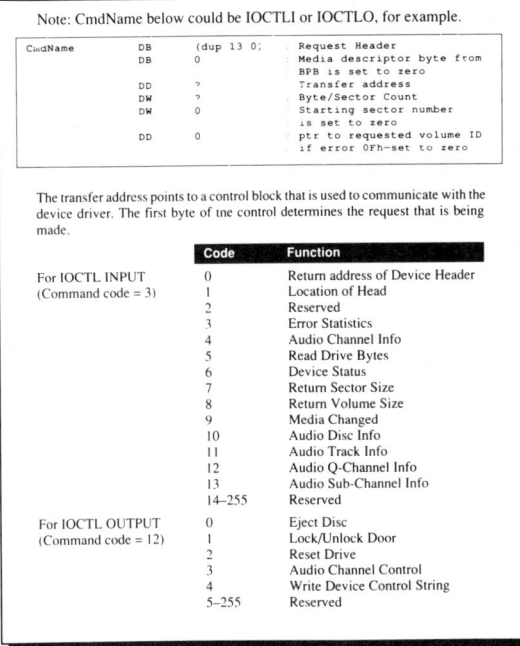

Figure 2-9. CD-ROM IOCTL input and IOCTL output, command code = 3 or 12

```
ReadL   DB      (dup 13 0)  ; Request Header
        DB      ?           ; Addressing mode
        DD      ?           ; Transfer address
        DW      ?           ; Number of sectors to read
        DD      ?           ; Starting sector number
        DB      ?           ; Data read mode
        DB      ?           ; Interleave size
        DB      ?           ; Interleave skip factor
```

Figure 2-10. READ LONG, command code = 128

field becomes the number of sectors to read, and the starting sector number is expanded to double-word length. This means it can now reference 4 gigasectors (or more than 8 terabytes).

This is part of how the CD-ROM's larger capacity is handled.

At the very least, CD-ROM device drivers will be able to return proper values for IOCTL calls and will be able to read cooked mode 1 data sectors using HSG addressing mode.

READ LONG PREFETCH attempts to anticipate where the next sector reads will take place. It is a hint from MSCDEX.EXE to the device driver that the sectors requested by this command will most likely be needed and the driver should attempt to cache the requested sectors or at least position the read head within the area they occupy. This minimizes the time that is required to seek the next location when reading data.

SEEK positions the read head at specific locations on a disc. All CD-ROM device drivers are required to support DEVICE OPEN and DEVICE CLOSE which are included for DOS compatibility. For CD-ROM drives with audio capability, PLAY would be used to play the audio section of a disc starting at a given location, and STOP PLAY would end audio playing.

CONCLUSION

In the final analysis, CD-ROM device drivers and their more familiar siblings have more similarities than differences between them. They are initialized in the same manner, they are accessed in basically the same manner (as far as the driver is concerned), and most of the systems issues are handled the same way for each.

For example, the ES:BX registers are used by both MS-DOS and MSCDEX.EXE to pass the far address of the request header when the driver's strategy routine is called. Once the request header has been passed to the strategy routine, it is dispatched to the appropriate subroutine. See Figure 2-11 for sample CD-ROM driver dispatch code.

```
; *** Offsets for cmd buffer ***
            public  drvtbl
drvtbl      label   word            ; Standard DOS device driver
                                    ; functions
            dw      error           ; *INIT (init. handled through
                                    ;  far jump
            dw      error           ; MEDIA CHECK
            dw      error           ; GET BPB
            dw      ioctl$i         ; *IOCTL INPUT
            dw      error           ; INPUT
            dw      error           ; NON-DESTRUCTIVE INPUT
            dw      error           ; INPUT STATUS
            dw      error           ; *INPUT FLUSH (Nothing for this
                                    ;  controller to do)
            dw      error           ; OUTPUT
            dw      error           ; OUTPUT WITH VERIFY
            dw      error           ; OUTPUT STATUS
            dw      error           ; OUTPUT FLUSH
            dw      ioctl$o         ; *IOCTL OUTPUT
            dw      devopen         ; *DEVICE OPEN
            dw      devclose        ; *DEVICE CLOSE
            dw      error           ; REMOVABLE MEDIA
            dw      error           ; OUTPUT UNITL BUSY
            public  drvtbl2
drvtbl2     label   word            ; Extended CD ROM device driver
                                    ; functions
            dw      read$           ; *READ LONG
            dw      error           ; reserved
            dw      pfetch$         ; *READ LONG PREFETCH
            dw      seek$           ; *SEEK
            dw      play$           ; *PLAY (for extended drivers)
            dw      stop$           ; *STOP (for extended drivers)
            dw      error           ; WRITE LONG
            dw      error           ; WRITE LONG NON-BLOCKING
            dw      error           ; WRITE LONG VERIFY

            public  ioi_tbl
ioi_tbl     label   word            ; IOCTL INPUT subfunctions
            dw      ret_addr        ; IOI_ret_addr
            dw      loc_head        ; IOI_loc_head
            dw      error           ; IOI_ioquery
            dw      error           ; IOI_err_status
            dw      rd_drv          ; IOI_rd_drv_bytes
            dw      dev_stat        ; IOI_dev_status
            dw      sect_size       ; IOI_ret_sectsize
            dw      vol_size        ; IOI_ret_volsize
            dw      media_changed   ; IOI_media_changed
            dw      audio_diskinfo  ; IOI_audio_diskinfo
            dw      audio_trackinfo ; IOI_audio_trackinfo
            dw      audio_qchaninfo ; IOI_audio_qchaninfo
            dw      error           ; IOI_audio_subinfo
            dw      upc_code        ; IOI_upc_code

            public  ioo_tbl
ioo_tbl     label   word            ; IOCTL OUTPUT sub-functions
            dw      eject           ; IOO_eject_disc
            dw      lock            ; IOO_lock_door
            dw      reset_drv       ; IOO_reset_drv
            dw      error           ; IOO_set_audio_param
            dw      wr_drv          ; IOO_wr_drv_bytes
            PAGE
; *** Device strategy routine ***
            public  strat
strat       proc    far
            mov     word ptr cs:[reqhdr],bx
            mov     word ptr cs:[reqhdr+2],es
            ret
strat       endp

; *** Device interrupt handler ***
            public  devint
devint      proc    far
; save registers
            push    ax              ; (1)
            push    bx              ; (2)
            push    cx              ; (3)
            push    dx              ; (4)
            push    si              ; (5)
            push    di              ; (6)
            push    ds              ; (7)
            push    es              ; (8)

            lds     bx,cs:[reqhdr]  ; dx:bx -> req header
            mov     al,ds:rqh_unit[bx] ; (al)= drive number
            mov     cs:drive_num,al    ; Save drive number
            mov     si,offset drvtbl   ; Assume it will be
                                       ; normal
            mov     al,ds:rqh_cmd[bx]  ; Get command in al
            cmp     al,DVRQ_NCMD_MAX   ; Check if normal
                                       ; command
            jbe     normal
            cmp     al,DVRQ_ECMD_MIN   ; Extended command?
            jae     ext                ; Yes
            jmp     error              ; Maybe
```

```
ext:
            cmp     al,DVRQ__EMCD_MAX  ; Extended command?
            jbe     ext2               ; Yes
            jmp     error              ; No
ext2:
            sub     al,DVRQ_ECMD_MIN   ; Convert to offset
                                       ; into table
            mov     si,offset drvtbl2  ; get address of
                                       ; table
normal:
            cbw
            shl     ax,1               ; Change to index
                                       ; into command table
            add     si,ax
            cmp     ax,0               ; Init. command?
            jz      init_this_dvd      ; Yes
                                       ; No
init_already_done:
            jmp     word ptr cs:[si]   ; dispatch to command
init_this_dvd:
            cmp     cs:init_dvd,0      ; Device driver init.
                                       ; yet?
            mov     cs:init_dvt,1      ; (Set the flag)
            jnz     init_already_done  ; Yes
                                       ; No
            jmp     far ptr doint      ; Perform the
                                       ; initialization
; *** IOCTL OUTPUT command handler ***
            public  ioctl$o
ioctl$o:
            mov     si,offset ioo_tbl
            mov     dl,IOO_cmd_max
            jmp     short ioctl

; *** IOCTL INPUT command handler ***
            public  ioctl$i
ioctl$i:
            mov     si,offset ioi_tbl
            mov     dl,IOI_cmd_max
            jmp     short ioctl
ioctl:
            les     di,ds:ioctl_xfer[bx]
            mov     al,es:[di]
            inc     di                 ; Skip past command
                                       ; code
            cmp     al,dl
            jbe     iolegal
            jmp     error
iolegal:
            cbw
            shl     ax,1
            add     si,ax
            jmp     word ptr cs:[si]   ; Dispatch to command
                       :
```

Figure 2-11. Sample dispatch code for a CD-ROM device driver

The combination of the front-end MSCDEX.EXE program and the low-level CD-ROM device drivers has the potential to make CD-ROM technology an integral part of the familiar MS-DOS personal computing world. All that remains is for developers to begin building applications to take advantage of this new environment.

Reprinted from the *Microsoft Systems Journal* by special permission. Copyright © Microsoft Corporation.

The Impact of CD-ROM XA

By Takashi Sugiyama

[Takashi Sugiyama predicts that the introduction of CD-ROM XA will have a broad impact on the development of the CD-ROM and CD-I industries. By freeing developers and publishers of target-system concerns, CD-ROM XA will stimulate the development of audio and graphic resource libraries and will facilitate the introduction of a new category of interactive multimedia CD-ROM applications.]

One of the most fascinating aspects of the CD-ROM business is its ability to provide unique opportunities for people from different industries, as well as countries, to work jointly to achieve a common goal. This kind of multilateral cooperation distinguishes CD-ROM from any other data storage or distribution medium available to date.

CD-ROM Extended Architecture (CD-ROM XA), announced jointly by Philips, Sony, and Microsoft in August 1988 is another significant step in further promoting such cross-industry cooperation, which is so essential for interactive multimedia applications development. CD-ROM XA is intended to provide a common platform for audio (and, eventually, graphic-image) resources, irrespective of target hardware or software environment, so that such resources can be efficiently distributed and shared as necessary to produce effective multimedia applications.

BACKGROUND OF CD-ROM XA

In looking back on the short history of CD-ROM development, it becomes immediately obvious that a series of standardization efforts played a significant role.

Very fast worldwide acceptance of Compact Disc Digital Audio, which was announced in the fall of 1982, is itself a product of successful standardization. Any compact disc purchased anywhere in the world is guaranteed to play on any compact disc player. Such compatibility is a must for successful consumer products. The fundamental concept of the Compact-Disc Interactive (CD-I) standard, which was first announced in 1986, resides in this philosophy of guaranteed worldwide compatibility of consumer products.

On the other hand, the CD-ROM format was announced in 1983 as a peripheral device format for computer products for which certain standards already existed. The important concept behind the CD-ROM format is to leave as much freedom as possible (without violating the fundamental physical characteristics of the compact disc format), rather than to lay down rigid specifications. Setting a standard almost always helps to provide wider acceptance of a new technology, but it can also act as an obstacle if it is set prematurely, preventing free competition and development of new ideas. The Yellow Book is a standard that lays down the minimum set of specifications necessary to support CD-ROM development in the computer industry.

After the initial development phase of CD-ROM, it became apparent that some type of standard for logical file format would help further growth of the market and be beneficial for all parties involved in the CD-ROM business. Hence came the High Sierra Format, which later became the basis of International Standard Organization ISO-9660. This standard was quickly followed by the MS-DOS CD-ROM Extensions, which made it possible to handle the large capacity of CD-ROM in a predominantly MS-DOS environment. These standards have greatly helped the recent growth of the CD-ROM industry.

In fact, there existed another standard in CD-ROM, namely Red Track audio (Compact Disc Digital Audio.) Until recently, this was the one and only commonly accepted standard for handling audio in CD-ROM. Even though the sound quality is certainly better than anything personal computer users have so far been able to experience, in reality few computer applications require such high-fidelity sound. Red Track audio also has an inherent restriction, in that no data can be retrieved from the CD-ROM while audio sectors are being played back.

With the advent of the interactive multimedia concept in the personal computer and CD-ROM industries, there has been a growing desire for standardized mid-fidelity audio that can be interleaved into a data stream on CD-ROM. The CD-I standard is born with such capabilities because its intended use lies mainly in the area of interactive multimedia applications. Unlike graphics, for which a number of significant standards already exist, there has been no standardization of audio, let alone interleaved audio, in the computer industry. It is apparent that a lot of

A PARADIGM FOR STANDARDS

In our high-tech world, we're confronted with non-standards every day. We have incompatible disk formats on our computers, incompatible plugs connecting our serial ports, telecommunication links with incompatible baud, and keyboards with incompatible layouts. When you find yourself trying to make a technology investment that won't be obsolete in a few years, ask the following questions:

Is there a standard that more than one company supports?

If the answer is no, prepare to have your investment be obsolete in less than a year.

What problem will this standard solve for me/my profession?

The answer should include "the ability to integrate data from unexpected sources, and exchange data with others using different hardware."

Why does a standard solve the problem?

It should reduce the need to select the "right" software or hardware up front, allowing for improvements in the performance and functionality of the software without affecting previously created data.

How does this standard address future requirements, given my predictions for the next five to ten years of use of the product?

Is future-proof a feature? How will the problem look different in a few years? How will manufacturers be able to extend the standard to accommodate new requirements in an upwardly compatible fashion?

By Greg Riker. From *Hypermedia Guide*. Copyright © 1988 by Mix Publications, Inc.

people, not only in the computer industry but also in interactive multimedia applications development, can benefit by the standardization of such mid-fidelity audio, especially interleaved audio. Is there a way to realize such standardization without sacrificing the beauty of the worldwide compatibility of CD-I? CD-ROM XA is the answer.

CD-ROM XA AS A "BRIDGE" FORMAT

CD-ROM XA can be thought of as a bridge format between CD-ROM and CD-I. It provides a de facto standard for the use of interleaved audio and, eventually, graphics in the Yellow Book environment, based on the specification defined in the Green Book for CD-I. In fact, making use of the multiple boot sectors of CD-ROM, it is possible to design a multimedia disc with common audio, graphics, text, and data resources to run on various suitably equipped systems. In essence, CD-ROM XA gives more freedom to software publishers as far as their target system is concerned.

BROADENS MARKET

The main impact of CD-ROM XA is in this freedom it provides. It can also be said that CD-ROM XA broadens the market opportunities for software publishers. For example, an application designed for CD-ROM XA in the MS-DOS environment can be made playable on future CD-I players sharing the same audio and graphics resources, or vice versa. It used to be necessary to determine the target system first in order to start an interactive multimedia development. It is still true to some extent, even with CD-ROM XA, but now it is possible to start designing the application conceptually and begin acquiring or accumulating audio and graphical resources immediately, leaving the decision of what target systems to play on until a later stage of development. Another way of putting this is to say that it should become possible to treat these resources

TAKASHI SUGIYAMA

Home: Yokohama, Japan
Job: Assistant Manager, PC Systems Division, Sony Corp.
Quote: *"CD-ROM will become the key factor of the 'personal information tools' of the near future."*

as objects whose characteristics are independent of the target systems.

IMPACT OF INTERLEAVED AUDIO

One of the key enabling technologies in the CD-ROM XA specification is ADPCM (Adaptive Delta Pulse Code Modulation) audio. Audio data is compressed with an encoding system in accordance with an algorithm specified in the Green Book. Because compressed data requires less space on the disc, yet the disc rotates at a constant linear velocity, there are unused sectors between compressed audio sectors. (In the case of Level B Stereo, only one in every four sectors are used for audio.) These leftover sectors can be used to store other data that are, in effect, interleaved with the audio data.

With interleaved audio, data can be retrieved while audio is played back in real time. Interleaved audio used in this way allows creation of more interactive applications. No longer do you have to wait for the graphics data to be fully

> *Now it is possible to start designing the application conceptually and begin acquiring or accumulating audio and graphical resources immediately, leaving the decision of what target systems to play on until a later stage of development.*

loaded into memory before audio can be played back. By interleaving graphics data with ADPCM audio data, for example, a user can get near-instant audio feedback at the click of a mouse or the push of a button, and loading of graphics data can take place while audio is played back. Even though the screen itself may remain unchanged for a moment, depending on how the application handles the graphics or textual data, immediate audio feedback gives the user an immediate sense of interactivity.

It is also possible to interleave several sources of audio data, or any other data for that matter, on the same track and to select a desired channel on the fly. There are many other ways of making use of interleaved audio, and it is up to the imaginations of applications producers to make full use of the capabilities of interleaved audio. [*For more information, see "Audio, CD-ROM, and CD-ROM XA" in Part 4.*]

COSTS ASSOCIATED WITH RESOURCES

Interactive multimedia applications typically require large amounts of audio and graphical resources. The cost associated with creation or acquisition of such resources is thought to be one of the most significant factors in any interactive multimedia project. With the introduction of CD-ROM XA, it is hoped that such costs will eventually be distributed over a larger number of units. Apart from the fact that applications can be made to run on multiple systems sharing the same resources, it will also become cost effective to form audio and image databases or libraries for public access as well as for internal use by multiple users.

FORMATION OF AUDIO LIBRARIES

Image resources are beginning to be accumulated as databases in some specific application areas, thanks to several standards that have emerged in the industry. One of the side effects of CD-ROM XA will be the formation of audio libraries and databases under a single standard. At the moment, there is no effective way to accumulate or distribute audio resources in a way that makes them suitable for handling by personal computers. With the CD-ROM XA ADPCM audio format, together with the new MS-DOS CD-ROM Extensions, audio segments can now be handled just like document files, without taking up excessive memory space but maintaining relatively high sound quality. For example, Level C Mono sound will take one-sixteenth the memory space of Red Track stereo audio. Considering the tradeoff between the memory requirement, sound fidelity, and cost of hardware, ADPCM is one of the most efficient algorithms available today. Like clip art libraries, clip sound libraries can become available on—what else—CD-ROM.

COSTS ASSOCIATED WITH HARDWARE

Another cost factor associated with CD-ROM XA is, of course, the hardware component. One of the reasons why the CD-ROM market has not become as big as everyone had hoped is often said to be the relatively high cost of drives. Drive manufacturers explain that the small volume of sales expected from the relatively small number of applications discs available do not justify lowering the price, but this is a typical chicken-and-egg situation. As history proves, setting a standard is one effective means of breaking away from such a situation, and the CD-ROM XA standard is one more step toward doing just that.

In addition, CD-ROM XA will hopefully stimulate a new category of interactive multimedia CD-ROM applications that will emerge as successful products, expanding the CD-ROM market as a whole and hence enabling the hardware price to come down further.

Interactive multimedia applications are only beginning to emerge, as are various forms of optical media. CD-ROM XA is a major step toward further accelerating the growth of these emerging industries. CD-ROM is, and will remain, the most inexpensive medium by far for delivering the huge amounts of information required for such applications. Every single one of us should be able to benefit from this development in the near future. An interactive system that greets you with "Good Morning, Dr. Chandra," may come into your hands well before 2001.

[Tagashi Sugiyama is Assistant Manager of Sony Corporation's PC Systems Division, where for the past five years he has helped plan new products and systems for personal computers. Sugiyama joined Sony in 1978, and has also worked on projects related to portable u-matic video tape recorders and digital video tape recorders.]

"XA" EXPANDS CD-ROM HORIZONS

The rapidly expanding CD-ROM industry received a major endorsement on August 30 [*1988*] with the announcement of the CD-ROM XA standard. This extended CD-ROM format, named CD-ROM Extended Architecture, incorporates much of the audio and graphics technology from the CD-I format. Jointly developed by Philips, Sony, and Microsoft, CD-ROM XA is intended to serve as a bridge between CD-ROM and CD-I.

Perhaps more importantly, this announcement confirms the growing momentum of CD-ROM in the face of new technologies. In recent months Tandy, Sanyo, Maxtor and others have garnered the headlines with press releases touting the new storage products they have under development. However, even if these were deliverable today, none can begin to compete with the cost, capacity, and distribution strengths of CD-ROM.

CD-ROM is now able to address the growing demands for multi-media applications on PCs. These applications require not only text and data, but also compressed sound, graphics, still pictures, and eventually animation. The two releases of CD-ROM XA will define these capabilities consistent with ISO 9660 and other CD-ROM standards; and unlike CD-I, CD-ROM XA is not dependent on specific operating systems or CPU's.

For CD-ROM publishers, the XA format offers tremendous opportunities. In many cases, standardized audio and graphics will allow publishers to add more value to their existing products. With up to 16 hours of interleaved audio capacity, CD-ROM XA will rapidly open up markets in education and training. In addition, publishers can develop multi-media products NOW that are compatible with any suitably equipped PC. These same discs can later be played on CD-I systems when they become available!

The message is clear and the news is good. CD-ROM is not only a dynamic format, but also the successful platform upon which future optical technologies are building. The growing CD-ROM development infrastructure is the core of the optical publishing revolution.

By Fred Meyer. From *CD Publisher News*. Copyright © 1988 by Meridian Data, Inc.

CD-I

THE DEVELOPMENT OF CD-I
By Gaston A. J. Bastiaens

**COMPACT DISC INTERACTIVE:
A DREAM AND A REALITY**
By Bernard J. Luskin

The Development of CD-I

By Gaston A. J. Bastiaens

[Gaston Bastiaens, Director of Philips Electronics Interactive Media Systems, was a natural choice to write this overview article about CD-I technology and its potential in the fields of entertainment, education, and information dissemination. Bastiaens predicts that CD-I will come into its own as a successful industry sometime in the nineties.]

Compact disc is one of the most successful products in the history of consumer electronics. Of the many reasons for this success the following three are the most important:

1. High-quality sound recording and reproduction that make it the world standard in the hardware and software industries.

2. The properties of the CD system: compact size, use of digital encoding, clarity and accuracy of sound, fast access, massive storage capacity, usefulness in many different environmental conditions, and so on.

3. A comprehensive and appealing disc catalog.

A successful product in the optical family is CD-ROM, now mainly used as a computer peripheral for fast retrieval of text and data. CD-ROM offers the computer world the enormous storage capacity of compact disc combined with the ability to program both the data and the controlling computer, whichever may be required by the individual application.

The CD-ROM standard issued by Sony and Philips in June 1985 defined the physical parameters of the actual disc—identical to that of CD Audio—as well as the actual data structure of the information stored on the disc.

Another feature of the CD-ROM standard is the definition of an alternative encoding technique that ensures error-free recording and reproduction of all data. This reliability is particularly important for critical data, including both computer programs and numeric data used in the computer and in the office environment.

While compatibility is not such a critical requirement in the computer world, there is nevertheless strong pressure from publishers for

GASTON BASTIAENS

Home: Eindhoven, The Netherlands
Job: Director, Philips Electronics Interactive Media Systems
Quote: *"The success of CD-I depends on the attractiveness and variety of available software. Together with the electronics industry, software providers will make CD-Interactive a successful and viable business in the nineties."*

interchangeability of CD-ROM discs. There is also a demand from the PC world for the addition of a standardized format for images and sound. For this reason Philips, together with Sony and Microsoft, proposed a new format—CD-ROM XA (Extended Architecture). This new format will meet the market needs, at the same time making it possible for CD-ROM XA discs to be produced in an MS-DOS environment and also be played on a CD-I (Compact-Disc Interactive) player.

THE CD-I DIFFERENCE

CD-I combines audio, video, text, and data into a single digital system. It uses the established 12-centimeter format of CD-Audio discs to store not only high-quality sound, but also pictures and graphics, text, and data, all interleaved together. Text and data are the types of information most widely used in the business and educational environments, but the methods of presenting and using this information can be enhanced by the addition of sound and pictures. When interactivity is added to the possibilities of moving video, the result, CD-I, becomes a powerful tool for training, sales, and presentation of information.

CD-I addresses three main areas of applications: entertainment, education, and information. Examples of software programs suited to CD-I include video-enhanced music, games, reference books, self-help materials, sports productions, children's programs, tourist and trail guides, and all manner of educational programs.

The CD-I standard includes encoding methods that enhance the delivery of sound and offer new video presentation. To reduce the space needed for sound and thus make room for other information, CD-I uses a new digital encoding technique called Adaptive Delta Pulse Code Modulation (ADPCM). Three levels of ADPCM are foreseen for sound—the highest level, A, being equal to the best high-fidelity stereo sound, but occupying only 50 percent of the disc, and the lowest level, C, being equal to speech level and using only 6 percent of the disc in mono. In addition to the general space savings provided by ADCPM, CD-I makes economical use of required sound space by allowing the audio channels to be used in parallel—for example, for different languages. Video program material, as well as text, data, and control-program code, can then be stored on the remainder of the disc.

For video information too, new digital encoding techniques achieve the fullest possible economy in recording, depending on the type of pictures required. Delta-YUV encoding is used for quality still pictures and for full-motion video inserts, while the limited number of colors needed for full-motion cartoons enables color lookup table and run-length encoding techniques to be applied. This encoding reduces the information space needed to store one fullscreen image from just over 300 KB for an uncompressed picture to 108 KB for a DYUV image and only 5 KB to 10 KB for an animated cartoon image. A 12-centimeter CD-I disc can thus contain more than an hour's worth of continuous full-screen, full-motion animation and a digital quality sound track. For user-manipulated graphics, every picture element, or pixel, is encoded in RGB 5:5:5, with 5 bits per color, making more than 32,000 color variations possible.

CD-I handles text just as easily as sound and video. Because CD-I generally tells and shows its story, text is usually used to support the main audio/video message. Text and controlware—the application program that runs the disc—take up little space in the disc track.

When played back, the interleaved data, sound, pictures, and text of CD-I are separated into the various decoding paths—audio, video, text, program data—in a continuous realtime process. The 68000 series microprocessor used in the CD-I player then assembles and synchronizes the various information types to present the program via the TV screen and the audio under user control. The CD-I operating system, CD-RTOS, and the application program stored on the CD-I disc, ensure that this all takes place smoothly.

CONCLUSION

The digital ADPCM format made possible the first revolution of the digital era. In terms of quality of sound, we have attained remarkable fidelity with compact disc.

The same will happen with video; the digital encoding techniques have prepared CD-I for this development, and the system can be adapted for IDTV/EDTV and HDTV. Future developments in video compression, together with higher bit rates on the disc, will develop the moving-video possibilities further. New developments in font reproduction also give text presentation an improved quality on the screen.

Of course, developments in technology will continue into the future. From a technological point of view, a great deal is possible.

HIGH-DEFINITION TELEVISION AND INTERACTIVE MULTIMEDIA

The ultimate market (for HDTV)...is more likely to be the larger and somewhat futuristic concept of the Home Information Center from which a consumer might access information from computers, optical discs, video and audio....

Multiple fiber optic ports in homes of the future would allow a child to do homework on a computer in one room while members of the family in other rooms use a computer to retrieve a library manuscript, watch a HDTV-quality movie (perhaps in three-dimensions) on a wall-sized thin screen and interactively dialogue with a professor delivering a televised lecture across the country.

By Tom Brown. Excerpted from "High-Definition Television: High-Powered Debate Rages" in the *Seattle Times*.

Like compact disc, CD-I is a software-driven product with broad applications in the fields of entertainment, education, and information. The success of the business depends entirely on the attractiveness and variety of available software, but because the system is based on a world standard, there is a great stimulus for software providers. Together with the electronics industry, they will make CD-Interactive a successful and viable business in the nineties.

[Gaston A. J. Bastiaens is the Director of Philips Electronics Interactive Media Systems, Eindhoven, The Netherlands. He is also Co-Director of the LIM (Limburgse Investeringsmaatschappij). Bastiaens graduated as an engineer from the K.U.L. (Koninklijke Universiteit Leuven).]

Compact Disc Interactive: A Dream and a Reality

By Bernard J. Luskin

[In this article, Bernard Luskin extolls CD-I, claiming that most of the obstacles facing the technology at its inception have been overcome. The way is clear for the development of affordable home interactive applications that will open up whole new areas of consumer experience.]

We are poised in 1989—three short years after the official announcement launching development of the Green Book specification at the Microsoft CD-ROM conference in 1986—on the threshold of a consumer product revolution. The interactive optical disc is emerging as a major means of access to entertainment, enrichment, and enjoyment in the home. Optical discs have propelled themselves through the 1980s, gaining impetus as they have been accepted into the consumer and professional marketplaces. The optical disc is evolving through a series of advancements, now gaining in sophistication of content as well as simplicity and diversity of use. We are preparing to enter a new era of disc technology and marketplace acceptance.

CD-I is clearly a revolutionary laser optical product, combining the familiarity of the digital audio disc with visual elements and with computer data to permit a breakthrough to easy-to-use interactivity.

Ever since the highly successful consumer launch of CD audio and the later emergence of CD-ROM, visionaries have been working their imaginations overtime, anticipating sales figures for products yet to be. CD-I is moving through this dream into the compact-disc family, and reality appears inevitably on the horizon. Today, the visionaries of CD-I have every right to be optimistic. The major obstacles have been overcome, and both the hardware and software technologies are here.

CD-I's strengths have been presented repeatedly. Primary on the list is the CD-I standard, the worldwide approach to title and market development. There is no VHS versus Beta issue here, no NTSC versus PAL, no MS-DOS versus OS-9. There is simply CD-I, the world's first attempt at a ubiquitous multimedia, interactive system for the home consumer.

Clearly, CD-I's capabilities put an enormous range of features at the disposal of CD-I designers. The numerous methods of creating and encoding material allow designers the flexibility necessary to create a diverse and exciting catalog of titles.

A major strength of CD-I is in the area of strategic marketing. Rather than being competitive with information-delivery systems currently on the market or anticipated to arrive, CD-I offers a twenty-first century approach. The "transparent player theory" guarantees that the consumer need not become bogged down in technical lingo to fully understand, utilize, and appreciate CD-I titles. Yes, there is a powerful 68000-family computer inside the CD-I player. But operation is intuitive and software driven; it is not predicated on a consumer's infatuation (or frustration) with a piece of machinery.

A number of obstacles are now being overcome as CD-I moves toward retail shelves. These obstacles are presented here in descending order of importance:

1. Component skills. The most critical obstacle to development of a "critical mass" of CD-I titles has been a dearth of individuals with appropriate skills. We must continue to develop and implement training methods that expand the pool of experienced CD-I designers, programmers, and others. American Interactive Media now has a Producers Group, in which all members are program developers.

BERNARD LUSKIN

Home: Santa Monica, California
Job: President, American Interactive Media
Quote: *"CD-ROM, CD-ROM-XA and CD-I will merge in the future with optical disc being the carrier of choice. CD will be to the 21st century what the book was to the 20th century."*

The group shares information and promotes a consistent approach to CD-I title development. Examples of companies and products represented in the group are Grolier Encyclopedia, the Smithsonian Institution, Berlitz Language Centers, Parker Brothers, Spinnaker, ICOM Simulations, Random House, Time-Life Books, and Capitol Video, to mention just a few.

2. Money. Prior to the emergence of a mature authoring environment, it was difficult to estimate production costs of titles and to plan for appropriate funding. In the early days of development, there was also the question of CD-I's viability in the consumer marketplace. Now that these issues are settling, financing of titles has become a more established process. Co-producers and co-developers are investing in varying degrees to ensure that they will be part of the consumer launch of CD-I.

3. Attitudes in the development community. As an unproven technology, CD-I suffered from early doubts about its validity. Once discs began to be demonstrated in 1988, reservations abated and an energized environment emerged.

4. Incentives. The lack of an existing player base was instrumental in creating a scenario in which return on investment of time, energy, and money was difficult to project. As the CD-I worldwide marketing plan has been finalized and the mass-marketing approach has been underscored, the incentive has increased. The players and the authoring platforms are here. Focus-group results are positive. Tools are being developed, and CD-I discs are now seen regularly in demonstration.

5. Documentation. Inadequate and inarticulate documentation of CD-I production methodology, particularly related to title-specific issues, was a direct result of the immaturity of the production environment. American Interactive Media has made great efforts to document methods, tools, and other elements of successful title creation in an attempt to allow others to benefit from the experience. Understanding of the software technology of CD-I is now increasing.

6. Communication gap. Communication of information and distribution of functional materials are closely related and are tied to documentation. Improved communication is already apparent in these areas.

7. Costs and results. Early cost models were based on numerous costly assumptions, again based on an immature production environment. Commercial authoring systems and sophisticated authoring tools are now in the marketplace, and soon a CD-I interpreter will significantly derease cost.

8. Personnel combinations. CD-I's power is that of a "best-of" media combination. The creation of successful CD-I discs requires the efforts of a team of producers, directors, visual and audio artists and technicians, interactive and multimedia designers, and subject-matter experts in a variety of fields. Publishers have been putting together teams of people with such diverse backgrounds for three years now.

9. Software sharing. Among the producers of CD-I noted earlier, sharing of methods, tools, and plans has now become common.

10. Distribution. Record store? Bookstore? Computer software outlet? Toy store? Electronics retailer? Direct mail? The question of where CD-I will have the most success in the marketplace becomes moot when one develops a plan that is responsive to the nature of the consumer marketplace. In fact, CD-I belongs in all of these outlets and will be sold there through the efforts of educated salespeople, through high-impact, hands-on demonstration, and through powerful promotion.

PolyGram International, now one of the largest entertainment software comanies in the world, has taken the lead in software distribution, and Magnavox, along with numerous other player marketers, is leading the way in the hardware arena.

11. Copyright laws. Copyright laws governing usage of music, programming code, and other elements of a CD-I disc have been worked through. Related issues, such as mechanical rates for music, are also being addressed in greater depth, and standards are emerging for the CD-I industry.

12. Retailer attitudes. Just another piece of equipment? Just another disc? Hardly.

CD-I is easily demonstrable as a valuable home-entertainment and education system. The emerging CD-I marketing plan will provide for dealer incentives that will go a long way toward removing doubt. The depth and quality of titles will do the rest.

13. Consumer attitudes. Consumer resistance to CD-I will be inconsequential. After all, here is a system that begins by playing one's favorite audio discs and expands to entertain and educate the whole family. The time is now, and all research points to readiness in the consumer market.

14. Consumer motivations. Consumer motivations are threefold: to correct a deficiency (by teaching a skill effectively and enjoyably), to gain personal growth, and to enable self-actualization. These principles underpin the essence of the psychological attraction of this type of product.

The perception of CD-I among consumers will be that of a technology that offers a wealth of immediately accessible knowledge and enjoyment. The experience of controlling one's own programming will enthrall today's couch potatoes by subtly encouraging engagement.

Titles in the areas of games, children's programming, music, enrichment/information, and so on will attract:

- The succeeder.
- The striver.
- The overachiever.
- The social climber.
- The status seeker.
- The technophile.
- The guilty parent.
- The young child.
- The latchkey child.
- The preteen.
- The rainbow chaser.
- The audiophile.
- The hobbyist.
- The pleasure seeker.
- The career changer.
- The childcare worker.
- The novelty seeker.
- The self actualizer.
- And more....

We are in a new era of software creation, with color television screens instead of green CRTs, uncrowded and appealing screen designs, new uses of scrolling and overlays, multiple planes, new types of viewports and menus to access and organize information, diverse fonts and font sizes, sophisticated graphics, high-quality screen resolution, multiple panes, and compact disc digital audio. These features offer a library of techniques never before available in an affordable home interactive system.

Software that lets the user set the pace and control the sequencing and that offers various steering alternatives and menus you never saw on your computer now opens broad vistas for the creation of a new consumer experience.

New technology means new rules. Emerging values, tastes, and interests will be the characteristics of the 1990s. The values of a new generation of Americans are reshaping virtually every product and service. As we move into the final decade of the twentieth century, we enter the era of the optical disc as the carrier of choice for the twenty-first century.

CD-I, the eclectic vision of software dreamers for thirty years, is now an emerging reality.

[Bernard J. Luskin is the President and Chief Operating Officer of American Interactive Media (AIM). Formerly President

of both Orange Coast College and of Coastline Community College in California, past Chairman of the Board of Directors of the American Association of Community Colleges, and former Vice President of KOCE-TV, Luskin has also held faculty positions at numerous universities, written seven books, and is a recipient of the UCLA Doctoral Alumni Association award for distinguished leadership in education.]

DVI

THE COMMERCIALIZATION OF DVI TECHNOLOGY
By Richard A. Stauffer

DVI AND ITS APPLICATIONS
By Sandra K. Morris
and Paula S. Zimmerman

The Commercialization of DVI Technology

By Richard A. Stauffer

[In this article, Richard Stauffer reveals Intel's game plan for DVI. Acquired in 1988 from General Electric, which had purchased RCA, developer of DVI technology, in 1987, DVI will probably be available as consumer-priced products in 1990. Commercial software development kits will be available in 1989 so that developers can produce applications in time for Intel's planned market rollout.]

In October 1988, Intel Corporation bought Digital Video Interactive (DVI) technology from General Electric. This purchase put in place the second important element in establishing DVI as the standard for CD-ROM-based interactive video. The first element was the technological breakthrough that allowed 72 minutes of full-screen, full-motion digital video and audio to be stored on a standard CD-ROM and to be played back on a standard PC equipped with DVI. This breakthrough was first announced when GE/RCA showed DVI at the Second Microsoft CD-ROM Conference in 1987. Now, with the Intel acquisition, DVI has a corporate backer with commitment to the PC market, the capabilities to manufacture advanced architectures such as DVI at low cost, and the strategic positioning to form the alliances necessary to build a standard. These are the final elements required to establish DVI as a broadly adopted platform for interactive video and audio products.

The years 1989 and 1990 will be important for CD-ROM markets, multimedia applications, and DVI technology. We believe the markets will evolve in three stages. In the first stage, DVI will penetrate emerging vertical markets currently served by more expensive, less flexible analog videodiscs. Over the next year, we expect to see the rollout of several major DVI CD ROM projects in vertical markets such as training,

RICHARD A. STAUFFER

Home: Atlanta, Georgia
Job: Marketing Manager, Intel Princeton Operation
Quote: *"DVI technology extends the functionality of CD-ROMs, allowing them to provide full-motion video, high-resolution stills, and audio with meaningful capacity. These added capabilities will allow CD-ROMs to penetrate a much broader set of markets. In 1990 many multimedia CD-ROM applications will be in full rollout in vertical markets such as travel, shopping, training, and public information. PC companies will begin offering CD-ROM-based audio and video capability in a fully integrated way, and the first desktop software incorporating interactive video will be introduced. Several consumer electronics companies will be developing and announcing the first hardware and software interactive video products targeted for the home."*

shopping, travel, real estate, and public information.

In the second stage, DVI technology will be incorporated as a standard component in personal computers. This will allow DVI PCs to be used in horizontal business and education applications as a standard way to access video and audio information on the desktop from CD-ROMs. For example, an analyst could get audio and video instruction on how to use a spreadsheet program through a video window while using the program. Or a company's annual report could be delivered on CD-ROM with motion video about the company and with animated grahics and charts, all accessible through the analyst's desktop PC. We expect this stage to begin in 1990.

In the third stage, DVI-based players will be used in the home for entertainment, education, and information. We can imagine an application in which the user simulates playing the great golf courses of the world or one in which a young child learns the alphabet through an interactive word book. By 1990, there will be many companies involved in full-scale development of hardware and software products for this market, for introduction in late 1990 or 1991.

Since its acquisition of DVI, Intel has put in place its plan for commercializing DVI technology. As mentioned earlier, the primary goal is to establish DVI as the standard technology for digital, full-screen, full-motion video in the PC environment.

THREE DVI PHASES

Intel's rollout plan has three phases. Phase One is best described as *Prepare for the Market*. In this phase, DVI will literally be moving from laboratory to marketplace. Intel has recently established a new operation in Princeton, New Jersey, called Intel's Princeton Operation. This operation will act as the primary location for developing DVI technology. Intel also attracted the DVI team to join in continuing the development of DVI. During Phase One, the team will move from the David Sarnoff Research Center to new Intel facilities in the Princeton area.

The Princeton Operation will also be completing development and testing during Phase One. The initial DVI product is a development kit that consists of a set of hardware and software that allows developers to produce DVI applications. The kit contains three basic boards with four piggyback boards that fill a total of four slots in a PC/AT or compatible computer. It also contains system software and authoring tools. DVI system software currently runs on Microsoft's MS-DOS operating system. Development kits have been in developers' hands for several months, and a number of companies have begun creating DVI applications in a beta test program. In the first quarter of 1989, we will expand this program.

Phase One will be completed with the introduction of fully tested DVI development kits in the second quarter of 1989.

Phase Two of DVI commercialization is *Implement the Strategy*. This phase will coincide more or less with the calendar year of 1989. First, we will be turning DVI into a low-cost, application-delivery platform by reducing costs of the powerful VDP chip set. The current VDP chip set, which is the real heart of DVI, is being custom designed with Intel tools to achieve the lowest possible cost. This custom-designed chip set will be completed near the end of 1989 and will be manufactured in volume by Intel for large-scale rollout in 1990. We will also be consolidating the basic three-board set into a single board. Both cost-reduction activities are currently under way.

The Princeton DVI Operation will work with key hardware and software companies to define a standard for computer and consumer electronics applications. The standard will provide a stable platform for long-term development of a large market in interactive video products. Two key players, Lotus and Microsoft, have already made statements about their participation in and support of this standard-setting process.

This standard will stimulate activity among independent software and hardware vendors worldwide. The Princeton DVI Operation will also encourage development of a large catalog of software titles to be available for Phase Three.

Phase Three of DVI commercialization, is what we term *Major Market Rollout*. This is expected to occur in 1990, coinciding with the completion of cost-reduced component and board technology. At that time, we expect to see the launch of a large and profitable industry providing interactive video products for training, education, information, design, and entertainment.

[Richard Stauffer is Marketing Manager for Intel's new Princeton Operation, the group responsible for commercializing DVI technology. In this role, Stauffer promotes application development for DVI technology and markets DVI to PC companies, consumer electronics companies, and system integrators. Prior to his current position, Stauffer managed GE's internal DVI Technology Venture.]

DVI and Its Applications

By Sandra K. Morris and Paula S. Zimmerman

[Sandra Morris's and Paula Zimmerman's enthusiasm for DVI technology is evident in this article, which describes some of the DVI applications currently being developed. After rollout, they anticipate that DVI will find its way into many markets in the commercial, education, and consumer arenas.]

March 2, 1987...Seattle, Washington... Microsoft's Second Annual CD-ROM Conference...a packed house of 1200 industry specialists and press.... The houselights dim and from the darkness the 25-foot projection screen comes to life with a montage of video imagery. The music of Mozart fills the air. All of this comes from a new, all-digital technology: full-screen, full-motion video with high-quality audio, playing from a standard CD-ROM. Then a host of interactive applications, from entertainment and education to training and design, unfurl live from a prototype Digital Video Interactive (DVI) system.

The response is unprecedented for a technical conference. The audience rises to applaud the work of a small group of dedicated scientists from RCA Labs in Princeton, N.J., scientists who have shown them that the future they expected to arrive in 1990, the future of the PC and interactive video, is here.

Computers allow us to stretch our own abilities; they are rich with the freedom that an all-digital environment brings. Video invites us to wonder at the richness and sheer beauty of the sights and sounds of the real world. Both types of communication are highly effective in their own ways. With DVI, these two technologies are united on a PC platform for the first time.

BUILDING BLOCKS OF DVI

DVI technology unites the interactivity of computers with the realism of full-motion video and audio. It is not only the best of both worlds, it is a new world: a world to see and to hear, and a world to transform. In order to accomplish this union, DVI takes images and sounds through three stages. First, they are *transformed* to the digital domain, so that they can be read and addressed by a computer. Next, they are *compressed* down to a size in which they can be stored on a hard disk or on a CD-ROM disc. Finally, they are *decompressed* and displayed in real time as an application is used.

But DVI does not stop with the union of computers and real motion video and audio. DVI also unifies audio, stills, synthetic video, animation, graphics, and text, collecting them in a single low-cost communications medium. The ability to mix and match an endless variety of these "building blocks" opens unlimited possibilities for applications.

The first building block of DVI is *motion video*. Up to 72 minutes of full-screen, full-motion video, with audio, can be stored on a CD-ROM. Using partial-screen video allows more minutes' worth to be stored, for example, at one-half screen, 144 minutes (almost 2 1/2 hours) of video can be stored. DVI compresses motion video at a ratio of more than 100 to 1: Less than 1 percent of the original data needs to be stored to recreate the original video. The image quality has also improved since March 1987 and now is somewhere between VCR and TV quality.

Full color *still images* are another fundamental DVI building block. At a 10 to 1 compression ratio, a developer can put 7000 high-resolution images or 3500 images with 20 seconds of audio describing each image on a CD-ROM. With medium resolution, a CD-ROM can hold up to 40,000 compressed images.

A third building block is *graphics*. The DVI chip set incorporates a very fast graphics processor, executing microcode stored in on-chip RAM at 12.5 million instructions per second. This means that a number of different operations, including video decompression, text, and dynamic graphics overlays, can be applied to each frame.

Last, *audio* is a key element of any multimedia application. DVI offers developers a

SANDRA K. MORRIS

Home: Princeton, New Jersey
Job: Application Market Development Group, Intel Princeton Operation
Quote: *"Being able to deliver all types of information—video, audio, graphics, and text—on a medium that can be widely distributed is a powerful learning tool. It is also a powerful research tool. It allows us to learn a tremendous amount about how people use all types of information to construct ideas and solve problems. The PC can now be used both to provide all of this information and to track the way it is used. As the PC is expanded to deliver all types of information, its capability as a 'laboratory of learning' is also expanded."*

variety of audio qualities ranging from near-AM to better than FM quality. Multiple audio channels can be mixed under software control. For example, volume can be adjusted to produce fade-in and fade-out effects. Audio and video stills can all be digitized and compressed on a DVI development system. Graphics and software can be produced on the development system as well.

A key advantage of DVI is the ability to integrate different types of information and to perform many functions at one time. This is where applications developers can work their own magic, harnessing DVI's power and channeling

PAULA S. ZIMMERMAN

Home: Princeton, New Jersey
Job: Application Market Development and Communications Coordinator, Intel Princeton Operation
Quote: *"By 1990, as digital, real audio, and video become more prevalent in computing, they will help bridge the gap between man and machine, making computers more accessible to people. People will be more comfortable working, learning, and playing in the computer's highly interactive world. 'A day in the life' will be more productive, more instructive, and more fun!"*

it into their own cutting-edge interactive applications. Covering a wide range of markets, the DVI pilot applications first demonstrated in March 1987 proved to be flagships for interactive video applications, capturing the imaginations of several industries from hardware manufacturing to applications development. For the most part, the technical implementation and technical design of the pilot applications were done by the DVI team. Design and production were a shared responsibility, as a well-established understanding of DVI was needed to begin and complete application design for the prototype DVI system. These first research projects helped to define the possibilities of DVI.

DVI PILOT APPLICATIONS

Flight Simulator, developed with Activision (now Mediagenics) and Imagineering, utilized DVI's three-dimensional and real-video texture-mapping capabilities to create landscapes with realistic terrain and buildings. It provides the user with both the full three-dimensional freedom of a computer environment and the realism provided by video texture-mapping. The demonstration of this capability has led to a great deal of interest in DVI-based vehicle simulators of all types. For example, Applied Optical Media is now developing a truck-driver training system for Du Pont Safety Services and the trucking industry. This application is discussed in more detail later.

Design & Decorate, developed by Intel Princeton Operation in conjunction with Videodisc Publishing, Inc. (VPI), is an interior-design and sales tool that creates realistic room designs. It also uses DVI's three-dimensional texture-mapped video capability. This pilot application has won praise within the home furnishings industry and is currently being commercialized through VPI. It has also helped make design and creativity developers more aware of the potential of DVI. Since the development of *Design & Decorate,* for example, Time Arts has ported their Lumena paint program to DVI.

Palenque, jointly developed by Intel Princeton Operation and Bank Street College of Education, is a multimedia educational exploration that uses surrogate travel and a museum motif for a database of images, sound, text, and graphics. Set in the rain forest of Mexico at an ancient Mayan site, this pilot application has spawned a wealth of interest in DVI as a tool for discovery learning and educational research, as well as mapping and travel applications. For example, the photographic technique of using fisheye still images to allow 360° panoramas under user control is already being applied to other DVI applications for surrogate travel.

Sesame Street: Words in the Neighborhood, developed by Intel Princeton Operation and Children's Television Workshop, is an interactive word book for children. It demonstrates DVI's multiple video and audio stream capability.

Ogilvy & Mather, one of the world's largest advertising agencies, has applied the multiple video and audio stream concept to its DVI research tool, which is currently in development.

DVI BETA APPLICATIONS

The DVI Beta program, under way since March 1988, was established to test the development kits before commercial release and to give key developers the opportunity to begin development of DVI applications well before product release. The spirit of the Beta program is one of entrepreneurship and, in many ways, partnership. While each organization participating in the Beta program has independently designed and implemented its own applications, the DVI team has stayed attuned to the organizations' software and hardware needs, assisting in the assurance of successful application development.

The Beta sites represent the first companies to do DVI development independently. They are building on the experiences of the DVI applications team and are continuing to define the design and implementation of DVI applications.

One of the most interesting places to be in the interactive video and personal computer industry in the past two years has been on the receiving end of the industry's response to DVI. There are many applications of DVI that trigger the "Aha!" reflex in groups and individuals searching for ways to solve problems confronting their industry. Our Beta site companies are a group of "Aha!" DVI applications developers. They were selected on the basis of technical strength and on the potential of their imaginative ideas about DVI and its capabilities [*see sidebar on the following page*].

At a 10 to 1 compression ratio, a developer can put 7000 high-resolution images or 3500 images with 20 seconds of audio describing each image on a CD-ROM. With medium resolution, a CD-ROM can hold up to 40,000 compressed images.

DVI AND ITS APPLICATIONS MARKET POTENTIAL

As DVI moves beyond the Beta test phase in 1989, it will find its way into many markets in the commercial, education, and consumer arenas. Many of these markets have received a head start from the DVI pilots and Beta applications, mapping the way for applications design, technical design, production techniques, and interactivity. The following is a summary of some of the key DVI applications markets and where they may be heading as DVI's first products beyond Beta are made available.

Training

Industrial and corporate training companies see in DVI a portable, flexible training system that provides both interactive video and graphics. Training workstations, consisting of a CD-ROM player, a large hard disk and DVI hardware in an IBM AT or compatible computer, or both, can be brought to the work site, thus reducing costs of transporting employees to training centers. Many work sites have an installed base of the necessary hardware and can reduce the costs of buying new equipment even further.

A second advantage for the training market is the amount of storage available on a DVI system as compared to other interactive-video technologies. Training is often complex, requiring more than the current one-half hour per side of laser videodisc. Three-quarters of the space taken up on the videodisc for quarter-screen images is wasted on the videodisc. With DVI, this space is available for more data in the form of video, text, audio, or still images.

DVI also allows some unique training methods. Split-screen capability allows users to compare either still or moving images, side by side. Techniques and procedures for everything from short-order cooking to delicate laboratory procedures can be compared for accuracy and results. High-quality graphics can be combined with video so that a trainee can examine subjects in ways possible only with such realistic synthetic video. Imagine a car-repair training application in which one-quarter of the screen is taken up by a motion-video sequence with audio, demonstrating the removal of a fuel pump. The student can stop the video and examine a realistic three-dimensional model of a

APPLICATIONS BEING DEVELOPED IN THE BETA PROGRAM

One developer, Applied Optical Media Corporation, is creating a *Truck Driver Safety* application for Du Pont Safety Services, a leading provider of high-technology safety-training programs for the industry. This application, installed in a full-size truck cab, simulates driving in highway, road, and loading dock scenarios, using real video from a driver's point-of-view. Views from rearview mirrors are also on the screen during use. DVI hardware and software are used to decompress a wide-angle view using the video from CD-ROM. The portion of the view indicated by the truck's current lane position is then displayed, with the view dynamically "skewed" to keep the horizon relatively fixed. Graphic objects overlaid on the video provide obstacles and simulate conditions such as passing, stopping, or yielding to another vehicle. DVI's unique ability to manipulate motion video can be used in other vehicle simulators as well.

In this instance, DVI provides realistic images, manipulates these images in real time to simulate changes in point of view, and provides real-time graphics overlays. While some or all of these capabilities are available in expensive simulators, DVI has made them all accessible to the trucking industry in a low-cost, standard PC environment.

Arthur Andersen & Co. Consulting Division is using DVI's unique real-time digitizing and compression of video (edit-level video) in its Computer Integrated Manufacturing work. The project focuses on process-improvement strategies that assist clients in gaining and maintaining a competitive edge in productivity. Using DVI's edit-level video, consultants can now capture a video of a manufacturing process, digitize and compress it in real time, and then analyze and recommend improvements. This application also permits the consultant to create summary findings, reports, and action plans. DVI is supporting all these activities in an integrated, PC-based workbench.

The low cost of DVI technology has allowed Cableshare, Inc. to improve its Interactive Television System. Hardware costs of the system are reduced by 80 percent, data speed is improved, and functionality is added by DVI. One application of this system is a real-estate sales tool that allows users to view homes for sale in a particular city on their television sets. Additional information about a particular property, views of additional rooms and the grounds, and the price, can all be chosen by the individual with a touch-tone telephone.

The graphics capability of DVI has been a major point of interest for a number of markets, including training and design. ECC International is combining DVI techniques like three-dimensional graphics, fisheye panorama, and the integration of dynamic video and graphics to create an Air Defense Training system that allows an operator to identify and track fuel pump in a second quarter of the screen, rotating it and viewing its moving parts in order to understand its shape and function. The student can also select a catalog of parts for text information on models or costs of fuel pumps. With DVI, the student can move from interactive motion video to graphics models to a text and picture catalog, all at one workstation. With this same software, the mechanic with DVI in a portable PC can receive on-the-job training in unfamiliar operations.

Retailing

Retailers and wholesalers have also expressed interest in DVI technology for point-of-sale applications. According to Touche-Ross, the installed base of in-store marketing systems will grow from 1500 to 50,000 by 1990. Retail applications that require buyers to configure or design their own purchases are ideal for a system using DVI. Applications for interior design (exemplified by *Design & Decorate*), for landscape design (allowing trees and shrubs to be placed, moved, and "grown" to show plantings as they mature), and for car design (providing an automotive configuration tool on the showroom floor) are examples of the possibilities.

Retailers are well aware of the captivating nature of motion video in advertising. Shopping malls, department stores, hardware stores, and grocery stores have all begun to use video kiosks to interest customers and to inform them about products. Although large volumes of motion

targets through actual terrain. ECC expects DVI to popularize desktop learning centers, supporting applications ranging from language training and cultural orientation to sophisticated electronics systems operations and repair.

Time Arts, Inc., developers of the popular paint package Lumena has also seen DVI as a platform for "the fastest and most natural-to-use PC paint package ever developed." An enhanced version of DVI Lumena is expected to be available to all developers of DVI applications. Time Arts, Inc. also expects DVI to bring dramatic performance improvements to three-dimensional solid modeling and animation.

The combination of motion video, stills, graphics, audio, and text in one compact and powerful environment has been the dream of computer industry visionaries for a number of years. As a proof-of-performance prototype Ogilvy & Mather is designing a multimedia tool to be used by their professionals. This tool is a teaching vehicle to inform, instruct, and educate Ogilvy & Mather professionals investigating consumer trends, motivation, and the influencing media. Information about these topics, including charts and graphs, motion video of focus groups and relevant current events, music, and promotional materials for a particular product can be seamed together by the researcher, who can then either create a presentation or integrate the information to formulate a new campaign. Ogilvy & Mather also sees DVI as a powerful way to sell products and services by way of electronic catalogs, point-of-purchase displays, and simulated shopping environments.

This brief overview is just a sampler of some of the current applications of DVI. Carnegie-Mellon University is creating an educational application for use by software engineers; Bethlehem Steel and Lehigh University are creating training applications for industrial workers; General Dynamics is creating conceptual applications for DoD customers; General Electric's Advanced Technology Laboratories is creating an Advanced Weapons Trainer; the National Geographic Society is planning to use DVI as part of the interactive exhibits in Explorers' Hall; and Murdoch Electronic Publishing is using DVI as a technology platform for its travel system, Jaguar. The features of these applications are as unique and as interesting as the ones described above, and they will open more doors to more developers and more industries. All told, the industries exploring DVI applications are diverse and their goals pervasive, from specific workbenches like Arthur Andersen & Co.'s Manufacturing Process Workbench to broad applications like the Time Arts Inc. paint package.

> *According to Touche-Ross, the installed base of in-store marketing systems will grow from 1,500 to 50,000 by 1990.*

video are best stored on CD-ROM, information that needs to be updated in a timely way can be downloaded to hard disk. Telephone updating would be possible for up-to-the-minute accuracy in product pricing. The customer could identify and research products, locate stores with the best sale prices, and even print out a shopping list, all at one kiosk.

The travel and real-estate industries can both benefit from showing motion video of locations to visit or buy, accompanied by a database of features of a property or nearby points of interest. Panoramic views of key rooms, of front and rear yards, and of the neighborhood can each be captured with a single 360° image, digitized and unwrapped in software, and put under user control. This approach cuts down on both production costs (one still in place of a motion-video pan) and on the storage space needed.

Education

In higher education, DVI can be used to create realistic simulations that enhance laboratory experience in the life and physical sciences. Large databases of material for history, social sciences, and the fine arts can enhance instruction, giving students and teachers access to a wide variety of material on one workstation. Educators at the college level are well aware of the value of visual media such as slides, films, and videotape, and they have adopted the personal computer as a standard tool for instruction, communication, and creativity for the intensive needs of the individual college student. DVI makes possible the marriage of visual media and computers; the computer provides the student with the ability to access real and synthetic video.

In the *Palenque* pilot, developed for home use by school-age children, sequential stills provide virtual travel through an ancient Mayan site. Graphic overlays give immediate visual feedback about available options. Arrows pointing forward or backward are always visible; arrows pointing right or left appear when turning is an option. A set of eyes appears when a 360° panoramic view is available. A hypermedia database accompanies the traveler through the Mayan site, providing movies, audio, still pictures, and text offering information about the rain forest and the Mayan people, maps of the area, and examples and explanations of glyph writing. The database is presented in the form of rooms in a museum. The entire interface is based on icons that are easily understood. The child using DVI has both the advantage of transcending the complex interface now associated with many personal computer applications, and the benefit of realistic video under his or her control.

THE FUTURE OF DVI: ENTERTAINMENT AND CONSUMER APPLICATIONS

By 1990 to 1991, the low price of DVI technology will make DVI available to the home consumer market. While the personal computer industry promised the home user the opportunity to learn, the reality is that the computer has never caught on for this home use. The personal computer was complicated, and although interactivity was appealing, the images and activities provided were not. The introduction of motion video, high-quality graphics, and real audio through DVI can make the interactive learning and entertainment markets come alive. Our *Sesame Street: Words in the Neighborhood* pilot demonstrates how television stock footage can be turned into an interactive word book for children, and testing has shown that children and parents find it extremely appealing.

Some of the same methods applied in training applications can be used to create how-to applications for the adult home user. For example, a photography application could effectively teach the use of a 35-mm camera. Images can be manipulated through DVI to simulate focus, composition, and lighting. Of course, real images can be used in this experience, and images in motion can be used for the "action shot."

Likewise, games for the home and the arcade can take on the flavor of real video images while retaining the power of the computer. Foreground video images can appear and disappear over video backgrounds on computer command. The possibilities of this, combined with video texturing, are limitless. Golf games, flight games, adventures, and mysteries are just a few that come to mind. DVI technology allows an approach that is drastically different from current interactive-video arcade games that provide only limited branching at specified points.

CONCLUSION

Market research indicates that the potential for existing limited technologies is good. We believe that the possibilities for an integrated medium are even greater. According to Disk/ Trend, sales of optical storage devices, including CD-ROM, will be approximately $1.3 billion by 1989. Frost & Sullivan, a research group in New York, predicts the market for all optical products could reach $2.5 to $4.5 billion by 1990.

Analysts also expect that the market will continue to grow as technology evolves, prices drop, and products proliferate. The power and versatility of DVI will make it a significant contributor to this market growth.

Each application market for DVI has unique needs. The flexibility of DVI allows a response to each that has not been available without a digital video/audio/graphics medium. It is this powerful simplicity that allows DVI to serve as the basis for the first truly universal communications medium.

[Sandra K. Morris is with the Application Market Development group with the Intel Princeton Operation. Her work focus is centered on the use of DVI technology in educational and training applications. Morris has acted as DVI's software Beta Program leader and as a project leader on several DVI application pilots.

Paula S. Zimmerman is responsible for application market development for the entertainment, design, and information/point-of-sale markets at the Intel Princeton Operation. She is also coordinator of Public Relations/ Communications for DVI.]

WRITABLE DISCS

COMPACT DISC RECORDING TECHNOLOGIES: THE STATE OF THE ART
By Ken C. Pohlmann

TANDY ANNOUNCES RE-WRITABLE CD TECHNOLOGY
By Abigail Shaw

Compact Disk Recording Technologies: The State of the Art

By Ken C. Pohlmann
From the *Laserdisk Professional*

[The writable-disc industry has added its share of acronyms to the CD roster. In this article, Ken Pohlmann explains the various technologies used to create write-once and erasable discs. He predicts that, although many people will buy optical recorders of one kind or another, writable discs will coexist peacefully with, rather than displace, CD-ROMs.]

The audio compact disk was the first optical storage technology to gain widespread name recognition. Indeed, no other consumer electronics product has ever achieved such rapid acceptance as the CD. It seems that anything linked to CD turns to gold. Thus manufacturers have been quick to introduce new members of the CD family, such as CD-ROM, CD-V, CD-I, CD-G, and even a miniature-sized CD, the CD-3. However, in all of these incarnations, the CD remains a playback-only medium.

That will soon change as parallel developments in optical disk technology merge with the CD format to produce both write-once, and fully erasable CDs. Although Tandy's announcement of development of an erasable CD technology has raised expectations, experts agree that a write-once CD will precede any erasable version, and indeed several technologies will vie for Tandy's share of that market. Let's examine the growing field of optical recording, to evaluate the technologies destined for the next generation of compact disks.

> *Although Tandy's announcement of development of an erasable CD technology has raised expectations, experts agree that a write-once CD will precede any erasable version, and indeed several technologies will vie for Tandy's share of that market.*

WRITE-ONCE DISKS

With a write-once disk, data can be written once, read many times, but cannot be erased. In other words, it is a permanent record, in much the same way that a photograph is permanent. A WO (write-once) disk (also referred to as WORM, or write-once, read many) may be implemented in a variety of ways. In some systems a laser writer burns pits in a thin film. Other mechanisms use lasers which cause bubbles to form in the medium. In other write-once systems, an irreversible phase change is used to provide a change in the index of reflectivity of the medium at the point where the laser strikes. In this way, the reading laser may differentiate between data.

Some systems using this method employ a thin metallic recording layer which changes its physical property from amorphous to crystalline when it is thermally heated by the writing laser. The phase transition alters the reflectivity of the recording layer at written spots, thus allowing laser reading of the data. An alternative to metal film is the use of polymer-dye binder bi-layer mediums. For example, colored dyes in a plastic medium over a reflective material can be written with infrared light and read with red light. In short, WO optical technology is not lacking for methods.

The question is, thus, which WO method will generally prevail, and which format specifications will be employed? The introduction of the CD format to write-once recording may solve both questions.

CD-WO

Philips and Sony, co-inventors of the CD, released specifications for a tentative writable CD format known as CD-WO (Compact Disk-Write Once) in February, 1988. The CD-WO format encompasses both CD-Audio and CD-ROM applications. A WO disk may contain both user-recorded and prerecorded material. To ensure compatibility among users, the format uses a pre-grooved disk. As with other write-once systems, a variety of materials may be used. The recording layer may have a decrease or increase in reflectivity when recorded to. In CD-WO, to simplify the servo system design, the high to low materials are used in a narrow pre-groove system, and low to high are used in an alternative wide pre-groove disk. The disk also contains CLV (constant linear velocity) clocking information (as a radial groove wobble) and timecode (as a modulation of the groove wobble) over the entire disk surface.

A CD-WO disk is structured with a defined sequence of data areas. Figure 2-12 shows the layout of a CD-WO disk without prerecorded tracks, and Figure 2-13 shows the layout of a disk with prerecorded tracks. The first area is a prerecorded lead-in area holding the TOC (table of contents). Next, there is the pre-grooved program area holding user-recorded information; the area consists of an optional prerecorded area user table of contents (UTOC), and recordable user area. Finally, there is a prerecorded lead-out area.

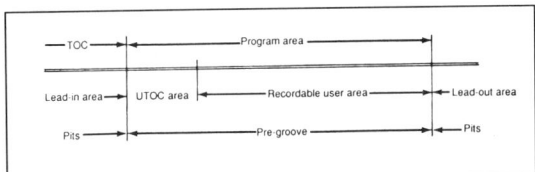

Figure 2-12. The layout of a disk without pre-recorded tracks

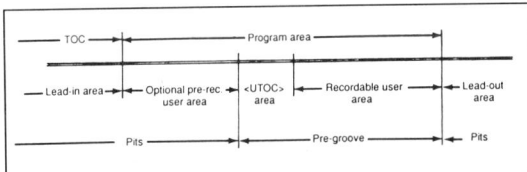

Figure 2-13. The layout of a disk with pre-recorded tracks

The prerecorded TOC in the lead-in area contains the start position of the optional prerecorded CD tracks, the position of the UTOC area, the start position of the recordable user area, the position of the lead-out area, and information on the physical parameters of the recording layer such as required laser recording power and the polarity of the recorded information (reflectivity increase or decrease).

All prerecorded data including the optional pre-recorded area is stored as CD pits. All user data is stored as a change in reflectivity. Both CD-Audio and CD-ROM data can be recorded in one track.

A single track numbering system is used for all pre-recorded and user-recorded tracks. A disk may contain a maximum of 99 tracks, of any duration. A disk may be recorded entirely at once, or discontinuously, over a period of time, new tracks starting at the end of previously recorded ones. In terms of disk dimensions,

> *Product introduction may follow the tentative specification announcement within 18 months. In short, we may see CD-WO sometime in 1989.*

scanning velocity, encoding, error correction, subcode, and data structure, CD-WO is identical to audio CDs. Disk capacity is identical to that of CD-Audio or CD-ROM: a CD-WO may hold about 74 minutes of audio, or about 650 MBytes of data.

Neither Philips nor Sony have announced dates for the introduction of CD-WO however it is possible that the time table of this roll-out may follow those of earlier CD incarnations. That is, product introduction may follow the tentative specification announcement within 18 months. In short, we may see CD-WO sometime in 1989.

ERASABLE DISKS

Several recordable/erasable optical media technologies have been introduced. These formats provide complete liberty in the reading and writing of data to optical disk. Several kinds of technologies have been developed. Among them are magneto-optical, phase-change, and dye-polymer recording. Magneto-optics is a system using a combination of vertical magnetic recording and laser optics; it is sometimes called "optically-assisted magnetic recording". Magneto-optical recording is sometimes referred to as MOR, and the disks as MODs.

Magnetic storage is an effective way to record and erase data, but suffers from basic problems such as medium and head wear. In addition, logitudinal magnetic storage limits the density of particles and the amount of information stored in an area. Optical storage offers longevity of medium and pickup and high data density, however optical properties of materials are not as easily changeable as their magnetic properties. Magneto-optical storage merges the record/erase properties of magnetic materials with the high density and contactless pickup of optical materials.

Magneto-optical recording

Magneto-optical recording utilizes a vertical magnetic medium. A vertical magnetic medium differs from a longitudinal medium in that magnetic particles are placed perpendicularly to the surface. This allows for much greater particle density, shorter recorded wavelengths, and, consequently, greater recording density. However, this recording density is not fully utilized by conventional magnetic heads whose recording flux fields cannot be focused sufficiently. In other words, the recorded area uses a far greater area than necessary. Optical assistance solves this problem.

With magneto-optics, a magnetic field is used to record data, but it is about one tenth the strength of conventional recording fields. By itself, it is too weak to affect the orientation of the magnetic particles. However, a unique property of magnetic materials is utilized: as they are heated, their coercivity (the magnetic field strength required to bring a saturated medium to erasure), suddenly drops close to zero. The temperature at which a material's coercivity drops suddenly is called its Curie point.

In the case of magneto-optics, at the Curie temperature the magnetic particles on the disk are easily oriented by a weak field. A laser beam focused through an objective lens heats a minute spot of magnetic material to its Curie point. At that temperature only the particles in that spot are affected by the magnetic field from the recording coil, and a very high-density recording results. After the laser pulse, the temperature decreases and the data is "frozen" into the magnetic layer, as shown in Figure 2-14.

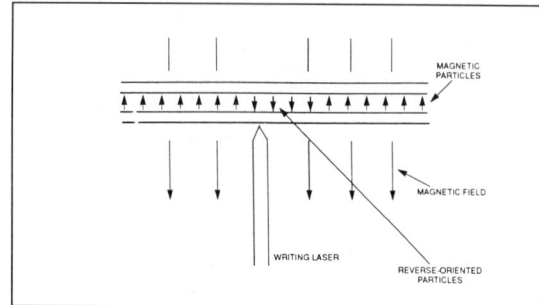

Figure 2-14. Data "frozen" into the magnetic layer after the laser pulse

Magneto-optical reading

Data readout utilizes the Kerr effect (sometimes called the Faraday effect), which describes the rotation of the plane of polarized light as it passes through a magnetized material. The reverse-oriented regions reflect laser light differently than the unreversed regions. To read the disk, a laser is focused on it and the angle of rotation of its reflection is monitored, as shown in Figure 2-15. An analyzer distinguishes between rotated and unrotated light and converts that information into a beam of varying light intensity. Data is then recovered from this modulated signal.

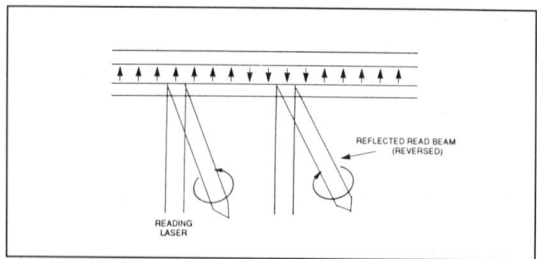

Figure 2-15. Reading the disk

The intensity of the reading laser is much lower (perhaps by a factor of 10) than the recording laser, so the magnetic information is not affected. To erase data and write again, a magnetic field is applied to the disk, along with the laser heating spot, as shown in Figure 2-16, and new data is written. In most systems an entire track must be erased on one rotation of the disk prior to writing new data. New data can only be written on the next rotation. Thus updating requires two disk rotations which slows data writing. Future developments may allow the writing operation to be accomplished in one pass, as with conventional magnetic media.

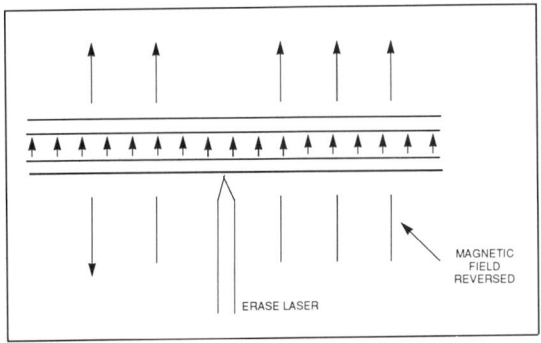

Figure 2-16. Applying a magnetic field and laser heating spot to erase data and write again

A magneto-optical system

An important aspect of any recording medium is its compatibility with media from other recorders. To achieve this within the high tolerances of a magneto-optical medium, blank disks may be manufactured with prerecorded and nonerasable addressing. The method is called hardware address sectoring, and uses a grooved disk in which address information is physically formed in the groove and detected by light beam reflection. Using this system, any magneto-optical drive will automatically track both address and data information contained on any magneto-optical disk. By superimposing the hardware addressing information on the recorded data signal, playing time is not sacrificed.

A magneto-optical disk retians the protective properties of other optical media. The recording layer is sandwiched between a transparent substrate and a protective layer. The laser light shines through the substrate, using its index of refraction to place surface dust and scratches out of focus with respect to the interior data. Although several magnetic materials are used, the ultimate selection will be based on orientation properties, signal-to-noise ratio, and long term stability. Magneto-optical disks use amorphous rare-earth transition metals such as alloy coatings of gadolinium terbium iron, terbium iron cobalt, and terbium iron. Special processing can make these reactive elements stable. Tests indicate that a magneto-optical disk could be erased/recorded over ten million times and would retain its data for ten years or more.

The optical head and magnetic coils of a magneto-optical system require sophisticated engineering both in terms of their own design and the hardware and software which controls them. In addition, a complete signal encoding chain is contained in every drive. Because of the similarity of tasks, it would clearly make sense for a magneto-optical drive to borrow some technology from the CD system and to emulate the CD format in terms of sampling rate and word length.

The CD system will be upwardly compatible with a magneto-optical system. Because much of the electronics are identical, all magneto-optical drives could also play back CDs, in the same way that a cassette machine can record or play prerecorded tapes. They could share a common optical head, and even the difference between CD and magneto-optical disks would be automatically detected because of the differences in reflectivity. Of course, to record magneto-optical disks, or to play back magneto-optical disks that are already recorded, a magneto-optical recorder will be needed. Magneto-optical recording systems are already in use, from a variety of manufacturers, embracing a variety of disk diameters and data formats. It is an open secret that both Philips and Sony have

REFERENCES

Bouwhuis, G., Braat, J., Huijser, A, Pasman, J., van Rosmalen, G., Schouhamer-Immink, K.A., *Principles of Optical Disc Systems*. Boston: Adam Hilger Ltd., 1985.

Compact Disc-Interactive: A Designer's Overview. ed. Philips International, Inc. New York: McGraw-Hill, 1988.

Isailovic, J., *Videodisc and Optical Memory Systems*. Englewood Cliffs, N.J.: Prentice-Hall, 1985.

Pohlmann, K.C., *The Compact Disc Handbook*. Madison, WI: A-R Editions, 1988.

Schouhamer-Immink, K.A., and Braat, J.J.M., "Experiments Toward an Erasable Compact Disc Digital Audio System." *Journal of the Audio Engineering Society*, 32:7/8, July/August, 1984, pages 531–38.

prototyped magneto-optical CDs, however product introduction is probably at least 2 years away.

PHASE-CHANGE TECHNOLOGY

Magneto-optics is not the only optical recording system being researched. Some systems use phase-change technology similar to that used in write-once systems. They use materials that exhibit a reversible crystalline/amorphous phase change when recorded at one temperature and erased at another. Typically, a high-reflectivity (crystalline) to low-reflectivity (amorphous) phase change is used to record data, and the reverse to erase.

Information is recorded by heating an area of the crystalline layer to a temperature slightly above its melting point. When the area solidifies, it has become amorphous, and the change in reflectivity can be detected. Because the crystalline form is more stable, the material will tend to change back to this form; thus when the area is heated to a point just below its melting temperature, it will turn to a crystalline state, erasing the data. A recording layer comprised of gallium antimonide and indium antimonide has been developed. It has a long shelf life, and is not affected by ambient temperatures and humidity. Over a thousand erasures can be achieved. Permanent recording may be achieved by simply increasing the power of the writing laser; this burns holes in the recording layer rather than changing its phase. Although in use, most observers believe that recordable phase-change technologies lag behind magneto-optical technologies in development.

CD-THOR

In another erasable technology, a dye-polymer recording layer is physically changed when recorded, and changed again when erased. The THOR-CD (THOR standing for Tandy High-intensity Optical Recording), announced in April 1988, uses this approach. A dye-polymer disk is made by sandwiching two layers of plastic materials coated with a dye that absorbs laser light. The media is written by laser heating. Laser light of a specific wavelength heats the two-layered material causing the lower layer to expand and push up the top layer. The top layer cools faster than the lower, and retains the raised bump. This can be recognized by the read laser.

Erasing and re-recording is easily accomplished: When the surfaces are again heated, this time with a laser with a different wavelength, the bump flattens out again, leaving the surface in its original form, ready for re-writing of new data. Data could be overwritten on a single revolution if the media passes under the smoothing laser just before it encounters the laser writing new data bumps. Significantly, because a pit is formed in the THOR-CD medium, the disk can be read by a conventional CD drive. Likewise, a conventional prerecorded CD can be played in the drive. Thus the new technology is backward compatible. However, an obstacle with this technology is that the recording surface can be erased only a few times, perhaps a hundred or less, before the layers become fatigued. While perhaps acceptable for some applications (e.g. consumer audio), it certainly is not for others (e.g. computer storage).

Tandy announced that THOR products may be available within 18 to 24 months, at a cost of $500 for an audio recorder. Although Tandy admits that it does not yet have a working CD-ROM prototype, those drives may follow a year after the audio recorders. That timetable and price point may also mirror the development of other recordable CD technologies. If anything, technology giants such as Philips and Sony, long-time advocates and technological pioneers of optical recording, may strive to better that projection, with their own technology. In either case, it seems clear that consumer recordable CDs are on the horizon, barring complications such as those thrown in the path of Digital Audio Tape by the record companies.

SUMMARY

For now, although not adhering to the CD format, optical disk recording is thriving. Both write-once and erasable systems are available from a variety of manufacturers, ranging from $1,000 to $100,000, and up. Perhaps the biggest obstacle facing the technology is the lack of disk and format standards. In time, standardization could be the biggest single benefit derived from the merging of the CD with optical recording technology.

And what is to become of good old CDs? Although a bright future certainly awaits recordable CD technologies, playback-only CDs will remain just as they are—an ideal medium for pre-recorded optical reproduction. While many people will certainly switch to optical recorders of one kind or another, one suspects that CD-Audio players and CD-ROM drives will keep going strong, just as another great prerecorded software transport, the turntable, persisted for a number of years.

Reprinted by permission of the *Laserdisk Professional,* **11 Tannery Lane, Weston, CT 06883.**

Tandy Announces Re-writable CD Technology

By Abigail Shaw
From *Optical Memory News*

[The Tandy High-intensity Optical Recording (THOR) technology announced in the second quarter of 1988 caused quite a stir. Not known for "vaporware" announcements, Tandy admitted that release of the first THOR product was a year or two away. Here, Abigail Shaw looks at the implications of this announcement and gives us some insight into the technology involved.]

On April 21, Tandy Corporation announced a "breakthrough" re-writable optical media which the firm contends is particularly suited to Compact Disc (CD) applications. The product is called Tandy Thor-CD. Tandy estimates that home CD recorders should be available within 18 to 24 months, at a cost of "less than $500 in the early years of development." In a demonstration at the announcement in New York, a Thor-CD disk on which music had been recorded was played on a standard CD player, and Tandy said that the re-writable disks will be playable on standard CD Audio players.

The technology announcement, which included an invitation to OEM purchasers to apply for a license to manufacture the media and/or drives, has two immediate implications: re-writable CD and CD-ROM players may be commercially available within a few years, and CD format re-writable media will be inexpensive enough to stake out a broad commercial market.

Re-writable optical drives have been announced for some months now, but all of the announced products are based on magneto-optic media technology. Tandy's media technology is neither magneto-optic nor phase-change (generally considered the second most mature re-writable media technology). In a surprising and bold market strategy, Tandy has released its own polymer/dye re-writable media technology.

Polymer/dye has been the subject of considerable research effort by at least three large firms for many years. Requiring a relatively simple production process, it has been viewed by many companies as offering the best potential for very inexpensive re-writable media production. By comparison, magneto-optic media is relatively expensive to produce, requiring sophisticated process control.

Despite polymer/dye's potential, however, no commercial announcements have been made before now. Although Tandy is understandably reluctant to discuss problems inherent in polymer/dye technology, leaders of research programs with other companies investigating this technology agree that polymer/dye media tends to "fatigue" after around 10,000 erase cycles, which means that at that point, error rates overcome current error detection techniques. In addition, raw error rates for production samples of polymer/dye media are generally higher than has been considered acceptable. Tandy has apparently overcome these problems in its research program, which is located in the santa Clara facilities which formerly house Memorex's research labs and which are now called Memtech, or, more formally, the Tandy Magnetic Media Research Center.

According to a representative, Tandy has "protected its patent position" on the technology. According to Tandy, it has reached an agreement with Optical Data, Inc. (ODI), Beaverton, Oregon, which has been developing a polymer/dye media for several years. Though the nature of the agreement has not been disclosed, Tandy has said that ODI's "bump forming media, which uses thermo-optical techniques" (Tandy's words) bears enough similarity to the Tandy product to justify an agreement, though Tandy categorically denies that ODI's technology has been licensed by Tandy's program.

It is meaningful that the immediate application described for the media technology is as a recorder for the home audio market. Audio data is more forgiving of high error rates than is

> *Erasable discs and drives will one day set the standard for data storage for mainframe computer installations, replacing today's magnetic media.*
>
> **By Alan Zeichick**
> **From CD-ROM Review**

coded data for computer applications. Also the limited erasure cycles observed with polymer/dye media are a small drawback, if any, for the home market, where users are unlikely to rewrite the media more than a few hundred times at the most. According to consumer electronics analysts, most consumers re-use erasable media much less than that.

The Tandy announcement also mentioned video applications, which should be easily graftable into the CD format (whether or not the recording device makes use of...DVI video compression chips, as some observers have suggested).

Tandy estimates that drives using its media for coded data applications would be available in 36 months. Tandy is allowing a year of additional development time for a computer data storage product, but the integration problems are minor enough to raise some questions about the generous time margin. For instance, will more sophisticated error correction techniques be needed? And will developers have to design an intelligent interface that bypasses the usual practice of rewriting the directory in a single location on the disk? This approach, which is said to be feasible, would minimize the number

PERSPECTIVE

Now where in this evolutionary structure [of information systems] does Tandy's erasable CD fit?

The reporters that call our offices [those of Rothchild Consultants] expect that we can lean back and read off some prepared text which answers the question. Instead, I will offer a warning: anyone who is confident that vast markets await the newest storage technology, especially in its "technology announcement" infancy, has not spent much time watching this industry. We have two to three years to speculate about Tandy's markets. If you are interested in trying your hand at predictions, look around and identify the problems the Tandy drive can solve, then add in the limiting factor of cost.

It may bring image processing to the office PC; it may automate some mapping applications; it may scare off piracy-fearful publishers of CD-ROMs; it may invade lap-top computers; it may replace VCRs in the home; it may install an Apple in every classroom; or it may have its moment of glory in the Christmas season, 1991, and vanish from view, replaced in our imagination by the erasable optical card, as yet unannounced.

By Abigail Shaw
From the *Laserdisk Professional*

of cycles required of any given track on the media. Until more is known about the composition of the polymer/dye recording layer, these questions cannot be answered.

Tandy's announcement included a reference to low-mass holographic heads, though representatives disclaimed any specific link to Pencom International, Sunnyvale, California, a firm which is developing such heads. Questions remain about whether current holographic heads can provide enough power at the media surface to work effectively with polymer/dye media. Optical drives using a less massive head will have substantially faster access times than drives with conventional heads.

The media technology that Tandy described is by no means limited to CD format applications. Tandy has focused on the audio area for several reasons made clear in its announcement. Robert McClure, President of Tandy Electronics Manufacturing, said that "there is a present and substantial market for a recordable CD Audio disk." By tapping that market immediately, Tandy and its licensees would be able to capitalize other, less immediate markets, such as re-writable 5-1/4" CLV disks using the CD file format, and even 5-1/4" disks using the higher-performance CAV format.

Of particular interest is Tandy's contention that Thor-CD will be inexpensive media. Tandy representatives said in private interviews that the production process will be "heavily leveraged on existing CD production techniques." To those familiar with that process, Tandy's statement indicates that substrates will be pressed with some format information in the injection molding machines now used to press data into CDs and CD-ROMs. The layers necessary to create a writable surface would be added after that. Read-only disks pass through a sputtering chamber which applies a thin aluminum layer, necessary to achieve the nearly 50% reflectivity that some CD and CD-ROM devices require for reading. Polymer/dye alone is unlikely to achieve reflectivity in that range. Reliable sources say that the Tandy media uses a reflective metal layer in addition to the polymer/dye. Tandy has said that Thor-CD media will "cost a small amount more to produce than CDs."

Tandy may plan to manufacture either drives (called recorders) and/or media using Thor-CD technology, though no details are available. Licenses are being negotiated on a case-by-case basis, as Tandy decides how best to handle the outpouring of interest created by the announcement. Three broad categories of licenses are available: Media, Recorder, and Component (presumably heads).

Reprinted by permission of Rothchild Consultants.

SECTION III

WHO'S DOING WHAT IN CD-ROM?

LIBRARY APPLICATIONS

EDUCATION AND TRAINING APPLICATIONS

RESEARCH AND REFERENCE APPLICATIONS

MEDICAL AND LEGAL APPLICATIONS

IN-HOUSE APPLICATIONS

HOME EDUCATION AND ENTERTAINMENT APPLICATIONS

LIBRARY APPLICATIONS

A STEP AHEAD: CD-PAC AT THE TACOMA PUBLIC LIBRARY
By Tom Watson

CD-ROM IN LIBRARIES: A PROMISE FULFILLED?
By Linda Langschied

THE LIBRARY MARKET
By Ron J. Rietdyk

WILL CD-ROM REPLACE MICROFICHE?
By Mark Vonderhaar

A Step Ahead: CD-PAC at the Tacoma Public Library

By Tom Watson
From *Wilson Library Bulletin*

[One of the most obvious applications of CD-ROM is for library catalogs. In this article, Tom Watson relates the experiences of the Tacoma Public Library, which decided to gamble on a CD-Public Access Catalog... and won.]

A patron using the new CD-ROM catalog at a branch of the Tacoma (Washington) Public Library was becoming visibly excited as she discovered what the machine could do. Finally she exclaimed, "I've got to show Ed!" and ran out to the car to get her husband. At another branch, where the new catalog had not yet been installed, a man became so frustrated with trying to use the old microfiche catalog that he threw his microfiche on the floor and announced with a huff that he was going to the downtown library to use the computer catalog.

A PROTECTED RISK

These kinds of stories, laughingly related by library staff, illustrate the success of Tacoma's bold, early commitment to a CD-PAC (public access catalog). The first computer stations went into service last fall, nearly 70 will be in operation this summer, and the total will surpass 100 next year. About 290,000 titles are listed. The installation hasn't always been trouble free, and a new challenge will be faced later this year when the CD-ROM units are linked with a central circulation system so catalog users can determine

THE FIRST CD-ROM PUBLICATION

In January 1985, The Library Corporation introduced the first commercial CD-ROM publication, the BiblioFile Catalog Production System. Because it was the first CD-ROM publication, there were no precedents to follow and no off-the-shelf components to use in its development. Consequently, nearly every part of the publication had to be developed from scratch.

By Brian Martin.
From *CD-ROM: Optical Publishing*.

a book's circulation status. But no serious problems have occurred, and reaction from the public and the staff has been overwhelmingly positive. Tacoma Public Library's "protected risk"—the way library director Kevin Hegarty describes the decision to be a CD-PAC pioneer—has already paid off handsomely.

Tacoma is one of the first public library systems in the country to put into operation the BiblioFile Intelligent Catalog, the CD-PAC product of The Library Corporation, of Washington, D.C. Each computer station includes a screen, keyboard, printer, and telephone receiver. The printer allows users to make a copy of any entry or series of entries. Those using the catalog for the first time can use the phone receiver to listen to an explanation of how the system works.

Advanced technology is certainly nothing new for Tacoma Public Library. It was also one of the first U.S. libraries to open a public computer laboratory, and it has had an automated circulation system since 1977. The circulation system has performed exceedingly well, according to library officials, but several years ago they decided they needed a more powerful system, with more capacity for expansion. In the summer of 1985, Tacoma put out a request for proposals for a new automated circulation system.

The evaluation committee eventually rejected all four proposals, since none of them really met the library's specifications. "Even more distressing," Hegarty said in a speech at the 1987 Pacific Northwest Library Association conference, "we discovered that the systems available were not even the equal, in terms of functionality, of the system we already had in place." As a result, it was decided the library would develop its own automated circulation system. That project is now nearing completion.

The RFP for the circulation system also sought proposals for an Online Public Access Catalog (OPAC). However, the OPACs offered by the bidders also seemed lacking in performance and capabilities, and were extremely costly as well. At this point, Hegarty became fascinated with the CD-ROM public access catalog that had just been introduced by The Library Corporation. This fascination soon developed into a working agreement that has been beneficial to both the library and the company.

PROVIDING THE MISSING LINK

Tacoma Public Library was an alpha site (preliminary testing) and beta site (secondary testing) for the Intelligent Catalog. Led by manager Lare Mischo, Tacoma's three-person automated systems staff has worked closely with Library Corporation in working out kinks in the product. Because of the library's development role, Library Corporation has given Tacoma an attractive price for the CD-ROM equipment, Hegarty says.

Having its own talented computer staff has been a huge advantage for Tacoma. That staff expertise and the reputation and commitment of Library Corporation are the main reasons Hegarty calls Tacoma's gamble on a relatively untested technology a "protected risk." Unless libraries have these kinds of protection, Hegarty says, he would not necessarily recommend they take such a risk.

Mischo and his staff, who call themselves the "droid technicians," in a reference to *Star Wars*, really seem like wizards when you learn that they not only help develop complex new systems, they pay for them, too. A few years ago Mischo developed *UNIFACE*, a software product linking bibliographic utilities and local automated systems. After selling several copies of *UNIFACE* (one happy customer is Tacoma Public Schools), the library sold the rights to Midwest Library Corporation. The payment for *UNIFACE* was viewed by library officials as "seed money for future automation work," says Mischo, and indeed it has been. This money will pay for all or most of the costs of the CD-PAC equipment and installation.

Hegarty says he prefers the CD-PAC over the OPAC for three main reasons: the CD-PAC is potentially more affordable, its search capabilities are far superior, and each CD-PAC station stands alone. With the more centralized OPAC, there's a greater possibility of down time for the entire system.

Tacoma's CD-PAC will soon become truly state-of-the-art. The new computerized circulation system should go into operation in early September, Mischo says, and at that time or shortly thereafter the CD-PAC units will be linked into that system so catalog users can determine the shelf availability of any library material. Tacoma Public Library and Library Corporation are working together on this interface, and have agreed to place this software in the public domain. The resulting computerized catalog that provides circulation status has been the "missing link" for libraries, says Hegarty. "It's going to revolutionize the marketplace," he predicts.

UP AND RUNNING

Installation of the Tacoma CD-PAC units, which began last summer, has been "pretty straightforward," says William Woodsmall, production manager for The Library Corporation. Several

BENEFITS OF CD-ROM

CD-ROM technology appears to be tailor-made for the library environment. It locks comfortably into the traditional types of storage media. It offers the librarian an opportunity to strengthen the traditional role of building collections, which is eroded by online information. Unlike online information that is supplied solely to and then disposed by an individual, CD ROM databases (discs) are added to the assets of the library which are available to everybody.

By Chung I. Park.
From *The COINT Reports*.

changes in the final product were made after testing at Tacoma, but such changes are typical. Probably the most significant changes were in the way the indexing is done, Mischo says.

Other suggestions made by the Tacoma staff have led Library Corporation to offer new options to future customers. For example, the innovative sound track explaining how to use the CD-PAC was originally projected through a speaker, but library staff found the noise too distracting. Now, users listen to the tape with the telephone receiver. Headphones are a third option that has been made available.

Another change proposed by library staff was that catalog users be given more than one choice for printing out a listing. Originally, only a short form of each catalog entry would be printed out, but now users can get a copy of the entire listing if they prefer.

Tacoma's introduction of the CD-PAC has been made more challenging by the fact that the library system is also undergoing a major expansion and renovation program. The construction is being funded by a $15.8 million bond issue, which will also pay for the new computerized circulation system. Since the main library building is being renovated as part of this project, that library has been temporarily relocated

LIBRARY TITLES

Title	Publisher	Telephone	Price
Access Pennsylvania High School Library Catalog, 3rd Edition	Pennsylvania State Library Pennsylvania Dept. of Education School Library Media Services 333 Market Street Harrisburg, PA 17126-0333	(717)787-6704	*
BIBLIOFILE Catalog Maintenance	Library Corporation P.O. Box 40035 Washington DC 20016	(800)624-0559	*
BIBLIOFILE Catalog Production	Library Corporation P.O. Box 40035 Washington, DC 20016	(800)624-0559	$1,750.00/ Startup package
British Library/ Bibliotheque Nationale Pilot Disc	British Library 2 Sheraton Street London W1V 4BH ENGLAND	01/323-7073	Free
CD-CATSS	Utlas International 2150 Shattuck Avenue Suite 402 Berkeley, CA 94704	(415)841-9442	$1,800.00/ Year
CDMARC Bibliographic	Library of Congress Cataloging Dist. Service Washington, DC 20541	(202)287-6100	*
CDMARC Names	Library of Congress Cataloging Dist. Service Washington, DC 20541	(202)287-6100	*
CDMARC Subjects	Library of Congress Cataloging Dist. Service Washington, DC 20541	(202)287-6100	$300.00/ Year *
Discon	Utlas International 8300 College Boulevard Overland Park, KS 66210	(800)33-UTLAS	$680.00/ Month
Enhanced BIBLIOFILE	Library Corporation P.O. Box 40035 Washington DC 20016	(800)624-0559	*
The Intelligent Catalog	Library Corporation P.O. Box 40035 Washington, DC 20016	(800)624-0559	$2,770.00/ Workstation

*Please contact publisher for price.

Title	Publisher	Telephone	Price
Iowa Locater, 3rd Edition	Iowa State Library Networking Dept. East 12th and Grand Des Moines, IA 50319	(515)281–4118	$50.00/ Quarter
The Kansas Library Catalog	Kansas State Library Statheouse 3rd Floor Topeka, KS 66612-1593	(913)296–3296	*
LaserCat	Western Library Network Mail Stop AJ-11W Olympia, WA 98504-0111	(206)459–6518	$1,300.00/ Year
LAsernet Database	State Library of Louisiana P.O. Box 131 Baton Rouge, LA 70821	(504)342–4923	*
LaserQuest	General Research Corporation, Library Systems 5383 Hollister Avenue Santa Barbara, CA 93111	(800)235–6788	*
Library Literature	H.W. Wilson Company 950 University Avenue Bronx, NY 10452	(800)367–6770	$1,095.00/ Year
MaineCat	Maine State Library Statheouse Station #64 Augusta, ME 04333	(207)289–5600	*
MCAT (Missouri Union Catalog)	Missouri State Library P.O. Box 387 Jefferson City, MO 65102	(314)751–3033	*
SuperCAT Library of Congress MARC: English	Gaylord Information Systems P.O. Box 4901 Syracuse, NY 13221-4901	(315)457–5070	$850.00/ Year
SuperCAT Library of Congress MARC: Foreign Languages	Gaylord Information Systems P.O. Box 4901 Syracuse, NY 13221-4901	(315)457–5070	$500.00/ Year
WISCAT	Wisconsin Reference and Loan Library 2109 South Stoughton Road Madison, WI 53716	(608)221–6161	$60.00/ Year

Compiled by Online Press Inc.

> *About ten years after personal computers began to invade libraries, libraries are counterattacking with a vengeance, invading personal computers through the agency of small shiny discs.*
>
> **Steven Sieck and Haines Gaffner**

in a downtown store. CD-PAC units went into service at this location at the same time it was opened. David Palmer, manager of the main library, says that in retrospect it would have been better if those two major changes had not happened at the same time. "But it worked out okay," he adds. Tacoma currently has six libraries open; when the construction project ends, there will be eleven.

Staff training has been vital in the changeover to the CD-PAC. Nancy Hagedorn, the library's computer operations supervisor, conducts the training for both the catalog and the new circulation system. For at least a week prior to each CD-PAC training program, staff members are given time to read the training manual and "play" with one of the units, Hagedorn says.

In a training session, she works with two to four people at a time, all gathered around the computer. Because staff members are somewhat familiar with the unit already and have plenty of questions, she says, "A quarter of the way through the training session, the script gets thrown away." Hagedorn will eventually train the entire staff, except for pages, on the CD-PAC.

Staff acceptance of the CD-PAC "was universal," says Palmer. "It helps everyone do their job better," Mischo adds. "And it's more fun."

PATRON APPEAL

Using a totally computerized catalog must surely be a drastic change for many library patrons, but perhaps this is what they've been waiting for all along. "The public has been very enthusiastic about the Intelligent Catalog," says Palmer. "They have almost unanimously taken it to heart." A few complaints have been made, but there have been far more expressions of thanks. Older people generally have more resistance to using computers than younger people, but even many elderly patrons love the new catalog. Palmer is especially pleased that people with bifocals find the CD-PAC easy to use; they had trouble with the old microfiche system because the angle of the screen could not be adjusted.

Perhaps the most popular feature of the new system, according to public and staff comments, is the instant printout of a catalog listing. No longer do patrons clutch stubby pencils and crumpled scraps of paper. The printer makes very little noise, and produces an easy-to-read printout.

The sound track feature appears to be less heavily used than one might expect. Many patrons figure out how to use the catalog from the information on the keyboard and the screen, or by asking library staff members. A brochure is also provided. Because there is no place for the telephone receiver to be set or hung, it just lies there next to the keyboard, and is easily knocked off. However, staff members note that some patrons have discovered the value of the sound track as a babysitting device. While they use the catalog, they let the receiver hang down to the floor and their two-year-old will sit and listen, fascinated, instead of running off into the stacks.

Updates of the CD-PAC are currently done quarterly, but the library soon expects to move to monthly updates, using a hard disk linked to the CD. It's conceivable that updates could be done even more frequently, Mischo says. Tacoma's old microfiche catalog was updated three times a year.

The Tacoma CD-PAC includes Reader's Advisory Assistance, based on software developed by the Del Mar Group, of Solana Beach, California. Used mainly in bookstores, this program generates an interest profile for the user, and then suggests related works that may be of interest. However, the library staff does not really promote this CD-PAC feature (most users don't even realize it's there), Mischo says, because it is primarily oriented towards helping bookstores sell books, and does not seem well suited for libraries. He adds that Tacoma Public Library and Library Corporation would both like to eventually enable the CD-PAC to provide more advice and recommendations to patrons who seek this kind of help.

BEST-READ CITY

The city of Tacoma has long lived in the shadow of Seattle, its larger, more cosmopolitan neighbor. But the city has much to be proud of, including its progressive library system and the reading habits of its residents. Library brochures proudly proclaim Tacoma's status as "America's Best Read City." For the past two years, surveys have shown that Tacoma has the highest per capita circulation of any municipal library system in U.S. cities of more than 100,000 residents. Hegarty says it appears the CD-PAC will increase circulation even more.

After hearing Tacoma library staff members talk about the CD-PAC, and observing patrons intently using the equipment, it's not easy to find fault with the system. Perhaps the worst thing that can be said is that it may be raising the noise level in the library. It's not the equipment that is noisy; it's the public. "Yesterday we had a man who yelled all across the library, 'This catalog is great!'" says Palmer. "And that's typical."

Reprinted by permission of the H.W. Wilson Company.

CD-ROM in Libraries: A Promise Fulfilled?

By Linda Langschied

[Linda Langschied shares a librarian's view of CD-ROM use in the library. She and her colleagues, she says, are still waiting for all the promises of CD-ROM to be fulfilled. She offers a few suggestions for improving CD-ROM systems so that they can live up to expectations.]

Three years ago, when CD-ROM made its debut in libraries, it generated some excitement. Why, then, did a recent *New York Times* article, citing the high cost of periodical subscriptions, note that some libraries were cancelling laser-based products? Why are libraries that got started in CD-ROM on grant monies reporting that, when funding runs out, they will not be able to absorb all of the CD-ROM subscriptions into their budget and will cull out the products with which they are least enamored? And why are some libraries simply not getting into the CD-ROM game at all?

From the vantage point of a university reference librarian responsible for automated reference services, I would say that CD-ROM thus far has been a source of unmet expectation. Librarians are still waiting for the original promise of CD-ROM to be fulfilled. Simply put, librarians are looking to CD-ROM for an affordable, easy-to-use end-user search system—one that will help library users become independent database searchers, help free librarians' time from intermediary searching, and offset the high cost of online database searching.

CD-ROM may ultimately fit this bill, but to date it has only partly met these expectations. While librarians may save time when online searches are redirected to patron use of CD-ROM, they must commit time to training users (most systems on the market *do* require some training) and to coping with the technical aspects of having an in-house database. Cost savings can be realized, but only on the databases that are heavily used in their online form. Some argue that it would be less expensive to offer unlimited online access to databases than it would be to pay for CD-ROM subscriptions. And getting started in CD-ROM, particularly in setting up the multiple workstations dictated by the current "one product, one station" attitude of the CD-ROM industry, is prohibitively expensive.

Still, CD-ROMs continue to emerge in libraries as new products are released and new configurations for them are devised. And despite the nay-saying above, I do believe that CD-ROM will prove to be a viable option for many libraries; indeed, a good number of libraries are already reporting on the popularity of CD-ROMs at their institutions. But many more libraries are playing wait-and-see, postponing their own purchases until they see proof at other institutions that CD-ROM delivers on its promise. For this to happen, I see the need for a great many improvements.

A LIBRARIAN'S ADVICE

I would like to share some of the ruminations I have about CD-ROM, those I dwell on alone over my computer and coffee and puzzle about with librarian colleagues. I would like to direct my comments to the producers and vendors of CD ROM products in hopes that a librarian's perspective might help inform their future decision making.

Be candid

Tell us what the system does and does not do. Are there fewer points of access or is less data available through the CD-ROM than through its online counterpart? Are there glitches you are experiencing now but are working out? Librarians will respond more favorably to a less-than-perfect product, particularly in these early stages of development, if they believe that they have been given an honest description of what they are purchasing and that the company is aware of, and dealing with, any problems. The fewer surprises that confront us when we initially use a CD-ROM system, the greater the likelihood of a favorable review when it comes time to consider renewing a subscription.

Librarians are looking to CD-ROM for an affordable, easy-to-use end-user search system — one that will help library users become independent database searchers, help free librarians' time from intermediary searching, and offset the high cost of online database searching.

Provide good support

The assumption of some CD-ROM producers that their systems are self-explanatory and self-sustaining has not always been borne out by experience. The least acceptable amount of support would be as follows:

1. Include a well-prepared, clearly written technical manual to guide installation and maintenance of the system is a must. Don't provide written documentation that is incomprehensible or, worse, provide none at all.

LINDA LANGSCHIED

Home: Trenton, New Jersey
Job: Coordinator of Online Reference Services, Rutgers University
Quote: *"CD-ROM has the enormous potential to become an integral element of reference services in all types of libraries. There is an immediate need for producers to further their efforts toward standardization, and to build good networking systems for CD-ROMs, in order to meet library criteria for ease-of-use and affordability."*

2. Give customers an 800 number so they can receive expert troubleshooting advice.

3. Provide support for *using* the system in the form of well-written, easy-to-use tutorials and help screens, as well as providing on-site training of librarians or a written user's manual.

Know your users

Remember that librarians, not technicians, will probably be responsible for bringing up and maintaining CD-ROM stations. I reiterate the need for good technical documentation and phone support. More importantly, though, producers must provide a system that is easy for nontechnical people to install and operate, and they need to show an awareness of the environment in which it will be used. For example, some libraries report having to deal with problems caused to resident AUTOEXEC.BAT and CONFIG.SYS files when they attempted to use a second CD-ROM system on a single station. For financial reasons alone, libraries might need to run more than one CD-ROM system from one station, and producers should be sensitive to these kinds of situations. Producers are well advised to extend user-friendliness to the library staff who are going to be responsible for the technical aspects of having CD-ROM in their midst.

Remember, too, that people, not programmers, will be the end users of CD-ROM products. This is probably the ultimate statement of the obvious, but I have experienced CD-ROM systems that nearly stymie me, and I am an experienced online searcher. It seems unlikely that the programmers had novice searchers in mind when they designed some of these systems. Ideally the user should, with a little practice, be able to conduct a basic search intuitively—that is, be able to search naturally, by feel, without having to summon up special help screens to proceed. For many libraries, it is a stated public-service goal to make patrons self-reliant library users. A CD-ROM system that requires much assistance from the librarian not only thwarts this goal but puts additional stress on the library staff and ultimately does not make a happy customer.

Standardize

Lack of standardized hardware, operating software, and search software presents one of the greatest obstacles to libraries embracing CD-ROM. Much of the high cost of CD-ROM can be traced to this issue as well, as librarians struggle to provide diverse machinery and software to accommodate individual CD-ROM products. True standardization would eliminate the many technical problems currently encountered and would solve the problem of users having to learn many different system interfaces. As yet, standardization remains yet another unfulfilled expectation.

IN SUMMARY

In the final analysis, cost will be the first, if not foremost, consideration for most libraries. Until some of the concerns stated above are addressed, libraries looking into the CD-ROM option will see a procedure that is both expensive and complicated. CD-ROM has the potential to become an integral part of library automated research services. Producers *have* made a good start, but the evolution of CD-ROM from a luxury purchase to a broad-based library tool depends on their making good the claims of affordability and ease-of-use. CD-ROM has a future in all kinds of libraries; producers need only make it happen.

[Linda Langschied is Coordinator of Online Reference Services at the Alexander Library, Rutgers University, New Brunswick, New Jersey.]

WHAT'S NEW, WHAT'S NEEDED

Vendors are doing a great deal to improve CD-ROM services, or make them more appealing to end users. Significant in the past few months has been the development of products with multiple search modes, so that the rank novice and the expert searcher can be served by the same CD-ROM system. More and more vendors are marketing systems that provide access to an online service for updating search results. We see more products that exploit the full capabilities of the technology in improved retrieval software; windowing and other graphics applications; saving of searches or search strategies for transfer to floppy or hard disks, or to online databases; post-processing of search results using built-in word processing or spreadsheet software; and combining optical and audio disc technology in the same package.

Several vendors are testing "jukeboxes" that allow one workstation to call for and search from any of several discs. Daisy-chaining one workstation to several players is now possible as well. Multiple access to the same disc is a feature that the industry has explored, but speed of searching is so slow that there is some doubt about marketing this for CD-ROM systems. At least one CD-ROM vendor and a large computer firm are working on remote access to CD-ROM stations through a network environment. They are at the point of establishing performance criteria for this means of access. There is little question that CD-ROM systems will be greatly enhanced if vendors can implement, and market at reasonable cost, some of the above-mentioned features.

By Nancy Crane and Tamara Durfee. From *Wilson Library Bulletin*. Reprinted by permission of H.W. Wilson Company.

The Library Market

By Ron J. Rietdyk
From the *Journal of the American Society for Information Science*

[In this overview of the library market, Ron Rietdyk analyzes the needs and attitudes of market participants and offers insights that could benefit those making decisions about future library CD-ROM applications.]

THE MARKETPLACE

Size

According to the American Library Directory of 1986 there are 37,138 libraries in the United States and Canada.

Types of libraries

1. University and Colleges—2,100
2. Academic Departments—2,000
3. Junior Colleges—1,380
4. Special—5,500
5. Public—16,600
6. Federal—1,900
7. Law, Medical, and Religious—3,500

Libraries outside the U.S.

An estimated 100,000 libraries in the rest of the world are potential CD-ROM users. Areas that lack an efficient datacommunication structure especially offer a new market to capture for CD-ROM.

Layers in the CD-ROM marketplace

Three groups of players are operating: librarians, publishers, end-users. Each has different attitudes towards CD-ROM. To be successful in this market it is necessary to understand these differences.

LIBRARIANS' ATTITUDE TOWARDS CD-ROM

General observations

A well-informed and organized marketplace: Librarians have learned about this new technology within the last year. In 1985 the main question at the exhibitions was: "CD-What?" Now the main question is "Why is database ABC or databank XYZ not yet available on CD-ROM?" Almost all the library organizations at the national and state level have been organizing or are planning conferences on optical media. [The ASIS 1987 Mid-Year Conference had as its theme "Laser Optical Disk and Video-Based Information Systems."]

Professionally trained in finding information: Librarians are trained to provide the user with the amount and level of information needed; they will look at the CD-ROM products as tools to fulfill this need. The librarians will closely examine a product in its smallest details.

Librarians do not like subsets or already existing products, especially if the only reason is the physical 600 MB limit of a CD-ROM disc. Librarians want to offer families of products that consist of a mix of databases from different vendors, e.g., a group of engineering databases, a group of medical databases, etc.

Slow and complex decision process: As most libraries have to serve a large heterogeneous user group and as they have a choice from an ever-increasing supply of information, librarians must select carefully the items for their collection. Most decisions are made through consensus by a group of librarians.

Tight budgets: A large part of the library world faces budget cuts of 10 to 15 percent in the coming years. Investments in PC equipment for CD-ROM and high subscription prices become real considerations. The reference desk at a library cannot easily demonstrate cost reductions from the use of CD-ROM. It is mainly the non-quantitative concept of providing better services to users that are the main reason for placing CD-ROM products in the library.

Yearly budget cycle: Most libraries prepare budgets a year in advance. If the current operating budget does not allow for the product, the order must wait until it can be incorporated in the new budget.

Loyal to suppliers: Usually a library continues the services of its regular suppliers. Only if services are very poor will libraries make a change.

CD-ROM benefits for the library

Fixed annual subscription: The unlimited usage of the data for a fixed price is clearly the biggest advantage for the library. The library can budget for it in advance without having to adjust the figure during the year.

More service to the end user: Making the data available directly to the end user with all search options, browsability, and experimentation without concern for cost is another advantage of CD-ROM.

No telecommunication facilities needed: Placing a disc in a machine and searching immediately is an easier and faster process than dialing into a local network, entering a vendor's database system, and giving passwords.

Less storage needed for print products in the future: Many librarians would like to reduce the large quantities of old print issues by replacing them on CD-ROM. For example the latest five year cumulative index of Chemical Abstracts exceeds 50 volumes of 3,000 pages each. Many libraries will run out of space in the next years if publication continues at its present rate. CD-ROM can help alleviate this situation.

Less dependent on intermediaries: In general there are online help screens, tutorials, and menu-driven software for the inexperienced user. While this user will have to learn to search efficiently and will in some cases find less information than the experienced user, he or she is the one who needs to judge the end result; it is very likely that by doing it personally, the end-user is better able to define his or her strategy than working through an intermediary.

CD-ROM obstacles for the library

Security: Giving a $2,000 database to a library user and free access to a PC with a printer can be done only if there is sufficient control and assistance in the reference area. In most libraries this is not the case. To manage the future collection of CD discs, special measures should be taken. SilverPlatter has designed a simple solution called MultiPlatter to solve this issue by separating the monitors/keyboards from the computer/CD-ROM drives.

Lack of standard retrieval software: We may be many years away from retrieval standards and the library world may have to live with this situation. There are no retrieval standards for paper products (index and contents structures all differ). This may be a good time to experiment and discover improvements. A much greater problem is the standardization of the contents of the data elements. Each database has its own definitions of descriptors, identifiers, subject headings, broader/narrower terms, etc. A strategy that works for searching database A does not work for database B. To tackle this problem SilverPlatter is even now writing different tutorials for each of our databases on CD-ROM.

Too few databases available: While the buyers are waiting for the vendors to offer more titles, the vendors are waiting for the buyers to purchase the equipment. (Schwerin describes this situation at some length in her article in [the same issue of the ASIS journal].)

Most libraries are interested in families of databases to appear on CD-ROM. One database may not be enough to answer their needs.

Too expensive: For many libraries the price of CD-ROM may be too high. The libraries either have to wait until prices come down or they have to be able to justify the higher expense by providing better service.

No place in the library budget: How does the library characterize CD-ROM? As a serial? New acquisition? Online service? Capital investment? We advise libraries to treat the discs as a subscription to a serial and place it within the materials budget.

Desire to keep the discs: In most cases the database on CD-ROM is licensed for a year to the library. If a library does not continue the subscription it must return the disc(s). Libraries, however, do not like to return an item which they feel they have paid for.

Training needed for users: Despite the menu-driven software some librarians think it is necessary to offer initial training to the end-users. However, a small research project in one of our test sites showed that a controlled group with no advanced training rated the system higher than the group that was trained for the system. Also, users are often satisfied with less information than an experienced searcher might obtain.

No multi-user facilities: Libraries like to share the expensive CD-ROM products with other users. Making discs available through a network by which terminals in other locations can access the CD-ROM is a possibility. However, the disc will always accommodate only one user at a time. The CD technology will not allow searching by more than one user and maintaining a reasonable response time.

We believe the best way to solve this problem is to have site licenses where libraries receive, for instance, 25 discs for a fixed fee.

Need to invest in equipment: Most libraries have no PCs available and thus have to make an additional initial investment to be able to use the CD-ROM product. In some cases a subscription which includes the PC can solve this problem.

Space needed for equipment: In some libraries the equipment can be installed only after a renovation. Some libraries build new rooms for these new microcomputer operations.

Exposes user to a universe of information larger than what is available locally: Reference databases may lead to some articles, which then have to be obtained from publications which the library may not have. This means additional interlibrary loan work.

INFORMATION PROVIDERS' AND PUBLISHERS' ATTITUDES TOWARDS CD-ROM

General observations

See more obstacles than benefits: The promotion of CD-ROM reminds publishers of the days when online searching began when they were called on to invest in a new technology with no way of knowing whether it would succeed. However, most feel they need to produce discs but will take very cautious steps in doing so.

Want to create new products: There is much interest in the creation of new products which can be extracted from already existing compilations but which will not compete with existing print or online revenue.

Want more technical facilities: For many publications graphics is an important feature. Publishers would like to see how graphics can be handled before moving further.

Also, for some publications one CD-ROM disc is not enough: multi-volume, single-file configurations are needed.

CD-ROM benefits for the publisher

Potential new markets: CD-ROM can add to their revenue through:

- Selling databases to countries that cannot be reached by online systems. Among our first users are libraries in Hong Kong and Australia; there are potential orders from China and India.

- Supplying databases to academic departments within the universities.

- Distributing databases to public libraries.

- Using the disc as a training tool for potential online searchers.

More control over their data: Publishers are reestablishing contacts with end users which had been shut off by the online vendors. Publishers can now gather feedback about the use of their data to show the effectiveness of a product.

Creation of new products: Using their vast amount of data, the publishers are able to create new subject-oriented ROM with their printed product by placing annual indexes on CD-ROM.

CD-ROM obstacles for the publisher

Fear of erosion of existing products: Replacement of their printed product by CD-ROM is the greatest fear of the publishers. For most library-oriented publishers, the income from the printed products is still the major source of revenue. Losing only a small percentage can mean a significant loss. Migration of online revenue is of lesser concern. Here the publishers like the possibility of gaining more control.

Piracy of data: A second major concern is the idea of having 20 years of work/data on one single disc which can be used by anyone who has paid the subscription fee. The idea that this disc can easily be used for downloading, repackaging, and reselling their information gives most publishers nightmares.

Unlimited usage: Some publishers are opposed to unlimited usage. They want (as with online) to be paid a variable usage fee depending on the time their data was used.

END-USERS' ATTITUDES TOWARDS CD-ROM

General observations

Little experience: Most library patrons have little or no search experience and will search infrequently. This puts a lot of pressure on the capabilities of the user interface.

Little knowledge of the database: The peculiar properties of the database are not easy to explain to end users. An online tutorial which is database specific is necessary to give the end-user the maximum benefit of his/her time with the system.

Advantages of CD-ROM for the end-user

Independence: Having personal access to the database itself and being able to refine or change searches in the process gives a great sense of freedom to end-users. End-users feel in control of their own searches when they do not have to depend on an intermediary who has to understand their needs.

Immediate gratification: Once they have found the references they are looking for, the users can either print or download the information for later use.

Information is free: With no clock ticking, users tend to spend more time with the system than originally planned. This leads to queuing problems in some of the libraries.

More interaction is possible: The ability to browse at one's own pace through the references and the dictionaries provides an intellectual stimulation that is not possible with the current online systems.

Obstacles in using CD-ROM

Many of these obstacles can be removed by use of training tools such as online tutorials which would help to solve the following difficulties:

- Need to learn about the database itself.
- Understanding that perfect search results are rare.
- Inadequate searching techniques may require more time at the terminal.

FUTURE PRODUCTS

For CD-ROM products to be successful in libraries it is necessary to remove the obstacles for the libraries as well as to guarantee the information providers a reasonable return on their investments. This can be done by offering technical solutions to libraries such as the MultiPlatter system which solves the security and disc control issues and by creating new products with the information providers.

The products offered presently are the first generation of a range of new CD-ROM based products. The existing products are derived or copied from existing online or printed products: they contain the same information but in a different medium. The next generation will be targeted for specific user groups and will contain data from multiple suppliers.

Since these new products will not be competing with already existing products, pricing can be competitive with prices ranging from $500 to $1,000 for quarterly updated subscriptions.

Reprinted from the January 1988 issue of *Journal of the American Society for Information Science* **(excerpted from "Creation & Distribution of CD-ROM Databases" by Ron Rietdyk). Copyright © 1988 by** *Journal of the American Society for Information Science.* **Reprinted by permission of John Wiley & Sons, Inc.**

Will CD-ROM Replace Microfiche?

By Mark Vonderhaar

[We end this section on library applications of CD-ROM with a discussion of the relative merits of CD-ROM and microfiche. Mark Vonderhaar analyzes the struggle for the "best storage medium" title and declares "no competition."]

From today's perspective, all indications point to microfiche and CD-ROM coexisting nicely, with both gradually yielding to the more advanced information publishing technologies of tomorrow. But of the two, microfiche will be the longer-lived and, possibly, more versatile medium to which next-generation technologies can be applied.

The silvery CD-ROM's appeal to our individual and collective imaginations springs mainly from its potential as a high-capacity digital storage device with random-access capabilities. Considering only these characteristics, it seems a short and safe leap to the conclusion that CD-ROM is destined to replace microfiche, the main present-day alternative to paper for mass storage.

However, many library administrators and records management experts question the assumption that radically different media are related by some sort of hydraulic principle: one medium in, another out, in a perfectly fluid displacement. Reality argues otherwise: Television has not replaced radio; cable TV has not consigned movie theaters to oblivion; videotape has not vanquished cable TV; and print media have survived and prospered through it all. In the library world, microforms have not rendered paper obsolete, and online systems have not replaced either paper or microforms. So, too, CD-ROM will find its place less as a competitor to established media than as a complement to them.

To be sure, CD-ROM is a superior medium for some types of publications traditionally distributed on microfiche. For example, large, widely disseminated databases containing information that is relatively stable—that is, valid for a week or longer—and for which minimum retrieval time is of paramount importance are finding an ideal delivery vehicle in CD-ROM. Thus, Micromedex's POISINDEX system uses CD-ROM to disseminate toxicological information that was formerly published only on microfiche. (Micromedex continues to sell the microfiche version of the database.) POISINDEX is typical in other ways of the small quantity of microform materials that have been converted to CD-ROM. Most such items tend to be composed mainly of quantitative data, and they readily lend themselves to loading into database and spreadsheet programs on PCs for further processing.

However, not all the material of this nature that is beginning to appear on CD-ROM was originally published on microfiche. Most large numeric databases begin life on magnetic tape. The Census Bureau's test disc containing data from the 1982 census of agriculture and retail trade and the U.S. Geological Survey's National Earthquake Information Center disc provide examples of databases converted from magnetic tape to CD-ROM. Because tapes are relatively time-consuming to duplicate, do not offer rapid random access, and do require expensive equipment and special expertise to manipulate, we can expect much more use of CD-ROM as a publishing medium for databases that now reside on magnetic tape and receive little or no circulation in that medium.

CD-ROM HAS ITS DRAWBACKS

On the other hand, the real strength of microforms from a librarian's perspective lies in their ability to capture rapidly, cheaply, and at ultra-high resolution massive quantities of information, especially information in page-facsimile

> *CD-ROM will find its place less as a competitor to established media than as a complement to them.*

form. Retention of the look and graphic content of the original printed page is an advantage—and sometimes a requirement—that is all too lightly dispensed with in many conversions to other media. While CD-ROM can serve as a medium for page images, it is inferior to microfiche in terms of the criteria that are significant for most applications.

Capacity

The first of these criteria is capacity. The impressive storage capacity of CD-ROM notwithstanding, it is not a true mass-storage device for page images. CD-ROM is a personal storage medium; it is not engineered to provide ideal performance as a retrieval device for high-resolution images of voluminous files. Depending upon the nature of the source material, the resolution chosen, and the kinds of data compression schemes used, it is possible to fit between 6000 and 20,000 page images on one CD-ROM. This is equivalent to only about 60 to 200 microfiche, assuming that a standard 98-frame grid is used. Given the drawbacks that come into play when CD-ROM databases extend over many discs, the open-ended capacity of a microfiche file is clearly a major advantage.

Cost

The second criterion is cost. The costs—including database definition, data conversion and editing, custom software design, documenta-

MARK VONDERHAAR

Home: Bethesda, Maryland
Job: Product Development Manager, Congressional Information Services, Inc.
Quote: *"In perhaps an apt illustration of McLuhan's theory of media as both transmitting and transforming information content, CD-ROM as a publishing medium reconfigures print information in a profound yet transparent way. CD-ROM has only begun to come into its own as the first medium to bring interactive searching of encyclopedic databases within reach of the individual researcher on a practical economic basis."*

tion, and user support—incurred in the production of a CD-ROM not containing image data are difficult to isolate, and they are grossly underestimated in many of the cost analyses that appear in print. Assuming that the producer of a page-image database wants the database to be searchable, all of the above costs must be incurred, plus the extra costs of the relatively slow process of scanning pages, checking them, and formatting them for the production of a disc.

Even for CD-ROM products that do not include images, prices tend to be higher than for equivalent products on microfiche. In the case of image-facsimile CD-ROMs, the difference in price is still greater. As part of the total expense of a CD-ROM system, a library must also consider the costs of computer equipment, space, training, supervision, and consumables, such as printer paper.

Resolution

The third criterion is resolution. Source-document microfilming makes use of silver-based film, which has unparalleled power to resolve fine detail, especially when the reduction ratio has been adjusted to reflect the nature of the material being filmed. A high-resolution camera image is in many ways more versatile than the original paper document. With the aid of electronic image-processing equipment, micrographic images can be converted into digital bit streams and quickly reproduced at a wide range of line densities. By way of contrast, once a digitally scanned page image is recorded on CD-ROM, its relatively low resolution severely constrains further processing of the image.

Durability

The fourth criterion—one that applies to all microfiche and CD-ROM products—is durability. Microforms are generally conceded to be the leading alternative to paper for long-term retention and archival storage. The stability of data stored on CD-ROMs over long periods of time is still open to question.

But the physical durability of CD-ROM might prove to be irrelevant. As a computer peripheral, a CD-ROM drive is a low-performance device. It would have a very different design were it not for the economies of scale that became possible by basing the product on the CD players manufactured for the high-fidelity audio market. Given the pace of change in computer technology, and even accounting for the life-extending effect of the standards now in place, the day will inevitably come when CD-ROM is followed by a better storage and retrieval device. Will today's CD-ROMs remain widely readable? Probably, although perhaps with growing inconvenience. Established information publishers no doubt would provide an upgrade plan for making the transition to any new digital storage medium. At the same time, there is no denying that microfiche, by their very simplicity, will remain accessible for the indefinite future.

At some point not too distant from the present, higher resolution will be desirable on digital media than can be provided by the 200 to 300 lines-per-inch scanning that is now the norm. Today's image-facsimile CD-ROMs will then fade into obsolescence. But microfiche, with the aid of computer-assisted retrieval equipment that is already on the market, could supply selected images for digital conversion at arbitrarily high resolutions. Or complete microfiche files could serve as the source for new generations of laser-optical products.

CD-ROM HAS ITS PLACE

None of this is to say that CD-ROM is inappropriate for facsimile applications. Depending upon the type of material and the value assigned to various factors, it could be the best option. Regulatory filings and scientific journals are two applications for which the benefits of CD-ROM might outweigh the costs.

Yet, microfiche today remains not only a viable medium for libraries; it is a dynamic one that has not yet reached its full potential. Broadened applications, higher quality production, and better reading and printing equipment have virtually reinvented the medium. CD-ROM is also an ascendant technology. It will be the preferred medium for some publications that would otherwise have appeared on paper, on microfiche, on magnetic tape, or online. Some information will continue to be published in CD-ROM and in other media, while CD-ROM will be the sole choice in other publishing contexts.

At Congressional Information Service, CD-ROM has been selected for electronic dissemination of large databases of index and abstract information that have previously appeared in print form. The indexes on CD-ROM will enhance access to microfiche files containing

> *As a computer peripheral, a CD-ROM drive is a low-performance device. It would have a very different design were it not for the economies of scale that became possible by basing the product on the CD players manufactured for the high-fidelity audio market.*

millions of pages of government documents. There is a future for both microfiche and CD-ROM, and it is one of synergy, of sophisticated information packaging, and of a broader array of choices for information consumers.

[Mark Vonderhaar works in electronic publications development for Congressional Information Service, Inc. CIS, based in Bethesda, Maryland, is a leading publisher of printed indexes, microform collections, and electronic database products that provide access to research resources in the fields of law, business, public policy, and the social sciences.]

EDUCATION AND TRAINING APPLICATIONS

FINALLY, THE REVOLUTION IN TEACHING
By Steven Frankel

USING CD-ROM TECHNOLOGY IN EDUCATION
By John Kernan

MAC BRINGS ANCIENT PHILOSOPHER UP TO DATE
By Frank Clancy

TECHNOLOGY TACKLES THE TRAINING DILEMMA
By Randy Ross

Finally, the Revolution in Teaching

By Steven Frankel
From the *Washington Post*

[Someday soon, children may be carrying CD-ROMs to school instead of books. Steven Frankel takes a look at the ways in which CD-ROM technology will enhance the educational process.]

Things haven't changed much in schools since the turn of the century. The occasional TV or computer may surface, but the most advanced technology in most classes today is still blackboard and chalk. The "real" business of teaching continues to be students reading from books, reciting in class and listening to the teacher.

Because of this track record, predictions that emerging technologies will have a massive effect on education are usually greeted with a big yawn. After all, if traditional methods have withstood radio, film, video and teaching machines, why should any other technology do any better?

But the technological revolution in education is finally at hand. Schools 10 years from now will be explosively different from the ones today. A new combination of existing products—microcomputers, compact disks, adaptive tests, satellite communications and artificial intelligence—will produce the first technological revolution this century that educators will be unable to ignore. This new synthesis will not go the way of educational television, programmed instruction and other innovations that were supposed to irrevocably change education. That's because when compared to conventional American education, the new techniques will be much cheaper and more appealing.

In fact, the annual savings in teacher labor alone could pay for the needed hardware. Labor comprises 70 percent of a typical school district's costs. If the new systems can cut this figure to 50 percent in the typical school system

> *Labor comprises 70 percent of a typical school district's costs. If the new systems can cut this figure to 50 percent in the typical school system that spends $4,000 a year to educate each student (Montgomery County and the District of Columbia are among the many that spend over $5,000), the resulting savings can provide each student with his own new individual instruction system funded from the regular operating budget.*

that spends $4,000 a year to educate each student (Montgomery County and the District of Columbia are among the many that spend over $5,000), the resulting savings can provide each student with his own new individual instruction system funded from the regular operating budget.

In other words, no capital investment in the form of bond issues should be required. This will make the concept immensely appealing to funding bodies, especially when it's coupled with the realization that even if a $500 system lasts only two years, the labor savings during that period will allow either reductions in tax rates or the kinds of improvements—such as class sizes under 15 or drastically improved teachers' salaries—that school systems have, until now, been unable or unwilling to fund.

Also, because the nation's teaching force is aging rapidly, attrition can provide the flexibility school systems will need to replace salary expenditures with outlays for equipment. Thus, from the perspective of the enthusiast for the new technology, there is not now and will not be in the future any teacher "shortage." Rather the next few years will offer a once-in-a-lifetime opportunity to radically change—without labor strife—the way our nation's children are taught.

The popular appeal of such systems will be equally hard to ignore. For, if thoughtfully designed, they'll provide instruction that is broader, more interesting and far more individually tailored to the student than teachers provide now. At the same time, the technology will permit students to extend themselves in ways we can't even conceive yet.

This is why interest in this new education technology will not fade away. If public school boards of education and administrators adopt the head-in-the-sand position they're famous for this time, other parties—from private enterprise to fundamentalist Christians—will quickly move in to fill the educational void.

THE CUSTOMIZED TEACHER

This is how the new education technology comes together. It starts with the computer-adaptive test. That is essentially a personal-computer program with a large bank of test questions ranked in order of difficulty. The computer starts by randomly selecting a fairly easy question. If the student's answer is correct, the program randomly selects a harder question next. If the answer is wrong, the next question will be easier.

Thus the program can quickly determine the highest level on the continuum of test items that the student can answer correctly. The computer then translates this into the student's score—either a grade reflecting the student's performance on the overall test or a judgment on his mastery of a given skill (e.g., adding whole numbers).

Computer-adaptive tests can usually reduce testing time by at least two-thirds—for example, giving an hour test in less than 20 minutes. This kind of a system also insures that almost all of the questions asked of a student are neither impossibly hard nor much too easy—keeping students' interest levels high and frustration rates low, probably contributing to better test performance.

But the biggest benefit of computer-adaptive tests comes when they are combined with compact disks (CDs). These are just like the ordinary music-playing compact disk, but when put into a player connected to an ordinary microcomputer, they can instantly access 500 megabytes, or megs, of text or computer programs.

To help you appreciate just how much text can be stored in 500 megabytes, that's 4,000 times as much storage as on the floppy disk of an Apple, or 100 million words, or 250,000 single-spaced typewritten pages.

But how does all this relate to an instructional revolution? The answer's obvious, once you realize that the complete text of the Encyclopedia Britannica consumes only 80 megs of text. Thus a single CD can contain all of the information included in the equivalent of six complete sets of Britanica, and a shoebox full of CDs could store as much information on most topics as the world's largest libraries.

> *Where educators today write texts, in the future they will write navigation scripts. We will not buy linear collections of book facts so much as an author's view of the data.*
>
> **Russell Lipton**
> **From *Computerworld***

ACCESSING THE CIVIL WAR

Now imagine an eighth-grade history class just a few years from now.

"Okay, class," says the teacher. "We're going to spend the next two weeks delving a bit more deeply into the real causes of the Civil War. Load your Houghton-Mifflin CD, 'The Compleat Civil War.' Go to the Newspaper section and identify stories in the 1859 and 1860 issues of The New York Times and The Abolitionist which might have influenced public opinion on slavery, in the North at least.

"Then go to the Economic Data section of the disk and build a spreadsheet showing the break-even point at which the decreasing cost of cotton and the increasing costs of slave labor would have made slavery an inefficient means of production.

"After that, go to the Texts section of the disk and read 'Uncle Tom's Cabin.' To contrast the image of slavery projected in that book with another view, return to the Newspaper section and find some of the articles appearing in southern newspapers in the 1850s relating to the business aspects of slavery.

"Finally, after you've done all that, go to the Adaptive Testing section and take the Events leading Up the Civil War exam. Your micro will use your results to lay out a reading program for you in the Texts and Journals sections of the disk. After you've done the reading, retake the test to make sure you've mastered the facts. Then put together an essay entitled 'Was Slavery the Real Reason Behind the Civil War?'"

An outlandish example? Not really. A 10-year compilation of the news sections of a dozen newspapers, along with 50 books and a few hundred journal articles can easily fit on a single CD. And there will be plenty of room left over for the software needed to access the disk, for word processing, for spreadsheets and data-base managers and for the adaptive-testing programs that will measure how well the students are understanding what they've been exposed to and guide them to the materials that the computer determines they need.

The software needed to support systems like these is already available. Grolier has recently released its "New American Encyclopedia" on a CD. Borland International has a $95 program called Turbo Lightning that can locate words or strings of text appearing anywhere on a disk in seconds. The two products together can

SCIENCE AND TECHNOLOGY TITLES

Title	Publisher	Price
Applied Science & Technology Index	H.W. Wilson Company 950 University Avenue Bronx, NY 10452 (800)367–6770	$1,495.00/Year
Compact Cambridge Life Sciences Collection	Cambridge Scientific Abstracts 7200 Wisconsin Avenue Suite 601 Bethesda, MD 20816 (301)961–6700	$1,250.00/Year
Encyclopedia of Polymer Science & Engineering	John Wiley & Sons, Inc. 605 Third Avenue New York, NY 10158 (212)850–6000	$3,200.00/Disc
General Science Index	H.W. Wilson Company 950 University Avenue Bronx, NY 10452 (800)367–6770	$1,295.00/Year
Haystack	Ziff-Davis Technical Information Co. 80 Blanchard Road Burlington, MA 01803 (617)273–5500	*
Kirk-Othmer Encyclopedia of Chemical Technology	John Wiley & Sons, Inc. 605 Third Avenue New York, NY 10158 (212)850–6000	$895.00/Disc
McGraw-Hill CD-ROM Science & Technical Reference Set	McGraw-Hill Book Company 11 West 19th Street New York, NY 10011 (212)512–2000	$300.00/Disc

* Contact publisher for prices.

produce a listing of every New American article in which "World War II" and "submarines" appear within 100 words of one another.

With such systems, learning can truly be individualized. For not only can the adaptive-testing programs monitor students' progress very effectively, but the banks of materials the programs can access are so huge that they can easily contain materials of many different levels of complexity. Thus—for the first time—we will really be able to meet all learners' needs.

But that's not all. Philips and Sony—the Dutch/Japanese duo that brought us first the cassette tape recorder, then the video tape recorder, and then the compact disk—have announced that by the end of 1987 they plan to mass market a new device called the CD-I (Compact Disk—Interactive). It will have all of the capabilities of the CD player with one important extra; CD-I players will have an extremely powerful processor built in—they will not need to be hooked into a personal computer. And they will sell initially for under $400.

Philips/Sony forecasts that within four years, the annual production rate for these players will be 24 million. If these projections are correct, before 1990 the CD-I will be ubiquitous in

Title	Publisher	Price
NTIS (1983–present)	OCLC 6565 Frantz Road Dublin, OH 43017-0702 (800)848–5878	$2,395.00
NTIS	SilverPlatter Information, Inc. 37 Walnut Street Wellesley Hills, MA 02181 (617)239–0306	$2,500.00/Year
Plus[37]	Phillips Electronic Instruments Inc. 85 McKee Drive Mahwah, NJ 07430 (201)529–3800	$5,000.00/Disc
Powder Diffraction File	International Centre for Diffraction Data 1601 Park Lane Swarthmore, PA 19801 (215)328–9400	*
Registry of Mass Spectral Data	John Wiley & Sons, Inc. 605 Third Avenue New York, NY 10158 (212)850–6000	$2,895.00/Disc
Science Citation Index	Institute for Scientific Information 3501 Market Street Philadelphia, PA 19104 (215)386–0100	*
Time Table of Science and Innovation	Xiphias 13464 Washington Boulevard Marina Del Rey, CA 90292 (213)821–0074	$150.00/Disc

* Contact publisher for prices.

Compiled by Online Press Inc.

> *We needn't worry about the broad commercial aspects of the technology at first. The sorts of people who watch PBS will lead the way in developing CD-ROM and CD-I. We need to concentrate on decision makers, get the technology in the schools, and hope that down the road future generations demand interactivity.*
>
> **James Burke**
> From *CD-ROM Review*

middle-class American homes. That's because a CD-I hooked up to an ordinary TV can play a movie just as a VCR does today, while at the same time replacing personal computers that allow adults to do much of their office work at home.

This concept is revolutionary enough. However, with the support of computer-adaptive tests, an unanticipated outcome of cheap, omnipresent CD-I players may be that schools, as we now know them, will be gulped down for dessert.

Now we can add to our Civil War lesson color, stereo sound, animation and motion—Matthew Brady's photographs, the Mormon Tabernacle Choir singing "When Johnny Comes Marching Home," and clips from movies such as "Gone with the Wind" and "The Andersonville Trial."

There's already been a CD-I disk demonstrated by Microsoft that teaches about whales. It mixes text, underwater photos, animated charts of migration patterns, narration and Judy Collins' humpback whale song.

Now we're talking about a $500, truly self-contained educational system that can be housed in an enclosure no larger than a ghetto blaster and that will be more appealing. After all, how many teachers can compete with Jacques Cousteau and Judy Collins teaching about whales?

WHAT WILL TEACHERS DO?

Want more? Add a $64 four-ounce modem to the package, and each student's system will be able to communicate with a master instructional computer system via telephone. This will permit teachers to monitor students' work and communicate with them directly, even if the students and teachers are thousands of miles away.

We can take this idea even further. By placing $400, three-foot-diameter, satellite-dish systems at locations where students would do their work, we could configure world-wide instructional systems. Students' work and inquiries could be sent to central locations via the modems, and live presentations and material not embedded on CD-Is could be transmitted via satellites to students at school or at home.

While this might seem unbelievable now, I predict that, if the CD-I systems become entrenched within the next decade, interactive satellite feeds will follow no more than five years after that.

Further, adaptive-testing systems will evolve to the point where today's systems will seem childishly naive. Ultimately, they will truly serve as the "mind" of each CD-I as programmers, realizing the immense potential of such instruction, embed artificial intelligence (AI) in their routines. These programs actually learn from experience and can apply rules and decision-making strategies that expert teachers have found to be highly effective.

AI-based adaptive-testing programs will be able to use students' responses over a long time to adapt themselves to individual students' moods, interests, reading levels and learning methods, as well as to their instructional levels and knowledge. When that point is reached, we'll really be able to talk about computer programs that "understand" students in a way few teachers, faced with classes of 25–40 students, can do today.

What, then, will teachers do? A CD-I-based course can sharply reduce the amount of time teachers spend with students. But it would focus that time on what teachers can do better than machines: motivating students and leading thoughtful discussions.

Whereas a high-school class might meet today with a teacher for four hours a week, CD-I classes would probably be structured around two hours of teacher-directed seminars and two hours dedicated to individual work on the CD-I. Sure, there will have to be adult supervision during the time students are working at their computers, but it could be provided by paraprofessionals earning less than half a teacher's pay.

Reprinted by permission of Steven Frankel.

Using CD-ROM Technology in Education

By John Kernan

[For today's children, who are caught up in an exciting world of video games, television, and music videos, school books may not offer much motivation to learn. John Kernan discusses how we can make learning fun by using the multimedia capabilities of CD-ROM and an intelligent user interface.]

One of the biggest challenges facing educators today is motivating children to learn. In most schools we are applying the same teaching methods we used fifty years ago. Yet look at how much the world has changed. Teachers are now competing with video games, television, and music videos. We must make education more stimulating and more visually interesting to capture students' interest and to motivate them to learn.

Exciting new educational tools can be created by combining CD-ROM technology with personal computers. This combination offers great promise for the future of education, but this promise can be fulfilled only if creative applications are designed to exploit the technology. Educators are not interested in technological innovations alone. They are interested in improving the education process, decreasing the dropout rate, and stimulating thought. If technology is a means to this end, then educators will embrace it.

In 1987, Education Systems Corporation (ESC) demonstrated its commitment to the future of CD-ROM technology. We were the first company to introduce a networked CD-ROM system in schools. Our product is a comprehensive curriculum of more than 1800 lessons in reading, math, and language arts. The lessons are stored on a single compact disc and are accessible from multiple student stations through a local area network. This system has gained widespread acceptance across the United States. We attribute this success to the superior instruction provided by the system, not to the technology, which is secondary from the perspective of our users. Yet it is the CD-ROM technology that made it possible for us to deliver our curriculum as an integrated system and to provide individualized instruction at reasonable cost.

In a nutshell, CD-ROM is an inexpensive mass storage medium. It is often used to distribute large volumes of information inexpensively. The amount of information made available by using microcomputers and CD-ROM would have required a mainframe computer only a few years ago. What does this technology have to offer education?

Currently, the two most common uses of CD-ROMs in education are for storing large reference databases and for storing comprehensive curriculum systems. Both types of information can be stored on a CD-ROM with almost instantaneous access. Databases can be compiled either from multiple information sources or from a single source. Likewise, comprehensive curriculum offerings can come from one publisher or from multiple publishers.

JOHN KERNAN

Home: San Diego, California
Job: President, Education Systems Corporation
Quote: *"CD-ROM will help make vast amounts of curriculum and reference materials available at reasonable cost to every student for use at his or her own pace. CD-ROM dramatically broadens our educational options."*

EVALUATING CD-ROM APPLICATIONS

Evaluating a CD-ROM application for use in a school is no different from assessing any new educational program. The questions are the same:

- Is the application relevant to the instructional program?
- Can it be integrated into the school's instructional plan?
- Does it relate to existing curriculum structures?
- Is adequate training and support provided?
- Will it enhance the ability to teach children?

CD-ROM frees us from some of the constraints associated with other storage devices. Application designs can capitalize on the luxuries afforded by this mass storage. The following features exploit the technology and can be used to add educational value to the information stored on compact disc:

- Networked access.
- Intelligent retrieval systems.
- Innovative user interfaces.
- Multimedia presentation.

To illustrate, let's look at an application that is currently being developed in partnership with Encyclopaedia Britannica, Inc. The application is a CD-ROM version of Compton's Encyclopedia, designed specifically for use by elementary and junior high school students. Compton's articles will be duplicated in their entirety in this new electronic medium.

NETWORKED ACCESS

Students will access articles stored on the compact disc from individual microcomputers connected to a file server and a CD-ROM drive. This networked environment allows simultaneous access to information from all computers in the network. As many as fifty students can read the same article in the encyclopedia at the same time.

Networking microcomputers with a CD-ROM player offers concurrent access to information stored on the compact disc. Such access leverages a school's usage of a reference database in a way that cannot be achieved by using a single printed version. Networked access also optimizes the hardware investment by allowing shared usage of expensive printers and a single CD-ROM player to support multiple computers.

INTELLIGENT RETRIEVAL SYSTEMS

Now we come to the real challenge. A ten-year-old student sits down at one of these networked microcomputers to write a composition on airplanes. How does this child locate the relevant information from the 550 megabytes of material at his or her fingertips? This is a shared challenge for all developers of educational CD-ROM applications.

Traditional Boolean search techniques can be too complex for a child to understand and use

EDUCATION TITLES

Title	Publisher	Price
A World of Language on CD	CALI, Inc. 526 East Quail Road Orem, UT 84057 (801)226–6886	$295.00/Disc
A-V ONLINE	SilverPlatter Information, Inc. 37 Walnut Street Wellesley Hills, MA 02181 (617)239–0306	$795.00/Disc
DIALOG OnDisc ERIC	Dialog Information Services Inc. 3460 Hillview Avenue Palo Alto, CA 94304 (800)334–2564	$950.00/Year
Education Index	H.W. Wilson Company 950 University Avenue Bronx, NY 10452 (800)367–6770	$1,295.00/Year
Education Library	OCLC 6565 Frantz Road Dublin, OH 43017-0702 (800)848–5878	$350.00/Year
ERIC	SilverPlatter Information, Inc. 37 Walnut Street Wellesley Hills, MA 02181 (617)239–0306	$650.00/Year
ERIC-Current Files	OCLC 6565 Frantz Road Dublin, OH 43017-0702 (800)848–5878	$425.00/Year

effectively. Incomplete and inaccurate queries are likely to result in no information or in too much information. Students need an intuitive retrieval system, one that is more responsive to the way they think about finding information.

ESC recognized the need for such a system to retrieve information from Compton's Encyclopedia. The electronic edition will use a relevance ranking system to present search results. Relevance is determined by awarding a score to each article that is based on the number of occurrences of the search terms or of related terms.

The student will enter a search request of one or more familiar words. The system will then establish a link between the search words and the index terms for the database. For example, a search term of *airplane* might lead to articles on the Wright brothers or World War I. The student can use the responses to narrow or broaden the query. The result is a human-scale response to a human-scale inquiry.

While the choice of retrieval techniques will vary by application, the objective of these techniques should be the same. Children require a natural, intuitive means of accessing massive

Title	Publisher	Price
ERIC-Retrospective Files	OCLC 6565 Frantz Road Dublin, OH 43017-0702 (800)848–5878	$900.00/Set
First National Item Bank & Test Development System	TESCOR, Inc. 12020 Sunrise Valley Drive Suite 260 Reston, VA 22091 (703)476–8000	$300.00/Month
International Encyclopedia of Education	Pergamon Compact Solution Athene House 66-73 Shoe Lane London EC4P 4AB ENGLAND	$1,950.00/Disc
Peterson's Gradline	SilverPlatter Information, Inc. 37 Walnut Street Wellesley Hills, MA 02181 (617)239–0306	$695.00/Year
Peterson's College Database	SilverPlatter Information, Inc. 37 Walnut Street Wellesley Hills, MA 02181 (617)239–0306	$595.00/Year
Science Helper (K–8)	PC-SIG Inc. 1030-D East Duane Avenue Sunnyvale, CA 94086 (408)730–9291	$195.00/Disc
Texas Education Encyclopedia	Quantum Access Inc. 1700 West Loop South Suite 1460 Houston, TX 77027 (713)622–3211	$2,000.00/Year

Compiled by Online Press Inc.

> *Children require a natural, intuitive means of accessing massive volumes of information. Intelligent retrieval systems are therefore a critical element in a successful CD-ROM application for schools.*

volumes of information. Intelligent retrieval systems are therefore a critical element in a successful CD-ROM application for schools.

INNOVATIVE USER INTERFACES

The user interface is an extension of the retrieval system. In a broad sense, it is what the student sees on the screen. It is how the student navigates through the system. The opportunity for innovation in the design of the interface is limited only by our imaginations. There is enormous potential for creativity in this area.

Children have different learning styles, personalities, and ability levels. These differences are often viewed as obstacles to the normal educational process, which is targeted at the average student. However, innovative user interfaces can turn this negative into a positive. The interface makes the information accessible and understandable to a wide range of users.

For example, the CD-ROM version of Compton's Encyclopedia will incorporate an online dictionary. When a student encounters an unfamiliar word in an article, he or she can request that a definition be displayed in a window on the screen. Another feature aimed at making the content more understandable is called "Take Another Look." This option allows students to view potentially difficult information from another vantage point. Complex concepts are converted to diagrams or are restated in simpler language for younger students or those with reading problems.

MULTIMEDIA PRESENTATION

Finally, the presentation of printed material in an electronic form should optimize the strengths of the new medium. In the case of CD-ROM technology, this means including multimedia presentation. By *multimedia,* I mean the combination of text, speech, music, color graphics, and animation. The mass storage capacity of CD-ROM allowed us to design multimedia lessons to create a multi-sensory learning environment for children.

Multimedia presentation will be used to make the Compton's project come alive. Many of the photographs, maps, charts, illustrations, and tables will be included in addition to the text of the articles. Animated sequences will be added to feature articles. Audio will be used mainly to pronounce glossary terms, but will also provide music.

CONCLUSION

Schools will accept CD-ROM technology when broadly available educational applications are able to take advantage of the technology. Cost is not the barrier to acceptance; the barrier is innovation in application design.

Networked access makes the information available to many users at the same time. Intelligent retrieval systems make the information accessible. Innovative user interfaces make the information understandable. And lastly, multimedia presentation makes the information exciting. In combination, these features make CD-ROM technology educational.

[John Kernan is President and CEO of Education Systems Corporation. Prior to joining ESC, he served as Group Vice President and General Manager of Gill Management Services, Inc., where he founded the Software Products Division. He was also Vice President of Product Development at DELTAK, Inc., the world's largest producer of video and computer-based education programs for adults.]

Mac Brings Ancient Philosopher Up to Date

By Frank Clancy
From *MacWEEK*

[Jim Bierman believes that if Aristotle were alive today, he'd be using HyperCard. As Frank Clancy explains, Bierman is bringing Greek philosophy alive on his Macintosh and hopes his work will be included in the CD-ROM Perseus Project.]

To reach Jim Bierman's house in the hills just outside this coastal city [*Santa Cruz, CA*], you take a narrow, private road that climbs steeply through a grove of redwoods, winding past llamas, cows, and a handful of scattered houses until you get to a grassy meadow.

On a recent summer day, Monterey Bay could be seen in the distance, stretching to the fog-shrouded horizon. A lone hawk and several turkey vultures circled lazily on updrafts of air. Inside his wooden house nestled in a hillside on the meadow's edge, Bierman was packing his bags: In two days, the professor of dramatic literature and theater at the University of California, Santa Cruz, would leave for Nicosia, the capital of the divided Mediterranean island of Cyprus, for an international symposium on ancient Greek drama. There he would deliver a lecture on Sophocles' "Oedipus The King," written in the fifth century B.C.

But the soft-spoken Bierman was more excited at the prospect of showing fellow scholars a more modern intellectual endeavor—his HyperCard study guide to Aristotle's "Poetics." The stack, Aristotle's Greek Tragedy Construction Kit, is aimed at college-level students of literature, theater and the classics, and it took Bierman much of the past year to develop. While planning his trip to Nicosia, Bierman had arranged, through Apple's Higher Education Department, for a Mac Plus to be available at the conference so that he could demonstrate the stack—an entertaining, accessible and intelligent program that uses diagrams, animation and graphics to augment Aristotle's original text and Bierman's explanations of the philosopher's work.

Relatively few college professors have thus far had the knowledge and interest to develop computer study aids in the field of literature: Of the 107 Mac programs in the spring catalog of Kinko's Academic Courseware Exchange (ACE) of Ventura, Calif., which is publishing Bierman's stack, only two are in literature. It is probably not surprising, however, that Bierman became intrigued by the prospect of using modern technology to study ancient writings because throughout his academic career, he has pursued an eclectic, often idiosyncratic array of interests.

The 46-year-old Bierman has studied, written about and taught 17th-century Spanish drama and the French playwright Molière. He has also researched the Miss California pageant and the Unification Church of the Rev. Sun Myung Moon. He has written some 20 plays, including one about the followers of Rev. Moon, called "Moonchild," that was produced as a made-for-television movie.

In the late 1970s, he designed and built his house. The two-story, gray wooden building is a near-perfect expression of its only occupant: unobtrusive and plainly furnished, wide open and airy, eminently practical and immediately appealing. Its northern wall and roof are insulated by earth; the southern wall, which faces the water, is glass. And inside, on a work table 20 feet from the glass wall that looks out over the bay, sits Bierman's Macintosh Plus.

Bierman cheefully described himself as a Macaholic. "When I got my Mac 128K [in 1984]," he remembered, "I became a diehard fanatic. I had to learn programming. I spent my summers learning C and Pascal."

Having studied at Princeton University in Princeton, N.J., where he earned his bachelor's degree; the Sorbonne University in Paris; and Stanford University in Palo Alto, Calif., where he earned his doctorate—learning Latin, French, Spanish, and Greek along the way—Bierman found computer languages to be fairly straightforward. He designed a font and two public-

> *Bierman expressed hope that his work on Aristotle will be included in the Perseus Project, an ambitious program sponsored by Bowdoin College and Harvard University using Macintoshes with CD-ROM disks to develop what promises to be the world's largest compendium of original source material and scholarship about ancient Greek civilization.*

domain computer-animation programs that were impressive enough for the computer science department at the university to invite him to teach a class on computers in art, an invitation he declined.

But it was HyperCard that pushed Bierman to more complex programming. In his Greek Tragedy Construction Kit, Bierman relies primarily on Aristotle's "Poetics," an attempt to systematically explore the elements of tragedy. The work of the Greek philosopher, who lived in the fourth century B.C., was the first example of Western literary theory and dramatic criticism ever published. "It's almost like a math," Bierman said. "You begin with definitions and axioms, and then you develop your hypotheses based on them. You constantly refer back to your definitions. Although he's talking about ethics and esthetics, he's very, very systematic."

Yet as anyone even remotely familiar with Aristotle knows, "Poetics" is an extremely difficult work, partly because the philosopher refers constantly to material found elsewhere, in and out of the "Poetics." (In one recently published edition, the notes take up twice as much space as the actual text.) For his stack, Bierman developed 70 separate full screens and more than 300 windows that allow the user to move fluidly between the original text and related material, including Bierman's analysis.

With Aristotle's definition of tragedy, for example, the user can immediately read the definitions of any of 11 key terms by clicking the mouse. For students of Greek, clicking on a translation of Aristotle brings forth the original Greek text. "What I hope to reflect," Bierman said, "is the elegance and deeply penetrating quality of Aristotle's thought. What I attempted to make was a piece of software that was itself elegant and deeply penetrating."

Bierman reminded himself throughout the development process that in order to succeed he could not simply publish a book on disk. "I love books," he said, pointing to a 15-foot-high, floor-to-ceiling bookshelf in his study. "But words on screen are more difficult to read than

TEACHING LANGUAGES WITH CD-ROM

The reality of CD-ROM is this: The potential is obvious in its memory capacity, present level of industry-wide standardization, and multimedia capabilities. Its limitations of cost, access of data, and difficulty in taking advantage of the multimedia capabilities seem to center around a continuing need for standards both in hardware and software.

In a way, CD-ROM also suffers from its own hype. Because CD-Audio became a household term, many have expected CD-ROM to maintain a constant upward growth since it was introduced. This has not happened. Ironically, one suggested reason for this is that of a backlash from CD-Audio popularity:

"In the CD-Audio market, high volume production has lowered retail hardware prices to under $200. As a result, it's difficult for many CD-ROM drive shoppers to justify paying up to $1000 for what seems to be merely an enhanced CD-Audio player.... The promise of low cost drives raises user expectations about CD-ROM and simultaneously stymies its initial growth." [Brian Brewer (from "Still Waiting for 'It' to Happen" in *CD-ROM Review*, January 1988)].

As negative as this may seem, CD-ROM is far from being a loser. Its inherent strengths and wide-spread industry support appear to ensure an eventual and secure, if slower-than-expected, niche in the computer world. At this point it would be effective for us in CALICO [*the Computer Assisted Language Learning and Instruction Consortium*] to determine how we can influence this coming acceptance and shape it for our purposes in teaching languages. Here are a few suggestions:

1. We need to cooperate in developing CD-ROM software. A first-time CD-ROM project can be overwhelming for one group to carry out. Why

on a printed page. With this program, every screen has to be engaging. I wanted the program to be beautiful. I think that's a tradition with Mac programs."

Using FullPaint from Ashton-Tate of Torrance, Calif., Bierman enhanced mythic images from ancient Greek vases that he found in an old French collection. His computer lexicon resembles the battered Greek dictionary he used at Princeton, complete with his freshman-year address on the inside front cover. And he wrote several animation routines that use mnemonic devices to emphasize important points.

Bierman expressed hope that his work on Aristotle will be included in the Perseus Project, an ambitious program sponsored by Bowdoin College and Harvard University using Macintoshes with CD-ROM disks to develop what promises to be the world's largest compendium of original source material and scholarship about ancient Greek civilization. But for his own next project, Bierman plans to jump ahead a couple of millenia from ancient Greece to

> *If Aristotle were alive today, he'd be using HyperCard. It's perfect for the way he thought: non-linear, non-sequential, and multileveled.*

write an interactive fiction game based on Shakespeare's "Hamlet."

If the reception afforded Bierman's computer version of Aristotle at the Cyprus conference is any indication, students of Shakespeare have something to look forward to. A few days after

---

not organize our efforts to produce software by sharing development costs among several institutions and commercial concerns?

2. We need to create a clearinghouse for information and ideas on CD-ROM in language teaching. The CD-ROM SIG is trying to gather knowledge and ideas about CD-ROM that we can make available to all CALICO members in order to encourage CD-ROM software research and production. Another possible approach is to have discussions (at the symposium or via modem or mail) on the most effective kinds of CD-ROM products for language teaching and the possibility of authoring systems for creating CALL [*computer assisted language learning*] lessons using CD-ROM discs as a source of multimedia input.

3. We need to encourage standardization. As effective as the Yellow Book standard is, we need more standardization in the area of indexing, search and retrieval software, and especially in multimedia applications. We should also encourage the development of effective network systems that allow one CD ROM drive to serve more than one computer station. CALICO has been given a mandate by the American Society for Testing and Materials (ASTM) to encourage standardization for applications of technology in language instruction. With such a mandate, we have a position of strength from which to push for standards for CD-ROM and all other areas of technology which can help us teach language better.

... The "Wait and See" option language teachers often take is not always the best; it can delay the acceptance of a useful tool. In CD-ROM we have an opportunity to directly influence the course of a growing technology. May we make the most of it.

By Verl Woodbury. From the *CALICO Journal.*

returning to Santa Cruz from Cyprus, Bierman reported that although the computer is virtually unknown in the Cypriot theater world, his stack was received enthusiastically—both for its use of the computer and his analysis of Aristotle. When the head of the Cypriot actor's union took Bierman to lunch, he made a point of bringing along his son, a computer programming student, who was intrigued by HyperCard. An East German director approached Bierman about translating his work into German.

But what Bierman seemed to have enjoyed most in Cyprus was the shared passion for Aristotle at the symposium. "Among Greek Cypriots," he said, "Aristotle's word is the ultimate authority. At the conference, people were quoting him from memory. It was great fun, an incredible experience to have people quoting the stuff I had on disk."

While Bierman has no illusion that every student will develop such passion through the computer, he does hope his stack will help them better understand the philosopher's work. He hopes, for example, that students will remember that the Greek word *hamartia*, often mistranslated as "tragic flaw," means an ig-

LANGUAGE AND LITERATURE TITLES

Title	Publisher	Price
Computer Library	Computer Library/Ziff Communications 1 Park Avenue New York, NY 10016 (212)503–4400	$695.00/Year
The Constitution Papers	Optical Media International Reflective Arts International 495 Alberto Way Los Gatos, CA 95032 (408)395–4332	$29.95
Dissertation Abstracts Ondisc: Archival Edition	UMI (University Microfilms International) 300 North Zeeb Road Ann Arbor, MI 48106 (800)521–3044	$5,495.00/System
Dissertation Abstracts Ondisc: Current Edition	UMI (University Microfilms International) 300 North Zeeb Road Ann Arbor, MI 48106 (800)521–3044	$1,695.00/Year
Essay and General Literature Index	H.W. Wilson Company 950 University Avenue Bronx, NY 10452 (800)367–6770	$695.00/Year
LISA	SilverPlatter Information, Inc. 37 Walnut Street Wellesley Hills, MA 02181 (617)239–0306	$995.00/Unit

norance of some particular fact—as with Oedipus, who did not know that the man he killed was his father.

It should be easy to remember. *Hamartia* was once an archery term meaning "a missing of the mark"; when clicking on the HyperCard screen in which Bierman defines *hamartia,* the user sees a black arrow move across the computer screen and land, with a resounding "boing," wide of an archery target. Like several other animation routines in Bierman's stack, it is simple but effective.

And for Bierman, visitors who point to a contradiction of using a computer to study the 2300-year-old "Poetics" are also wide of the mark. "If Aristotle were alive today," Bierman said, "he'd be using HyperCard. It's perfect for the way he thought: non-linear, non-sequential, and multi-leveled."

Reprinted from *MacWEEK,* August 23, 1988. Copyright © 1988 by Ziff Communications Company.

Title	Publisher	Price
MLA International Bibliography	H.W. Wilson Company 950 University Avenue Bronx, NY 10452 (800)367-6770	$1,495.00/Year
National Newspaper Index on InfoTrac	Information Access Company 362 Lakeside Drive Foster City, CA 94404 (800)227-8431	$4,000.00/System per Year
OCLC Compact Disc Cataloging System	Online Computer Library Center 6565 Frantz Road Dublin, OH 43017-0702 (614)764-6000	*
Pravda 1987 on CD-ROM	ALDE Publishing 4830 West 77th Street P.O. Box 35326 Minneapolis, MN 55435 (612)835-5240	$249.00/Disc
Readers' Guide Abstracts	H.W. Wilson Company 950 University Avenue Bronx, NY 10452 (800)367-6770	$1,995.00/Year
Readers' Guide to Periodical Literature	H.W. Wilson Company 950 University Avenue Bronx, NY 10452 (800)367-6770	$1,095.00/Year
The Visual Dictionary	Facts on File, Inc. 460 Park Avenue South New York, NY 10016 (800)322-8755	*

* Contact publisher for prices.

Compiled by Online Press Inc.

Technology Tackles the Training Dilemma

By Randy Ross
From *High Technology Business*

[In the last article of this section, Randy Ross explains why more and more corporations are investing in training programs and extolls the virtues of interactive training. Although videodisc is still preeminent in the field, CD-ROM, CD-I, and, eventually, DVI will slowly gain ground as their respective technologies stabilize.]

Training has been a problem for businesses since business began. In the earliest days, people learned from one-on-one instruction; craftsmen served apprenticeships and the children of the wealthy learned essential skills from private tutors. Head-to-head training is still probably the most effective method ever developed, but it's useless for teaching large numbers of students. When the Industrial Revolution created a need for an educated work force, schooling came to the masses in classrooms governed by a new type of educator—bespectacled Miss Crabtrees wielding chalk in one hand and a hickory switch in the other. Such classes could handle large numbers of students, but quality suffered because Miss Crabtree had to slow down lessons to accommodate the weaker students.

At last technology is providing solutions to the training dilemma, with methods that don't compromise quality for quantity. New methods rely on "interactive" technologies that adjust to the individual student, just as an attentive tutor would. And they're fast. Experts claim that computer-based training and interactive video can cut training time in half.

Both computer-based training and interactive video rely on computer technology to gear training to students' needs. For instance, a worker learning how to repair computer equipment may be presented with a lesson followed by a quiz. An incorrect answer on the quiz cues the computer program to send him to a remedial section that helps him find the correct answer. However, people who understand the material can race through from start to finish at a faster pace. Such learning programs are interactive because a student's responses determine the sequence of the training interactions. Also, workers can tackle training at any time, as long as a personal computer or interactive-video monitor are at the ready.

When large companies need to reach many employees scattered across the country, teleconferencing and business-owned TV networks are rapidly becoming the method of choice. Private broadcasts let a company's best instructor reach all the pupils at the same time....

These advanced training technologies come not a moment too soon. Faced with increasing international competition, businesses need well-trained workers now more than ever, especially businesses that depend on complicated and often confusing technologies. What's more, in this cost-sensitive era when companies must get by with slim staffs, training can play an essential role in getting the most from the remaining workers.

The need for training will only intensify. Business and industry is changing so fast that, among today's workers who make it through the year 2000, about 75 percent of them will need retraining. Young people now entering the work force will change occupations about four times during their careers, and at least two of those occupations don't exist yet, according to the *Training and Development Journal.* Combine a shrinking pool of entry-level workers with the 23 million American adults who are considered functionally illiterate, and it's clear that more corporations will offer basic education in the workplace.

Already, U.S. businesses spend about $30 billion on education and training each year, according to an estimate from the American Society for Training and Development. Training

> *Faced with increasing international competition, businesses need well-trained workers now more than ever, especially businesses that depend on complicated and often confusing technologies.*

expenditures should increase 5 percent per year for the next five years, predicts Stuart Krasny, president of California-based SK&A Research.

Those training dollars pay for a range of approaches—no-tech methods such as seminars and workbooks; low-tech techniques, including videotape and film, and high-tech alternatives such as interactive computer software and laser-disc systems.

Among the high-tech methods, computer-based training—interactive systems consisting of a computer and training software—accounts for a whopping 30 percent of the corporate training dollar, Krasny says. Interactive-video systems, which use a computer, video-disc player, and a 12-inch laser disc, now take only about a 2 percent slice, but are growing. By 1992, interactive video will cut into demand for instructors and videotape, and account for about 8 percent of the training market, according to Krasny.

Similarly, teleconferencing, which transmits lessons to several remote sites simultaneously,

> *Young people now entering the work force will change occupations about four times during their careers, and at least two of those occupations don't exist yet.*

accounts for about 2 percent of corporate training expenses. Krasny expects that figure to double to 4 percent over the next four years. By that time, even more advanced training technologies should be in place. Systems being developed by such heavy-weight researchers as General Electric and Sony Corp. will use compact discs with digitized images to give workers access to large databases.

Even though machines may never match the love Miss Crabtree put into her lessons, high-tech training methods handle many tasks more efficiently. A 1984 study conducted by IBM showed interactive video to be about three times more effective at teaching than an instructor, and consultants claim that computer-based training teaches one-third faster than do standard, instructor-led classes.

Another benefit of machine instruction is that it increases one-on-one interaction. The oft-quoted axiom holds that we recall 25 percent of what we hear, 45 percent of what we hear and see, and 70 percent of what we do. Interactive video and computer-based training force students to participate, which can be a feat in itself. "In first grade, people learn how to get by without paying attention," notes Gloria Gery,

author of *Making CBT Happen* (the "CBT" stands for computer-based training).

Other advantages of high-tech teaching include consistency, efficiency, and economies of scale. "Trainers are human, and have good days and bad days," says Thomas Reeves, assistant professor of instructional technology at the University of Georgia. A machine that delivers a prerecorded lesson has no such variation—management can be sure that each employee receives the same information every time. In addition, by eliminating tangents, interactive technology can reduce class time by one-third, says Ruth Clark, a California-based training consultant.

Further, students can save their companies time and money by using self-paced instruction that lets them skip lessons they already know and focus on unfamiliar material. Faster learners get back on the job sooner; slower learners can redo a lesson until they get it right, without appearing incompetent in front of peers or wasting class time.

Even though interactive video is dwarfed by the number of computer-based training systems installed, it represents an up-and-coming training method. The technology uses a video disc read by a laser, similar to audio compact discs that play music, but packed with images and controlled by a microcomputer. A student uses a keyboard to respond to questions, options, or problems presented by the program on the disc.

The major benefit of interactive video is its ability to provide television-like, full-motion pictures. These are hard to beat when teaching behaviors, such as how to act on a sales call, or for demonstrating hands-on skills that are difficult or dangerous to undertake in real life. Video simulations are used to teach everything from how to handle a nuclear-power-plant disaster to emergency medical care.

However, the high cost of hardware and video production typically limit interactive video to organizations with deep pockets, such as governments and large corporations. "If you're not training [at least] a thousand people,

I'm not sure you can justify [customized] interactive video," says Charles Hall, sales manager for Interactive Medical Communications of Waltham, Mass. Interactive-video hardware can add about $4,500 to the cost of a personal computer, or total about $9,450 for an integrated system such as the IBM InfoWindow. Major hardware suppliers include IBM, Sony, and Matrox Electronic Systems Ltd. of Dorval, Quebec. Custom-made interactive-video software can cost about $200,000 to $450,000, according to Richard Michaels, vice president of Learncom, a company in Cambridge, Mass., that makes training software.

When it's available, generic, off-the-shelf software can be considerably cheaper. Interactive Medical Communications, a $12-million company that makes only interactive-video products, offers a series of generic programs that teach Occupational Safety and Health Administration standards, for about $1,700 per program. The company also rents hardware; a complete package can cost as little as $125 per trainee.

For companies that can afford the up-front investment for hardware and software, the long-term payoff from interactive-video training can be substantial. A system used by the U.S. Army cuts training time by almost 50 percent for computer repairmen who must learn to maintain and repair disc drives in Digital Equipment's VAX minicomputers. Formerly, an instructor needed three days to train 15 people, giving each student time on the computer. The interactive-video system lets instructors teach 15 people in less than two days. Instructors can cost $400 a day, so this can represent a substantial savings.

Such savings in time and expense account for the sudden pickup in the popularity of interactive video. Applied Learning Inc. of Naperville, Ill.—probably the biggest player in the frag-

AUTOMOTIVE TITLES

Title	*Publisher*	*Price*
Automated Parts Catalog	ADP 1950 Hassell Road Hoffman Estates, IL 60195-2308 (312)397–1700	*
Chrysler Parts Catalog	Bell and Howell 5700 Lombardo Center Suite 220 Seven Hills, OH 44351 (216)642–9060	*
GM Parts Catalog	Bell and Howell 5700 Lombardo Center Suite 220 Seven Hills, OH 44351 (216)642–9060	*
Honda/Accura Parts Catalog	Bell and Howell 5700 Lombardo Center Suite 220 Seven Hills, OH 44351 (216)642–9060	*

* Contact publisher for prices.   **Compiled by Online Press Inc.**

mented training industry, with about $200 million in annual sales—has seen its interactive-video revenues jump from $3 million in 1985 to an anticipated $80 million this year. "Interactive video is replacing live education," says company president William Roach.

The U.S. Army has been a major benefactor of the technology and recently signed a hardware contract with Matrox that could be worth as much as $223.5 million over the next five years. At Fort Benning in Georgia, an interactive-video system simulates tank warfare, eliminating hazards to soldiers and damage to expensive equipment. On one occasion, trainees using actual tanks drove into a river and several people drowned, recalls Thomas Reeves, assistant professor of instructional technology at the University of Georgia. The tanks also wore paths in the ground that were easy to follow, allowing drivers to cheat. No such problems arise during a computerized simulation.

Interactive video is also making significant inroads in sales training, because it can demonstrate body language and other visual cues important in approaching a customer. Massachusetts Mutual Insurance Company of Springfield, Mass., uses a system that trains agents, and then videotapes their performance in various sales situations. Agents may retape the exercise as many times as they like, then show it to a supervisor for a critique. The $15,000 system includes a touchscreen monitor, a laser-disc player, a color camera and video recorder/player, and an IBM AT personal computer, all housed in a portable cabinet.

The Massachusetts Mutual system cuts training time by about half, says Jane Curtis, director of field development. At one field office, the system contributed to a 40 percent increase in agent productivity, as measured by sales results.

Because laser-disc video systems offer greater interaction, they could eventually replace videotape in the training industry. However, it will be at least five years before disc systems make serious inroads. At the moment, videotape is the training industry's most popular technology. A survey by Minneapolis-based Lakewood Research found that 80 percent of the trainers polled use videotape, compared to 35 percent who use computer-based training systems, and 3.9 percent using interactive video.

ACTV of New York is developing an interactive videotape system that may help the older technology hold on even longer, particularly as companies seek to maximize the return-on-investment of their tape equipment before buying laser-disc hardware. The ACTV system is being developed for the consumer market, but may find its way into training by the end of the decade, says Rockley Miller, editor of *The Video Disc Monitor* newsletter. The device can read one of several parallel tracks on the videotape, allowing the program to branch into various areas in response to student inputs. The interactive tape would run on a conventional videotape player equipped with a "black box" to read the specially coded tape.

Nevertheless, the technology still has limits for training, says Miller. In particular, videotape can't hold a still image for very long, and the tape cannot easily go backward when a student's performance indicates the need for review—something that's a snap with random-access video discs.

Computer-based training systems lack the visual capability of interactive video, but their lower cost makes them attractive alternatives for teaching cognitive tasks such as memorizing a body of knowledge or learning the steps of a procedure. Generally, computer-based training consists of either custom or generic software on a floppy disk that runs on a conventional personal computer. Custom programs can cost $40,000 to $70,000, about one-fifth the price of comparable interactive-video software, says Michaels of Learncom, which also sells off-the-shelf software ranging from computer literacy to project management for less than $200.

Prudential Insurance Company of America uses a computerized training program to prepare agents for the National Association of Security Dealers licensing exam. The company hired Longman Financial Services Institute Inc. of Southfield, Mich., to develop the program. When agents were taught in classroom lectures, only about 68 percent passed the exam, says John Murray III, Prudential's vice president of research. With the computer-based training program, the pass rate jumped to almost 90 percent. The program has also helped Prudential deal with rapid agent turnover: Its agents are more content after passing the exam, because the license lets them sell products such as mutual funds and variable annuities that boost commissions.

Computer-based training also is used extensively for management training, especially for exercises that simulate business situations. Such exercises let managers practice running various divisions of a company—operations, finance, research and development—without making real-life judgment errors that could damage the company. During a typical simulation, participants divide into teams that are given the responsibility of running a fictitious company. The computer program crunches through the data and provides quick feedback on the imaginary company's profits and competitive position, based on the management decisions made by the players.

When immediacy is an issue, teleconferencing continues to be the best way to get the word out. On the evening of last October's stock-market crash, several financial services and brokerage firms, including Merrill Lynch, used private television broadcasts to contact brokers scattered across the country. "In situations like that, the savings cannot be measured," asserts Elliot Gould, publisher of the industry newsletter *Telespan*.

More tangible savings from teleconferencing come from reductions in training-related travel. Using a business TV network, companies can broadcast training programs to employees at their workplaces.

Although business TV is widely considered a successful training technology, its high price limits it mainly to large companies. Installing a private network can cost more than $1 million, plus ongoing operation and production costs. And even though satellite-telecast programs reach large, dispersed audiences, they are basically an extension of the auditorium-lecture approach. Interaction between lecturer and worker is limited to the few telephone calls that may get through to the studio. "A trainer could not possibly handle all the calls. He probably

> *CD-I could be useful for teaching sales people who must sell a wide array of products from a catalog, such as those from large department stores or auto-parts dealers.*

gets a tenth of 1 percent," says Ron Zemke of *Training* magazine.

In the near future, training will be delivered on adaptations of compact-disc players. Like video discs, compact discs store data as a digital pattern of pits on the disc's surface. A laser reads the pits, which are then decoded and presented as pictures on a screen, sound through a speaker, or data on a computer monitor.

Compact discs, which are technically the same as the 4¾-inch CDs used in home stereo systems, can store vast amounts of data—one disc can hold the equivalent of the information available on 1,500 floppy disks.

Compact disc-interactive (CD-I), being developed by Philips, in cooperation with Matsushita and Sony, combines limited interactive video with large databases. SK&A Research's Krasny says CD-I could be useful for teaching sales people who must sell a wide array of products from a catalog, such as those from large department stores or auto-parts dealers. In addition, at about $2,000 for a complete system, CD-I hardware would cost about one-third the price of a comparable video-disc system. CD-I is expected to hit the consumer market in mid-1989, and possibly the training market in another year after that.

General Electric is developing an alternative to CD-I that can deliver moving pictures, but experts say the picture quality is not up to snuff. This technology, called digital video interactive (DVI), uses add-on boards to coordinate a personal computer, a CD-ROM drive, an amplifier, and speakers. The add-on boards could add approximately $7,000 to the cost of such a system. DVI technology, which is expected to reach the consumer market in 1990, can accommodate more full-screen, full-motion video than CD-I.

Although compact-disc technology represents the next wave of training technology, it's still too early to speculate on when it will arrive. The training industry has been slow to accept interactive technologies, and, as one executive put it: "You can't hit them up every year with a new gadget." The acceptance process could be accelerated when CD systems are able to provide acceptable moving images; until then, many software developers may ignore CD technologies.

But even the most sophisticated, readily adoptable, technology will not put Miss Crabtree on the unemployment line. In the future, instruction may involve a machine that delivers the lesson and a person who handles problems and can therefore spend more time with trainees. The bottom line: Miss Crabtree will become more efficient and her students will become more productive.

Reprinted with permission from *High Technology Business* magazine, September 1988. Copyright © 1988 by Infotechnology Publishing Corp.

RESEARCH AND REFERENCE APPLICATIONS

ARCHIVING THE ARCHIVES
From *Computerworld*

O.E.D., IN A GIGABYTE TASK, TO TRANSFER TO COMPACT DISKS
By Francis X. Clines

CD-ROM AND THE BIBLE
By Bob Hall

FROM ONLINE TO ONDISC: A THREE-YEAR UPDATE
By Rick Meyer

STACKING UP CANDIDATES AT ABC
By Steven Levy

Archiving the Archives

From *Computerworld*

[No more paper at the National Archives? Although it's not possible to do away with paper altogether, a small task force is prototyping ways to put 15 billion page images into a searchable database that will facilitate research and preserve fragile paper documents from the wear and tear of repeated handling.]

According to Bill Hooton, director of the National Archives' optical digital image project, the archives' charter reads, "To store, maintain and make available to the public the records of the federal government." With hundreds of thousands of such records, that's a tall order to fill.

Hooton, 36, started in DP at the Internal Revenue Service in 1970, became interested in videodisk for image storage and retrieval and eventually designed a paperless IRS using optical disks. After that ambitious trial project was under way, he moved to the National Archives as part of its high-tech task force. Currently, he is installing the test system that will put the fragile 19th-century personnel documents of Tennessee's Confederate soldiers into an optical storage system put together by Unisys Corp.'s System Development Group. Hooton, who is also chairman of the Digital Image Application Users Group, spoke recently with Kelly Shea, a *Computerworld* assistant editor, about the nuances of the Archives' system.

What needs will an optical imaging system fill at the national archives? The biggest need is that we're completely out of space. So we either have to build a new building and/or we have to do something with the existing space.

Number two is a real preservation issue—we don't want to handle those original documents. It's also a real pain in the neck to try to get at the information—of course, any kind of manual filing system would be, especially in terms of the six or seven billion page images of permanent records that we have. And those are the ones we have to keep forever. We have about 15 billion, if you count everything.

So those are two issues, and of course, trying to automate the retrieval is another one.

> *It's also a real pain in the neck to try to get at the information — of course, any kind of manual filing system would be, especially in terms of the six or seven billion page images of permanent records that we have. And those are the ones we have to keep forever. We have about 15 billion, if you count everything.*

When this system is up and running, will you put as many documents as possible on it? Well, not necessarily on this system. This is really an isolated system, intended to be a research test bed. That's why it's so flexible. If we went with a much larger system, we would probably redesign it.

How many users will be able to access this system? At one time, we'll have four pure retrieval terminals, with the possibility of about eight, because any of these high-resolution monitors—which are also used for quality control and indexing—can be used for anything else. They're strictly controlled by the user profile on the password.

Have you followed the traditional rules of DP acquisition with this system? Oh yes. There's only one benefit to doing a research test as opposed to a pure production DP-type of an operation, and that is that you don't have to do a cost-benefit analysis before you buy it. Because by definition you are trying to get that information.

Have there been any major problems so far? When do you plan to have this test running? The date right now for installation completion is Dec. 7. I expect it will be before that.

Everything is going extremely smoothly, much more smoothly than anything I've ever been involved with. This is a $1 million system—actually it's a $4 million system, but we paid $1 million for it because it's advertising for Unisys.

I think the reason things are going so smoothly is that Unisys realizes that they'll either get $30 million worth of advertising if it's a good system, or they'll have to close their doors if it's a bad one.

I'm in a position to tell the world, and I plan on telling the world. So they're working devilishly hard to try and make it a beautiful system. They have done that, and things have been on time, and it's really nice so far. I reserve the right to change my mind on that, though.

How will MIS shops interface with such systems? That's a big political problem these days. It was a big political issue originally at the IRS, because they've got a huge DP division nationwide—we're talking thousands of people. At the IRS, people didn't know where the system fell. Was it a file management system? Was it a DP system? It didn't really fall under a DP procurement, because it didn't manipulate data, it only stored it. Nobody really wanted it at first, but as soon as it caught on then everybody wanted it.

Users don't usually want to do this type of procurement through the normal, huge DP organization because it doesn't get done quickly. It gets put in with all the other thousands of projects and doesn't go anywhere. If it's kept on the user side, driven by the user side and looked at as more of a records management kind of thing, it usually gets done much faster. So that's where people are opting to try and put it. But more and more now I see that it's going as normal DP.

Do you think that that's better? Should it be under the guise of MIS? Oh I don't know. It all depends on whether it's going to be integrated in with the existing mainframe; if so, then it really should be under DP. If it's a little stand-alone, office-size thing, it should not be under DP, I don't think.

Will the archives' system eventually be integrated with DP? Well, right now we don't have DP. We don't have anything like that. We've got a few people, we've got some small branches and things like that, but we don't really have a large organization. We are trying to reorganize, and eventually we will probably have one giant DP group like everybody else does. But right now it's not a problem. Everything's just being run by this small, high-tech staff that I'm on.

A lot of people say that this is a technology looking for a market. Is it? I think it was always a technology looking for an application. And I think that users now can look at those test pioneers who took the ball and ran with it at the beginning and say, "Look, it really did work. We don't have to go with some kind of test system for our application. We have a big application, and we can go with a production system." And

> *Federal sources said the Defense Department accounts for nearly half of the federal government's information-technology purchases. The Health and Human Services Department, the Treasury, the National Aeronautics and Space Administration and the Energy Department are the biggest purchasers among civilian agencies.*
>
> **From the *Wall Street Journal***

that, I think, is what's going to turn it around. So it just took time. It always takes time.

**Reprinted from *Computerworld.*
Copyright © 1988 by C.W. Publishing Inc.,
Farmingham, MA.**

GOVERNMENT TITLES

Title	Publisher	Price
CD-FICHE	USA Information Systems, Inc. 3303 Duke Street Alexandria, VA 22314 (800)USA-8830	$3,250.00/Year
CIS Congressional Masterfile, 1789-1969	Congressional Information Service, Inc. 4520 East-West Highway Suite 800 Bethesda, MD 20814-3389 (800)638-8380	*
Construction Criteria Base	National Institute of Building Sciences 1015 15th Street N.W. Suite 700 Washington, DC 20005 (202)347-5710	$970.00/Year
DIALOG OnDisc NTIS	Dialog Information Services Inc. 3460 Hillview Avenue Palo Alto, CA 94304 (800)334-2564	$2,700.00/Year
Enflex Info	ERM Computer Services Inc. 855 Springdale Drive Exton, PA 19341 (800)544-3118	*
The Federal Procurement Disc	ALDE Publishing 4830 West 77th Street P.O. Box 35326 Minneapolis, MN 55435 (612)835-5240	$495.00/Disc
Government Documents Catalog Subscription (GDCS) CD-ROM	Auto-Graphics, Inc. 3201 Temple Avenue Pomona, CA 91768 (800)325-7961	*
Government Publications Index on InfoTrac	Information Access Company 362 Lakeside Drive Foster City, CA 94404 (800)227-8431	$2,500.00/System per Year
GPO on SilverPlatter	SilverPlatter Information, Inc. 37 Walnut Street Wellesley Hills, MA 02181 (617)239-0306	$950.00/Disc

*Contact publisher for prices.

Title	Publisher	Price
Index to U.S. Government Periodicals (IGP)	H.W. Wilson Company 950 University Avenue Bronx, NY 10452 (800)367–6770	$995.00/Year
Le Pac: Government Documents Option	Brodart Automation, a division of Brodart Company 500 Arch Street Williamsport, PA 17705 (800)233–8467	$2,900.00/Year
Marcive/GPO CAT PAC	Marcive, Inc. P.O. Box 47508 San Antonio, TX 78265 (800)531–7678	$995.00/Year
Microsoft Stat Pack	Microsoft Corporation 16011 N.E. 36th Way P.O. Box 97017 Redmond, WA 98073-9717 (206)882–8080	$149.00/Disc
Optext	VLS, Inc. 310 South Reynolds Road Toledo, OH 43623 (419)536–5820	$1,390.00/Year
PAIS on CD-ROM	Public Affairs Information Service, Inc. 521 West 43rd Street New York, NY 10036-4396 (212)736–6629	$1,795.00/Year
Parts-Master	National Standards Association Inc. 1200 Quince Orchard Boulevard Gaithersburg, MD 20878 (800)638–8094	$6,650.00/Year
TLRN-CD2	Innovative Technology Inc. 7927 Jones Branch Drive McLean, VA 22102 (703)734–3000	*
U.S. Government Printing Office Monthly Catalog (GPO)	H.W. Wilson Company 950 University Avenue Bronx, NY 10452 (800)367–6770	$995.00/Year

*Contact publisher for prices

Compiled by Online Press Inc.

O.E.D., in a Gigabyte Task, to Transfer to Compact Disks

By Francis X. Clines
From the *New York Times*

[Proud owners of the compact-print O.E.D. and the even prouder owners of the 12-volume version can't begin to imagine the etymological delights that the O.E.D. on CD-ROM has in store for them. In this article, Francis Clines gives us a behind-the-scenes look at what's involved in maintaining this 130-year-old reference work.]

Gigabyte is the latest word at the Oxford English Dictionary, a measure of the 1,000 million bytes needed for what will be a major event in the history of both computerization and lexicography: the transference and updating of the entire 16-volume O.E.D. onto three compact disks.

Here [*Oxford, England*], in a humble old stone building along one of the university roads, workers are preparing to free the O.E.D. giant—the largest and most historically authoritative dictionary of the language—for a romp across the fluorescent fields of the modern computer.

The task is so mammoth that to put the same work of 22,000 pages and 500,000 definitions and usages onto conventional computer floppy disks would require more than 3,000; compact disks are far roomier.

The first two disks containing the basic 12-volume dictionary, minus its 4-volume supplement, will be ready by the end of the year, and Oxford University Press is already expecting wide subscription from the world's libraries. Even more may it appeal to the computerized layman eager to put aside the magnifying glass that is the proud tool of the current owner of the printed O.E.D. and turn to the keyboard for a trip through the language that should prove faster and offer fresh leeway for whimsy.

The multiple search powers of software, for example, would permit someone to track a particular German-rooted word and then tangentially inquire into how many such German words came into the language in a given century, or two or three. Or a reader checking on a gastronomical word could impulsively inquire into all the words involving cookery that have been traced to late 15th-century French. One beauty of the O.E.D. is that no entry is ever discarded, only listed as obsolete with change. Another is that each entry has the earliest possible printed reference from history.

MORE WAYS OF REFERENCE

"It will be very exciting, opening up more doors, more ways of reference," said John A. Simpson, the co-editor and chief wordsmith at O.E.D. He appreciates the instant retrieval and 40 different typefaces at hand with the new software, but he basically gets through each day by jotting down words he hears into a crammed pocket pad: a usage for "mimosa," the drink of champagne and orange juice, and the birth of "blik," a notion referring to a slant or perception.

He is the sort of researcher who will visit New York and ask the waiter in an Italian restaurant exactly what he meant when he uttered the perfunctory, "Enjoy." Is it from the Italian and if so where can there be found the printed historic reference that the O.E.D. requires? "You've got to make a fool of yourself sometimes," Mr. Simpson says.

There is the search for new words, with one worker thoroughly dissecting a book version of the movie "Platoon" for the latest vulgarisms while another is tracking the origins of "Teflon President" and "Big Mac." There is the search into the past for the oldest available reference in print on a word. Mr. Simpson was delighted to discover "annualist" was referred to by Coleridge in an 1828 letter that will force the discarding of the 1829 reference point in the original O.E.D. He similarly treasures the discovery that "Catch-22" originated differently in an earlier work when the writer Joseph Heller referred to it as "Catch-18." "But Catch-18 didn't catch on," Mr. Simpson said.

Such curiosity by himself and 40 others involved in the lexicography of the O.E.D. is only part of the work that will produce a computer dictionary with main headings for 300,000 words plus an additional 200,000 subsidiary usages—an increase of 25 percent over the original O.E.D. But by the Oxford press's patient plan, this will be only a modern stepping-stone toward an even more ambitious vetting of the language already being researched to produce a totally revised dictionary that is planned for the O.E.D.'s second century of life. The initial computer disks will result in a new printed edition of the O.E.D., too, in 1989, but the main bonus of the conversion to the computer will mean that the dictionary can be fluidly updated as the new century arrives, rather than locked into its last printed version.

ENTER OEDIPUS LEX

Oedipus is the acronym for the 5-year, $13-million entry into the computer age, the last four letters referring to Integration, Proofing and Updating System. Workers call it Oedipus Lex, just as some of its readers fondly term the dictionary GOD (Great Oxford Dictionary). But the O.E.D. is big enough to bear minor sacrilege as much as mundane smut, with the inclusion of latest rough vulgarisms long accepted. One staff debate focuses on whether to cite a royal family member's recent vulgar imperative to shoo some annoying photographers.

The first O.E.D. was planned here in 1858 and published in 12 volumes from 1884 to the final book in 1928. By then supplements were needed that themselves stand as a separate masterwork in four volumes that were finally

> *The task of computerizing the Oxford English Dictionary involved a total wordage of more than 60 times that of the complete works of Shakespeare.*

finished last year, but with such words as "AIDS" and "black hole" already arising too late for inclusion in the printing.

The initial computerized O.E.D. will represent a partial updating, with the four-volume supplement to be added to the disks by 1989, along with Mr. Simpson's enlargement of that by about 5,000 recent words—an "interim" deed only for lexicographers who work across decades. No prices have yet been announced for the first disks. The printed O.E.D. currently costs about $1,600, or $240 for the compact-print edition.

Once a century of work is safely on the computer, Oxford University Press will focus on the complete revision of the dictionary through the 1990s, with scores of thousands of additional words already being researched for inclusion from the ever spiraling, living, breeding language that is both bane and joy at the O.E.D. Fifteen trusted volunteers aid in this task, receiving about 30 cents for each carefully researched word that is accepted.

The refreshing fact at teatime at the O.E.D. is that the earnest band working on this project spends little time discussing the technology of glyphs and software and indulges in far more fanciful chats about words.

Sara Tulloch, the senior assistant editor, was sipping coffee and chewing on "perestroika," a Russian word that "seems to be coming on" as the new Soviet leaders talk of basic restructuring. She knows exactly when the great Russian buzzword "glasnost" finally entered English on its own rather than as translated to "publicity" or "openness."

Mr. Simpson was casually denying entry to variations beyond the basic "yuppie" word. "Buppies, duppies, guppies, whatever," he said. But he was yielding to "televangelist." "Don't like the word myself," he said as the teatime words were flying out like endless rain into a paper cup.

From the *New York Times,* October 17, 1987. Copyright © 1987 by The New York Times Company. Reprinted by permission.

REFERENCE TITLES

Title	Publisher	Price
ABI/INFORM Ondisc	UMI (University Microfilms International) 300 North Zeeb Road Ann Arbor, MI 48106 (800)521–3044	$4,950.00/Year
Academic Index on InfoTrac II	Information Access Company 362 Lakeside Drive Foster City, CA 94404 (800)227–8431	$4,000.00/Year
Art Index	H.W. Wilson Company 950 University Avenue Bronx, NY 10452 (800)367–6770	$1,495.00/Year
Biography Index	H.W. Wilson Company 950 University Avenue Bronx, NY 10452 (800)367–6770	$1,095.00/Year
Book Review Digest	H.W. Wilson Company 950 University Avenue Bronx, NY 10452 (800)367–6770	$1,095.00/Year
Books In Print Plus	Bowker Electronic Publishing 245 West 17th Street New York, NY 10011 (800)323–3288	$995.00/Year
Books In Print with Book Reviews Plus	Bowker Electronic Publishing 245 West 17th Street New York, NY 10011 (800)323–3288	$1,395.00/Year
Books Out-of-Print Plus	Bowker Electronic Publishing 245 West 17th Street New York, NY 10011 (800)323–3288	$395.00/Year
CD WORD: Multilingual Dictionary	Dai Nippon Ichigaya-kagacho Shinjuku-ku Tokyo 162 JAPAN 03/266–2111	*
CD-ROM SourceDisc	Diversified Data Resources Inc. 6609 Rosecroft Place Falls Church, VA 22043 (703)237–0682	$89.95/Disc

*Contact publisher for prices.

(continued)

REFERENCE TITLES *continued.*

Title	Publisher	Price
Cumulative Book Index	H.W. Wilson Company 950 University Avenue Bronx, NY 10452 (800)367–6770	$1,295.00/Year
Facts on File News Digest CD-ROM	Facts on File, Inc. 460 Park Avenue South New York, NY 10016 (800)322–8755	$695.00/Disc
Gale GlobalAccess: Associations	Knowledge Access International, Inc. 2685 Marine Way Suite 1305 Mountain View, CA 94043 (415)969–0606	$2,295.00/Entire state
General Periodicals Index (Academic Library Edition) on InfoTrac	Information Access Company 362 Lakeside Drive Foster City, CA 94404 (800)227–8431	$7,500.00/Year
General Periodicals Index (Public Library Edition) on InfoTrac	Information Access Company 362 Lakeside Drive Foster City, CA 94404 (800)227–8431	$7,500.00/Year
Humanities Index	H.W. Wilson Company 950 University Avenue Bronx, NY 10452 (212)588–8400	$1,295.00/Year
Ingram-Books In Print Plus	Bowker Electronic Publishing 245 West 17th Street New York, NY 10011 (800)323–3288	$1,200.00/Year
Ingram-Books in Print PLUS	Ingram Distribution Group Inc./ R.R. Bowker Company, Inc. 347 Reedwood Drive Nashville, TN 37217 (800)937–8100	$300.00
International Books-in-Print	Saur Verlag KG Postfach 711009 Possenbacherstrasse 2B 8000 München WEST GERMANY (8979)10480	*
Kojien: Japanese Dictionary	Dai Nippon Ichigaya-kagacho Shinjuku-ku Tokyo 162 JAPAN 03/266–2111	*

*Contact publisher for prices.

Title	Publisher	Price
Magazine Index/PLUS on InfoTrac	Information Access Company 362 Lakeside Drive Foster City, CA 94404 (800)227–8431	$4,000.00/System per Year
McGraw-Hill Science and Technical Reference Set	McGraw-Hill Book Company 11 West 19th Street New York, NY 10011 (212)512–2000	$300.00
Merriam Webster's Ninth New Collegiate Dictionary	Highlighted Data, Inc. Washington-Dallas International Airport P.O. Box 17229 Washington, DC 20041 (703)241–1180	$199.95/Disc
Microsoft Bookshelf	Microsoft Corporation 16011 N.E. 36th Way P.O. Box 97017 Redmond, WA 98073-9717 (206)882–8080	$295.00/Disc
Multilingual Dictionary Database	Sansyusya Publishing Company Ltd. 1-5-34 Taito-ku Tokyo 110 JAPAN	*
Multilingual Dictionary of Science & Technology	Sansyusya Publishing Co. Ltd. 1-5-34 Taito-ku Tokyo 110 JAPAN	*
The New Electronic Encyclopedia	Grolier Electronic Publishing Inc. Sherman Turnpike Danbury, CT 06816 (800)356–5590	$395.00/Product
The NewsBank Electronic Index	Newsbank, Inc. 58 Pine Street New Canaan, CT 06840-5408 (800)223–4739	*
Newspaper Abstracts Ondisc	UMI (University Microfilms International) 300 North Zeeb Road Ann Arbor, MI 48106 (800)521–3044	*
Periodical Abstracts Ondisc	UMI (University Microfilms International) 300 North Zeeb Road Ann Arbor, MI 48106 (800)521–3044	$1,175.00/Year

*Contact publisher for prices.

(continued)

REFERENCE TITLES *continued.*

Title	Publisher	Price
Programmer's Library	Microsoft Corporation 16011 N.E. 36th Way Box 97017 Redmond, WA 98073-9717 (206)882–8080	$395.00/Disc
Publishers International Directory	Saur Verlag KG Postfach 711009 Possenbacherstrasse 2B 8000 München WEST GERMANY (8979)10480	*
Resource/One	UMI (University Microfilms International) 300 North Zeeb Road Ann Arbor, MI 48106 (800)521–3044	$795.00/Year
Social Sciences Index	H.W. Wilson Company 950 University Avenue Bronx, NY 10452 (800)367–6770	$1,295.00/Year
The Electronic Whole Earth Catalog	Broderbund Software 17 Paul Drive San Rafael, CA 94903-2101 (800)527–6263	$149.95/Disc
The Original Oxford English Dictionary on Compact Disc	Tri Star Publishing 475 Virginia Drive Fort Washington, PA 19034 (800)872–2828	$950.00/Disc
TOM	Information Access Company 362 Lakeside Drive Foster City, CA 94404 (800)227–8431	*
Ulrich's Plus	Bowker Electronic Publishing 245 West 17th Street New York, NY 10011 (800)323–3288	$395.00/Year
Verzeichnis Lieferbarer Buecher: German Books-in-Print	Buchhandler Vereinigung GmbH Grosser Hirschgraben 17-21 Postfach 10042 6000 Frankfurt am Main 1 WEST GERMANY	*

*Contact publisher for prices.

Compiled by Online Press Inc.

CD-ROM and the Bible

By Bob Hall

[From the O.E.D., we turn to the best-selling book of all time: the Bible. Through the centuries, the Bible has been transcribed from medium to medium, and scholars have been quick to expand their research activities to take advantage of whatever capabilities a new medium offered. With the publication of the Bible on CD-ROM, says Bob Hall, whole new discoveries await them.]

One could go on forever discussing the Bible. Simply stated, it is the best-selling book in the world. CD-ROM raises new questions about this book: Which Bibles? How many of them on a single CD-ROM? Which search engine? The most common question is, "Is there a market for such a product?"

Consider the following: There are more than 345,000 churches in the United States alone; this is certainly a potential marketplace. More than 142,000,000 people profess membership in a church, and more than 48,000,000 declare full or confirmed membership.

The number of churches with a computer system grows steadily each day. Churches have discovered the use of computers within the ministry. Many of the more than 530,000 clergy in the United States have discovered the power of the computer. From portables for writing sermons "on the go" to full mainframes for church management systems, we see the computer becoming a part of the church. Steve Hewitt, editor of *Church Computing Magazine,* stated, "A two-year-old list of churches yielded over 18,000 positive responses indicating the churches had computer systems." It has been estimated that of the more than 187,000 churches with 200 or more members, at least 75 percent have computer systems.

The Bible is a natural for CD-ROM. Only CD-ROM can offer both the clergy and the lay person the storage required for multiple versions of the Bible and for other related information. With CD-ROM's storage capacity, powerful indexes, and search capabilities, the Bible can finally be fully explored.

Traditionally, the clergy and students of the Bible have used reference books, different translations of the Bible, and, often, commentaries and dictionaries. Normally, this procedure

BOB HALL

Home: Oklahoma City, Oklahoma
Job: Director of CD-ROM Technology, Ellis Enterprises
Quote: *"I think CD-ROM is here to stay, but we'll see it grow in leaps and bounds when the game industry gets active in the field and the first adventure game comes out on CD-ROM."*

requires several books, marked pages, abundant notepads, and the patience to search and cross-reference the material. The King James version of the Bible occupies 3 to 5 megabytes of disk space, so anyone wanting to search more than one version of the Bible using a computer's hard disk quickly runs out of space.

With CD-ROM, however, several versions, dictionaries, concordances, and other related material can be combined for theological explorations. The CD-ROM search engine has the responsibility of remembering where the information is located and of retrieving it for the user.

Computer-assisted biblical study has been a reality for some time, but the larger databases have been available only on mainframes. CD-ROM means that the large databases and collections of biblical information can now be made available to many more people.

The Bible has been painstakingly preserved for almost nineteen centuries. It has reached us on handwritten manuscripts, passing through the hands of many devout copyists and translators. It has been written on various media throughout the centuries: papyrus, skins, paper ...and now on CD-ROM.

[Bob Hall is Director of CD-ROM Technology for Ellis Enterprises, Inc., a CD-ROM publishing company. Prior to joining Ellis Enterprises, he owned a computer store. He has extensive background in computer programming and systems integration.]

From Online to OnDisc: A Three-Year Update

By Rick Meyer

[Three years after the publication of The New Papyrus, *Rick Meyer answers the questions he posed to online vendors and database producers about the burgeoning CD-ROM market. All indications are, he reports, that the future seems to hold the peaceful coexistence of CD-ROM and online services, not the battle that was once anticipated.]*

Three years ago, the Microsoft Press book *The New Papyrus* heralded the arrival of the CD-ROM business. In a chapter entitled "From Online to OnDisc," I identified key questions that online vendors and database producers would face in entering the CD-ROM market:

- Should products derived from online data target "information intermediaries," such as librarians, or should they target end users?
- Would CD-ROM attract new customers, or would existing customers substitute CD-ROM for print publication or online use?
- Would substitute use be more or less profitable?
- What expected usage should form a basis for pricing?

In three years, CD-ROM markets have taken shape enough to provide some tentative answers.

CD-ROM PROVIDERS

For the purpose here, the online business can be defined as the business of distributing electronic-retrieval access through telecommunications networks to databases containing publicly available, professionally oriented and work-related information. Information providers in the online business have a variety of market-proven databases that already exist in searchable,

RICK MEYER

Home: Los Gatos, California
Job: Product Manager, Dialog Information Services, Inc.
Quote: *"CD-ROM is exciting large numbers of new users about electronic information retrieval in general, users who will become new customers for online services as well as additional CD-ROM products. The next challenge is to develop hybrid online/ondisc services where the choice of local or remote storage of databases becomes a matter of convenience and economics."*

machine-readable form. As expected, proven online databases have been among the first and most popular CD-ROM products. The business is generally divided between the database producers, who compile and index databases, and the online vendors or distributors, who publish these and other databases in an online service with consistent retrieval software.

Several of the top online distributors have introduced CD-ROM products. Mead Data Central, the vendor of the LEXIS and NEXIS online services, acquired Micromedix, a small publisher of CD-ROM products for medical emergency services. At the time of writing, however, Mead has not introduced CD-ROM versions of any of the major legal and general reference material in LEXIS or NEXIS.

On the other hand, Dialog Information Services, the vendor with the largest number of databases and with tens of thousands of users, has developed the DIALOG OnDisc product line from eight of its online databases, including such mainstays as Medline and ERIC. The data are licensed from government sources and from private-sector database producers.

In addition, BRS Information Technologies, an online vendor emphasizing online medical information has introduced a single product derived from the government medical database, Medline. And H.W. Wilson provides fourteen CD-ROM discs integrated with its online service.

Vendors using CD-ROM as yet do not include the consumer-oriented online services such as CompuServe and THE SOURCE.

Although they have started modest CD-ROM efforts, the online distributors continue to devote the large majority of their resources to their successful and growing online products.

In addition to online distributors, many database producers and other publishers who have distributed their information through online distributors as well as through other media, such as paper and microforms, have taken a very active interest in CD-ROM. Aside from granting CD-ROM rights to online publishers, some of the larger and more self-sufficient publishers have also developed CD-ROM products themselves with the help of service bureaus such as Reference Technology and Laserdata.

Information Access Company, publisher of such databases as Magazine Index and Computer Database, pioneered optical publishing with its highly successful InfoTrac products based on videodisks, and it has moved the InfoTrac products to CD-ROM, also with great success. These products, targeting academic and public libraries, are replacing microfiche rather than online versions of the same data.

Another early success has been Compact Disclosure from Disclosure, Inc. This is a product containing selected company information derived from SEC filings. The company is building on its initial product by providing additional discs containing the full text of the same SEC filings. As with InfoTrac, CD-ROM is replacing Disclosure's microfiche delivery medium.

Other successful online products that have been independently introduced on CD-ROM by their publishers include ABI/Inform and Dissertation Abstracts from University Microfilms, the Books in Print series from R.R. Bowker, and Compustat PC Plus from Standard & Poor's (which also publishes S&P Corporations with Dialog).

The biggest financial success story of CD-ROM is Lotus Development's One Source/Datext products. In mid-1988, Lotus projected 1988 sales of $60 million for its CD-ROM products. These products are not the exact counterpart of any online files, but they contain data derived from some of the top online business databases. Nor were the products developed by an online vendor or by the database producers themselves; they come, of course, from a top microcomputer software company seeking to complement its best-selling Lotus 1-2-3 speadsheet and capitalize on its existing franchise with financially oriented professionals.

THE ECONOMIC OUTLOOK

An estimate of the total CD-ROM information market has been provided by LINK Resources in its "CDROM Industry Review and Outlook, 1987-1992." LINK defines two segments of the CD-ROM market, professional database publishing and libraries, which are also the chief markets for online services. LINK projects that the dollar value of CD-ROM information products in these segments for 1988 was $143.1 million, derived from sales or leases of 609,000 discs.

Individual vendors of professional CD-ROM databases report that their successful CD-ROM titles sell in quantities of hundreds per year; some successful vendors may have reached quantities in the low thousands. Most products are sold on an annual subscription basis at

Individual vendors of professional CD-ROM databases report that their successful CD-ROM titles sell in quantities of hundreds per year; some successful vendors may have reached quantities in the low thousands.

CD-ROM TITLES ABOUT ONLINE SERVICES

Title	Publisher	Price
Online Hotline News	ALDE Publishing 4830 West 77th Street P.O. Box 35326 Minneapolis, MN 55435 (612)835–5240	$199.95/Disc

Compiled by Online Press Inc.

yearly prices generally ranging from the high hundreds to the low thousands of dollars, although Lotus One Source and Compustat prices are much higher.

CD-ROM USAGE

Usage situations vary widely. CD-ROM already has wide acceptance in library markets, where PC workstations are set up for use by library patrons with some assistance from library staff. The success of these installations, combined with the resulting disc shuffling and patron queueing problems, has led to a strong interest in putting the discs in a centralized CD-ROM network server for access from a number of workstations.

The strongest impact of CD-ROM on other information media is apparently on microforms. This area shows the only clear cases of product replacement, although overall vendor revenues have not necessarily declined. Several database producers are projecting measurable impact on paper indexes as well and are adopting pricing strategies designed to discourage cancellation of equivalent print subscriptions.

The impact of CD-ROM activity on the online information business has been complex. CD-

BUSINESS TITLES

Title	Publisher	Price
Busi/Stats	Hopkins Technology 421 Hazel Lane Hopkins, MN 55343-7117 (612)931-9376	$59.00/Disc
Business Indicators	Slater Hall Information Products 1522 K Street N.W. Suite 522 Washington, DC 20005 (202)682-1350	$2,200.00/Year
Compustat PC Plus	Standard and Poor Compustat Services 7400 South Alton Court Englewood, CO 90112 (303)740-4510	$12,000.00
DIALOG OnDisc Canadian Business and Current Affairs	Dialog Information Services Inc./ Micromedia Ltd. 3460 Hillview Avenue Palo Alto, CA 94394 (800)334-2564	$1,450.00/Year
Microsoft Small Business Consultant	Microsoft Corporation 16011 N.E. 36th Way P.O. Box 97017 Redmond, WA 98073-9717 (206)882-8080	$125.00/Disc
STANDARD & POOR'S CORPORATIONS	Dialog Information Services Inc./Standard & Poor's 3460 Hillview Avenue Palo Alto, CA 94394 (800)334-2564	$4,250.00

Compiled by Online Press Inc.

ROM has not noticeably reduced the growth rate of the online industry as a whole, nor have individual CD-ROM databases hurt their online counterparts in all cases where information was available. The sales of online electronic information services to libraries and information centers, still the core market for most services, continues its healthy growth of about 20 percent annually, despite rapid penetration of CD-ROM products in the same markets.

Potential explanations for CD-ROM's lack of impact on online delivery are not hard to find. Both online and disc information sources have large untapped potential markets. Vendors' customer bases are in the tens of thousands at most, out of the millions of professional knowledge workers who could benefit from access to electronic information. In this market of low penetration, the growth of one vendor's product is not necessarily at the expense of a "competitor's" market share. In fact, because many CD-ROM products are being used by library patrons and other end users who have had no previous experience with electronic information retrieval, a wide range of users is discovering electronic research in general. This exposure leads to an interest in other databases, including the thousands of online databases that are not, and may never be, available on disc because, compared with online distribution, CD-ROM is limited in size and currency and thus unsuitable for some online databases.

The appeal of actual CD-ROM products in online markets is largely due to factors that are not inherent in the technology. First, most CD-ROM products have flat annual pricing as opposed to online's usage-sensitive pricing. Once a CD-ROM product is paid for, the incentive in an institutional setting is to facilitate access to the product, and this access can easily expand to new end users. With online's pay-as-you-go pricing, the incentive is to carefully limit access to trained individuals so as to control costs.

The typical CD-ROM and online pricing models are evolving simultaneously. Technologies for metering CD-ROM access have been introduced, permitting online-style pricing. Some online vendors are experimenting with flat-rate pricing, often for their larger customers. As a result, the price structure differentiation between online and CD-ROM products is likely to blur with time.

CD-ROM products originated in the PC environment, so the retrieval software typically includes menus, windows, online help, and other appealing ease-of-learning features. In contrast, to maintain compatibility with a common denominator of terminals and terminal-emulation software, the user interfaces of even menu-driven online services do not use the PC's full capability to simplify access.

Online vendors are, however, also introducing PC "front-end" software to provide increased ease of use and convenience. At the same time, 1988 saw the introduction of several technologies designed to allow CD-ROM to be shared by multiple workstations over a network in a type of "local online" configuration.

> *CD-ROM has not noticeably reduced the growth rate of the online industry as a whole, nor have individual CD-ROM databases hurt their online counterparts in all cases where information was available.*

MAPS AND CENSUS TITLES

Title	Publisher	Price
1982 Census of Agriculture	Slater Hall Information Products 1522 K Street N.W. Suite 522 Washington, DC 20005 (202)682–1350	$1,200.00/Disc
Census Test Disk 2	U.S. Bureau of the Census Customer Services Washington, DC 20233 (301)763–4100	$125.00/Disc
Consu/Stats I	Hopkins Technology 421 Hazel Lane Hopkins, MN 55343-7117 (612)931–9376	$49.00/Disc
County, metro area statistics	Slater Hall Information Products 1522 K Street N.W. Suite 522 Washington, DC 20005 (202)682–1350	$1,200.00/Disc
DeLorme's World Atlas	DeLorme Mapping Systems P.O. Box 298 Freeport, ME 04032 (207)865–4171	*
The Electronic Map Cabinet	Highlighted Data, Inc. Washington-Dallas International Airport P.O. Box 17229 Washington, DC 20041 (703)241–1180	$199.95/Disc
EtakMap National Transportation Network	ETAK, Inc. 1455 Adams Drive Menlo Park, CA 94025 (415)328–3825	*
GEOdisc State Atlas Series	Geovision, Inc. 270 Scientific Drive Suite 1 Norcross, GA 30092 (404)448–8224	$1,995.00/Disc
GEOdisc U.S. Atlas	Geovision, Inc. 270 Scientific Drive Suite 1 Norcross, GA 30092 (404)448–8224	$495.00/Disc

*Contact publisher for prices.

Title	Publisher	Price
MetroScan: El Dorado County	Digital Diagnostics, Inc. 601 University Avenue Suite 255 Sacramento, CA 95825 (916)921–6629	$350.00/Year
MetroScan: Placer County	Digital Diagnostics, Inc. 601 University Avenue Suite 255 Sacramento, CA 95825 (916)921–6629	$350.00/Year
MetroScan: Sacramento County	Digital Diagnostics, Inc. 601 University Avenue Suite 255 Sacramento, CA 95825 (916)921–6629	$600.00/Year
MetroScan: Yolo County	Digital Diagnostics, Inc. 601 University Avenue Suite 255 Sacramento, CA 95825 (916)921–6629	$300.00/Year
Place-Name Index	Buckmaster Publishing Route 3 Box 56 Mineral, VA 23117 (703)894–5777	$295.00/Year
POPLINE	SilverPlatter Information, Inc. 37 Walnut Street Wellesley Hills, MA 02181 (617)239–0306	$750.00/Year
Population Statistics on CD-ROM	Slater Hall Information Products 1522 K Street N.W. Suite 522 Washington, DC 20005 (202)682–1350	$1,200.00/Disc
Supermap 1.0 1981 Australian Census	Chadwyck-Healy Ltd. Cambridge Place Cambridge CB2 1NR ENGLAND 0223 311479	*
Supermap 1.1 1980 U.S. Census County Level	Chadwyck-Healy Ltd. Cambridge Place Cambridge CB2 1NR ENGLAND 0223 311479	$990.00
Swedish Census Data	National Land Survey of Sweden 80112 Havle SWEDEN 026/100340	*

*Contact publisher for prices.   **Compiled by Online Press Inc.**

Some of the most successful products, from Lotus, Dialog, and Wilson are really hybrid services that incorporate timely online information with highly accessible, but less current, CD-ROM information.

As product pricing and user interfaces merge, and as professional databases of all kinds are increasingly accessed from local-area networks, the choice of online or disc as an information-access medium becomes a matter of convenience and economy. The CD-ROM versus online battle that was widely anticipated three years ago has not materialized. The future seems to hold the peaceful co-existence, and perhaps even marriage, of these complementary media.

[Rick Meyer is CD-ROM Product Line Manager of Dialog Information Services, a subsidiary of Knight-Ridder, Inc. He is responsible for business and product planning and product development of the DIALOG OnDisc CD-ROM product line. Prior to joining Dialog, Meyer was Senior Product Manager at MicroPro International Corporation, publisher of WordStar word-processing software.]

Stacking Up Candidates at ABC

By Steven Levy
From *Macworld*

[In the last article of this section, Steven Levy gives us a fascinating peek at MAGNA, the ABC network's HyperCard-based secret weapon for 1988 presidential-election coverage. MAGNA is an example of what can be done to create high-powered, interesting resource materials—new-generation reference works with that new-media touch.]

At this summer's political conventions, a third ABC anchor sat between Peter Jennings and David Brinkley—a Macintosh II, loaded with ABC's secret weapon in its coverage of the 1988 presidential campaigns. The secret weapon is MAGNA, one of the most extensive feats of HyperCard programming to date. It was designed and maintained by the network's election specialists, with some help from Apple. With MAGNA, the entire ABC team was able to access information instantly on anything—from where Dukakis stood on Star Wars to who the key votes were in the Iowa delegation. Most striking, the data was fully accessible to Jennings himself, who could mouse his way into an up-to-the-minute delegate count, a recap of what happened on Super Tuesday, or even a record of his own notes on a given topic.

MAGNA (which stands for Macintosh ABC General News Almanac) is an interlocking set of HyperCard stacks holding thousands of campaign facts. It marks the deepest incursion that personal computers have made into the electronic news business. A virtual showcase of the powers of HyperCard, MAGNA not only allows computer innocents to get facts quickly and intuitively, it permits easy changes in the data. MAGNA, for instance, can reflect a rapidly changing situation—a floor demonstration at a political convention or an election-night tally. It allows Macs to shovel information to ABC personnel as smoothly as Holly Hunter fed facts to William Hurt in *Broadcast News*.

David Bohrman, ABC's senior political producer for election coverage, realized that HyperCard could replace the thousands of 5-by-7-inch cards the networks were using for covering major events like presidential campaigns. Once Bohrman convinced his bosses to allow him to centralize the innumerable facts gathered in the course of the campaign on HyperCard, ABC cut a deal with Apple to lease ten Macs, some laser printers, a flatbed scanner, and several copies of HyperCard software. In addition, Apple provided support, including some programming on the interlocking system of around 130 stacks and over 5000 cards.

But most of the design and the HyperTalk work was done at ABC. One look at the attractive, clearly arranged cards tells you they were designed by experts in presenting visual information on screen. During the primary season, for instance, one card contained digitized faces of all the Democratic candidates: click on the face of Dukakis and you got a card that linked you to his current delegate count (automatically updated), his stance on any given issue, his personal background or information on his staff and finances.

At the conventions, layouts of the arenas in Atlanta and New Orleans were cross-referenced

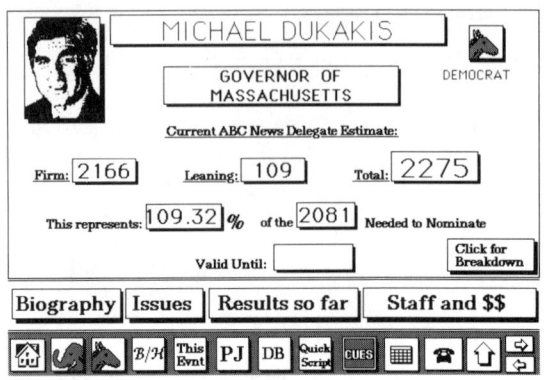

Further information about a candidate

according to where each state delegation sat, and which reporter was assigned to each area. The schedules and images of key players were stored in stacks so correspondents could find them in an instant. And ABC linked up the appropriate data from Mediagenic's City to City program so that information on hotels, restaurants, and emergency services was also accessible.

When we spoke to Dave Bohrman in June, he was already savoring the edge MAGNA gave ABC over its competitors. "My counterpart at CBS caught a glimpse of the system in Iowa," he said. "He was extremely envious. He's trying to get Macs [at his network], but it's too late." Bohrman thinks this type of technology will eventually be standard in electronic journalism. And besides HyperCard use, Macs have been making themselves indispensable at ABC in other ways. One night, the Mac II was even called into service as a makeshift TelePrompTer.

For now, watch for MAGNA on election night, where, as Bohrman notes, "millions of people will see the results of HyperCard." From there, anything could happen. If HyperCard works for Peter Jennings, perhaps the winner of the 1988 election will consider using a set of stacks when answering queries in his first presidential press conference.

The HyperCard-based MAGNA system, showing digitized faces of the Democratic candidates

Reprinted by permission of *Macworld*, from the September 1988 issue, published at 501 Second Street, San Francisco, CA.

CD-ROM: NEWSPAPER APPLICATIONS

CD-ROM is warmly welcomed in the newsroom. Many newspapers are getting services from Data-Times, a company which is offering a complete production service to its newspaper clients who have built up a staple archive and want to convert their established databases from magnetic tape to CD-ROM. One disc can store roughly three years' worth of copy from a large daily newspaper. This is an attractive medium for packaging their morgue. Says Miller [1]: "it is the possibility of selling newspaper data on disk that excites some managers." And Miller illustrates its markets: "Potential users could include real estate companies that might want to track developments in a certain areas of a city, corporate officials who want to track activities of competitors, attorneys who want to research individuals or organizations, politicans who want to scout out potential contributors or marketers who want to cull sales prospects."

Its immediate benefits come from internal use of CD-ROM within the newsroom. For example, *The Washington Post* is planning to distribute their database on CD-ROM to avoid telecommunications problems for some of their bureaus.

Additionally, some news companies are looking into storing news photos on compact disk, according to Miller.

The applications of CD-ROM seem to be pervasive. "Given the normal resistance to change and industry's reluctance to buy 'new, improved' hardware," Gale says, "this is happening so fast" that CD-ROM is on the verge of becoming a necessity for information management [2]. One probable reason why CD-ROM is easily accepted is that it does not demand any change of information searching behavior. Discs are physically delivered via the old familiar way of shipment; CD-ROM databases do not have to be maintained through a real-time interaction between multiple participants. Any changes and updating of information can be achieved through replacement of discs in a less costly manner; it takes 47 days to transfer 550 MB of data via 1,200 baud line at the cost of $18,000, while one CD-ROM disc can be delivered in 24 hours for $10.75 [2].

[1] Miller, Tim, "SilverPlatter: dishing up data for libraries." *Information Today*, June 23, 1986.
[2] Gale, John C., "Use of optical disks for information storage and retrieval." *Information Technology and Libraries*, December 1984; pages 379–382.

Reprinted from Vol. 6, No. 5 of *The COINT Reports* (excerpted from "CD-ROM: Revolution Maker, With an Annotated Current Bibliography," reported by Chung I. Park) by permission of Info Digest. Copyright © 1986 by *The COINT Reports*

MEDICAL AND LEGAL APPLICATIONS

TESTING THE NEW TECHNOLOGY: MEDLINE ON CD-ROM IN AN ACADEMIC HEALTH SCIENCES LIBRARY
By Beryl Glitz

FROM VARIABLES TO VIDEODISCS: INTERACTIVE VIDEO IN THE CLINICAL SETTING
By Mary Anne Sweeney and Claire Gulino

INTEGRATING COMPUTERS INTO LAW FIRMS
By Nora Leven

Testing the New Technology: MEDLINE on CD-ROM in an Academic Health Sciences Library

By Beryl Glitz
From *Special Libraries*

[In the first article in this section, Beryl Glitz discusses the criteria that are important for stand-alone medical database systems, as she reviews the UCLA Biomedical Library's test of MEDLINE on CD-ROM.]

The UCLA Biomedical Library was asked in the fall of 1986 to test Cambridge Scientific's *Compact Cambridge/MEDLINE*, a six-month portion of the 1986 MEDLINE file on compact disc. This paper will describe why we decided to test this product, what preparations we made for its use in the library, and how our patrons responded to this new type of bibliographic tool. I believe that the questions we asked, both philosophical and practical, are the questions that all libraries should be asking about this new technology. In conclusion, I will discuss the implications this type of technology has for the future of library service.

Our library is one of the largest and busiest health sciences libraries in the country open to the general public, as well as to the university community. We perform a large number of computerized literature searches, most of them on the MEDLINE database. In the academic year 1985/86, of a total 1,895 searches, 1,469 of these or 78 percent were on MEDLINE. In the last two or three years, many of our patrons have become interested in doing their own searches, and we have begun an active educational program for end user searching. Because so many of our patrons need MEDLINE, usually demand rapid delivery of database search results, and some, at least, seem interested in doing their own searching, we felt that MEDLINE on CD-ROM would be an important new tool for our library. We were therefore eager to evaluate this product.

Our library is an extremely busy one: typically 2,500 individuals enter the library daily. Despite the high volume of activity at the reference desk, we can only schedule one librarian each hour. Therefore, we must always consider the possible impact on public service staff when we contemplate the introduction of any new tool or service. We were thus very anxious to learn just how "user-friendly" CD-ROM technology might be: Could our patrons learn to use it with no more help from a reference librarian than would be provided if they were using the printed *Index Medicus*? Also, we needed to know just how library users would react to CD-ROM and whether it would be a useful and appropriate new reference tool. We assumed that users would in fact appreciate and use this new technology. Our final questions centered on the quality of the search process and results for the library user. Would CD-ROM provide appropriate and sufficient access to a complicated database like MEDLINE? Could new users access the system easily and retrieve what they wanted? Could experienced users bypass the more simplistic searching method once they knew the system?

PREPARATIONS FOR TESTING

With these questions in mind we began our preparations for testing MEDLINE on compact disc. Before the equipment and software arrived, we identified several management questions we had to address, questions which apply to the testing of any new technology:

1. What equipment would we need to run the test. What would the producer supply and what must we provide?

2. Where should we locate the equipment, in this case a CD-ROM work station, in the library?

3. Which hours of the day should we make this new tool available?

4. How could we best prepare the reference desk staff to cope with the new tool?

5. What kind of help should we be prepared to give our patrons when they used the equipment?

6. How should we publicize a new tool like CD-ROM so that it was indeed used?

7. How could we best obtain feedback from the patrons who used the new tool?

The first issues were easy to resolve. Cambridge would supply the CD player and MEDLINE disc, the search software, connecting cable, and the interface card for the PC. The library had available an IBM-PC with 512K of memory, two disk drives, and an empty expansion slot. We also had an IBM Proprinter to use as part of the work station. We decided to locate the CD-ROM station close to the reference desk so that staff could more easily promote the use of MEDLINE on CD-ROM with our patrons and be able to observe its actual use. Since we had no idea how much help patrons might need and because we could not secure the equipment very well, we decided to make the service available only during the hours that the reference desk was staffed.

In order to help prepare reference desk staff, a memo was sent to all librarians who worked at the desk detailing the when, where, and how of equipment setup; our objectives in doing the test; our plans for staff orientation and training; and our ideas for publicity. We were very aware of the importance of keeping staff up to date with plans for any new tool or service and of providing adequate opportunities for them to learn about new equipment and its possible impact on them.

In terms of patron assistance, we felt strongly that this should be kept to a minimum. If CD-ROM was indeed going to be feasible in our library environment, then patrons must be able to use it with little help from the reference staff. In order to create a realistic test situation, we wanted to prepare a handout that would show patrons how to get started and how to perform searches with a minimum of help. We decided to wait until we had a chance to use the system ourselves before drafting the exact instructions for the handout.

To publicize the service, we wrote a brief article for our monthly acquisitions list, a vehicle we often use to tell patrons about new services or instruction programs. This list goes to faculty and staff who pay a subscription for it. We also sent out a flyer to all the second-year medical students at UCLA and informed our Library Advisory Committee. We placed a large sign in direct view of everyone entering the library, which advertised the availability of MEDLINE on CD-ROM.

Finally, we designed an evaluation form that would tell us how our patrons reacted to CD-ROM. With this form we hoped to learn the following: who our CD-ROM users were, how much previous searching experience they had, how easy it was for them to learn to use the system and the equipment, how satisfied they were with their search results, whether or not they used the more advanced method of searching, if they would use a system like this again, and if they thought the library should buy such a system. On the form, we also asked for a short description of their search and their comments.

A PHYSICIAN'S PERSPECTIVE

The ultimate research subject in the Information Age is information itself. A great deal needs to be learned about systems for acquiring, organizing, storing, and distributing the world's knowledge about health and disease. Vast and fundamental changes are being made in methods of scholarly communication. These changes are evolving principally through the marketplace. They urgently need scientific examination.

By Nicholas E. Davis. From "The National Library of Medicine and the American Medical Information System: A Physician's Perspective," in the October 1986 issue of the *Bulletin of the Medical Library Association*. Reprinted by permission of the Medical Library Association. Copyright © 1986 by the Medical Library Association.

SETTING UP THE WORK STATION

Although we were now ready to perform our test, there were delays in receiving the CD-ROM equipment. I think this is a common problem in dealing with manufacturers, so libraries should

> *If we had had any doubts that our patrons might not use CD-ROM or not appreciate it, they were soon dispelled.*

be aware of this when making their overall plans. When the equipment finally arrived, several staff members tested it. From their reactions and suggestions and from reading through the manual that came with it, we decided on the basic information our patrons would need to get into the system and to start searching. We decided that we would create a single sheet of instructions, telling people how to know when the system is functioning properly; how to get help; how to choose options from the menu and briefly what those options meant; how to correct errors, truncate, and return to previous screens; and how to print out their search strategy and exit the program. On the instruction sheet we would also remind them about using medical subject headings in their searches, tell them that they should consult the user manual for further help, and ask them to fill out an evaluation form. We did not want to go beyond that; if we had to provide more information, then the system was not user-friendly.

We decided to keep the search manual at the reference desk since we only had one copy. We located the box for completed evaluations next to a supply of blank forms beside the CD player, hoping that patrons would not miss them! In the instructions we asked users to print out their search strategies and include them with their evaluations. We had hoped to learn about their searching techniques from the printouts. A separate set of instructions was prepared for all the reference librarians, which also described the kinds of help we should be giving patrons and encouraging everyone working at the desk to try the system. We held an orientation session for desk staff, which included a demonstration of the system and practical details on setting up and storing the equipment. Now we were ready to go public!

If we had had any doubts that our patrons might not use CD-ROM or not appreciate it, they were soon dispelled. We were, in fact, rarely lacking in test candidates, and people were very good about completing their evaluations. We had a few questions about which subject headings to use in a search and some problems with running out of data storage space because previous users had not erased their search statements. Most of the questions and difficulties, however, dealt with printing. The printer itself gave us a lot of problems with jamming and error messages. We also experienced some queuing problems when several patrons wanted to print out lengthy search results. The rest of the equipment functioned smoothly, and people just sat down and used CD-ROM without much consultation with desk staff.

EVALUATION RESULTS

Overall we received 63 completed evaluation forms during the two weeks we had the system available. We are not sure if this reflects the actual number of users; we did do our best to encourage everyone to complete the form. Not all 63 people answered every question, but many people included comments.

Of the 63 who responded, 24 percent were faculty, 18 percent were staff, 40 percent were graduate or professional school students, 5 percent were undergraduates, and 13 percent gave no affiliation. Since our library is open to everyone, including the general public, we did not restrict access to CD-ROM to any group of library users.

In the area of previous search experience, 65 percent of the respondents said they had never done a computer search before. Of the 33 percent who had, several listed the library's online catalog as their searching experience. Clearly a lack of experience did not prevent people from trying this new method of searching the literature. Neither did it prevent them from quickly learning how to use it. An overwhelming 83 percent said they found the system easy to learn and easy to use once learned. Only 13 percent found it difficult to use. Though the basic search system was obviously not a problem, only 25 percent used the more advanced searching method. Many people made comments on the searching methods; most centered on the slowness of the system. Users obviously did not like waiting for what seemed a very long time while the system searched, especially when they used the advanced method. And they were even more unhappy at having to wait a long time only to then be given another search option rather than actual results. We realized of course that some of the slowness was due to using a PC rather than an XT or AT, and libraries need to take this into consideration when setting up CD-ROM equipment. Several people also complained that they did not know if the system was still actually operating while it searched. They would have liked some indication, e.g., a flashing message, that it was still working. Another frequent complaint about the search system was its lack of flexibility. It seemed that most users did not find out how to combine search statements, so could not modify their searches. This capability was not included in our search manual and could only be learned by reading through six help screens!

As to user satisfaction, 57 percent indicated that they were satisfied with their searches; 30 percent said they were not satisfied. It was interesting to note, however, that 85 percent of those who were not satisfied still said they would use the system again, and 63 percent of them went on to suggest that the library purchase it. We were a little suspicious of these responses, however, when we looked at the search strategies we received. Unfortunately, there were not as many of these strategies

> *Clearly a lack of experience did not prevent people from trying this new method of searching the literature. Neither did it prevent them from quickly learning how to use it.*

handed in as we had hoped because of printer problems. However, we discovered that people were retrieving either huge numbers of citations on very broad subjects or just one or two on a topic that clearly had more information available in the database. One respondent who did attach her search strategy and who said she was satisfied with her search had actually retrieved 826 citations, while another "satisfied" user found nothing on his topic.

Apart from not being able to combine search statements, a major problem that several people had was not using medical subject headings but relying on text words and, thus, missing many pertinent citations. In retrospect, we feel that we should have phrased our question on user satisfaction differently. When people responded positively we did not really know if they were satisfied with actual search results or satisfied with being able to do the search themselves. A more appropriate way of asking for user satisfaction would be to ask how many citations were retrieved, how many were wanted or expected, and whether or not those retrieved were pertinent.

IMPACT OF ELECTRONIC PUBLISHING

Although most types of libraries will feel the effects of the shift to electronic publishing, medical libraries will be among those most affected because of the enormous amount of publishing done by medical workers and its importance to the field, the reliance of researchers on journal literature rather than on monographs, and the emphasis on speed and accuracy of reporting research data.

> By Brian Aveny and Sheila Conneen. From "The Atomization of Information," in the January 1986 issue of the *Bulletin of the Medical Library Association*. Reprinted by permission of the Medical Library Association. Copyright © 1988 by the Medical Library Association.

In spite of questionable retrieval, slow response time, and many printer problems, an overwhelming 85 percent of all respondents said they would use the system again, only 6 percent said they would not, and 74 percent felt that the library should purchase the system. Several people, though critical of some features, felt that the library was "on the right track" in providing such a tool. A few respondents complained that the system did not cover a long enough period of time, despite all we had done to inform patrons that the disc was only a small demonstration. Clearly CD-ROM was a hit with our users even when they did not really get what they wanted from it.

IMPLICATIONS FOR THE LIBRARY

What did we learn from testing this new technology in the library and what are the implications for any library in providing new, technological tools like CD-ROM for their patrons?

1. There seems to be little doubt that patrons like doing their own searching and are obviously willing to try out new, electronic searching methods, even with little or no previous experience.

2. Using tools that don't give people exactly what they want but do print out their results may be preferable to paging through printed indexes and laboriously writing down citations.

3. People don't necessarily understand what a system can really provide for them and will underutilize it if its features are not readily and easily apparent.

4. While people need systems that are easy to learn and use, they must be provided with problem-specific help where and when they need it so they can use all available features without having to read through lengthy help screens or printed manuals.

5. Since it is difficult for people to understand the coverage of electronic tools, like CD-ROM, which are so different from a printed tool, providing the user with enough information about what they are searching is extremely important.

6. Databases designed like MEDLINE, which are searched more effectively using specific subject headings, must be easily searchable with those headings, and, if patrons insist on entering text words, as we know they do, the search software must be able to accommodate this and automatically convert text words to appropriate subject headings.

7. If CD-ROM technology is to be useful in large, academic libraries, which cater to many types of library users, then CD-ROM systems must be truly user-friendly to everyone, with search capabilities flexible enough to accommodate many levels of ability. For experienced users, menu-

driven methods must be easily bypassed in favor of a more rapid and responsive method that assumes a greater knowledge of searching skills.

8. Busy library users, like health practitioners, may be patient with new technology at first, but their patience may wear thin when the novelty is over. If CD-ROM systems are to be truly user-friendly, these search systems must provide rapid retrieval and communicate with the user so that he or she knows when a response is due. Also, hardware must be easy to operate so that citations can be quickly printed or downloaded so that the system can be freed for the next patron waiting.

What does all this mean for the library? It behooves us to take an active part in testing new technology, such as CD-ROM, so that we can make sure the manufacturers will develop the kind of systems that we and our patrons really need: user-friendly systems that provide rapid and easy access to information and which are not a drain on our already overburdened public service staff. Technology like CD-ROM holds great promise for libraries, but it is librarians who must help ensure that the promise is fulfilled.

Reprinted from *Special Libraries,* **v. 79, no. 1 (Winter 1988), pages 28–33. Copyright © 1988 by the Special Libraries Association.**

From Variables to Videodiscs: Interactive Video in the Clinical Setting

By Mary Anne Sweeney and Claire Gulino
From *Computers in Nursing*

[In this article, the authors demonstrate the usefulness of health tutorials on interactive videodisc as a way of turning clinic waiting time into an educational and informative patient-teaching opportunity. It is not hard to project from their detailed discussion the role multimedia CD-ROMs might play in similar environments.]

The video monitor shows a young pregnant woman standing by a window. The voice of the narrator says:

This is my friend Maria. In a few months, she's going to have a baby. This will be her first child. Maria has always thought that she would breastfeed her baby, but now she's wondering what to do. Her grandmother says that breastfeeding is good, but some of her friends are bottlefeeding their babies. Maria wants to do the best thing for her baby, but she is not sure what that is. What will Maria do?

Maria appears to be deep in thought. After a slight pause, the narrator continues the story:

Will she prepare for breastfeeding, or prepare for bottlefeeding? Help Maria decide. Touch your choice now.

The program stops and waits until the patient indicates her choice by touching a picture on the bottom portion of the screen. A red box on the right side contains a picture of a baby bottle and a blue box on the left side contains a picture of a nursing mother. The patient must become actively involved in the decision making for the program to proceed. The patient selects the segment she wishes to see next and is asked to make breastfeeding or bottlefeeding choices for Maria at a number of other decision points throughout the course of the story. The first patient spends 15 minutes of her time in the clinic waiting room watching a customized bottlefeeding version of this educational program on infant feeding. She now has several specific questions to ask her health care provider about the care and feeding of the baby she will soon deliver. After the first patient leaves for her appointment with the nurse-midwife, another patient moves into the chair in front of the television screen. The voice of the narrator repeats the initial message about Maria. The second patient chooses the breastfeeding version of the program and gathers information about feeding her baby.

Modern technological advances enabled both patients to access information that was tailored to their individual needs, yet neither patient was aware that she was directing both a microcomputer and a videodisc player. A light pressure on the screen was all that was needed to initiate the desired segment of the story at each decision point. When the red rectangle was touched, Maria's story resumed in a fraction of a second, and detailed her preparations for bottlefeeding. The easy touch-screen format eliminates the need for typing skills and the use of color, symbols, and auditory directions reduces the necessity of reading skills. The only piece of electronic equipment visible to the patient was the television monitor. This interactive video program was successful in turning idle waiting time in a bustling community health center into a useful patient-teaching opportunity. Such

> *This interactive video program was successful in turning idle waiting time in a bustling community health center into a useful patient-teaching opportunity.*

"high tech" methods of instructional delivery were not designed to replace professional caregivers, but to provide patients with standardized information that they could use to initiate a dialogue about infant feeding issues with clinic personnel. Clinic nurses can build on this baseline knowledge and give more personalized and detailed instruction. This article describes the steps that were taken to create a videodisc for prenatal patients and to make this application available to patients in a community-based setting.

INTERACTIVE VIDEO

Microcomputers offer tremendous potential to the clinical educator. They are especially suited for teaching applied skills when coupled with a videodisc player. The videodisc brings to the screen clear views of the patient, the equipment, or the setting, rather than relying on the printed word or computer-generated graphics to get the message across. Videodiscs can store up to 54,000 frames of visual material with two accompanying sound tracks. The ability to use any combination of still frames, slow motion, real-time action, or fast forward or reverse

> *The overall story line was crafted by media consultants who had expertise in translating factual information into a visual format. Scriptwriting was a difficult task even for the experienced professionals.*

A videodisc looks like a shimmery phonograph record, but it has visual information encoded and stored in some 50,000 concentric grooves. As one educator notes, "Played at approximately 30 frames per second, the disc contains enough storage for an entire movie with video resolution far surpassing broadcast television" [2]. The most popular format, the optical or laser videodisc, is read by shining a laser onto the concentric bands and decoding the reflections [3]. The result of the computer-video interface has been described by Levin [4] as follows:

"It enables the learner to participate actively in the unfolding of an educational television presentation that is individualized to the learner's own interest level, knowledge base, and learning rate. The learner is in control, as with a book, but the information is presented through vivid personalities, multiple sound and music tracks, and colorful still frame images or motion picture action...[yet] unlike a book...[it] spontaneously reacts differently according to the immediate decisions of the student."

movement allows the authors of the programs creativity. Learners, on the other hand, are required to participate in the action. The first few minutes of watching the emergency room activities revolving around a young man with a gunshot wound in one of the videodiscs created by Intelligent Images [1] clearly demonstrates the active decision making possible in videodisc simulations. The video scenario pauses while diagnostic or therapeutic choices are made at critical points, and the program branches off to different video scenes according to the selections made by the user. The computer is the conduit between the video sequence or computer graphics display and the user. In other words, users select the action that they would take next in a clinical situation, and the computer locates the appropriate video footage and shows it on the screen in a matter of seconds. The speed of the execution of this process with the videodisc makes it seem more lifelike and fast-moving than interactive video that uses slower-winding videotapes.

The microcomputer is used to do the things it does well: recording and storing information, keeping track of time, controlling the flow of information, giving direction to the various machines, and accepting input from several types of devices. The instructions that are executed by the computer can be produced in a number of ways, but one of the most popular methods of producing interactive video programs is through use of an authoring system [5].

The few published reports on the use of interactive video programs in health-related settings focus primarily on the education of professionals rather than patients [6] [7], and none mention the use of more than one audio track. The interactive video program described in this article was developed during the course of a binational research project that was funded for a 2-year period. The basic elements of the three phases of program production and implementation are described in the following sections.

THE PREPRODUCTION PHASE

The preproduction phase of the project was the longest, and it consisted of three separate activities. The intial step involved the implementation of a research study to determine the key factors that influence the infant feeding decisions and practices of Hispanic women. Nearly 200 Hispanic women who gave birth in any of four hospitals in Tijuana, Mexico, and San Diego, California, were interviewed. Data were collected on prenatal influences on the choice of infant feeding method within 24 hours of delivery, and the actual feeding practices of the new mothers were tracked throughout the first postpartum year. Interviews were carried out when the children reached the ages of 6 weeks, 3 months, 6 months, and 1 year [8] [9]. The study served as a baseline needs assessment of a representative group of Hispanic patients. Patients in low- and middle-income groups were surveyed since they were targeted as the prime potential audience of such an educational program.

The second activity involved the preparation of a script for the videodisc production. The script was based on information gathered from many sources, including the research subjects, the literature, subject matter content experts, consultants who were part of the research project, practicing nurses in clinical sites and, finally, the previous clinical experiences of several members of the research team. The overall story line was crafted by media consultants who had expertise in translating factual information into a visual format. Scriptwriting was a difficult task even for the experienced professionals. Several drafts were extensively rewritten before all the participants approved of the final product. The information gathered as a result of the research study was used consistently in making decisions about the script as well as the overall production. For instance, subjects in the study were asked to use a five-point scale to rate the impact of a variety of factors on their choice of

REFERENCES

[1] "Clinical Simulation." *Medical Disc Reporter,* 1985:1(1), page 5.

[2] Leonard, W., "Interactive Videodiscs: Computer Instruction of the Future?" *Collegiate Microcomputer,* 1987:5(2), pages 197–200.

[3] Schwartz, M., "An Introduction to Interactive Video Systems." *Computers in Nursing,* 1984:2, pages 8–13.

[4] Levin, W., "Interactive Video: The State-of-the-Art Teaching Machine." *The Computing Teacher,* 1983:11(2), pages 11–17.

[5] Schwartz, E., *The Educator's Handbook to Interactive Videodisc,* Washington, D.C.: Association for Educational Communications and Technology, 1987.

[6] Fishman, D., "Development and Evaluation of a Computer Assisted Video Module for Teaching Cancer Chemotherapy to Nurses." *Computers in Nursing,* 1984:2, pages 16–23.

[7] Quy, N., and Covington, J., "The Microcomputer in Industry Training." *Technological Horizons in Education Journal,* 1982:9(3), pages 65–68.

[8] Gulino, C., Sweeney, M.A., and Small, M.A., "An Investigation of Breastfeeding Practices in a Binational Population." *Proceedings of the Eleventh Annual Transcultural Nursing Conference.* Salt Lake City, UT: Transcultural Nursing Society, 1986.

[9] Sweeney, M.A., and Gulino, C., "The Health Belief Model as an Explanation for Breastfeeding Practices in a Hispanic Population." *Advances in Nursing Science,* 1987:9(4), pages 35–50.

[10] Miller, R., "CD-ROM and Videodisc: Lessons to Be Learned." In S. Lambert and S. Ropiequet, *CD-ROM: The New Papyrus,* Redmond, WA: Microsoft Press, 1986, pages 37–42.

an infant feeding method. The process involved rating multiple items on a comprehensive list of informational sources. Choices included friends, relatives, the media, educational programs, support groups, and health care professionals. The influence of the patient's mother and grandmother was clear because of the high scores both parties were given. Thus, an important decision about the narrator's voice was made quickly. It had to be familiar and friendly as opposed to authoritative in a professional way, and it had to sound like an older woman who could be either a mother or a grandmother. The low ratings in the survey assigned to the nurses and to friends of the same age group only reinforced the decision to cast an older grandmother figure as the storyteller of the Spanish sound track of the videodisc. All of the variables in the research study were reviewed with the script production team and, thus, the research findings became the starting point for program development.

An off-camera narrator was used to relate the information because of the language and translation issues. It was decided that the individuals in the film would converse softly with each other while the narrator presented the story line. This arrangement permitted the use of both soundtracks located on the videodisc. Thus, a bilingual disc was conceived with one audio track in Spanish and the second in English.

The third preproduction activity involved the design of the videodisc map (Figure 3-1). Even though the script for "The Story of Maria" was divided into 19 segments, the map contains 21 possible steps since two segments may be inserted in a different sequence depending on the branching choices that are made. Patients can personalize the instruction by moving through different pathways of the story according to the choices they make at decision points. A fairly simple and straightforward branching program was selected for this project to keep the attention of the learners and to minimize future maintenance problems for the clinical sites.

THE PRODUCTION PHASE

Program production was completed within 6 weeks. The initial segment involved decisions and activities that needed attention before taping, such as casting parts, scheduling taping locations, and gathering realistic equipment and props. The taping took place in several locations over a 3-day period. The taping was done by the same media consultants who worked on the script. The taping was the most expensive part of the entire project because the quality of the picture was a major concern. Broadcast quality videotape was used to ensure that the transformation from videotape to videodisc would provide a crisp, clear picture on the monitor. The organization of the cast and their substitutes was a challenge since the script called for an infant at different stages of development (three different infants were cast in the role of the growing baby Christina). Each infant needed a handy substitute in case of inclement temperament. Editing the videotape was the last step in this phase of the production.

In addition to the selection of the best visual sequences, the editing included insertion of graphics (primarily still-sequence artwork), background music, and the scripted narration. The artwork consisted of line drawings, anatomical diagrams, and the red and blue rectangles with icons that were inserted at the decision points for the touch-screen choices. The narration was added to the tape in two different recording sessions, one in English and the other in Spanish. Since approximately one-third more words are needed to verbalize the same ideas in Spanish than in English, the Spanish sound track caused some editing problems because of its length.

THE POSTPRODUCTION PHASE

A "check" or "proof" videodisc was made from the edited version of the 1-inch master videotape (Optical Disc Corp., Cerritos, CA

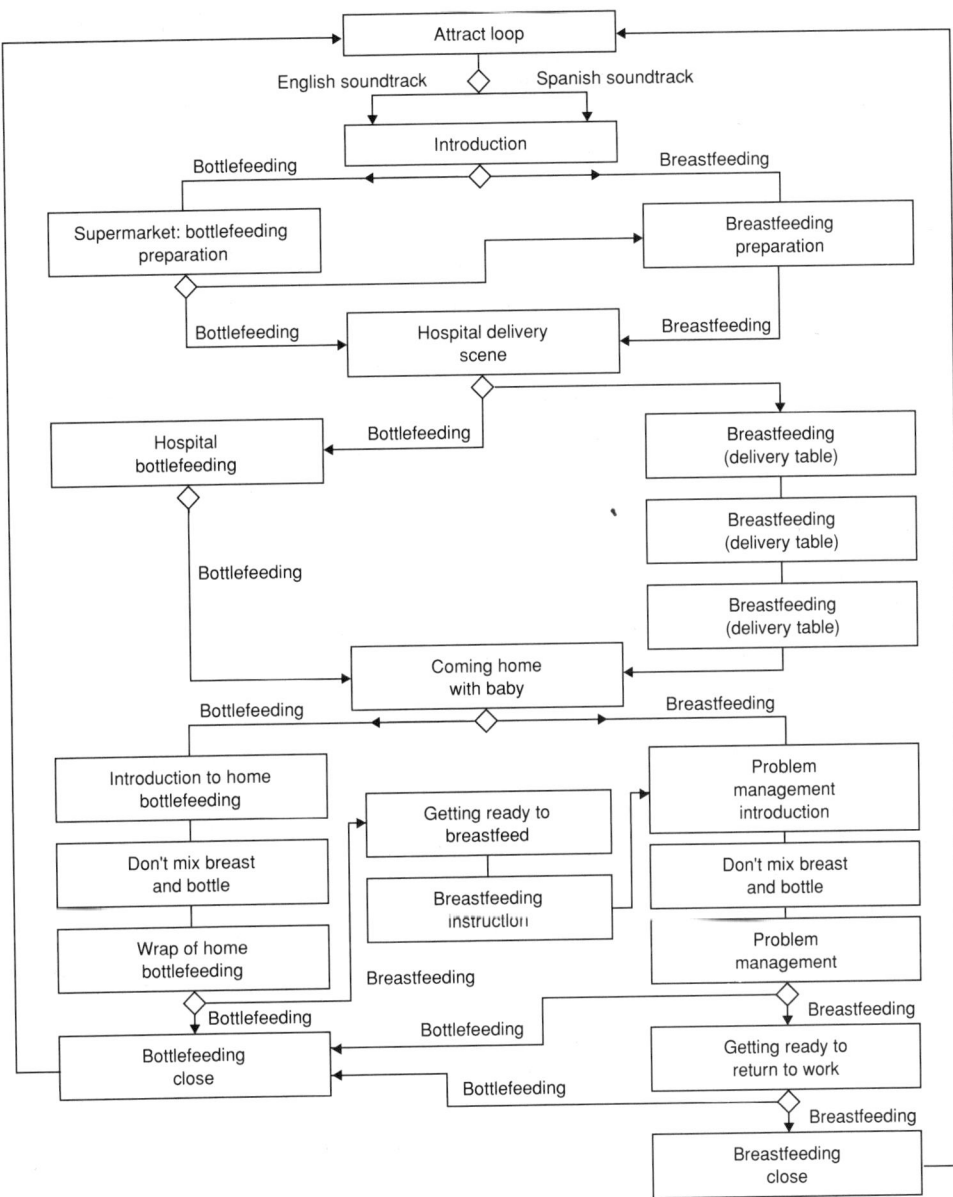

Figure 3-1. Videodisc map. The attract loop is a portion of video and audio that runs constantly until the screen is touched by the viewer. As soon as the screen is touched, the program is set in motion. This feature is designed to attract attention and to encourage the patient to get involved with the program. Eight decision points (◊) were placed at the end of each section to allow the viewer to decide whether to view the segment on bottlefeeding or breastfeeding. A still frame of video will appear on the screen at each decision point.... Verbal instructions describe each choice and the two areas of the screen are defined by both color and graphics. A light touch to the designated area of the screen directs the action to one of the two story sequences. If the screen is not touched within 45 seconds, the program automatically returns to the attract loop. After the final frame of the bottlefeeding close or breastfeeding close, the program automatically returns to the attract loop.

90701). This version of the videodisc costs a small portion of the amount of the final mastering of the disc and permitted the authors to sample the program to determine whether further editing was needed. It was also available for immediate use in the computer programming activities. The initial quality of the video on the proof disc was inferior to that of the final mastered version, and the glass disc was fragile and had to be handled and stored carefully. The picture quality of this proof disc deteriorated rapidly with repeated use in programming sequences of the videodisc map, but this step was a necessary prelude to mastering the final videodisc version. The mastering of the final version of the videodisc and the production of the copies was done by the 3M Corporation (Minneapolis, MN) in a 2-week period. The nearly indestructible copies should withstand repeated use in the clinical setting.

The next task in the postproduction phase was the development of the instructions for the computer since it would handle communication between the patient and the videodisc. For instance, when the patient touched the red box containing the icon of the baby bottle, the location of the signal was translated by the computer into a request to have the videodisc machine play a designated segment contained in the videodisc map....

The computer programming was carried out by using a menu-driven authoring system (a software package) developed specifically for generating interactive instructions (© 1985, Quest authoring system, Allen Communications, Inc.). A number or "address" is located in the upper left corner of each frame of the video program. The individual frame is followed by similar, yet slightly different, still pictures or frames. When played at a rapid speed, these frames produce a smooth motion sequence or moving picture. The videodisc has room for 54,000 individual frames, so the potential for a great deal of programming exists. The computer program directs the action to the precise locations according to its set of instructions, and then tells the videodisc player to display one image or a sequence of images. Many frames are needed to display even a brief video motion segment. The special computer program devised to run "The Story of Maria" for this patient education project was placed on a single floppy disk.

The computer hardware used in the project and the approximate costs of the major production items are listed in Table 3-1. Although a number of options were available when hardware selection was carried out, the decision was made to purchase all components from a single vendor (Allen Communications, Inc., Salt Lake City, UT 85116). This step ensured such important factors as the compatibility of parts and the adjustments necessary for touch-sensitive screen control. Market conditions change quickly, and several companies now offer similar configurations. Some of the equipment has even decreased in price since the project hardware was acquired. The budget figures can fluctuate widely depending on many factors, such as the availability of in-house equipment, programming expertise, and capabilities for necessary components such as videotaping and production of artwork.

THE NEXT STEPS AND FUTURE ENHANCEMENTS

The next stage of the research project involved an extensive study of the impact of the interactive video program on patients and staff.

The preliminary pilot testing of the interactive video program with primiparous patients in community health clinics has shown that patients of differing educational levels can use the program with ease. Beta testing of the program is underway in two community health centers in southern San Diego County. The patient advances through the program by touching the screen and no interaction is required with the hardware on the upper shelf of the cart. An additional computer program is currently being developed with the same authoring system that will be designed as a continuing education program for the nursing staff. This additional use of the videodisc will broaden its applicability and lower the cost per person for its use. The continuing education program for nurses will be in the form of an assessment test with corrective feedback for incorrect responses. Some of the visual feedback will be obtained (recycled) from the artwork and action sequences located on "The Story of Maria" videodisc, and added information will be generated from newly devised computer graphics.

Videodiscs and their associated hardware configurations have been available since 1980. As Miller [10] pointed out, most new technologies move through three basic stages in their early evolution. The first stage is one of unbridled optimism in which the technology is viewed as a panacea for all types of problems. Stage 2 is a pessimistic depression that sets in when the technology cannot live up to early expectations. The third stage focuses on areas of real benefit and real value. The authors hope that "The Story of Maria" interactive videodisc program is a part of the third stage of this new technology, and that it has real value for both patients and clinicians. Readers are encouraged to explore new areas and enhance patient education by taking advantage of this computer-based technology.

Reprinted by permission of J.B. Lippincott Company, publishers of Computers in Nursing, no. 6(4).

APPROXIMATE COST OF INTERACTIVE VIDEO PROGRAM DEVELOPMENT AND PLAYBACK

Item	Cost
Videodisc production costs	
Scriptwriting, taping, and editing of 1-inch broadcast quality videotape	$40,000
Artwork	200
Proof or check videodisc	350
Videodisc mastering plus printing of 18 copies	2,500
Total	$43,050
Hardware costs: production	
IBM PC XT with a hard disk, 512K RAM	$2,500
Zenith ZVM 135 13-inch high-resolution color monitor with RS 232 serial port cable and microtouch touch screen controller mounted inside	2,350
Pioneer LD-V 1000 disc player	
Microkey model 1100 to control and synchronize graphics overlay and interface	1,265
Tecmar Graphics Master High Resolution Graphics Card adapted to Microkey	560
Quest comprehensive authoring system, IBM/Videodisc touchscreen version	1,295
Total	$7,970
Hardware costs: playback	
IBM PC XT or IBM System 2 model 30	2,200
Zenith touch screen monitor as above or a comparable monitor such as the IBM InfoWindow	2,350
Microkey needed with the Zenith	1,265
Videodisc and presentation diskette for the program	*
Total	$5,815

*Price to be determined after beta testing is completed.

HEALTH AND SAFETY TITLES

Title	Publisher	Price
CCINFOdisc: Series A1 and A2: Chemical Information	Canadian Centre for Occupational Health & Safety 250 Main Street East Hamilton, ON L8N 1H6 CANADA (416)572–2981	$114.00/Year
CCINFOdisc: Series B Occupational Health and Safety Information	Canadian Centre for Occupational Health & Safety 250 Main Street East Hamilton, ON L8N 1H6 CANADA (416)572–2981	$114.00/Disc
Health Index on InfoTrac	Information Access Company 362 Lakeside Drive Foster City, CA 94404 (800)227–8431	$2,000.00/System per Year
Health/Stats	Hopkins Technology 421 Hazel Lane Hopkins, MN 55343-7117 (612)931–9376	$49.00/Disc
Material Safety Data System	National Safety Data Corporation 259 West Road Salem, CT 06415 (203)859–1162	$750.00
OHS MSDS ON DISC	Occupational Health Services, Inc. 450 Seventh Avenue Suite 2407 New York, NY 10123 (800)445–6737	$5,000.00/First year

Compiled by Online Press Inc.

MEDICAL TITLES

Title	Publisher	Price
AfterCare Instructions	Micromedex, Inc. 660 Bannock Street Suite 300 Denver, CO 80204-4506 (800)525–9083	*
AIDS Supplement	Digital Diagnostics, Inc. 601 University Avenue Suite 255 Sacramento, CA 95825 (916)921–6629	$350.00/Year
BiblioMed	Digital Diagnostics, Inc. 601 University Avenue Suite 255 Sacramento, CA 95825 (916)921–6629	$950.00/Year
CANCER-CD	SilverPlatter Information, Inc. 37 Walnut Street Wellesley Hills, MA 02181 (617)239–0306	$1,750.00/Year
CancerLIT	Online Research Systems Inc. 2901 Broadway Suite 154 New York, NY 10025 (212)408–3311	$1,995.00/Year
Compact Cambridge CancerLit (Cancer Literature)	Cambridge Scientific Abstracts 7200 Wisconsin Avenue Suite 601 Bethesda, MD 20816 (301)961–6700	$995.00/Year
Compact Cambridge MEDLINE	Cambridge Scientific Abstracts 7200 Wisconsin Avenue Suite 601 Bethesda, MD 20816 (301)961–6700	$1,250.00/Year
Compact Cambridge Drugs Database	Cambridge Scientific Abstracts 7200 Wisconsin Avenue Suite 601 Bethesda, MD 20816 (301)961–6700	$1,950.00/Year
Compact Cambridge PDQ (Physicians' Data Query)	Cambridge Scientific Abstracts 7200 Wisconsin Avenue Suite 601 Bethesda, MD 20816 (301)961–6700	$950.00/Year

*Contact publisher for prices.

(continued)

MEDICAL TITLES *continued.*

Title	Publisher	Price
Compact Library: AIDS	Medical Publishing Group 1440 Main Street Waltham, MA 02254 (617)893–3800	$875.00/Year
Compact Med-Base	Online Research Systems Inc. 2901 Broadway Suite 154 New York, NY 10025 (212)408–3311	$3,495.00/Year
COMPREHENSIVE MEDLINE/ EBSCO CD-ROM	EBSCO Electronic Information P.O. Box 13787 Torrance, CA 90503 (800)888–EBSCO	$1,000.00/Year
CORE MEDLINE/EBSCO CD-ROM	EBSCO Electronic Information P.O. Box 13787 Torrance, CA 90503 (800)888–EBSCO	$1,400.00/Year
DIALOG OnDisc MEDLINE	Dialog Information Services, Inc. 3460 Hillview Avenue Palo Alto, CA 94304 (800)334–2564	$1,250.00/Year
DOSING & THERAPEUTIC TOOLS	Micromedex, Inc. 660 Bannock Street Suite 300 Denver, CO 80204-4506 (800)525–9083	*
Drug Information Source	American Society of Hospital Pharmacists 4630 Montgomery Avenue Bethesda, MD 20814 (301)657–3000	$1,950.00/Year
DRUGDEX System	Micromedex, Inc. 660 Bannock Street Suite 300 Denver, CO 80204-4506 (800)525–9083	*
Eidetic	Eidetic Knowledge Systems 50 Valley Stream Parkway Malvern, PA 19355 (215)889–9780	$600.00
EMERGINDEX System	Micromedex, Inc. 660 Bannock Street Suite 300 Denver, CO 80204-4506 (800)525–9083	*

*Contact publisher for prices.

Title	Publisher	Price
Health Planning and Administration	Online Research Systems Inc. 2901 Broadway Suite 154 New York, NY 10025 (212)408–3311	$1,995.00/Year
IDENTIDEX System	Micromedex, Inc. 660 Bannock Street Suite 300 Denver, CO 80204-4506 (800)525–9083	*
LILACS	PAHO (Pan American World Health Organization) 525 23rd Street N.W. Washington, DC 20037 (202)861–3366	*
MARTINDALE: The Extra Pharmacopoeia	Micromedex, Inc. 660 Bannock Street Suite 300 Denver, CO 80204-4506 (800)525–9083	*
MAXX: Maximum Access to Diagnosis and Therapy	Little, Brown and Company 34 Beacon Street Boston, MA 02108 (617)227–0730	*
MEDLINE: BRS/Colleague Disc	BRS Information Technologies 1200 Route 7 Latham, NY 12110 (800)468–0908	$995.00/Year
MEDLINE Knowledge Server	Aries Systems Corporation 79 Boxford Street North Andover, MA 01845-3219 (508)689–9334	*
MEDLINE on SilverPlatter	SilverPlatter Information, Inc. 37 Walnut Street Wellesley Hills, MA 02181 (617)239–0306	$950.00/Year
NATASHA: National Archive on Sexuality, Health & Adolescence	Knowledge Access International, Inc. 2685 Marine Way Suite 1305 Mountain View, CA 94043 (415)969–0606	$495.00
The Nurse Library	Ellis Enterprises Inc. 225 N.W. Thirteenth Street Oklahoma City, OK 73103 (405)235–7660	$700.00/Year

*Contact publisher for prices.

(continued)

MEDICAL TITLES *continued.*

Title	Publisher	Price
Oncodisc	J.B. Lippincott Company East Washington Square Philadelphia, PA 19105 (215)238–4200	$1,950.00/Year
OSH-ROM	SilverPlatter Information, Inc. 37 Walnut Street Wellesley Hills, MA 02181 (617)239–0306	$900.00/Year
The Physician Library	Ellis Enterprises Inc. 225 N.W. Thirteenth Street Oklahoma City, OK 73103 (405)235–7660	$1,000.00/Year
Physicians' Desk Reference on CD-ROM	Medical Economics Company P.O. Box 551 Oradell, NJ 07649 (800)526–4870	$595.00/Year
POISINDEX System	Micromedex, Inc. 660 Bannock Street Suite 300 Denver, CO 80204-4506 (800)525–9083	*
TOMES System	Micromedex, Inc. 660 Bannock Street Suite 300 Denver, CO 80204-4506 (800)525–9083	*

Compiled by Online Press Inc.

Integrating Computers into Law Firms

By Nora Leven
From *Puget Sound Computer User*

[They say you can't teach an old dog new tricks, but in this high-technology age, even "yellow pad and pencil" lawyers need to move on in order to move up. In the last article of this section, Nora Leven discusses the computerization of legal offices.]

CEOs do it. Accountants do it. Even doctors do it. But many lawyers just flat-out refuse. We're not talking about buying malpractice insurance or paying alimony. No, it's much worse than that; it's typing.

It's sitting down at a keyboard and using your fingers to hack out words and figures. You can try to trick some people by taking the keyboard off a typewriter and plunking it down on a computer, but the true die-hards won't be fooled. Typing is typing, and typing is what secretaries do, they say, not what high-powered, $150-an-hour lawyers do.

"It's an image problem," explained David Hambourger, director of the Law Office of the Future project for the American Bar Association (ABA) in Chicago. "Many lawyers have an aversion to typing, or don't think they should have to type. You're supposed to have uncluttered walnut bookshelves in your office, not a computer."

In just the past two or three years, though, that image problem with a keyboard is showing signs of reversing. "Now it is just beginning to be viewed as a status symbol," Hambourger said, "that you know how to work a computer and that may give you an advantage over someone who doesn't. It's now perceived as a way to take control."

Still, very few lawyers have computers on their desks, although computers can be found in other areas of the typical law office—namely on

> *It is just beginning to be viewed as a status symbol, that you know how to work a computer and that may give you an advantage over someone who doesn't. It's now perceived as a way to take control.*

the secretary's desk. By ABA estimates, close to 75 percent of the 240,000 law offices in the country probably use word processing, either on a desktop computer, with a dedicated word processor, or on some form of mag-card typewriter. Just 10 percent, however, use a computer for time accounting and billing and other applications.

"Lawyers have never been ones to automate quickly or to bring new management tools into their office," noted Richard Robbins, director of the ABA's Legal Technology Advisory Council (LTAC). "Most have electric typewriters and that's as far as they go. We're still in the old days with most of them buying yellow pads and pencils. It's tradition, but it's changing rapidly because the competitive environment is so strong in most places that lawyers have to [automate] to save money and serve their clients."

The amount of technical support and encouragement from the ABA belies the slowness of the legal mind to adopt new technology. There's Robbins' LTAC, which tests and recommends software packages for the ABA membership, and Hambourger's Law Office of the Future project, an advisory arm that has developed a communications and menu program called *Lawlink*. There's also ABA-Net, an electronic-mail system set up for membership use.

So with all this help available, it's hard to believe that a little thing like an image problem with typing can put the kibosh on an entire profession's acceptance of what has become almost commonplace in every other industry. In fact, according to Hambourger, typing is only one of the many reasons lawyers have been taking technology continuances. Aversion to typing might be just a convenient excuse; a bigger problem is lack of relevant information, he said.

"While there's an attempt to make technological information useful to lawyers, there has historically been a lack of clear explanation of the basics, like what is a computer and what is the difference between [different amounts of memory]," Hambourger said. A lot of people in the computer industry take that knowledge for granted, he said, adding that while lawyers are very good at puzzling through details on a complicated case, they have not been especially prone to do so for the sake of automating their own offices. "Lawyers have little patience for picking up a [general computer magazine] and trying to figure out how it all can apply to them," he said.

Another problem, according to Hambourger, is lack of hardware and software compatibility. "Unless you're a larger firm with a computer-knowledgeable staff person, which most law firms are not, you're left in the air to do your own buying," he said. "Trying to figure out which things work together is very difficult; there's a lack of standards for lawyers to follow to make sure their word processing will work with a time-and-billing program."

Finally, like all business people, lawyers are concerned about the cost justification of automation. This concern spans two levels: one is the justification of the dollar investment in hardware and software, and the other is the time investment in getting trained in and acclimated to the new machinery and procedures. The time and dollar investment usually does pay off, Hambourger said, but for most lawyers the benefits just aren't clear right now. "I hear from time to time that the computerized offices can reduce staff or that they can bill more time, but there's no hard and fast evidence; for the most part, you can't see a causal connection, and that makes the cost difficult to justify."

The benefits are there, though, he said, but they tend to be more intangible—at least at first. Accomplishing more work faster and maintaining a sense of control are difficult benefits to quantify, Hambourger explained. Billing more time is how those intangible benefits get translated, but it may take some time to realize that fatter bottom line.

LITIGATION SUPPORT

In the meantime, those other intangible benefits can at the very least make life easier for an attorney while at the same time impressing clients. One area coming into its own with the help of technology is what's known as litigation support. This involves finding, assembling and retrieving all the information and data involved or related to a particular case. As one case can often involve a number of lawsuits, litigants, witnesses and lawyers, handling all the documents for the trial preparation and proceedings can be an impossible task without the help of a computer.

The largest and most well-known example of computer-assisted litigation support is the Coordinated Asbestos Insurance Trial, which involved more than 50,000 personal-injury lawsuits, 100 law firms, 60 insurance companies, more than a million pages of documents and close to half a million exhibits. The case, which went to trial in 1985, was so large it had to be held in a San Francisco auditorium.

American Legal Systems, a New York City-based company specializing in computerized litigation support, installed 30 terminals in the auditorium-cum-courtroom. The terminals were connected to the firm's IBM mainframes in

> *I hear from time to time that the computerized offices can reduce staff or that they can bill more time, but there's no hard and fast evidence; for the most part, you can't see a causal connection, and that makes the cost difficult to justify.*

Dallas, which contained the huge files of case-related information. As the trial proceeded, the judge and the lawyers on both sides could gain access to the voluminous documents and exhibits pertinent to that day's arguments.

That case, while certainly larger than most, is indicative of a growing trend of monumental product-liability cases. In 1985 alone there were more than 13,000 such cases, with average jury awards approaching $1 million. Those involved in providing computer software and services to the legal profession know that as our society becomes more and more litigious, the reliance on computers to handle the ensuing tidal wave of information also grows.

Equally important to preparing and managing documents and exhibits in a trial is integrating historical data with the facts of the current case. Lawyers often conduct legal research, looking for past precedent-setting cases or relevant statutes that may help them win their case.

There are two ways to do this research: manually or through data-base searches.

According to Robbins, data-base searching is the number-one application of computers in law firms, even bigger than word processing. "Many lawyers have been doing this for 20 years now; it's the oldest and most accepted usage of computers," he said.

INCREDIBLE SHRINKING LIBRARIES

While legal data bases may not totally replace law libraries, they may shrink their size simply by virtue of reducing the amount of shelf space necessary to store the volumes of case histories and statutes. More and more law firms are now

LEGAL TITLES

Title	*Publisher*	*Price*
Decision Series: California Decisions	ROM Publishers Inc. 1033 'O' Street Mezzanine Level Lincoln, NE 68508 (402)476–2965	$2,695.00/Year
Decision Series: Federal Decisions	ROM Publishers Inc. 1033 'O' Street Mezzanine Level Lincoln, NE 68508 (402)476–2965	$5,400.00/Year
Decision Series: Federal Supplemental Decisions	ROM Publishers Inc. 1033 'O' Street Mezzanine Level Lincoln, NE 68508 (402)476–2965	$5,780.00/Year
Decision Series: Northwest Regional Decisions	ROM Publishers Inc. 1033 'O' Street Mezzanine Level Lincoln, NE 68508 (402)476–2965	$2,690.00/Year
Index to Legal Periodicals	H.W. Wilson Company 950 University Avenue Bronx, NY 10452 (800)367–6770	$1,495.00/Year
LAW MARC	UTLAS International 8300 College Boulevard Overland Park, KS 66210 (800)33–UTLAS	$750.00/Disc
LegalTrac on InfoTrac	Information Access Company 362 Lakeside Drive Foster City, CA 94404 (800)227–8431	$5,000.00/System per Year
The Texas Attorney General Documents	Quantum Access Inc. 1700 West Loop South Suite 1460 Houston, TX 77027 (713)622–3211	$600.00/Disc

Compiled by Online Press Inc.

even creating their own data bases from their own file cabinets, using scanning and compact-disk technology, Hambourger noted.

"There's more use of CD-ROM [Compact Disk, Read Only Memory] technology," he said. "Huge cases can be scanned into machines. It won't do away with paper, but it will reduce the number of file cabinets a firm may need, and make it easier to find all the pieces of paper that go with each case."

Of course, not everything can be done electronically. There are certain documents that require signatures, and with electronic mail, there's the problem of proving that the document was actually sent should one party claim he never received it. "Whole areas of law will have to change to recognize the technology," Hambourger said. "As it stands now, though, most everything still requires a documented paper trail."

Still, computers can help lawyers whittle down the time it takes to actually create all that paper. Many forms are used in law, especially in the real-estate and tax specialties, and boilerplate word processing can make the creation of those forms a much more efficient process. As a complement to the forms programs, computerized time tables remind lawyers when the form needs to be filed, as well as performing other calendar and scheduling functions.

Like the boilerplate forms, other aspects of law are similarly mechanical and repetitive. Deciding whether a client's tax situation is appropriate for subchapter-S corporation status, for example, or processing through a real-estate closing are both applications well suited for what are being called "expert" or "substantive" systems.

Such systems take the lawyer through a series of questions that result in the program making a recommendation. "All the rules that apply to a legal decision can be reduced to a flow chart," Hambourger explained. "These systems mean that more people in the firm will be able to make these decisions, not just the experts.

LEGAL APPLICATIONS

"CD-ROM is an ideal medium for many legal applications," says Befeler [1]. Attorneys have to constantly review a tremendous amount of printed texts that typically include volumes of court decisions, statutes, digests, law reviews, loose-leaf services, citations, legal encyclopedias, treaties, law journals, legal forms, and patents/trademarks. All of these reference materials could be stored on several CD-ROM discs and they are ready for retrieval at attorneys' fingertips.

"The combination of CD-ROM storage devices and user-friendly text retrieval software running on a personal computer has opened up a new realm of information retrieval for the legal and acccounting fields," Befeler says. "And it couldn't happen to a more appropriate group."

[1] Befeler, Michael G., "Laserdisc System from Reference Technology: Multiuser Technology for High-Use Environments." *Library Hi Tech*, 1985: 3(2) pages 55–59.

By Chung I. Park. From *The COINT Reports*. Copyright © 1986 by The COINT Reports.

You'll still need the firm's expert in tax law, for example, to check the decision to file for subchapter-S, but it takes the burden off the expert by not having to be involved in every minor detail."

These systems free lawyers to devote more time to creative legal thinking, Hambourger said. "Rather than spending time worrying about filing depositions, the checklists allow the paralegals and legal assistants to take over that responsibility, and the expert systems take some of the details off the expert lawyer's shoulders. What we need is to find the right way to introduce these programs so they will be accepted."

Reprinted by permission of *Computer User*, MSP Publications, 12 S. Street, Suite 400, Minneapolis, MN 55402. All rights reserved.

IN-HOUSE APPLICATIONS

CORPORATE MANAGEMENT INFORMATION SYSTEMS AND CD-ROM
By Robert B. Fisher

DEVELOPING CD-ROMS IN-HOUSE FOR CORPORATE USE
By Douglas Iles

IN-HOUSE CD-ROM PUBLISHING: IS IT CATCHING ON?
By Fred Meyer

Corporate Management Information Systems and CD-ROM

By Robert B. Fisher

[In our first article about in-house CD-ROM applications, Robert Fisher discusses how MIS managers view the technology and describes one successful corporate implementation of CD-ROM.]

Reading this *Yearbook* makes one thing obvious: CD-ROM is a very powerful medium for information distribution. With the potential to hold over 600 megabytes of data in the form of text, graphics, audio, and video, CD-ROM has revolutionized the way information is organized and delivered. Because CD-ROM discs and drives are similar to their counterparts for playing and distributing CD audio, the costs of using CD-ROM are much lower than they would be if the medium had been developed independently.

This article examines how managers of corporate management information systems (MIS) view this powerful new technology. It also addresses the way CD-ROM is being used successfully by the auditing staff of Arthur Andersen & Company. These two topics will show that both users and vendors of CD-ROM must be committed to this technology if it is to receive broad acceptance.

CD-ROM technology was first used in libraries for cataloging and for reference materials.

Many publishers found that they could improve the efficiency of the alternative media for their applications—paper, microfilm, and online systems—by using CD-ROM. Some of the early adopters of this technology were The Library Corporation, with its Bibliofile product, and Brodart Automation, with its Le Pac product line. In 1986, a few early products were ready for use by libraries. Today, when you attend a convention for the American Library Association, you cannot move down an aisle at the show without seeing several CD-ROM products.

The early products for the library market were quickly followed by a group of products for the financial database market. In January 1986, Datext Corporation started publishing information on publicly traded companies. Their product was an instant success and was quickly followed by products from Disclosure, Lotus, and Standard & Poors.

Despite the early growth of CD-ROM in these and other markets, one group has lagged behind. This group, somewhat of a sleeping giant in the CD-ROM marketplace, is the MIS organization of large corporations.

In early 1988, Philips and Du Pont Optical (PDO) decided to find out how this group of potential users felt about CD-ROM technology. Our survey team contacted more than 200 members of MIS senior management at large industrial companies and at prominent service organizations and financial institutions. These were firms with annual sales ranging up to $70 billion and employee totals pushing past 300,000.

The questions we asked this largely conservative audience provided some surprising and

FINANCIAL TITLES

Title	Publisher	Price
Business Periodicals Index	H.W. Wilson Company 950 University Avenue Bronx, NY 10452 (800)367–6770	$1,495.00/Year
CD/Banking	Lotus Development Corporation One Cambridge Center Cambridge, MA 02142 (800)554–5501	$16,000.00/Year
CD/Corp Tech	Lotus Development Corporation One Cambridge Center Cambridge, MA 02142 (800)554–5501	$7,500.00/Year
CD/Corporate	Lotus Development Corporation One Cambridge Center Cambridge, MA 02142 (800)554–5501	$17,500.00/Year
CD/International	Lotus Development Corporation One Cambridge Center Cambridge, MA 02142 (800)554–5501	$1,950.00/Year
CD/Investment	Lotus Development Corporation One Cambridge Center Cambridge, MA 02142 (800)554–5501	$11,000.00/Year

encouraging answers, revealing that a large percentage of MIS managers are taking CD-ROM very seriously.

Two-thirds of the managers surveyed said they were happy with the technologies they are currently using for information distribution. One-third of the group was considering the use of CD-ROM, but less than 5 percent are currently using CD-ROM.

NUMBER ONE ENEMY—PAPER!

One thing was clear: All the managers in the survey group agreed that they had one common enemy, PAPER—more specifically, the cost of handling, storing, and distributing paper. When asked about the problems they had with their current information distribution systems, 38 percent of those surveyed mentioned the cost of managing paper as their number-one problem.

In spite of the problems with paper, however, the usage rate is very high. We looked at the monthly distribution of paper and found that, on average, they distributed more than 9.1 million pages of computer-generated paper per month. More than 20 percent of those surveyed, distributed more than 11 million pages a month.

With this information, it was not surprising that, when asked about problems these managers would like to see addressed or corrected, paper topped the list. Nearly 50 percent of those surveyed said they wanted to reduce the storage and distribution costs of paper.

Title	Publisher	Price
CD/Newsline	Lotus Development Corporation One Cambridge Center Cambridge, MA 02142 (800)554–5501	$2,000.00/Year
CD/Private+	Lotus Development Corporation One Cambridge Center Cambridge, MA 02142 (800)554–5501	$6,500.00/Year
CDX (Corporate Data Exchange)	LaFountain Research Corporation 15 Park Row Suite 700 New York, NY 10038 (212)766–3777	*
Compact Disclosure	Disclosure Incorporated 5161 River Road Bethesda, MD 20816 (800)843–7747	$3,700.00/Year
Company Accounts Register of the Belgian National Bank	Bureau Marcel van Dijk 250 Avenue Louise Suite 14 1050 Bruxelles BELGIUM 02/648–6697	$2,500.00/Year

*Contact publisher for prices.

(continued)

MAY I HAVE THIS DANCE?

In its early years, from around 1983 until 1985, CD-ROM was like the high school cheerleader everyone was afraid to ask out for a date.

However, once users discovered that this attractive phenomenon had a personality, its dance card began to fill up with applications and new ideas. For instance, MIS and PC managers are finding that CD-ROM provides a means of distributing 600 million characters of data—equivalent to 175,000 pages of ASCII text, plus indices—to any end user with a microcomputer and a $700 drive.

By Barbara Sehr. From *Computerworld*. Copyright © 1988 by C.W. Publishing, Inc.

VIEW OF CD-ROM

As mentioned above, one-third of the MIS managers surveyed are interested in CD-ROM. We asked them to tell us what benefits they expected to derive from using CD-ROM. The low-cost distribution of data, the ability to have archival information available locally, and the ability to reduce hardcopy distribution costs were cited most frequently as the most important benefits of using CD-ROM. Other reasons included the ability to deliver images and text together and the ability to free mainframe storage capacity by reducing the need for online systems.

Clearly, not every MIS manager is sold on CD-ROM. Those active in the industry have a number of things to do to turn this situation

FINANCIAL TITLES *continued.*

Title	Publisher	Price
Corporate & Industry Research Reports (CIRR)	SilverPlatter Information, Inc. 37 Walnut Street Wellesley Hills, MA 02181 (617)239-0306	$1,250.00/Year
Disclosure/Spectrum Ownership Database	Disclosure Incorporated 5161 River Road Bethesda, MD 20816 (800)843-7747	$2,000.00/Year
Econ/Stats I	Hopkins Technology 421 Hazel Lane Hopkins, MN 55343-7117 (612)931-9376	$49.00/Disc
Million Dollar Directory	Dun's Marketing Service 3 Sylvan Way Parsippany, NJ 07054-3896 (201)455-0900	*
One Source	Lotus Development Corporation One Cambridge Center Cambridge, MA 02142 (617)577-8500	$11,000.00/Year
The Telerate Expert	Telerate Systems, Inc. One World Trade Center 104th Floor New York, NY 10048 (212)938-5400	$850.00/Month

*Contact publisher for prices.

Compiled by Online Press Inc.

around. Nearly 50 percent of the people we surveyed stated that they were unfamiliar with CD-ROM and were unable to evaluate possible applications for CD-ROM. Because the MIS marketplace tends to err on the side of conservatism, this may explain why 16 percent of the MIS managers surveyed admitted they are reluctant to try any new technology. Other objections to CD-ROM included the perception that CD-ROM was too slow for their needs compared to on-line systems and that it is too expensive a technology.

Many of these barriers to using CD-ROM are being lowered. For example, costs continue to drop for developing applications, and speed of accessing data continues to be reduced. It is important that those of us in the business of supplying the industry educate our potential customers about the continually growing advantages of using CD-ROM.

CD-ROM SUCCESS STORY

We also asked MIS managers who did not see a need for CD-ROM to tell us what it would take to change their minds. Almost half said that, before they would use CD-ROM, they would need a better understanding of how the applications would fit their business, and that they would like to see evidence of success stories. One company that has a success story to tell is Arthur Andersen & Company of Chicago, Illinois.

Arthur Andersen, one of the world's largest public accounting firms, is taking advantage of CD-ROM technology to distribute information to its auditors. The disc the firm distributes

TAX TITLES

Title	Publisher	Price
PHINet-American Federal Tax Reports	Prentice Hall Information Network 1 Gulf & Western Plaza 18th Floor New York, NY 10023 (212)373–8600	$2,500.00/Disc
PHINet-Private Letter Rulings	Prentice Hall Information Network 1 Gulf & Western Plaza 18th Floor New York, NY 10023 (212)373–8600	$2,500.00/Disc
PHINet-Revenue Rulings and Procedures	Prentice Hall Information Network 1 Gulf & Western Plaza 18th Floor New York, NY 10023 (212)373–8600	$2,500.00/Disc
PHINet-Tax Court Reported and Memorandum Decisions	Prentice Hall Information Network 1 Gulf & Western Plaza 18th Floor New York, NY 10023 (212)373–8600	$2,500.00/Disc
Tax/Stats	Hopkins Technology 421 Hazel Lane Hopkins, MN 55343-7117 (612)931–9376	$49.00

Compiled by Online Press Inc.

ROBERT B. FISHER

Home: Farmington, Michigan
Job: U.S. Sales Manager, Philips and Du Pont Optical
Quote: *"I think we are now over the 'hump.' There is enough momentum building behind the development of applications for CD-ROM technology that it's a certainty it's here to stay."*

contains proprietary software and a full library of technical information: SEC regulations, FASB and AICPA pronouncements, and internal standards and procedures. This database is being used by auditors working out of more than 200 offices in 49 countries. Today, these products are distributed to Arthur Andersen auditors as a combination of paper, online CD-ROM databases, and floppy disks.

Arthur Andersen looked at several options for distribution of its hybrid database. CD-ROM became an apparent choice early on during the evaluation process, explains John Konvalinka, chief information officer for Arthur Andersen. "We found that CD-ROM fit the profile of our chosen database and users very well. The database is large and stationary. Our auditors are decentralized, working at clients' locations or our field offices." Arthur Andersen investigated write-once optical media, but soon discarded this as an option when the economics of drives, media, and duplication made CD-ROM clearly the right choice.

Jack Dreiss, a partner in charge of product research and development for Arthur Andersen's Accounting and Audit Division, felt that the hardest part of the development process was taking the many inconsistent forms of media and converting them into a common format. "Our information for the CD-ROM comes from many environments with as many inconsistencies as there are sources."

Once the first prototype CD-ROM was made, the challenge for Arthur Andersen was to ensure that it would be in a position to make the second disc. "The issue was creating a publishing process," Dreiss emphasized. "There was, and still is, a lot of care and feeding required to maintain and manage the database. If you don't manage this task, the database will be outdated before you are ready for the next release."

One other concern Dreiss mentioned is a problem all developers face when working with a new and evolving technology: the stability of the vendors that companies like Arthur Andersen must work with. The vendors' software solutions for CD-ROM tend to be the products of small companies with a short product history and very little depth of personnel and customers. Dreiss put it simply, "We're using version 1.0 of our software today. We need to make sure our software vendor will be around for versions 2.0, 3.0, and 4.0."

In spite of these issues, the key to the success at Arthur Andersen and other companies using this technology was their determination to make CD-ROM work early on in the development process. By making the commitment, such companies can support their development with the resources required to make the application of a new technology a success. Without this commitment by senior management, the project could easily be delayed.

One unanticipated fruit of Arthur Andersen's efforts to apply CD-ROM technology has been the development of in-house skills that the firm may be able to market to its clients. "CD-ROM is an important part of a program our clients must consider for their electronic publishing strategy," Konvalinka remarked. "We feel the skills and methods we've developed for the approach and management of CD-ROM can be very useful."

SUMMARY

Taking advantage of a new technology requires dedication from both the vendors to the industry and the users.

Arthur Andersen's success with CD-ROM is important to the industry. The firm has led the way by showing how efficient this technology is for information distribution. Just as important, Arthur Andersen has shown other potential users of CD-ROM how to make it work: by applying the necessary people and resources to ensure that the application of a new technology had enough resources. Without such commitment, Arthur Andersen's use of CD-ROM would have been less successful.

Vendors to the industry must also be dedicated to encouraging and supporting early developers. Managers in information systems groups are becoming aware of CD-ROM. Once they are exposed to CD-ROM, they quickly become aware of its efficiency in information distribution. Vendors of the new technology must be willing to invest resources to help educate potential users. Without this commitment, the growth of applications using CD-ROM will not meet its full potential.

[Robert Fisher is U.S. Sales Manager for Philips and Du Pont Optical (PDO) — a joint venture between Philips N.V. and E.I. du Pont de Nemours — which develops, manufactures, and markets optical media. Fisher has been with PDO since its inception in 1986.]

> *According to one recent journal article, more than half of the Fortune 500 companies are formally reviewing or have initiated a CD-ROM project.*
>
> **Lou Hoffmann**
> **From *CD Publisher News***

Developing CD-ROMs In-House for Corporate Use

By Douglas Iles

[How does a corporation transform an idea into a CD-ROM product? Doug Iles takes a look at the in-house CD-ROM development process, emphasizing the importance of planning.]

Although horizontal CD-ROM products targeted for the commercial sector have garnered the headlines, there is a ground swell of CD-ROM development activity behind the scenes. This activity consists of corporations transforming massive amounts of paper and electronic information into CD-ROMs.

Hewlett-Packard is one of the corporations at the forefront of this trend. With the introduction of the HP LaserROM service in September 1987, Hewlett-Packard became the first company to distribute customer-support information on CD-ROM.

Drawing from the experience of launching HP LaserROM, this article will touch on some of the key issues associated with in-house CD-ROM publishing. Regardless of the number of CD-ROMs that you plan to publish and update, the critical question remains the same: How does a corporation take an idea presented on paper and transform it into a real CD-ROM product?

For starters, it's important to realize that the early stages of a CD-ROM project play a critical role in its long-term success. Although CD-ROM is now a mature technology, there is a good chance that it will be viewed as emerging or embryonic by senior management. This means that even one false start can sometimes doom a CD-ROM project by giving it the label "unproven, cutting-edge technology."

With that in mind, an effective way to build momentum for a CD-ROM project is through a prototype disc. Unlike a specification that can take months to build, a prototype demonstrates how CD-ROM can specifically benefit your corporation and the people it serves. Equally important, a prototype shows that the technology is available today. This show-and-tell approach creates an impact that cannot be duplicated by a slide show or a report.

Beyond strengthening the recommendation, a prototype builds a bridge to the prospective users of your CD-ROM product. By interacting with a real product, albeit a prototype, these users can provide valuable feedback on the application. Furthermore, by establishing some benchmarks with the prototype, you can begin to gauge what type of productivity gains will be realized from the proposed CD-ROM.

Keep in mind that you do not have to create a CD-ROM production environment to develop a prototype. There are service bureaus that are ideal for handling the CD-ROM data preparation process on a one-time basis. Thus, the development of a prototype does not require a major investment. The following represents a breakdown of the costs incurred in producing a prototype for HP LaserROM:

Task	Cost
Internal data preparation	$40,000
Outside data preparation (service bureau)	30,000
Retrieval software and user interface	2,500
Mastering	3,500
Six discs	150
Approximate total	$76,150

Many corporations already maintain their potential CD-ROM-bound information in a structured, electronic form, and this will reduce the costs associated with internal data preparation.

After reviewing the information generated by the prototype and any other reports and studies, a sound recommendation can be developed. As mentioned earlier, your prototype will establish productivity gains, and these gains should be emphasized in the recommendation to illustrate that CD-ROM adds value to the information through such capabilities as electronic searches.

Once a decision is made to create a CD-ROM in production quantities, the next step involves building an in-house CD-ROM publishing environment based on standards. An entire book

DOUGLAS ILES

Home: Mountain View, California
Job: Applications Support, Hewlett-Packard
Quote: *"In addition to major corporations using CD-ROM as a distribution medium, we can also look forward to new and exciting technologies emerging in the field of knowledge transfer for which CD-ROM has been a catalyst."*

could be written on this topic, but one point should be emphasized here: Implement standards early in the process.

The most effective CD-ROM publishing environments are automated, and automation can be achieved only through standards. For example, a corporation might be dealing with text that originates from several different word-processing programs, a typesetting system, voice mail, and mainframe computer programs, to name a few. There must be a common bridge (standards) among these varied formats and CD-ROM.

In a sense, the CD-ROM development process is like manufacturing, except that the product is information instead of tangible goods. And, as in any manufacturing process, shrinking the labor costs of the process significantly reduces overall costs. Toward this end, there are numerous available off-the-shelf CD-ROM retrieval-software/user-interface packages that reduce or even eliminate the need for software engineering. To further simplify the CD-ROM publishing process, Hewlett-Packard and Meridian Data recently announced a turnkey CD-ROM publishing system.

It's also worth noting that the CD-ROM production environment should be merged into the more traditional paper publishing environment, a task that is easier said than done. Traditional publishing groups within corporations have followed the same mission statement for years—to create hard copy—and it is difficult to change such an entrenched style. Planning is needed to develop an environment in which the CD-ROM production group and the traditional publishing groups coexist peacefully. This planning relates back to the issue of standards and to the idea of a single electronic source that fuels both the printing and the CD-ROM production process.

From a global standpoint, getting a CD-ROM project off the starting block in a large corporation requires a nucleus of people willing to champion the cause. It takes a collective effort. This means that, in the early stages, a person championing CD-ROM might best serve as a catalyst, sparking others within the company to embrace CD-ROM.

[Doug Iles is responsible for the development of Hewlett-Packard's CD-ROM production environment, which updates and distributes information on a CD-ROM subscription basis. Prior to joining Hewlett-Packard, he was Vice President of Construction Time Share, with responsibility for the company's computer operations. With 20 years experience in the computer industry, Iles has held executive engineering positions with Pacific Gas and Electric, Bank of America, and Honeywell Information Systems.]

CD-ROM MAKES IT BIG IN THE AUTOMOTIVE INDUSTRY WORLDWIDE

Automobile manufacturers in Japan, America and Europe have discovered CD-ROM, and by the looks of it, CD-ROM applications for the automotive industry could become a very lucrative market.

In Japan, Hitachi and several Japanese car manufacturers teamed up to develop an Automotive Parts Data Retrieval System capable of storing more than 1 1/2 million parts for more than a hundred different car models. Used to locate and order parts, it is claimed to beat microfiche and computer printouts hands down in terms of cost, speed, space and accuracy. The PC-based system can also produce estimates, invoices and re-order documentation locally. By linking the system to the headquarter's computer, online enquiry and ordering facilities may be added.

In the U.S., the Ford Motor Company is developing a CD-ROM based service bay diagnostic system (SBDS) that will first discover what's wrong with a vehicle, then automatically display the specific parts and repair procedures needed to remedy the problem. SBDS has been tested at five pilot sites so successfully that Ford plans to install the system in five hundred sites by 1989. Full installation at all 5,000 Ford dealerships is planned to be completed by the early 1990s.

Ford's SBDS works like this. Using hardware developed by Hewlett-Packard, SBDS is hooked up to a car's on-board computers. Then, artificial intelligence technology in the form of an expert system diagnoses the problem. The diagnosis is communicated to the CD-Guide hypertext search and retrieval system, developed by Office Workstations, Ltd. (OWL) of Edinburgh, which automatically accesses a CD-ROM holding each vehicle's parts, service procedures and fault-finding information. Technicians can access this information using a simple touchscreen interface that takes only a few minutes to learn.

Also in the U.S., Chrysler and General Motors are using a CD-ROM-based system developed by Bell & Howell to provide their sales and support staff with immediate access to the 325,000 parts and 30,000 pages of technical information needed to perform maintenance and repair procedures.

**Reprinted from *The Electronic Library*
by permission of Learned Information,
Oxford, England and Medford, New Jersey.**

In-House CD-ROM Publishing: Is It Catching On?

By Fred Meyer

[In the last article of this section, Fred Meyer examines recent industry developments that have sparked the growing momentum of in-house CD-ROM development, and gives us some examples of successful in-house uses of CD technology.]

While commercial CD-ROM "titles" such as Microsoft *Bookshelf* and the Grolier *Academic Encyclopedia* have garnered the spotlight, another CD-ROM publishing trend has been taking shape. Companies of all sizes, as well as government agencies, are implementing in-house CD-ROM publishing environments to distribute large amounts of information on disc. There are a number of factors fueling this trend.

For starters, the cost of creating CD-ROM applications continues to spiral downward. CD-ROM development systems, such as CD Publisher from Meridian Data, enable organizations to handle the CD-ROM data preparation process on microcomputers rather than on costly mainframe- or minicomputer-based systems.

Also, the cost of disc production has been dramatically reduced. Today, the price of a CD-ROM master is approximately $3000 (with a three- to five-day turnaround), and as few as 50 discs can be replicated for approximately $12 per disc. These numbers represent a 200 to 300 percent decrease from the market prices available in 1987.

Even one of the largest obstacles to in-house CD-ROM development, the data conversion process, has been greatly streamlined. For example, there are artificial-intelligence-based data conversion tools that can take information with embedded typesetting codes or information from an OCR system and convert it to an acceptable format for CD-ROM development. If the information targeted for CD-ROM resides on paper, there are systems that greatly simplify the process of converting paper information into electronic form.

FRED MEYER

Home: Capitola, California
Job: President, Meridian Data, Inc.
Quote: *"CD-ROM, CD-ROM XA, and CD-I are destined to fundamentally change our perception of information. Not only does CD make information accessible to all, but CD also delivers on the multimedia promise. A world standard with immense capacity and low cost, CD will be the mainstay of the electronic publishing revolution."*

Another important development involves the recent introduction of CD-ROM networking products that enable an organization to place multiple CD-ROM drives (and discs) on a standard local area network. These CD-ROM networking products will have an enormous impact on the marketplace because they send the per-user cost of a CD-ROM application plummeting. It takes a significant purchasing decision to put 5000 CD-ROM drives on 5000 desks. On the other hand, it's much easier to justify the cost of a few dozen CD-ROM drives and networking gear.

Last, a CD-ROM infrastructure is now firmly entrenched. This means organizations can rest assured that their CD-ROM investments are protected by industry-accepted standards. The Yellow Book, a standard created by Philips N.V. and Sony Corp. that specifies the physical format for storing digital data on a compact disc, established the framework for CD-ROM. Later, an industry ad hoc committee, called the High Sierra Group, proposed a standard for the logical file structure. This proposal was approved with few changes by the International Standards Organization (ISO 9660) and ensures that the operating system, CD-ROM drive, and disc will be compatible regardless of manufacturer. On the hardware side, manufacturers are producing CD-ROM drives in a standard half-height, 5 1/4-inch form that fits right into a personal computer.

CD-ROM AS PRODIGY

Prodigies such as CD-ROM also require special handling by trained professionals. Sometimes, these professionals are hard to find.

Many companies already using or considering CD-ROM are faced with the problem of getting the specialized help necessary to create CD-ROM programs. Developing this capability in-house has always been an expensive and somewhat scary proposition, but alternatives are now available.

Many are taking advantage of the growing number of firms which work with the publisher to create and format CD-ROM programs. These firms may not have the intimate knowledge of a company's application requirements, but they specialize in working with the people who do.

In addition, some in-house systems now permit simulation of CD-ROM programs on several hard disks. With relative ease and at a low cost, companies can now work out any problem that may exist in a program, observe the way it will perform it its final CD-ROM form, and create the properly formatted tape required to produce the final product.

By Roger D. Hilde. Excerpted from "The Problems and Promises of a Child Prodigy," *CD-ROM Review.*

Collectively, these factors are the catalyst behind in-house CD-ROM publishing. Unlike the CD-ROM service bureau business, the market for in-house CD-ROM publishing is expected to skyrocket in the coming years (see Figure 3-3).

Equally illuminating, a survey at the nationwide CD-ROM Developers' Seminar conducted by Meridian Data, Philips and Du Pont Optical, and Microsoft Corporation showed that nearly every Fortune 500 company has already initiated some type of CD-ROM project. In the vast majority of cases, the number-one objective of these projects was not to generate revenues. Instead, these industry leaders expected to strengthen their customer support services, better educate their field staff, or make more accessible the information that otherwise resides on a mainframe computer.

For example, Cummins-Engine Co., a diesel engine manufacturer, publishes a master price book of parts information that its field people use to repair engines. The 60,000 pages of text and graphics is now published on CD-ROM. Cummins-Engine decided that CD-ROM was the only reasonable, cost-effective way to distribute image data. The result is that the company's field technicians can electronically search and retrieve information instead of laboring through microfilm searches.

On the government side, the United States Geological Survey (USGS) was one of the early

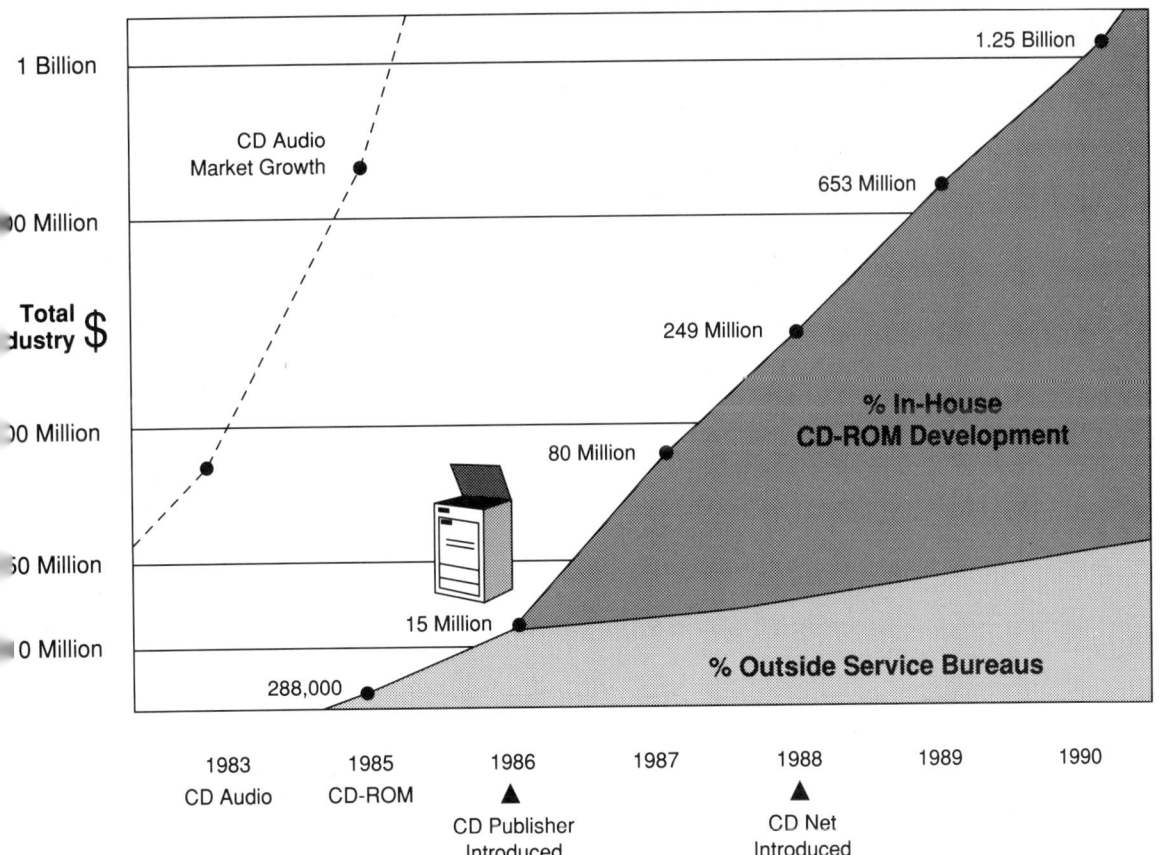

Figure 3-3. Comparison of growth rates for CD-ROM service bureau business and in-house CD-ROM publishing

advocates of CD-ROM. Realizing that map data on magnetic tape and in hard-copy form carries certain limitations, the USGS turned to CD-ROM. Today, the agency distributes a range of geological information on CD-ROM, both as ASCII files and as digitized map images.

In the computer marketplace, Hewlett-Packard already distributes customer support documentation for three different computer systems on CD-ROM. Furthermore, company plans call for eventually placing more than one million pages of documentation on disc.

The organizations pioneering in-house CD-ROM publishing—organizations like Cummins-Engine, the USGS, and Hewlett-Packard—have successfully proven that CD-ROM is more than a convenient way to distribute information. The key lies in the fact that CD-ROM adds value to information by providing an electronic search capability.

While it's always difficult to predict the success of an emerging technology, there's no doubt that in-house CD-ROM publishing is gaining momentum. Regardless of its industry, any organization can benefit from adding value to the information it already possesses. And that's exactly what CD-ROM accomplishes.

[Fred Meyer is co-founder and President of Meridian Data. Formed in 1984, Meridian Data manufactures and markets optical product development tools, CD-ROM networking systems, and mass storage subsystems. Prior to forming Meridian Data, Meyer co-founded two companies that gained a reputation for interactive videodisc delivery systems and application development.]

BOEING, BOEING

If you're planning to fly in a British Air 757 in the near future, you may not be sure of the food quality, but you'll know that on the ground, the mechanics and engineers have the latest in technology to service the latest in aviation technology.

The Boeing 757 is one of the latest breed of passenger aircraft. It's roomier, quieter, uses less fuel, and requires fewer people to fly it than its predecessors. But the aircraft is just as difficult, if not more so, to maintain. Until recently, high-tech had stayed away from this part of the shop, where maintenance personnel refer to a 14-volume, 140-pound set of manuals.

But CD-ROM has changed all that.

A CD-ROM-based maintenance manual, developed for Boeing by KnowledgeSet and Sundstrand, combines a high-resolution personal computer display with vector graphics to bring 757 maintenance into the modern era. The manual offers all of CD-ROM's traditional advantages—large amounts of information in a small space, fast search and retrieval, powerful searches, and data integrity.

It is presently being tested by British Airways. When used commercially, Boeing will update the disc every 90 days at first, then over longer periods as the plane ages and new procedures and notes become less common.

By Roger Strukhoff. Excerpted from "Boeing, Boeing," *CD-ROM Review.*

HOME EDUCATION AND ENTERTAINMENT APPLICATIONS

CD-ROM AND PUBLIC TELEVISION
By Rod Daynes

THE MEDIA LAB
By Stewart Brand

CD-ROM and Public Television

By Rod Daynes

[Here Rod Daynes teases us with visions of future offerings from WGBH/Boston, public television's most innovative program developer. As futuristic as some of his scenarios may seem, like a good science-fiction writer, Daynes tints his descriptions with enough of the here-and-now to leave us with a feeling not of "What if...?" but of "When...?"]

You have finally decided to do it: build that bookcase for the rec room. On a book rack by the checkout counter of your local hardware store you see a book on furniture building. There is a familiar and trusted face on the cover—Norm Abram, master carpenter on the PBS television series "This Old House." As you thumb through the pages you notice bar codes here and there, and you see a compact (video) disc inside the jacket. "Ring it up," you say, and a few minutes later, with the book in front of you on your workbench, you insert the disc into the half-height CD drive in your portable TV. You turn to an illustrated section on a particularly tricky procedure in the book, pass your "wand" (bar-code reader) over the bar code, and there is Norm on the TV, showing you exactly what to do. You can freeze the procedure, walk through it in slow motion (forward or backward), or instantly branch to a different view, to an index, or even to a help program.

This vision of the potential of public television is brought to you courtesy of WGBH/Boston, America's leading public-television organization. Although the Public Broadcasting Service (PBS) comprises more than 300 stations, WGBH provides more than 30 percent of prime-time scheduling. WGBH invented the mini-series with "Masterpiece Theatre." Its "NOVA" is the longest-running science-documentary series in the history of television. Other award-winning programs include "Frontline," "Vietnam: A Television History," "Eyes On The Prize," "ZOOM," "Mystery!," Evening At The POPS," "Degrassi Junior High," "The American Experience," and a number of how-to programs including "This Old House," "Victory Garden," and the now-classic cooking show, "The French Chef," with Julia Child. At any given time more than 100 major national projects are under development at WGBH, including costume dramas, documentaries, children's programs, music, and more.

ROD DAYNES

Home: Wenham, Massachusetts
Job: Director of Project Development—Telecommunications, WGBH Educational Foundation, Boston
Quote: *"The next step in these technologies is an industry-wide adoption of a publishing model."*

You have just seen a "NOVA" program on the most significant Nobel Prize awards for physics. You now turn to your personal computer, which is equipped with a CD-ROM drive. Through simulation, you are able to re-create some of the pivotal experiments that led to each prize.

As a major television-producing organization, WGBH's policy toward new technologies, such as CD-ROM, is to put the content before the technology—to select the medium or media best suited to the story we want to tell. As new programs and series are developed, WGBH designs multimedia applications at the treatment level. Instead of "re-purposing" an existing program to fit a new medium, we now design for shooting original footage that, from the beginning, is meant for an interactive application. This approach makes the task of creating multimedia much easier and more versatile. In addition, we are able to include footage and background data, storable on CD-ROM, that we could never include in a one-hour time slot. The purpose is to communicate a message and to accommodate the "linear" broadcasting format, which is certainly not the only way to present a topic.

It is the harvest season. You have just seen a PBS documentary on the life and times of the pilgrims, showing where they came from and what they were like. There is a full-color trade book on the subject, and you can get stackware for your Macintosh that allows you to travel in time back to 1627 to "Plimoth Plantation," participating in events and actually conversing with the pilgrims themselves about their world view. Your time machine, the Mac, has a "20th century" button that gives you access to additional data, such as modern essays on the pilgrims, graphics showing land elevations and site plans, the route of the Mayflower, and reproductions of old documents. Together, the old and the new give you a much richer perspective on one of the cornerstones of American history.

To survive, public broadcasters must adopt a new-media publishing model that enables them to look at new forms of distribution for programs in addition to cable and VCR markets and to do some innovating on behalf of public television's commercial broadcasting counterparts. This is our role. We welcome the new technologies, especially those whose applications can help us better understand ourselves and the universe we live in. This role is not one with which public television is unfamiliar. In 1979, the Corporation for Public Broadcasting (CPB) provided funding to public station KUON at the University of Nebraska for the investigation of the full potential of videodisc technology and subsequently created a worldwide clearinghouse on new media. Today, CPB is looking into the potential of interactive broadcasting from both a research and a creative perspective. The goal is to develop technologies and program concepts that finally enable you to talk back to television...and receive an intelligent reply. CD-ROM and new optical disc technologies will play a central role in public television as we look to the future.

[*Rod Daynes is Director of Project Development—Telecommunications at WGBH Educational Foundation in Boston, where he develops projects for a wide range of new media, including the interactive optical technologies (such as videodisc, CD-ROM, and CD-V), hypermedia, and HDTV. Prior to working for WGBH, Daynes was President of Pacific Interactive, the West-Coast division of Online Computer Systems, Inc., and cofounder of Interactive Technologies Corp., a San Diego-based company dedicated to the development of interactive videodiscs for training.*]

The Media Lab

By Stewart Brand
From *HyperMedia*

[This article guides us through the fantasy-like world of the Media Lab, a futuristic experimental environment at MIT, where techniques that may well become the stock-in-trade of entertainment application developers of the future are currently being explored and developed.]

Note from the Editor of HyperMedia magazine: At MIT's Media Lab the goal is for the audience to take over—to make mass media individualized media. Nicholas Negroponte, director of the Media Lab, has a vision of the future that includes personalized computers, televisions, even books that know the user so intimately that the dialog between machine and human brings about ideas unrealizable by either partner alone—machines so perceptive they can respond to the user's voice, gestures and the subtle movements of an eye.

Stewart Brand is your tour guide on this "Hitchhiker's Guide to the Hypermedia Galaxy." Brand is best known for founding, editing and publishing the Whole Earth Catalog (1968–1985) and the CoEvolution Quarterly (now called Whole Earth Review; 1973–1984), but he has also had a longstanding involvement in computers and the media arts.

Following his degree in biology from Stanford in 1960, and two years as a U.S. Infantry officer, Brand became a photojournalist and multimedia artist, performing at colleges and museums. In 1968 he was a consultant to Douglas Englebart's pioneering Augmented Human Intellect program at SRI, which devised now-familiar computer interface tools such as the mouse and windows. While editor in chief of the Whole Earth Software Catalog (1983–1985), Brand organized the first "Hacker's Conference," which has since become an annual event. He is currently researching learning in complex systems. Brand lives with his wife, Patricia Phelan, on a tugboat in San Francisco Bay.

The Media Lab: Inventing the Future at MIT is an exclusive and coherent report of developments on the leading edge of hypermedia. The research and analysis presented by Brand amount to a tour de force of the new media. This book is a result of his recent three-month participation at the Media Lab.

In the basement the inventor of the white-light hologram that flickers from America's credit cards is demonstrating the world's first projected hologram. It's an 18-inch Camaro parked in midair, and the sponsors from General Motors are pleased. One of them steps from the front of the car around to the back and then *has* to reach into it. His hand grasps nothing. The information is in his eye, not in the air.

Out in the Wiesner Building's sunny atrium, 7-foot-long computer-controlled helium blimps are cruising the five-story space learning to be like fish—feeding, schooling, seeking comfortable temperature habitats.

On the third floor, body tracking is in progress; a figure in black leather and studs is twirling in sensitive space. The studs are position indicators (infrared-light-emitting diodes) being sensed and translated by a computer into an animated figure on the room-size screen dancing in perfect echo to the human. The computer is paying attention and remembering: this is how humans move.

On the fourth floor a violinist strokes once more into a difficult piece, trying it with a slower tempo. The piano accompanist adapts perfectly, even when the violinist changes tempo in the middle of the piece. The uncomplaining player is an exceptionally musical computer.

In the Terminal Garden on the third floor a visitor pretends to be a schoolchild and types "hedake" into a computer. A computer voice says aloud, "Headache," and shows the word spelled correctly.

That's only a small sample of the variety of endeavors going on in the Wiesner Building, but it gives a glimpse of major themes in Media Lab research. Everything mentioned involves communication, empowers the individual, employs computers (the Camaro was not photographed from a model but generated out of pure computer bits), and makes a flashy demonstration.

STEWART BRAND

Home: Sausalito, California
Job: Researcher, Global Business Network.
Quote: *"Where's CD-ROM headed? We don't know yet; that's why we're interested."*

DEMO OR DIE

Students and professors at the Media Laboratory write papers and books and publish them, but the byword in this grove of academe is not "publish or perish." In Lab parlance it's "demo or die"—make the case for your idea with an unfaked performance of it working at least once, or let somebody else at the equipment. "We write about what we do," comments director Negroponte, "but we don't write unless we've done it." The focus is engineering and science rather than scholarship, invention rather than studies, surveys or critiques.

The Lab is a fascinating visit, drawing no end of visitor traffic. On one somewhat heavy day, a year after opening its doors, the Lab was toured by 40 computer scientists from China, the chief scientist from IBM, 35 Japanese architects, 15 members of a Japanese study mission, the secretary of state from West Germany, and the president of the German Newspaper Federation.

Industrial sponsors of the Lab come to see if they should buy in ("For less than $200,000 it's not really worth our time," Negroponte observes). Journalists come looking for "The Story" and go away confused but still with plenty to write about. Distinguished visitors come because this is the kind of technological excitement that America and MIT want them to see, and it's one of the few places where so much is so concentrated.

They see the demos and are suitably dazzled or puzzled, but what draws them here is they've heard or sensed that the Media Laboratory has a Vision, capital V.

NEGROPONTE, THE AMPHIBIAN

Consider the visionary.

"You'll find that your left cuff link will be communicating with your right cuff link via satellite," Negroponte teases an audience. "With flatpanel technologies every license plate, wine label or price tab will be a display." Asked about computers, he replies, "There will be many more MIPS in the nation's *appliances* than in its computers." What about broadcast, the broadcasters ask him. He breaks it to them ungently. "Sports and elections probably will remain synchronous and shown live. The rest won't. The rule might be: if you can bet on it, you won't see it out of real time. As for the motion picture industry, it is the smokestack industry of today's information world."

Nat Rochester, a senior computer scientist for IBM and the central negotiator for IBM's early and large involvement with the Media Lab, told me, "Nicholas combines very great technical knowledge and creativity with an artist's eye and skill, and really world-class salesmanship. If he were an IBM salesman, he'd be a member of the Golden Circle—that's the inner group that's made ten Hundred Percent Clubs; from then on they're completely privileged. If you know what good salesmanship is, you can't miss it when you get to know him."

Indeed, this is no rumpled, tweedy, musing scholar. *Fortune* magazine observed that he "looks more like a matinee idol than a walking paradigm of the state-of-the-art technologist." Negroponte does look a bit like a young Robert Wagner. He's meticulously groomed and dresses sharp. The child of an old Greek shipping family, he grew up in Switzerland and the stylish circles of New York and London.

At age 43 Negroponte is young for his responsibilities at MIT. He rose fast by virtue of the quality of his research on computer interfacing, the single-mindedness of his effort—the

ENTERTAINMENT TITLES

Title	Publisher	Price
Film Literature Index	H.W. Wilson Company 950 University Avenue Bronx, NY 10452 (800)367-6770	$695.00/Year
Variety's Video Directory Plus	Bowker Electronic Publishing 245 West 17th Street New York, NY 10011 (800)323-3288	$295.00/Year

Compiled by Online Press Inc.

Media Lab is essentially his life work—and the way he's built on a peculiarity of his university. MIT is more merrily in bed with industry and government than any other academic institution in the world. Professors are not only permitted, but encouraged to devote up to 20% of their time, "a day a week," as they say, to outside consulting and other profitable business interests such as starting companies.

Negroponte found it easy to mix with the chairmen, directors and chief executive officers of major corporations and government research offices. Months on the road every year, he's acquired a business sense of the world. At the university he's an exotic with the moves of a jet-set executive and a businessman's get-on-with-it rigor. But in corporate boardrooms and on trade organization stages he's the prestigious professor, representing the lofty intellectual perspective and long view of the university. Negroponte is an amphibian, comfortable in both worlds, giving an amphibian's value to both worlds, taking an amphibian's advantage of both worlds. Nevertheless, in his origins and fundamental loyalty he's an academic.

He gets the public attention of a media maven as Marshall McLuhan did, but Negroponte is different in major ways. He doesn't comment in order to comment—his only books are two somewhat specialist tracts from the MIT Press, and another one available solely in Japan, in Japanese. He comments in order to get money to invent, to enable the entire apparatus of the Media Lab and its people to invent.

Negroponte's vision: all communication technologies are suffering a joint metamorphosis, which can only be understood properly if treated as a single project, and only advanced properly if treated as a single craft. The way to figure out what needs to be done is through exploring the human sensory and cognitive system and the ways that humans most naturally interact. Join this and grasp the future.

It worked. Negroponte and former MIT president Jerome Wiesner toured and lectured and demoed and bargained for seven years, and

> *They see the demos and are suitably dazzled or puzzled, but what draws them here is they've heard or sensed that the Media Laboratory has a Vision, capital V.*

raised the requisite millions. High aluminum walls, countless computers, attractive salaries were generated out of tense, soaring proposal words: "...New theories about signals, symbols, and systems will evolve from the merger of engineering, social science, and the arts..." "...a place where people will be expected to be equally familiar with lumens, leading and lambda calculus. Graduates will be required to pursue studies in epistemology, experimental psychology, filmmaking, holography and signal processing, as well as in computer science." Unlike the other 45 laboratories at MIT, the Media Lab was aspiring to become an academic department as well.

The noblest phrase, and customarily the meanest practice, on any campus is "interdisciplinary." Yet sponsored research volume for the Media Lab in fiscal 1985 to '86 was $3.7 million; for 1986 to '87 it was $6 million. That's in addition to the academic budget provided by MIT of about $1 million each year.

Buying what? The boundaries keep shifting, but when counted in early 1987 the Lab was divided into 11 groups:

1. Electronic Publishing gets $1 million, most of it from IBM. In the Terminal Garden are the electronic books and self-

personalizing electronic newspapers, magazines and TV broadcasts. Walter Bender runs the Garden.

2. Speech works with $500,000 mainly from the Defense Advanced Research Projects Agency (DARPA) and Nippon Telephone and Telegraph. Chris Schmandt invents such things as phones that know your friends and can converse with them on your behalf.

3. The Advanced Television Research Program is led by William Schreiber. Some $1 million comes to it from a consortium of television worriers—ABC, NBC, CBS (initially), PBS, Home Box Office, RCA, 3M, Tektronix, Ampex, Harris. Investigation centers on how gorgeous you can make television if you let the TV set have some computer intelligence.

4. Movies of the Future gets about $1 million from Warner Brothers, Columbia, 20th Century Fox and Paramount, who suspect that computer digitalization will change their industry. Andy Lippman presides over the recording of "paperback movies" on compact discs, and other ambitions.

5. The Visual Language Workshop, headed by design prize-winning Muriel Cooper, is trying to cure the chronic ugliness of computer graphics and visual design, working with $250,000 from Polaroid, IBM and a German print technology firm called Hell.

6. Spatial Imaging, otherwise known as holography, gets about $500,000, mostly from General Motors and DARPA. The leading light is Stephen Benton, who came from a couple decades of working at the right hand of Polaroid founder Edwin Land.

7. Computers and Entertainment is a fuzzy set containing a fantasy called the Vivarium sponsored by Apple Computer, featuring Alan Kay, along with Marvin Minsky trying to godfather the next generation of artificial intelligence, and other fecund activities. Just as the Media Lab is considered by some to be MIT's lunatic fringe, this group is the Lab's lunatic fringe, and gets about $300,000 accordingly.

8. Animation and Computer Graphics, led by David Zeltzer, operates with $300,000, mostly from NHK and Bandai. The group is seeking the animator's holy grail: real time computer animation. "Real time" means live—the animation is created "on the fly" in the computer. It manages that by imitating some techniques of life itself.

9. Computer Music, running on $150,000 from the Science Development Foundation, is in the process of becoming a major music research center exploring "music cognition" as well as new performance modes. Barry Vercoe and Tod Machover are in charge.

10. The School of the Future, also called Hennigan School, led by Seymour Papert, gets a hefty $1 million, most of it originally from IBM, some from LEGO (of LEGO blocks), some from Apple Computer, MacArthur Foundation and the National Science Foundation. The idea here is to find out what happens when you really put computers in a grade school.

11. Human-Machine Interface operates on $200,000 from DARPA, the National Science Foundation and Hughes. Richard Bolt's machines can read your lips and eyes, which can feel like they're reading your mind.

The idea is that these disparate activities shall intersect like the teething rings diagram, and their people will collaborate gladly, defying hallowed academic custom. In fact, the lab is full of collaborative alliances which are generating much of the best work. But that's a little boring. What are the problems in utopia?

THE BOGGLE FACTOR

It is the dark side of demos. It begins with sensory overload. Too much coming too fast to sort out. Too many named new things. Too much that needs explanation to even understand what it is, much less what it's for or what's remarkable about it. Too much that appears too consequential or inconsequential to take lightly figuring out which is which. And it's all connected, so any piece of confusion infects everything else. You don't know what to be impressed by. You start to look for reasons to trust your guides, because the potential for being bamboozled is total.

In fact, the Media Laboratory is scrupulously trustworthy, but one would like that to be self-evident, and there's no way it can be. I stayed boggled most of the three months that I worked at the Lab. I'm not boggled when I go there now, and I don't think someone who's read [*The Media Lab*] would be. It just takes time to build the context to digest the considerable news of the place.

The Media Lab aims to reframe the way the individual addresses the world and the world addresses the individual; is that handwave preceding a creation or substituting for it? Sponsors have put millions into the place expecting long-range but nevertheless commercial inventions or information; are they getting their money's worth? If there is a clear idea at the heart of the Lab's research goals, will it emerge crystalline and focusing or blend back into the blur of technological drift? What is that clear idea exactly?

The Media Laboratory is a huge public bet by MIT, by the myriad sponsors, by the researchers who are risking major portions of their careers. The idea that communications technologies are converging in the world, the idea of convening communication disciplines at MIT under one conceptual roof, the specific people that are gathering to work on it...they all have to be right to get a win. Demo or Die.

Reprinted by permission of Viking Penguin Inc. From *THE MEDIA LAB: INVENTING THE FUTURE AT MIT* by Stewart Brand. Copyright ©1987 by Stewart Brand. All rights reserved.

SECTION IV

THE MAKING OF A CD-ROM

DEVELOPING A CD-ROM PRODUCT
MULTIMEDIA PERSPECTIVES
HYPERTEXT PERSPECTIVES
RETRIEVAL-SYSTEM PERSPECTIVES
PREPARING TEXT
PRODUCING GRAPHICS AND IMAGES
JAZZING IT ALL UP
PREMASTERING/ MASTERING PERSPECTIVES

DEVELOPING A CD-ROM PRODUCT

CHANGING THE PUBLISHING MODEL WITH OPTICAL MEDIA
By Richard A. Bowers

THE APPLICATION DEVELOPMENT PROCESS
By John Einberger

DESIGNING A CD-ROM INTERFACE
By Linda Stone and Rachel Rutherford

THE IMPORTANCE OF PRODUCT TESTING
By Tim McManus

WHY YOU NEVER GET A STRAIGHT ANSWER WHEN YOU ASK HOW MUCH IT WILL COST!
By Chris Bowman

Changing the Publishing Model with Optical Media

By Richard A. Bowers
From *Electronic and Optical Publishing Review*

[Richard Bowers' enthusiasm for optical technology is evident in this introductory article, in which he urges CD-ROM publishers to adopt a new mind set when developing products—a mind set usually associated more with theater than with publishing.]

First came the story-teller. Each one worked alone, related his tales of history and adventure. Later many story-tellers came together to collaborate in telling a single story, each player taking a part in the tale. Theater grew to become the great collaborative art of our civilization.

The business of publishing also grew from a more or less one-man operation to a collaborative effort. The man with the press was frequently also the author and illustrator of the works he manufactured. Now many individuals work together, to play roles in the authoring, illustrating, production and distribution of published works of all kinds.

The work of the stage players took on new dimensions with the advent of a new technology, technology that could record all those fleeting moments of drama for repeated viewings. The craft of play-making became the craft of movie-making and television. Theater itself did not change, but it spawned a new class of art.

The publishing industry is about to experience a similar expansion. New recording and delivery technologies, like CD-ROM and other

RICHARD A. BOWERS

Home: Columbus, Ohio
Job: Director of Development, Applied Information Technologies Research Center
Quote: *"CD-ROM and its optical cousins are more than exciting opportunities for profit. The combination of digital optical media and advanced computing techniques permits us the first tentative steps toward a major new understanding of how we can—and will—use information of all types in the future. We will be dealing with more than books and tapes and motion pictures, but a new paradigm that combines all information types into a new medium that can deliver all types in unique new ways."*

optical media, will enable publishers to create new types of products to tell their stories differently. And, perhaps more importantly, to tell new kinds of stories not able to be told before.

Publishing, as an art and as a business, is at the threshold of an expanded horizon. A most obvious change is in the production process for this new class of products. The physical activities required to make a product will be very different. The remainder of this article deals with the specific requirements of the process for creating an optical publication.

But there is a fundamental, more subtle change in the model we know as 'publishing'. It is a change in the way we look at conceiving and designing information products. Publishing, in an optical environment, becomes less a business of preparing static presentations of information, and more the packaging of content, with process, with user involvement.

It means, in short, that optical publishing can assume many of the advantages and benefits of theater. Creating a product development and marketing strategy that takes advantage of the unique manipulative potential of a computer for presenting information in useful, interesting, and perhaps entertaining ways, can be a productive approach. The theatrical analogy gives the designer a new perspective from which to make decisions.

A changing model also encourages the publisher to take a new view of the nature of the service he provides to the customer, and prepare for new opportunities that are not obvious from a traditional print viewpoint.

Just as the advent of film and videotape created new breeds of playwrights/screenwriters, technicians and deal-makers, so the advent of CD-ROM, videodisc and other options for electronic publishing is going to create new kinds of writers, editors and deal-makers. We will have a larger cast of characters that may look like publishers, but are not traditional players on today's publishing scene.

The process of adopting a new view of publishing—information delivery—as a result of technological change is not an easy one. For the traditional paper publisher, it first requires learning a new jargon. All the items that once contributed to the mystique of publishing, like *picas, chases* and *plates,* are to be supplemented by words like *byte, disc drive,* and *CRT.*

Then there is the new medium to consider—a computer screen is a very different presentation device than paper. The environment in which a product can be used is also different—much more highly structured requiring the use of a complex piece of hardware as an access tool.

Two of the most important considerations for assembling an optical publication revolve around the nature of the medium and its potential for adding value to information, and the character of the customer using the product.

First, the nature of a good electronic publication is a very different creature than printed or even online products.

In the print environment, a page—like this one—is created once. It is designed for maximum utility and to be pleasing to the eye, but once done, it is done. The printed page is a static thing, the reader either accepts it, or doesn't use the publication.

Even online products are relatively rigid in the way data is presented on the CRT. A standard record layout is used. The customer usually has the option of modifying the presentation by excluding pieces of the standard record but cannot really manipulate the presentation without down-loading and using other software.

In a CD-ROM environment, the product can be far from a passive object. In many ways, this new kind of information product can be alive, and take on an active role in the search for information and the final presentation of the results. Searching is an interactive process in which the product can give meaningful feedback about the results of the search request. The text can be presented in windows or in segments on the screen. The user can change the way the presentation appears. Portions of the found text can be extracted, and manipulated.

All this capability is directly under control of the publisher of the product. The publisher makes the decisions that affect, in every way imaginable, the usefulness, and, finally, the success of each optical publication. It is the richness of alternatives that the optical publisher must prepare to deal with.

New applications can incorporate sound, or combinations of graphics or even processes (such as software). Each additional component adds to the complexity of the design, but can make a significant contribution to the value of the final product. Each also adds a new dimension to the presentation, and design decisions once more hark back to theatrical roots: Will the new capability enhance the message, or get in

> *The publisher makes the decisions that affect, in every way imaginable, the usefulness, and, finally, the success of each optical publication. It is the richness of alternatives that the optical publisher must prepare to deal with.*

the way, is the screen too busy, can the user follow the action and keep all the characters straight?

Value is added to information in other formats by 1) making it available, and 2) organizing it in a meaningful way, either through its physical arrangement or through overlaid features like indexes. Optical media permit new kinds of organizational techniques and vastly expand the amount of information that can be collected, and thus can add significant value over other presentation media.

Secondly, the customer has very different perspectives and expectations for an optical product compared to a print product.

The customer approaches a computer with a different mindset than the user of a printed product. Whether or not an experienced computer-user, the customer brings a high level of expectation, and at least some understanding of the limitations of the medium. An understanding, for example, that he cannot roll this medium up and stick it in a hip pocket, and likely will not take it into the bathroom for light reading exercises.

In addition, the new customer for optical publishing is going to expect a substantial pay-off in value for the hassle of changing his habits and having to learn new methods and tools for getting to information.

The potential customer base is only just now becoming aware that the capabilities of optical media exist. There is no identifiable segment of optical publication users—yet. There is even a confusion of labels—or roles—in discussing the CD-ROM customer: can he or she be characterized as a user as in the computer sense, or as a viewer as in the television sense?

The success of any business depends on understanding the customer and the customer's needs as they relate to the product or service being offered. In the world of optical publishing, there must be an iterative process to achieve that understanding. Products will be introduced, customers will react and products will be modified. Placing customer reaction in the context of the total collaborative effort—that is, not simply reacting to content, or to media, or to presentation, but playing an acknowledged role in the process—will result in stronger lines of information product packages.

CHALLENGES IN OPTICAL PRODUCT DESIGN

The most critical decisions in product development are those that are made in assembling and organizing the content, and designing the presentation of the information to the user, com-

FIVE GOALS FOR CD-ROM PUBLISHERS

Publishers must *add value to the information* as they put it on CDs.... Either through more systematic or intelligent organization, or because the data appear in forms that help people solve problems (like Microsoft's Stat Pak spreadsheet files), these products ought to somehow add value to the information itself. Some products will have software front-ends that impose organization on "raw" data sets, although many of the best products will probably include some structure in the information itself (pointers, links, levels, etc.).

Products must be *relevant and complete*. One of the advantages of CD-ROM is size. Complete versions of many bodies of knowledge will fit on a single CD-ROM (e.g., entire encyclopedias, huge data sets, etc.). Developers can also combine multiple tools or information sources on a single disk for "information synergy"—another type of added value.

Software and hardware are going to have to be *fast*. A key advantage to online information is that you can access it far more quickly than in any other form. We don't want to be kept waiting. For *very* high value information in high risk environments (e.g., securities information for large investors), we're willing to wait a while for accurate information. But in more casual reference, entertainment, education, and training applications, people will not use the software if they can't do it quickly and easily. So "user-friendliness" is also an area in need of improvement. Nobody likes "KGB" user interfaces, even though some people will put up with them if the information is valuable enough.

CD products should be as *integrated* with other applications and parts of a total system as possible. In entertainment applications we want CDs to be connected with audio, video and computer systems all at once—in the home entertainment center of the future. With business applications we want to be able to cut and paste into other applications, import data from CDs, combine CD data with magnetic data between updates, and use in audio, video, graphics and desktop publishing programs, etc. In education, we'd like to be able to do a little of each.

CD products should be *compelling and interactive*. This is perhaps obvious; but it should also have been obvious in educational software, and there is a lot of boring, minimally interactive computer-based instruction out there!

By Dr. Carl Binder. Excerpted from "The Emerging Industry," published in the Spring 1988 issue of *Optical Insights*. Reprinted by permission of Dr. Carl Binder, Optical Insights, and the Boston Computer Society. Copyright © Dr. Carl Binder.

monly referred to as the "user interface." These decisions drive the remainder of the production effort.

Two key design decisions are important in assembling an optical product:

- Selecting the content—the mix of all the data—whatever its type or source, and determining its relationships within the package.

- Designing an appropriate "package"—the organizational scheme and access method—which takes advantage of the unique character of the optical media, and also provides the customer with a usable, meaningful collection of information.

One of the features of optical media is that the applications designer is freed from much of the traditional concern about physical space for the storage of programs and data. A CD-ROM contains substantial space for the program code required to manipulate very sophisticated presentations of large amounts of data. In addition, this space can be used for data structures that contribute intelligence to the search process, or unique attributes of data that might otherwise not be available.

DESIGN ISSUES

Consider these issues when making design decisions for adding value to information to create an optical product:

1. The nature of optical media makes it possible to organize information in at least two special ways:

   — Large volumes of similar material, such as large bodies of text, or of bibliographic abstracts, etc.

   — Mixtures of traditional formats, such as text, sound, sophisticated graphics and so forth.

> *A person viewing a CRT is probably thinking "application software" (if they are experienced computer users) or "television" (if they are not).*

A good optical application is probably going to be one which takes advantage of one or both these unique characteristics.

2. Consider the presentation of the information product as theater. Remember that a person viewing a CRT is probably thinking "application software" (if they are experienced computer users) or "television" (if they are not). Take advantage of the interactivity to make the product interesting, use multiple media formats where appropriate (sound, graphics, etc.), find natural ways to involve the user in the information process.

When you hear or see references to retrieval software, replace the word "retrieval" with "presentation." The optical publisher has the opportunity to "present" data in a meaningful, responsive way rather than simply retrieving and displaying it.

3. Modifiability—the ability to change and make information personal—is an important aspect of the "information process." It is also an important characteristic of some

print products, in that the reader can make notes in margins, highlight words and so forth. Technology may yet provide us with good solutions for recording information on the published product (through new write-once capabilities). But provision can be made, in any case, for the attachment of comments to a fixed product.

Many of the retrieval packages currently available have this capability. The ability to pull out paragraphs and make them available for further word-processing and manipulation, to capture numerical data into a spreadsheet, to move a graphic into a document—are all important features to the active user of information.

4. Altogether new product concepts and special data types. As new data are considered for publication, and as new presentation styles prove effective, and as the customer base begins to absorb the technology and understand their needs more distinctly, it becomes necessary and exciting to experiment and try new approaches. A new, improved type of presentation may require only a change in software.

NEW PUBLISHING OPPORTUNITIES

Publishing opportunities for this new medium are unlimited, but several classes can be identified. A new commitment to explore other traditional media and markets from new perspectives is vital to uncovering profit potential using optical media.

Here are just a few broad application areas that are relatively easy to envision. The actual execution of marketable products in these areas, or any other, is the challenge addressed by the remainder of this article.

1. *Traditional, existing products which can be enhanced by new access methods or the combination of media formats to achieve their original goal.* There are many examples of this type of opportunity, but consider the area of education and training as a starter, such as the training program that combines sound with text and graphic presentations. Or the programming training product that provides source code, compilers, basic and advanced training procedures, all on a single CD-ROM.

2. *New alliances among owners of content to create comprehensive, cohesive presentations in specific areas of interest.* For example, in a specific area of science, individual publishers of a textbook, an encyclopedia, a dictionary, several journals, vendors of a statistical or other software package and non-publishing companies with specialized, relevant information could all combine to produce a unique information product about a narrow field.

3. *Non-traditional new sources of publishable content.* Where trigonometry tables and other such reference material have been staples, new "raw" source information could become important research tools. There is a multitude of government data sources, such as Landsat data, that have had no practical use because there have been no adequate storage mechanisms available to make delivery or use practical. Warehouses of financial information, available in small time slices, for large statistical samples on a horizontal or longitudinal basis, could become major new research tools.

4. *Non-traditional uses for published content.* Knowledge bases for use with expert systems of a variety of applications are not far in the future. Control information for systems of manufacturing robotics, or environmental control in "smart" buildings are the tip of the iceberg of applications that could utilize access to a large body of information in optical format.

5. *New markets for content from traditional sources.* Vertical applications for information content, packaged with appropriate presentation software, can open up opportunities not available previously. For example, computer documentation—hardware, systems and application software, internal procedures—available to a single large industrial customer or across a manufacturer's customer base, provides a new market for specialized material currently available only from a variety of sources in non-uniform formats.

CONCLUSION

The publishing community has always been very creative in locating content and targeting the product toward the market in a variety of paper forms. Now product developers need to take into account the determination of media and presentation processing decisions as well. These new dimensions of decision-making present significant opportunities and challenges.

CD-ROM and other optical media are tools that will require time for learning appropriate uses and applications. New and radical ideas must be created and nurtured. For all we know, the new Shakespeare of the optical "stage" may be sitting at a desk in a nearby firm, ready to invent the optical stories, scripts and special effects to capture the imaginations of readers for the next 400 years.

Reprinted from *Electronic and Optical Publishing Review* by special permission from Learned Information, Oxford, England and Medford, New Jersey.

The Application Development Process

By John Einberger

[In this article, John Einberger outlines the complete CD-ROM development process. At each step, he lists questions to ask and things to consider, giving developers valuable advice about planning and designing a CD-ROM title. For those who would prefer not to undertake this task alone, we've included a short article about how to hire a consultant to assist you.]

The production of a CD-ROM is a substantial task. The process takes a great deal of careful planning, analysis, and patience. Placing information on CD-ROM is conceptually much like preparing a manuscript. A number of steps must be followed in order to have a successful product. The difference between success and failure often lies in the absence of established procedures and sophisticated tools that automate the production process of a CD-ROM. This situation, however, is rapidly changing as the CD-ROM industry matures. The critical ingredient in the success of any project is having competent project management that understands the process and commands the resources to make the product happen. This article discusses the questions surrounding the selection of appropriate hardware and software, the steps necessary to produce a CD-ROM-based product and, finally, some of the salient issues of project management.

WHAT IS CD-ROM?

CD-ROM is, first and foremost, a publishing medium; it is best suited for the distribution of large amounts of information that, ideally, is relatively stable with updates occurring no more frequently than once a month. Anything that can be represented digitally can be played back from a CD-ROM, so almost any type of information can be placed on it—from textual data to graphics, audio, and video.

Development of a CD-ROM disc involves many interrelated tasks, all of which must be coordinated. Figure 4-1 is a diagram of these tasks and their relationship to one another. Two parallel paths are represented: The path down the left side depicts the workstation development activities, and the right side represents the data-preparation activities.

DATA PREPARATION

Data preparation is a term that describes the techniques of capturing and processing data to be placed on a CD-ROM disc. Preparing data for CD-ROM publication is the most critical and, often, the most time-consuming stage in the CD-ROM production process. The immensity of this step is consistently underestimated, often by an order of magnitude. To do everything right the first time requires a thorough understanding of the data structure, good formatting and indexing tools, talented technicians, and infinite patience. In Figure 4-1 the steps on the right side, down to and including *Logical Formatting,* are collectively referred to as *Data Preparation.* The last step is referred to as *Mastering.*

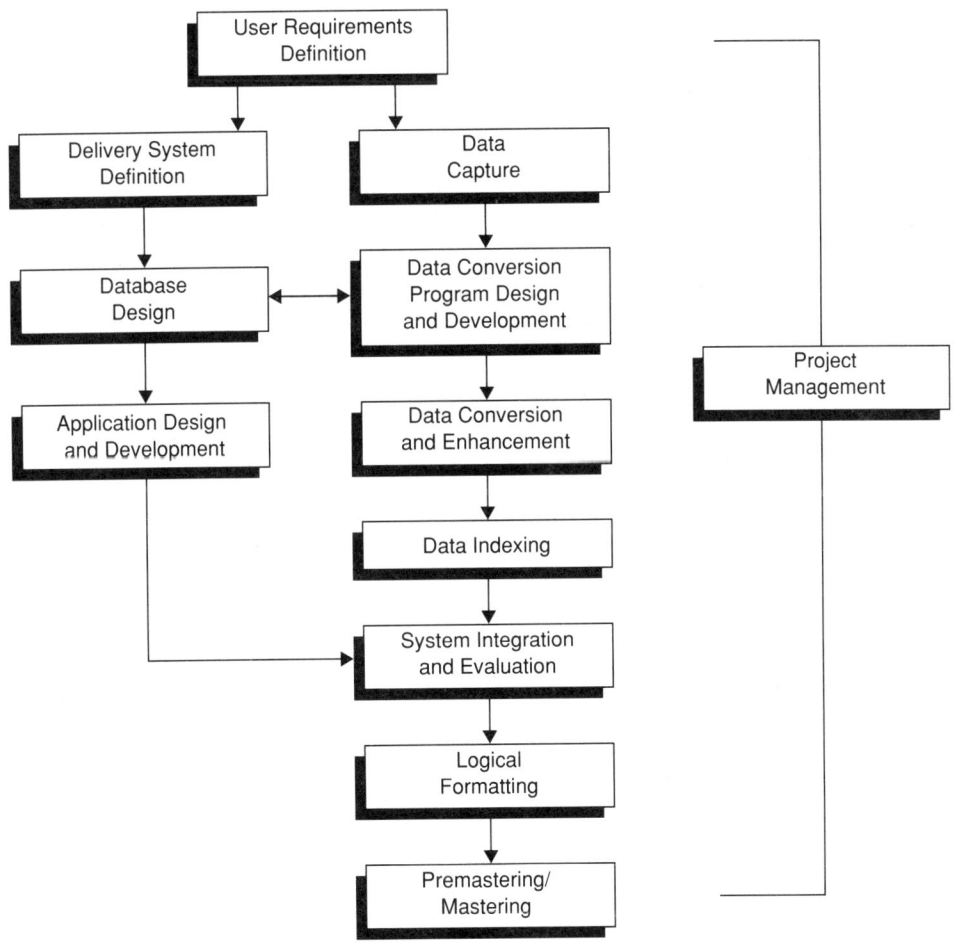

Figure 4-1. The application development process

DEVELOPING A CD-ROM PRODUCT 243

STEP 1: USER-REQUIREMENTS DEFINITION

Before beginning any project, you need a complete analysis of the intended customer base in order to make informed decisions about the features and functions that will be required. This crucial first step sets the stage for all future decision making. The tasks that go on during this step include market analysis, competitive analysis, a determination of distribution channels, pricing analysis, and project sizing, including an estimate of the time and resources required. It is at this step you should ask yourself the tough questions about the business case for doing this project. For example:

1. What form is the existing data in?
2. To whom is the data set valuable?
3. How is the data being used in its present form?
4. How would delivery on CD-ROM make the data more valuable, less expensive to deliver, or more useful?
5. What is the development payback period?
6. What type of profit margins can you expect on this product?
7. Can this data be combined with other related data to provide a product that is not yet available?
8. How can the data be transformed most efficiently for use on a CD-ROM?
9. Do tapes have to be converted, does data need to be keyed in, or is a feasibility study needed on techniques like OCR or image raster scanning?
10. What is the update cycle and how will it be handled?
11. How will you package the product? This question includes disc-label artwork, documentation, and the physical package.
12. Will the controlling software be on the CD-ROM disc or on diskette?
13. Will you license the product or sell it outright?
14. How will you distribute the product?
15. Who are your competitors, and how have they priced their products?
16. Will you include product guarantees?

The result of this first step should be a plan that spells out the business case for the proposed product. If you are unable to convince yourself and your business partners of the product's viability, now is the time to stop.

STEP 2: DELIVERY-SYSTEM DEFINITION

This step focuses on the issue of the hardware and software platforms used to deliver the data to the end user. Here it is important to recognize that existing CD-ROM drives are relatively slow devices and, therefore, not suitable for use with multiuser minicomputers or mainframes. The target delivery system is almost always a microcomputer workstation. In defining the delivery system to be used with your product, consider these questions:

1. What types of software (operating system, file manager, and so on) are required to make the data useful and exciting?
2. What "look and feel" will your user interface have?
3. Who will provide and maintain the software?

4. Which computer hardware platform will the retrieval system be based on?

5. Will computers currently installed on the customer site be used, or will your product include the hardware?

6. Are there special hardware requirements, such as high-resolution displays, mice, laser printers, or compression and decompression hardware? If so, will the potential customer accept the added price of this equipment?

If you decide to market the hardware with the product, you will face many issues that go beyond the scope of this article. Here, however, are a few good questions to consider:

1. How will you handle hardware delivery? Will you sell the hardware outright, lease it, or package it with a product subscription?

2. Where will you obtain the equipment? Will you get it from a system integrator or directly from the manufacturer?

3. If you decide to use hardware that is not already designed to work with the retrieval system you have chosen, how will you resolve hardware/software conflicts or hardware/disc playability issues?

4. Who will provide maintenance?

STEP 3: DATABASE DESIGN

Database design is the most critical step. A design that is inadequate in meeting the requirements will almost certainly yield an unsuccessful product. Avoid retrieval methods designed for small magnetic-based systems; they often break down when used on databases of 600 MB or more. Remember, a CD-ROM is not the optical equivalent of a Winchester disk. The key to efficient and optimized CD-ROM access is the design of data structures that minimize the number of seeks and that read large amounts of data at one time. Questions to consider are:

1. Who are the intended users of the data, and are they computer literate?

2. How is the data indexed and used today?

3. Will this CD-ROM product replace a paper, online, or microform product?

4. Which features/functions of the present product must be duplicated in the CD-ROM product?

5. How is the data currently organized, and is this organization appropriate for use on a CD-ROM?

6. How is the data structured? That is, is it free text or structured?

7. How much data is there?

8. How "clean" is the data?

9. What is the retrieval performance expectation?

10. How frequently is the data updated?

11. What form of data enhancements are necessary?

Figure 4-1 shows a connection between database design and data conversion. This line represents a series of fundamental trade-offs that must be made when structuring a database. These trade-offs are as follows:

1. *Data preparation versus retrieval.* The issue to be considered here is whether to place more burden on the retrieval engine at the time an inquiry is made or to spend more time during data preparation and build appropriate indexes into the index scheme. For example, full-text indexing systems often use a thesaurus to find documents with word equivalents. One

JOHN EINBERGER

Home: Boulder, Colorado
Job: Vice President, Software Development, Micro Decisionware
Quote: *"Our current method of storing and retrieving information is generations old and inadequate for the ever increasing volume. We have in our hands today a new media which holds the potential of expanding man's quest for knowledge."*

approach to implementing this feature is to expand the inquiry with synonyms at retrieval time. An alternative approach is to expand the indexes during data preparation to include the equivalents. These approaches differ in that the expansion is done each time an inquiry is made under the first scheme and done only once under the second. The price paid under the first scheme is slower retrieval times; under the second, more storage space is required.

2. *Space versus performance.* This is a classic data-processing trade-off. On the one hand, you can provide for improved user performance by furnishing extra indexes, but these indexes consume additional storage space and take away space for data. On the other side of this issue, you can provide minimum indexes (consuming minimum space), but then you have to ask the user to wait while the computer performs the necessary searches.

3. *Update versus remaster.* With volatile data, it is often necessary to supply updates before the next scheduled disc-mastering cycle. Such updates are frequently made by sending out floppy disks with the new material and asking each end user to copy the data onto the computer's hard disk. When a new CD-ROM disc is sent out, the update data has already been included with earlier information, so the user can delete the old data. More frequent disc updates of rapidly changing data would eliminate the need for sending intermediate data on floppy disks.

STEP 4: APPLICATION DESIGN AND DEVELOPMENT

This step has the same properties as many software-development projects. It is beyond the scope of this article to detail this process. Any good text on software development will guide you through the task. The basis for the design and development should be the requirements collected during Step 1.

STEP 5: DATA CAPTURE

Data to be placed on CD-ROM can come in many different forms. It may be binary data, text on printed pages, photographs, photocomposition tape, aperture cards, or word-processing files, or it may not yet exist in machine-readable form. This stage in preparing information for CD-ROM involves creating and converting all dissimilar forms of data into a format that can be manipulated by a computer. The task can be very large and use many outside vendors. For example, the keyboarding of data is best left to those who have expertise in this area. Conversion of photocomposition tapes and scanning of images can be done in-house, however, if the proper equipment and resources are available. A key lesson to be learned during this step is tagging the data as early in the data-preparation process as possible. Activities that occur during this stage include:

1. Digitization of audio data.
2. Keyboard entry of text data.
3. Optical character recognition of text data.
4. Scanning or digitizing or both of photos, line drawings, documents, and so on.
5. Document decomposition.
6. If possible, tagging of structural and formatting information (for example, with SGML—Standard Generalized Markup Language).

STEP 6:
DATA-CONVERSION PROGRAM DESIGN AND DEVELOPMENT

After the data is captured and converted to a machine-readable form, it is often in a format that is incompatible with the retrieval and indexing software. Therefore, this data must be reformatted and coded to be read, displayed, and indexed. For example, the formatting codes stored on a photocomposition tape must be translated so that they can be displayed in the screen environment of the retrieval software. In addition, words, paragraphs, pages, and chapters in the original data may have to be recoded so that they can be indexed for later retrieval.

It is absolutely essential to have a thorough understanding of the data before beginning this task. The most common mistake is in obtaining a sample of the data and assuming that the complete data set is identical. This is frequently not the case. Make sure your sample data is truly representative. The best way to do this is to have the complete data set in hand when you start.

STEP 7:
DATA CONVERSION AND ENHANCEMENTS

During this step the conversion programs developed in Step 6 are actually run against the complete data set. Normally, you will correct any and all errors you can at this time. During the indexing phase that follows, all typographical errors, redundant data, and improper coding overlooked in error checking will be indexed and processed along with the good data. A good rule to follow is to catch errors as early in the production cycle as possible. When errors are found and corrected later, the project cost increases.

When your documents or images require more space than you have available on the disc, you may want to compress them. Compression is usually done at this stage in the production process. It is important to remember that compressed data must eventually be decompressed to be displayed or printed. Both processes require special software, and some techniques require hardware. This compression/decompression can add to the overall cost of production and, ultimately, it may add to the user's cost.

If you want to ensure that your data cannot easily be copied, you can scramble it with some method of encryption. This scrambling is another process that is performed during the data-conversion step, either by software or by special hardware. Encrypted data also requires software, hardware, or both for decryption.

These are the activities that usually occur in the data-conversion step:

1. Conversion of magnetic media, such as photocomposition tapes, word-processing files, and binary data, to remove, translate, or add formatting information required by the retrieval system.

2. Reblocking of data to conform to retrieval and indexing systems.

3. Image compression.

4. Data encryption.

5. Programmatic insertion of display formatting tags.

6. Data clean up.

7. Identification of imbedded cross references.

STEP 8: DATA INDEXING

Data stored on CD-ROM is indexed for fast retrieval. The slow access time of CD-ROM precludes storage of unindexed data. Like a book index, a retrieval index lists the location of data stored on the disc. The indexing method and the retrieval software are closely related because the retrieval software must be able to read the index. Both are strongly influenced by the type of data. For example, a full-text application requires, at the very least, an indexing method that lists the location of every word. It may also need an index to chapter heads, sentences, or paragraphs. Structured databases require a different form of indexing to make them useful. Activities that occur during the indexing stage include:

1. Text inversion.

2. Key-field indexing.

CONSULTANTS: HOW TO FIND AND TO HIRE

The goal of a good microcomputer consultant is to wind up unemployed as soon as possible, having used a wide variety of skills to work his or her way out of a job.

The consultant must be a good technician, aware of the latest technology and how it can be used to solve the client's problems. To identify the problems, the consultant must be a good listener and a good communicator. He or she must also be a loyal and impartial champion who can represent the client in choosing the best available system within a budget, and a shrewd adviser who can save the client's time, money and sanity.

How does one locate such a talented person so willing—for a fee, of course—to be used and abandoned? And how does one take advantage of such a person to the fullest extent?

Define the goals

The first step is to define, in as much detail as possible, what the consultant is expected to do. What, specifically, are the goals? What are the deadlines, budgets and other constraints on the project? The problem may be simply that you feel you ought to be getting more out of your computer, but don't know how to go about it. This is a reasonable anxiety, but try to be as exact as possible.

Next, ask others who may have had the same problems or interests if they have used consultants, and if so, if they can recommend anyone. Failing this, check the listings for consultants in newspapers, the phone book and computer magazines. If you already have a computer system, see if the dealer who sold it to you offers a consulting service.

The Independent Computer Consultant Association is a national organization of consultants who agree to adhere to a code of professionalism and ethics. The association has a telephone referral service, (800) 438–4222 or, in New York City, (212) 690–7790.

Jeffrey M. Sachs, president of the association and head of Alembic Computer Systems Inc. in Mesa, Ariz., said a client should check out the consultant's background, experience and reputation. Ask for references, and call them. Don't ask just about the consultant's technical competence; ask how it was to sit down and work with the consultant.

The decision often comes down to a gut reaction, Mr. Sachs said. Do not hire the first consultant you interview. Shop around for competence, experience, price and personality.

Should one choose a consultant from a big firm or a small one?

The smaller computer consulting firm usually has a quicker reaction time and greater flexibility. The

3. Image/sound indexing.

4. Resolution of cross-references.

5. Compression of index files.

STEP 9: SYSTEM INTEGRATION AND EVALUATION

At this stage, you bring everything together and test the complete system. The application program developed in Step 4, along with the data prepared in Steps 5 through 8, should all be loaded onto a simulation system that allows all aspects of the data and software to be run together. The types of tasks that are accomplished are as follows:

1. Debugging of the application.

2. Verification of data integrity.

3. Optimization of placement of data on disc.

4. Evaluation of retrieval performance.

5. Quality assurance of data content.

Often, the testing done during this stage yields some unexpected results that necessitate further work on either the application program or the data. But it is better to discover any shortcomings now, rather than after a disc has been made and sent to customers.

---

consultant may be the owner or partner of the firm, with a vested interest in doing a good job. Your project may be a mere training exercise for the big firm, while it could represent a substantial portion of the yearly income for a small outfit. Even so, the cost may be less because small firms have lower overhead. On the other hand, Mr. Sachs noted, many small firms are just starting out and may be vulnerable to start-up failures, and losing a consultant in the middle of an important project can be devastating.

Large firms have the time and personnel to handle larger projects, but their size requires more rigid standards and structure. There is a perceived lower risk factor associated with the loss of any one consultant. If one individual cannot handle the job, simply call for another. Large firms may also offer support services such as clerical assistance.

When conducting an interview with a larger firm, request that the person who will be managing or overseeing the project is present. Make sure you understand how the consultant plans to go about the work.

Ask if the consultant has a financial interest in any particular products or companies. Many consultants are also dealers, and by selling the client a product he carries, he profits twice. A good consultant will disclose this up front. "What's best for the customer is the primary reason for a recommendation, not whether he can make a buck," Mr. Sachs said.

The bottom line

Some consultants operate on a flat fee basis, while others charge by time and material. Avoid time and material agreements unless the project has a fixed cutoff date, Mr. Sachs advised; otherwise it can turn into a blank check. "We recommend time and material only to experienced clients," usually to augment an existing data processing staff, he said. In a flat fee agreement, make clear what you will accept as a finished product.

Draft a contract that spells out which services are to be provided, fees, whether the consultant's travel, phone and other expenses are going to be paid, and, in cases involving the design of custom software, who owns the results. Questions of warranties, and liability in the event of disastrous consequences, should be addressed, as well as the protection of confidential data examined during the consulting process.

Mr. Sachs added that there is one thing you should not expect from a consultant: a miracle. There is no magic wand, and solving a major computer-related problem takes time, dedication and a team effort.

By Peter H. Lewis. Reprinted by permission of the *New York Times*. Copyright © The New York Times Company.

> *In managing large projects, it is worth spending the time to investigate alternatives, if only to improve your understanding of the processes that await you.*

STEP 10: LOGICAL FORMATTING

We proceed now to the side of data handling that is more routine because it deals with a task that comes up virtually every time a CD-ROM disc is produced. During this step, all forms of data—text, images, structured databases, sound, or whatever—converge into a unified structure. The primary activity during this step is the building of the logical structure that allows the file manager to locate and retrieve data from the disc. Formerly, this step was unique to each data-preparation house because there was no standard for a logical format. Now that the High Sierra format has been so widely adopted (for approximately 95 percent of all discs made), this stage in the process has become standardized.

The steps in logical formatting are:

1. Building of the logical structure required by the file manager; this is usually either High Sierra or ISO 9660.
2. Building of the disc image.
3. Blocking of data to mastering facility requirements.
4. Creation of ANSI-labelled, 9-track tape.

STEP 11: PREMASTERING/ MASTERING

After the ANSI-labelled magnetic tapes are created, they are sent to a disc mastering plant. Technicians process this data, adding error detection and correction information. There is no logical checking of the data during this premastering; whatever data is on the tapes will later be mastered to the CD-ROM. Here is a summary of premastering activities:

1. Verification of tape readability.
2. Calculation of level 3 (layered ECC) error detection and correction bytes.
3. Writing of data to magnetic disk.
4. Calculation of levels 1 and 2 error correction.

After the error correction and detection information has been added, the data is used to record the information by exposing a photoresist-coated glass master to a laser beam. A metal-plated stamper molded from the developed glass master is then used to stamp out identical polycarbonate discs. This step is almost always done by a mastering plant because there is a significant capital investment required to purchase and run the laser lathe and clean room necessary to perform this task successfully.

PROJECT MANAGEMENT ISSUES

The production of a CD-ROM title is a large project. In managing large projects, it is worth spending the time to investigate alternatives, if only to improve your understanding of the processes that await you. When you have a choice of several methods for accomplishing a particular step, analyze them all, even if you are already biased toward one. For example, consider both OCR and rekeying to capture text; for premastering, investigate both desktop systems and service bureaus. A project manager helps immeasurably in bringing together a complex project on time and within budget. Assistance you can obtain from a competent project manager includes:

1. Assistance with application development, data capture, and hardware procurement.

2. Conversion of data structures or media. For example, conversion from EBCDIC to ASCII, handling of unlabeled tapes, uploading from floppy disks or similar media, conversion to particular file formats or indexing structures, and so on. ANSI-labelled tapes (ANSI X3.27-1978) are almost always considered the standard input medium because they are the standard means of information exchange in the computer industry and are the most practical for large volumes of data.

3. Project scheduling. Of concern here is the ability to set realistic schedules and then manage to meet them. The schedules should contain measurable milestones.

4. Scheduling and management of production issues with the mastering facility.

5. Operational procedures necessary to ensure proper reporting and sign-offs prior to beginning each phase of the project.

Be careful not to underestimate the complexity of making a CD-ROM disc. Spend some time talking to companies that have already made a disc and listen to their stories. Understand the market need, so that you can provide the right product, at the right price, to the right customers. CD-ROM technology is real and is here today, awaiting the creative innovator who can bring a successful product to market.

[John Einberger is Vice President of Software Development at Micro Decisionware, Inc. He is responsible for the development of software used to access mainframe databases from personal workstations. Prior to joining MDI, Einberger was Vice President at Reference Technology Inc., where he was instrumental in forming and chairing the High Sierra Group, which formulated an international standard for the logical format of CD-ROM discs.]

Designing a CD-ROM Interface

By Linda Stone and Rachel Rutherford

[While focussing specifically on HyperCard, this article pinpoints many key issues that apply to interface design for any platform. For developers of Macintosh products, the authors list several useful resources.]

Is it easier to find a product by driving around looking for a place to buy it? By reading a map? By asking for directions? By riding with someone who's driving there? Or by having the item delivered to your door? These five alternatives illustrate five *interfaces* for finding something you seek. The resounding success of door-to-door rapid-delivery services demonstrates the rewards of developing a good interface. To users of CD-ROM discs, finding information can seem as easy as calling for a delivery, if the interface is designed well.

The interface is what the user sees and interacts with. A simple, intuitive, aesthetically appealing, and useful interface is rarely designed in one attempt. Usually, designers go through many cycles of repeated development and user testing before evolving an interface that is attractive and effective. Because good interfaces are born through repeated iteration, designers need tools that let them create protoypes completely and rapidly. One such tool, used as an example throughout this article, is Apple Computer's HyperCard software, which allows for a smooth migration through the various design and development phases. In some cases, what begins as a HyperCard prototype can grow into a final piece by fleshing it out and fine-tuning it.

What gives a tool such as HyperCard its power as a CD-ROM front end is that designers can quickly:

- Produce rich, vivid graphics.
- Change the location, appearance, and content of text that the user sees.
- Create realistic prototype interfaces.
- Change ineffective or unattractive interfaces completely.
- Create final interface front ends to existing CD-ROM data.

Currently, HyperCard is often used to build front ends for existing retrieval engines. This gives developers the ability to change the CD-ROM interface easily without having to rework the engine software.

DESIGNING AN EFFECTIVE INTERFACE

Developing a powerful, effective, and memorable interface is both an art and a science. A background in film can be more helpful than familiarity with printed media. The following skills contribute to success:

- General architecture (structure of information, navigation).
- Visual or graphic design.
- Programming/"scripting."
- Content expertise.
- Writing expertise.

There are seven stages in the design and development process.

Stage 1: Define the problem

- What problem are you trying to solve, and what will success look like? Before launching into a needs assessment, clearly identify the problem to be solved and the characteristics of a successful solution. Too often we launch into a thorough definition of objectives without having a sense of how they relate to the bigger picture.

Stage 2: Analysis/needs assessment

- Who is the audience?
- What is the subject matter, and how will the development team get access to it?

LINDA STONE

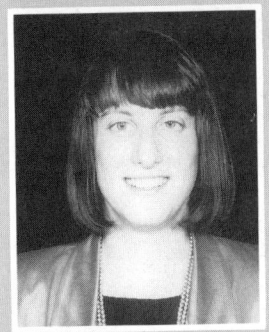

Home: San Francisco, California
Job: Market Development Manager, Business Multimedia Marketing, Apple Computer, Inc.
Quote: *"With the integration of text, graphics, video, speech, animation, music and sound, we are approaching an important critical mass. As we become more sophisticated information architects, we can help to make communicating more joyful and participatory. Information dumping will be replaced by knowledge transfer. The barrier between teaching and learning will begin to dissolve as we become sharers and contributors, rather than just consumers of multimedia information."*

- How will the audience use this subject matter? At this point, it makes sense to focus on audience characteristics and on what, exactly, needs to be covered.

Stage 3: Develop a vision

- What will your users want to experience? Think of all the real-world models that might apply: film, video, books, television, architecture, geography, automobile repair... This is a time to think broadly. Let all the information you gathered in the analysis phase rest in your subconscious. Take a step back and let the ideas flow.

> *A really good interface is one that's so obvious and so integral to the content that the user never perceives it as an interface.*
>
> **Laura Buddine**

Stage 4: Design

- Brainstorm. What type of environment/metaphor suits both the audience and the content? If no metaphor seems to fit, don't force one. Instead, focus on providing consistent backgrounds and visual landmarks. How will you present the subject matter, and how will the user navigate or search through the material? You provide the structure, but allow the user to choose the path. User control is a critical element of a compelling interface.

- Design the interface. Consider text, graphics, and sound.

Stage 5: Development

- Build a prototype. Taking a thin slice of your vision and building it enables you to answer two questions: "Is it technically doable?" and "Will the interface work?"

- Test the prototype with real users. When testing, always watch the users interact with the interface. What you observe is as important as what they articulate. Don't say anything: Ultimately, you won't be there with each user.

- Incorporate what you have learned from user testing and build the rest of the interface. The cycle works like this: build, test, modify. Frequent repetition of this cycle enhances your chances of success.

Stage 6: Production

- Build a final production version. During production, the focus shifts from improving the interface to building a robust version. With HyperCard, many people rebuild their set of "cards," or stacks, from scratch to get clean production versions.

Stage 7: Test

- Test the interface to be sure it works on all target machine configurations.

- Check for consistent sound, visual effects, and animation.

- Proofread the text.

- Be sure everything works and nothing breaks.

- Check to ensure your interface contains no virus contaminants.

Interface design should be an iterative and fluid process. Many development teams are accustomed to a more linear process: teaming an instructional designer with a content expert, passing their work on to a graphic designer for enhancement, and then handing it off to a programmer to put it all together. With a tool like HyperCard, however, once the problem has been defined and you've conducted a needs assessment, every team member needs to be involved. The iterative nature of the development process allows for ongoing design review and fine-tuning. Users can work with and give input during the development process rather than waiting for a final piece that is difficult to modify.

Because the development phase of the process is so fluid and iterative with a tool like HyperCard, managing logistics can be challenging. Who will be responsible for the master version? It's helpful to appoint a "stackmaster," or stack librarian, who tracks versions and coordinates with all team members to manage effective integration of their work. HyperCard makes a powerful interface tool because it is easy to tailor and change, and because it can be used to build both the prototype and the final interface.

HYPERCARD DESIGN RESOURCES

One of the best sources of prerelease Apple documentation and developer support information is the Apple Programmer's and Developer's Association (APDA). You can write or call for membership information at:

*Apple Programmer's and Developer's
    Association
290 SW 43rd
Renton, Washington 98055
(206) 251–6548*

Even if you are not developing a commercial application, you are welcome to become a member.

Another rich source of software, newsletters, and experts is the Apple User Group Connection. If you live in the United States, call (800) 538-9686, extension 500, for the names, addresses, and telephone numbers of up to three Macintosh user groups in your geographic area. Apple also has a HyperCard User Group, AHUG. You can obtain more information by calling or writing:

*AHUG
20525 Mariani Avenue M/S 27-AHUG
Cupertino, California 95014
(408) 974–1707*

You can also join one of the following two large user groups, regardless of where you live.

RACHEL RUTHERFORD

Home: Mountain View, California
Job: Designer of Demo Discs, Apple Computer Interactive Discs, Apple Computer, Inc.
Quote: *"As the computer, music, publishing, graphic designer and video industries merge, expectations grow. People want information to be as sensory as television and as responsive as a human. We need to give the world both the technical skill to merge these media and the design skill to make the end product simple and elegant."*

*The Boston Computer Society
One Center Plaza
Boston, Massachusetts 02108
(617) 367–8080*

*Berkeley Macintosh User's Group
1442–A Walnut Street #62
Berkeley, California 94709
(415) 849–9114*

There are a variety of books on HyperCard available in retail bookstores. We also recommend looking at books and resources in the fields of film, video, television, graphic design and typography, and animation.

Three books from Apple are especially applicable to CD-ROM interface design:

Human Interface Guidelines: The Apple Desktop Interface, published by Addison-Wesley and available through retail bookstores or the

Apple Programmer's and Developer's Association. This book focuses on standard Macintosh application design, features a section on general interface and visual design principles, and includes a broad bibliography of recommended reading.

HyperCard Stack Design Guidelines, forthcoming from Addison-Wesley. A preliminary draft is currently available through the Apple Programmer's and Developer's Association. This book describes user-interface and visual-design principles for HyperCard stacks.

AppleCD SC Developer's Guide, available through the Apple Programmer's and Developer's Association. This is a technical book, covering interface, networking, and implementation issues for developers wanting to use the AppleCD SC drive.

[Linda Stone is currently a Market Development Manager in Business Multimedia Marketing at Apple Computer, Inc. She has an M.Ed. from the University of Washington and has been involved in the computer industry since 1982.

Rachel Rutherford is a designer of interactive color-animated Demo Discs in Apple Computer, Inc.'s Interactive Design Group. She is also the author of Apple Computer, Inc.'s HyperCard Stack Design Guidelines, *forthcoming from Addison-Wesley.]*

The Importance of Product Testing

By Tim McManus

[Gone are the days when product testing had all the characteristics of an afterthought. Here, Tim McManus gives us an overview of testing procedures at Lotus Development Corporation, emphasizing the need for integrating quality assurance and quality control from the very beginning of a project.]

Although premarket product testing is important in any industry, it takes on an especially significant role in the CD ROM market. Because the market is relatively young and vendors are striving to establish themselves, quality and commitment to high-quality product-testing standards are key differentiating elements for the vendor who would be a leader in the CD-ROM industry.

CD-ROM products require frequent data and software updates, so product testing must continue beyond the conception and development stages. In some cases, as in the financial services industry, CD-ROM products must be updated as often as every week, sometimes even nightly, because the vendor's competitiveness depends on the quality and accuracy of the information provided. As a result, the CD-ROM developer must not only adopt a rigorous testing procedure prior to a product's introduction, but must also determine a method for ensuring that the product updates are of the utmost quality.

QUALITY ASSURANCE AND CONTROL

Several aspects of a CD-ROM product must be tested—the way the information is indexed and integrated with the software (data links), the way the software handles the information, and the quality of the data itself. Thus, for example, testing of the Lotus One Source products at Lotus Development Corporation has been broken down into two major functions, Quality Assurance (QA) and Quality Control (QC). These functions are under the jurisdiction of the Product Marketing Manager, who is also responsible for identifying market need and appro-

TIMOTHY J. McMANUS

Home: North Andover, Massachusetts
Job: Director of Marketing—Compact Disc Information Services, Lotus Development Corporation.
Quote: *"Today and in the future, customers will not buy CD-ROM products; they will buy integrated solutions."*

priate product offerings and for guiding the development process. The Product Marketing Manager works closely with QA at each step of the development process.

Quality assurance begins when the product is conceived and continues through the design, development, testing, and initial introduction of the product. It is important that QA personnel understand how the product is designed and developed, in order to know which elements require rigorous initial testing and which will require ongoing testing as the product is updated.

Because the quality assurance people have an intimate understanding of the product specification, they perform "reality tests" at each juncture of development to ensure that the product concept is viable and well executed. They also form the critical link between groups of developers working on different aspects of the product to ensure that the final product is tightly integrated.

Quality assurance also assists developers in evaluating the feasibility of new product ideas. These ideas often come from customers, who perceive a need for a new function or a new feature in an existing product and communicate that need to (at Lotus) the Product Marketing Manager.

If the QA/Product Marketing Manager relationship did not exist at Lotus, the development process would not be as smooth. Pieces of a product that had been developed separately might not fit correctly when finally brought together. Feedback from customers might not be well integrated in new designs; and products might not come to market in a timely fashion. This combination of integrated development and customer feedback is both the control and the catalyst for bringing a product concept successfully through the development process.

In contrast to QA, QC at Lotus is responsible for checking the final CD-ROM product each time it is prepared for updates. An automated testing process uses keystroke macro programs, such as Lotus Metro macros and Lotus 1-2-3 macros, to test the product updates at various levels: the network level, the in-house publisher level, and the final published level.

Quality Control, with the production department, has also automated the process for reporting errors when they occur in the testing process. By taking advantage of electronic mail and electronic bulletin boards, QC is able to notify developers immediately when an error is found and therefore allow more time to be spent in solving problems than in identifying errors.

Quality control not only tests the operations of the product, but ensures that the right data is in the right place. Without QC, there is the potential for data inconsistency. In the information-services industry, such a mistake is disastrous. Imagine an investment banker searching financial reports labeled *1986* that are, in fact, from 1976. Quality control ensures that all information on the disc is complete, correct, in the appropriate place, and labeled properly.

ALPHA AND BETA TESTING

Product testing should take place at different stages during the development process. This testing should begin during the initial development stage and progress into the Alpha and Beta stages. At Lotus, the Alpha program is used to share new product designs with a few customers, to allow them the opportunity to provide input at the design stage of the product. In doing so, Lotus is able to determine whether its products are meeting clients' needs.

The Beta program begins just prior to product introduction and serves as the stress-test in the CD-ROM product cycle. This final program aids both the developers and the marketing department in fine-tuning a product before its first shipment.

CD-ROM vendors must provide customers with a high-quality product. Rigorous product testing, such as the Lotus Quality Assurance and Quality Control programs, enables the developer to ensure the highest quality possible by minimizing product errors and responding to customer needs as quickly and comprehensively as possible. In a growing, volatile market like the CD-ROM industry, the quality of a product is a clear, differentiating factor among vendors.

> *Quality assurance begins when the product is conceived and continues through the design, development, testing, and initial introduction of the product.*

[Tim McManus is Director of Marketing of the Compact Disc Information Service at Lotus Development Corporation. He is responsible for all marketing activities for the Lotus One Source product line. Prior to working for Lotus, McManus was Vice President of Sales and Marketing for Datext, Inc., which was acquired by Lotus in 1987.]

Why You Never Get a Straight Answer When You Ask How Much It Will Cost!

By Chris Bowman

[Developing a CD-ROM project budget can be difficult. Requests for estimates may yield a wide range of figures, all supported by lengthy lists of assumptions and caveats. In this article, Chris Bowman tells us why.]

Asking how much it will cost to produce a CD-ROM is likely to elicit the same response as asking an airline ticket clerk if your flight will arrive on time. A probable answer is: "It depends." As you may already have discovered, the cost of CD-ROM development can range from the price of a Yugo to that of a fleet of Porsches.

Why is it that service bureaus and other vendors cannot come up with standard rates for CD-ROM development without adding a long list of exceptions and qualifiers? Simply put, it is because no two projects are the same. The factors that affect costs are numerous, and most are impossible to assess without actually seeing the data. Any vendor who quotes a price without evaluating a data sample is only guessing at the ultimate cost.

FACTORS AFFECTING COST

What are some of the factors affecting the cost of a CD-ROM project? The first consideration is text conversion. Because CD-ROM is an emerging technology, in most cases information providers must convert existing databases for use on CD-ROM. Information that traditionally has been delivered on paper or on microfilm exists in a wide variety of formats. Converting that data to a format that will allow an inverted index to be created can be a complex and costly task.

Custom engineering is another factor that influences the final cost of a CD-ROM project. A retrieval system that requires custom engineering can significantly affect both the time and the cost to develop the project. For example, taking a retrieval system designed for reference manuals and trying to modify it to search data in a phone directory is a major undertaking. Some retrieval systems, such as KnowledgeSet's KRS, have been designed for specific applications such as technical documentation. So look for the system whose features most closely meet your requirements.

Assuming that the CD-ROM developer has selected a retrieval system that meets all specifications and does not require custom engineering, there are still the following factors to consider:

- How large is the database? The amount of stored data determines the cost of data preparation and can also determine whether the entire database can fit on a single CD-ROM disc. Multiple CD-ROMs mean greater costs for premastering, mastering, and replication.

- Is the data in machine-readable form? To be indexed and stored on CD-ROM, data must be machine readable. Otherwise it must be scanned or keyed in—a process that can be expensive and time consuming.

- If the data is in machine-readable form, does it contain typesetting code (such as Penta or troff)? If so, these codes (or tags) probably have to be removed, with a resulting increase in expensive programming fees.

- How consistent is the data format? Headings should be used in a consistent manner throughout the database, and tables and figures should be labeled consistently.

CHRIS BOWMAN

Home: Menlo Park, California
Job: Director of Marketing, KnowledgeSet Corporation
Quote: *"The acceptance of CD-ROM will be driven by corporations that embrace the technology's application-specific solutions, not by off-the-shelf products."*

- Are there cross-references within the database? If so, they should be consistently identified so links can be created during data preparation.

- What about graphics? The cost will be affected by the number and nature of drawings or photographs and by whether or not they are currently in magnetic form or must be scanned. The format of raster drawings (CCITT Group 4, Run Length Encoded, and so on) will affect the amount of storage space required on the disc and the speed of display and printing.

To put it simply, the more surgery performed on the data, the greater the cost.

- Finally, what are the hardware issues? The cost will be affected by your system requirements, especially if device drivers need to be written for a special graphics display or input device. Costs can also escalate if your system requires image decompression and you want hard copies.

The answers to these questions may not be obvious to someone just beginning to explore CD-ROM, while a seasoned veteran will realize that some of the issues are oversimplified. But this discussion is not meant to be a development checklist; it is simply an introduction to the dynamics of analyzing the cost of CD-ROM development.

THE BIGGEST HURDLE

The fundamental hurdle lies in the wide variety of formats in which data currently exists. Few information providers are currently authoring for CD-ROM, but as more of them begin to do so, standards for data formats will emerge and the process of preparing data for mastering will become more straightforward.

One of the most exciting developments in hastening the acceptance of CD-ROM is HyperCard and Apple Computer's commitment to positioning it as a CD-ROM authoring tool and front end. As the number of databases created in "stacks" increases, the life of the CD-ROM developer will become simpler because a stack will become a standard data format on the Macintosh. Unfortunately, even if there were a HyperCard equivalent in the MS-DOS and UNIX worlds, it's unlikely that a hardware vendor would support the product the way Apple has by bundling it at no charge with the Mac.

THE BOTTOM LINE

So where does all this leave the person considering CD-ROM? There are no simple answers. If the price seems too good to be true, it is probably just that. Unless a database consists only of free text—without subheadings, stored in ASCII, with no graphics—one is likely to face many of the issues raised here, and even a few not mentioned. It's better to do some homework in the beginning than to revise the budget six months into the project.

A final word of advice for simplifying the process and keeping costs down: Be willing to compromise on your functional requirements. Don't try to specify the ultimate utopian retrieval system. It doesn't exist, and attempting to build it will cost you the price of that fleet of Porsches!

[Chris Bowman is Director of Marketing at KnowledgeSet Corporation, a leading developer of retrieval systems for CD-ROM. His responsibilities include corporate business planning, marketing communications, and product marketing. Prior to joining KnowledgeSet, Bowman served in marketing management positions with Apple Computer, Inc., the Atari Corporation, and Tandy Corporation.]

MULTIMEDIA PERSPECTIVES

DESIGNING AND PRODUCING A MULTIMEDIA CD-ROM
By Laura Buddine

HYPERCARD: A TOOL FOR MULTIMEDIA PRESENTATIONS
By C. Joseph Williams

SCRIPTING FOR INTERACTIVE MULTIMEDIA CD SYSTEMS
By Mark Dillon

Designing and Producing a Multimedia CD-ROM

By Laura Buddine

[The multimedia technologies are the rising stars and starlets of the CD-ROM industry. Offering the glamor of horizontal mass markets and home penetration, they are the stuff that interactive designers' dreams are made of. Some designers, like Laura Buddine whose article on multimedia design and production starts this section, have been doing a lot more than just dreaming.]

Until recently, the lack of commonly accepted standards for quality audio and visual displays has hindered the development of multimedia CD-ROMs. Yet the potential success of CD-ROM really lies in multimedia. Few horizontal market applications need multiple megabytes of text, but an application rich in pictures and audio, although it takes a vast amount of delivery capacity, has an equally vast potential audience. A picture may be worth a thousand words, but a digitized picture takes the space of ten thousand. Thankfully, in 1988, the progress made in CD-I and DVI, along with the announcement of the CD-ROM XA standard and Apple Computer's CD-ROM specifications, made development of multimedia titles for horizontal markets a near-term prospect.

THE CRITICAL FACTOR: UNDERSTANDING THE USER

The success of any project is determined by how well it meets its defined goals. Fundamentally, success then becomes an issue of identifying and

> *The success of any project is determined by how well it meets its defined goals. Fundamentally, success then becomes an issue of identifying and understanding the people who will use the application.*

understanding the people who will use the application. This is the most important issue in the entire process of design and production.

The importance of understanding the user is easy to see in the context of an educational title. You must understand your target student to know whether or not the subject is useful and to know at what grade level it should be presented. How is the student receiving the material now, and what are the problems that your application can solve? Where does interactivity provide value to the student, and where does it simply add complexity? What portions of the subject are best understood from audiovisual explanations, where is text appropriate, and where do you need an interactive module for hands-on learning? How long do you expect the title to be used by the student before the material is mastered, and how do you maintain interest?

Our company, Tiger Media, Inc., makes entertainment titles for the consumer market. Although the context is different from the education example above, we must ask the same questions. What type of household will be the early purchaser of a multimedia delivery system? (Our titles can be implemented on CD-I, CD-ROM XA, DVI, Apple CD-ROM and any similar audiovisual delivery system, and we call all of these "New Media.") Who in the household will be involved with the purchasing decision, and who will use the application? What content is attractive to these consumers? How can interactivity add value to that content? How much interactivity is acceptable, and how much is too much for our consumer? How long do we expect a consumer to use the title before it is exhausted? At what price point does the perceived value exceed the cost? Can we sell enough copies during the product's lifetime to make it profitable?

At this writing, there are not yet any New Media delivery systems in the consumer market. So to determine our target market, we made a detailed study of the historical demographics of "market innovators" and "early adopters" from the home computer, video game, CD audio, and VCR markets to determine who buys new entertainment technology when the price is high and the software offerings are limited. We cross-correlated this with a study of current TV "zapping," the almost interactive use of a remote control that is a strong indicator of boredom with current TV entertainment. These studies gave us a good guess at the type of households most likely to purchase New Media systems.

From the understanding of the market's needs and wants (and your target user is your market, even for an industrial application) comes the design, the budget, and the implementation plan. But your market understanding is something you must constantly re-evaluate. At this point, you know what you *think* the market will want. In order to *really* serve the market, you must begin testing your assumptions as soon as you have something you can communicate to potential users. Your testing should continue throughout all phases of design and production.

DESIGNING FOR THE TARGET MARKET

The identification and understanding of your target user will determine the content, presentation level, and interactive approach of your initial design. In our case, although we determined that our market would be upscale urban households, we found that about 35 percent had no school-age children and about 20 percent did not include any computer users. We decided to create a title for adults and to attempt a design that would be entertaining and challenging in content but with a level of interactivity not much more involved than changing channels. One of our first designs was a mystery title, a popular adult genre that lends itself strongly to interactivity, but that can also be challenging in content without intense and demanding interaction.

The next step in design is to define the "interactive mechanism," the way the interactive portion will work. There are a few basic mechanisms that can underlie a lot of very different products. One mechanism is hierarchical or tree-structured, which lends itself strongly to HyperCard designs; but this is not the only mechanism. We've identified about eight, and combinations and hybrids of these can yield even more options. The mechanism we chose for the mystery game is a set of parallel tracks across which the user can move—what we call a "maze in time and space."

The content and the mechanism must fit naturally together. We find it helpful to think of mechanisms in terms of game designs, even if the title isn't a game or any type of entertainment at all. What is the payoff to the user, and is it worth the interactive effort you're asking for? When you think of design this way, it becomes evident that not all materials are appropriate for interactive presentation. Make these materials linear segments, and save the interactivity for the areas where it adds real value.

The user interface must fit the content, the mechanism, and the target user as naturally and as unobtrusively as possible. A really good interface is one that's so obvious and so integral to the content that the user never perceives it as an interface. This point is especially important in entertainment and in educational products for children and for adults who don't use computers. If the user needs a map to navigate, make finding the map part of the prologue, so that the map becomes integral to the story. If your application allows the users to examine objects, let them choose the objects by pointing. Use menus only when they're unavoidable, and be sure that your icons are self-evident to your target user.

LAURA BUDDINE

Home: Downey, California
Job: President, Tiger Media, Inc.
Quote: *"In the next few years, all of the technical issues of how to make interactive multimedia will be solved. The creative issues—what to make that people will really want to buy—will be challenging us for the next century."*

DESIGNING FOR PRODUCTION

The two major constraints as you move into production design are technical and budgetary. You may have dreams of the ultimate interactive program, one that pushes CD-I or DVI to the limit and requires a "Star Wars" budget. Save your dream for a few years, and concentrate on

> *Our designs generally start as what we'd like to do and, through an iterative process, become what we can afford to do.*

something you can produce within today's constraints.

We presently design all of our products to fit within what we call the "safe subset." We can produce versions of any product for any competent New Media system—CD-I, DVI, CD-ROM XA, Apple CD-ROM, and so on—without any change in the design. The safe subset excludes technical areas that we don't completely understand, and there are still some of these, even after two years of work. This approach prevents us from using some of the neat features in CD-I or DVI, but it gives us the broadest possible potential market and ensures that our designs are producible today.

Unless you're designing your application for a single manufacturer's delivery system, it's a good idea to avoid designs in which the seek performance is critical. In our safe subset, we design for many operating systems, displays, and CPUs, and we try to avoid *all* performance-sensitive designs. This consideration, plus the necessity of rewriting the control program for different systems, points us toward products with strong audiovisual content and small, simple control programs.

Strong audiovisual content combined with strong control programs is a good approach for avoiding the technical issues, but it can run you smack into budgetary constraints. Art and photography are *expensive,* and these discs can hold a lot of pictures. If you license stock photographs at magazine rates, the cost for a disc with three hours of content could run as high as $500,000. Clearly, some creative approaches are needed to solve this problem. There are some alternatives, such as negotiating a block license, shooting your own photographs, or hiring artists on a project basis, but unless you already own the visual material for a project, you can expect the cost of art and photographs to be the major portion of your budget.

Because we hope to make a profit from our products, designing the final production is a constant process of testing against the budget. We can afford to invest more in a reference product with a five-year life than we can in a game that will be old in 18 months. Our designs generally start as what we'd like to do and, through an iterative process, become what we can afford to do. Sometimes, this reduction pushes the design beneath our standards of acceptability, and we must put it on the shelf to wait either for a larger market or until we convince someone else to help pay for it.

PRODUCING THE MULTIMEDIA PROJECT

If you've done a good job in the design phase, production should be similar to producing a well-planned video. (Just as with a video, you'll do some redesign during the production process.) There are three major areas of difference between our products and video, however: assuring continuity in an interactive script; working with art in the digital domain; and debugging and testing requirements.

You can't go to your local software store for an interactive scripting tool. For our mystery title, we created a very large paper chart of the mechanism, which covered two walls of the largest room in our office. As we developed the story elements, we stripped the modules in with tape and identified them with Post-it notes. The tape was moved many times and the modules were rewritten as we walked (almost literally) through the various ways the modules could be put together into a story.

When we were convinced that the basic continuity was sound and that the game was challenging but winnable, we created a prototype of the title on a Commodore Amiga. The Amiga has speech synthesis capability, so it could read the script aloud to us as we tested the game play. After five weeks of testing and script modification, we recorded the final audio with 12 actors, using only one day in the studio. The Amiga prototype was our most valuable continuity tool, and we highly recommend this solution to the multimedia producer. Such a prototype is one of the very few tools that are truly inexpensive and easy to make.

Digitization and manipulation techniques for art could fill a volume the size of this yearbook, and you still might not find the answers for your particular combination of source art, digitizing equipment, image-processing software, and target machine. The best advice is to test. With our safe subset approach, we find it much easier to start with flat art than with digitally created pictures because we can always redigitize if necessary to support a different graphic display. For line art with solid color fills, we digitize in black and white and colorize on the computer. Remember that, in most cases, it is much easier to start with clean art than it is to fix a flaw after digitizing.

The technical aspects of programming, synchronization, and mastering are beyond the scope of this article. Your programmer should be part of your design team from the mechanism phase on. Both of you will be involved in the constant testing, debugging, and redesign. For this to go smoothly, he or she must understand the product's goals as well as you do.

Your early testing, both internally and with potential users, will be fun. There's no more exciting day than when a prototype is working and you begin to get a sense of how your application will actually play. Before it's finished, you'll have been through it so many times with so many people that you'll almost hate it. There will be a great temptation to minimize the testing—to test only internally rather than with users, or to postpone major testing until the product's almost complete. Don't succumb to this temptation, or you may be faced with the unpleasant choice between an unsuccessful product or a major and costly rework.

A FINAL NOTE

If your targets are educational, industrial, or corporate markets, you may feel that the entertainment examples in this article don't have much application to your multimedia projects. Ultimately though, it is the entertainment value that makes using multimedia worthwhile. People learn quickly and retain more when the presentation is stimulating and fun. The entertainment inherent in a rich, interactive multimedia application gives us an exciting new medium for effective communication.

[Laura Buddine is founder and President of Tiger Media, Inc., a New Media entertainment company producing multimedia CD-ROM and CD-I products. She is also co-author of The Brady Guide to CD-ROM, *Prentice Hall, 1987.]*

HyperCard: A Tool for Multimedia Presentations

By C. Joseph Williams

[In this article, Joe Williams advocates the use of HyperCard to support all stages of development of a multimedia product, from design through development, and finally, during production. He argues that a single tool is necessary to facilitate communication among project team members and to make production of multimedia titles generally more efficient.]

It wasn't too long ago that computer output consisted only of uppercase letters, numbers, and a few special characters. Computer operators complained when they had to provide lowercase capability because it meant physically changing the print-train mechanism and jobs ran slower. Images in those days, other than those produced on multimillion-dollar machines, were carefully laid out by someone so that shading was suggested by printing or overprinting these alphanumeric characters. These effects were usually created just to show that they could be done, rather than for any useful purpose.

Today, we're moving quickly from desktop publishing to desktop presentation to desktop multimedia applications. We have hundreds of fonts in any style and any size we care to choose. With outlining applications and word-processing programs we can create, revise, and produce printed materials. Graphics can be quickly scanned, cleaned up or modified, and resized. With page-layout, painting, and presentation programs we can produce printed newsletters and color slides. Improved sound circuitry and increased internal memory allow computers to produce or replay sound far beyond the simple beeps of the past. With music composition and performance software we can place notes on a staff, accept stereo input, or drive music synthesizers. The increased storage capacity of CD-ROM and videodisc enable photograph-quality images and full-motion video to be displayed under computer control. With improved authoring tools and display technologies, computers are being used not only for creating, but also for delivering presentations.

The problem facing today's designer is no longer "Can I use a particular font?" or "Can I use sound, graphics, or animation?" A variety of hardware and software tools make it possible to produce almost any multimedia design element desired. Instead, the problem has become "How can I communicate a design idea *effectively* and *efficiently* to the people who have the talent to make the best possible use of these tools?"

A NEW GENERATION OF TOOLS

When we talk about tools for multimedia presentations, we're usually referring to the tools used in the production of a "final" version of a presentation. But graphics, sound, animation, and interactive-control tools are rarely used by a single individual; a team of people with these different talents is usually required. It's too early in the era of desktop multimedia to have defined a standardized process like those of the film and animation industries, but tools—and systems of tools—are needed to support the various stages of multimedia design, development, and production. Most important are tools that facilitate the communication required among the team of people involved in these stages.

In the past, designers created multimedia presentations by completely specifying the design, development, and production steps, usually on paper, and then handing the detailed descriptions to the technicians who actually created the final presentation. New tools are changing that process. Such tools support the design, development, and production stages by providing an easy way to create and communicate text, graphics, sound, animation, and interactive-control requirements to the production team. These tools can be used throughout the design, development, and production stages, and allow the processes to be more evolutionary and collaborative, rather than completely prespecified.

One available tool that can be used to support all stages of multimedia development is Apple's HyperCard software. HyperCard allows a user to create text and graphic frames and to connect the frames through links. Using the built-in HyperTalk language, a user can control sound, specify animations, and produce special effects.

DRAFTING AND SKETCHING TOOLS (DESIGN)

When a multimedia designer creates a concept, the designer must be able to present it to others

JOE WILLIAMS

Home: Cupertino, California
Job: Senior Instructional Designer, Apple Computer, Inc.
Quote: *"We must explore and demonstrate what's possible using interactive multimedia because people can't want what they don't know is possible."*

> *With [new kinds] of hardware as the departure point — as loony as it might seem to say today — look for HyperCard to become a museum piece. It will be like the old crank motion picture cameras: quaint, but evocative of the time when something exciting and important was just beginning.*
>
> **Peter Black**
> From "Technology Ahead of Its Time,"
> *MacWEEK*, August 1988

the mind of the designer and no treatment, however well written, can fully convey the look and feel of a multimedia presentation to a reader. What's needed is a tool that allows early creation of a prototype illustrating the presentation's graphics, sounds, and interaction.

This ability to produce a prototype is essential in a major project that will be created by a team of writers, illustrators, graphic designers, sound composers, and programmers. It's important to convey the general direction to these people early. Written descriptions on paper are inadequate for conveying the look, feel, and structure of a multimedia presentation to a variety of people with these different backgrounds and responsibilities.

Because it's easy to use, HyperCard can be used to model an initial idea for a multimedia presentation. The designer can sketch or scan placeholder graphics, play digitized sample sounds, simulate interactions, and write both the on-screen text and descriptions of more detailed directions and intentions. From such a model, members of the team can get an idea of where graphics will occur, what text will be present on the screen, what animation is desired, and the sequence or structure of the user interaction. In team meetings with projection displays, concepts and corrections can be made directly to the prototype.

as soon as possible in a form that's easily understandable. The designer needs feedback on whether the concept meets the requirements of the intended audience, has the right content, is possible to produce technically, and has an appropriate, understandable structure and method of interaction.

In the past, a *treatment* was used to get this initial feedback. A treatment is usually a short, written description that communicates the look and feel of the presentation to management, marketing groups, and team members. This can include descriptions of images, sounds, text, and user interactions. But the complete concept is in

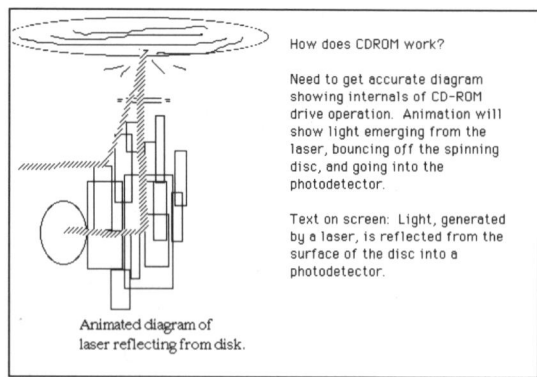

Figure 4-2. An initial sketch of a CD-ROM drive in operation

Figure 4-2 shows a multimedia designer's initial sketch, in HyperCard, of a CD-ROM drive's operation. The designer quickly sketches ideas for a graphic and describes its purpose and possibilities.

PROTOTYPING TOOLS (DEVELOPMENT)

A multimedia presentation evolves from the designer's initial prototype. HyperCard allows the same stack to be revised and expanded as the presentation is developed. During the development phase, team members can use HyperCard to explore alternative layouts, images, navigation, interactions, or sounds for the presentation. The alternatives can be mocked up exactly at the point where they would occur in the presentation, so separate productions are not required to show each alternative.

The HyperCard prototype is an interactive electronic storyboard that communicates the "feel" of the user interaction and navigation techniques. HyperCard also provides storyboarding in printed form. A storyboard can be used to communicate the status of the production and to bring new team members quickly up to speed. HyperCard's ability to print screens in various sizes lets team members compare the progress of frame development at a single glance or to review the overall structure of a presentation by physically arranging the frames to show sequences and branches.

The HyperCard prototype also permits user testing at various points in the development stage. As an evolving production, the prototype is ready to be reviewed by content experts, other designers, and samples of the target audience. New ideas can be tested as soon as they're added, and improvements can be implemented easily and quickly.

Figure 4-3 shows a later version of the CD-ROM operation illustrated earlier. In this version, a graphic that more closely resembles the final version has been hand-drawn and scanned. A "Show Me" button has been added to let the reviewer see animation effects.

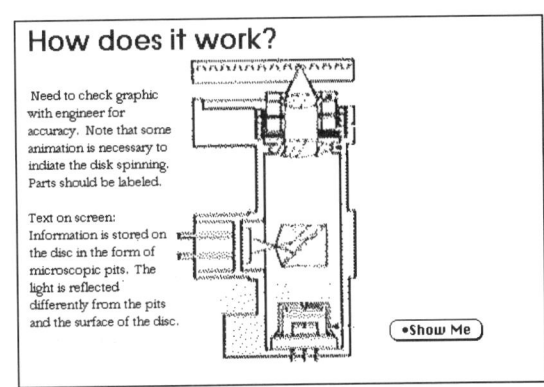

Figure 4-3. A modified version of the CD-ROM drive sketch

REVISION TOOLS (PRODUCTION)

HyperCard makes it easy to implement revisions during the final production phase. As a production evolves, continual adjustments must be made to the words appearing on screen, to the size and layout of graphics, to the timing of animations, to user interactions, and to sound placement. Often, these last-minute adjustments, which can be made only after all elements are in place, ensure the quality of a presentation. Without a tool like HyperCard, revisions often cannot be made because of the difficulty of changing graphics and text or of reprogramming sounds and interactions.

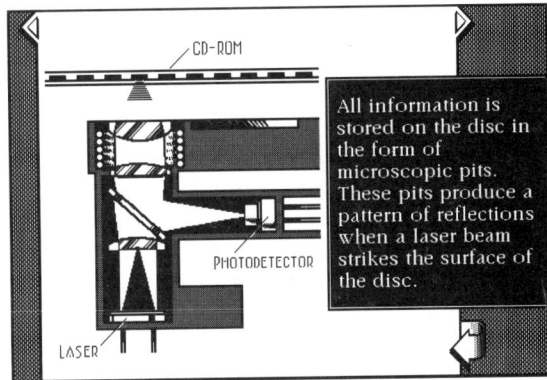

Figure 4-4. The final version of the CD-ROM drive sketch

Figure 4-4 shows the final version of the frame demonstrating the operation of the CD-ROM drive. This is one frame in an animated sequence showing the path of the light beam as it is produced by the laser, reflected off the spinning disc, and then received by the photo-detector.

TOOLS AFFECT THE PROCESS

Multimedia is the coordination of various design elements to produce a single effect. The process of creating multimedia presentations is one of collaboration among a team of people with different skills and talents. Various tools are now available to support the different team members and their specific production requirements. What is required to make the process more efficient is a single tool that supports all facets of the multimedia development process, including communication among team members.

HyperCard is one such multimedia development tool. As the field of multimedia presentation grows, both the tools and the processes in which they're used will become more efficient and effective. Tools that are both powerful and simple to use will make the multimedia development process streamlined, creative, and robust.

Buckminster Fuller, in his book *Education Automation,* foresaw the day when the ideas of the world's greatest minds would be captured and enhanced on an ongoing basis with images, sound, and interactivity. This evolutionary and revisionary process is the great advantage of computer-based multimedia presentations over traditional multimedia technologies and is possible only if easily used tools exist to support it.

[Joe Williams is a Senior Instructional Designer at Apple Computer, Inc., and is currently working on multimedia presentations. Prior to working at Apple Computer, he worked with the University of Alabama in Birmingham, Chevron, Inc., and Bank of America designing instructional materials on the use of computers.]

Scripting for Interactive Multimedia CD Systems

By Mark Dillon

[Drawing on his background as a film director, Mark Dillon discusses the parallels and differences between creating movies and creating multimedia products. He suggests that the interactive designer will become the movie director of the twenty first century. Picking up on this theme, we include an excerpt from a book by Ted Nelson, who insists that interactive designers should first determine the effect they want to produce in their audience and then look for ways to produce that effect.]

Because the technical aspects of CD-based technologies (such as CD-I and CD-ROM XA) are still a challenge, creative issues are not attracting the attention or concern they deserve. As encoding, authoring, and emulation become routine and economical, this imbalance will be corrected. Just as a computer "paintbox" cannot make you an artist, an "authoring system" cannot make you an interactive designer—it will only allow you to become one.

CD-I (and any other interactive, multimedia mass memory technologies) requires more intimacy between the audiovisual arts and software design than has occurred in the past. Software has frequently come to the service of the arts. Computerized lighting effects, computer-generated graphics, and the MIDI interface, for example, have propagated new modes of expression from very old forms (theater, graphics, and music). Graphics have come to the service

MARK DILLON

Home: Fresno, California
Job: Executive Vice President, American Interactive Media
Quote: *"CD-I is moving information into the home and audio visuals into the office."*

Even the fundamental word *script*—as verb or as noun—does not comfortably describe the design document for an interactive multimedia CD program. Producers in the audiovisual or video media think in terms of screenplays, while computer programmers are more likely to conjure up images of flowcharts and data files. (As a film director, for example, I find it difficult to see images as "data." Those in my profession call them "presentation assets.") As a result, the miscommunication between those responsible for the multimedia aspect and those responsible for the interactivity can be tremendous.

Thus, from a filmmaker's point of view, a script is a familiar, well-established, convention. Marbling the words to be spoken are sparse annotations that provide clues to the director indicating location, time of day, and perhaps the mood of the speaker. From these meager instructions, a film of $1,000,000 to $50,000,000 or more can be made. Studio executives "see" the picture. A producer creates a budget. A director begins scouting locations, casting, designing sets, and planning the special effects and the thousands of additional elements that make a movie.

Not only is film a linear medium to watch, it is a linear medium to create. With some reasonable slippage and overlap, a film is written, prepared, shot, and edited. At each step different individuals contribute their creative skills. The writer controls the script while it's in the word processor. The director controls the script while the film is in the camera. The editor, by and large, controls the film when it leaves the camera. And by this time the script is history. The production is now a film, not a script. The producer? The producer hires (and fires) everyone else and then gets out of their way....

In this process, a film script starts skimpy and grows. At each phase, artists add their creative energies, bringing the script to life. A movie combines the ideas of different people as the project is handed over to them, each in their time. A telling sign of the teamwork and collaboration is the comfort each of the craft guilds

of computers: PARC-based interfaces, CAD-CAM, and some computer games all rely on graphics to perform old tasks in a better way. But all in all, software has not yet been considered an art form.

Interactive multimedia programs, however, mesh audiovisual data with software design so completely that these components can and should be indistinguishable. Here, creativity is defined as the way data, design, and programming are fused into a single product. The creator of this new art form is the interactive designer. Unlike the painter or programmer, working alone in his garret or garage, the interactive designer is the creative focus of a talented team—more like a film director of the twenty-first century.

Unfortunately, this potentially idyllic marriage of technology and art is hampered by some very practical problems. Just how do groups of programmers, artists, cameramen, and actors work together on a day-to-day basis to produce such a product? The traditions of film production and software design provide imperfect models.

takes in thinking that it is really the driving force behind a good movie.

So why can't a puny little $250,000 CD-I title be produced from such a script? Because an interactive production is not produced with the same linearity as a film. Because it requires a design specification that contains creative decisions made up front, instead of during the actual shooting or in post-production. This difference in focus dramatically relocates the seat of creative power in an interactive multimedia CD production. The name above the title is now that of the interactive designer.

Actual production of audio, video, and graphics occurs in parallel. Nobody, by that time, has the overview available in film and consequently nobody is in a position to take the creative control customary in filmmaking. This greatly changes the timing of input by photographers, graphic artists, and writers. Creative participation must occur up front, during the design specification process, not during implementation.

Then, too, a film editor is the person who assembles the final sequence of all audio and video elements. This is the last person who can fix mistakes that occurred in all the preceding production phases. But there is no editor in an interactive production. The person who assembles the final sequence of all audio and video elements is the viewer who can't fix anything. The closest thing to an editor in an interactive production is the programmer who, while implementing the design specification, must recognize problems and work with the designer to correct them. In any case, these efforts are derived from the design document.

An interactive design specification is developed by a team of art directors, writers, producers, and subject-matter experts. It is not a skimpy document. It is large, detailed, and difficult to change, and this is where creators of interactive productions often begin having trouble—particularly the programmer.

Good programmers often work best by themselves rather than as part of a team. Many I know listen to what you want, go away, and come back some time later, ready to show you *their* version of what you said you wanted. But by the time code is being generated in an interactive production, tens of thousands to hundreds of thousands of dollars have been spent on presentation assets. This is no time for a programmer to decide to redesign the program, change functions, or add them. To do so will waste dollars already spent and possibly require that more be spent. A programmer creates a control script that will manipulate pictures, sound, and text. For productive (and economical) results, these images, graphics, and sounds must be described and labeled in the design specification before it reaches the programmer.

We have identified three steps in the design specification process that permit the creative process to cause presentation assets to be specified, produced, and then made available to the programmers so that they know what to do with them and how to find them. (Finding is not a trivial matter. Presentation assets may total 2 to 5 gigabytes of storage.) The steps are: *Treatment, Node Map,* and *Screen Breakdown.*

STEP 1: TREATMENT

The treatment is the least specific of the steps. It is a sophisticated (often electronic and machine-readable) napkin sketch. It must describe the interactive paradigm of the production—that is, provide the overall look and feel of the program. The treatment must identify the various parts of a program and, particularly their relationships to each other. The treatment deals with the metaphor and interrelationships of a production.

STEP 2: THE NODE MAP AND DESCRIPTIONS

A node is a timed sequence of one or more informationally related screens, with one discrete entry point and one or more exit points. It's a basic chunk of interactivity. The node map is a graphic representation—looking much like a flowchart—of all the nodes in a production and their interconnectivity.

Node descriptions are coupled to the map. Node descriptions contain a rough storyboard frame that suggests the graphic content of a node and include text descriptions of the activities that go on within the node.

HyperCard and FileMaker are two excellent programs for creating node descriptions because they allow the designer to branch between nodes in a computer instead of flip between pages in a book.

STEP 3: SCREEN BREAKDOWNS

Screen breakdowns take higher-level nodes and detail them down to every image—its audio, graphical, and logical components. From this detailed breakdown work orders for presentation assets can be created, database structures for their eventual storage can be designed, and the programmer can begin implementing the control code that anticipates the presentation assets.

INTERACTIVE SYSTEMS AND THE DESIGN OF VIRTUALITY

Our approach to a computer design we call "the design of virtuality." By virtuality we mean the *seeming* of an object or system, its conceptual structure, its atmospherics and its feel.

Every object has a virtuality, a seeming. Natural objects are more or less what they seem to be; man-made objects are not. The virtuality of a house, or an automobile, is what the designer made it—the structure and qualities that were chosen, and the techniques by which they were realized.

The closest analogy to the design of interactive computer systems, I think, is the making of movies. What counts is *effects,* not techniques. We are not concerned with just *how* a certain effect is to be achieved, so much as with what effect is wanted.

An effect is something intended to take place in the mind. Suppose the movie effect desired is *a sense of a monster approaching.* This can be done by showing a man in a lizard suit—yaargh—or animated puppets, or by showing the fright of a person who sees the monster. In other words, a variety of techniques may be selected toward a common effect.

The design of an interactive computer environment, similarly, should not be based on particular hardware, or a particular display device, or a programming technique. It should be based on the intended effect *in the mind and heart of the viewer.* ("Heart" here is added because we are too seldom mindful of the emotional component in a user's reaction.)

Another way of saying this is that the "systems analysis" for an interactive system should deal with the mental space of the user's experience.

The process is a cycle: study, and design. First we must study the approximate structure of whatever we are designing, and *roughly* what it is about. Then we design, that is, look to see how the computer's capacities may be made to assume a similar conceptual shape....

There is one other key constraint in system design: conceptual simplicity. If any but highly-trained people are to use a system, it must be extremely simple. It must be simpler by far than anything computer people are accustomed to designing—a factor of ten, let us say, simpler than what a computer hacker considers "simple."

Popular lore in the computer field holds that simple systems are not "powerful"—where powerful seems to mean "allowing concise macro-language programming." (This is evidently the view of those who consider TECO a powerful text editor, or, indeed, a text editor.) We believe that true power, meaning easy and focussed control by the user on what he means to do, is not merely compatible with simplicity, it requires it.

By Theodor H. Nelson. Excerpted from *Replacing the Printed Word: A Complete Literacy System,* **by special permission.**

LEADING THE TEAM

Enforcing these three steps is very difficult. There is a tendency for team members to want to get going and not wait for the design specification to be completed before presentation assets are made or code is written. It can be very frustrating to do all this talking and planning before actually getting into production. For programmers, writers, or artists, these new relationships within an interactive design team can be misunderstood and resented.

It is the clear vision and strong voice of the interactive designer that makes the difference between a team and a committee. It is the designer's challenge to communicate a vision of the product to the other artists on the team who provide the creativity and insight that must go into the design specification if the production is to work.

[Mark Dillon is Senior Vice President of Production at American Interactive Media (AIM). Prior to joining AIM, he served as Vice President at Interac Corporation, a high-end interactive videodisc systems company which he helped found in 1983.]

HYPERTEXT PERSPECTIVES

THE CHALLENGE OF HYPERTEXT
By Steven Jong

A HYPERTEXT INTERFACE TO CD-ROM
By Jim Culbertson

HYPERTEXT PROBLEMS
By Jef Raskin

The Challenge of Hypertext

By Steven Jong
From *Proceedings: 35th International Technical Communications Conference*

[Hypertext is not a new concept. For many years, it sat in the wings, waiting for an appropriate technology to be developed. Now, as Steven Jong explains, it is causing writers and editors to rethink their crafts. This general discussion of hypertext was written with its implications for software documentation in mind. Nevertheless, the article gives the reader unfamiliar with hypertext an overview of the concept and a feel for its potential in the CD-ROM environment.]

WHAT IS HYPERTEXT

Hypertext is a means of connecting information in a non-linear manner, with a computer automating the process of moving from one piece of information to another. This is an accurate, if somewhat dry, definition. But the reality of hypertext is difficult to describe on paper. It is as if the traditional conventions of signaling departures from the main line of text—the parenthetical reference, the note, the footnote, the commentary, the cross-reference, the sidebar, the table of contents, the index, the glossary—were suddenly to become active, direct portals into related information that the reader can choose either to enter or bypass.

Hypertext provides an entirely new set of tools for technical communication:

- Links from any piece of information to any other.
- Searching functions that shift the burden of finding information from the reader to the machine.
- "Browsing" functions to scan through information rapidly.
- Full bit-mapped graphics, including animation.
- Digitized sounds, including voices.

It promises, or perhaps threatens, to transform the way in which information is stored, retrieved, and used.

HISTORY OF HYPERTEXT

Vannevar Bush, science advisor to President Roosevelt, conceived in 1945 a "memex" machine that stored and linked vast amounts of data [1]. Memex users could enter, search, and examine data, establishing links and recording "associative trails" that they could later follow or give to others to follow. He pointed out that information by itself is not valuable unless it is accessible: value is created by pathfinders through the information. For example, the *Encyclopaedia Brittannica* has separate guides that suggest particularly fruitful paths to take through the volumes. Closer to home, it is common for third-party authors to write books telling computer users how to read through product documentation.

As chronicled by Conklin [2], Bush's seminal idea was expanded upon by Douglas Englebart in the 1960s at the Stanford Research Institute, which implemented the NLS/Augment system. Ted Nelson is credited with coining the term *hypertext,* and during the 1970s designed the Xanadu system at MIT. Along with Bush, Englebart and Nelson are considered the fathers of hypertext.

PRODUCT SURVEY

After this period of experimental gestation, several commercial products have been born. Four are described here.

The Symbolics Document Examiner [2] provides online access to the entire Symbolics computer manual set. Readers can set "bookmarks" on topics and return to them later. Readers can also use a keyword search feature.

The Tektronix NEPTUNE system [3] allows multiple browsing methods—using a graphical tree, using successive lists, or using keywords.

OWL International's Guide for Apple Macintosh and IBM PC computers [7] provides "straight" hypertext, with some graphics support. Future versions of Guide are planned to operate under the DOS, OS/2, and UNIX operating systems, and on the Atari, Amiga, and Apple IIGS computers [4].

Most exciting of all is Apple's HyperCard for the Macintosh computer. HyperCard implements the vision of hypertext, then extends it to include not only "hypermedia," the combination of text, graphics, and sound [2], but "hyperfunctions," the addition of programs that can be executed from hypertext.

The conceptual model of HyperCard is the common index card, representing one record in a database. Each HyperCard card serves as a viewport into a database, called a *stack. Buttons* link one card to another, and allow you to go to the next, previous, and home cards as well. Buttons also let you jump to another stack, or run a program. The overall effect is like sticking index cards or notes all around your work area: everything is equally accessible.

HyperCard is a highly interactive, highly visual environment. It freely mixes text and graphics. It permits sophisticated, television-inspired "wipes" from one card to another. The response time when moving from card to card, or searching for a particular card, is excellent. Information organized for cards is of necessity broken into convenient chunks that are easy to absorb.

CHALLENGES FOR TECHNICAL COMMUNICATORS

If hypertext technology catches on, it may force both writers and readers decisively into the paperless age, not only in the computer field, but almost everywhere. Why? Hypertext offers readers the best hope of conquering huge manual sets: they can at last get to the information they need. Hypertext means the end of "quick-reference" information that we now assemble in cards or booklets: hypertext is at once more accessible, more concise, and more complete. Hypertext negates all our attempts at progressive-disclosure writing: the order in which information is presented is now entirely in the hands of the reader. Hypertext ends our struggle to produce audience-specific documentation: readers can build personalized documentation for themselves. Clearly, our challenge will be to adapt to this new environment.

Fortunately, the transition to hypertext is not accomplished just by putting text online and turning on the software. No matter how they are read, information databases must be designed for effective presentation. And as Bush pointed out forty years ago, someone must forge the links between information. These tasks require skill, understanding, and creativity. This is where we must concentrate our efforts.

We should embrace hypertext, and use it to its full advantage. The following discussion examines some traditional documentation problem areas and suggests hypertext analogues. In each case, the hypertext version is more effective than anything we can do with ink and paper.

Hyperwriting

With hypertext, we can write at full efficiency, by documenting a piece of information only one time and thereafter linking to it whenever and wherever it is needed. Eliminating duplicate information reduces our workload, and makes updates easier and less prone to error. Yet thoughtful cross-referencing will still ensure readers full access to the information.

Converting traditional encyclopedic reference material into hypertext will be a trivial operation. Put one procedure, call, statement, or command on each card, with links to the subtopics "summary," "syntax," "arguments," "description," "examples," and "related information." Readers can summon up details on whatever topic they like. Links to examples can be "live"; that is, jumping to an example can cause a demonstration program to run, illustrating both the form and the effect of the code. Cross-references to related information can actually take the reader to the related information. Summary tables can be linked to fuller descriptions of each table item.

REFERENCES

[1] Bush, Vannevar. "As We May Think." *Atlantic Monthly*, 176, July 1945, pages 101–108.

[2] Conklin, Jeff. "Hypertext: An Introduction and Survey." *Computer*, 20:9, September 1987, pages 17–41.

[3] Delisle, Norman, and Schwartz, Mayer. "NEPTUNE: A Hypertext System for CAD Applications." *Proceedings of the ACM International Conference on Management of Data — SIGMOD '86*, 1986, pages 132–143.

[4] DeMaria, Russel. "Hypertext-Based Guide Helps Users with Interactive Program Development." *PC Week*, 4:50, July 28, 1987, pages 61–70.

[5] Jong, Steven. "Issues in Online Documentation." *Proceedings of the 29th ITCC*, 1982, pages T-36–T-39.

[6] Kay, Alan, and Goldberg, Adele. "Personal Dynamic Media," *Computer*, 10:3, March 1977, pages 31–41.

[7] OWL International, Inc., *Guide*, 1986.

Perhaps more challenging will be task based material. Consider a configuration task that consists, at a high level, of four steps:

1. Logging in.

2. Starting a configuration program.

3. Responding to configuration program prompts.

4. Performing a verification procedure.

If all goes well, the process can be simple. But what if the user doesn't know how to log in, should an explanation be included? How much should prompts be explained, and how thoroughly (and how often) should valid responses be specified? What if the responses depend on the hardware or software environment; should there be a series of "IF-THEN" clauses (which are known to be highly confusing)? What if verification fails? Documenting such contingencies turns what ought to be a simple task into a complex-looking one.

With hypertext, procedures can be at once simple and fully realized, because all side paths are documented using links. The straight path is unencumbered by detours, yet the ancillary information is instantly available. Readers who don't know how to log in can jump to the actual discussion of login. All prompts can be explained in complete detail. Trails can be established for every possible hardware platform, and the reader can select the one that is appropriate. Possible errors can be dealt with only if they arise. All levels of readers will be well satisfied.

Progressing one step further, we can in fact merge introductory, tutorial, reference, and task-based documentation into one entity. These are nothing more than different approaches to communicating the same set of information. By breaking information down into the right chunks, we can assemble hypertext trails that can introduce, teach, inform, or lead a reader, all at the reader's own discretion.

Hyperillustrating

Apple Computer's HyperCard, by extending the concept of hypertext to embrace graphics, gives us techniques that transform illustrations just as

HYPERTEXT AND HYPERSPACE

In promoting the development of CD-ROM and related optical technologies, software and hardware designers can sometimes lose sight of the most important issue surrounding this new tool: Of what value is all the world's information on disc if you cannot readily access it?

Knowledge is information with structure. Hypertext lets you create that structure by making associative links between small, concentrated frames of data in the same way your mind makes links between the information it processes and remembers. You determine the amount and type of information you gather about a topic by traveling from one unit to another, in any order you choose. Do you need more detail? Jump to a lower level. Less detail? Return to a higher level. The ideal system maintains a trail of the jumps you make, so you can return to your point of origin at any time.

Building a concise framework for the collection of great quantities of information can be difficult, however. Browsing through a hypertext document, you can easily be distracted by equally interesting but unrelated or nonspecific topics. Before you know it, you may find yourself lost, disoriented, balancing on the edge of hyperspace, a black hole in the middle of who knows where. If the system you're using isn't well defined, you may never find your way back to your original set of links.

How do you avoid hyperspace? If your hypertext system has no "road map," the following strategies may help you keep your bearings:

- *Notting*: As you jump from topic to topic, develop a talent for identifying information you will *not* use. Scan titles and topic sentences quickly, "notting" out the text that is of no value. Use judgment and common sense in selecting the level of detail to pursue and ignore any extraneous details.

- *Linking*: Before you jump to a different item of information, ask yourself whether the link you are about to establish is the most logical. Is there a connection between this frame and the one you plan on jumping to? Concentrate on the order in which you access frames as well as their content, and you'll find it easier to retrace your steps to the highest level of the knowledge.

- *Framing*: Frame new information you've obtained by reviewing it in the context of what you already know. Searching with a specific frame of reference is less likely to lead you astray than searching the unknown.

By Julie Sickert, a freelance muse living in Torrance, California.

radically as text. For example, software illustrations, which are often dull, can become useful and even exciting learning aids:

- "Live" procedural maps can jump readers to actual procedures.
- Comments on program listings can "pop up" on command.
- Flowcharts can be cross-linked to fragments of the actual code.

Hardware illustrations, too, can be supercharged:

- Callouts can "pop up" on command.
- Procedural drawings can be animated, step by step.
- "Exploded-view" diagrams can actually explode.
- "Rotated" perspective drawings can actually rotate, in steps.

Hyperediting

No matter what the media or presentation, technical information needs technical editing. Inconsistencies will be much more apparent when readers can jump from module to module instantly. As with paper documentation, ensuring consistency of presentation between hypertext modules, even those written by different people at different times for different databases, will be a major task.

Another editing task updated for hypertext will be ensuring adequate and reasonable linkage between pieces of information.

Other hyperactivities

Hypertext can trigger a revolution in computer-based training. Hypertext technology makes it practical to design courseware that conforms with precision to the needs of many different students. Each student can select an appropriate level of detail, and follow a different trail through the same database. HyperCard, especially makes it simple to design courseware that branches whenever a student answers a question. Its visual tools are also far superior to those of current course-building software.

Oh, yes. When the work day is done, hypertext makes it easy for us to produce intricate, interactive adventure/fantasy games for the amusement of our colleagues!

A FEW PITFALLS

The excitement over hypertext doesn't mask some few shortcomings in existing products, and some few weaknesses in hypertext in general.

Bush's original conception made it simple to enter new information in bulk. Existing hypertext products, particularly HyperCard, make it difficult to enter existing data files.

Reader annotations are a crucial element of hypertext. Readers should be able to add notes to hypertext as if they were writing in the margins of a book. In current hypertext products, this function is difficult, if not impossible.

Given the nature of hypertext, the more powerful the searching functions, the better. But searching for unlinked text in a hypertext database is no more efficient than brute-force searching in large text files. Single- and multikey searches will be a powerful enhancement of hypertext. As yet there is also no way to search for images and portions of images unless they are pre-indexed.

It is easy for readers to get "lost in hyperspace" [2] if they lose track of what trail they are following. Hypertext requires some means of orienting readers. Kay and Goldberg [6] have suggested that this can best be done visually, using graphical maps.

Hypertext lives on the computer screen, and does not translate well to paper. When a trail of modules is printed, it becomes flat, like a flower preserved under glass. Unless access to computers increases dramatically, hypertext will remain something of an elitist tool.

Finally, all of the problems forecast for online documentation [5] are possible with hypertext. They include:

- Problems inherent in reading from a computer screen.
- The potentially huge space on disk occupied by hypertext.
- Contention over ownership of the hypertext "code."
- Resource disputes over who creates the programmatic tools.
- The need for verification.

Reprinted by permission of the Society for Technical Communications. From the proceedings of the 35th International Technical Communications Conference (ITCC). Copyright © 1988.

A Hypertext Interface to CD-ROM

By Jim Culbertson

[From a general discussion of hypertext, we move to an article that focusses on the implementation of hypertext in the CD-ROM environment. Jim Culbertson uses Guide to illustrate how hypertext takes advantage of the capabilities of the computer to avoid the constraints of paper-based documents.]

CD-ROM technology provides a new and economical way to distribute and locally store large quantities of relatively static information. In terms of information storage, CD-ROM is a medium that competes with paper. CD-ROM provides the advantage of increased density of stored information, while paper provides the more familiar material. As a medium, CD-ROM will be successful in replacing paper to the extent that it offers advantages that outweigh any learning effort required by the user in mastering a new way of finding information.

THE NEED FOR A NEW INTERFACE

To date, most applications have attempted to promote CD-ROM by removing the need to learn how to use a new interface. This has been accomplished by imposing the more familiar structure of paper-based materials on the new medium. Whether this is a conscious strategy or a response to years of training and "education," is not clear. After all, our entire educational system is geared to communication via paper. We

JIM CULBERTSON

Home: Seattle, Washington
Job: Director of Product Marketing, OWL International
Quote: *"Hypertext provides a new way to structure and access large free-form documents, removing the last major obstacle to the rapid growth of CD-ROM technology."*

are trained to think in terms of the constraints of this paper medium and to overcome these constraints in structured and predictable ways. We learn a set of rules—an interface—that governs the creation and use of information in such a way that the creator of the information can overcome the limitations of the paper medium in ways understandable to the reader. For example, we use tables of contents and indexes to help the reader find desired information. We use abstracts or executive summaries to provide an overview for the reader who wants a quick synopsis, and we use footnotes and bibliographies to aid those who seek more information than we have presented.

Unfortunately, the result of imposing this familiar interface on CD-ROM is that the new medium is constrained largely in the same way as the paper it attempts to replace. While the interface problem is reduced, the benefits of the new medium are not allowed to surface.

The biggest challenge facing CD-ROM today is finding a new interface that is both simple to use and better suited to the capabilities of the medium. CD-ROM has capabilities entirely different from those of paper and demands an interface more suited to its own strengths and weaknesses. While this difference means that we must rethink the interface and requires somewhat more effort on the part of both the creators and users of information, it also gives CD-ROM the opportunity to provide benefits that paper cannot and, therefore, opens up the opportunity to succeed in areas, which up to now, were inaccessible.

One of the differences between paper and CD-ROM with a computer interface is that the computer can make a document multidimensional and interactive. A computer system permits close interaction between reader and document, allowing individual readers to adapt the appearance of a document to their own needs. If the computer is exploited to give people a better way to read documents, there is a good chance that they will come to prefer screen-based documents to paper-based ones.

HYPERTEXT

Hypertext systems, particularly in combination with a windowing environment, can provide an interface that is both simple to use and well suited to the advantages of CD-ROM. Hypertext does not work under the same constraints that have bound paper-based documents. Hypertext documents need not be read linearly beginning with the first word and following through to the last word. They do not force all readers to read the same level of information, nor do they require great effort if a reader wants to explore an additional level of detail or related background material. Hypertext documents need not be limited to text and fixed images, but can include sound and moving images as well. Further, hypertext documents can be interactive. The level of detail presented by a document can change in response to input from the reader—something not remotely considered in paper-based systems. In short, hypertext was designed with the abilities of the computer, rather than the constraints of paper, in mind. As such, it facilitates the generation and review of documents that take advantage of the computer interface and the unique benefits of CD-ROM.

Simplicity is the key

But providing all these benefits is only half the equation. The balance of the interface equation demands that the solution be simple; learning to create or read hypertext CD-ROM documents must not require a large investment of time and effort. The well-implemented hypertext system will ease the creation and use of these documents. As Dr. Peter Brown, professor of computer science and author of numerous books and articles on human/computer interfaces, once said, "Ideally, the system should be as simple to use as a television set."

The ideal hypertext system should make extensive use of a windowing environment to keep the interface as graphical and as simple as possible. A pointing device, such as a mouse, or a touch-sensitive screen would facilitate interaction with the document and provide an easy way to trigger such events as requesting an additional level of detail, gaining access to a referenced document, or viewing a video image. The system should support a range of type styles and sizes, as well as high-resolution graphics to provide the ability to create visually attractive and interesting documents. The ability within a windowing environment to display multiple documents at one time and to connect different documents or parts of the same document easily also add to the diversity and appeal of hypertext CD-ROM documents.

Guide

One such hypertext product available today is Guide, from OWL International. This product was designed for computer-based documents and makes extensive use of a graphical interface. The mouse is used to customize the document to the level desired by the reader. All that the reader need do to identify the areas in

> *If the computer is exploited to give people a better way to read documents, there is a good chance that they will come to prefer screen-based documents to paper-based ones.*

which he or she would like more detail is position the mouse pointer on the appropriate button and click.

Figure 4-5 is a screen with an open hypertext document. Note that it contains both text and images; some of the text has been emphasized with bold type styles. Except for the window bars and header, this could easily be a paper document. To one reader, this level of information may be sufficient and he or she will continue on in the document, scrolling down with the scroll bar. For another reader, however, there is much more to be learned. Suppose the user is interested in more information about the "Forebrain." The reader need only locate the mouse pointer on that word and click (see Figure 4-6).

Another level of information is presented to the user (see Figure 4-7); the document has been instantly modified to suit the needs of the reader. Note that the new text contains a reference to a supporting article. The interested reader can access the referenced document, again by pointing and clicking.

The referenced article is opened in another window and the relevant material is presented. Still curious, the reader can continue to probe to

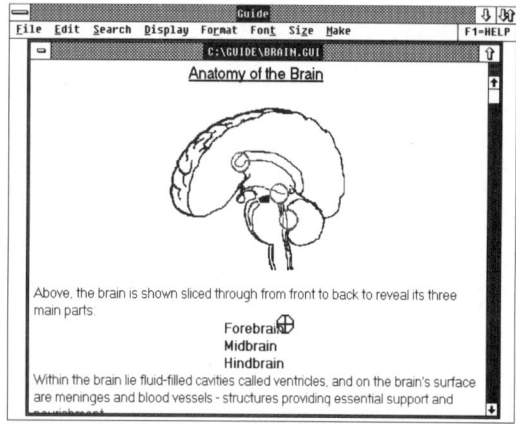

Figure 4-5. An open hypertext document

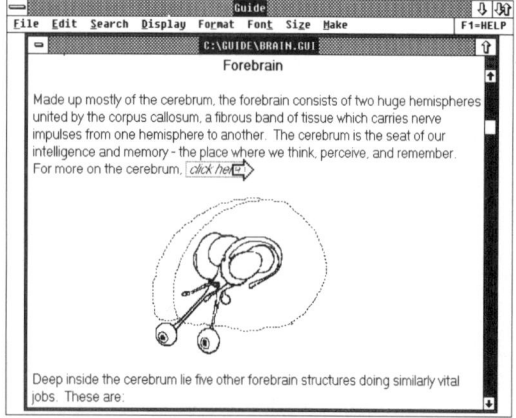

Figure 4-6. The expanded document

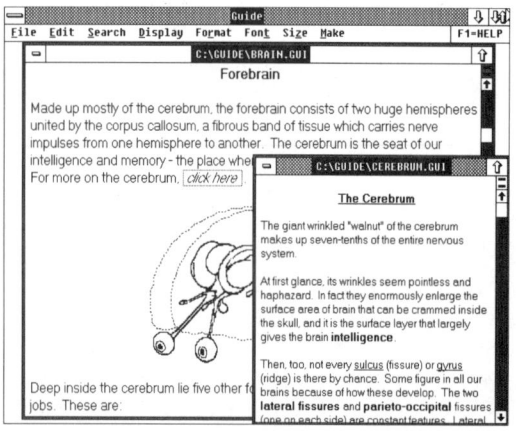

Figure 4-7. The next level

deeper levels and explore other related information. When sufficient knowledge has been acquired, returning to the original spot in the document is as easy as closing the newly opened windows or clicking on the backtrack icon. Most impressive is that the process doesn't get any harder. Bringing up a moving video image with full audio is no more difficult than opening a reference document—it's just a matter of pointing and clicking.

EASE OF AUTHORING

Some will be concerned that authoring such a document would be difficult and time-consuming. It isn't. Text that already exists can be imported as an ASCII file, graphic elements can be cut and pasted. And links, whether they are to other documents, to other applications, or to the next level of information in the same document, can be made simply by selecting options from the pull-down menus. It's as easy as pointing and clicking.

With an easy-to-use interface, the pieces of the puzzle come together to reveal a new kind of document and a new way to communicate. The combination of a windowing environment, a well-implemented hypertext document, and CD-ROM technology have much to offer both the creator and the user of information.

While learning to use a new interface can never be eliminated, it can be intuitive and painless. And the benefit of hypertext is enormous because the interface redefines the way information is communicated.

[After obtaining a BA at Princeton University and an MBA at UC Berkeley, Jim Culbertson worked in marketing at Intel and Microrim before joining OWL International as Director of Product Marketing.]

Hypertext Problems

By Jef Raskin

[Is hypertext the panacea predicted by visionary Ted Nelson almost two decades ago? Not necessarily, cautions Jef Raskin in the concluding article of this section. Here, he waves a flag of caution for hypertext developers, pointing out some fundamental problems and offering a few solutions.]

The literature in hypertext is generally effusive and non-critical. Even Conklin's survey article in *IEEE Computer,* September 1987, concludes gushingly with his hopes that "the reader comes away from this excited, eager to try using hypertext for himself, and aware that he is at the beginning of something big, something like the invention of the wheel, but something that still has enough rough edges that no one is really sure that it will fulfill its promise." However, some of those rough edges are surface manifestations of deep cracks that extend into the heart of any sizable hypertext project.

Working with a hypertext system can be like playing computerized adventure games. The games ostensibly avoid requiring that you learn special commands by allowing you to frame your desires in English. This sounds very inviting, but whenever your response varies from the stylized vocabulary and grammar that the game recognizes, you run into a wall of incomprehension. The game spins off a subgame of guessing which words the developer thought useful or significant. Synonyms in English may or may not be synonyms to the game; you often find that though what you said is correct, it doesn't work. To enjoy the games, you must come to accept that figuring just how to emasculate your vocabulary and grammar is part of the game.

What is really happening in these games is that the players are learning a set of computer commands by trial and error. In an adventure-style sword battle your knowledge of fencing is of no use, but your knowledge of the system developers' frame of mind is.

HYPERTEXT

In a hypertext system you might be reading about monarch butterflies gathering in Monterey,

JEF RASKIN

Home: Pacifica, California
Job: Entrepreneur
Quote: *"It's not the medium, but what you do with it."*

California. The dream of hypertext goes like this: you point to the word "monarch," and a picture of the butterfly comes onto your screen. You touch one of the legs of the butterfly and up comes the details of the leg. You then activate the "go back to where I was" button and continue reading. Upon pointing to the word "California," the delve deeper button might give you a map of California with Monterey called out, and so forth. Your display might be linked to data sources, reference librarians, zillions of megabytes of data, all available in microseconds.

It sounds wonderful. But is it?

HYPERPROBLEM 1: IS WHAT YOU WANT THERE?

Take the passage where the text mentioned a gathering of monarch butterflies. Say you point to "monarch" and you find yourself in the midst of a discussion of the divine rights of hereditary rulers. You go "up" and try "butterfly" but get a general description of the lepidoptera. Maybe what you want is there, and maybe it isn't. Maybe it's referenced in the way you are thinking about it, maybe it isn't. In a big system, instead of information at your fingertips, you get a fishing expedition.

HYPERPROBLEM 2: WHAT ARE YOU POINTING AT?

Say you point to the tip of a leg of a picture of the butterfly. Seems simple. But it is not clear if you are pointing to the tersus, the whole leg, to legs in general, to butterfly legs, or to the whole insect. If the portion the machine "thinks" you are pointing to is highlighted in an attempt to avoid the ambiguity, then you will be left trying to find the right place to point to get exactly what you want, as happens often with today's computerized drafting systems. The problems don't end there: if you want to learn about symmetry, you might highlight the whole insect since butterflies are beautifully symmetrical, and yet the system cannot divine what you want further information about.

HYPERPROBLEM 3: WHICH ITEMS HAVE FURTHER INFORMATION?

Not every item or detail in a picture will have a reference attached to it. How will you tell which do and which don't? I tried a medical hypertext system where you could point to a structure in a dissection and get further views. It seemed fine when demonstrated by the designer who knew which body parts had further data behind them, but when I tried to use it and pointed to structures that I was curious about, most of the time the system could give me no information and did nothing.

WHERE TO GO FROM HERE

Users and designers of hypertext systems must remain sensitive to the problems outlined here. The three hyperproblems are as yet unsolved in general, although specific implementations have gotten around them by various techniques, primarily by limiting the number and scope of possible queries.

Like adventure games, badly designed hypertext forces you to second guess the link builder rather than paying attention to the subject at hand. Knowledge of the system will often be more valuable than understanding your field. As the students of a poor teacher learn to give not the right answers but those the teacher wants, users of hypertext systems designed without attention to the details outlined here will spend much of their time pleasing the system instead of themselves.

[Jef Raskin is C.E.O. at Information Appliance Inc., a firm that designs human interfaces. When he was Manager of Advanced Systems at Apple Computer, Inc., he created the Macintosh project. Before joining Apple, Raskin founded a computer documentation company and a model airplane company and was conductor of the San Francisco Chamber Opera and the San Diego Ancient Music Society. He was a professor and computer center director at the University of California at San Diego and a visiting scholar at Stanford University's Artificial Intelligence Laboratory.]

RETRIEVAL-SYSTEM PERSPECTIVES

WHAT'S NEW WITH RETRIEVAL TECHNOLOGY
By Lyndon S. Holmes

DESIGN CONSIDERATIONS FOR CD-ROM RETRIEVAL SOFTWARE
By Edward M. Cichocki and Susan M. Ziemer

EVALUATING TEXT STORAGE AND RETRIEVAL SOFTWARE
By Paul Nieuwenhuysen

What's New with Retrieval Technology

By Lyndon S. Holmes

[In this article Lyndon Holmes describes three kinds of retrieval systems and speculates about the development of a hybrid system that will offer users several ways to find the information they seek.]

CD-ROM has opened up the potential for almost instantaneous access to phenomenal amounts of data. Going beyond the capacity of a single CD-ROM disc, users are already installing multiple-disc CD-ROM configurations, both for stand-alone and network access. But a gigabyte of text is a *large amount of text:* a billion characters, a thousand million letters, twenty million words, thirty million pages...a thousand novels. When, typically, all we want is to find a single nugget of knowledge, how do we find it easily and quickly under these proverbial mountains?

Retrieval technology, particularly that used on microcomputers with CD-ROM, offers a variety of techniques for accessing large text databases; some are innovative, some traditional. As the sizes of databases have increased, the concomitant sophistication of these technologies has recently made some exciting steps forward.

Today's retrieval technologies can be grouped into two major areas: *targeted* and *navigational*. In targeted searching, the user provides an *a priori* specification of what is required. The specification typically consists of one or more words or terms to be found in the database. Most of the commercially available online and CD-ROM retrieval systems use targeted searching techniques. In contrast, navigational searching (frequently referred to as *hypermedia,* or *hypertext access*) requires no prior specification. Instead, the searcher navigates into and through the database, using links and structures created by the database author. Databases that are structured on Apple Computer's

LYNDON HOLMES

Home: North Andover, Massachusetts
Job: President, Aries Systems Corp.
Quote: *"In our complex world, knowledge creates progress. We aim to make the world's knowledge universally accessible. That's all."*

HyperCard are classic examples of navigational databases.

TARGETED SEARCHING

Most targeted retrieval systems provide basic key-word searching. This allows the user to specify one or more words, which must be in a document, in order to find the document. Some such systems allow you to specify word adjacency or proximity to limit searching to certain portions of a document (for example, title, abstract, or index terms), or they allow you to truncate words to retrieve variant forms or to combine words using Boolean logic and to combine search result sets. These tools require the user to invest considerable time learning both the concept of term searching as well as the particular searching syntax of the system. For a casual user, this can be a formidable task.

A further, significant characteristic of this implementation of targeted retrieval is that it tends to encourage failure. If the search specification contains only a few words, many documents will be found, and the user becomes frustrated while scanning through much irrelevant material. Conversely, a very explicit specification containing many words typically ends up finding nothing. Either way, the user can easily become discouraged and give up.

PROBABILISTIC RETRIEVAL

During the past decade, much theoretical study and research has been undertaken by information scientists in the area of probabilistic retrieval, and it is in this area that answers to the problems of targeted searching now seem to be appearing.

Probabilistic retrieval operates on the premise that the author of a document and the searcher respectively use independent vocabularies to characterize their work or their search. However, statistical probability indicates that, in a sufficient number of cases, a significant overlap will exist between these two vocabularies. The overlap will be sufficient to provide a reasonable likelihood of cross-matching the searcher's and author's vocabularies, thereby enabling the searcher to retrieve a document of likely interest.

This technique offers several benefits. First, the matching process no longer has a binary outcome, as is characteristic of traditional Boolean retrieval logic. Instead, the matching creates a gradation, or likelihood measure, of any particular document matching the search specification. Thus, in the absence of exact matches with the search specification, close or nearby matches can be offered as alternatives without requiring the searcher to identify and execute highly complex search algorithms. Second, the documents identified in a probabilistic search can be ranked or ordered by their likelihood of relevance to the search specification. This means that the document result set can be presented to the searcher in order of likely relevance, thereby reducing time spent scanning irrelevant materials.

The effect of probabilistic retrieval is enhanced by the fashion in which the searcher establishes the search specification. Ideally, this specification can be made with a natural-language-style expression rather than with a formalized search language. For example, it's a lot easier for the searcher to type "Do helmets reduce injuries in bicycle accidents" than to create the more traditional expression "TW=HELMET$ AND TW=BICYL$ ACCIDENT$ and TW=REDUC$ INJUR$". For those unfamiliar with traditional search systems, the latter means: Find documents containing any derivatives of the word *helmet,* and containing *bicycle accident* or *bicycle accidents* or *bicycling accidents,* and so on.

Of course, the real challenge with this type of retrieval is maximizing the functional flexibility of the retrieval system (that is, adaptation to the human searcher) while preserving reasonable response times on an economical hardware configuration with a database that has practical value to the searcher.

It's exciting to observe that we're now seeing the first generation of a new retrieval technology that exhibits these characteristics.

NAVIGATIONAL SEARCHING

Navigational, or hypertext systems are intrinsically easier to use than targeted systems, but provide a characteristically narrower view of the database. The user chooses a single entry point and from there follows one or more threads through the database. Depending on the entry point chosen, the items found along the thread may or may not be pertinent to the searcher's interest. To search exhaustively, the user must serially choose all possible entry points and all thread divisions that may occur—again, a formidable undertaking.

A database can contain many nodes of information that have relevance for the searcher. In a navigational searching environment, discovery of all these nodes depends on the author's having created links among all of them. If sufficient links do not exist, the searcher will not find the nodes.

> *The problem is not electronic. It is not "software," meaning procedural obstacles to implementation. The problem is conceptual. If such systems are to be promulgated to a wider public—no longer just in-house—they must be clear and simple to use, yet offer powerful new features. They may not merely be a clumsy imitation of paper systems.*
>
> **Theodor H. Nelson**
> From *Replacing the Printed Word: A Complete Literary System*

This need for adequate linkages places a new burden on the author. Now the author must create not only the intellectual content (the traditional authoring task), but also a road map pointing out intellectual relationships among the nodes. This task shares some of the characteristics of creating an index for a printed document—it is time-consuming and relatively

> *The value of a navigational document to the searcher is directly related to the richness of the linkages that the author creates. The value of the document becomes directly dependent on the investment made by the author, rather than upon the mechanical processing of the hypertext environment.*

uninteresting to many authors, and often is done in a desultory fashion, if at all. And the author must anticipate the needs of the searcher by creating the links that will be important to the searcher, rather than those that are important to the author.

So the value of a navigational document to the searcher is directly related to the richness of the linkages that the author creates. The value of the document becomes directly dependent on the investment made by the author, rather than upon the mechanical processing of the hypertext environment.

"TARGETED HYPERMEDIA" RETRIEVAL

Although such systems are not yet commercially available, we can anticipate an integration of the probabilistic and navigational knowledge-finding styles. Such a system will provide both targeted and browsing access to the knowledge base. Probabilistic retrieval will provide numerous access points into the knowledge base. It will also permit automatic creation of many of the navigational links between nodes in the knowledge base. The author will focus less on creating links and more on defining a thesaurus of terminology (perhaps analogous to the preparation of a glossary), which can then be used to generate automatic semantic links between nodes. This will eliminate the tedium of manual link definition and once again allow the author to focus on the intellectual content of the work.

How far away is this capability? Because we already have commercially available probabilistic and navigational products, it's likely we'll see the first true "targeted hypermedia" knowledge system within the next five years, perhaps sooner than that. In combination with the capacity and economies of CD-ROM, we may then see a revolution in knowledge dissemination rivalling that created by the printing press a half millennium ago.

[Lyndon Holmes is President of Aries Systems Corporation, headquartered in North Andover, Massachusetts. Aries Systems publishes CD-ROM databases and an innovative retrieval software package called Knowledge Finder, for the Apple Macintosh. The company specializes in the health care market and offers a variety of MEDLINE databases on CD-ROM.]

Design Considerations for CD-ROM Retrieval Software

By Edward M. Cichocki and Susan M. Ziemer

From the *Journal of the American Society for Information Science*

[The following discussion of retrieval-system design, while geared to a more technical audience, nevertheless offers valuable insight into the factors that can make a difference between successful and unsuccessful designs.]

CD-ROM differs from magnetic media. While there are only a few parameters that the designer must consider, these have a significant impact on the design of a CD-ROM retrieval system. The first is that CD-ROM is a Constant Linear Velocity (CLV) medium rather than a Constant Angular Velocity (CAV) device. CAV discs rotate at a constant speed, which makes the drive mechanism fairly simple, but requires that data be more closely packed closer to the center of the disc. In contrast, CLV discs have a constant storage density, with pit spacing the same on outer tracks as on inner ones. Although this makes the drive mechanism more complicated, the reading optics can expect data of constant format at constant delivery rate. The capacity of a single CD-ROM is 550 to 580 MBytes (the data equivalent of the 60–74-minute playing time inherited from the CD-Audio derivation of the disc).

Another consideration is that CD players have a slower access—seek—time than the drives for magnetic disks. The values are 500 to 1000 ms for CDs and 50 ms or less for typical Winchester drives. This is because data are more closely packed on the CD, requiring more precise head positioning, and to the CLV nature of CD. Because the reading is done optically, however, seeks to nearby positions can be done very quickly, since in such a case the mirrors on the head can be rotated slightly rather than having the head move. Thus seek times can be minimized if related data are kept in close proximity.

One must also take into consideration the data transfer rate of a CD-ROM drive, which is also slower than magnetic media drives (about 150 KBytes/s as opposed to 100–300 KBytes/s). This data transfer rate is quite comparable to that of a floppy disk, but only about half of what can be achieved with Winchester technology. Thus, though storage density of a CD-ROM is very high, there are penalties in both seek time and data transfer rate.

The final difference is extremely important. CD-ROM is a read-only storage medium. While this implies real restrictions in terms of the overall utility of the medium as a one-for-one replacement for magnetic media, it is a true advantage in the use of CD-ROM for storage of databases, because the designer can arrange data in confidence that its organization will remain unchanged.

GENERAL DESIGN CONSIDERATIONS

In light of the advantages—incredible storage capabilities—and the disadvantages—slow access and average transfer rates—the designer of a CD-ROM retrieval system must devote much thought to the format of the data. Regardless of the data structures decided upon, the following points apply.

Minimize seeks

The designer must do whatever he or she can to minimize accesses to the disc. In the case of many databases and information retrieval systems, there is some *a priori* knowledge of the data and their use. For example, in menu-driven systems, some amount of information is present about the general order in which data will be retrieved, and data can then be placed in relation to that order. Further, if large amounts of related data are placed proximately, sequential reading can be done without head placement. Finally, indexes can be designed to be shallow and broad such that much index information can be quickly retrieved by one seek followed by sequential reading.

Transfer large amounts of data

Although data transfer rate is slow for CD-ROM, seeks are much slower as compared to magnetic disks. It is desirable therefore to transfer as much data as possible following each seek. The CD Standard requires storage of information in 2 KByte blocks. If system buffering is employed, the designer will not have control of the number of data moves to transfer a given amount of data. If an application calls for 30 Bytes of data, for example, the CD Operating System (OS) will automatically move 2 KBytes to an intermediate buffer and then make another move of the 30 Bytes. Instead, the system should be designed to call for the full 2 KBytes, then use an offset pointer to the 30 Bytes, saving that extra data move. In general, the designer should avoid system buffering and generate his own buffering method, using large RAM buffers and an algorithm based on caching data on a Least-Recently Used (LRU) basis.

Computer memory (RAM) is now about the least expensive component of the system, and therefore can be used somewhat extravagantly. The designer should lean toward generous RAM usage, at least insofar as reasonable hardware configurations permit. On a PC level machine, this means that the presence of at least 640

KBytes of RAM is basic, and that 1 MByte is not too much; on a minicomputer 4 to 8 MBytes are desirable. The major memory should be used for the storage of index information, since most moving about is done in indexes. Also, the primary level of index should reside permanently in memory. Lower level index information can be kept in LRU buffers. The other major use for memory is to store the currently browsed text since a user will spend some time in or near the current record.

Proximal storage

Related data should be stored proximally on the disc. This means that it frequently will be necessary to intersperse index information with the text of the database. Also, since data are typically presented to the user in the form of screens—and many records require two or more screens for presentation—all the screens for a given record should be kept together. This implies a considerable amount of preprocessing before pressing the disc; since the medium is read-only, the initial structure will never be undone by use. This form of layout differs from that used for magnetic media. Run-time processing is frequently done for databases stored on magnetic media—for example, assembling N elements from a relational database for the generation and presentation of a record. The number of seeks incurred by such run-time processing on optical disc could devastate response time, thus much preprocessing must be done.

Many types of preprocessing can be performed. Any necessary character conversions, unit addition, data cleanup—such as using the same precision for all decimal numbers and other similar processing for display—should be performed before the data are stored on CD-ROM. Usually, the huge storage capacity of CD-ROM offsets the penalties that accrue from such preprocessing. For example, it may seem wasteful to store units with each number in a dataset, when the run-time software could assign the unit (e.g., meters) to each value of a given datatype; however, storage capacity is so high with CD-ROM that even such redundant storage is possible and is more than offset by the improvements in run time. This technique should be carried out as far as is possible with the database and software used. If the system being developed has any level of known screen formats, for example, those should be generated during preprocessing. The amount of preprocessing possible will, however, always be a function of the system being used.

Data access method

In general, information retrieval from databases can be viewed as accessing data from a file in one, or some combination of, three methods. The first is by single key; this method is very common in applications such as credit checking databases. The key may be unique (or at least assumed to be unique), such as a Social Security Number, or it may be duplicative, such as a surname. The second method is by multiple keys, common in applications such as personnel files. In this case, any of the keys may be unique or duplicative, and it is likely that the retrieval system will depend on some level of Boolean combination of keys ("find all records for personnel with a college degree and seven years experience").

The third method is full text retrieval, in which every word in the datafile can be regarded as a key (with the possible exception of trivial words such as articles and conjunctions which usually are eliminated via a Stoplist). This method typically is used in such applications as bibliographic database retrieval systems, where words in a natural language such as English are used as the query terms to access information. In this method, the usual technique is an inversion of the initial database so that each unique word is stored once, with a list of locations of that word stored after it. Location may merely be a record number or may be so sophisticated as to include record number, paragraph, sentence, and position within sentence.

If such complex pointers are used, Boolean operations are possible as are relational operations such as adjacency. Inverted files are often stored so as to be read left-to-right and right-to-left, to permit truncation on either side of query terms.

Depending upon which of these three methods is used, the specific techniques available for maximizing CD-ROM performance differ. The balance of this article discusses those specific design considerations with special emphasis on inverted file structure, since that is the most powerful of the methods and the one most likely to be employed with large textual databases. In practice, it is likely that a complete system will contain some combination of all three methods. For example, a text retrieval system usually has a feature that permits the user to look at the term index to find such things as variations in spelling; this feature may well be implemented through a single key method even though the basic system is primarily an inverted file system.

DESIGN CONSIDERATIONS FOR SPECIFIC CD-ROM RETRIEVAL MODES
Single key mode

Minimizing the number of seeks can be accomplished by hashing, if the keys are unique or have a very low level of duplication. A hashing algorithm translates the key, such as a Social Security Number, to the disc address of the pertinent record. Because one considers the data to be static when working with a CD-ROM medium, the designer should spend the necessary time to design a hashing algorithm that provides an even distribution of addresses. The optimal condition is to have an absolutely flat distribution (an example is a dictionary in which the number of words starting with "A" equals the number of words starting with "B" equals the number of words starting with "C", etc.; while it is unlikely that a natural language dictionary

RETRIEVAL SYSTEMS

System	Company
Bibliofile	Library Corporation P.O. Box 40035 Washington, DC 20016 (800)624–0559
Bluefish	Lotus Development Corporation 55 Cambridge Parkway Cambridge, MA 02142 (617)577–8500
BRS/Search	BRS Information Technologies 1200 Route 7 Latham, NY 12110 (800)468–0908
CAIRS	Info/DOC P.O. Box 17109 Dulles International Airport Washington, DC 20041 (703)979–5363
CD Answer	Dataware Inc. 2 Greenwich Plaza Suite 100 Greenwich, CT 06830 (203)622–3908
CD-GUIDE	OWL International 2800 156th Avenue S.E. Bellevue, WA 98007 (206)747–3203
Compact Cambridge	Cambridge Scientific Abstracts 7200 Wisconsin Avenue Suite 601 Bethesda, MD 20816 (301)961–6700
Compact Disclosure	Disclosure 5161 River Road Bethesda, MD 20816 (800)638–8076
Customized Software Development	Bresler Associates 4276 22nd Street San Francisco, CA 94114 (415)282–5448

would have this property, it is possible to design a hashing algorithm to approximate that condition). Self-adjusting hashing algorithms have been reported in the literature; they reprocess the input file in iterative fashion until an optimal hash is reached. These algorithms are especially worthwhile if the data are to be updated periodically and discs repressed, since the basic characteristics of the data distribution will differ after each update, and a hash that was initially optimal may no longer be so.

An almost unavoidable consequence of hashing is the possibility of collisions (more than one key hashing to the same value). One way to handle this is to use data buckets capable of holding multiple records; usually this will waste storage space because collisions will occur only for some keys. However, this condition may be acceptable if total database size does not use the full capacity of a CD-ROM. Another solution is to have an overflow area linked to the data buckets, to which collisions are relegated; since another seek is necessary to reach the overflow area, this technique is tenable only if the number of collisions is relatively small. The final solution is to use open addressing, which typically results in considerable scattering of the data; this can be a problem if the data are spread across multiple files or if multiple databases are to reside on a single disc.

Hashing usually provides excellent retrieval performance because in most cases (other than collisions) a record can be retrieved with only one seek. Some space is sacrificed to allow for collisions, but space is what is most available on CD-ROM. The trade-off in choice of the method used to handle collisions will be a function of the hashing algorithm employed and the degree to which space can be traded for seek time.

The general rules for transferring as much data as possible after each seek and storing data proximally apply to this mode. Even if a record is too big to store in memory, as much as possible should be taken. Use memory to cache

System	Company	System	Company
Customized Software Development	Del Mar Group 722 Genevieve Suite M Solana Beach, CA 92075 (619)250-0444	DLS/Search	Digital Library Systems 5161 River Road Building 6 Bethesda, MD 20816 (301)657-2997
Customized Software Development	Online Computer Systems Inc. 202512 Century Boulevard Germantown, MD 20874 (301)428-3700	Docufind	Emanuel Data Systems 1865 Palmer Avenue Larchmont, NY 10538 (914)834-5722
Delve	Group L Corporation 481 Carlisle Drive Herndon, VA 22070 (703)471-0030	Dragnet	Access Softek 3204 Adeline Street Berkeley, CA 94703 (415)654-0116
Dialog OnDisc	Dialog Information 3460 Hillview Avenue Palo Alto, CA 94304 (800)3-DIALOG	FIND: Filed Indexed Documents	Acctex Information Systems 131 Steuart Street Suite 600 San Francisco, CA 94105 (415)543-4290
Dialog	IS/R Systems 850 Bear Tavern Road Suite 207 West Trenton, NJ 08628 (609)883-6286		

(continued)

records on a Least Recently Used basis, and, to the extent possible, preprocess the data. For single key applications, this typically involves predetermination of display format.

Multiple key mode

One way to treat multiple keys is to store information redundantly, under each key, and use hashing, thus avoiding indexes. This effectively reduces the problem to be analogous to Single Key Mode (though the software will have to handle combination of sets); the design considerations of the previous section are pertinent. Redundant storage is possible if there is a small number of keys and if total file size multiplied by the number of keys is still less than the total real estate of the disc. Good access performance is to be expected, but, of course, the penalty in storage use is quite severe in this case, since the full amount of data is stored two, three, or more times redundantly.

If storage space is insufficient, the best technique is to hash to index buckets. Each of the index buckets contain the index entries and pointers to the records. Hashing is used to make the initial seek number minimal, but additional seeks are necessary to get to the records from the index buckets. This avoids redundant storage of records; it will entail some wasted space in data buckets or overflow areas—the same situation of collisions applies if one hashes to index bucket addresses as if one hashes to record addresses; and it will usually require at least two seeks to reach any record.

All of the other general conditions apply to this mode—transfer as much data as possible after a seek, cache as many LRU records as possible, store related records proximally, and preprocess data. In the case of multiple keys, the preprocessing can, in some applications, become quite sophisticated. If the designer has operational data on frequency distribution of key use, for example, he can use this data to organize the indexes.

RETRIEVAL SYSTEMS *continued*

System	Company	System	Company
Findit	Reteaco, Inc. 716 Gordon Baker Road Willowdale, ON M2H 3B4 CANADA (416)497–0579	FYI 300 Plus	FYI Inc. 4202 Spicewood Springs Road Suite 101 Austin, TX 78755 (512)346–0134
FreeForm	Micro Dynamics, Ltd. 8555 16th Street Suite 802 Silver Spring, MD 20910 (301)589–6300	GIS Retrieval Information System	AXSES Boutilier Point Halifax, NS B0J 1G0 CANADA (902)826–2440 (826)429–6521
Ful/Text	Fulcrum Technologies, Inc. 331 Cooper Street Ottawa, ON K2P 0G5 CANADA (613)238–1761	HP Laser-RETRIEVE	Hewlett Packard/Meridian Data 4450 Capitola Road Suite 101 Capitola, CA 95010 (408)476–5858
		HyperSearch	Discovery Systems 7001 Discovery Boulevard Dublin, OH 43017 (614)761–2000

Inverted file mode

The design considerations for inverted files also apply to single or multiple key mode when there is much duplication of keys. The most powerful technique in this instance is the use of B-trees for indexing. B-trees are hierarchical indexes, in which each entry in Level One is greater than or equal to all entries in Level Two which it points to, and so on for additional levels. Using our simple dictionary analogy again, let us assume that you want to make a two-level B-tree index for the words: access, algorithm, bit, byte, file, heuristic, list, nanosecond, pointer, record, stoplist, and write. The first level of the index would contain byte, nanosecond, and write. Under byte would be access, algorithm, and bit; under nanosecond would be file, heuristic, and list, etc. If you were searching for "algorithm," your entry to the first level would get you, via binary search, to the "byte" entry and then drop you down for a binary search of the second level of the three words under "byte" until you found "algorithm." This can be taken as far as necessary, but typically, use of B-trees minimizes the

> *Looking back 10 years from now, we will view the retrieval methods we use today as cryptic and complex. Right now, they're better than ever. We are truly at the dawn of a new era.*
>
> **Jerry Fand**
> From *CD-ROM: Optical Publishing*

System	Company
Impact	Auto-Graphics Inc. 3201 Temple Avenue Pomona, CA 91768 (800)235–7961
KAware2	Knowledge Access International, Inc. 2685 Marine Way Suite 1305 Mountain View, CA 94043 (415)969–0606
Knowledge Finder	Aries Systems Corporation 79 Boxford Street North Andover, MA 01845-3219 (508)689–9334
KRS	KnowledgeSet Corporation P.O. Box 51125 Pacific Grove, CA 93950 (408)375–2638
Le Pac	Brodart Automation, a division of Brodart Company 500 Arch Street Williamsport, PA 17705 (800)233–8467
Marcon	AIRS Inc. 335 Paint Branch Drive College Park, MD 20742 (301)454–3832
Media Mixer	Software Mart, Inc. 4131 Spicewood Springs Road Suite I-3 Austin, TX 78759-8608 (512)346–7887 (512)346–1393
MediaBase	Crownshield Software 1105 Commonwealth Avenue Boston, MA 02215 (617)787–8830
Meta-Morf	Thunderstone (EPI, Inc.) P.O. Box 83 Chesterland, OH 44143 (216)449–6104

(continued)

number of levels of index. Each seek provides a large number of key comparisons, and much of the tree is eliminated with each seek. One of the problems with B-trees is that the whole hierarchy has to be rebuilt when a record is added in an update, so B-trees are somewhat costly in magnetic disk environments in which frequent updates occur. However, for CD-ROM, where a one-time creation produces a disc that will have a considerable lifetime, it is usually worth the effort to use B-trees. True, they will have to be entirely recreated when the update is made, but the whole disc has to be remastered and repressed at such a time anyway, so the investment in rebuilding the B-tree is usually not a large portion of the total cost of updating.

B-trees have some disadvantages, too. There will be at least as many seeks required as there are levels in the tree—this can be reduced to *number of levels* minus one if the primary level is kept in memory and data are used as the lowest level. Because each index bucket contains all the elements of the next level of index (or record pointers at the lowest level), some runtime processing will be required with a binary search, to get the proper element out of an index bucket. Finally, because of the hierarchical relationship, the LRU algorithm for caching must be quite sophisticated. These disadvantages can be minimized to some extent. Because the data are static, every bucket can be filled to 100 percent of its capacity with no worry about overflow. This means that the designer must build the indexes on the basis of all the information available and may well have to spend considerable time analyzing the database to answer questions such as:

- How many unique terms are to be inverted?
- How many total occurrences of terms will there be?
- What will the key look like in terms of size and distribution?

RETRIEVAL SYSTEMS *continued*

System	Company
MicroBasis	Information Dimensions, Inc. 505 West King Avenue Columbus, OH 43201-2693 (614)424–6314
OPTI-Search	Amtec 3700 Industry Avenue Lakewood, CA 90714-6050 (213)595–4756
Personal Librarian	Personal Library Software 15215 Shady Grove Road Suite 204 Rockville, MD 20850 (301)926–1402
Phonedisc	Digital Directory Assistance Inc. 5161 River Road Building 6 Bethesda, MD 20816 (301)657–8548
QA Gateway	Quantum Access, Inc. 1700 West Loop South Suite 1460 Houston, TX 77027 (713)622–3211
Research	TMS, Inc. 110 West 3rd Street P.O. Box 1358 Stillwater, OK 74076 (405)377–0880
Search CD450	OCLC, Inc. 6565 Frantz Road Dublin, OH 43017 (614)764–6063
SearchExpress	Executive Technologies, Inc. 2120 16th Avenue South Birmingham, AL 35205 (205)933–5494
SilverPlatter Search and Retrieval Software	SilverPlatter 37 Walnut Street Wellesley Hills, MA 02181 (617)239–0306

- How many levels of indexing are necessary?
- What is the optimal index bucket size?
- How much RAM will be available for use by the index?

Efficiency can also be obtained by maintaining in memory as much of the primary index as possible. Use the first seek to go to the primary index level and then load as much as possible of that index into memory (remember, data transfer rates are reasonable). Another measure is to use large buckets. Although that may seem to be counterproductive because of the necessity for run-time processing to do the binary searches through the data in a bucket, the increase in processing time is slight; there is only a log N increase in the number of compares when the number of data elements goes up by N. This technique results in a shallow and flattened B-tree structure.

Again, the general rules about data transfer, proximal storage, etc., apply; the rule regarding proximal storage pertains to indexes as well as data. The designer should lay out the indexes so that levels are contiguous to each other on the CD-ROM. This will minimize seek time from level to level. With this technique, the designer will have to do his or her own LRU buffering, and must keep track of the levels from which the various index buckets in the cache have been taken. Design for a CD-ROM is a challenging activity, but the work will pay off in superior performance when the disc comes back from the replicator.

In addition, there are two other considerations that are somewhat unrelated to index design for inverted files, but which are applicable to most applications that use this design. First, Boolean searches can get lengthy, even on a mainframe with magnetic storage and certainly more so on a PC with CD-ROM. Many sets may well have to be combined for a given query.

System	Company
Silversmith	Taunton Engineering, Inc. 505 Middlesex Turnpike Billerica, MA 01821 (617)663–3667
SONAR	Virginia Systems 5509 West Bay Court Midlothian, VA 23113 (804)739–3200
Status	CP International 521 Fifth Avenue New York, NY 10175 (212)949–8051 (212)883–8912
TextWare	Unibase Systems, Inc. 333 Main Street Suite 300 Park City, UT 84060 (801)649–4440
VAX/VTX	Digital Equipment Corporation 2 Mount Royal Avenue UPO 1-3 Marlboro, MA 01752 (617)480–4816
What?	Highlighted Data P.O. Box 17229 Washington, DC 20041 (703)241–1180
Where?	Highlighted Data P.O. Box 17229 Washington, DC 20041 (703)241–1180
Wilsondisc	H.W. Wilson Company 950 University Avenue Bronx, NY 10452 (212)588–8400
Window Book Technology	Box Company 63 Howard Street Cambridge, MA 02139 (617)576–0892
Zyindex	Zylab Corporation 233 East Erie Street Chicago, IL 60611 (312)642–2201

Compiled by Online Press Inc.

> *The Ten Minute Rule: Any system which cannot be well taught to a layman in* ten minutes, *by a tutor in the presence of a responding setup, is too complicated. This may sound far too stringent; I think not. Rich and powerful systems may be given front ends which are nonetheless ridiculously clear; this is a design problem of the foremost importance.*
>
> **Theodor H. Nelson**
> From *Dream Machines,* **Microsoft Press**

Thus, the user should be given a status report to know that the system has not died but is still working on the problem. One can also disguise the fact that time is passing by using camouflage techniques such as printing query results by each term rather than waiting until all the logic of the Boolean expression has been evaluated, then displaying the final result.

The second issue is to consider the use of data compression. Again, such intensive processing may not seem to be worthwhile, yet there are real advantages. Full text systems typically operate on *large* databases, and many such databases are too big to fit on a single CD-ROM despite its storage capacity. Data compression permits storing even more on a single disc. Because the disc is meant to be used by many people many times, the price for compression may well be worth the effort. Finally, data compression techniques permit encryption at very little incremental processing cost, so if security of proprietary data is an issue, this procedure becomes even more beneficial.

CONCLUSION

The designer of retrieval systems based on CD-ROM (and, most probably, using a PC-level computer) must consider the physical characteristics of this medium. CD-ROM is not just another disc; design considerations developed for magnetic media do not apply. Well-conceived design and extensive preprocessing will result at processing time in more satisfied users. Well-designed and well-executed retrieval systems for CD-ROM databases can perform as well as the state-of-the-art online systems.

Reprinted from the *Journal of the American Society for Information Science.* Copyright © 1988 by John Wiley and Sons, Inc. Reprinted by permission of John Wiley and Sons, Inc.

Evaluating Text Storage and Retrieval Software

By Paul Nieuwenhuysen

Excerpted from *"Criteria for the Evaluation of Text Storage and Retrieval Software."*

[Intended as a checklist for the evaluation of management systems for bibliographic descriptions, this article offers anyone charged with selecting a retrieval system a comprehensive and detailed reminder of the areas to investigate and the questions to ask.]

INTERACTIVE INFORMATION RETRIEVAL

Displaying the index

1. Can a list of index terms be displayed on the screen, for instance to give a new or inexperienced user an idea of the contents of a database, or to give the users an idea of the contents of a new database?

If yes:

— Can the number of postings be viewed?

— Can the retrieval/search module of the program also display eventual relationships between terms (e.g., narrower terms, synonyms)? In other words, to which degree can the thesaurus (if present) be integrated with the database?

Finding and combining terms

1. Is it possible to search using these Boolean logic operators or equivalents:

    — AND? (Intersection)

    — OR? (Union)

    — NOT? (Exclusion)

    Some programs require the explicit use of these operators or equivalent commands such as *, +, −, etc.; other programs offer the Boolean combinations implicitly, menu driven.

2. Proximity searching:

    — Can adjacency of two search terms be used as a search criterion?

    — Can the user specify that two search terms must appear within a given number of words of each other?

    — Can occurrence of two search terms in the same field be used as a search criterion?

    — Can occurrence of two search terms in the same paragraph be used as a search criterion?

3. Is the number of operators for Boolean combinations or other search operators in one command line, search statement or option unlimited? Or is it limited to only one or two? In practice, this limitation is not important in many cases.

4. Can parentheses be used in the combination of search terms, to indicate the order in which the program should execute the operations?

5. Truncation and wildcard searching:

    — Is truncation available at the end of a search term, i.e., on the right side?

      If yes: Must the user specify explicitly right side truncation? Other programs always assume right side truncation, which can be easy, in particular for small databases.

      If yes: Can the user specify the number of characters to be truncated?

    — Is truncation available at the beginning of a search term, i.e., on the left side?

      If yes: Can the program then give a quick response by using a special index to cope with left truncations? (Or does the program only use a slower sequential search algorithm in the case of left truncation?)

    — Is embedded truncation (or "wildcard" searching) available?

      If yes: Can the user specify the number of characters to be masked?

    — Is it possible to use more than one form of truncation simultaneously?

    — Is it possible to use truncation and wildcard searching with Boolean operators and proximity searching?

6. Can searching be limited to specified files and fields?

7. Can the user search for terms which are not included in an index (for instance by simple, sequential, string searching)?

8. Can the number of hits for a search term be displayed?

9. Can multiple-term search commands be entered ("stacking")?

    If yes: Can the number of hits for each term be displayed?

10. Can the user execute a phonetic search? (This can be effective, for instance to search for names of persons, chemical substances or biological systems, when the user does not know exactly the spelling used in the database.)

11. Can the user search with weighted-term logic, so that he can attribute more or less weight to the various items in a query?

12. If the program accepts in the input phase other characters beside the 7-bit pure, plain ASCII character set

    — Can these "strange" characters then also be used directly in the search terms?

    — Can the "strange" characters be searched by using corresponding characters (if these exist) from the standard ASCII set, in the search terms? For instance: searching for letters modified with an accent or otherwise, by using the same letters without the accent or other modification, e.g., searching for "ü" by using "u" and/or "ue" in the search term.

13. Does the program make a distinction between lowercase and uppercase letters in search terms? This will only be useful in special applications.

14. Can the program distinguish numbers from characters to allow more sophisticated retrieval with operators such as

    — Smaller than?
    — Greater than?
    — Equal to?
    — From...to...?
    — Etc?

15. Can the user directly go on with a search on the basis of previous search results, without having to type the new search term when this is based on those search results, but by simply pointing to part of the displayed information, using the keyboard or a mouse? For instance, searching and retrieving a particular document can yield an interesting keyword or author associated with that document, which can then serve as a new search term in a search restricted to a certain field.

16. When the user has selected a number of records from a database, can the program then create a sorted list of terms, words or numbers occurring in that set of selected records? (Such lists of terms can be useful to analyse the contents of the selected records in an efficient way and to discover other, new, useful search terms which were overlooked in the previous search. For instance the host system ESA-IRS offers this feature with a set of "ZOOM" commands.)

    If yes: Can the sorting be based on

    — The number of times that the term occurs in the complete set of selected records?

    — The number of times that the term occurs in a part only of the set of selected records, to shorten the required calculations?

    — A more sophisticated weight factor calculated by the program from (on one hand) the number of times that the term occurs in the set of selected records, and on the other hand the total number of times that the term occurs in the complete set of records, i.e., in the whole database? A sorting based on such weight factors can be more useful because it reflects better the order of relevance of the terms in that particular set of selected records.

17. Can the program perform analyses on the contents of a set of selected records?

    If yes:

    — Can the results then be displayed graphically? (For instance in histograms or piecharts.)

REFERENCES

Schultz, Louise, "Computerized Literature Files," *Medical Electronics*, September 1983, pages 72–78.

Rowbottom, Mary, "First Steps in Choosing Information Retrieval Packages," *Library Micromation News*, 4, April 1984, pages 13–16.

Hubbard, Abigail, "Reprint File Management Software," *Online*, 9:6, 1985, pages 67–73.

Leggate, Peter and Dyer, Hillary, "The Microcomputer in the Library: III. Information Retrieval from External and Internal Databases," *The Electronic Library*, 4:1, February 1986, pages 38–49.

Murphy, C.E., "Microcomputer-based Catalog Creation Software Options for Small Libraries," in: *AGARD Lecture Series No. 149: The Application of Microcomputers to Aerospace and Defence Scientific and Technical Information Work*, NATO, Advisory Group for Aerospace Research and Development, 1986, pages 3–7.

Pollard, Richard, "Microcomputer Database Management Systems for Bibliographic Data," *The Electronic Library*, 4:4, 1986, pages 230–240.

Puglia, Vincent, "TBMS: Database power unleashed," *PC Magazine*, 25, November 1986, pages 211–230.

Besemer, H., Citroen, Ch.L., van de Lustgraaf, B., Mastenbroek, O., Nieuwenheysen, P., Parmentier, E.A., van Ramhorst, G.G., and Sieverts, E.G., *Vergelijking van programmatuur voor gebruikers van online informatiesystemen. Resultaten van een software onderzoek van de VOGIN werkgroep Programmatuur, Apparatuur en Datatransmissie (PAD), (2nd edition. 2nd revised print.)* VOGIN (The Netherlands Association of Users of Online Information Systems) 1987. Distributed by PUDOC, Postbus 4, 6700 AA Wageningen. 94 pages. ISBN 90-72037-02-2.

Besemer, H., Citroen, Ch.L., de Jong, A.J.C.M., Kuperus, A.J., van de Lustgraaf, B., Mastenbroek, O., Nieuwenhuysen, P., Parmentier, E.A., van Ramshorst, G., and Sieverts, E.G., *Microcomputer Applications for Online and Local Information Systems: A Test and Comparison of 30 Software Packages. (Report of a software evaluation by members of VOGIN.)* VOGIN (The Netherlands Association of Users of Online Information Systems) 1987. Distributed by Johan van Halm and Associates, P.O. Box 688, 3800 AR Armersfoort, The Netherlands. 107 pages.

Besemer, H., Besselink, H.E., Hainebach, R., de Jong, B., Mastenbroek, O., Nieuwenhuysen, P., Parmentier, E.A., van Ramhorst, G.G., Scheepsma, G., Sieverts, E.G. and Vis, G.V., *De microcomputer voor beheer van online en lokale informatie. (Een gebruikersgids, gecombineerd met resultaten van een software onderzoek van de VOGIN werkgroep Programmatuur, Apparatuur en Datatransmissie, PAD.)* VOGIN (The Netherlands Association of Users of Online Information Systems) 1988. Secretary of VOGIN, Bibliotheek Technische Universiteit Delft. Postbus 98, 2600 Delft, Nederland. Distributed by PUDOC, Postbus 4, 6700 AA Wageningen; price is 20 guilders, 96 pages ISBN 90-72037-03-0.

Newton, S.J., *Text Filing and Retrieval Systems — A Practical Evaluation Guide*, Manchester: National Computing Centre Publications, 1983.

Hamilton, Catherine D., Kimberley, Robert, and Smith, Christine H., (eds.), *Text Retrieval: A Directory of Software*, Gower Publishing Company, 1985.

Kimberley, Robert and Rowley, Jennifer, *Text Retrieval: A Directory of Software, 2nd Edition*, Gower Publishing Company, 1987.

— Can the results then be transferred more or less automatically to a more specialised program to present data graphically?

18. Can the search history, i.e., a list with brief descriptions of sets created during the search session, be displayed?

19. Can search statements, i.e., queries, be saved on a

    — Temporary basis, during the present search session?

    — More permanent basis?

    If yes: see below under "Search Profiles."

OUTPUT FACILITIES

The following applies to output to a visual display unit, to a printer, or to a disk in machine readable form.

1. Can the user select and specify the fields required in the output? (In other words, can the user specify that some fields of the records be omitted from the output?)

2. Can the user define how the records must be sorted in the output?

    If yes:

    — What elements may be used to define the order? For instance, can the contents of any field be used?

    — Which options exist for the alphanumerical sorts? For instance, alphabetical sorts based on letters or based on words can be different; numerics may sort before alphas.

    — Can certain unimportant but confusing elements be discarded in the sorting algorithm? For instance, can articles at the beginning of a field be discarded in an alphabetical sorting algorithm?

    — What is the maximum number of sort levels? For instance, when the contents of the field that defines the sorting is identical for some records, is another sort level useful to execute the sorting of those records?

3. Can the fields in the output be indicated by their name and or meaning, or be an abbreviation of this (often called a "tag")?

4. Can the program eliminate duplicate records?

5. Can the program highlight or mark the search terms within the body of the retrieved record (document)?

    If yes: To which extent can the user then choose the type of indication? For instance, by placing search terms between asterisks or other uncommon characters, by capitalizing, underlining or double underlining search terms, or (in case of a video display only) by highlighting the search terms.

6. Can retrieved records, i.e., documents, in this context of text retrieval, be ranked in relation to the number of hits contained?

7. Can the following outputs be produced:

    — Key word in context (KWIC)?

    — Key word and context?

8. If an extended character set can be used during input, containing other characters than those belonging to the standard, plain, pure 7-bit ASCII character set:

    — Can the "special" characters then be displayed too?

    — Can the program then convert the special characters to corresponding characters or combinations of characters which do belong to the 7-bit ASCII set? (This can be useful for transfer of data to a printer, to other computer systems or to networks, which cannot handle the extended character set used by the program.)

— Can the program then cope with the special characters in the sorting algorithms to sort output containing extended characters?

9. Can the output of a record be cut off automatically if the size of the complete record exceeds a certain threshold which can be specified by the user?

10. Can the output of the contents of a field also be cut off automatically if its size exceeds a certain threshold which can be specified by the user?

11. Can the user define the order in which the fields are placed in the records in the output?

12. To which extent can the user define the output regarding layout, paragraph formats, size and font of the characters?

13. In the case of output on paper, can the user place running heads on top and/or on the bottom of each page?

14. Can output formats specified by the user be stored on disc as "report definitions" or "style sheets"?

   If yes: How many of these formats can be stored?

SEARCH PROFILES

See also above for the criteria concerning "Finding and combining terms" and "Output Facilities."

1. What is the maximum number of terms and/or lines in a stored search profile?

2. Can a profile be amended, i.e., can terms be
   — Added?

— Deleted?

— Modified?

3. Are outputs of profiles produced
   — At intervals specified by the program?
   — At intervals specified by the user?
   — At the request of the user?
   — Automatically, when new records are added to the database?

SECURITY/PRIVACY/ AUTHORIZATION

1. Are passwords
   — Essential?
   — Possible?

   If yes: Can access be prohibited completely to
   — Whole database(s)?
   — Specified files?
   — Specified records within a file?
   — Specified fields within records?

   Can access be restricted to
   — Read-only facilities, i.e., consulting with no amendment/editing/input of whole database(s), specified files, specified records within a file, or specified fields within the records?
   — Consulting and editing the contents of the database(s), but without the possibility of changing the structure of the database(s)?

2. Is the user notified that facilities/records are not available?

3. Is the user notified of his/her last access or of previous accesses?

4. Can passwords be changed? Is data encryption a feature?

CHEAPER, LIMITED VERSIONS

1. Can multiple copies of a read-only version be bought at a price which is considerably lower than that of the complete version? (This can be useful to distribute data in electronic form; in particular, such a version can be used for electronic publishing of bibliographies.)

    If yes: Is distribution then restricted by the software supplier to a well defined user-community (such as a company) or not?

2. Does the producer also supply a cheaper version of the program which offers the user only an already established, fixed database structure suited for a specific application, and which does not allow changes of this structure?

INTEGRATION WITH OTHER PROGRAMS

1. Can the package be integrated with other programs? For instance, the program for text retrieval can serve as a module for cataloguing and/or public access catalogue (OPAC) in an integrated software package for library management. The integration with programs for word processing has already been mentioned above.

2. Can the package import data from other programs? (For instance, it may be desirable to export data from a spreadsheet into a text database.)

Reprinted from *The Electronic Library* by permission of Learned Information, Oxford, England and Medford, New Jersey.

PREPARING TEXT

WHAT'S INVOLVED IN TEXT DATA PREPARATION?
By Joyce Cox

CHARACTER ANALYSIS
By Ben Templin

CD-ROM TEXT PREPARATION WITH SGML
By Bill Zoellick

What's Involved in Text Data Preparation?

By Joyce Cox

[Text data is currently the backbone of most CD-ROM applications. In this article, Joyce Cox briefly discusses the generic steps necessary to prepare text for the indexing and other manipulations required by specific retrieval systems.]

As the CD-ROM industry moves toward exciting multimedia applications, text data is assuming some of the characteristics of the proverbial wallflower. It seems homely and unchallenging, and it doesn't capture the imagination the way graphics and sound do. However, all applications include text of some sort, so all CD-ROM title producers have to contend with the processes involved in preparing text data. This article presents a brief overview of these processes.

STEP 1: GETTING IT INTO THE COMPUTER

The first consideration is to ensure that the text is available in a machine-readable format. If it isn't, you have two options:

- Key in the text. This method can be cost effective if you seek out typists with flying fingers and impeccable accuracy. If the volume of data warrants it, you might want to contact some of the service bureaus who specialize in keyboard entry. Costs are usually calculated per thousand characters and accuracy is guaranteed by a method such as double entry (where two typists key in the same data and their files are compared using a utility program).

- Scan the printed pages. This method involves passing pages through a scanner equipped with optical-character-recognition (OCR) software, which converts letters scanned as bit-mapped images to ASCII codes. OCR is still not reliable

JOYCE K. COX

Home: Bellevue, Washington
Job: President, Online Press Inc.
Quote: *"The technological breakthroughs that made it possible to place over 600 MB of information on a small plastic disc are interesting. But I am much more excited by the potential applications that will be produced as people stretch their creative abilities and imaginations to find ways to use all that storage space."*

enough to dispense with a proof-and-correction pass, so you either need to make sure that this pass is included in estimates from scanning companies, or you need to budget time and money for proofing as a separate step.

STEP 2: IMPOSING STRUCTURE

Traditionally, publishers of printed information have mixed and matched typefaces and have varied type sizes and weights to add sophisticated levels of structure and "eye appeal" to the printed page. The structure helps readers follow the logic of a discussion and orients them as they move from one topic to another. The eye appeal has the psychological effect of capturing and retaining interest.

Most of today's CD-ROM title developers are rightly concerned more with how to make their data easily accessible than with how to make it look pretty. However, up to a point the two considerations are one and the same. The more distinctions you make between elements, the more sophisticated the methods you can use to index and retrieve information. And once the information is retrieved, the more visual cues you give readers to help them move through the information on the screen, the easier your product is to read and the more likely readers are to use it. At one end of the scale, the distinctions between elements might be nothing more than a hierarchical system of headings. At the other end, your title's text data might include various levels of indent, the use of line rules, boxes, and other topic dividers, and "rich text" formatting such as bold or italic fonts or colors.

So the second consideration in preparing text for CD-ROM is to make sure your data contains the formatting instructions necessary to implement the structure required by your retrieval system and to display the information the way you want on the screen. If your data doesn't, you have two options:

- Algorithmically insert codes. In some cases, programs can be written to insert codes based on a file's structural cues. For example, all strings of words in capital letters might be interpreted as first-level headings.

- Manually add the instructions. In the case of OCR-generated files, for example, you may need to insert codes for rich-text formatting that were not picked up during the scanning process.

Having to impose structure where none previously existed can be a time-consuming, costly task. But if your files have already been structured for some other purpose, such as typesetting or online retrieval, don't assume that you can eliminate, or perhaps even significantly reduce, the time and money you should allocate to this step. If the existing structure is well-documented and totally consistent across all the files you intend to include in your CD-ROM product, conversion to the structure needed for CD-ROM presentation may be a simple matter of writing a custom program and clocking machine time. Conversion of poorly documented or inconsistent structures, on the other hand, can take unpredictable amounts of time and eat up huge chunks of the product-development budget.

A common source of data for CD-ROM titles is the photocomposition files used to produce the printed version of the information. These files are created by the "front-end" systems that give typesetting machines instructions on how to output the text. The instructions are in the form of codes, or tags, that establish the font, typesize, leading, and column width the typesetting machine is to use for any particular element. It is these tags that give the data its structure.

The tags of some systems are easier to decipher than others. For example, some systems relegate most instructions to format files that can be read like the source code for computer programs. Other, usually older, systems require that the typographer embed all formatting codes in the file itself. Embedded codes can be harder for the person developing conversion algorithms to evaluate. In any event, the implementation of the instruction set of any particular front-end system is subject to the interpretation and skill of the individual typographer, and may change from one file to the next if more than one typographer was involved in the project.

Critical to the smooth execution of this step in the text-preparation process is a thorough knowledge of the files. Up-front analysis of a representative sample of the data you will be working with and of the printed output, if available, goes a long way toward eliminating the surprises that can cause deadline slippages and budget over-runs.

DATA PREPARATION HOUSES

State	Company	State	Company
AL	Disctronics Inc. 4905 Mooresmill Road Huntsville, AL 35881 (205)859–9042 FAX: (205)859–9932		Optical Media International 485 Alberto Way Los Gatos, CA 95032 (408)395–4332
CA	3M Corporation 420 South Bernardo Avenue Mountain View, CA 94043 (415)969–5200		Tiger Media 10810 Paramount Boulevard Suite 201 Downey, CA 90241 (213)862–5591
	Disctronics Inc. 1120 Cosby Way Anaheim, CA 92806 (714)630–6700 FAX: (714)630–1025	CO	Lasertrak Corporation 6235-B Lookout Drive Boulder, CO 80301 (303)530–2711
	Meridian Data, Inc. 4450 Capitola Road Suite 101 Capitola, CA 95010 (408)476–5858		Reference Technology Inc. 5700 Flatiron Parkway Boulder, CO 80301 (303)449–4157

(continued)

A photocomposition source file coded with troff typesetting commands

STEP 3: ADDING CROSS REFERENCES

Much of the value-added aspect of CD-ROM products lies not only in their search functions but in their capability of linking related items of information, both within and across documents. You forge these links during data preparation by inserting cross-referencing codes, using two methods:

- Insert tags with a program. If the text is highly structured—dictionaries, encyclopedias, and maintenance manuals fall into this category—you can probably code most cross references algorithmically. But do allow time for proofing and for manual adjustments. Rarely can a program insert

DATA PREPARATION HOUSES *continued.*

State	Company	State	Company
GA	Denon America 1380 Monticello Road Madison, GA 30650 (404)342–3425	MD	AIRS Inc. 335 Paint Branch Drive College Park, MD 20742 (301)454–3832
IN	Digital Audio Disc Corporation 1800 North Fruitridge Avenue Terre Haute, IN 47804–1788 (812)462–8160 FAX: (812)466–9125		Online Computer Systems 20251 Century Boulevard Germantown, MD 20874 (800)922–9204
	SANYO Laser Products, Inc. 1767 Sheridan Street Richmond, IN 47374 (317)935–7574 FAX: (317)935–7570	NJ	Denon America 222 New Road Parsippany, NJ 07054 (201)575–7810 FAX: (201)575–2532
ME	Shape Optimedia Route 109 & Eagle Drive Sanford, ME 04073 (207)324–1124 FAX: (207)490–1707	NY	Magnetic Press, Inc. 503 Broadway New York, NY 10012 (212)219–2831 FAX: (212)334–4729

tags where you want them, and not where you don't want them, with 100 percent accuracy.

- Manually insert tags. If the text you are dealing with is not highly structured, manual cross referencing may be unavoidable. For example, if you are preparing the text of a book, you will be able to algorithmically cross reference all occurrences of *see Chapter 6 for more information*. However, cross referencing *see the following chapter* or *see the section entitled "Driving on the Wrong Side of the Road"* is beyond the power of most programs.

Having created links for all appropriate cross references, you need to verify that every target

A format file containing formatting instructions for the Magna typesetting front-end system

State	Company	State	Company
OH	Discovery Systems 7001 Discovery Boulevard Dublin, OH 43017 (614)761–4159	TX	Memory Technology Inc. 2800 Summit Avenue Plano, TX 75074 (214)881–8800
OK	TMS, Inc. 110 West 3rd Street Stillwater, OK 74076 (405)377–0880		Software Mart 4131 Spicewood Springs Road Suite I-3 Austin, TX 78759–8608 (512)346–7887 FAX: (512)346–1393
PA	American Helix Technology Corporation 1857 Colonial Village Lane Lancaster, PA 17601 (800)535–6575 FAX: (717)392–7897	VA	Nimbus Records Inc. P.O. Box 7305 Charlottesville, VA 22906 (804)985–1100
NC	Philips and DuPont Optical Kings Mountain Highway 29 Grover, NC 28073 (800)433–3475 FAX: (302)479–2512	WA	Online Press Inc. 14320 N.E. 21st Street Suite 18 Bellevue, WA 98007 (206)641–3434

(continued)

(the item being cross referenced *to*) is unique and that every source (the item being cross referenced *from*) has a corresponding target. A program can tell you if a source is pointing to nowhere or if two or more targets have the same tag. However, you need to allocate time for manually resolving any problems the program might identify.

CONCLUSION

This has necessarily been a somewhat simplistic discussion of the basic processes involved in the preparation of text for CD-ROM. Because the time and manpower you need to allocate for these processes can vary depending upon the kind and condition of the source data, you should schedule analysis of your text-preparation needs early in the product development cycle.

[Joyce Cox is President of Online Press Inc., which provides traditional and CD-ROM publishing services ranging from the development of entire publishing systems to the production of specific paper-based and online publications. Formerly Managing Editor of Microsoft Press, Cox has fifteen years' experience in helping make technical subjects accessible to nontechnical audiences.]

DATA PREPARATION HOUSES *continued.*

State	Company
WA	OWL International 2800 156th Avenue S.E. Bellevue, WA 98007 (206)747–3203
	ScanText Inc. 1525 132nd N.E. Bellevue, WA 98005 (206)451–3350
Australia	Disctronics Inc. 9 Dehavilland Roade Braeside, Vic 3197 AUSTRALIA 03/587–2633 03/587–2901

State	Company
Canada	AXSES Boutilier Point Halifax, NS B0J 1G0 CANADA (902)826–2440 FAX: (826)429–6521
	Reteaco, Inc. 716 Gordon Baker Road Willowdale, ON M2H 3B4 CANADA (416)497–0579
Wales	Nimbus Records, Ltd. Wyastone Leys Monmouth NP5 3SR WALES 0600/890 682

Compiled by Online Press Inc.

Character Analysis

By Ben Templin
From *MacUser* magazine

[Although this article focusses on OCR packages for the Macintosh, many of Bill Templin's comments concerning this technology apply equally well to packages for the IBM.]

Morris Q. writes law books on a typewriter. He's done it that way for 30 years and wouldn't switch to a word processor any sooner than he would trade his bow tie for the latest in splashy Italian silk. It's Morris's publisher who's left to hire typists to input the text in the computer and proofreaders to make sure the manuscript is typed correctly.

Such work is common even in the age of desktop publishing, when the distinction between writer, typesetter, and publisher is increasingly blurred. But using typists to rekey information is, in management parlance, labor-intensive. A more elegant solution is optical character recognition (OCR).

WORD PICTURES

OCR is like printing in reverse. You start with hard copy and end up with an electronic file. Unfortunately, the middle steps aren't quite as easy as choosing a document and clicking a command. The average system digitizes a page into the computer's memory by using a scanner. The scanner acts like a camera to create a picture of the text. OCR software then looks at each image of each letter and matches it to an ASCII text character. In other words, it turns the picture of a word into an actual word that can be read into a database, spreadsheet, or word processor.

OCR isn't a radically new technology. The idea has been around ever since someone asked who would be the unlucky stiff to type all the company files into the computer. However, OCR has been slow to arrive to the Macintosh because of poor results during early tests. OCR often falls short of the mark when trying to recognize letters that look similar. For instance, the letter *i* is often mistaken for *l*, or the letter *c* for *e*. Some of the lower-end packages are little better than a 35-word-per-minute typist who can't

> *Is a word worth a thousand pixels? In optical character recognition, the answer is yes — if you don't mind that it's misspelled.*

spell. However, the past year has seen technical enhancements, more product introductions, and a corresponding drop in cost.

The software reviewed here varies considerably in price and performance. Some are packages that come bundled with a scanner. Others are programs that hardware manufacturers offer their customers at an additional charge. Still others come from software companies and work with a variety of scanners. What they have in common is what they won't accomplish. With the exception of ReadStar II Plus, none of these programs satisfactorily reads typeset text. You won't be able to convert a published book or magazine article into a word-processing document. But all of them can handle text typed on a typewriter, and some work with dot-matrix or laser printer output as well.

OCR doesn't work well with typeset material because the hardware can't provide an image with enough resolution for the software to isolate each letter from the one next to it. Most Macintosh scanners digitize images at 300 dots per inch (dpi). While this is more than enough information for the human eye, the computer can't always discern the subtle nuances between letters with such little information.

Some of the software packages compensate for hardware shortcomings with options that enhance the resolution. For instance, brightness and contrast controls adjust for poor quality that's a result of colored paper, third- or fourth-generation copies, or light printing.

Another option is to filter out stray marks on the page. Even one pixel's worth of dirt above the letter *o,* for example, might be interpreted as an ascender and cause the program to misread the character as a *b.* To avoid confusion, some programs have an automatic filter that removes

OCR HISTORY

The human eye has always been the model for optical character recognition technology. When you read, your eyes scan a line of text; the lens focuses the light on the retina; and the retina then "digitizes" the image and transmits it to the brain. In fact, many of the early developments in optical character recognition stemmed from efforts to build reading aids for blind and visually impaired people. One of the first patents on record for a reading machine for the blind is dated 1809.

OCRs have been under research and development for over 100 years by various individual scientists. C.R. Carey of Boston, Massachusetts, developed the first retina scanner in 1870, using a mosaic of photocells to scan characters; P. Nipkow of Poland developed a scanning disk in 1890 that was a forerunner of modern television cameras; Emmanuel Goldberg of Chicago converted scanned text into Morse code; and others added to or refined the technology.

In the early 1950s, the widely publicized work of Mark Sheppard, the inventor of GISMO ... A Robot Reader-Writer, generated widespread interest in optical character recognition. In 1954, Jacob Rabinow developed a prototype machine foreign accent marks. Other programs require that you use an eraser tool and clean up the accents and dirt yourself before sending the page through the OCR process.

COMPATIBLE PARTNERS

You'll want to make sure that the OCR package you buy also controls the scanner you own. All the packages reviewed control at least one scanner directly. (For detailed information on compatibility, see the accompanying chart.) Some programs, like Read-It!, claim to work with any scanner because they open the image files that most scanners support—TIFF, PICT, bit map. However, that approach is time-consuming because you have to use two applications (the scanner's imaging software and the OCR program) to accomplish your task.

Another factor that can cut down on time spent is the amount of control an OCR package offers before scanning. One of the obstacles in effective OCR is isolating text from other extraneous elements on the page, such as graphics, letterheads, and rules. No OCR program for the Macintosh has enough smarts to distinguish a graphic as such on its own. When encountering a graphic, most OCR programs will try to parse it as text, which results in a long wait and lots of gibberish.

To get around this, most programs allow you to define the single rectangular area of the page that you want scanned. Although this limited solution lets you eliminate most letterheads, more complex pages with multiple graphics still require you to isolate text from graphics after a page is scanned and before it is sent through the OCR process.

At least one program, however, gives you control over the page without the extra step between scanning and OCR. Microtek's MacinTEXT lets you mask out any part of the page to exclude graphics. More importantly, it also lets you define separate areas on the page that are to be run through the OCR program. This is particularly useful if you are processing multiple copies of the same form. You can, for instance, designate only the fields that were filled in by a typist and not worry about processing the form's instructions each time it is scanned.

The one problem with defining areas before scanning is assuring that the page is physically aligned to the electronic grid. If the page is off by even a fraction of an inch, you might end up cutting off part of a line of text. The easiest way

---

that was able to read uppercase typewriter output at a "fantastic" speed of one character per minute. Many large companies, including IBM and Bell Laboratories, also worked on optical character recognition techniques during this period.

Sheppard and Rabinow both went on to start their own companies and were instrumental in developing optical character recognition tools for the government, banks, and publishers. During the late 1960s, the technology underwent many dramatic developments, but for the most part OCRs were still considered exotic and futuristic. Systems that cost millions of dollars were not uncommon, and even relatively low-priced systems ($50,000) did not become commonplace in the business office until this decade, when the widespread use of personal computers dramatically changed the role of OCRs.

By Tom Stanton. Excerpted from "Peripheral Vision: A Guide to Optical Character Readers," *PC Magazine.* **Copyright © 1985 Ziff Communications Company**

to center a page precisely on a scanner is to use a document feeder. These add-ons, which are offered by most scanner manufacturers at an additional charge, feed pages along a set path with more accuracy than human hands.

Document feeders also prevent "skew" problems. Skew occurs when a page is put through the scanner cockeyed. If the baseline of the text isn't at a 90-degree angle to the edge of the paper, the letters appear to travel uphill or downhill. This confuses the OCR's matching tables. A certain amount of skew (1 to 2 degrees) is usually allowable during OCR, but a safer bet is to use a document feeder.

SETTING THE TYPE TABLES

Part of the problem with OCR is that the desktop publishing world now contains so many different typefaces. As a result, it's difficult for a program to recognize them all. For instance, the lowercase Courier letter *g* differs from the *g* in other faces—so much so that it could easily be mistaken for Prestige Elite's *q*.

OCR packages approach the font problem in a variety of ways. Some packages include type tables that you load into memory before running the OCR program. This assumes that you know what font was used on the page you are trying

OCR PACKAGES FOR THE MACINTOSH

Features	MacinTEXT	ReadStar II Plus	TextScan	Read-It!*	Publish Pac
Typewriter fonts†					
Artesian	yes	N/A	N/A	no	no
Bookface Academic	yes	N/A	N/A	no	no
Bold	no	N/A	N/A	no	yes
Courier	yes	N/A	N/A	yes	yes
Elite	yes	N/A	N/A	yes	yes
Gothic	yes	N/A	N/A	no	no
Letter Gothic	yes	N/A	N/A	yes	yes
Madeleine	no	N/A	N/A	no	yes
OCR-B	no	N/A	N/A	yes	yes
Pica	yes	N/A	N/A	no	yes
Prestige Pica	yes	N/A	N/A	yes	yes
Prestige Elite	yes	N/A	N/A	yes	yes
Title	no	N/A	N/A	no	yes
Victoria	yes	N/A	N/A	no	no
Learning mode	no	yes	yes	yes	no
Scanners (direct control)	Microtek	Microtek, Canon	Canon	Microtek, Canon (MacScan)	DEST
Pre-scan control					
Brightness	yes	yes	yes	yes	no
Contrast	yes	yes	no	yes	no
Define page	yes	yes	no	yes	no

to read. If you're dealing with documents that were typed ten years ago, the typewriter might not still be around. Other packages, like Publish Pac, take an "omni-font" approach. Here you don't need to tell the program what font it is trying to read; the program looks at the general characteristics that most letters have in common.

Still other systems require you to build the font files yourself. As you read a page, you teach the program to recognize certain characters that it then remembers and saves in a separate file. ReadStar II Plus is one such program. Some programs mix the two approaches. ReadIt! comes with font files that you can then customize for the peculiarities of your particular typewriter.

MacinTEXT and Read-It! include some standard Apple LaserWriter fonts. The question is, of course, why run a page through an OCR program if it was generated on a Mac in the first place? There might be a small need for Apple fonts if your system crashed and your only backup was hard copy, but that would be rare and certainly not the best way to back up your data.

The reliance of OCR packages on computer fonts has gone to even more ridiculous lengths. The technology has actually spawned two fonts

Features	MacinTEXT	ReadStar II Plus	TextScan	Read-It!*	Publish Pac
Mask out graphics	yes	no	no	no	no
Define OCR areas	yes	no	no	no	no
Filter dirt	yes	no	no	yes	no
Post-scan control					
Define OCR areas	yes	yes	yes	yes	yes
Eraser tool	no	yes	no	no	no
Saves text in					
Text	yes	yes	yes	yes	yes
MacWrite	no	no	no	no	yes
Word 3.0	no	no	no	no	yes
Formatting					
Indents	yes	no	no	yes	yes
Insert tabs for space	no	no	no	no	yes
Text flows/line for line	Line for line	Text flows	Line for line	Line for line	Text flows
Compensates for hyphenated words at end of line	no	yes	yes	no	yes
Editing within OCR program	yes	no	yes	yes	no
Statistics	no	yes	no	yes	no

*Also supports several brands of typewriters
†Font styles may vary between makes of typewriters

of its own. The fonts, named appropriately enough OCR-A and OCR-B, are optimized to increase the recognition rate. At first it seems ironic that the fonts even exist, but there is a reason. A retail store, for instance, can use the font for labeling products and prices. When an item is bought, the tag is scanned to update the inventory. However, bar code technology is more reliable and faster than OCR, and its widespread use has virtually eliminated OCR's chances in that market.

CHARACTER ASSIGNATION

Before an OCR program even attempts to match characters, it has to separate the letters into individual bit maps. This is known as *parsing*. For monospaced fonts, parsing is simple. Each character in a monospaced font is of equal width, regardless of how big the character actually is. To parse the letter you only need to draw a square around each character. This is as if you superimposed a piece of graph paper over the image.

Proportional fonts, on the other hand, vary the space according to the width of the letter. Fonts that are typeset often contain kerned letters. This is where the space between two letters is tightened (or sometimes loosened) for readability (or artistic concerns). To parse a kerned font, the OCR program must lasso that part of the letter that hangs over another. Some letters are kerned so tightly that they actually touch. Since OCR programs usually can't distin-

TESTING RULES AND RESULTS

The tests were conducted using a Macintosh II with 2 megabytes of memory and a 40-megabyte hard disk that had 12 megabytes of free space. The scanners were all SCSI-driven. The sample consisted of a seven-page typed document that used a monospaced Prestige Pica font. The document was 1,261 words long and had a total of 8,323 characters.

At first glance, it looks like MacinTEXT is the winner for speed and accuracy. However, the file it generated contained a carriage return at the end of each line. Publish Pac was a close second, but is in many ways more desirable since it formats documents with "running text"—only inserting a carriage return at the end of each paragraph.

Although ReadStar II Plus, Read-It!, and TextScan have lower accuracy rates, it should be noted that these programs are based on "learning" a font as they process it. When an unknown character is encountered, the program stops and "queries" the user for the correct character. A different document was used to teach these programs the font being used until satisfactory results were obtained. The test document was then run with the program's "query" capability turned off. The accuracy would have been better if the "stop and check" mode had been activated, but then again, it would have taken more time too.

The decision to buy a program should be based on particular needs. If you must accommodate a wide variety of fonts, one of the "learning" OCR programs might prove to be the best choice. However, you'll have a much easier time processing documents if the font you need to OCR is supported by MacinTEXT or Publish Pac.

Results	Words per minute	% of accurately read characters	% of accurately read words
MacinTEXT	325	99.53	96.91
Publish Pac	203	99.07	93.82
Read-It!	63	98.30	88.65
ReadStar II Plus	150	96.90	78.98
TextScan	150	96.91	79.54

guish between the two bit maps, they compensate by allowing you to designate two letters for one image. ReadStar II Plus is the only program among the five reviewed here that is sophisticated enough to lasso kerned text. In fact, in some ways it works better with typeset text than it does with typewritten pages.

MATCH GAME

After the type is parsed, it must be read. You can do this in several ways. Matching bit maps to ASCII characters breaks down into two basic methods: matrix matching and pattern extraction. Matrix matching searches a type table for an exact pixel-by-pixel duplicate of the bit map. Pattern extraction examines the structure of a letter rather than its shape. The idea is to isolate strokes and loops that are characteristic of a letter. Pattern extraction is more appropriate for proportional typefaces. It's also slower. Most packages use a combination of the two methods: Using matrix matching for monospaced fonts and pattern extraction for proportional type is a common solution.

Actually running an OCR program can be as simple as choosing a command and waiting for the text to appear (MacinTEXT and Publish Pac) or as complicated as teaching the program the font as it processes a document (ReadStar II Plus, Read-It!, and TextScan). In the latter case, this usually consists of looking at the bit map of a character and typing it on the keyboard. The theory is that after you've processed enough documents, the font will become known and you can switch the program into automatic mode. In practice, you get the best results when the "query" function is active—even after extensive learning sessions.

Getting a wrong match is commonplace. How an OCR program reacts to an unknown character is sometimes more critical than the fact that it actually made a mistake. Most respond by putting in an uncommon character—such as when you try using a spelling checker on the document. If the unknown character falls

OCR FUTURE

It appears 1989 will be the vintage year for OCR products on the Macintosh. A combination of automatic recognition and learning mode will be the new style. Some interesting rumors concern hardware products. It appears Xerox has recently acquired DataCopy, which has a line of scanners for the Macintosh and an OCR software product that recognizes typewritten material only. Xerox already owns Kurzweil, pioneers in OCR technology for microcomputers, though never for the Mac. Kurzweil and DataCopy have been combined into one division. Their development teams are cooperating, so it appears likely that we will eventually see an OCR product for the Macintosh from their combined efforts. My guess is that the most likely product will be a card for the Mac II that automatically reads typewritten and typeset material.

The other company to watch in this area is Calera (formerly Palentir). At last September's Seybold Desktop Publishing show, they introduced a card for the IBM PC AT that gave it advanced OCR capability. It was priced at about $3500. They are known to be working on a Macintosh version, but its release date and features haven't been announced.

By Scott Beamer, who has published over 100 articles in the popular Macintosh magazines.

in the middle of a word, most checkers will see that single word as two words. This makes it difficult if not impossible to replace the misspelled word with the correct one. The more versatile OCR programs let you assign your own character. This way you can use an uncommon alphabet character (like the uppercase *Z*) which is compatible with a spelling checker but which will seldom spell a real, though incorrect, word.

TextScan goes even one step further. It lets you make global changes to a recognized character immediately after a document has been OCR'd. If all *l*s were recognized as *!*s, for instance, TextScan lets you correct the mistake without changing what should be an exclamation point into the numeral 1.

FORM VERSUS FUNCTION

Another critical element in OCR is how well the software maintains the original formatting. A program can have an outstanding recognition rate but still require extensive editing because the layout isn't maintained. For instance, it's difficult for most programs to distinguish between an end of a line and an end of a paragraph, so every line is given a carriage return. This means you'll have to strip out all the extra returns if you want to rework the document in a word processor. Also, most programs won't compensate for words that were hyphenated at the end of a line. The exceptions to these problems are Publish Pac and ReadStar II Plus. Both programs insert a carriage return only at the end of a paragraph. They also rejoin words that have been hyphenated at the end of a line (this can be a mixed blessing if the correct spelling of a word already contains a hyphen).

WHAT'S NEW, BUT NOT NEW

OCR technology is moving forward rapidly. What was unavailable last year is now within easy reach of most consumers. Yet some critics contend that OCR will be out of date by the time it gets up to speed. They say it's a matter of attrition: As the Morris Q.'s of the world give way to more modern methods, there will be less of a need for OCR. Still, there remain millions of pages of documents in company file rooms waiting to be input into computers. Furthermore, as FAX/modems become integrated into Mac IIs and SEs, the demand for OCR will also increase. A FAX creates an image of a document that is then sent over the phone lines. OCR answers the need to then convert those documents into ASCII for document processing.

As it stands, optical character recognition on the Macintosh won't win any spelling bees, but in most cases it's significantly faster than the average typist. In fact, in a small desktop publishing operation, it might be an economical alternative to hiring a typist to input manuscripts.

Reprinted from *MacUser*, September 1988. Copyright © Ziff Communications Company.

CD-ROM Text Preparation with SGML

By Bill Zoellick

[Some people look to standards like SGML to simplify the preparation of data for CD-ROM. Widespread acceptance of this markup method would indeed facilitate the use of the same files for different purposes, as Bill Zoellick explains.]

When you look at a page of text, you are seeing more than letters and words; you are aware of the page's *structure*. Titles stand out because they are centered and, often, printed in a different typeface. Your eye can pick out headings because they, too, are often in a different typeface and because of the way that white space is arranged around headings. Tables stand out because they are so highly structured, broken into rows, columns, column headings, and so on.

All of this structure that is so immediately obvious to your eye is invisible to a computer if we simply feed it a stream of letters, tabs, and spaces. But it often happens that the computer needs access to text structure just as much as it needs access to characters. We solve this problem by inserting *markup* into the text stream. The markup usually consists of special sequences of characters, called *tags*, used to indicate the beginning and end of text structures. We might, for example, indicate that the following text segment consists of a first-level heading, a paragraph, and a list by inserting marks like this:

<h1>About Markup</h1>

<p>Text-processing and word-processing systems typically require additional information to be interspersed among the natural text of the document. This additional information, called markup, serves two purposes:</p>

<list>

<li>Separating the logical elements of the document.

> *An increasingly large number of publishing tools can make use of SGML, and therefore an increasingly large number of options are open to you as you move SGML-based tags and text from system to system.*

<li>And specifying the processing to be performed on those elements.

</list>

The processing system must be able to differentiate between markup tags and the actual text of the document. In this example, tags are distinguishable from text because they are enclosed in angle brackets.

Over the years publishers, typesetters, and designers of formatting and page-composition software have devised a great many different markup schemes. In a sense, the escape sequences sent to your printer to make it do boldfacing, italics, and changes of font are markup schemes. The information stored in a Microsoft Word or WordPerfect file that keeps track of indentation, spacing, and changes in font represent another type of markup, even though most users see only the results of the markup on their screen or on the printed page, rather than dealing with the markup directly. There are also systems in which the use of the markup is explicit—those such as troff, Scribe, TeX, and other kinds of text-formatting software. Individual publishers and typesetters have often developed their own private markup schemes for use within their own organizations.

SGML

This diversity of markup schemes creates an interchange problem. Files marked up for use on one system often cannot be used directly on another system. "Converting" the files for use on another system simply by stripping out the tags and transferring the characters and spaces in ASCII form is not really an acceptable solution because the structure of the text is often just as important as the individual letters and spaces. The obvious solution or, at least, so it seemed a number of years ago, is to get everyone to agree upon a single, standard markup scheme.

Unfortunately, attempts to agree upon a single, universal set of markup tags were about as successful as attempts to get everyone to speak Esperanto. As reasonable as the proposal to create a standard tagging scheme might seem, the fact is that different types of applications, different types of work environments, require radically different approaches to markup. So the proponents of a standard tagging scheme backed off one step: If we all cannot agree upon a single tagging scheme, how about agreeing upon a standard way of describing tagging schemes? In other words, your system and my system can use different tagging schemes, and they can interchange documents using these different schemes, as long as we agree upon a method for communicating the key information we need to use each other's tags. The questions are:

- How do you differentiate the tags from the text?
- What is the set of legal tags?
- What are the legal relationships between these tags?

SGML, which stands for Standard Generalized Markup Language, is the tool that has emerged for accomplishing these tasks. SGML is, in fact, a language, just as COBOL and Pascal are languages. But rather than describing algorithms and procedures as these languages do, SGML describes markup systems.

The heart of an SGML description is a Document Type Definition (DTD). A DTD is a formal, rigorous description of all the tags that can legally occur in a document and of the permissible arrangements of these tags. A DTD might tell us, for example, that the tags describing the list items in our example above (<li>) are permitted to occur only within the context of a list (delimited by the <list> and </list> tags).

A DTD is a description of a tagging scheme. Different markup systems have different DTDs. A tagging scheme described with an SGML DTD is called an SGML *application*.

SGML Applications

It is important to distinguish between SGML itself and its applications. Keeping this distinction clear is complicated by the fact that, while SGML is, as its name implies, a standard (ISO 8879), so are some SGML applications. The most notable standard application, AAP Markup, was developed by the Association of American Publishers (AAP) for tagging books, articles, and serials.

Another important SGML application is the tagging scheme developed by the U.S. Department of Defense as part of the Computer Aided Logistics System (CALS) initiative. This markup system, described in MIL-M-28001, is a set of tags used in technical documentation for weapons systems.

Other SGML applications are in use by the Canadian Department of National Defense, Hewlett-Packard, and others. The Hewlett-Packard system (HP Tag) is used as a direct input to CD-ROM production.

BILL ZOELLICK

Home: Boulder, Colorado
Job: Consultant
Quote: *"The CD-ROM industry is moving from being an industry apart to being an integral, well-defined part of the publishing industry as a whole. CD-ROM is finally emerging as yet another publishing medium, one that is particularly well suited for delivering certain kinds of information effectively and inexpensively."*

SGML Publishing Systems

A carefully designed SGML tagging scheme can be the backbone of a true publishing database. In other words, a good tagging system can allow a company to treat its information as a resource, rather than as just an archive. The tagging system can facilitate sophisticated, flexible information retrieval, extraction and rearrangement of material for producing different publications for different audiences, and presentation of the material on different types of print and electronic media. This last point is particularly important for CD-ROM production, in which so much of the data-preparation cost is often associated with backing the material out of a format designed for paper-based publication.

Why use an SGML-based tagging system rather than some other tagging scheme? There are several answers to this question:

- Use of SGML to describe your tagging scheme guarantees that your tags can be understood by other SGML-based software. An increasingly large number of publishing tools can make use of SGML, and therefore an increasingly large number of options are open to you as you move SGML-based tags and text from system to system.

- SGML is a formal, rigorous description of your tags and therefore provides you with an automated way of verifying that all the tags in the document do, in fact, conform to the rules you have established. Such verification of tag validity and consistency is often difficult or impossible with less formal *ad hoc* tagging systems.

- A number of companies make SGML *parsers*. The better parsers in this group provide you with a mechanism that reads through all the tags in a document, recognizes them, and can then use the tagging to do useful work, such as translation to specific output formats. Use of a good parser in combination with SGML-based tagging can help you avoid writing special-purpose translation and conversion software from the ground up.

Once you have decided to use an SGML-based system, either by defining your own tagging scheme and DTD or by using an established system, such as AAP Markup, how do you get the tags into the text? There are several answers, each appropriate for different circumstances:

- You can insert the tags by hand.

- If you are creating the text for the first time, you can use an SGML-based editor that inserts the tags as you create the document.

- If you have text that is already marked in a highly structured way, you may be able to use a code-for-code translator to create most of the SGML tags.

- If you are working with less structured input, such as that coming from word-processing systems or from optical character-recognition devices, you can purchase software that uses artificial intelligence techniques to actually recognize the text structure in much the same way that your eye and brain do.

For more information about the SGML standard itself, contact the Graphics Communication Association, 1730 N. Lynn Street, Suite 604, Arlington, Virginia 22209. For more information about SGML-based products, consult publications, such as *The Seybold Report on Publishing Systems,* that deal specifically with the publishing industry, and contact the vendors listed there.

[Bill Zoellick is a consultant working out of Boulder, Colorado. Prior to consulting, he served as Vice President of Avalanche Development Company, a software firm applying artificial intelligence technology to the problem of preparing data for use in electronic publishing and desktop retrieval systems. Zoellick is the author of a widely used textbook on file structures and the co-editor of a book on optical publishing. He has also written numerous articles on information retrieval, CD-ROM file systems, and CD-ROM software technology.]

PRODUCING GRAPHICS AND IMAGES

ENVISIONING INFORMATION
By Edward Tufte

DIGITAL IMAGE STORAGE ON CD-ROM
By Michael D. Martin

IMAGE MANAGEMENT ON CD-ROM
By Bruce Benge and Calvin Aiken

Envisioning Information

By Edward Tufte
From *The 1988 Personal Computing Forum*

[What makes a good graphic? In this section's first article, which is adapted from a presentation made at the 1988 Personal Computing Forum, Edward Tufte shows us outstanding examples of graphics that work. As he explains why, he outlines some of the basic principles of information design.]

Let's begin with a remarkable story, an example of why many graphics are a lot better than talk, talk, talk.

This is the story of the trial of John Gotti, the alleged Mafia leader in New York who was acquitted [*in 1988*]. The jury had met for several days and then they asked the court to let them take another look at a piece of evidence that Gotti's lawyers had introduced. It was the chart shown on the following page. They saw the chart again and then immediately voted to acquit John Gotti and his colleagues.

The chart shows the crimes that the federal witnesses against Gotti had committed. And if you look at it, you'll see a remarkable example of a spreadsheet. We have here the seven informants—who are now, by the way, all in the witness protection program—who testified against Mr. Gotti and his colleagues. We have their names across the top of the chart and down the first column we have their crimes.

There are some interesting design principles at work here. First, the more obnoxious crimes have been placed in the visually more prominent positions, either at the top of the first column—murder and drugs—or at the bottom, where a special crime has been created—pistol whipping a priest.

Now we can read this chart, of course, in two directions. It uses the flatland of the paper quite well. We spread the crimes out one way and the informants out the other way, and we can then read down the columns and look at the activities of some of these gentlemen.

CRIMINAL ACTIVITY OF GOVERNMENT INFORMANTS

CRIME	CARDINALE	LOFARO	MALONEY	POLISI	SENATORE	FORONJY	CURRO
MURDER	X	X					
ATTEMPTED MURDER		X	X				
HEROIN POSSESSION AND SALE	X	X		X			X
COCAINE POSSESSION AND SALE	X		X	X			
MARIJUANA POSSESSION AND SALE							X
GAMBLING BUSINESS		X		X		X	
ARMED ROBBERIES	X		X	X	X		X
LOANSHARKING		X		X			
KIDNAPPING			X	X			
EXTORTION			X	X			
ASSAULT	X		X	X			X
POSSESSION OF DANGEROUS WEAPONS	X	X	X	X	X		X
PERJURY		X				X	
COUNTERFEITING					X	X	
BANK ROBBERY			X	X			
ARMED HIJACKING				X	X		
STOLEN FINANCIAL DOCUMENTS			X	X	X		
TAX EVASION				X		X	
BURGLARIES	X	X		X	X		
BRIBERY		X		X			
THEFT: AUTO, MONEY, OTHER			X	X	X	X	X
BAIL JUMPING AND ESCAPE			X	X			
INSURANCE FRAUDS					X	X	
FORGERIES				X	X		
PISTOL WHIPPING A PRIEST	X						
SEXUAL ASSAULT ON MINOR							X
RECKLESS ENDANGERMENT							X

© From The 1988 Personal Computing Forum

If you look at the middle column for Mr. Polisi, you'll see that he has a streak going.

There's an intellectual among the crowd—Mr. Foronjy, the second column from the right. No violence for him. It's gambling and perjury and counterfeiting and tax evasion and a little theft and insurance fraud. But nothing violent.

So from this chart, the jury can see different kinds of patterns. This is a marvelous example of the power of graphics, particularly in a courtroom setting.

In a courtroom, we have an endless flow of talk, talk, talk that can't be controlled by the "user." The wonderful thing about good graphics is that they are user-controllable; they are also a wideband channel. In addition, good graphics allow us to reason while looking at the material. We can customize it and edit it individually. Graphics bring a freedom to the user; they take the control of the information out of the hands of the editors and publishers. I'll discuss this more later, as I talk about envisioning information.

THE PURPOSE

We envision information in order to communicate, to reason about, and to preserve that information. This has all been going on now for about 6,000 years. We can't let any NIH [Not Invented Here] syndrome influence us when it comes to showing information. People have been doing it now for 6,000 years.

In the course of my work, two themes have been central to my thinking about how to show information visually. The first is that we begin with very complex information. The world is complex, or in statistical jargon, it is a multivariate world, a high-dimensional world. And yet our display devices are endless two-dimensional flatlands, whether they be paper, or a computer screen, or anything else.

Thus one of the two central tasks of envisioning information is to escape flatland. There have been design strategies, going back to Galileo in 1610, for escaping flatland and adding dimensionality to paper.

And the second thing at the heart of envisioning information is to try to find design strategies that help you increase information density.

To summarize then, the heart of the matter, whether we're dealing with a paper display or with a screen display, is to try to increase its information resolution—to escape the dimensional flatland of paper and screen and to increase the density of the information.

What I would like to do in the rest of this article is to look at some examples, to suggest some techniques for enriching flatland and increasing information density, and to look at some general principles. These ideas are relevant to escaping the KGB interface, as it has been described, which is an embarrassment to everybody in the industry.

THE SECRET

To begin, let us revisit Napoleon's March. I expect many of you have seen the next graphic, but it's such a miracle that I'd like to describe it briefly again. This graphic, of course, shows the War of 1812. It was done by a Frenchman named Charles Joseph Minard in 1869. In the upper right-hand corner is Moscow and over at the left is the Polish-Russian border. The width of the gray line—the river of troops flowing in—is the size of Napoleon's army at any point on the map. It is moving from left to right.

They begin with 422,000 soldiers—the gray band at the far left. It is bitterly cold. They reach Moscow greatly reduced to 100,000 soldiers. Moscow is on fire, sacked, and deserted. They retreat.

The dark line at the bottom is the path of the retreat, moving from right to left. The line grows ever thinner. Notice that, just a little bit to the left of the middle of the graphic, the auxiliary troops rejoin and fatten up the line briefly. But then you see a sharp discontinuity in the line. That is about where half of the surviving army falls through the ice of the Berezina River and drowns.

The comparison is enforced in this graphic. That's the essential task of reasoning about information. The comparison is enforced when we compare the bank of 422,000 soldiers that started with the 10,000 that survived—one in 42. This is a graphical *War and Peace,* drawn by a visual Tolstoy.

Minard tied the path of the retreating army to the temperature scale drawn at the bottom of the graphic. And so we have the position of the army and various temperatures. It is extraordinarily cold. You can read some of those temperatures, and in my book, *The Visual Display of Quantitative Information,* where this graphic is in color, you can see all the details.

This graphic is a miracle of information design. On the flatland of the paper, without ever making a big thing about it, Minard has put six dimensions of data: the size of the army, its location in two-dimensional space, its direction, time and temperature. No mumbo-jumbo; this is transparent design. We can contemplate what happened to Napoleon. If one of my colleagues in Yale's sociology department were to do this, there would be a lot of mumbo-jumbo about "multivariate-spatial-temporal analysis" and so on. This, thank heavens, is free of the jargon.

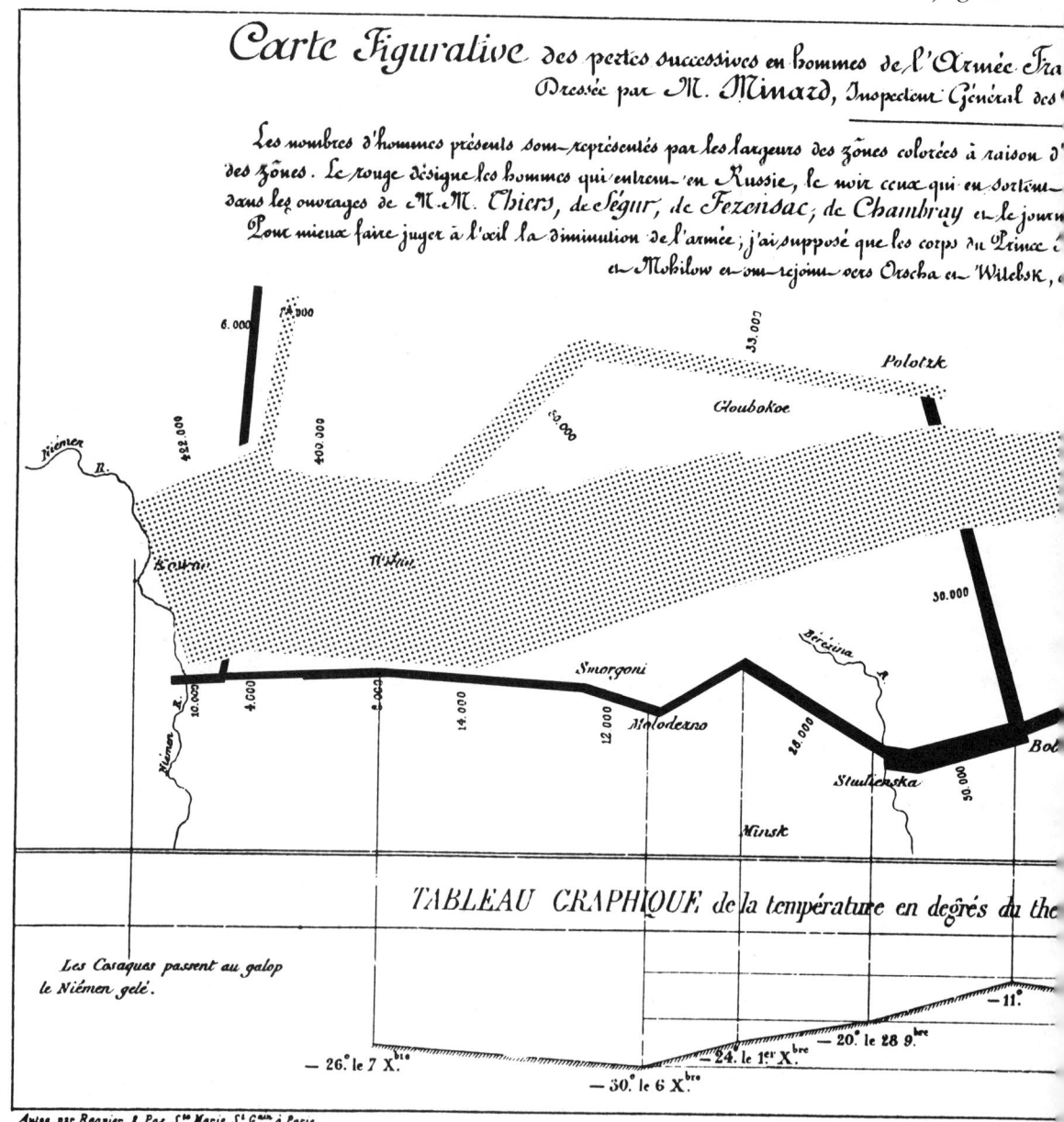

There is a design secret here, in this genius of a performance. It's all captured in the one person who did this graphic—in Minard. He was a great engineer, he was a historian, he could count, he designed many bridges in France. But most of all, this graphic was driven by its substance: Minard hated war. He produced the graphic as an anti-war poster. And so you have, caught up in this one person, all the talents necessary for good information design. You have somebody who could see and somebody who knew the substance. Both of these talents are absolutely necessary to skilled information design.

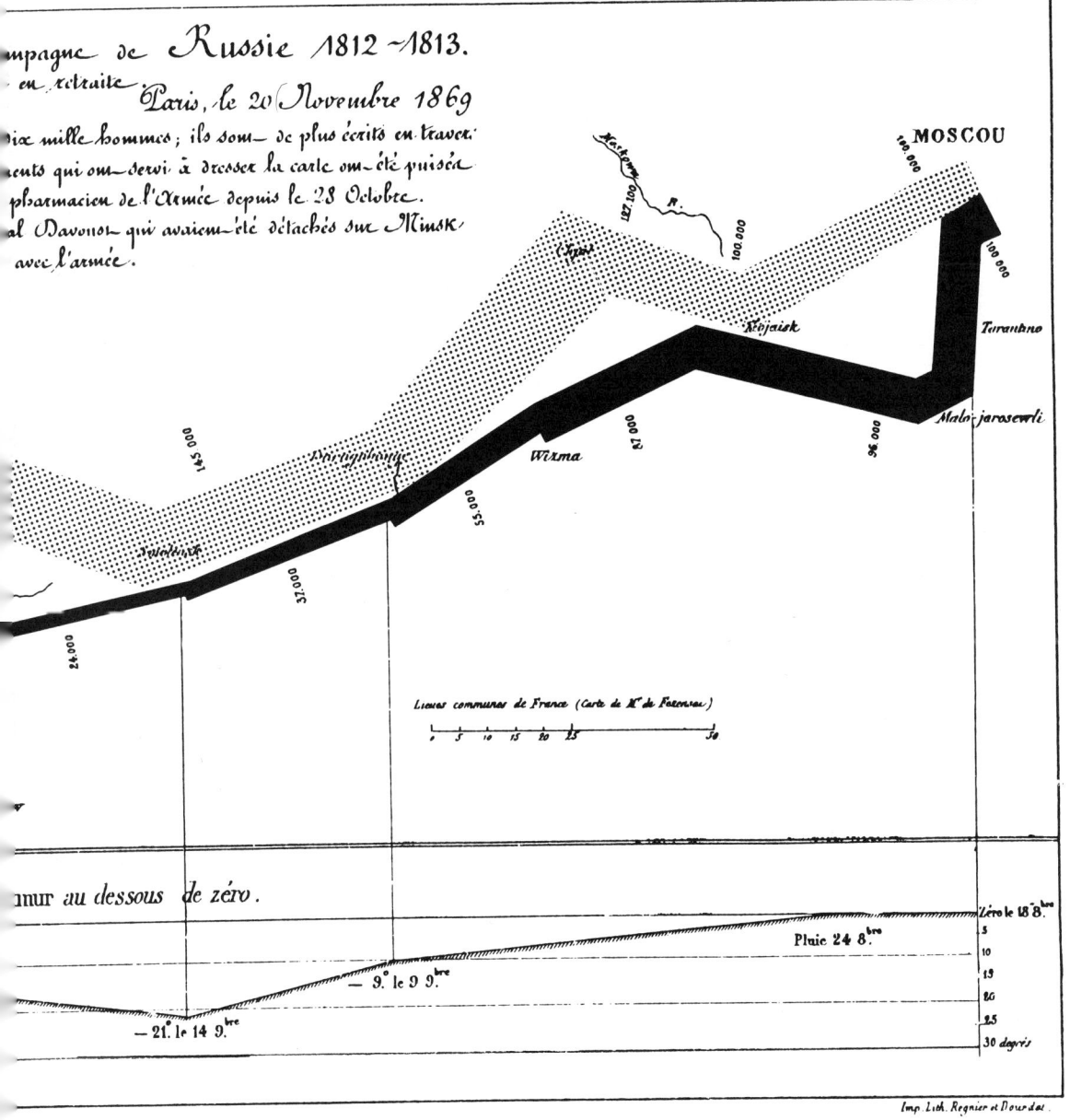

THE POTENTIAL RESULTS

A second classic of information design is the next graphic, a map of central London in 1854. It is no accident that many of our best examples of good graphics are maps. You see Oxford Street at the top. The black dots mark the houses where one or more people died of cholera during an epidemic in 1854.

Dr. John Snow, an epidemiologist, plotted all those deaths on the map. In addition, because he had a substantive idea about the cause of the deaths, he plotted with X-marks all the water pumps in that area. Then he looked carefully at the map. And if you look equally carefully, you'll see almost at the middle of Broad Street a pump just to the right of the "D" in "Broad." Snow thought, on the basis of this map, that that pump was contaminated. He ordered the handle of the pump removed, and the epidemic which had taken more than 500 lives ended. That is information design.

Think what Snow did here. His original data was a stack of death certificates sequenced over time. He reordered them. He took them out of that one-dimensional sequencing, he reordered them with a causal theory in two-dimensional space, and he came to this remarkable result.

DESIGN STRATEGIES

The example of the cholera epidemic and the next example, the Anderson map of New York, illustrate an extremely rich principle in showing information.

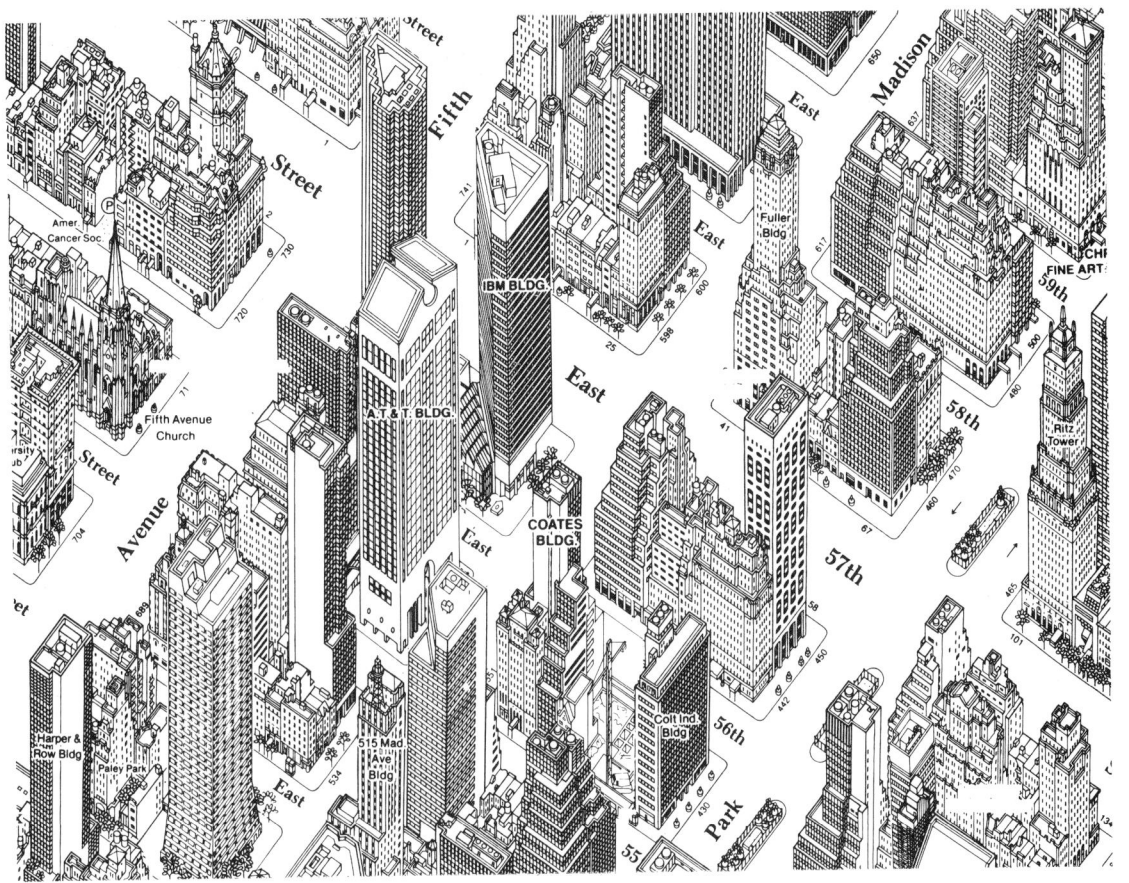

There's enormous detail in this map. We see the AT&T building with the Chippendale top, we see the IBM building on 57th and Madison with the atrium, and so on. We see where we may have been in New York, where we may have walked. This map suggests a remarkable design strategy; that is, in many cases in order to clarify you need to add detail. What happens here is that the detail of each window—the microstructure—grays into the texture of the wall. When we "read" this map from a distance, we see surfaces and blocks and structure. When we read it up close, we see the floor on which we worked last summer and, oh, there's the window of the manager, and so on. So in many cases, to simplify and to clarify the reading of graphics, add detail.

Most important here, though, is the micro-macro structure of the reading. This structure allows each user who comes to this map to read his or her own story—to personalize, to customize, to edit. With extremely high-density designs like this, you tap into the immense human capacities of selection and editing and all that they involve—choosing, remembering, forgetting, looking, sorting. These immense capacities are brought to bear as users add their personal information—their micro-information.

This example is just like a good aerial photograph of your hometown. When you show the photograph to other people, everybody is delighted about it, but they're all delighted for different reasons. They look at their houses, the neighborhoods where they went to school, and so on and so on.

PRODUCING GRAPHICS AND IMAGES

A contrast is the clunky, low-density computer disaster shown in the next graphic, a bar chart. What this graphic says—and it says nothing about substance—is "I used a Tinker Toy graphics program on the computer." It says nothing about the data. What it says is "My type is so heavy-handed that I have to encode everything with abbreviations. I have mindless moire vibrations. I have more numbers on the Y-axis than there are data points shown."

This chart should have been done as a table. Tables are especially good for small data sets—under 20 numbers. Graphics start to get powerful with maybe 200, 300, or 400 numbers. They start to get really good with 100,000 numbers. The world record is 6.6 million numbers. You can see this record holder, a picture that has 100,000 numbers per square inch, in the first chapter of my book.

Alas, low information density, because of low-resolution screens and low-resolution type designs, seems to have infected the whole industry. I once looked into the information resolution and information density of books, following up on my research on data density in *Visual Display*. The *World Almanac* runs 230 typographic characters per square inch, a typical telephone book runs about 170 or 180 characters per square inch, the bestselling *Mobil Travel Guide*, 150 characters per square inch, and so on. And then I looked at a good many computer manuals from all sorts of different companies. Well, I have discovered, I think, that people who write manuals are paid by the page! We're getting 20 characters per square inch in a good many of the commercial manuals. This compares with that bestselling book, *The Magic of Michael Jackson,* which runs 60 characters per square inch—not a deep book!

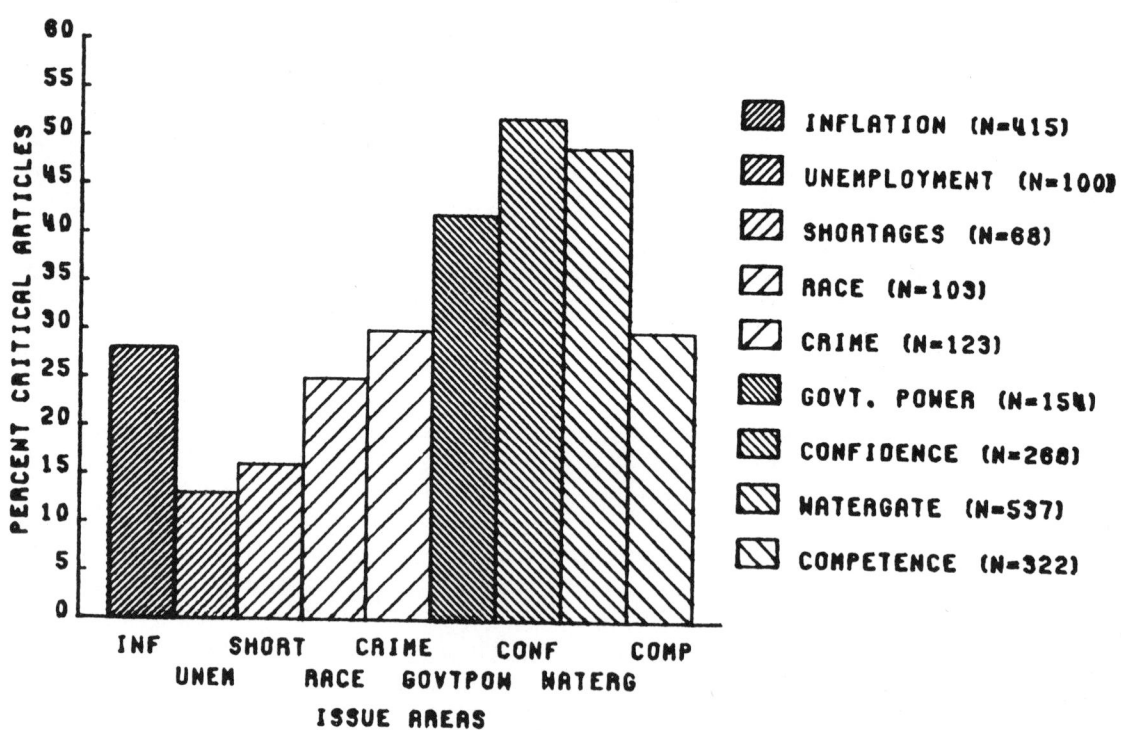

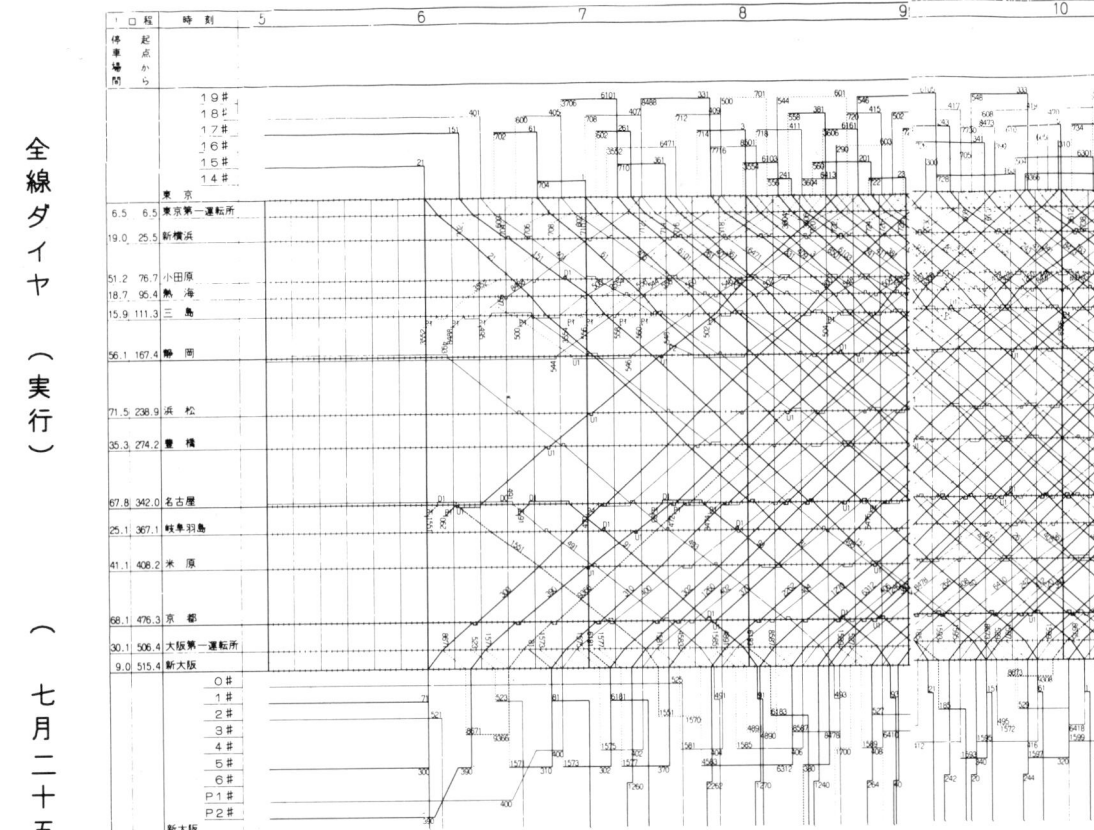

Let me show you another example of micro-macro design—an extraordinary example from the control room of the Japanese National Railroad (JNR). This is the control room from which the high speed Shinkansen—the bullet trains—are run. This up-to-date graphical time table, which is about six feet long, is a visual method of running an extremely complex system. The control room is filled with computers, but they still look at things on paper and print these schedules every day.

When I visited this control room, I was looking at some of the monitors and I saw times—the scheduled time of arrival and departure for the trains and then the actual time. And then I saw a little red dot next to one of the times, and I asked what it was. They said, "Well, we record the arrival and departure time of every train at every station and if any of those times—every arrival, every departure, every station—is off by more than 30 seconds, the red light goes on and there will be trouble."

When I came home, I called a friend at Amtrak and I said, "Tell me, what's your definition of 'on time'?" And he said, "Well, if the train makes it to the last station"—there's more—"within 30 minutes of its scheduled time, then the train is considered to be on time." So in Japan: every stop, in and out, within 30 seconds. Amtrak: last stop within 30 minutes.

PRODUCING GRAPHICS AND IMAGES 351

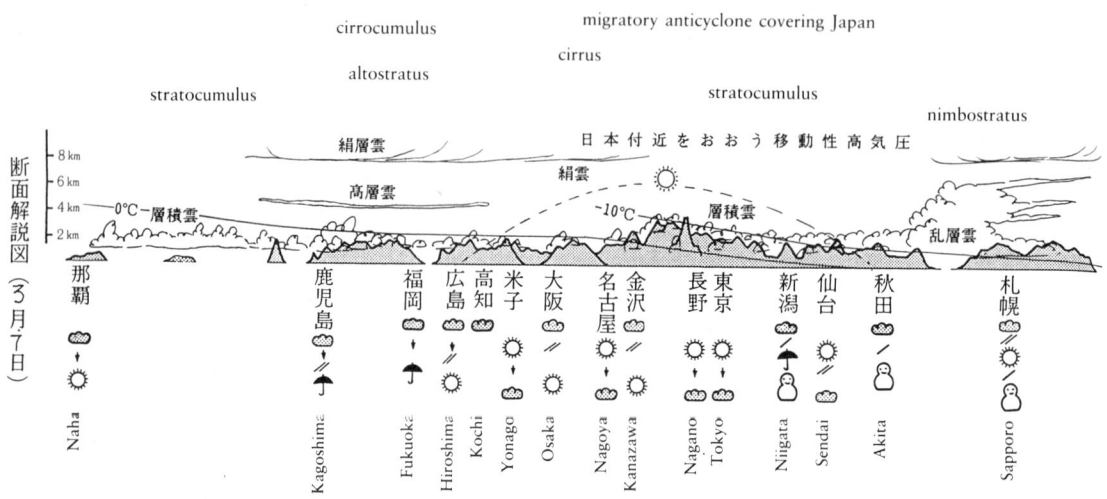

Let's look at one final Japanese example—an illustration that escapes flatland, so to speak, by changing the perspective. Instead of the standard model weather map, we have an ocean-eye view, showing the mountains and the clouds over the country, with contour lines for temperature. This is a marvelously simple, deft, smooth way of showing information. Of course, it helps if you're doing this for a long, thin country.

SOME PRINCIPLES

I'd like to conclude by pulling together some of the principles I've just discussed. The first one is the notion of information resolution and of designing so that we increase the information resolution of our extraordinarily low-resolution devices. The human eye easily accommodates 150 million bits of information. We have enormous powers of selection and editing. We should ask our users to rely on their eyes, rather than asking them to rely on their memory as they scroll, change screens, and so on. There are enormous gains to be made in increasing information resolution, whether through design or through technology. And much can be done with design.

A fine example of increasing resolution is in HyperCard, where a function shows the last 42 screens you've looked at in little postage card form. Good idea! It allows you to review and pick and choose. The screens are all in view at once to help you recall what you did.

Now, what about confusion in the face of all this information? The essential thing to remember is that confusion and clutter are design failures, not information attributes. The problem is never with the information or with the user. It's a function of whether you get the arrangement right—of skilled information design.

This leads me to my next point: When it comes to information design, never underestimate the audience. For example, in my jury trials I have heard attorneys say, "Well, we have only one college-educated person in this courtroom and it's a very complex case. Maybe we'd better have color graphics. Do something like *USA Today.*" My view is that that kind of contempt—that kind of patronizing attitude toward the audience—will leak through. [*In* The Elements of Style] Strunk and White say that no one can write decently who is condescending or patronizing.

This same kind of contempt shows up in some manuals, especially introductory manuals, which can be a bizarre mix of baby talk—sort of Mr. Rogers style: "Can you see the light on the top of the box?"—and words that never existed until the manual was written. Think of the message this mix conveys to the user. It's saying "When we talk your language, we use baby talk. But when we talk our private jargon, it's no more Mr. Nice Guy." The contempt is transparent.

My fourth point is one I've already discussed: the powerful idea of micro-macro design, of escaping flatland by a hierarchy of readings—by the microscopic reading, by the macroscopic reading.

My fifth and my last point is that the best analogy—I refuse to use the word *metaphor*—for visual interface is the map. There is in map-making—in cartography—enormous visual craft combined with the hard-headed engineering quality of surveying. Mapmakers have got their interface right. They know how to handle topography and color, how to layer information, and how to use extremely high densities of information.

CONCLUSION

Just because we are on the frontiers of technology does not mean that we are on the frontiers of design. We want to borrow from history—from the 6,000 years of human effort dedicated to information design. But we want a skepticism toward the routinely received doctrines of information design. For instance, one such doctrine is: To simplify, reduce the amount of information. And yet we see many situations where to clarify, we should add detail.

To conclude, I want to tell you a story about skepticism. This is the story of a professor who went off to England to give a talk. He was a philosopher and he spoke about the use of language. He had studied the world's languages and said that in some of them, a double negative means a negative—a reinforced negative. For instance, when the President of the United States said, "There ain't no smoking gun," he really meant that there wasn't one. The double negative was a reinforced negative. And sometimes, of course, a double negative is a positive; the signs cancel each other out. But, the professor said, though the meaning of a double negative might vary depending on context, one thing was for sure: In absolutely none of the world's languages did a double positive ever mean a negative.

Well, sitting in the back of the room was a feared "counter-example" person, Sidney Morgenbesser. He heard the theory that in none of the world's languages did a double positive ever mean a negative come floating to the back of the room. And without missing a beat, Morgenbesser said, "Yeah, yeah."

Originally published in *The 1988 Personal Computing Forum*, by EDventure Holdings Inc. Adapted by special permission. Copyright © 1988 by Edward Tufte. Copyright © 1988 by EDventure Holdings Inc.

Digital Image Storage on CD-ROM

By Michael D. Martin

[In this article, Mike Martin describes the Planetary Data System project and its investigation of image storage and compression techniques. The project's goal was to find an efficient means of cataloging and distributing the thousands of images collected during spacecraft planetary flybys to scientists and engineers for analysis and research.]

NASA's planetary exploration program has resulted in the collection of nearly 150,000 digital images of the planets of our solar system and their satellites. Only Neptune (which will be studied by Voyager 2 in 1989) and Pluto have not yet been visited by unmanned spacecraft.

The image collection is just one of many data sets acquired by instruments aboard planetary spacecraft. It has a special significance because the images support a broad range of scientific studies. In addition to their scientific value, many of the images present vistas of incredible natural beauty. Views of the complex ring system of Saturn, erupting volcanoes on Io, the swirling red spot on Jupiter, and a gigantic Martian canyon that would span the continental United States have dramatically changed mankind's perception of the solar system.

IMAGE DESCRIPTION

Most of these images have been acquired by camera systems that produce a rectangular array of picture elements. Each picture element, or "sample," within this array measures the brightness of the target object. This brightness is usually represented by an 8-bit integer value (0 to 255) representing an intensity ranging from black (0) to white (255). The size of the image array varies from 200 lines by 200 samples for the earliest Mariner 4 images of Mars to 1056 lines by 1204 samples for the Viking Orbiter images of Mars.

Most camera systems include a high-power telescope. These telescopes are so sophisticated that the Voyager camera system could resolve an object the size of a tanker truck from a distance equivalent to the number of miles between New York and Los Angeles. The cameras also include a filter wheel for obtaining images at various wavelengths. By taking images of the same scene through red, green, and blue filters, it is possible to reconstruct full color images from monochrome data. Sequences of images are often taken in swaths, which can be pieced together by hand or by computer processing to produce mosaics showing large areas of planetary or satellite surfaces. Images of the same scene, taken from different viewing angles, can be combined to produce three-dimensional "stereo" images for topographic analysis.

During the 1960s and 1970s, only a handful of facilities in the world were capable of processing or displaying digital images. Analysis was performed with prints of standard processed versions of the images, which were distributed to about a dozen sites involved in planetary image analysis. Special digitally processed versions of images could be obtained by contracting the services of the Image Processing Laboratory at the Jet Propulsion Laboratory (JPL), or the U.S. Geological Survey, Flagstaff, Arizona. This processing normally includes radiometric correction to account for irregularities in the vidicon system, and geometric correction (warping), to account for the viewing conditions of the image. Digital filtering and contrast stretching are also frequently used to extract information from the images.

IMAGE STORAGE

The image collection produced by each mission was stored on magnetic tape in a mission-dependent format. In the early 1980s JPL carried out a restoration program that copied the 12,500 original tapes to 1200 new tapes in 6250-bpi for-

MIKE MARTIN

Home: Pasadena, California
Job: Project Engineer for Planetary Data Systems, Jet Propulsion Laboratory
Quote: *"CD-ROM will allow each researcher to have a complete set of applicable data at hand for immediate analysis, bringing about an unprecedented era of scientific discovery in the next decade."*

mat. This effort allowed us to preserve the data for future analysis and made it possible to produce two additional copies of the archived images (at a cost of $50,000 per copy), which were delivered to the U.S. Geological Survey and the National Space Science Data Center to support continuing research. This effort led to an important discovery regarding the processing of 10- to 15-year old tapes. Although the old tapes were read successfully, they could be read only once because the act of reading them destroyed the oxide coating. The moral: never "scan" old tapes without first copying them to a new medium.

In a related effort, JPL also produced a 35-mm "film" by photographing high-quality prints of all the planetary images, plus a large number of lunar images. The resulting film was used to produce two laserdiscs, each containing 54,000 images per side. Two hundred copies of these discs were distributed to science analysis sites for use as a "browse" catalog of the image collection.

Uranian Ring System. This 96-second, wide-angle exposure, taken while Voyager was in the shadow of Uranus, enhances the visibility of micrometer-size particles. The short streaks are smeared images of background stars.

While these steps dramatically increased the availability of the planetary image collection to the science community, weeks or months were still required for user access to the digital data, and the only form of distribution was magnetic tape. This, at a time when more users were obtaining workstations capable of doing sophisticated image processing and analysis at their own facilities. It was also apparent that microcomputers would become a display and analysis tool, but that most would not have access to magnetic tape drives for receiving the digital data.

In 1984, the pilot Planetary Data System project was charged with the task of finding an efficient, cost-effective method of widely distributing these large data sets. The distribution of the Voyager 2 images of Uranus (to be acquired in early 1986) was selected as a pilot project. Several optical technologies were explored, including digital laserdiscs, write-once optical discs (WORM), and CD-ROM.

In 1985, the results of this testing were presented to the Voyager Imaging Team and CD-ROM was selected as the target medium. Major factors in this decision were inexpensive replication, standardization of the CD-ROM recording format, and inexpensive reader cost. Budgets were allocated for the production of 10 discs, 9 of which would contain the 7000 images anticipated from the Uranus encounter, along with one catalog disc. In early 1987, about a year after the Uranus encounter, the first NASA CD-ROM containing 800 of the most interesting images of Uranus and its satellites was produced and distributed.

While the expense of the Uranus production effort was reasonable, the extrapolated cost of converting the entire planetary image archive collection to CD-ROM format approached $2 million (200 discs at $10,000 each)—an overwhelming and prohibitive amount given the budget outlook at the time. To reduce the magnitude of the task, the use of data compression was explored. A simple scheme was developed that resulted in a compression factor of 3 to 1. This allowed the entire Uranus image set to be placed on 3 discs instead of 9, so the remaining discs could be used to distribute images from earlier Voyager encounters with Jupiter and Saturn. The use of image compression also reduced the total number of discs required for the complete image archive to about 60, making the production task a palatable effort to factor into NASA budgets, especially when expected reductions in CD-ROM mastering and replication costs were taken into account.

The first three Uranus discs are expected to be completed by the end of 1988. In early 1989, three Jupiter and two Saturn discs containing the most scientifically interesting images from the Voyager 1 and 2 flybys will be produced. These five discs will represent about one-fifth the total number of images from the Jupiter and Saturn encounters. The conversion of 50,000 Mars images from Viking Orbiter missions will also begin in 1989. It is expected that 5 to 10 Mars discs will be produced in the first year, and

PHOTOS GO ELECTRONIC

The traditional photograph just doesn't fit in today's high-technology workplace. Automated offices handle text with ease, but photographs remain hard to print, complex to manipulate, expensive to process, and difficult to transmit over telephone lines.

The Japanese-led Electronic Still Camera Conference has devised a new set of specifications that promise to standardize products that create stop-action video pictures much like ordinary photographs. These electronic images, however, will be much easier to use in business because they can be stored and manipulated by computer.

The first business products are already available—Sony says it has already sold more than 5,500 units of its Mavica imaging system in the United States. Other still-imaging products could begin to penetrate the consumer market as early as this year.

A group of Japanese companies, initially led by Sony, has been working on electronic still-image cameras and recorders since the 1970s. Last year, with the participation of Sumitomo 3M and such U.S. companies as Kodak and Polaroid, the 43-company conference established specifications for a new generation of electronic imaging systems that use special microchips called charge-coupled devices to record the images in an analog format, patterned after videotape.

Such systems store 25 images on a two-inch floppy disk. If users are willing to settle for half the clarity, they can squeeze 50 images onto a disk.

Unfortunately, even the sharper images, which offer the 483-line resolution of a television picture, cannot compare with the quality of a typical 35-mm photograph. In a few years, the advent of high-definition television may correct this imbalance, but meanwhile, supporters say, electronic imaging's flexibility should help compensate for its lack of definition. They say the current level of resolution is good enough for use by daily newspapers and even by weekly news magazines.

The heart of a still-image system is the deck that holds the disks—equivalent to a home tape deck or VCR—but users can add peripheral devices for new functions. Sony's Mavica system, for example, lets users rearrange images on disks and copy them from one disk to another, transmit images over telephone lines, store as many as 8,000 digitized photographs on a 16-gigabyte optical disk, make instant four-color separations for printing presses, and print glossy images.

Several manufacturers, including Sony, have introduced cameras that make pictures directly on floppy disks. Other camera companies, such a Minolta, offer special backs that attach to their conventional cameras, replacing the film with a charge-coupled device and a floppy disk.

However, one of the beauties of the standardized format is that users don't really need a special camera. Still-imaging decks can grab images from any available video source—video cameras, video recorders, or directly from broadcast television.

Sony, Matsushita/Panasonic, Minolta, Fuji, Konica, and Casio introduced still-imaging products in Japan a few years ago, and Sony, Canon, and Kodak followed in the U.S. market last year. Most manufacturers aimed primarily at broadcasters, publishers, and computer-graphics users. But proponents predict large corporations that regularly send images from one office to another represent an even larger market.

Eventually, the technology is expected to fulfill its potential in the consumer market. Andrew Wilson, editor of the trade magazine *ESD*, predicts that if high-definition television can sufficiently improve picture quality, still-video imaging could capture at least 60 percent of the worldwide photography market.

But most traditional camera companies are afraid of cannibalizing their sales of film cameras. So far, Casio's $800 still-imaging camera is the only product aimed mainly at consumers, and is available only in Japan. Other companies are waiting for prices to fall from today's $3,000 to $4,000 for a deck and $10 per disk.

Some companies aren't willing to wait much longer. Kent Ekberg, project manager for still-image systems at Sony America, expects several leading manufacturers, perhaps including Sony, to introduce home systems by the end of this year. Even though consumers will be able to view their photos immediately on television screens, they will probably have to take their disks to the local photo store for printing.

By Robert Chapman Wood. From *High Technology Business*. Reprinted by permission of High Technology Business magazine. Copyright © 1988 by Infotechnology Publishing Corporation.

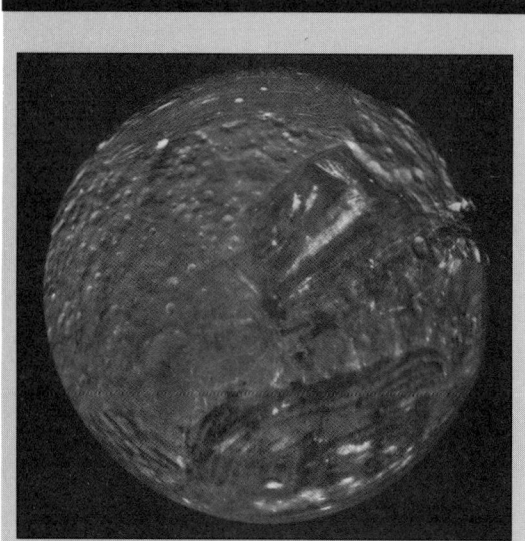

Miranda. Nine images were combined to create this mosaic of Uranus' moon Miranda. The moon's surface consists of two strikingly different types of terrain: old, heavily cratered areas and young, complex regions characterized by scarps and ridges.

that the entire task will take 3 years, with a resulting 30 discs. Late in 1989, Voyager 2 will have its last planetary encounter, photographing Neptune and its satellite Triton before heading into interstellar space. The Neptune images will be distributed in early 1990, with production of the remaining 20 Jupiter and Saturn discs also beginning in that year. One goal of the Planetary Data System is to have all the existing data converted to CD-ROM format before the anticipated deluge of data from new missions scheduled to be flown in the 1990s.

The next new planetary mission, Magellan, will be launched in 1989. It will use a radar imaging system to systematically map the surface of Venus. Current plans are to distribute all of the important Magellan data on a set of 100 CD-ROM discs, with the first appearing in 1990. The later Galileo mission, which will send an orbiter and probe to Jupiter, will also be launched in 1989, but will not arrive at Jupiter until the mid-1990s. Another, the Mars Observer mission, will be launched in the early 1990s and will perform extensive reconnaissanse of that planet in preparation for a Mars Rover and potential manned landings in the next century.

IMAGE COMPRESSION

The goal of the compression effort was to find a simple but effective compression technique for planetary images. To preserve data integrity, the technique used had to be "lossless"—that is, capable of producing an exact replica of the original image. Underlying all the development work was a desire to use well-documented techniques, with minimal effort required to develop decompression software.

Digital images are good candidates for compression because the data values naturally cluster to produce a distribution of values like that shown in Figure 4-8 and 4-9. Differences between adjacent sample values along a single line of the image are small, as are differences between adjacent lines. This clustering can be seen by producing an image "histogram," which graphs the frequency of occurrence of each sample value in the image. Simple Huffman coding, which substitutes short bit patterns for frequently occurring values, often reduces the image volume by 50 percent. Its efficiency depends on the height and spread of the image histogram. In the process of testing various approaches it was determined that the height of the histogram could be substantially increased and the spread reduced by subtracting each sample value along a line from its neighbor (see Figure 4-9). Thus, a row of samples with values 10, 10, 11, 12, 12, would be converted to 10, 0, +1, +1, 0. The combination of previous-sample differencing with the Huffman coding scheme generally doubled the efficiency of the compression, providing an overall compression factor of better than 3 to 1.

The Huffman technique involves building and storing a table of frequencies of sample differences to be used in decoding the image. In some applications this table can be standardized—for example, in CCITT FAX formats. This standardization offers two benefits: the decoding table does not need to be transferred with the compressed data (saving about 1 KB per file), and the software that performs the decoding can be simplified to decode in a fixed manner. This technique could not be expected to work well with raw images, but it might be viable because the previous sample step normalized images so that the most frequently occurring value was always 0, followed by +1 and −1, followed by +1 and −2, and so on. Tests on a variety of different images, however, indicated that, even with the sample differencing, the variation from image to image made the fixed decoding table undesirable.

In normal Huffman coding applications, an entire file is compressed as a unit. Thus, the entire file must be decompressed to access any portion. Then the required portion can be extracted from the decompressed file. This procedure always requires that decompression start at the beginning of the image and makes it difficult to display the image "on the fly" as it is being decompressed. However, instead of utilizing the entire image, many image display applications focus on a "screen-sized" subset. If the image format is 1000 × 1000, but the display size is 512 × 512, this technique requires the processing of several times more data than are needed. In addition, a data error at any point in the file will corrupt all data beyond that point.

To avoid these problems it was decided to compress the planetary images on a line-by-line basis, using variable length records (as specified in the ISO CD-ROM standard) to store each compressed line. The first sample of each line is stored intact, followed by the compressed differences. Thus, the decompression process can begin on any line of an image. Also, corrupted lines result only in the loss of a single line. The overhead for this scheme is a 2-byte length indicator on each line, plus about 1 byte of unused storage on each line resulting from the requirement that lines contain an even number of bytes.

Another consideration in compressing images is the "background" data content that may be encountered. Some types of images contain a large number of unvarying lines, usually either all black or all white. In these cases a good compression scheme is run-length coding, in which a flag value is stored to indicate that a run of samples will follow. The flag value is followed by a count byte and then by the sample value of the run. This technique, combined with Huffman coding, is being used in producing an

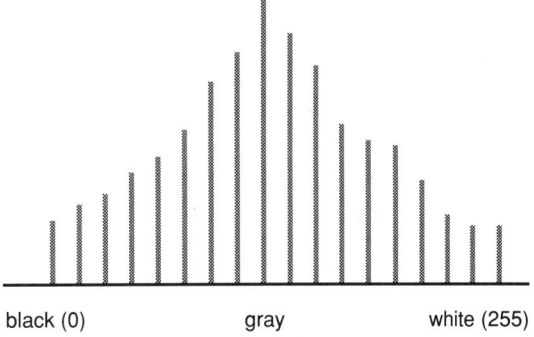

Figure 4-8. An image histogram

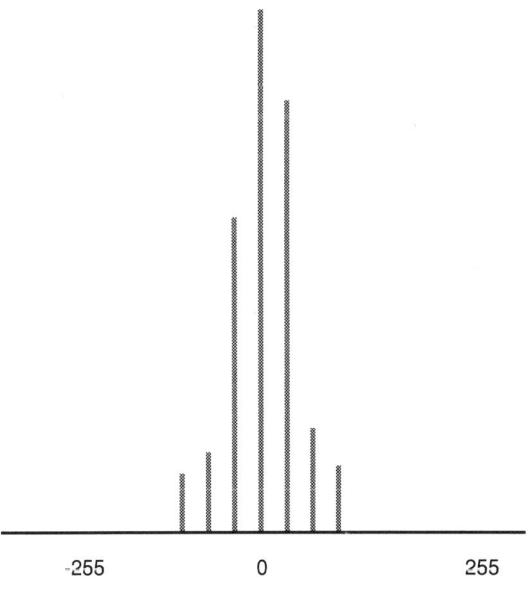

Figure 4-9. The histogram after sample differencing

archive of ocean images for NASA and yields a compression factor of 5 to 1.

To allow users to access the compressed images in many environments, the software to decompress the images is provided as stand-alone programs and as subroutines that can be called by a user's program to decompress lines of data on the fly. The software is provided in both C and FORTRAN. The subroutines were designed for portability, and will work on the VAX VMS, the IBM PC (with Microsoft C and Microsoft FORTRAN), and UNIX (Sun) systems.

BROWSE IMAGES

The decoding software must load the decompression table and then process each line in turn to recover the original values. This process takes about 60 seconds for a 640-KB file on an IBM PC AT or a VAX 11/780. In normal usage the user would select frames of interest based on a catalog search and then decompress and view the images sequentially to determine which were needed for further analysis. It was realized that this would be a cumbersome process, with a 60-second delay for decompressing each image. The solution was to produce a low-resolution "browse" image that could quickly be displayed for evaluation during the search phase. For the 800 × 800 Voyager images, a subsampling factor of 4 was used to produce a 200 × 200 browse frame. While the subsampling reduced the data volume by a factor of 16, the images retained enough detail for the user to determine the utility of the image in most types of scientific study. Both decimation and averaging were considered for use in producing the browse images, with decimation chosen by a review board of scientists.

CATALOG INFORMATION

Three types of supplementary information are needed to process planetary images: the format of the image, the camera state at the time of the observation, and the viewing geometry.

The image format includes the number of lines, the number of samples or picture elements within each line, and the number of bits used to represent each sample. The image format pa-

IMAGE PUBLISHING

There are several very important situations in which large numbers of images must be distributed, usually with some annotation or other support information, to large numbers of users. Examples include

- Engineering drawings for aircraft.
- Patent drawings.
- Engineering, architectural, and product standards.

Paper and microform have been the only media available for this purpose, and they do not do the job. Users look at the shelves full of binders crammed with engineering standards and walk away. The documentation for an airplane can weigh more than the airplane. Updates arrive and may not be inserted. Active users tear out the sheets they need most, and then other users can't access the information.

The cost and sluggishness of automated microform systems makes them unlikely to be useful to professionals with anything less than constant need to review the stored information. Indexing of microform is just as primitive as that of paper.

With the low cost of CD-ROM hardware, it is possible to distribute large image publications on plastic and realize the following benefits:

- Far lower "printing" cost (below $10 for several thousand engineering drawings).
- Much faster and better supported access to desired information, by the use of database management and other sorting and indexing techniques running on the user's computer.
- Portability of the image base, enabling such useful innovations as taking the documentation in live form along in the vehicle.

rameters are generally fixed for a given spacecraft and camera system.

The camera state parameters include the filter identification, exposure interval, and camera electronics settings. These parameters are necessary for performing radiometric calibration on the image. The camera state parameters are embedded in the engineering data returned with the image by the spacecraft and can be extracted fairly easily.

The viewing geometry is necessary for performing geometric calibration and is also a primary tool for searching and sorting images. It includes such parameters as the latitude and longitude of the center and corners of the image, the distance from the spacecraft to the target, the lighting conditions at the target, and the viewing angle. Determination of viewing geometry is a very complex procedure requiring the combination of several pieces of information. The inputs to the calculations include the exact instant that the camera is shuttered, the direction in which the camera is pointing, and the positions in space of the spacecraft and the target body (spacecraft and planetary ephemeris).

If images were transmitted immediately from the spacecraft to Earth, the calculation of shutter time would simply require subracting the time it takes the signal to be transmitted (one-way light time) from the time the image is received on Earth. Most images, however, are tape-recorded on the spacecraft for later playback to Earth. Thus, the shutter time must be computed by correlating the spacecraft clock count associated with an image with Universal Time Corrected (UTC). Determining the camera direction is complicated because most spacecraft maintain proper orientation by fixing sensors on bright celestial objects (the Sun and Canopus are often used). As the spacecraft drifts off its proper orientation, the sensors record a drop in intensity and trigger small gas jets, causing the spacecraft to drift back in the other direction. This technique is called "limit cycling," and the position within these limits must be taken into account when computing camera direction. The positions of most planetary bodies are known with extreme precision, and the spacecraft position is determined very precisely using optical and radio-tracking techniques.

- Use of the image material for interactive instruction as well as reference, by including the appropriate index and branching keys on the disk.

Given that CD-ROM stores digital data with no restrictions, several methods are available for recovering images. These include

- Digital facsimile methods, following the CCITT Group 3 or Group 4 standards, or similar methods of scanning and compression, for which a typical image recovery time is 1/3 second (A4, $8 \times 8/mm^2$, GIII compression).
- Digitized television, using any of the several standards for digitizing the composite video signal, for which a typical image recovery time is two seconds ($3f_c \times 8$ bits).
- Pixel maps in monochrome or color, to whatever level of resolution, for which a typical image recovery time is ten seconds (1000×700 pixels, 16 colors).
- Videotex protocols such as Prestel and NAPLPS, for which image recovery time is well below one second for most practical cases.

By Rothchild Consultants. Reprinted by permission of Rothchild Consultants. Excerpted from *CD-ROM and OROM Products, Applications, and Markets.* Copyright © by Rothchild Consultants.

> ### YOU DON'T HAVE TO BE A SCIENTIST...
>
> The University of Colorado LASP recently published the first three discs of a multiple-disc set of data from NASA's Voyager spacecraft. Sure to be of interest to amateurs and professionals alike, *Space Science Sampler Volumes 1 and 2* contain breathtaking images of Uranus taken by the Voyager 2 spacecraft, and *Voyages to the Outer Planets Volume 1* offers a collection of scientific data on the Earth and our solar system.
>
> **Joan Lambert**

In the CD-ROM design effort, it was decided to include the format and camera parameters in an ASCII label at the beginning of each image. An example of the labels for an uncompressed Voyager image is shown in Figure 4-10. Because the viewing parameters are subject to change over time as more precise measurements of event time, camera direction, and spacecraft position are determined, it was decided not to record them with the images. Instead a special disc will be produced for the "volatile" information and will periodically be updated as new information becomes available. This disc will also contain the latest versions of calibration data and software.

The labels indicate that each image file is composed of three "data objects": a histogram, an engineering table, and the image itself. As you can see in Figure 4-10, the format of the engineering table is fairly complex, and is defined in an external file called ENGTAB.LBL. A group of engineering parameters that are appended to each image line is defined in another file, named LINESUFX.LBL.

For each disc-volume set (Uranus, Jupiter, Saturn) an ASCII table containing the label values for all images is also provided on each disc. This table contains the values in fixed-length fields separated by commas, with all text fields enclosed in quotation marks. This format can easily be read into almost any data management system, so the user can build a customized catalog for searching and retrieving images.

PROCESSING SOFTWARE

Access to the image files on a CD-ROM disc is fairly straightforward for IBM PC and compatible computers. This is not the case, however, on VAX and UNIX minicomputers, which are used extensively for image analysis. While the CDREADER has been a standard fixture on DEC workstations for several years, the operating system supports only UNIFILE format CD-ROM discs, not the more popular High Sierra format. In order to provide user access to CD-ROM files, FORTRAN access routines were developed by the USGS, Flagstaff, Arizona.

Software to perform radiometric and geometric calibration of planetary images has been developed by the Image Processing Laboratory (IPL) at JPL, and by the U.S. Geological Survey (USGS), Flagstaff. These systems are called VICAR (Video Image Communication and Retrieval), and PICS (Planetary Image Cartography System), respectively. Both software systems run on VAX minicomputers. A version of the VICAR software is also being converted at Arizona State University to run in the UNIX environment. These systems also provide standard image processing capabilities (filtering, stretching) as well as production of digital mosaics and other special functions.

Because many planetary users were expected to access the CD-ROM images on personal computers, an IBM personal computer image display program (IMDISP) was developed. This program can be used to display planetary images on CGA, EGA, PGA, and VGA displays, however, only the PGA and VGA displays provide enough gray levels (16) to produce adequate displays for planetary-image analysis. The user response to IMDISP has been very favorable, and more than 500 copies of IMDISP have been distributed to scientists and engineers around the country.

```
NJPL1I00PDS100673816              = SFDU_LABEL
/*          FILE FORMAT AND LENGTH
RECORD_TYPE                       = FIXED_LENGTH
RECORD_BYTES                      = 836
FILE_RECORDS                      = 806
LABEL_RECORDS                     = 3
/*          POINTERS TO STARTING RECORDS OF MAJOR OBJECTS IN FILE
^IMAGE_HISTOGRAM                  = 4
^ENGINEERING_TABLE                = 6
^IMAGE                            = 7
/*          IMAGE DESCRIPTION
SPACECRAFT_NAME                   = VOYAGER_2
MISSION_PHASE_NAME                = URANUS_ENCOUNTER
TARGET_NAME                       = MIRANDA
IMAGE_ID                          = '1705U2-001'
IMAGE_NUMBER                      = 26846.17 /*FLIGHT DATA SUBSYSTEM (FDS)
IMAGE_TIME                        = 1986-01-24T16:43:57Z
EARTH_RECEIVED_TIME               = 1986-01-27T23:01:48Z
INSTRUMENT_NAME                   = NARROW_ANGLE_CAMERA
SCAN_MODE_ID                      = '1:1'
SHUTTER_MODE_ID                   = NAONLY
GAIN_MODE_ID                      = LOW
EDIT_MODE_ID                      = '1:1' /*FULL RESOLUTION
FILTER_NAME                       = CLEAR
FILTER_NUMBER                     = 0
EXPOSURE_DURATION                 = 1.9200 <SECONDS>
/*          DESCRIPTION OF THE OBJECTS CONTAINED IN FILE
OBJECT                            = IMAGE_HISTOGRAM
 ITEMS                            = 256
 ITEM_TYPE                        = VAX_INTEGER
 ITEM_BITS                        = 32
END_OBJECT
OBJECT                            = ENGINEERING_TABLE
 BYTES                            = 242
 ^STRUCTURE                       = 'ENGTAB.LBL'
END_OBJECT
OBJECT                            = IMAGE
 LINES                            = 800
 LINE_SAMPLES                     = 800
 LINE_SUFFIX_BYTES                = 36
 SAMPLE_TYPE                      = UNSIGNED_INTEGER
 SAMPLE_BITS                      = 8
 SAMPLE_BIT_MASK                  = 2#11111111#
 ^LINE_SUFFIX_STRUCTURE           = 'LINESUFX.LBL'
END_OBJECT
END
```

Figure 4-10. Voyager image label parameters

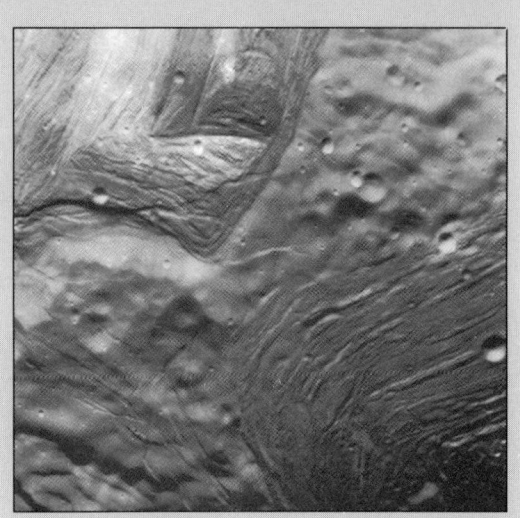

Miranda's Terrain. Evidence of a variety of geologic processes is seen in this patch of Miranda's surface. The entire picture spans an area about 220 kilometers (140 miles) across.

Many of the calibration programs from VICAR have been converted to operate on an IBM personal computer, and a menu-driven shell for accessing them is currently being developed. We are also in the process of developing a similar display program for the Apple Macintosh II color display.

SUMMARY

The use of CD-ROM discs to store and distribute planetary science data promises to usher in a new era of scientific discovery. Each scientist will have a complete set of relevant data close at hand, providing the ability to perform in minutes analysis tasks that previously might have required weeks or months of preparation. The CD-ROM archive is also expected to end problems associated with the maintenance of large magnetic tape collections.

The CD-ROM development task described in this article is the result of the efforts of individuals representing several organizations. These individuals include Eric Eliason, Branch of Astrogeology, United States Geological Survey (USGS), Flagstaff, Arizona; Randy Davis, Laboratory for Atmospheric and Space Physics, University of Colorado, Boulder, Colorado; Charlie Avis, Jet Propulsion Laboratory, Pasadena, California; Robert Mehlman, Institute of Geophysics and Planetary Physics, University of California, Los Angeles, California; Dennis McMacken, Information Systems Division, USGS, Flagstaff, Arizona. Funding for this task has been provided by the Voyager project and the Planetary Data System (PDS).

[Mike Martin is Project Engineer for the Planetary Data System, a NASA project designed to enhance the utilization of scientific data gathered by the planetary exploration program. He has worked for the Jet Propulsion Laboratory, California Institute of Technology, since 1971, supporting scientific analysis of data returned by the Mariner, Viking, and Voyager missions.]

Image Management on CD-ROM

By Bruce Benge and Calvin Aiken

[In this article, the authors draw on their experience with CD-ROM image-management systems to offer some insights into the issues facing developers. Although they touch on some of the aspects of image processing discussed in the first article in this section, their primary focus is on the practical choices developers have to make and the trade-offs they need to consider.]

For several years developers have been creating prototype applications using black and white images coming from a CD-ROM. Our attention was drawn to this area by client requests for a low-cost system that would manage both text and images. Several important issues and challenges are associated with the process, and some of these are presented in this article in a synoptic form.

IMAGE QUALITY

The first question that must be considered by an application developer is "What image resolution should I use?" The answer should be governed only by the desired image quality: The higher the image resolution (usually dots per inch, or *dpi*) the larger the raw image. For example, a 200-dpi image creates a half-megabyte raw raster file, a 300-dpi image creates a one-megabyte raw raster file, and a 400-dpi image creates a two-megabyte raw raster file. Note, however, that, whereas uncompressed images grow with the square of the resolution, a smaller penalty is associated with compressed images, which grow linearly with resolution.

In answering the resolution question, the developer must also consider the display devices—both monitor and printer. Monitors can display images from 40 dpi to 300 dpi, and printers can print images from 100 dpi to 600 dpi. The resolution at which images should be scanned is critical. Higher resolution requires more storage space and more expensive monitors

BRUCE BENGE

Home: Stillwater, Oklahoma
Job: Marketing Manager, TMS, Inc.
Quote: *"It became obvious to us that if we told our customers that they had to buy a $1000 board for each image workstation, we would have a serious image problem. We therefore went to work and came up with a fast software solution to decompress, scale, and display images."*

and printers for display. Lower resolution leads to loss of image quality. Many of the issues examined in this article have an impact on the application developer's choice of image resolution.

Many application developers agree that images scanned at 300 dpi are satisfactory for their image-management applications. The reason for this is threefold: One, the quality of the image being displayed on most of the graphic monitors is good; two, relatively inexpensive 300-dpi laser printers are available; and three, the storage needs are not excessive. Thus, 300-dpi resolution provides a good trade-off between quality and cost.

ACCESS TIME

CD-ROM is ideally suited for storing digitized images because of its large capacity and the static nature of most images. The major problem with CD-ROM technology is the slow access time—150 kilobytes per second is the current maximum access speed. Because a 300-dpi, $8\frac{1}{2}$-by-11 inch image in uncompressed form represents 1 megabyte of data, the CD-ROM application requires about 7 seconds just to read the data from disc. Additional time is needed for scaling and for displaying on a monitor or for printing. Because this access time is generally unacceptable, the developer must compress the image before storing it, even if storage space is not a major consideration.

COMPRESSION/ DECOMPRESSION METHODS

Depending on image content, compression algorithms can produce average compression ratios of at least 5 to 1, and some can produce ratios of up to 40 to 1. By compressing images, the application developer can store many more images and thus increase the utilization of storage capacity of the CD-ROM disc. Also, the compressed image file can now be read in less than a second, thereby improving access time considerably. But now, another issue affects the application developer's image-management solution, and that is the ability to decompress the compressed file. This issue could affect hardware requirements and does affect the access time for displaying the image.

There are three ways to choose a compression/decompression scheme. The first is to use a proprietary method. This sometimes gives better compression ratios and decompression speed, but ties the application to methods that are not generally accepted within the industry. The second option is to use vectors. Vector images, used mainly in the CAD/CAM industry, have high compression ratios (smaller compressed images) and are easy to scale to prescribed monitors. However, they have major disadvantages: Very few inexpensive personal-computer monitors or printers can print a vector image directly, and the conversion of vector images to raster images for display is slow. The third choice is to use the CCITT facsimile standards, both Group 3 and Group 4. These standards are widely used because their compression ratios are respectable, the images can be displayed on almost any monitor or printer, and a wide variety of software and hardware packages that use these standards are available. In addition, the images can be shared between companies, and they can be sent to facsimile machines over the public telephone network.

SCALING

Images generally don't fit on all monitors and printers without scaling. Therefore, we again need to consider the issue of desired image quality. Image-management tools use scaling methods in order to fit an image to a specific display device. Scaling is an important issue when a variety of monitors and printers can be used; there are two methods.

One method of scaling involves *bit dropping,* or *bit duplicating.* With this method, bits are systematically deleted from or added to the image. For example, scaling 50 percent would mean dropping every other bit and line in an image. The scaling works, but image quality for display may suffer. Another potential limitation of this method is that the number of scaling modes is usually very limited. For example, the method might support only 1:2, 1:4, 2:1, 3:1, and 4:1 scaling ratios. This limitation affects the ability of the application to display an image that is readable in its current form or needs only some minor improvements or adjustments.

The other method is *intelligent scaling.* This method analyzes the bit stream and decides which is the best bit to drop or to duplicate. This scaling method attempts to maintain transitions (such as small lines), yet keeps about the same ratio of white bits to black bits. Intelligent scaling tends to provide a wider range of scaling ratios, thereby providing more flexibility in application development and in maintaining the desired image quality. A drawback is that intelligent scaling is slower than bit dropping or duplicating.

CALVIN E. AIKEN

Home: Stillwater, Oklahoma
Job: Software Engineer, TMS Inc.
Quote: *"It makes sense to put bitonal images on a CD-ROM as long as it is done intelligently. If done wrong, application and system performance will suffer."*

SPEED

Most users are not affected by compression time. Images are compressed before the CD-ROM is made, so users are not directly affected by the time the process takes, except to the extent that compression time affects the cost of making the CD-ROM. There are several hardware/software configurations available that scan and compress images at different speeds. Generally, hardware solutions are more efficient, but also more expensive, than software solutions.

End users *are* affected by CD-ROM reading time, decompression time, scaling time, and display and printing time. Factors that affect speed are the source and saize of the compressed image; the speed and type of personal computer, monitor, and printer being used; the choice of decompression board or software decompression package; the method of scaling; the user interface; the application software; and memory speed. Many users want the image to be displayed in less than 6 seconds and printed in less than 25 seconds—goals that can be achieved with many of the current software and hardware packages available in the market place.

IMAGE-MANAGEMENT APPLICATION SIZE REQUIREMENTS

Application developers must also consider the memory requirements of the image-management software tools. Most packages require some RAM space for executable code and buffers. Some packages also require secondary storage space on the hard disk for temporary files of images. The best approach, if speed is an issue, is to allow for decompressing the image into memory and rescaling the image for display; the trade-off is that this approach requires large amounts of RAM or the use of EMS boards.

MONITOR AND PRINTER SUPPORT

Image-management tools provide various levels of monitor and printer support. In some cases, the application developer provides all monitor and printer support. In other cases, the developer provides embedded device drivers, but these cannot be updated easily, especially in the case of hardware boards that have direct monitor or printer interfaces, or both. A third approach is to provide loadable device drivers. Here, the application developer has the option of using existing drivers or of writing new device drivers needed for a specific application. This approach usually provides the greatest number of options and a known upgrade path.

MIXED-MODE SCREEN

Most application developers want to add alphanumerics to their displays of digitized images. Some monitors and printers allow for dual-plane display, but this ability is limited to certain character sets and character sizes. An alternative method of handling this is to convert alphanumerics to raster for addition to the display of digitized images. This conversion allows us to use monitors and printers that do not have a dual-plane display capability.

APPLICATION DEVELOPMENT SUPPORT

Many of the current image-management tools give the application developer low-level hooks for image manipulation. But with this type of approach, the developer must create the support routines necessary for image management. A second way to provide the developer with this support is to give the application linkable code that performs high-level functions, such as ZOOM(x), MOVE(x,y), and ROTATE(x). Such libraries of functions are much easier to use and also provide a path for quicker application development and future upgrades.

SUPPORT

Two types of support are also necessary. The software tools used by the developer must be supported by good technical manuals, telephone consultation, and good source code examples. In turn, the application developer must ensure that end users of the information product are well supported.

HARDWARE SOLUTIONS VERSUS SOFTWARE SOLUTIONS

A comparison of hardware and software solutions is provided in the following list of advantages and disadvantages:

Advantages	*Disadvantages*
Hardware	
Fast compression.	Requires a personal-computer slot.
Fast decompression.	Scaling is usually limited.
Usually has dedicated interfaces for scanners, printers, and monitors.	Harder to change and update for new hardware platforms and new operating systems.
Sometimes has extra memory for holding decompressed images.	Costs more—from $400 for a board supporting only decompression and compression to $6000 for a fully functional image-management system.
Improved hardware chips are being introduced; for example, the AMD VCEP and T134020.	Hardware is basically I/O bound, so faster chips only marginally speed up the system.
Expected life of a board is 5 to 7 years.	
Software	
Doesn't require a slot.	No special interface provided for printers, monitors, and scanners.
Easy to change and upgrade as standards change.	Not as fast as hardware at compression; production scanning and compression station may need a hardware solution.
More portable to other hardware platforms and operating systems.	
Can provide fast decompression and will become even faster as CPUs are speeded up. Current speeds for software decompression, scaling, and display match those obtained on many boards.	Does not allow for additional memory chips.
May be able to use EMS RAM for decompression, so that redraws require only scaling.	May become I/O bound on some personal computers.

SUMMARY

With the availability of low-cost software solutions for decompression, scaling, and display, we can expect an increasing number of applications that use bitonal images. Each application is different, and no approach is ideal for all applications, but the following generalizations apply in most cases:

- Resolution should be driven by the application, not the solution.

- Compression/decompression methods should follow standards to provide industry acceptance and multiple sources for compression and decompression solutions.

- Scaling should be intelligent.

- Compression should be hardware based on production systems.

- Software is an alternative for office environments.

- Decompression and scaling should generally be software based because the cost of hardware can be saved. Hardware should be considered an alternative only for applications needing very fast viewing and fast printing.
- Loadable device drivers are needed to cope with the wide variety of display devices (monitors and printers) utilized by end users.
- Application-support libraries must be provided for quick application development.

[Bruce Benge is Marketing Manager of the Image Products Division of TMS, Inc., Stillwater, Oklahoma.

Calvin Aiken is Technical Product Manager of the Image Products Division of TMS, Inc.]

JAZZING IT ALL UP

TECHNOLOGY AHEAD OF ITS TIME
By Peter Black

MULTI-IMAGE: A CREATIVE MODEL FOR MULTIMEDIA PRODUCERS
By Tom Corddry

ESSAYS IN ANIMATION
By MacroMind, Inc.

MAKING THINGS MOVE: REGENERATIVE ANIMATION IN FRAME-BUFFER DISPLAY SYSTEMS
By Jay Fenton

AN ANIMATED TOPIC
By Dan Cody

AUDIO, CD-ROM, AND CD-ROM XA
By Suzanne Ropiequet

MAKING THE MOST OF SOUND ON CD-ROM
By Bryan Brewer

Technology Ahead of Its Time

By Peter Black
From the "Mac Soapbox" column of *MacWEEK*

[Peter Black starts out this section with an upbeat overview of the potential of "infoware"—the new medium of ideas, sights, and sounds that CD-ROM is about to become.]

A lot of hardware companies are spending big bucks on technologies for which there is no market. On the face of it, this seems loony.

Apple introduces a CD-ROM player with practically nothing to play on it. Philips and Sony commit vast funds to the development of compact disc-interactive (CD-I), a new consumer technology that plays compact discs with fancy graphics, audio, and text. RCA and Intel spend a pile of money developing chips that will allow digitally encoded and compressed video to be played back in real time.

Didn't anybody tell these people that most of us already have bought videocassette players?

But these guys aren't crazy. They are gamblers, betting on a fundamental shift in the nature of the use of computers.

To date, microcomputers have been used for such tools as spreadsheets, databases, and word processors. You put the information in, you add the value, and you take it out. But all that will probably change in the next few years. That shift will take us from software to infoware.

The personal computer is about to become something more than a toolkit. It's about to become a medium of ideas, sights, and sounds. And that means software will change, too. Infoware will be information packaged as software.

And it's going to come home. Infoware will not be limited to business applications like electronic yellow pages and parts inventories—though you can bet that those applications will show up very soon. It will be CD-based encyclopedias and interactive Dr. Spock. There will be flight simulators with satellite image-based maps of terrain, and there will be exploration games with such depth and detail of imagination as to put "Alice In Wonderland" to shame.

All in all, infoware will stretch the present generation of computers to its limits.

PETER BLACK

Home: Santa Monica, California
Job: President, Xiphias
Quote: *"Computers and video have been destined to marry for a long time. Over the next five years, the nuptials will be complete."*

The IBM PS/2 series will prove woefully inadequate to meet the demands of infoware. The Video Graphics Array is barely acceptable, and that is the best available to most IBM users. Fancy graphics ideas also will have to run on CGA and EGA boards, which means there really can't be fancy graphics at all. And there is not a PC or PS/2 that can issue anything more complex than a beep. IBM simply does not supply a platform for infoware.

The Macintosh is a different story. The worst graphics performance is the monoplane Macintosh Plus/SE display, and it's not at all bad. With the Mac II, things start to get interesting. The forthcoming QuickDraw improvements should solidify the Macintosh's claim as the premier microcomputer graphics platform.

The Mac's sound facilities parallel its graphics. The SE and the II have been intelligently designed for sound. And as Impulse and Farallon have improved their sound sampling gear, the Macintosh is a perfectly decent place to record and play back voicework, incidental music, and sound effects.

In short, the Macintosh is where the interesting stuff will happen for the next year or so. But look forward to high-fidelity audio rather than the AM-radio-grade sound the Mac offers now. Also, plan on graphics that rival and surpass the standards set by broadcast TV instead of the static, posterized effects (lacking subtlety) to which the Mac is currently limited.

And with that kind of hardware as the departure point—as loony as it might seem to say today—look for HyperCard to become a museum piece. It will be like the old crank motion picture cameras: quaint, but evocative of the time when something exciting and important was just beginning.

Reprinted from MacWeek, August 9, 1988. Copyright © 1988 Ziff Communications Company.

Multi-Image: A Creative Model for Multimedia Producers

By Tom Corddry

[Is your CD-ROM product crying out for motion video sequences that you simply cannot squeeze onto your disc, no matter which compression technology you try? Veteran event producer Tom Corddry offers a solution: sophisticated multi-image techniques that create the effect of motion video without hogging storage space.]

CD-ROM came into the world offering three promises:

- To distribute great quantities of information in a compact and inexpensive form.
- To provide powerful tools for finding and retrieving just the right information from within this vast store of data.
- To present the information it finds in rich and memorable ways.

This article is about the third of CD-ROM's promises—richness of presentation. Thanks to *Monday Night Football,* we all know what richness means: It means video. Yet video, in all its full-color, full-frame, full-motion glory, devours memory. By video standards, CD-ROM's vaunted storage capacity is inadequate.

Compression—squeezing more data into less memory—partly solves the problem. DVI technology, for example, promises to compress video enough to support up to 100 minutes of video per disc. This is a brilliant accomplishment, but even with such compression, a product that contains a lot of video is no longer the great storehouse of information we all expect,

TOM CORDDRY

Home: Seattle, Washington
Job: Executive Producer, Microsoft's Fourth International Conference on CD-ROM
Quote: *"For an information product to succeed, it must be so attractive that people will forego other activities in order to spend time with it. It must be able to compete with such entrenched information-intensive activities as attending meetings, watching television, reading, using the telephone, playing poker, going to concerts and plays, even daydreaming. This is stiff competition.*

"I see a bright future for CD-ROM products that offer markedly better selections of information, better interfaces, better searching capabilities, and better information presentations than what we have seen so far. As for the rest, I'd rather daydream, or play poker."

THE MULTI-IMAGE MEDIUM

Think of A-V as "video lite," if you wish, but think of it seriously. A-V has long been an underrated medium, but it has been transformed by the advent of the personal computer. Over the past ten years, A-V has become a graceful new medium called *multi-image*. With the PC to provide precise, reliable synchronization, multi-image has attracted some exceptionally creative people who, by experimenting, have learned how to create moving presentations with still images. Creating in multi-image is different from creating in video or in film, and the differences can offer valuable lessons to multimedia producers.

Multi-image is not widely known because multi-image presentations, which require from two to two hundred separate slide projectors, are cumbersome to set up and display. Hence, they are typically produced for small group showings—annual meetings, product introductions, or exhibits.

On the other hand, many of the creative problems multimedia producers face today have been faced and solved by multi-image producers. They can, for example, create effective interaction between audio and a series of still images, or between one image and the next. Multi-image producers have also faced and solved the "read my lips" problem. In a still image, lips don't move; thus, unlike video, multi-image cannot fall back on the tried-and-true talking head shot.

Multi-image producers have also learned to function with cost-per-minute budgets comparable to those available for CD-ROM production; the same cannot be said of many motion picture or video producers. Because multi-image presentations are often assembled from elements of diverse origin, multi-image producers have grappled with a number of the intellectual property issues now facing multimedia producers. Multi-image producers, like multimedia

because so much memory is dedicated to video's 30 frames per second. Fortunately, there's a less ravenous way to perform the storytelling functions video performs: A-V (audio-visual), the sequencing of still images with synchronized audio, as in a slide show. At roughly 12 frames per minute, instead of 30 frames per second, this A-V approach to multimedia uses memory about 150 times more efficiently than video.

CD-ROM producers, are also called upon to cover topics in short time periods, rather than in an hour or two, as is common in television and motion pictures.

Here are three axioms from the world of multi-image that might prove useful to multi-media producers:

- Leave out as much as possible. A few superb images are more effective than a profusion of adequate ones. Because you are not forced to march to the next image every 30th of a second, you can choose to stay on one aesthetic mountaintop until you are ready to move directly to the next.

- Put heavy emphasis on a strong audio track. Unlike film or video producers, who assemble the pictures first, and then enhance the pictures by adding audio, multi-image producers typically build the sound track first and then attach pictures to it.

- Make one point clearly, with the simplest possible structure. Then stop.

GETTING THE PICTURE

To learn more about what multi-image creative techniques can do for you, seek out a few good multi-image producers and ask to see samples of their work. To give you starting points, I've listed AMI, the multi-image producer's trade association, and the names and addresses of four producers who have produced excellent presentations [see the Resources box]. AMI has local chapters in many cities, and holds festivals on local, regional, and international levels. From time to time, the organization sponsors touring collections of award-winning productions. These tours offer you an excellent way to learn a lot in a short time.

[Tom Corddry is the Executive Producer of Microsoft's Fourth International Conference on CD-ROM. He spent five years as Associate Creative Director with Watts/Silverstein, and has experience in writing, producing, and directing events, speeches, and presentations in print and on film, video, and interactive videodisc.]

RESOURCES

Association for Multi-Image (AMI)
8019 North Himes Avenue, Suite 401
Tampa, Florida 33614
(813)932–1692

Gipstein Multimedia
25 Huntington Avenue, Suite 614
Boston, Massachusetts 02116
(617)266–8485

Donna Lawrence Productions, Inc.
P.O. Box 4608
Louisville, Kentucky 40204
(502)589–9617

LSI Communications
801 Arch Street
Philadelphia, Pennsylvania 19107
(215)574–2000

Watt/Silverstein, Inc.
1921 Second Avenue
Seattle, Washington 98101
(206)443–4200

Essays in Animation

By MacroMind, Inc.

[Screen dumps from the galleries of animation art offered as demonstrations in the VideoWorks II package cannot begin to convey the results now being achieved by creative people and their computers. But, as illustrated here, animation has the potential, both as a substitute for motion video and as an artistic and educational medium in its own right, to capture and hold the interest of young and old alike.]

MAKING CONTACT

 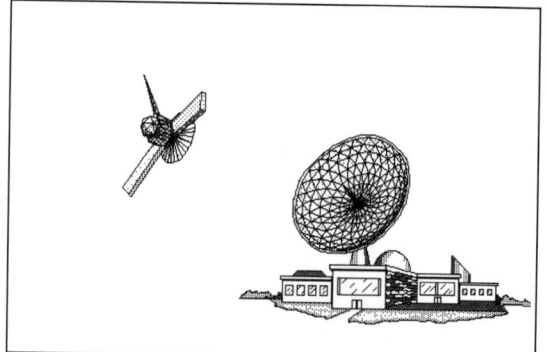

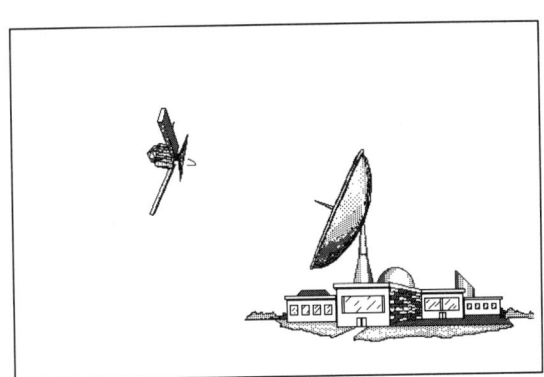

Reprinted by special permission of MacroMind, Inc.

WALKING THE DOG

THE CHICAGO BULLS

FAST FOOD

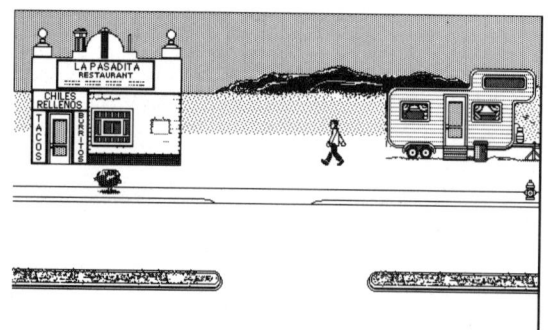 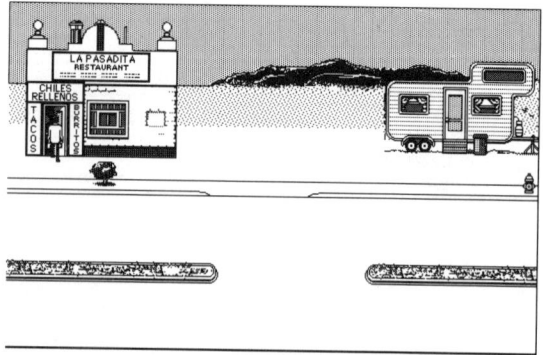

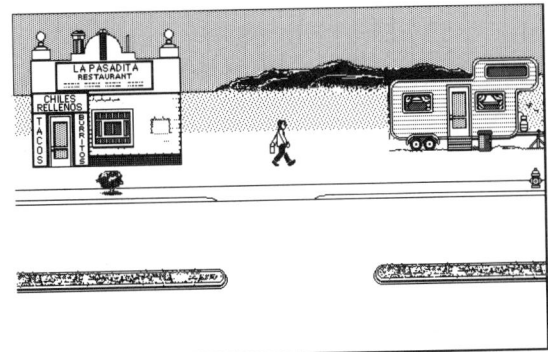
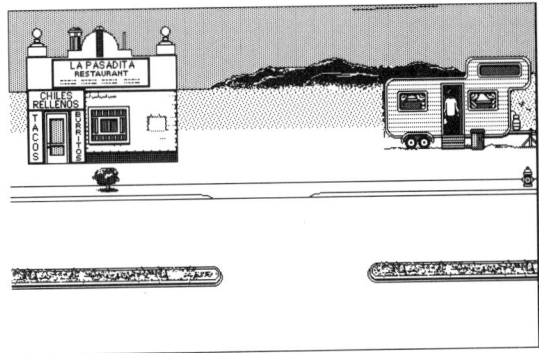

Reprinted by special permission of MacroMind, Inc.

Making Things Move: Regenerative Animation in Frame-Buffer Display Systems

By Jay Fenton

[In this article, Jay Fenton gives us insight into the programming techniques that are used to create smooth animation sequences.]

Early graphics systems functioned by tracing through a display list of images in memory and drawing these "primitives" onto an XY-addressable cathode ray tube (CRT). Most of the rendering work was done by hardware. A program merely had to change the values of display-list parameters to affect animation.

The use of vector CRTs has been superseded by the use of the video frame-buffer technique. With this approach, images are stored as large arrays of pixels, which are converted into video signals by a direct-memory-access process. Unlike with vector CRTs, the picture does not have to be re-created for successive video frames.

Even in a frame-buffer system, display lists are useful. You can have a process examine a display list and react to changes between one video frame and the next by drawing the changes on the screen. Typically, the bandwidth available for changing the frame-buffer images is considerably less than required for the display rate. How do you get around this problem? Here are a few solutions:

- Double buffering. Some systems allow programs to change the frame-buffer read address. This allows programs to prepare one frame while displaying another and switch back and forth between the two during the vertical interval.

- Hardware sprites. Other systems relegate the frame buffer to displaying background information while miniature frame buffers, called "sprites," display the foreground cels. Programs can change the position and appearance of the sprites, which are usually limited in number as well as in size and color.

- Direct rendering. Still another option is to draw the animation directly on the screen. This can produce side effects, the most common being "beam collision," which results when drawing is out of sync with the vertical scan. A partial, incorrect image is then presented. Some systems permit drawing only during the vertical retrace interval, when a collision is impossible. How do you avoid this glitch on other systems? If the image is not too complicated, you can scan-synchronize the changes.

- Regenerative animation. Systems that cannot support hardware double buffering can often take advantage of regenerative animation, a technique that combines double buffering with direct rendering. The idea is to prepare offscreen an updated version of a region of the display and then copy it onto the screen. Fortunately, even if copying is not synchronized with the vertical scan, the resulting beam collision is barely perceptible.

The Apple Macintosh does not officially support hardware double buffering, so both direct rendering and regenerative animation are used extensively by developers of Macintosh applications. Often direct rendering is used to create tracking outlines and to scroll and refresh areas

JAY FENTON

Home: Los Angeles, California
Job: Staff Engineer at Apple Computer, Inc.
Quote: *"Compact disc computer media are not going anywhere until consumers can write on their discs. Someone should be able to sell their old Volkswagen Bug and raise enough money to buy an entry-level authoring system. It will be individuals, laboring for love, that will deliver the software.*

"Consumers are cynical about standards. Too many of them bought eight tracks and Betamax machines. Everyone will lose a CD-ROM standards war."

of the screen using the update-event mechanism. Regenerative animation is used when required to avoid flicker and beam collisions.

The Macintosh Operating System (MOS) is designed primarily for direct rendering, so this technique presents no problems for developers. The use of regenerative animation, however, requires the developer to layer custom code above MOS and Quickdraw, which manages the display list and accomplishes the updating. Many developers have added this layer, using similar but incompatible methods. This incompatibility is unfortunate because it represents duplicated effort.

Having implemented this added layer in several different ways in many different programs, I have developed some techniques that may be of interest to others considering implementing regenerative animation in their programs. In particular, I'd like to describe the system used in Playground 1, a prototype object-oriented animation, music, communications, and programming environment I have developed here at Apple.

THE PLAYGROUND SOLUTION

With Playground, the displayed image is represented by a display list that is an array of handles to display objects. Each display object is a record whose fields, called "slots," describe the width, height, position, and appearance of a primitive graphic object. Playground supports objects such as boxes and circles, as well as text strings and composited pictures, but the program relies on the Quickdraw graphics package to do the actual drawing.

In addition to descriptive slots, each object has a time-stamp slot that is updated whenever any of an object's other slots are changed. Playground accomplishes animation by means of a noticing process, which walks down the display list, checking each object's time-stamp slot to see if that object has changed. If it has, the screen areas affected are noted on a "dirty" rectangles list. If any of these rectangles overlap, they are combined together into a larger rectangle, so that the result of the check is a list of non-overlapping, rectangular screen areas that must be regenerated.

For each dirty rectangle, Playground creates a list of all the display objects that intersect the rectangle. The program sorts this list by z-coordinate and, starting from the bottom of the list, draws the objects into the offscreen buffer using the painter's algorithm. When the image of the rectangle is complete, Playground uses CopyBits to transfer the contents of the offscreen buffer to the screen.

To make all this work, Playground must keep track of where each object was, as well as where it moved to. This is done by maintaining a separate list of the values noted for this object at the end of the previous update cycle. When the object moves, the old bounding rectangle from the separate list is combined with the new bounding rectangle to give the dirty rectangle.

This scheme is designed for situations where the foreground moves while the background stays the same. The scheme's efficiency deteriorates if everything changes and must be regenerated from scratch. However, there are many ways to improve the scheme to maintain efficiency. You can:

- Enlarge dirty rectangles so as to align them with word boundaries, thereby minimizing shifting.

- Combine adjacent but non-overlapping rectangles. This pays off if the cost of updating the area between the rectangles is less than the cost of updating each dirty rectangle separately.

- Separate foreground images from their background, by caching geometric primitives as bitmaps and caching intermediate compositions.

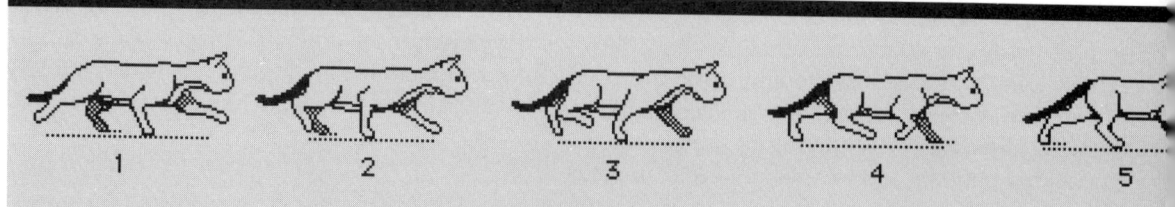

- Test whether objects are obliterated by those in front of them. If they are, do not bother drawing them. Be aware that this technique may not pay off in enough savings in drawing time to justify testing in real time.

- Use a range-searching algorithm to determine which subset of the display list intersects a given rectangle. A simple linear search results in an $M \times N$ computational complexity, where M is the number of dirty rectangles and N is the length of the display list. You might want to try a variation of the quadtree representation instead.

- Precompute the frames and compress them in such a way that they can be decompressed rapidly. The idea here is to trade space for time. One compression approach is to compare a frame with the one before, find the regions of the screen that change, and store new data only for the changed regions.

- When playing back a prerecorded sequence, run as far ahead of real time as possible, generating frames before they are needed. Idle time and memory is thus put to good use.

The display-list rendering routine I have described reacts to changes made in the display list by higher-level software. Only certain slots change over time, and the changes usually occur in predictable patterns. You can identify these patterns by using simulation code to dynamically generate the changes, or by playing back recordings of changes to the objects on a change list. Insights about the patterns can then be used to compress the change data. But obviously, the more compressed the change data becomes, the harder it is to edit. You might consider compressing the data for storage and expanding it for editing.

Playground uses regenerative animation to implement as much of the user interface as possible. However, some components of the toolbox, such as the Control Manager and Text-edit, insist on using the direct-rendering technique, so you must either fake these managers out, ignore them, or follow their lead. For example, I forego regenerative animation for scroll bars, edit fields, and menus, retaining direct rendering.

I find that using a general-purpose regenerative-animation package like Playground simplifies the construction of application programs. Because regenerative animation can be efficient when properly implemented, I would like to see facilities for regenerative animation incorporated into future operating systems.

[Jay Fenton is currently working with the Apple Computer Vivarium Project in Los Angeles, building an authoring system for children, called Playground. Fenton has been involved with the microcomputer industry since the middle 1970s. He started out writing an operating system for pinball machines for Bally. He has written several coin-operated and home videogame programs, including GORF and the Bally Arcade. After the video game boom ended, he moved to home computers, authoring such classics as MusicWorks and VideoWorks.]

Reprinted by special permission of MacroMind, Inc.

An Animated Topic

By Dan Cody
From *Sky* magazine

[Before computer animation programs migrated to the personal computer, this specialized technique required access to sophisticated and expensive equipment. The most advanced animation techniques are still the domains of film makers, as Dan Cody explains in this article. But some day…]

Sometime soon, parents everywhere will be dragging the kids away from the Saturday morning cartoons and off to the theaters for a dose of Charles Dickens and his heavy-handed Victorian morality.

No, wait a minute. It's the kids who will be dragging Dad and Mom away from Dallas, Denver, and tropical vice to follow the twisted intrigues of Oliver Twist, Sikes, and Fagin in that 19th-Century version of a prime-time soap.

Whoever does the dragging, they're all in for a typical Disney-esque treat. The movie is *Oliver*, still in production at the Disney magic factory. It's an Americanized, animated retelling of the Dickens' tale, in which the hero becomes a top cat among a gang of rambunctious dogs roaming the streets of modern-day New York.

Aside from being another full-length, animated Disney feature—usually a box-office success—the film represents a major step forward in movie-making. It combines the old with the new on several levels—a classic story told in traditional form, but cast in a contemporary setting and enhanced by a technology still new enough to inspire awe. And it does so on an unprecedented scale.

CARTOONS AND COMPUTERS

In the climactic scene, Sikes, in the persona of a big-time gangster driving a limousine, pursues Fagin, a bag person putting around town in a motorized shopping cart. The hair-raising chase speeds through the New York subway system, and it is in this scene that the animator's art joins the programmer's science to create a hybrid form of animation. The characters are the animator's. The tunnel, the train, and cars are the computer's.

Oliver is not the first Disney movie to employ animation and computer graphics in tandem. *The Great Mouse Detective,* released in 1986, contained some brief footage combining the two, but the scene from *Oliver,* about five minutes long, marks a point of no return for Disney, a commitment on the part of the studio to apply new technologies to the time-honored tradition of animation.

Different definitions

Animation is one of those art forms that has been set free by technology, not only at Disney, but throughout the animation industry. It has escaped the narrow boundaries that once limited it to fuzzy bunnies, crafty coyotes, and pudgy pigs. A vast number of techniques now come under the animation label—from the simple pen-and-pencil drawings to lively lumps of clay to the digitized, high-resolution computer graphics that made the *Star Wars* trilogy leap off the screen.

Consider, for example, how the Motion Picture Academy of Arts and Sciences defines animated films when voting the Oscars: "An animated film usually falls into one of two general fields...character or abstract. Some of the techniques of animating films include cel animation, computer animation, stop motion, clay animation, puppets, pixilation, cutouts, camera multipass imagery, kaleidoscopic effects, and drawing on the frame itself."

TV TECHNOLOGY

Outside of Hollywood, much of what the public sees in new animation technologies comes through television commercials, where the budgets exist to produce the ideas dreamed up by independent filmmakers who are the avant-garde of animation. Here, computer animations or frame-by-frame video systems are making stars out of squares like Max Headroom. Other techniques, such as the imaginative clay animations created for Kentucky Fried Chicken and other advertisers, are also drawing kudos.

However, in animation especially, the old maxim applies: the more things change, the more they stay the same. Nowhere is this more true than back at the Disney studios, where anthropomorphism is the eleventh commandment.

"We use the computer as a tool," Disney spokesman Howard Green says. "It can't do the type of personality-animation Disney is famous for. Not yet. Maybe never. The personalities of the characters are something that can only come from the human artist who is the actor.

"But, beyond that, we are committed to a new $12-million R&D program we're calling

> *An animator must be fascinated with the way things move. He or she must be a keen observer of the world. An animator must be something of an actor. The ability to give a cartoon figure character depends on the ability to feel a character within oneself.*
>
> **Kit Laybourne**
> **From *The Animation Book,***
> **Crown Publishers, New York**

> *Animation is one art form that has truly been set free by technology, not only at Disney, but throughout the entire industry.*

CAPS (Computer Animation Production System). It's just now being installed and will utilize the computer to a much larger extent in the future, particularly in post-production operations like cel painting or other technical applications. We're very committed to the new technologies here and they're very exciting. However, it's important to stress that the hand-drawn characteristics of Disney animation will not change."

Creating an environment

When *The Great Mouse Detective* was in production, animator Phil Nibbelink and computer programmer Tad Gielow teamed up to produce a computer animation sequence that subsequently became part of the film; that led to CAPS and what promises to be some startling new effects in films to come.

"I've always enjoyed doing chase scenes," Nibbelink says. "But it was frustrating because with animation we're restricted to flat artwork. We can only truck in and out or pan left and right. But with the computer, we're able to create an entire environment and move in, around, and through it.

"That scene we did from *The Great Mouse Detective* was where the characters were running through the clock gears of Big Ben, jumping from tooth to tooth. With the computer, the camera could swoop alongside of them, go in front, and create a kind of helicopter footage that would be impossible in normal animation."

EARLIER DIMENSIONS

In the early years of animation, a technique called the "multiplane camera" was what gave the Disney features a surprise look of three-dimension reality. The system was a complex camera that could shoot several levels of background, with the artwork physically separated in space by pieces of glass.

"We haven't been able to do that of late because of the expense involved in creating all the artwork required and the fact that it takes about ten people to operate the camera," Nibbelink continues. "Artistically, with the computer, it will be possible to composite an infinite number of levels compared to the three or four cels we now do with animation alone. As a result, the audience will see a much more realistic environment, have a better sense of 3-D, and see much lusher production values. That's still a couple of years away, but it will allow animators to do things we never could before."

That laborious artwork required and the expense it entails have historically limited animation to a few studios. Typically, it takes about 24 individual drawings or cels to create one second of motion on film. That translates to an animation cost alone of over $300,000 per 30-minute episode. But with the new technologies, animation companies have flourished. Where once there were three, there are now more than a dozen. Domestic production alone now exceeds 1,000 half-hour programs per year.

HANNA-BARBERA

The most prolific of these is Hanna-Barbera Productions. Its founders, Bill Hanna and Joe Barbera, first collaborated on the *Tom and Jerry* cartoons for MGM in the 1940s. They later established their own animation studio, which since has become part of Taft Entertainment (which also includes two other animation companies, Ruby-Spears and Southern Star).

The impact that Hanna-Barbera has had on the animation industry and on the minds of a generation of American children is immeasurable. Currently, more than 225 H-B television series or specials are being carried in syndication or in first-run and rerun telecasting on the three major networks. The company recently introduced a home videocassette series based on Bible stories; in the works for 1987 are nine two-hour movies featuring such Hanna-Barbera creations as Scooby-Doo, Top Cat, the Wacky Racers, Yogi Bear, Galtar, Heidi, and The Flintstones.

An awesome addition to the Hanna-Barbera animation complex is a cluster of three VAX 11/780 computers with an astonishing six billion bytes of memory. The huge system has already started cutting into the production time and costs that have limited even Hanna-Barbera's efficient cartoon assembly line.

A personal art

But even in this case, where the production is almost exclusively for television and does not require the high-resolution film necessary for theatrical release, the animator is still the dominant figure. For all its power, the computer cannot yet produce the kind of movement that shapes a character's personality. On the other hand, the computer does excel in its function as a tool by easing the drudgery of work—for example, the repetitious coloring of each cel and background. It also digitizes the artwork, assembles individual frames into the proper sequence, and records the finished product (with sound to be dubbed later) onto broadcast videotape.

"Animation," says Hanna-Barbera spokesperson Sarah Baisley, "is a highly personal art, one which will never be totally replaced by computers, for the animated actor is really the talented animator. It's his skill that brings personality to the cartoon; a machine will never accomplish this task."

DRAWING FROM TWO PHILOSOPHIES

Echoing that philosophy is Yutaka Fujioka, who heads TMS, the huge Japanese animation conglomerate. "To study Disney is to understand how to communicate with an audience," he says. "Japanese animation tends to be more realistic. Which is not to say that it is superior to American animation, just that it has grown in a different direction. Our objective is to combine the best of both art forms and hopefully emerge with something new."

To that end, the parent company has established its American arm, TMS Entertainment/Animation Futurists, in Los Angeles. In doing so, it has also launched a unique cross-culturalization program certain to fertilize the creativity of future animators. In making the *Mighty Orbots* (now seen on ABC), American writers, animators, and other artists travel to Tokyo to work on the production, while their Japanese counterparts come to the U.S.—a system of management interplay now filtering through the automotive industry and one that will be extended to other animation projects.

New technologies

The Japanese studio has also vigorously pursued the development of new technologies to produce its 16 feature movies and more than 3,000 half-hour segments in prime-time television around the world.

For example, one device is a multiplane camera controlled by a computer that positions characters, objects, and backgrounds painted on up to seven separate layers of celluloid, so a realistic illusion of depth is achieved. A halogen light system, buried in the basement beneath the towering mechanism, enables the cameramen to create realistic backlighting effects. Simultaneously, on a platform two-stories high,

> *Creativity and imagination are elements inherent in all of us, and the kinds of ideas best suited for animation can be encouraged through various disciplined forms of playfulness.*
>
> **Kit Laybourne**
> **From *The Animation Book,***
> **Crown Publishers, New York**

a video camera allows them to observe the effect shot by shot, rather than by relying on viewfinders.

TMS has also developed a break-through 3-D system. While still requiring special glasses to enjoy the 3-D effect, the picture, without glasses, is equally sharp and distinct—with no double image or blurring.

Much of the TMS technical achievement is being focused on *Little Nemo,* its first theatrical feature for worldwide release, due within the next two years. The $15-million production is an adaptation of the classic comic strip about a boy who enters the magical world of his own dreams.

While the computer is still incapable of fully replicating the animator's art, there are those in the computer-graphics field who feel it may be only a matter of time before a new generation of "artistic scientists" are creating at the keyboard.

ANIMATION AWARDS

In March, the National Computer Graphics Association will present its annual awards for achievements in animation. More than 300 entries are under consideration (double the number submitted last year), in ten different categories.

Dean Ross Eaker, publisher of *Computer Pictures Magazine,* is chairman of the animation competition committee. His message is that, "Around the world a revolution is occurring in the way startling images are being created by a new wave of innovators at the keyboards of computers. And while the outcome of revolutions generally remains unsettled for a long time, we can be certain of one thing: each of us will be affected in some important way by this ongoing dramatic development in human communications."

In 1980, film critic and animation historian Leonard Maltin published *Of Mice and Magic: A History of American Animated Cartoons,* at a time when the marriage of computers and animation was barely a nodding acquaintanceship. Even then, Maltin was prescient in his conclusion that:

> *"Animation is a limitless medium, and anything is possible with time, tools, and thought."*

From SKY magazine, January 1987.
Reprinted by permission of Bernie Ward,
Lake Worth, Florida.

Audio, CD-ROM, and CD-ROM XA

By Suzanne Ropiequet

[From animation, we move to sound, and specifically to the audio made possible by the new CD-ROM XA format. Here, Suzanne Ropiequet explains how the new format will be implemented and suggests ways that it might be used.]

Although CD-ROM's heritage lies in the CD audio world, audio hasn't yet played much of a role in CD-ROM applications. This is largely because there has been no standard way to store and play anything except full-fidelity digital audio on a CD-ROM. A new CD-ROM format known as CD-ROM XA (Extended Architecture), proposed by Sony and Philips in cooperation with Microsoft in August 1988, should help make the use of audio more appealing to many CD-ROM developers because it will provide a standard way to play digital audio using a personal computer.

INTEGRATING CD AUDIO AND CD-ROM FORMATS

Most compact disc enthusiasts know that a single CD can store up to 73 minutes of the highest quality digital audio. The disc format for storing digital audio, often called the Red Book format, is an international standard that specifies where and how the data is placed on the disc. Because all compact discs adhere to this standard format, they can all be read by all CD players.

CD-ROM discs can also contain CD audio, which can be played by any CD-ROM drive with CD audio playback circuitry. However, integrating CD audio into a CD-ROM product can be both a design challenge and a technical challenge. The design challenge stems from the newness of the concept, the technical challenge from the differences between the ways that CD-ROM data and CD audio data are prepared and stored.

The specifications for all compact discs call for data to be stored sequentially on one or more contiguous spiral tracks. CD audio is stored in 2352-byte blocks (composed of ninety-eight 24-byte *frames*) and CD-ROM data (images, programs, and so on) are stored in either

> ## CD-ROM DATA MODES
>
> Mode 1's 2048-byte sectors contain an additional 288 bytes of error correction/detection information, whereas Mode 2's 2336-byte sectors contain none. Product developers generally use the Mode 1, 2048-byte sector format for any uses, such as computer programs, compressed images, and text that require bit-perfect data. They use the Mode 2, 2336-byte sector size for data, such as uncompressed images, that won't suffer from a few missing bits here and there.

2048-byte (Mode 1) or 2336-byte (Mode 2) *sectors*. Because these three formats differ, they are all stored in separate tracks on the disc. Mode 1 and Mode 2 CD-ROM data are placed on their own separate tracks, and each selection of CD audio data is placed in one of up to 99 additional tracks.

Full-fidelity CD digital audio requires a great deal of disc space—about 176 KB per second of audio. It is so dense with information that it completely fills the drive circuitry or *bandwidth* when it is read from the disc, thus preventing any other data from being read at the same time.

From a designer's point of view, these factors mean that:

- Each audio selection must be accessed separately.

- The drive cannot send images or code to the computer *while* the sound is playing; it has to wait until the sound is finished (plus a second or two more as the head jumps back to the track containing the images and other data).

These constraints limit the amount of audio that designers can use, and they require all images or programs to be loaded before the audio is played—a workable strategy only when the images that must be synchronized with an audio passage can be loaded completely into memory. Problems with this approach occur when the image sequence is too big to fit in memory — a common occurrence when dealing with high resolution, full color images.

For example, let's say the program is to play a musical segment in sync with a full-color slide show, but has only enough memory to preload half the images at a time. In this case, it would have to preload the first set of images, branch to the CD track and play it, return to the program to load the next set of images, and then branch back to the same CD track to play the remainder of the music.

This sequence may sound simple enough, but it isn't an acceptable solution if the application needs "seamless" audio, and here's why: It takes a CD-ROM drive head about a second to seek to a new location on a disc. In addition, each image also takes time to load, and remember that the transfer rate is only 150 KB per second. If the second image sequence in this example consisted of ten 128 KB images, the listener would hear a pause of about 9 seconds between the two music segments.

One way around a problem like this is to ensure that all the images are preloaded either by changing the design or by adding more memory. Another approach is to combine, or *interleave*, the audio and data in a single track. This technique is used in the CD-I format and is soon to be included as CD-ROM XA, an extension to the existing CD-ROM format.

CD-I (GREEN BOOK) FORMAT

The CD-I audio format, ADPCM, is a special variation of the CD-ROM format that is specifically designed for audiovisual applications. In essence, ADPCM takes CD-ROM Mode 2 and breaks it into two forms, Form 1 and Form 2. These forms are almost identical to CD-ROM Modes 1 and 2, except for one very important aspect: Both forms reside in a single track. (You may recall that the CD-ROM specification allows only one mode per track.)

Placing Mode 1 data (programs, compressed images, text) in the same track as Mode 2 data (audio) allows the different types of data to be processed in real-time as they are read from the disc. The two forms are interleaved on the track so that every few sectors of Form 1 data alternate with Form 2 data. The interleaved sectors are read alternately and sent to either the audio or video outputs at the rate of about 150 KB per second. By the time they are played and displayed, the effect is a completely synchronized audiovisual sequence.

CD-ROM EXTENDED ARCHITECTURE

To encourage CD-ROM developers to begin creating audio-enriched multimedia applications, Sony and Philips, in cooperation with Microsoft, proposed CD-ROM Extended Architecture as an extension to the CD-ROM standard. CD-ROM XA represents a bridge between CD-I, a proprietary viewing device, and CD-ROM working in a standard personal computer system.

CD-ROM Extended Architecture (CD-ROM XA) defines a format for storing compressed audio along with other data on a CD-ROM disc, and the way in which the stored information is read from the disc. Using this standard format, publishers will be able to develop multimedia CD-ROM products that will work on any personal computer system that is equipped with the appropriate XA hardware.

The CD-ROM XA specification will allow several fidelities of audio to be interleaved on the same track as the image, text, and program data, and then played back at the same time the images are being transferred to memory and displayed.

Interleaved audio is an important addition to the CD-ROM standard because, until its introduction only full-fidelity digital audio could

ADPCM

ADPCM stands for Adaptive Differential Pulse Code Modulation. ADPCM audio is decompressed to PCM audio, which is the encoding format used by Red Book audio.

be stored on a CD-ROM disc, and then only on a separate track. In CD-ROM XA, audio signals are combined with text and graphics data in a single track so that they can be read at virtually the same time. This eliminates the need to move back and forth from an audio track to a data track while playing a multimedia event.

How does interleaved audio work?

In concept, interleaved audio will work in the CD-ROM XA environment along the lines described below.

When an application requests an interleaved file from the disc, the CD-ROM drive will read the data one sector at a time and allocate it to its assigned data transfer *channel*. This channel is specified in a header at the beginning of the sector. The information can be assigned and transferred, in up to 16 channels for audio and 32 channels for data.

DATA STORAGE FORMATS		
CD Audio	*CD-ROM*	*CD-I*
CD audio	CD audio	CD audio
	Mode 1 (2048 bytes of data)	—
	Mode 2 (2336 bytes of data)	Form 1 (CD-ROM Mode 1 with extra 8-byte header)
		Form 2 (CD-ROM Mode 2 with extra 8-byte header)

SUZANNE ROPIEQUET

Home: Redmond, Washington
Job: ISV Account Manager, Multimedia Systems Group, Microsoft Corporation
Quote: *"The average person is far more interested in products that entertain, educate, amuse, or help them do their job than in the technology that makes these products possible. When the delivery mechanism for the CD-ROM technology finally becomes transparent to the consumer, and the programs themselves become the focus — then we will see an incredible market for CD-ROM."*

The CD-ROM XA specification allows each channel to contain either computer data (program code, text or graphics) or audio (voice or music). The number of audio channels is limited by the amount of data bandwidth each audio channel uses. Higher audio grades require more space and allow fewer channels, while lower audio grades take up less space and allow more channels. For example, two channels of full-fidelity CD digital stereo audio (CD-DA) fill the entire bandwidth, whereas CD-ROM XA's lowest fidelity mono audio fills only $1/16$ of the data bandwidth, allowing 16 channels.

In CD-ROM XA, audio signals are "compressed" to take up less space on a disc, which means that they also use less bandwidth than full-fidelity CD digital audio. Instead of using the full bandwidth of data that CD-ROM makes available for the audio signal, CD-ROM XA's compressed audio uses only one-fourth or one-eighth of the total bandwidth. The remaining transfer bandwidth is then available for interleaving text and graphics information with the audio.

The CD-ROM XA controller will intercept the data as it comes off the disc and send the data portion of the file to system memory and the audio portion to an audio processor located in the drive controller circuitry. Because the CD-ROM XA audio will be stored in a compressed form (ADPCM encoded format), it must be decompressed and then converted to an analog format to be played back. This decompression and conversion will be handled by the audio processor.

What happens to the interleaved images?

Because the CD-ROM XA specification allows the program to transfer data while playing audio segments, images can be sent directly to the screen, or they can be preloaded for later display or animation.

This ability to transfer data while the audio is playing avoids the long delays that would otherwise be caused by the slow transfer rate of the CD-ROM drive. With this ability, a properly scheduled multimedia sequence appears seamless. However, the author of the multimedia event is responsible for working out the timing so that the data required for each effect is loaded in time. If an image is sent to the screen before it is fully loaded from the CD-ROM, it will appear to be torn or distorted in some manner.

What audio fidelities will CD-ROM XA support?

In its proposed form, the CD-ROM XA specification offers three audio fidelity options: full-fidelity CD digital audio, and two additional compressed sound fidelities referred to as levels B (medium high fidelity) and C (speech quality). Missing from the sequence is Level A audio, which is used only in CD-I systems.

Level B audio: Level B audio is roughly equivalent to the best FM radio broadcast, but without the static and other interference associated with radio communication. It is more than adequate for most CD-ROM applications requiring better than average sound quality.

One second of Level B stereo audio requires about 42.8 KB of disc space, much less than the 176 KB required for a second of CD-DA. A Level B stereo audio disc would play for four hours, and a Level B mono disc would play for eight.

Level B audio can be interleaved with other data on the disc. Because Level B stereo uses only 25 percent of the drive's bandwidth, the rest of the space can be used to transfer other data stored on the disc at the same time the audio is playing.

Level C audio: Level C audio is usually considered to be close to AM radio quality, again without the noise normally associated with radio. Most developers who have worked with this level say that it is quite adequate for voice applications.

One second of Level C mono requires only about 10 KB. Thus, a disc filled with Level C stereo would play for about eight hours, its monoaural counterpart for more than sixteen hours.

Level C audio can also be interleaved with other data. Level C mono uses about 6 percent of the drive's bandwidth, allowing a lot of other data to be stored and transferred while the sound is playing. Because this level uses so little of the disc and drive resources, it is often the best choice for applications that use synchronized audiovisual effects and animation.

Although the 32 data channels can be interleaved in any configuration on a CD-ROM XA disc, the normal configuration when using Level C mono audio is 1 sector of audio for every 15 sectors of computer data. This configuration provides a transfer rate of $^{15}/_{16} \times 150$ KB/sec = 140.63 KB/sec for the data when audio is being played.

BANDWIDTH

The term *bandwidth* refers to the amount of data that can be transferred through the data channels. The actual data transfer rates for the three audio formats are as follows:

CD-ROM Mode 1: 2048 bytes × 75 sectors/sec = 153.6 KB/sec

CD-ROM Mode 2: 2336 bytes × 75 sectors/sec = 175.2 KB/sec

CD digital audio: 2352 bytes × 75 sectors/sec = 176.4 KB/sec

SWITCHING AUDIO CHANNELS IN REAL TIME

Like radio or television channels, a data channel is not necessarily "played" all the time. It is played only if the control program says so. In other words, if a sequence of four sectors is assigned to data channels 1, 2, 3, and 4, and the control program says to use only the information in channels 1 and 2, then the data in sectors 1 and 2 will be used and the data in sectors 3 and 4 will be lost.

So far we've focused mainly on interleaved audio and images. But audio can also be interleaved with more audio. Because of the way that CD-ROM XA stores interleaved data, it is possible to switch instantly between audio channels in the same file. This allows the program to provide a variety of audio responses appropriate to the actions of the person using the program. If the following audio segments were stored in eight channels of a CD-ROM, the program could switch between channels to produce a much larger selection of sentences. (In this example, 64 sentences could be formed.)

1. The dog is OLD.

2. The cat is COLD.

3. The fox is BOLD.

> **RESOURCES**
>
> Meridian Data, Inc.
> 4450 Capitola Road, Suite 101
> Capitola, California 95010
> (408)476–5858
>
> Microsoft Corporation
> 16011 NE 36th Way
> Box 97017
> Redmond, Washington 98073
> (206)882–8080
>
> Online Computers
> 20251 Century Blvd.
> Germantown, Maryland 20874
> (301)428–3700
>
> Optical Media International
> 485 Alberto Way
> Los Gatos, California 95032
> (408)395–4332
>
> Philips DuPont Optical
> 1409 Foulk Road, Suite 200
> Wilmington, Delaware 19803
> (302)479–2500
>
> Sony Technology Center
> 1003 Elwell Court
> Palo Alto, California 94303A
> (415)965–4492

4. The goat is GOLD.

5. The frog is BROWN.

6. The bird is FAST.

7. The cow is BIG.

8. The horse is SMALL.

For example, by telling the system to play channel 3 until after the word *is* and then switch to channel 6, we could create the sentence *The fox is FAST*. In a language-training program, the user could select an animal and a modifier, and the application would change channels automatically to use the word correctly in a sentence. Without this ability to switch between channels, either all 64 possible sentences would have to be stored on disc, or all of the words would have to be stored in system RAM and constructed in real time.

To take proper advantage of this powerful feature, the timing of the start of the variable words must be lined up when the interleaved file is built. If one word in a group is longer then the others, space must be inserted to realign the timing before the next point at which a channel change is allowed. In the example described above, all of the last words (OLD, COLD, BOLD, and so on) would have to start at the same point in time.

In this example we are using only 8 of the 16 channels that are flowing off the disc. There is no reason why we couldn't fill the remaining 8 channels with more sentences or with other types of data. If we were to fill them with image data, it would be sent to the computer while a sentence was being played.

TOOLS FOR INTERLEAVED AUDIO

When this article was written, the CD-ROM XA specification had just been proposed. At that time, no tools were available to help the author determine the most efficient disc layout and interleave factors for compressed audio data and images. There is no question that tools will begin to appear as soon as the specification is finalized and made public, although it is not yet clear who will provide them. If you plan to use audio in your future products, look to the companies listed in the "Resources" box for guidance.

CONCLUSION

Interactive multimedia applications are the next major milestone in the future of personal computers. The potential for computers to communicate, educate, entertain and enhance personal and business productivity will be significantly improved when industry-standard personal computers are able to support interleaved ADPCM audio. CD-ROM XA is an open standard that will allow peripheral manufacturers to incorporate ADPCM decoders into their CD-ROM drives and in so doing, allow software developers to add high-quality audio to their PC applications. Its announcement demonstrates the emerging role that personal computers will play in multimedia information products.

Special thanks to Bob Ogdon of Ogdon MicroDesign, Inc., Lakewood, Colorado, producers of the first CD-ROM XA prototype demonstration, for his help in compiling this article.

[Suzanne Ropiequet is currently a Product Manager for Microsoft Corporation. She has been involved in the CD-ROM industry since 1985, as Editor of Microsoft Press's first two CD-ROM books and Program Director of Microsoft's first three CD-ROM conferences.]

Making the Most of Sound on CD-ROM

By Bryan Brewer

[In the concluding article in this section, Bryan Brewer acts as an audio advocate, offering advice on the dos *and* don'ts *of implementing sound into CD-ROM products.]*

As CD-ROM matures, we'll begin to see more multimedia discs, especially those that include good-fidelity *audio* along with text and images. The technology holds great promise for many types of discs:

- Reference works (talking books, databases of nature sounds, music encyclopedias).
- Entertainment titles (flight simulators with sound effects, adventure games with speaking characters).
- Presentation programs (product demos, point-of-sale advertising, mail-order catalogs).
- Training applications (narrated software tutorials, foreign-language teaching aids).

How do you make the most of sound on these types of CD-ROM applications? "Just hire an actor to read a script" is how a developer once described to me his version of adding sound to a CD-ROM application. True enough—the process can be that simple. But the quality of the audio production will show it; and you might miss the opportunity to apply interactive audio techniques in ways that can truly enhance the overall value of your disc.

If sound is going to play a role in your multimedia CD-ROM, here are some basic guidelines that will help you maximize the interactive value, production value, and entertainment value of your efforts. I've also included my responses to some of the "Yes, buts…" that I've heard about sound on CD-ROM."

MAKE AUDIO AN INTEGRAL PART OF THE USER INTERFACE

Programs of the 1980s each have a certain look and feel. The 1990s will see the concept expand to the look, feel, and *sound* of the user interface. Don't use audio halfway. Make the disc talk. Any interactive program provides abundant opportunity to have real human voices speak to the user—to guide, to correct, to persuade, to warn, to encourage—to exploit the full range of human conversational techniques.

"Yes, but... the client/user/buyer doesn't want sound coming from a desktop computer." This response is conditioned mostly by the poor quality of sound we have become accustomed to hearing from computers. It's no wonder that people are unenthused after hearing irritating beeps, tinny-sounding music, and barely intelligible synthesized speech.

To sell sound on CD-ROM, present the delivery medium in the same context as audio tapes, videotapes, and interactive videodisc. You don't hear objections to sound output from these widely used media. And headphones can minimize disruption to other workers in an office.

USE PROFESSIONAL VOICE TALENT TO PORTRAY A MIX OF CHARACTERS

The characters you create to present spoken information to the user are the "soul" of your multimedia program. If you rely on a neutral, lecture-type voice reading a safe script, you're likely to induce boredom and the desire on the part of the user to "change the channel." Distinctive audio characterizations will add spark and life to your program and will energize your users' emotional responses.

And don't necessarily limit yourself to just one or two characters. Most successful media presentations have a set of characters with different roles. The local newscast (radio or TV) has an announcer, an anchorperson, a sportscaster, a weather forecaster, and additional reporters. A talk show has a main host, a sidekick, and various guests. Most dramas have a protagonist, an antagonist, and supporting roles. Use these types of paradigms to establish characters that can interact appropriately with the user (and each other) to add entertainment value to your production.

"Yes, but... we're not in the entertainment business. It's too risky." Sure—you may not be able to please everyone with your choice of characters. But using them is far better than settling for middle-of-the-road drabness that's almost guaranteed to put people to sleep. Wake up and join the media culture of the twenty-first century.

USE VOICES, SOUNDS, MUSIC, AND AUDIO EFFECTS TO ACHIEVE HIGH PRODUCTION VALUES

There's a lot more to creating effective narration than putting an actor in front of a microphone. You must pay attention to the overall sound design to imbue your recorded segments with the desired aural textures. Get a competent audio producer who can give effective voice direction, specify the right sound effects, choose appropriate music, and supervise audio effects processing such as reverb, panning, and equalization. (If you don't know what these terms mean and how to apply them, then *be sure* you find a producer who does.)

Like good writing or video production, good audio takes a lot of editing to produce satisfying results. Here's where extra time can make a big difference. Don't skimp on this or on any of the other phases of audio production if you want your product to sound professional.

"Yes, but... it takes a lot of money to produce good audio." Yes, that's part of the price of admission to multimedia CD-ROM. Of course, there are ways to get good results on a tight

BRYAN BREWER

Home: Seattle, Washington
Job: President, Earth View, Inc.
Quote: *"Multimedia CD-ROM will find its first widespread use as an interactive training medium for business and government applications. It combines some of the best aspects of computer-based training and interactive videodisc, and it can be applied in a cost-effective manner to solve real-world training problems."*

budget, but you can't stretch the dollars too thin. Audio is one area in which low quality is very hard to hide.

(*Note*: Even though the compact disc is a digital storage medium, it is not necessary to record or mix your audio with digital equipment. Good analog recording equipment can produce very clean sound and can be less expensive than digital recording.)

COORDINATE THE AUDIO PLAYBACK WITH THE SCREEN DISPLAY

This point may seem obvious, but it requires extra attention if the sound and images are not to be stored together. In a video or a film, the accompanying soundtrack is always played in synchrony with the images. It's stored that way. This is also true of interleaved audio that is mixed with graphics or text for a synchronized audiovisual playback. In non-interleaved multimedia CD-ROM, images may be displayed from the computer's memory under program control while the sound is played directly from the CD.

If the same audio is always played with the same images, coordinating the two should be no problem. If you plan to match an audio segment with two or more visual segments, or vice-versa, then you need to coordinate the timing among all the allowable combinations. Remember that audio is the real-time medium and should be the controlling factor in coordinating timings. (Hmmm... better think that script through again so we don't have to go back and re-record some audio.)

DON'T WORRY ABOUT WHICH AUDIO FIDELITY LEVEL TO USE

I've seen too many discussions about interactive audio degenerate into needless debate about the choice of level of audio fidelity. CD-ROM XA provides three levels and CD-I provides one additional level, and they all sound good. Unless you're dealing with sonic information (such as quality musical performances or audio test data) that requires the reproduction of high frequencies, your choice of audio fidelity level will be dictated by how much space is left on the disc for the audio. If your images, text, and software take up $3/4$ of the disc, and you need two hours of audio, you can use Level B mono, or you can use Level C stereo or mono.

The choice of audio fidelity level for interleaved audio is likewise a matter of data storage. Storage requirements for Levels B and C range from $1/4$ to $1/16$ of the bandwidth, and your choice depends on the density of the interleaved graphics or text.

"Yes but... won't the lower fidelity sound worse?" Believe me, with ADPCM, you can fool most of the people most of the time. Focus on content and design. They are what most people will remember about the audio on your disc.

DESIGN FOR SOUND FROM THE BEGINNING

If you want to make a truly integrated multimedia CD-ROM, you need to raise the audio consciousness of the designers and producers on the product team. This means including audio considerations in all phases of the project, from design to production to testing (and don't forget marketing). The scriptwriter and the audio producer need to understand how audio segments are going to be used in the scheme of user interaction. The programmer and visual artist need to know how audio will be synchronized into audiovisual presentations. The project manager and marketing staff need to know what role audio will play in order to properly position and sell the product.

Sound on CD-ROM can be easy, entertaining, and effective. It can add drama, excitement, and realism to your multimedia production. We are still in the early stages of development of interactive audio. You have the opportunity to let your imagination and creativity made a mark on the industry. I encourage you to "go for it."

[Bryan Brewer is President of Earth View, Inc., a Seattle-based company specializing in interactive audio applications of the compact disc. Earth View's first CD audio product, The Fine Art of Relaxation *by Joel Levey, was released in 1988. In addition to serving as contributing editor to* Digital Audio *magazine and* CD-ROM Review, *Bryan is the author of articles in* CD-ROM The New Papyrus *(1986, Microsoft Press) and* CD-ROM Optical Publishing *(1987, Microsoft Press), and is co-author of* The Compact Disc Book *(1987, Harcourt Brace Jovanovich).]*

PREMASTERING/ MASTERING PERSPECTIVES

DETECTING AND CORRECTING ERRORS ON CD-ROM
By Linda Helgerson

CONVERTING THE DATA FOR CD-ROM
By Linda Helgerson

THE PDO SHOW
By Roger Strukhoff

Detecting and Correcting Errors on CD-ROM

By Linda Helgerson
From *CD Data Report*

[First published in 1985, this article offers a concise, nontechnical description of the CD-ROM error detection and correction schemes that result in one error on one out of 20 million discs.]

A discussion of error correction and CD-ROM can be quite simple or inordinately complex, because, in fact, it is both. The simple explanation is that by the time the user views data from a CD-ROM disc on a CRT, any errors have been detected and corrected.

The complex description involves how such a feat is accomplished. For those readers who could care less about the process—only the results are important—we suggest you stop reading here, because data integrity for CD-ROM can exceed specifications for all other digital data storage media. For those determined to become intimately knowledgeable with the finite details, we suggest the four papers on error correction found in the Audio Engineering Society's conference proceedings, *Digital Audio,* published in 1983. This article is designed for readers whose interest level is somewhere between.

The need for stringent error correction is obvious in CD-ROM, but the need to know specific details about how it is accomplished may be less obvious. Error correction schemes for encoding and then decoding digital data have only been in existence some 25 years. Since 1970, most work has involved refinements in detecting and correcting various kinds of errors randomly dispersed or found in patterns, and also in applying error correction theory to real-world applications.

The standards for compact audio discs, established by N.V. Philips and The Sony Corporation in 1980, were based on earlier theoretical research combined with enhancements to meet future requirements of digital audio playback on compact disc. The same standards are used for CD-ROM during the encoding segment of the mastering process and in the decoding circuitry of the CD-ROM drive or in the host computer software. Extra space (288 bytes) is available on a CD-ROM disc for added error detection codes (EDC) or error correction codes (ECC).

The chart shown in Figure 4-11, supplied by N.V. Philips, illustrates the data integrity loop for CD-ROM media. With the EDC and ECC encoding, the bit error rate (BER) is equal to 10^{-15}. The BER in a replicated disc is 10^{-5} to 10^{-6}. The CD-ROM drive includes two decoding mechanisms, one that detects and corrects errors according to the compact audio disc standard described above and a second one that checks and corrects according to the additional error detection and layered error correction encoded during premastering.

As the chart indicates, the data integrity strategy involves the combination of two encoding and two decoding processes, which together improve the BER to 10^{-15} at the user level, or in lay terminology, provides error-free data on the screen to a degree that data errors become a non-issue.

MAKING SENSE OF THE NUMBERS

Error correction involves issues that come from the technical community, not the user community. Users are often confused as to what numbers such as 10^{-5} or 10^{-18} really mean. Jargon can also be a problem—seek errors, burst errors, C1 or C2 uncorrectable errors are not household words. Since methods for detecting and correcting errors are algebraic or statements of probability, understanding the process can be difficult. Demystifying error detection and correction is nonetheless important.

First, the numbers. In communications transmission, the acceptable error rate is 10^{-4}. For magnetic tape, the acceptable level is 10^{-5}. The error rate for CD-ROM is somewhere between 10^{-12} and 10^{-18}, according to Bert Gall, manager of product planning at Philips Subsystems & Peripherals Inc., which is better than transmission and mag tape rates by a factor of thousands. Sounds good, but what do the numbers really mean. If the expected error rate were 10^{-16}, that would mean there would be one nonrecoverable error in every 10 quadrillion (10 quadrillion = 10 million × 1 billion).

An error in this sense means that the data cannot be recovered or reconstructed during decoding for accurate viewing by the user. Since there are one-half billion bytes on a CD-ROM disc, this would mean there is one noncorrectable error on one disc every 20 million discs. In other words, the user would see an error on the screen if lucky enough to acquire that one-in-20 million disc. In such instances, the editors suggest the user call the supplier and demand another disc. Even in such a case, cleaning the disc and removing dust particles or fingerprints might resolve the problem.

RANDOM BIT ERRORS

There are different kinds of errors and therefore different methods for detecting and correcting each type of error, but all the methods must be combined into one compatible correction scheme. Random-bit errors are just that—bit errors that have no correlation with other bit errors. The materials used in production may have small defects or damage. Despite the clean room and highly accurate replicating equipment, foreign particles may be imbedded in the plastic coating. Or the disc's playing surface may be scratched while it is out of the drive. These minute imperfections are randomly spread over the disc and cause errors in the data.

The first method used to detect and correct single random glitches is called parity, or oversampling. A method also used in magnetic computer storage, this decoding process checks for and corrects one- or two-bit errors. It also flags errors of two or more consecutive bits for a later decoding and correction process. If the data does not conform to appropriate algebraic patterns, the right data pattern or value is substituted. If the error is unable to be corrected during this stage, it is detected or identified as an error for later correction.

BURST ERRORS

Burst errors refer to groups of consecutive bits that are in error. The CD-ROM standard recommends that burst errors have less than seven bits per error. These errors more often result from scratches and fingerprints on the disc than from defects or damage in the mastering and

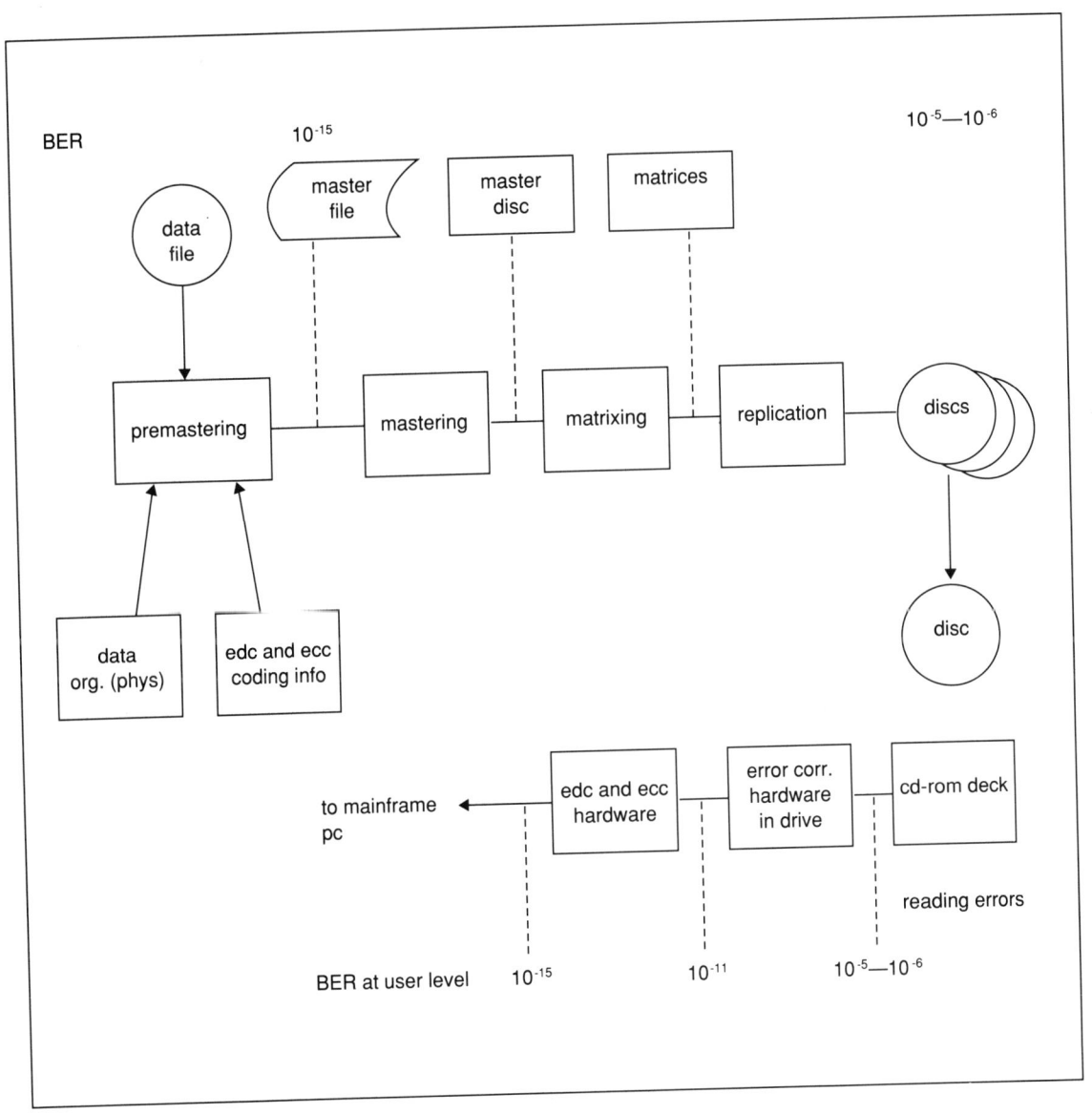

Figure 4-11. *The data integrity loop*

GLOSSARY

Block error correction: scheme by which additional recovery methods are applied to a block of data during premastering to ensure recovery of an entire physical block of user data (2048 bytes). EDC and ECC are used to detect and correct block errors.

Burst error: an error of a group of consecutive bits; normally occurs as a result of fingerprints and scratches on the surface of the disc; burst errors are detected in C1 and corrected in C2; the possibility of this happening is 10^{-12} or one bit error in a trillion bits; see CIRC.

C1: A Reed-Solomon code that corrects random bit errors and detects burst errors of 2 bits or more for correction by C2.

C2: A Reed-Solomon code that corrects burst errors and detects further uncorrectable errors, which can then be corrected or recovered by the additional EDC and ECC.

CIRC: Cross Interleave Reed-Solomon Code; a series of two different block codes (C1 and C2) combined with data delay and rearrangement techniques. As a result of CIRC, data integrity is 10^{-12} or better.

THE REED-SOLOMON CODE

The error correction scheme, established by Philips and Sony in 1980, utilizes the correction code developed in 1960 by Irving S. Reed, professor of electrical engineering at the University of Southern California, and Gustave Solomon of Hughes Aircraft and the University of California at Berkeley. In fact, two Reed-Solomon codes are used.

C1 refers to the first correction code, described above, which is used to correct random bit errors and to detect burst or multiple errors. C2 is the second Reed-Solomon correction code used to correct up to two burst errors of varying sizes and patterns as flagged by C1. The word "code" used in this sense refers to an algebraic formula for encoding and later decoding a block of data (1 block = 288 bits). Errors unable to be corrected using C2 are also flagged in the output. The possibility of this happening is around 10^{-8}.

The use of the two Reed-Solomon codes is combined with an additional technique—cross interleaving—which reduces the possibility of improper decoding and actually enhances error correction. The cross interleave method requires two block codes, such as C1 and C2. Before and between these two codes, two simultaneous manipulations occur. Some of the data is delayed and the remainder rearranged before encoding with one error correction code, and then another pattern of data is delayed afterwards.

CROSS-INTERLEAVING

This combination of delaying and rearranging data in different patterns during encoding (and reversing the process during decoding) separates possible errors that may be too large or that occur consecutively, thereby enhancing

replication process. Burst errors are detected during the first check described above and are corrected primarily by the second correction code. They can be long or short, random or sequential. Regardless of the type of burst error, the correction scheme must be able to identify and handle all possible types and patterns of errors and yet make certain the correction process itself does not cause new errors or affect one of the other correction codes. Therein, of course, lies the complexity.

correction using the two Reed-Solomon codes. The resulting correction scheme is known as Cross-Interleave Reed-Solomon Code or CIRC.

Although more detailed explanations of error correction are certainly possible, even a simple discussion should reassure potential users of CD-ROM technology that there is sufficient insurance against nonrecoverable errors.

Reprinted from the April 1985 issue of *CD Data Report* by special permission.

Converting the Data for CD-ROM

By Linda Helgerson

[This second article by Linda Helgerson, also first published in 1985, describes the premastering processes that prepare CD-ROM data for mastering and replication. These processes are usually handled by facilities equipped to manipulate the huge file sizes that may be involved.]

Information providers who are considering converting their databases to the CD-ROM format are faced with at least two new requirements. First is the structure of the files, now a priority discussion item in the CD-ROM standards meetings described elsewhere in this issue [March 1985 issue of *CD Data Report*]. The second requirement is the preparation of the data for subsequent conversion to CD-ROM. This conversion process includes premastering and data modulation encoding.

To convert the data, the mastering facility must receive the digital data from the information provider in a certain form:

1. The digital information must be placed on an open reel of magnetic tape that is
   - .5 inch wide (12.7 mm).
   - 2400 feet maximum length (732 m).
   - and 1.5 mil thick.

2. The digital information must be recorded on a 9-track tape using the Phase Encode System with a density of 1600 or 6250 BPI.

3. The digital information must be divided into units of 2048 bytes (2K) per sector in the order they are to appear on the final disc, for a maximum capacity of 540 MB per disc, or 270 blocks of 2K units of user data.

Rearrangement of data of this magnitude requires at least a minicomputer. Firms such as The Library Corporation, LaserData, and Reference Technology provide this service. Certain mastering houses are also planning to provide this data preparation service to customers.

Once the data is reorganized into units of 2048 bytes, the files require additional manipulation for mastering to the compact disc format. This step, according to Denon vice president Robert Heiblim, is "the most grueling task." It essentially involves adding 288 more bytes of system data to each user data block for a total of 2352 bytes:

12	bytes added for the synchronization pattern
4	bytes added for the block address (minute/second/block/mode)
2048	bytes of user data from magnetic tape
4	bytes added for error detection
8	bytes added for blank space
276	bytes added for additional error correction code (ECC), improving the error rate by 100 times beyond that of compact audio disc
2352	bytes = 1 block (270 blocks of user data per disc)

Once the blocks of user data are premastered by sync, header, EDC and ECC, then the data modulation process begins. The purpose here is to adjust the data in the proper proportion so that a) the bit density is increased while the resolution is maintained, b) errors in one block are not spread to other blocks, c) the DC signal content is reduced to low frequencies as required by the servo mechanism, and d) the data transfer rate of 150 bytes per second is maintained as the data is read from the disc.

To achieve these requirements, the 8-bit binary data is converted to 14-bit modulated data (called Eight-to-Fourteen Modulation or EFM) and then three additional bits are added (called merging bits) between each of the 14-bit sets, as shown in the N.V. Philips figure below [see sidebar]. The selection of the appropriate merging-bit pattern is computed automatically during mastering and is limited by the requirements for a) a minimum of three bits between transitions or at least two "0"s between "1"s, and b) a maximum of 11 bits between transitions, where a 1 = transition.

This brief explanation of data modulation during the mastering phase is purposefully

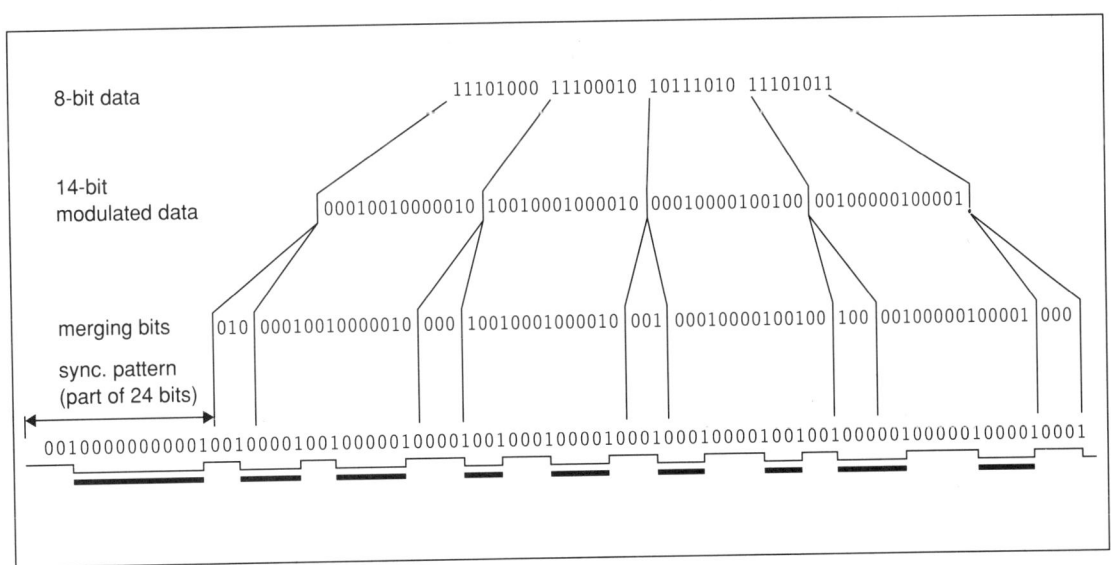

A "1" is represented by the transition from a land to a pit or a pit to a land.
"0s" are represented by the run length between transitions, i.e., length of a pit or land.

oversimplified. No further conclusions can be drawn with more detailed description. Further explanation, however, is available from N.V. Philips, the license holders of the mastering technology.

The importance of these processes should be clear nonetheless. The conversion of data from magnetic tape through premastering and mastering is an exacting and highly specialized process. Nothing short of perfection is required. To fill this market, a growing number of firms are acquiring the requisite capital, ordering and installing the necessary equipment, and some are already producing discs using the processes as described.

On the one hand, it is important for information providers to understand that there is a great deal more to CD-ROM than the latest announcement of a CD-ROM drive. On the other hand, it is comforting to know that the technology to produce discs is already here, not something promised for the distant future.

Reprinted from the March 1985 issue of *CD Data Report* by special permission.

The PDO Show

By Roger Strukhoff
From *CD-ROM Review*

[In this article, Roger Strukhoff gives us an overview of the mastering process by recounting his tour of the PDO facility in Kings Mountain, North Carolina. He reports that, like other mastering facilities, such as 3M and Disctronics, PDO is waiting for the expected rise in demand for CD-ROM products.]

Start naming big companies, and before long you should have mentioned Philips, the Dutch electronics giant and inventor of the compact disc, and DuPont, one of the largest chemical companies in the world. Combine them in a compact disc joint venture and you have the Philips and DuPont Optical Co., or PDO.

PDO was formed March 21, 1986, as an equal partnership. Today it is, not surprisingly, a major force in the compact disc industry. Its plant in Hannover, West Germany is one of the two largest in the world—Sony's Digital Audio Disc Corp. plant in Terre Haute, Ind. is the other—yet Hannover is only part of the PDO story.

PDO also is involved in larger videodiscs and write-once disks. The company is working with Eastman Kodak to develop a 14-inch optical write-once disk standard. Research also continues in erasable, or in PDO parlance, "reversible" technology.

The company makes various types of video discs in a Blackburn, England plant, and most recently "cloned" the Hannover compact disc plant in an existing factory structure in Kings Mountain, N.C. (The Hannover plant was built by PolyGram, now a subsidiary of the Philips organization.)

The Kings Mountain facility encompasses 160,000 square feet in a pastoral Piedmont setting, about an hour's drive west of Charlotte. It began CD production in December 1986. When *CD-ROM Review* visited earlier this year, the plant was gearing up for a capacity of 30 million discs per year. Plans call for a capacity of 60 million per year, with its current employment of 250 rising to about 400.

Compact discs are the only type made in Kings Mountain. CD-ROM played a minor role in total capacity early in 1987, but there is plenty of room to grow with the demand. CD-ROMs we saw in production during our visit included a leading financial database service.

The Kings Mountain plant has the Hannover plant's traditional layout, with premastering and mastering taking place in one side of the building and replication in the other. Clean rooms rated at less than 100 particles per cubic foot—standard in the industry—are found in the mastering and replication processes.

CD-ROM manufacture can be broken down into a number of constituent parts, the number varying with how close one wishes to analyze the process. Broadly speaking, the steps are data generation, data preparation, premastering, mastering, and replication. Once data has been selected and organized, the pieces of the puzzle include:

- Premastering, in which data is formatted on a tape.

- Mastering, where a laser burns data onto high-quality optical glass.

- Electroforming, where the glass master is used to create a stamper disc.

- Replication, where the stamper prints its image onto plastic compact discs.

- Testing and packing, where the final CDs are checked for flaws, bundled up as required, and set on the loading dock for distribution.

Figure 4-12 provides a more detailed look at the PDO process of CD-ROM creation.

The injection molding technique is typically found in CD-Audio plants, and is accordingly common to CD-ROM manufacture. It is in contrast to the "2P" photo-polymerization process patented by 3M (*CD-ROM Review,* August 1987, pages 33–37).

STRICT GUIDELINES

Inspections at every step are a feature of the compact disc maufacture.

Specifications for CD-ROM data preparation are defined by Philips and Sony. The recording format specifies that data modulation must meet four key criteria:

1. High bit density without resolution problems.

2. Self-clocking data, since clock pulses must be regenerated from the data stream after it has been read from the disc.

3. Minimal error propagation.

4. Minimum power requirements necessary to read the data.

At the mastering stage, the argon-ion laser writes to a 0.12-micron layer of photoresist that has been baked onto the glass. An alkaline solution flows over the resist layer after exposure to the laser, dissolving the photoresist in the exposed areas.

This stage is similar in principle, but with smaller tolerances, to optical microlithography techniques used in integrated circuit production. The "pits" burned into the glass master average 0.6-micron in width—about 1/40,000th of an inch. A separate laser monitors the process and can stop the process if necessary. The completed master is then inspected by eye and by microscope.

FATHERS AND MOTHERS

A silver coating is applied to the master, followed by electroplating of a nickel shell. The nickel copy is separated from the master, destroying the data on the master. Called the "father," the nickel copy is a "negative" of the master. The father can then be used for replication in some low-volume runs, but more often, the father is used to create electroplated "mother" positives. The mothers produce negative sons, which are used as stampers in mass replication.

One stamper may be adequate for the relatively low volume CD-ROM jobs that exist today.

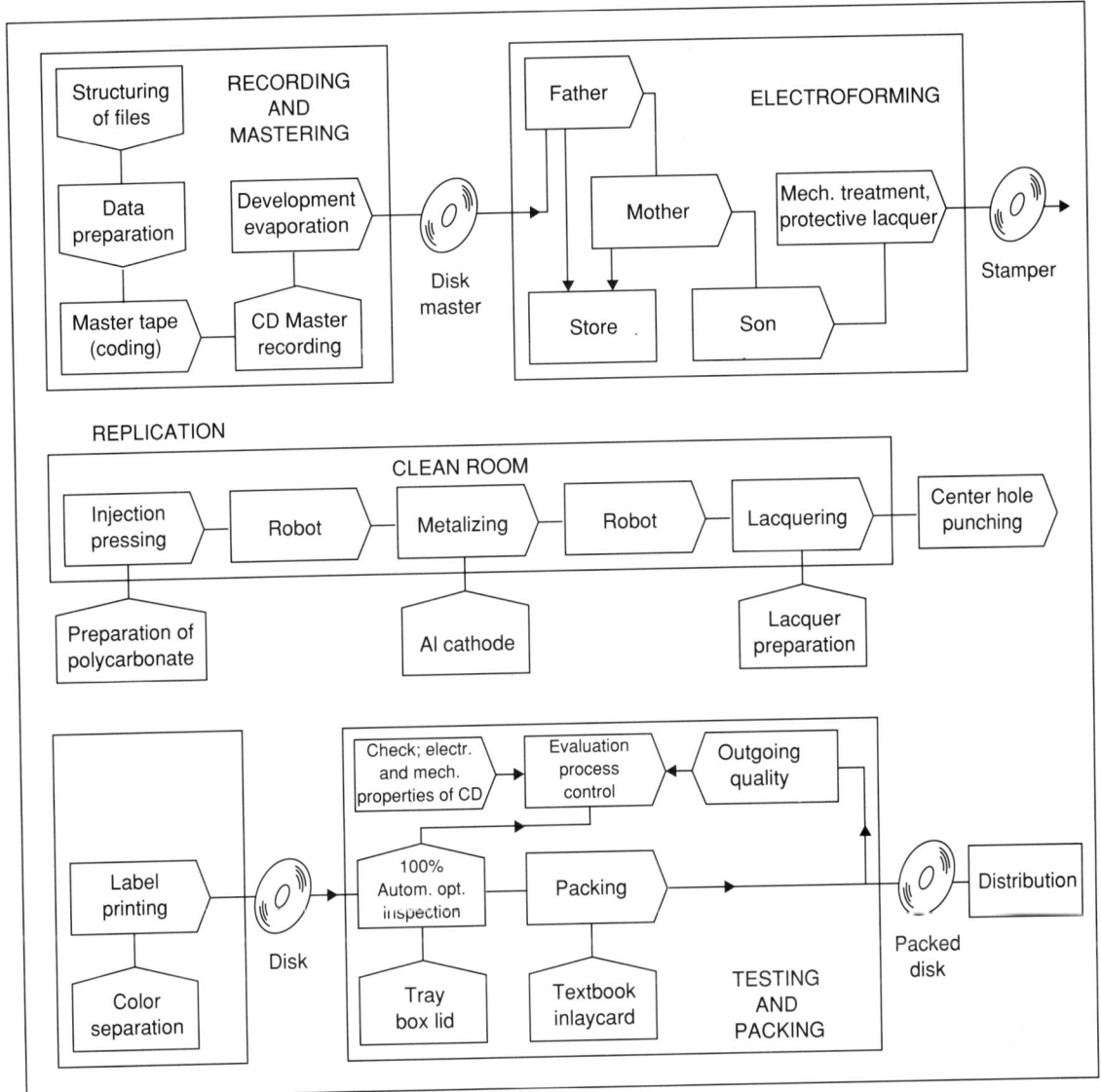

Figure 4-12. A detailed look at how PDO creates a CD-ROM

Typically, a stamper will last for about 6,000 copies.

In the injection molding process, a warp of more than 0.4 millimeter is not tolerated. Bubbles large than 0.1 to 0.2 millimeter are unacceptable and "orange peel" structure and "waviness" must be less than 0.001 millimeter. Polycarbonate for this process is purchased in 1,000-pound bags of "kernels."

Once the discs have been molded, they are metallized with an aluminum reflecting layer about 60 to 70 microns thick. Again, microscopic irregularities are unacceptable. A protective layer of lacquer, which must be compatible with the aluminum layer below it and a label coating above, is then applied. The label is applied by silk screening.

Center hole punching, like injection molding, is also an exact process. Positioning is determined optoelectronically. Finally, all finished CDs are visually inspected before they leave Kings Mountain.

This plant classically represents high-tech manufacturing; no smokestacks, just a little bit of steam emanating from an exhaust vent located near the front of the plant. The majority of energy expenses are for the clean rooms, and the loudest noises come from the clean room pumps.

The factory is well-lit and clean throughout. Well-appointed executive offices line the front of the building. A computerized nerve center keeps track of production.

PDO's big Carolina [*mastering and replication facility*] isn't scheduled to reach full capacity until sometime in 1988. For this plant, like the CD-ROM industry in general, there's plenty of room to grow.

Excerpted from "The PDO Show." Reprinted from the September/October 1987 issue of *CD-ROM Review* by special permission. Copyright ©1987 by IDG Communications.

MASTERING/REPLICATION FACILITIES

Country	Company	Notes
AUSTRALIA	Disctronics Inc. 9 Dehavilland Road Braeside, Vic 3197 Country Code: 61* 03/587–2633 FAX: 03/587–2901	
ENGLAND	Disctronics Inc. 24 Queen Anne's Gate London SW1H 9AD Country Code: 44* 1/222–6878 FAX: 1/222–4407	
FRANCE	Moulage Plastique de l'Ouest RC Mayenne 61B2 53700 Averton Country Code: 33* 043/032 735 FAX: 043/037 933	
JAPAN	Dai Nippon Printing Company Ltd. 1-1 Ichigaya-kagacho 1-chome Shinjuku-ku, Tokyo 162 Country Code: 81* 03/266–2111 FAX: 03/235–2594	
	Sanyo Electric Company Optical Disk Products Department Ohmori Ampachi-cho Ampachi-gun, Gifu-ken 503-01 Country Code: 81* 058/464–4971 FAX: 058/464–4976	
SWEDEN	CD Mastering AB Box 9173 20039 Malmo Country Code: 46* 040/946 570 FAX: 040/949 660	
	Toolex Alpha Esplanaden 1 P.O. Box 176 17225 Sundbyberg Country Code: 46* 046/828–9030	

*Dial this code before the telephone and FAX numbers

(continued)

MASTERING/REPLICATION FACILITIES continued

Country	Company	Notes
SWITZERLAND	ICM Ltd. Muehlebachstrasse 27 8800 Thalwil Country Code: 41* 01/720–7942	
USA	3M 3M Center Optical Recording Department Building 223-5S-01 St. Paul, MN 55144 (612)733–1110 FAX: (612)733–0158	
	Capitol Industries/EMI 3 Capitol Way Jacksonville, IL 62650 (217)245–9631	
	DADC 1800 North Fruitridge Avenue Terre Haute, IN 47804 (812)466–6821 FAX: (812)466–9128	Mastering fees range from $1500–3500.
	Denon America 1380 Monticello Road Madison, GA 30650 (404)342–3425	Mastering fee includes premastering. Prices include insertion of customer-provided booklet, shrinkwrap, bulk packaging, and drop shipment.
	Denon America 222 New Road Parsippany, NJ 07054 (201)575–7810 FAX: (201)575–2532	Mastering fee includes premastering. Prices include insertion of customer-provided booklet, shrinkwrap, bulk packaging, and drop shipment.
	Discovery Systems 7001 Discovery Boulevard Dublin, OH 43017 (614)761–2000 FAX: (614)761–4258	No advance notice required. Mastering done in as little as 1 day for extra charge.
	Disctronics Inc. 4905 Mooresmill Road Huntsville, AL 35881 (205)859–9042 FAX: (205)859–9932	As fast as 1 day turnaround time available. Extra charge for jewel box cases, booklets, shrink wrap.
	Disctronics Inc. 1120 Cosby Way Anaheim, CA 92806 (714)630–6700 FAX: (714)630–1025	As fast as 1 day turnaround time available. Extra charge for jewel box cases, booklets, shrink wrap.

Country	Company	Notes
	JVC Disc America Inc. 2 JVC Road Tuscaloosa, AL 35405 (205)556–7111	
	Memory Technology Inc. 2800 Summit Avenue Plano, TX 75074 (214)881–8800	
	Nimbus Records Inc. P.O. Box 7305 Charlottesville, VA 22906 (804)985–1100	
	Philips and DuPont Optical Kings Mountain Highway 29 Grover, NC 28073 (800)433–3475 FAX: (302)479–2512	The mastering fee given is approximate, depending on the volume, contract, and customer. Includes 50 discs at no extra charge, the use of a CD Publisher for 1 day, and the Philips quality guarantee— if any sector of any disc is bad, you will receive a free master.
	Sanyo Laser Products 1767 Sheridan Street Richmond, IN 47374 (317)935–7574 FAX: (317)935–7570	Per-disc fee depends on quantity.
	Shape Optimedia Route 109 & Eagle Drive Sanford, ME 04073 (207)324–1124 FAX: (207)490–1707	
WALES	Nimbus Records, Ltd. Wyastone Leys Monmouth NP5 3SR Country Code: 222* 0600/890682	
WEST GERMANY	eps Electronic Printing Service Carl-Bertelsmann-Strasse 161 4830 Gütersloh 1 Country Code: 49* 05241/805 415 FAX: 05241/78521	Prices are in DM. Shorter turn-around on special request.

*Dial this code before the telephone and FAX numbers

MASTERING/REPLICATION FACILITIES *continued*

Country	Company	Notes
	Philips and DuPont Optical Customer Pressing Department Klussreide 26 3012 Langenhagen 1 Country Code: 49* 0511/730–6331 FAX: 0511/731 802	
	Sonopress Gmbh Data Replication Carl-Bertelsmann Strasse 161 4830 Gütersloh 1 Country Code: 49* 05241/803 074 FAX: 05241/75863	

Compiled by Online Press Inc.

SECTION V

CD-ROM AND THE LAW

PROTECTING INTELLECTUAL PROPERTY RIGHTS

LIABILITY ISSUES

PROTECTING INTELLECTUAL PROPERTY RIGHTS

WHO OWNS CREATIVITY? PROPERTY RIGHTS IN THE INFORMATION AGE
By Anne W. Branscomb

DOWNLOADING FROM CD-ROM
By Brian Kahin

END USER LICENSES: WHY AND WHAT
By Henry W. Jones III

A LOOK AT TWO "CREATIVE" ANSWERS TO ELECTRO-COPYING
By Nicholas A. Veliotes

LAWSUITS OVER LAW RESEARCH
By Stephen Labaton

Who Owns Creativity? Property Rights in the Information Age

By Anne W. Branscomb
From *Technology Review*

[Intellectual property rights and mechanisms for their protection are the topics of this overview article. Anne Branscomb explores the issues as they pertain to the new computer technologies, arguing that a new rationale and a systematic approach to protection would serve the computer industry in general and the CD-ROM industry in particular better than the current ad hoc approach.]

The desire of individuals—and corporations—to profit from their own intellectual creativity has often clashed with the public's wish for relatively free access to ideas and innovations. Over the centuries, many different legal mechanisms have been invented to strike a balance between the two. However, what suited the age of print and mechanical inventions is proving inadequate to that of the computer program, expert system, and distributed database. The attempt to force these new technologies into outmoded categories can create absurd and contradictory situations that threaten to undermine public confidence in the principle of intellectual property rights itself.

> *Copyrights and trademarks — the bête noire of the industry. A lot of lawyers are going to be rich before this battle is over. There is no precedent for many issues, and let's hope companies try to solve problems without litigation.*
>
> **Janet Tiampo**
> From "Evaluating the Industry,"
> *CD-ROM Review,* March/April 1988

Software is a good example. Copyright is designed to protect literary expression. But what makes a computer program a literary work? Is it the code written to make the program function? Or is it, as Lotus argues, the look of the screen and feel of its commands?

To make matters even more confusing, software manufacturers simultaneously employ other legal protections to safeguard their intellectual property rights, because they are doubtful that any one will prove effective. The principle of trade secrets underlies the "shrink-wrap license" to which every software user supposedly agrees upon opening the package of a new program.

Some computer programs are also eligible for patents, most notably software embedded in computer hardware. And while operating systems that are not built into hardware have traditionally been excluded from patent protection, the U.S. Patent Office has recently been considerably more lenient toward such applications.

As the forms of protection increase, the gap between legal precedent and everyday behavior grows wider. The new technologies make copying intellectual property easier and legal protections much more difficult to enforce. Some degree of unauthorized copying has become accepted social practice—despite the legal prohibitions against it: journal articles are photocopied at universities, recorded music is taped onto blank cassettes, and computer software is commonly reproduced.

Although disputes about technology and intellectual property are usually cast in narrow legal terms, they are intimately related to public attitudes. Realistic legal rules depend upon a social consensus about what kind of behavior is acceptable and what is not.

"TO PROMOTE SCIENCE AND THE USEFUL ARTS"

The idea of intellectual property rights has been around since the late Middle Ages, but the roots of U.S. intellectual property law go back to the Constitution: "The Congress shall have the Power...To promote the Progress of Science and useful Arts, by securing for limited Times to Authors and Inventors the exclusive Right to their respective Writing and Discoveries."

As this language suggests, the fundamental goal of intellectual property rights is not to benefit the creators of works but to further the public good. Authors and inventors are given a limited right to their work as an incentive to create and disseminate ideas and information. Thus, intellectual property law makes protection conditional on public disclosure.

For example, copyright law covers original "works of authorship" as long as they are "fixed" in a "tangible medium" such as a book.

Copyright protects the literary expression of an idea, rather than the idea itself, from unauthorized copying for the life of the creator plus 50 years (or, for corporations, for a total of 75 to 100 years). Other authors can make "fair use" of a copyrighted work—for example, quoting a passage in an article or review—without asking the original author's permission. More extensive use requires permission and often the payment of a royalty.

Patent law protects inventions or discoveries that are registered with the U.S. Patent Office. Unlike copyright, a patent protects not only the expression but the actual useful features of a product or process for 17 years. A design receives protection for 14 years. Patent rights grant a monopoly, good against those who independently discover the same design or product. But rights can be licensed to other users.

However, a patent is much harder to get than a copyright. To be eligible for patent protection, a work must have distinguishing features that are innovative, useful, and not obvious. And the application process often takes two years or more.

Not all forms of intellectual property protection require public disclosure. The oldest and probably most common form of protection is secrecy. Trade secrets are protected by contracts designed to ensure confidentiality on the part of licensed users. To be enforceable in court, the information considered a trade secret must be used commercially and relevant to a firm's competitive advantage. Also, the firm must have evidence that it has actively attempted to keep the information secret.

THE INTELLECTUAL PROPERTY SYSTEM BREAKS DOWN

These traditional mechanisms for balancing public and private claims worked relatively well during the industrial era. As long as the publication of books and journals depended on a relatively small number of commercial printers, it was easy to identify copyright violations. As long as most industrial innovations had a relatively long life, the patent process successfully protected their economic value. And as long as most violations took place either within a single nation or between nations with relatively compatible legal systems, effective sanctions could be easily enforced.

Recently, however, three interrelated factors have eroded the effectiveness of traditional protection mechanisms: the development of new information and communications technologies, the globalization of the marketplace, and the privatization of information providers.

The traditional categories of intellectual property law depend on a set of clearly defined "products" or "processes"—literary works, inventions, designs, etc. But with the new technologies, boundaries between media are blurred and intellectual assets become increasingly abstract and intangible. The same work or even parts of a work can be stored and presented in a variety of forms—not only paper, but magnetic tape, floppy disc, or laser disc. The work can be made available to large numbers of people via broadcasting, computer networks, or telephone lines. Databases can be packaged and re-packaged. Pieces of music or video images can be electronically re-mixed, reformatted, or otherwise altered. And easy-to-use technologies like video graphics and desktop publishing allow more individuals and small businesses to enter the information marketplace than ever before, making enforcement of intellectual property rights nearly impossible.

The globalization of the world economy, caused partly by the new technologies, has also contributed to the breakdown of the old system. International conflicts over intellectual property have always been a problem, as developing countries, anxious for economic growth, have been unwilling to extend protection to foreign works. This was true of nineteenth century America, and it is true of much of the Third World today.

But the increasing integration of the world economy has multiplied both the incentives for international violations of intellectual property rights and the economic harm of such violations. Today, the products of newly industrialized countries such as Korea or Taiwan are sold all over the world. "Borrowing" intellectual property allows these countries to successfully compete in markets for many advanced products without bearing the cost of research and development.

Finally, the growing trend toward using market mechanisms to gather and disseminate information has disrupted the traditional public infrastructure for sharing intellectual assets. For example, before the breakup of the regulated Bell Telephone system, Bell Labs was the equivalent of a national basic-research laboratory, supported by corporate cross-subsidies. Today, institutions like Bell Labs face growing pressures to pay their own way. The federal government has mandated that agencies such as the National Technical Information Service and the National Library of Medicine become self-supporting through user fees. And even universities are turning to patent rights and copyright royalties to recoup their investment in faculty research and development.

LET ME SCAN JUST THIS ONE PICTURE...

Computers present all kinds of ethical difficulties for the unwary. It sometimes seems that with every advance of the technology, another opportunity develops for the innocent user to go astray.

We're running into that right now with scanning illustrations into desktop-published documents. We're right on the edge of it with the large-scale use of research material from CD-ROMs. And we're creeping up on genuinely troubling problems about the integrity of images we process through our computers for many uses.

When you and I are pulling together documents on our desktop publishing systems, the ease of running graphics of all sorts through that tidy little scanner at our elbows is highly seductive. When we're worrying about holding the long gray-scale of a photo, we often don't worry much about the *source* of that picture.

If it's a drawing, photo, or other creation of our very own—say a snap you made with your 35mm of George Hamill, the guy over in shipping about whom you've written this story for the company newsletter, you're in good shape.

But what if you need a nice long, skinny graphic for the bottom of the first page of the newsletter... and you just happen to spot a nice long, skinny photo of a sunset in this month's *Life* magazine?

In a couple of minutes, you can run that image through the scanner, maybe tweak the gray scale a little, and presto—you've got your artwork.

You've also got one foot in court. Because that photo was copyrighted by Time Inc., publishers of *Life*, who in turn probably bought only limited rights to the photo from the photographer who made it—who also has a cause of action against you.

The moral: we can't go around borrowing (read: lifting, using, stealing) art wherever we find it.

LAW AND ETHICS

The practical will argue that you probably won't get caught. Sure. Is "probably" good enough? What about your conscience? Will this kind of unfortunate "what's mine is mine, and what's yours is mine, too, if I can get it" attitude become ingrained, part of the PC culture?

On to CD-ROMs. I wrote here a month ago about how much I like Microsoft's new *Bookshelf* reference disk. It's clearly part of a first wave of comprehensive reference works on disk. When we can so easily cut and paste from the disk to our own work, what are the ethical and legal requirements for our use and *attribution* of that material?

I searched in vain through the blizzard of paperwork in the *Bookshelf* box for details on how the material can legally be used. I found nothing. I suspect that was less an oversight than a tacit admission that Microsoft and the companies from which it licensed the material hadn't themselves figured out how we ought to be able to use their material.

The extent to which we can bring into a larger document a few paragraphs of reference material—not so identified—and in effect claim it as our own work is a big issue, too.

THE HIGH COSTS OF COPYING

Thus, at the very moment when information is becoming a valuable commodity, protecting the economic value of intellectual assets is proving more difficult. While the loss of income is difficult to ascertain, etimates range anywhere from $20 billion to $60 billion each year.

Most serious is the deliberate commercial pirating of both low- and high-tech products in foreign countries. For example, videotaped copies of Hollywood films are often illegally released in foreign markets before the U.S. release. The Motion Picture Association of America estimates the loss at about $6 billion annually. And illegal publishing of books and technical manuals abroad costs the American publishing industry about $1 billion every year. In Korea alone, nearly 1 million U.S. titles have been pirated.

Other violations of intellectual property rights—for personal rather than commercial use—are more difficult to track. The rule of thumb in the software industry is that at least one unauthorized copy exists for every authorized sale of a software program. According to the Software Publishing Association, software

---

THE COST OF COPYING

This season's political wars have reminded us of the high cost of plagiarism. Will the ease of electronic research aggravate the problem? What constitutes—either legally or morally—"fair use" of electronic research materials?

Finally, the big one: As we get the ability to do serious manipulation of graphics on our PCs, who's going to stop the unscrupulous among us from, say, cropping the Reverend Jesse Jackson out of a photo and electronically inserting a perfect-fit image of, oh, maybe Ed Koch?

That's already possible with larger systems. The classic example so far was *Rolling Stone* publisher Jann Wenner's removal of a pistol and shoulder holster from a cover photo of "Miami Vice" heartthrob Don Johnson. And it's leading to serious questions.

The American Society of Magazine Photographers, interested in members' financial stakes in their images as well as the integrity of those images themselves, is kicking up a lot of dust about this. Good for them.

SETTING LIMITS

Magazine editors and art directors are talking about what the limits ought to be for this kind of ex post facto manipulation of images. Many are eager to use the exciting new tools being made available to them and, rightly confident of their own ethical integrity, wrongly assume that everyone else in their trade will also act responsibly.

Computer systems capable of that kind of undetectable manipulation of photographs cost a lot more than today's PCs. But the technology is barreling down on our systems at high speed; in a couple of years we'll be faced with the opportunity to snatch images of famous people from magazine pages, mix and match them in improbable combinations and settings, then electronically paste them into our desktop-published pages.

If some, unchallenged, are engaging in wholesale theft of others' work now, by lifting images wherever they find them, and if others are already slavering at the possibility of "writing" electronically cut-and-pasted term papers for a fee, and if that image-manipulation software and computer power winds up on our desks, as it inevitably will....

Too often ethical constructs seem distant abstractions, angels-on-pinheads exercises for the kind of people who read Plato and Kant the way you and I read *Garfield* and *Peanuts*.

But these are real issues, and if we let ourselves slip so far over the line that we ignore or condone the kind of innocently motivated lifting of artwork that has begun to appear in the desktop publishing community, we're going to lose a lot more than our innocence.

Let's start asking the hard questions now. In public.

By Jim Seymour
Reprinted from *PC Magazine*,
January 12, 1988. Copyright © 1988
by Ziff Communications Company.

manufacturers lost approximately $1 billion in sales to piracy (both for profit and for personal use) in 1986. Lotus claims that over half of its potential sales of 1-2-3 are lost—at a cost of about $160 million every year. And Wordstar estimates that in 1984 it lost $177 million in potential sales, compared with $67 million in revenues from actual sales of the program.

Such reports need to be taken with a grain of salt, as they assume that every user of an unauthorized copy would buy the program in question were the copies to disappear—an unlikely proposition. Still, the numbers suggest the scope of the problem.

Violations of intellectual property also have public costs. Widespread copying is one factor in high software prices, as firms try to recoup their investment in a program as quickly as possible. If unauthorized copying could be eliminated, it is likely that the costs of software could be greatly reduced—a net gain for society as a whole.

Owners of intellectual property have tried a variety of methods to combat unauthorized copying. In some cases, technology itself seems to offer a solution. To stop satellite-dish owners from capturing broadcast signals without subscribing to local cable services, programmers scramble their signals. Today, the most popular programs cannot be received by satellite unless viewers pay a monthly fee to gain access to the special code of each cable channel.

However, technical protections can spawn their own technical countermeasures or result in a consumer blacklash. For example, the practice of "copy protection," once widespread in the software industry, has given birth to special programs whose sole purpose is to override copy-protection code. And consumer dissatisfaction with the inconvenience of using copy-protected software has led most software companies, Lotus included, to give up on copy-protecting their programs altogether.

On the international front, the federal government has encouraged trading partners to enact intellectual property laws or expand coverage of laws that already exist. Under recent provisions in trade and foreign aid laws, countries whose copyright and patent practices do not conform to U.S. standards can be penalized, even to the point of restricting their imports to the U.S. market. The federal government is also promoting a multilateral agreement on intellectual property as part of the Geneva Agreement on Tariffs and Trade.

So far, such efforts have had only limited effect. The sanctions available to federal trade officials are miniscule compared with the enormous profits foreign companies can make by using U.S. processes and designs in the international market. Even money damages and confiscation of goods are simply absorbed by pirate firms as a cost of doing business.

COPYRIGHTING THE USER INTERFACE?

In the absence of effective protection, owners of intellectual property have tried to fit their products into any and all of the available legal categories. The results are legally contradictory and confusing to the general public. They also undermine traditional rationales for intellectual property protection.

For years, the legal status of computer programs was unclear. Although the U.S. Copyright Office began tentatively registering software under its "rule of doubt" provision in 1964, many analysts suspected that computer code written to be read by a machine rather than a human couldn't qualify for copyright. And the Patent Office considered most programs a collection of algorithms—which like other mathematical equations, are excluded from patent protection.

So the computer software industry relied primarily on trade secrecy. This has worked reasonably well for larger computer installations with custom-made software. However, the mass distribution of easily available software made possible by the personal computer created a new legal situation.

Any personal computer user has seen the long and complicated agreement, usually set in type so small that it is barely legible, on the cover or inserted underneath the outer protection of most software diskettes. This is the shrink-wrap license to which the purchaser is assumed to agree upon opening the package. Most such licenses stipulate that the buyer cannot "use, copy, modify, merge, translate, or transfer" the software "except as expressly provided in this agreement."

The shrink-wrap license treats software as a trade secret. This poses an immediate practical problem. To consider a computer program used by millions of people as a trade secret offends common sense—the fact that so much copying takes place indicates how few users take the agreement seriously. What's more, at least one court has held such licenses legally invalid.

In 1980, Congress amended the 1976 Copyright Act to explictly include software, partly because there seemed no other adequate mechanism for protecting what was clearly a valuable asset. Since then, the courts have steadily extended copyright protection for software. At first, it applied only to the source code, written in a programming language such as Fortran or Cobol. Later court cases established that a program's object code, the sequence of 0s and 1s read directly by the computer, was covered as well. In 1986, the flow diagrams that encapsulate the logic and sequence of the program were also included under copyright.

That same year, in *Jaslow vs Whelan*, the Third Circuit Court of Appeals affirmed a lower court ruling that copyright protection extends to certain "non-literal" features of the program. The court decided the screen design and commands of the program represented the time and effort the computer software programmer had expended in understanding the needs of the application in question—an inventory system for dental laboratories. The conclusion was that such laborious intellectual analysis should be protected. This has set the stage for the "look and feel" cases currently under consideration.

> *At the very moment when information is becoming a valuable commodity, protecting the economic value of intellectual assets is proving more difficult.*

At the same time that copyright protection is being expanded, software firms are again turning to patent protection. Court cases have redefined the status of computer programs under patent law, considering operating systems just like other industrial processes and therefore eligible for patents. In 1986, the artificial intelligence firm Teknowledge received patents on two new software products.

THE DANGERS OF AD HOC PROTECTION

There are a number of dangers inherent in this ad hoc approach. First, it is contradictory to claim that a computer program is a trade secret and yet deserves copyright protection, which assumes broad public dissemination. And saying that the same software can come under both copyright and patent law similarly defies people's sense of what belongs in what category.

Second, ad hoc measures run the risk of shifting the emphasis toward too much protection, even to the point of threatening innovation itself. Protecting the "look and feel" of a computer program could become a serious obstacle to standardizing software applications and could prove extremely costly as well.

> *The new technologies make copying intellectual property easier and legal protections much more difficult to enforce.*

For example, should the federal district court in Boston decide that the look and feel of Lotus 1-2-3 can be copyrighted, then every maker of computerized spreadsheets will have to create distinctively different screen designs. This could mean that the techniques and skills acquired by using Lotus spreadsheets wouldn't be transferable to other spreadsheet programs. Individuals and firms would face increased training costs, and even the most innovative software would encounter substantial barriers to entering the spreadsheet market.

Third, as communications technology becomes more complex, the ad hoc approach will become even more cumbersome. For instance, a single "read-only" compact disc (CD-ROM) can store a 20-volume encyclopedia. What uses of the CD-ROM are permissible within the limits of current law? Can users print the entire 20 volumes, or is this a violation of copyright? If so, how much of the encyclopedia can they reprint? Can portions of the encyclopedia be transferred to another computer, or does this constitute making a copy? Can portions be displayed in the classroom, or might this legally qualify as a performance or retransmission? May the contents be simultaneously networked to many locations, such as different classrooms at a university?

Some lawyers argue that since different mechanisms protect different rights, the proliferation of mechanisms covering the same intellectual asset is both effective and reasonable. So, for example, design of the laser videodisc may be patented; the process by which it is manufactured may be a trade secret; the content of a specific disc can be copyrighted; the commercial name under which the product is marketed will be a trademark; the talent whose performance is captured on the disc will be subject to performance rights; and the work, if retransmitted by a cable system, may be subject to royalties.

The problem is that such an elaborate system is costly and, when it comes to competing in the world economy, a distinct disadvantage. The price of a product must reflect not only the high costs of research and development but also the legal fees necessary to document legal protections and enforce them.

TOWARD A NEW RATIONALE OF PROTECTION

As long as the United States depends on the private sector to create and disseminate information, we need a simpler, less costly system for protecting intellectual property. Such a system should recognize that effective protection of intellectual property is not just a legal matter. It is also a function of public attitudes and opinions. No law, no matter how carefully worded, can prohibit widespread practices that the public considers acceptable.

While ethical standards for using new information technologies are still in an early state of development, it seems clear that the public favors flexibility—as long as the original owner of the copied product enjoys no commercial advantage. The rationale seems to be that if you can loan your friends books, why not let them copy your software programs and musical tapes?

A public opinion poll conducted by the Congressional Office of Technology Assessment found that 70 percent of those questioned thought copying a record, tape, software, or TV program in one's personal possession is permissible. About half agreed that such copies should be publicly available, for example, in a library. However, some 80 percent opposed circumventing commercial offerings such as pay TV or cable television. And nearly all deplored the reselling of databases for personal gain.

Both Congress and the courts have begun to take these attitudes into account. Under the Cable Communications Act of 1984, satellite-dish owners do not have to pay to capture the broadcast signals of copyrighted programs, as long as those programs are not available to them on cable television.

And in the now-famous "Betamax" (*Sony Corp. vs Universal City Studios*), the Supreme Court recognized that it would be fruitless to try to turn the tide aganst the massive purchase of videocassette recorders able to record television programs for later use. Although collecting copied programs for a personal video library might violate the Copyright Act, the Court made a distinction between commercial exploitation and copying for "private use."

Owners of intellectual property are beginning to realize that they must cultivate public awareness and sympathy to protect capital investment. Numerous trade organizations are selecting this route and allocating more dollars to public education than litigation. For example, the Association of Data Processing Service Organizations has initiated a "Thou Shalt Not Dupe" campaign to discourage corporations from copying programs. The association has sent out hundreds of thousands of brochures urging companies to adopt a sample policy statement against copying. Similarly, the recently formed American Copyright Council is launching an advertisement campaign on the legalities of copyright infringement. And in addition to prosecuting flagrant cases of cable piracy, the cable television industry is spending millions of dollars advertising the impropriety of tapping into cable lines.

However, initiatives like these do not address systematic commercial pirating or complicated

> *Too often, the lawyers and legislators who write and litigate intellectual property laws have only a superficial understanding of the technology in question.*

conflicts between innovation and imitation such as the look-and-feel lawsuits. Here, we need to articulate a new rationale for legal protection.

The starting point should be an understanding that information technology makes the form a product takes easy to separate from the intellectual assets that go into it. This suggests that copyright law, with its focus on the expression of an idea rather than on the idea itself, is inappropriate for protecting what is really valuable in the new kinds of intellectual property.

More suitable would be a system that emphasized the actual use of intellectual assets. For example, the entertainment industry has developed its own legally binding arrangements to determine who benefits from the use of entertainment programs. Standard contracts govern the division of earnings among all those necessary to produce works for continued use on radio, television, and videotapes. Perhaps the software industry could develop similar mechanisms.

Another possibility is a modified form of patent rights with registration procedures, monopoly time limits, and rules for licensing all shaped to the unique realities of the computer industry.

Of course, such efforts may eventually demonstrate that simple and effective protection of new kinds of intellectual property is largely impossible. If so, policymakers will have to reevaluate recent trends toward the privatization of information. When the private creators of intellectual assets cannot be adequately protected for their efforts, then new kinds of public support may be necessary.

Whatever the specific mechanisms for addressing the problems of intellectual property protection, those who are creating the new information and communications technologies—and who best understand their capabilities and limits—need to play a more active role in policy debates. Too often, the lawyers and legislators who write and litigate intellectual property laws have only a superficial understanding of the technology in question.

One possibility would be to create teams of technical experts to serve as negotiators or mediators in complex technological controversies. Or professional associations could develop codes of ethics for what constitutes acceptable—and unacceptable—borrowing of others' intellectual work.

Only when we hear from technologists will we begin to meet the real challenge of intellectual property rights: encouraging creativity while preventing exploitation inimical to investment and the rational allocation of R&D funds.

Excerpted from "Who Owns Creativity? Property Rights in the Information Age," May/June 1988 issue of *Technology Review* by special permission.

Downloading from CD-ROM

By Brian Kahin
From *Optical Insights*

[Picking up on some of the issues raised in the previous article, Brian Kahin's article looks at the use of contracts as a supplementary form of intellectual property protection.]

FROM ON-LINE TO CD-ROM

Database publishers confront the opportunity to publish on CD-ROM with some trepidation. In the on-line environment, they are paid as a service, roughly in accordance with use. Traditionally, this was done through connect-time charges, although recently many have also instituted "hit" charges—i.e., charges keyed to quantity, such as the number of records accessed.

As long as database publishers were paid on a measured basis, there was only intermittent concern about downloading practices. Many publishers did not develop policies on downloading. Others limited downloading to hard copy—which was what users got in the days of dumb printer terminals.

A CD-ROM, however, is not normally subject to metering. Information can be downloaded at a very high rate (especially compared with dial-up lines), and there is no record of how much or just what information has been captured by the user. A CD-ROM can be moved from one location to another at will; it can be used without authorization by many different users.

What does copyright law say about this? And, whatever it says, is there any way to enforce it?

The principal right of the copyright owner is the exclusive right to "reproduce the work in copies." Simply displaying a work does not, under copyright law, amount to producing a copy, but displaying a work on a computer monitor requires generating what amounts to a copy in the video display register. A special section (Section 117) was added to the Copyright Act in 1980 to accommodate the internal copying that necessarily occurs in the execution of a computer program. However, a "computer program" is defined in the Copyright Act as "a set of statements or instructions to be used directly or indirectly in a computer in order to bring about a certain result"—which appears to exclude retrieved data.

ONE OF CD-ROM'S DEADLY SINS

Another aspect of the license agreements of most of the CD-ROM products which we wish would be eliminated is the requirement that subscribers return the product if the subscription is cancelled for one reason or another. This practice discourages us from cancelling print subscriptions. What if we discontinue the print product and CD-ROM is not successful enough for the producer to continue with it? Where are we left then? We realize these questions indicate a note of pessimism, but let's face it: the technology is new and its long-term success is not yet proven. If the license agreements merely stipulated that the subscriber could keep the last disk received if the subscription were cancelled, we could rest a lot easier. PAIS is to be commended for its understanding of this dilemma. So is H. W. Wilson for its policy of allowing users to keep all disks rather than requiring subscribers to return superseded ones.

Excerpted from "The Seven Deadly Sins of CD-ROM" by Jean Reese and Ramona J. Steffey, the Laserdisk Professional.

FAIR USE

While Section 117 may not apply to data, it seems reasonable to assume that incidental copying of data in the course of displaying it would qualify as "fair use" under Section 107 of the Copyright Act. This is the section which permits quotation for critical reviews, parodies, photocopying for personal use, etc. The Supreme Court applied the principles of fair use in the "Betamax case" (Sony v. Universal Studios) to determine that home copying of free off-the-air television programs for time-shifting purposes did not violate the rights of the copyright holders.

Whether or not fair use provides a defense against an infringement claim requires an analysis of many factors in the context of the particular case. Because of this uncertainty, committees of producers and users have worked out guidelines for what can be safely considered fair use in education for two situations: off-air taping of television programs and photocopying printed materials for classroom use. However, there is as yet no effort to work out guidelines for downloading from databases.

It seems likely that fair use permits some downloading beyond copying into the video display chip, but what? And does it differ for CD-ROM and on-line delivery? Most people cannot read at 1200 baud, let alone 2400 baud, and surely the use of hit charges is acknowledgment that more is going on than meets the eye. But can users download records into electronic files, edit and massage them, and use them in an in-house publication?

CONTRACTS

Copyright protection is very powerful in that it can automatically provide attorney's fees and statutory damages (assuming the work is registered with the Copyright Office). But the uncertainty around fair use and other areas leads producers to consider contract law as a supplementary form of protection. Thus, when database producers specify policies on downloading, they are seeking to impose contractual limitations on downloading.

However, there must first be a valid underlying contract if these limitations are to be effective. This is the same problem that software publishers have confronted in shrink-wrap licensing: How can there be a contract if the user doesn't see the licensing agreement until after the package has been purchased?

In the on-line environment, things are different. The user does expect to be buying a product. The user expects a service, and the terms of that service (including the vendor's restrictions on downloading) can be conveyed on-line before the user starts incurring charges.

CD-ROMs are usually leased—not sold. A mass market has not yet developed, so most transactions are direct from publisher to user, rather than through a distribution chain. Publishers, most of whom are on-line publishers as well, are aware of the time-limited value of their information and the need to market timeliness to users. They are wary of diluting their market by allowing discarded, slightly dated discs to trickle down to would-be customers. They have also learned from the lessons of shrink-wrap licensing. Instead of selling discs subject to a license, publishers are leasing discs, with licensing restrictions part of the lease and with the disc to be returned to the publisher at the end of the lease term.

To benefit from this arrangement, the publisher must, of course, make it clear from the outset that the CD-ROM remains the publisher's property and that the user is subscribing to a service for a period of time. Aside from certain benefits under copyright, leasing means that contractual restrictions on transfer or use of the disc are more enforceable, because they will not be subject to attack as unreasonable restraints on alienation. (A common-law principle of long standing which says, in effect, that if you own something, you should be able to do what you want with it.) This provides publishers with the ability to dictate restrictions on downloading that can be enforced in court.

The problem, however, is determining when the restrictions have been violated. If portions of the downloaded database are repackaged and sold on the open market, that's easy. But then the real violation is in the republication, not the downloading. As with unauthorized duplication of software, the best (and maybe only) opportunity to catch in-house violations may be the disgruntled employee. But here, unless there is downloading of large portions of a database, it will be hard to establish copyright liability, and the rewards of suing on contract (based on the publisher's own downloading policies) are likely to be minimal. Most importantly, filing suit against one's customers does not sit well with other customers or potential customers. Unless, perhaps, the violation is egregious—and that, in its way, may be as hard to determine as fair use.

From *Optical Insights*, Spring 1988 issue. Copyright © 1988 by Brian Kahin.

End User Licenses: Why and What

By Henry W. Jones III
From *CD-ROM Review*

[Do you read the warranties that come with appliances? Have you scrutinized the subscriber agreement regulating your use of online electronic database services? Do you know the terms of the license agreements for the software that your company uses? Usually, the answer is no.

For CD-ROM developers, publishers and remarketers, however, end user agreements are extremely important.]

INTELLECTUAL PROPERTY

Most consumers believe the legalese in end user agreements is merely defense armor for vendors who fear product glitches, or lawsuits by irrational customers. History has proven the consumer's assumption is correct.

Many are familiar with the 1986 lawsuit filed by a Florida construction company against Lotus Development Corp., seeking more than $250,000 in damages, even though the customer admitted using Lotus' Symphony product incorrectly. The plaintiff's erroneous spreadsheet calculation resulted from his failure to follow product documentation, not product defects. But what many computer law specialists also know is that Lotus lacked the desired armor—they failed to correctly draft and typeset the end user agreement included with Symphony.

Adequate defense armor is just one consideration for creating end user agreements for technology products. Another is the "value added" in videodisks, databases, most software, and all CD-ROM products, based on the intellectual property (copyrights, trade secrets, trademarks, and sometimes patents) created by the developers. Such proprietary rights considerations are usually irrelevant for traditional, non-technology products.

The content and form of end user license agreements are an important, multifaceted issue for companies involved in CD-ROM.

One decision to be faced is whether to obtain a signed contract before shipping, versus using a "shrink-wrap" approach (i.e., including the contract on the outside of the product, under clear polyethylene wrapping, with conspicuous language stating that "by opening this product, you agree to the contract terms below").

An important business planning and sales issue is determining what specific rights are granted to, or withheld from, customers. For example, will it be the customer's choice whether he or she may use your CD-ROM disc on a local area network (LAN)? Or, should a LAN license be offered, at a higher fee?

An end user agreement can also spell out policies regarding technical support, transferring the product to a third party at a later time, and whether the product may be supplemented by the customer's programming and data.

It is not a "standardized" document that merely recycles legal "boilerplate." All the various rights, obligations, procedures, and information must be clearly set forth, and must interrelate smoothly. In this regard, designing, writing, and "debugging" an end user agreement is much like creating and refining a database or computer program.

KEY ISSUES

Several issues must be considered when making the business decisions and drafting the contract language for a workable agreement:

1. Copyright protection

Federal courts are currently split on the proper legal standard for determining when a "compilation" of data deserves protection under the 1976 Copyright Act (see "CD-ROM and Copyright," *CD-ROM Review,* December 1987, page 64).

Because this issue could eventually have an adverse effect on CD-ROM developers, and because a dispute could arise involving your product in one of the "unfavorable" federal court circuits, an end user agreement can supplement proprietary protection for the software and data on your disc.

HENRY W. JONES, III

Home: Atlanta, Georgia
Job: Attorney, Morris, Manning, & Martin Law Firm
Quote: "CD-ROM companies and projects will mutate and proliferate, as have software companies. As a result, there will be no 'standard operating procedures' for managing product development, distribution, and licensing. This increases the challenge to identify and manage the legal issues that directly impact companies' survival and profitability, such as securing potential proprietary rights, avoiding contract interpretation disputes, avoiding inadvertent infringement, and avoiding product defect claims. The out-of-court settlement of the West Publishing v. Mead Data litigation muddies the question of whether entrepreneurial companies can penetrate one particular major market: placing court decisions on CD-ROM in lawyers' libraries."

Specifically, an end user *license* should track the rights provided by copyright legislation, and prohibit (or specify the permitted circumstances for) the customer's copying, modifying, and publicly distributing, displaying, or performing your product (assuming this matches your business policies).

If you permit customers to reproduce portions of your disc's contents, such partial copies often must contain a proper *copyright notice* stating the rights of your company or its content supplier. Make sure your contract requires that customers affix this copyright notice to such partial copies.

2. Trade secrets

The legal standards for "trade secrets" protection, primary risks in this area, and operational procedures designed to protect trade secrets, are fairly complex, and cannot be adequately addressed in a single article. The watchword, however, is that vendors have an obligation to identify and protect the product innovations they deem to be proprietary. Your contract should spell out the proprietary nature of the disc's contents, prohibit the customer from making such proprietary contents available to unauthorized third parties, and perhaps recite that your work is maintained in confidence by your company and was developed through significant investment and effort.

If you fail to put your customer on notice concerning this legal claim, and fail to place such restrictions on the customer, then this omission may be seized upon later by a third party (e.g., a competitor) as a valid legal defense for misappropriating your technology.

3. Customer relations and dispute avoidance

It may be difficult to believe, but contracts can serve as marketing tools. Early in your agreement, explain your company's procedures regarding technical support. Specify which hardware, operating systems software, peripherals, and other components are necessary for using your product. Make the customer aware of a separately-available product maintenance or update contract, and consider offering additional, customized services.

Because CD-ROM is still a new technology, some customers will make inaccurate assumptions regarding what the product is, how it works, and what you are offering. Avoiding customer misunderstandings and unpleasant surprises goes a long way towards maintaining marketplace good will and avoiding unnecessary expenses on litigation.

4. Warranties and liabilities

Product defect claims, and planning for and defending against them, are an inevitable element of the current American business environment. This risk is particulary acute in CD-ROM technology (see "What, Me Warranty?" *CD-ROM Review,* May 1988, page 58).

In drafting the end user agreement, companies must determine whether some customers might be deemed a "consumer" under an extremely broad, liberal definition found in what is commonly known as the Magnuson-Moss Act. If so, it is important to include "magic language" specified in that federal statute advising customers that the vendor's warranty disclaimer and liability limitation may be superseded by state law, and is, therefore, inapplicable.

The Uniform Commercial Code may also apply to your end user transactions. This "uniform sales law" stands in 49 states, and requires that any disclaimer of the implied warranties of "merchantability" or "fitness for a particular purpose" be "conspicuous."

Legislative history and past court rulings concerning these issues mean companies must carefully select their contract wording, typeface and type size, and the location of the disclaimer paragraph in the contract.

5. The "battle of the forms"

The vendors' "standard sales contracts" often clash with the customer's "standard purchase orders." Your customer's "fine print" often includes provisions unacceptable to technology vendors, such as unrealistic, lengthy warranties, and recitals that the customer obtain all proprietary rights in the product. If the customer's contract controls the transaction, then your company's rights may be permanently damaged.

Your objective is to make your end user agreement override the customer's boilerplate. This is why many contracts include provisions regarding "only written amendments," and attempt to expressly invalidate the effect of any purchase order or related correspondence.

6. Dispute resolution

Your agreement should specify the "operating system" that will govern your company's relationship with your customers. Due to the unexpected and unusual provisions of the law in certain states (e.g., California), vendors should specify the law of their state as the "governing law" for contract interpretation and enforcement.

Several related provisions are even more important when drafting your end user agreement:

- Venue. By specifying that any contract-related lawsuit must occur in your city, you can reduce the expense of a legal dispute (and often increase it for the hypothetical adverse customer, thereby creating additional incentive to resolve a dispute short of litigation).

- Arbitration. Due to the expenses, delays, and other frustrations associated with litigation, a carefully-drafted arbitration clause can be a good alternative for resolving disputes, particularly those regarding product customization and other technical issues. However, since you may need speedy access to the judicial system to protect your proprietary rights, arbitration should be inapplicable to these types of problems.

- Attorney Fees. Making "the loser pay" both sides' attorney's fees and costs also can be a disincentive to litigation. In most cases, however, it is necessary for such a provision to appear in the contract.

This article appears solely for educational purposes.

Reprinted by permission of and Copyright © 1988, 1989 Henry W. Jones, III, Esq., Atlanta, GA. USA. All rights reserved.

A Look at Two "Creative" Answers to Electro-Copying

By Nicholas A. Veliotes
From *Publishers Weekly*

[The illicit downloading of copyrighted material represents a significant loss of royalty revenue to publishers and authors alike. This article describes two experiments to plug the royalty drain. Another solution has been proposed by Personal Library Software, whose ROI desktop information system allows publishers to actually meter CD-ROM database usage (see Part Six: The CD-ROM Marketplace).]

Some of the most dramatic challenges for American publishers are coming from the mind-boggling array of new technologies that constitute "electro-copying."

Imagine a future in which one copy of a reference work, probably stored on CD-ROM diskettes, resides in a computer to which the whole world has dial-up access.

Using computers that exist today, hundreds of people could simultaneously "read" (and copy) the same part, or different parts, of the work. Obviously the manufacture of the CD-ROM amounts to the making of a copy of the work and requires permission from the copyright owner. It must be clear that individuals with no relationship to one another, acting independently, who electronically peek at different portions of the work amount to "the public," and that the copyright law covers such activities.

An equally serious electro-copying problem—when rights are clearer but enforcement remains difficult—is represented by the ability of users of such systems to copy, on demand, the extract that they have viewed, or even the entire work. Technology can assist here, provided that the designers and operators of the system make users accountable for their copying.

Two interesting experimental programs are exploring ways of using the new technologies to provide their own answers to the copyright questions they create.

ADONIS is a consortium of journal publishers investigating the possibilities of supplying their publications in machine-readable form to document-delivery centers that will print out individual articles on demand. The consortium was formed about eight years ago in response to the photocopying explosion of the 1970s and grew out of a desire to see if the new optical technologies could be used to fill requests for articles more cheaply than the cumbersome and labor-intensive photocopying procedures. If these economies could be achieved, royalties could be paid to the copyright owners without increasing users' costs.

The first phase of the project ended in discouragement in 1984 when it was found that the cost of replicating the disks and the cost of the workstation needed to utilize the system were prohibitive. However, with the advent of CD-ROM, these costs were drastically reduced, and the consortium regrouped. The current ADONIS project, which will run through 1989, supplies 219 biomedical journals published in 1987 and 1988 on CD-ROM. The disks are delivered approximately once a week to major document-supply centers in Europe, the U.S., Mexico, Australia and Japan, and are used to fill requests for individual journal articles. ADONIS, thus far, has produced valuable new technological insights into the workings of such a publisher-generated system.

THE UMI EXPERIMENT

An experimental system now being developed by University Microfilms International offers intriguing possiblities. Developed to provide an integrated information system to the library, business and professional communities, the project marries an abstract and index database to full text. Workstation hardware utilizes system software called BART (billing and royalty tracking) which records the volume, issue and page being accessed and copied, producing complete records for compensating the copyright owner.

This compensation can be accomplished in the form of a pre-purchased "debit card"—much like a transit fare card—with a specific monetary value from which will be debited royalties and fees each time a copy is made. A compensation system of this type could be used at universities. In a coporate setting the compensation could be arranged by allocating the copying to specified account numbers. A coin-operated workstation might be used at public libraries. The system seems to offer a flexible and eminently practical way of insuring that copyright holders are equitably compensated for the use of their materials.

The pilot program is now running at four universities—Eastern Michigan University, the University of Michigan, Michigan State and Northwestern—and should provide some interesting marketing insights for publishers.

Reprinted by permission of
Publishers Weekly. **Copyright © 1988**
Reed Publishing U.S.A.

Lawsuits Over Law Research

By Stephen Labaton
From the *New York Times*

[Aware of the implications for optical databases, the CD-ROM industry kept a close eye on a West Publishing v. Mead Data *lawsuit that sought to determine whether the organization of a database, rather than the data itself, could be copyrighted. In a somewhat less than precedent-setting finale, the suit was settled out of court before a ruling could be issued. Though the exact terms of the settlement were not immediately disclosed, it is believed that a sum of money changed hands and that Mead obtained a license for specific uses of the data indexing system that has made West Publishing texts essential components of any legal library.]*

COMPUTER SERVICE CONTROL IS AT STAKE

Over a century ago, Henry Wheaton and Richard Peters fought in a celebrated case for the right to be the reporter of the United States Supreme Court's decisions. Now the modern-day equivalent of the Wheaton-Peters fight is playing itself out in a bitter feud between the two largest computerized research services used by lawyers, judges and academics: Lexis and Westlaw.

Their parents, Mead Data Central Inc. and the West Publishing Company, have filed lawsuits in Ohio and Minnesota, where the two companies are respectively based. The outcome could determine which company will gain control of the highly competitive and fast-growing market for computerized legal research.

The trial in a copyright case brought by West Publishing, parent of Westlaw, ended last Friday in Minneapolis and a ruling is expected by June. Two other actions, involving charges by each company that the other violated various antitrust statutes, will begin next year.

ACCUSATIONS TRADED

Lawyers for West say that Mead Data, a unit of the Mead Corporation, has committed nothing short of theft by stealing the reference system for organizing judicial opinions in thousands of

West volumes. Mead Data has countered by accusing West of engaging in a series of monopolistic practices and censorship that has the effect of limiting the public's access to the courts.

The stakes in the dispute are considerable. Both sides expect that the winner would control a market that last year was worth more than $200 million in sales and is now dominated by Lexis. That market, according to executives of Mead Data and industry analysts, is projected to grow by 20 to 30 percent annually for the next few years.

Having succeeded in supplying services to many of the largest law firms, the two companies are looking to smaller firms and particularly to solo practitioners, which make up about half of the bar. While a decade ago such lawyers had to spend upward of $20,000 to start a decent law library, the sophisticated computerized services now make it possible to practice without a single volume.

Experts in antitrust, copyright and First Amendment law are also watching the Westlaw-Lexis suits closely because they offer a number of significant, yet novel, legal questions, particularly in the field of intellectual property. In addition, the cases have enormous import for laws that govern protection of computer software, laws still considered to be in their infancy.

Already, more than a dozen articles have been written about the dispute in scholarly law journals around the country.

"It's a great case," said Floyd Abrams, an authority on First Amendment law who is representing Mead Data, whose other computerized products include Nexis, a news service. "It is a case that squarely pits the past against the future."

Vance K. Opperman, West's main lawyer, sees the feud somewhat differently. "Plagiarism is the highest form of flattery and they have flattered us more than most people," he said.

Although the dispute began in 1985 as a relatively straightforward copyright case, its roots go back much farther, to customary practices by

> *The stakes in the dispute are considerable. Both sides expect that the winner would control a market that last year was worth more than $200 million in sales.*

the judiciary and by West that have lasted for decades.

In its narrowest sense, the copyright case in the Federal District Court in Minneapolis involves the use by Lexis of a system of citations called "star pagination."

BLACKSTONE'S SYSTEM

The standardized reference system, devised by Sir William Blackstone in England in the 18th century, makes life easier for lawyers and judges. It involves references by a publisher of court decisions to the same page numbers used by the officially recognized publisher of decisions.

Star pagination, so named because it consisted originally of page numbers surrounded by asterisks, enables jurists writing a memorandum, brief, or opinion to make reference to the official page number of a precedent in a decision, even if they are actually researching the case by using rival texts.

In almost every Federal and state jurisdiction, West Publishing's books have evolved into the official or standard volume. A secretive company based in St. Paul and owned by 14 senior executives, West dominates the legal-publishing field. By some estimates, the company last year

> *Plagiarism is the highest form of flattery and they have flattered us more than most people.*
>
> **Vance K. Opperman
> Lawyer for West Publishing Company**

had revenues of about $400 million. There were no reliable estimates available of Westlaw's revenues.

For most of its 106-year history, West has been the sole or primary publisher of state and Federal court opinions. It became the leading publisher in large part by making a major innovation at around the turn of the century.

AN INDEXING INNOVATION

It developed a way to synthesize judicial opinions into neatly definable principles of law, much the way the Dewey Decimal System is used to help to find books in libraries, thus enabling a lawyer or judge to quickly find a case and a precedent to support an argument. Called the West key number system, the indexing innovation is the usual way most older lawyers who are less skilled in computers do research.

Last year the company received 150,000 opinions from about 3,500 Federal and state court judges. One way it persuades judges to send in their decisions is by giving them free copies of its publications, routinely engraved with the recipient's name.

West also promises those judges a form of immortality: Their decisions are memorialized in the thousands of yellow volumes—standard fare in legal libraries.

"Everyone likes to see their opinions published," said one prominent Federal appeals judge in Manhattan. He added that the clerks of his court as a matter of routine send decisions to St. Paul.

Legal stylebooks insist that cases cited by lawyers and judges include the volume and page number of the West publication where the decision and principle of law can be found.

LEXIS STARTED EARLIER

Lexis, however, has dominated computerized legal research because it began its service earlier and its system was considered much easier to use by lawyers than the early version of Westlaw. While Mead Data does not break out the revenues of Lexis, all of its services last year generated revenues of $231 million.

No information is available on the market share held by the two companies, although by all accounts Westlaw has been gaining on Lexis.

Three years ago, Lexis announced that it was about to begin a star pagination system that makes reference to the precise pages of corresponding text in West publications.

West, fearful that such a system would make its volumes obsolete and hurt Westlaw's sales, countered swiftly. The company obtained an injunction barring Lexis from using star pagination until the outcome of the case.

West does not maintain in the action that it has a copyright on the judicial opinions: the Copyright Act of 1976 and judicial decisions starting with the 1834 Supreme Court case of Wheaton v. Peters have prohibited anyone from obtaining a copyright for the texts of decisions by a government body.

Rather, West maintains that the "arrangement" of the cases is protected by copyright and therefore Lexis's move to print corresponding pages is an impermissible infringement. It points to numerous lower court cases that have upheld copyrights of compilations of factual materials, such as telephone books.

INJUNCTION GRANTED

In October 1985, Federal District Judge James M. Rosenbaum granted West's motion for a preliminary injunction after finding that the arrangement was probably protected by copyright law and that Lexis's pagination system was an illegal infringement. A Federal appeals court upheld the injunction, although both opinions have sharply divided the academic community.

In the recent trial, Mead argued that the arrangement could not be copyrighted because it was tantamount to public property and also because it failed to meet the legal requirement for copyrighted material—that of being original.

Lawyers for Mead Data also say that by giving West a monopoly over an officially recognized form of citing cases, the Federal court would limit the public access to the judiciary.

West, however, contends that its staff of 3,400 expends considerable labor organizing, arranging and editing the decisions and that the material may therefore be protected by copyright. Its lawyers have also said that if Lexis were allowed to use star pagination West's printed volumes could become obsolete.

"If we lose, it would be disastrous," said Mr. Opperman, West's lawyer and the son of Dwight D. Opperman, West's president and chief executive. "It would mean that authors are not safe. A lot of creative activity would dry up."

"Nothing in the First Amendment requires that somebody give away a product free of charge," he added. "If there is anyone out there that doesn't have access, West would be happy to sell it to them."

Reprinted from the April 20, 1988 issue of the *New York Times* by special permission. Copyright © 1988 by The New York Times Company.

LIABILITY ISSUES

WHAT, ME WARRANTY?
By Henry W. Jones III

LIABILITY INSURANCE AND MALPRACTICE
By Joseph J. Mika and Bruce A. Shuman

What, Me Warranty?

By Henry W. Jones III
From *CD-ROM Review*

[From protection against illegal use, we move to protection against liability suits. How can you limit your liability exposure and safeguard your business without shirking your responsibilities to those who buy your products? Hank Jones has some suggestions.]

CD-ROM entrepreneurs must plan in advance to capture profits from their products. But profits are not merely a function of sales, it's what's left over after *liabilities*.

One major threat to profits for technology-related companies is products liability exposures. For example:

- Publishers of books, maps, databases, and other information technologies have been held liable by the courts for errors in their products.

- Lotus Development Corp. was sued by a Florida general contractor for $250,000 in damages, on the assertion that the design of the Symphony product permitted users to inadvertently commit errors in their business calculations—even though the user admitted using the software contrary to the instruction manual. The case was dismissed after the plaintiff apparently decided not to undertake the lengthy and expensive effort required for modern commercial litigation. However, most "computer law" specialists note that Lotus was significantly and unnecessarily exposed—due to a mistake in the warranty provision of the contract attached to the product.

- In the initial public offering made by Oracle Corp., a leading software vendor, the *first* "risk factor" set forth for potential investors was the possibility of bugs.

ASSUME NOTHING

A common misconception is that contract "boilerplate" will always provide the protection that business people seek.

> *More courts are viewing computer-related products as special cases, and finding that more liberal rules will apply when customers bring law suits alleging product defects and related damages.*

Another erroneous assumption is that judges and juries understand and appreciate the complexities involved in designing, developing and using computers, software, and other technology tools.

Minimizing this revenue risk can be a good investment for companies designing, developing, or distributing CD-ROM discs. By implementing straightforward steps in product development, contracting, employee training and marketing, companies can improve their profit potential as well as their industry reputation, customer relations, and overall economic health.

NEW LEGAL ENVIRONMENT

To understand and appreciate the following preventive law steps, it is necessary to recognize recent changes in product liability law which have significantly modified the business environment.

Recent court rulings have poked wide holes in the contract "boilerplate" on which business people formerly relied. For example, in the case of *RRX, Inc. vs. Lab-Con, Inc.*, a vendor was unable to deliver the "exclusive remedy" promised in its contract. In September 1985, the federal appellate court held that this glitch erased its contractual protection against consequential damages. As a result, the vendor was required to pay cash damages to its customer in excess of the fees that were received, even though the vendor was found to have acted in good faith, and attempted to remedy the problem (two key technical employees left the company).

In addition, more courts are viewing computer-related products as special cases, and finding that more liberal rules will apply when customers bring law suits alleging product defects and related damages.

WHAT TO DO

There are a number of relatively easy, inexpensive and effective steps that any company involved in the CD-ROM industry should implement:

Step 1: Product design

Profit protection and preventive law steps start at product design, not at the shipping dock. For example, program customer reminders into your disk content, so that they will appear appear on the monitor screen to suggest that users back up copies of their data, store and evaluate the parameters of their searches, and implement other "safe use" procedures.

The disc's data and software components should be "modularized" and "commented" to reduce a company's ongoing dependence on a particular individual or design team. Remember the old problem of mobility in the technology industry: "here today, gone to Maui."

Companies should also conduct extensive internal product testing as well as relying on outside business partners and skilled, long-standing customers. Implementation of alpha and beta testing may be necessary to avoid later charges of negligence in product completion. Implementation should be documented in a company's files.

Step 2: Contract upgrading

Vendors should "upgrade" and "debug" their customer and remarketer contracts to adapt to changes in the legal environment.

In most states, a *disclaimer* of implied warranties must be *conspicuous* under the law (i.e., the Uniform Commercial Code, which usually governs the sale of goods, and often applies to licensing of technology products). Conspicuous means the disclamatory language must be in capital letters, underlined, or in boldface type.

Product *performance* warranties should be specific. Will your warranty policy depend on the user having a particular configuration of hardware, certain peripherals, or a particular *version* of the appropriate operating system software? If so, make sure it's in the contract.

The *remedies* offered by a vendor for product problems should also be specific. For example, must the user have first returned a registration/warranty card? Should the user send in information regarding data input, data output, and the specific nature of the problem?

Provisions specifying remedies should be separated (or "unbundled") in the contract from liability limitation and warranty disclaimer provisions. This modular approach results from the new court rulings removing any cap on damages in instances where there occurs a "failure of an exclusive remedy."

It may be prudent to offer some actual, reasonable cap on your liabilities, rather than an absolute bar to any liability whatsoever. This approach may side-step tempting a judge to find the contract "unconscionable" and, therefore, unenforceable in the event of later litigation.

Step 3: Marketing and distribution

Mature companies have their advertisements, sales literature and instruction manuals reviewed by company counsel. Such materials often are held to constitute express warranties by the vendor to all potential customers.

> *For vendors whose products might be used by consumers rather than businesses, special contract language may be necessary to comply with federal and state consumer protection legislation.*

Contracts with distributors, dealers, OEMs, VARs, and other remarketers should include detailed provisions defining the business partner's obligations regarding product claims, advertising, sales practices, use of customer contracts approved by the vendor, and indemnification against any overselling. As a follow-up step, smart vendors will periodically monitor the activities of such remarketers.

Other steps

Many technology companies are taking other steps to manage this portion of their business.

"Errors and omissions" insurance, specifically created to cover electronics companies, is offered by the St. Paul's Fire and Marine Insurance Co. and other carriers. Directors and officers of companies many want "E&O" insurance and indemnifications from their companies as well.

For vendors whose products might be used by consumers rather than businesses, special contract language may be necessary to comply with federal and state consumer protection legislation.

Technical support, sales, and other employees should be trained regarding the meaning and effect of key contract provisions, and encouraged to alert specified managerial personnel regarding the existence of bugs or threats of lawsuits by dissatisfied customers.

By recognizing and managing this parameter of the business environment, CD-ROM companies and entrepreneurs can look not only to sales, but also profits.

This article appears for educational purposes only and should not be deemed legal advice.

Reprinted by permission of and Copyright © 1988, 1989 Henry W. Jones, III, Esq., Atlanta, GA, USA. All rights reserved.

Liability Insurance and Malpractice

By Joseph J. Mika
and Bruce A. Shuman
Excerpted from *Legal Issues Affecting Libraries and Librarians*

[CD-ROM publishers are not the only people who need to be concerned about liability issues. The information technologies are spawning the new profession of "information broker." As this article points out, information brokers should be aware of the malpractice risk to which they may be exposing themselves.]

LIABILITY AND INSURANCE

When entering the profession, librarians rarely think about the impending responsibilities they might incur. Yet much of what we do may lead us into situations that are potentially open to liability suits filed by our clients and employees. Liability, as defined in legal terms, means bound and obliged in law, or equity, responsible, answerable; or responsibilities, duties, obligations that are based in the law.

The patron who falls on a slippery floor, the individual who takes issue with our reference service, the parents upset by material they term "pornographic" provided by the children's librarian, the employee angry over denial of a raise or promotion who brings suit against the director for financial mismanagement, or the person who accuses a librarian of malpractice and sues the board of trustees; these are just a few examples. The scope of liability extends to library directors, employees, and the boards or individuals governing the library.

As professionals, we are seen by our clients as experts in information retrieval, reader's service, and information management. The patron's initial reaction is to accept the information we provide as factual, as gospel, as an accurate statement or record. Our clients normally do not question the accuracy of the information, nor do they seek a second opinion. However, when that information causes action leading to damaging results, a client may consider suing the librarian for professional malpractice or liability.

Recently the public has become much more aware of their rights and their redress if a product or a service rendered is not up to standards. Ralph Nader not only opened the eyes of consumers; he also exposed librarians to review. Librarians as well as giant corporations are now equally open to public scrutiny. Clients are becoming increasingly aware of their right to *accurate* information and their right to sue because of actions taken on the advice of librarians or based upon library data that proves to be faulty.

Who sues whom

State laws, regulations, and statutes establish guidelines that boards of directors or trustees must follow. Noncompliance opens an officer or director deemed negligent to financial damage and personal liability. Individuals pursuing a legal claim against librarians soon realize that very little can be gained financially by suing the professional (our salaries fail to do a very good job of supporting *ourselves,* much less provide a windfall for patrons). They therefore seek recompense from the library, or, more accurately, from the trustees or directors. Trustees are considered to be prominent citizens, well-to-do, or the spouses or heirs of wealthy individuals who have a "special" interest in community affairs and the library, and suing trustees should be more lucrative than suing the librarian. More commonly, complainants conclude, "We'll sue them all, including the librarian."

Before accepting a post as library director or trustee, each individual should inquire about liability insurance coverage. One should analyze the specific coverage, not simply raise the issue. If the library lacks an attorney who can explain the policy, you must analyze it yourself.

MALPRACTICE

Malpractice is defined as "the treatment of a case by a surgeon or physician in a manner contrary to accepted rules and with injurious results to the patient; hence, any professional misconduct or any unreasonable lack of skill or fidelity in the performance of professional or fiduciary duties" (*Webster's New International Dictionary, 2nd edition*). It is interesting to note that the definition relates to medical practice, a profession with which librarians often wish to be compared. Since the medical profession, along with the legal profession and others, is experiencing an increase in malpractice suits, malpractice should also be of concern to librarians.

In "Malpractice Liability: Myth or Reality" (*Journal of Library Administration* [Winter 1980] 3–7) Nasri defines malpractice as "any professional misconduct or unreasonable lack of skill in the performance of professional duties through intentional carelessness or simple ignorance." The concern is real, at least in Illinois. In November, 1986, the state legislature mandated that "a public employee acting in the scope of his employment is not liable for an injury caused by his negligent misrepresentation or the provision of information either orally, in writing, in a book or other form of library material." (Illinois Public Act 34-1431; sec. 2-210).

Information brokers and fee-based suppliers of information would appear to be more at malpractice risk and loss of income than the librarian in the school, academic, or public environment, and therefore would have more to lose by engaging in practices that may be unethical or illegal.

The matter of degree must also be considered. Does it make a difference whether the question I answer incorrectly is "How high is Mount McKinley?" or "What information can you provide me on the establishment of my own business?" If the height of the mountain is wrong, does it compare with providing inaccurate and/or out-of-date information that prevents a patron from establishing, or delays the start-up of, a business, involving considerable effort, time, and financial investment?

An interesting article on the information practitioner and malpractice is provided by Anne P. Mintz ("Information Practice and Malpractice...Do We Need Malpractice Insurance?" in *Online* (July 1984) 20-26).

Fortunately, the first actual case of librarian malpractice entailing subsequent lawsuit has yet to appear in the literature, although Allan Angoff wrote a very believable report of a fictional case in *American Libraries* (September 1976: 449), "Library Malpractice Suit: Could It Happen to You?" The lack of library malpractice suits may have to do with our clients' innate belief that we try to provide accurate information or as accurate as possible, and that we attempt to mislead no one intentionally or willfully. Or perhaps our clients figure that our free services entail occasional inaccurate information; after all, you get what you pay for, don't you? More likely, it is again, a realization that any claim against a librarian would realize more in personal satisfaction than monetary gain, and is just not worth the time and effort.

Excerpted from "Legal Issues Affecting Libraries and Librarians" in *American Libraries,* February 1988. Reprinted by permission of Joseph J. Mika and Bruce A. Shuman. Copyright © Joseph J. Mika and Bruce A. Shuman

SECTION VI

THE CD-ROM BUSINESS

MARKET PERSPECTIVES

PUBLISHING PERSPECTIVES

PRICING A CD-ROM

FINANCING YOUR CD-ROM ENDEAVORS

CREATIVE COLLABORATION

CD-ROM INDUSTRY PROFILE

THE FUTURE

MARKET PERSPECTIVES

THE BUSINESS OF SOFTWARE
By Doug Houseman and Anna O'Connell

MARKET RESEARCH: HIGH TECH LOOKS BACK TO THE FUTURE
By Dan Woog

THE EUROPEAN CD-ROM MARKET
By Julie B. Schwerin

HIRING A PUBLIC RELATIONS AGENCY
By Denise M. Topolnicki

RECRUITING AN AD AGENCY
By W. K. Schoonmaker

THE ABC'S OF LIST SALES
By Linda Hanson

PLEASE, TAKE MY CARD
By Echo M. Garrett and Webster E. Williams

The Business of Software

By Doug Houseman and Anna O'Connell
From *The APDAlog Newsletter & Catalog*

[We start this section with some down-to-earth advice to software developers that is just as appropriate for publishers of CD-ROM products. In this article, the authors briefly discuss the three key decisions that publishers must make before embarking on development of any product: Who is the Product for? how much should you charge? and how will you distribute your product?]

MARKETING: RESEARCH AND DECISIONS

Before a product can be financed, brought to market or even properly designed, that product must have a market. A market is the audience who will buy and use your product. If it is a CAD program the market will be very different from the market for a medication tracking program. Knowing what the market is and who is in it will help you to write a proper specification that will address the needs of the users who will (hopefully) make up your market.

Market segmentation

The first phase of market research is to figure out the general segment of the population of the world who will use the software you are writing. Is it the educated persons of the world, or those without a high school education where reading may not be a universal skill? Is the market overwhelmingly male or female, is it young or old, do they share a common set of skills and knowledge? What is the average earning power of the individuals who will buy this or will it only be sold to corporate buyers?

If you can rapidly narrow your focus to a set of persons with a few common characteristics, you will simplify the writing of your program specification by at least an order of magnitude. A target market could be as broad as all owners of micro computers or eventually as narrow as mechanical engineers who work on space station design. Remember that the very broad audiences are hard to target, and writing flexible enough software for a broad audience is also very tough (and competitive!). Conversely, as the size of the audience narrows, the complexity and specialization of the software also increases. Writing software to a customer specification and then later broadening the appeal and use of that software to the whole industry is normally twice as hard as writing a broader, industry targeted product in the first place.

Market data

You should eventually be able to produce the following information on your target market: How large is it in terms of both people and available money for your product, what type or shared skills does it have, what is the age of the persons in the market, where are the target users located? If it is a natural group, how does it communicate among its membership? Also important is how that market buys its software products and what software reviews are most influential. In many cases you will already know much of this, through those people on your staff who represent the segment(s). Even if you know, however, it is important to verify your knowledge.

Most of this information can be found in the public library with about 3–5 evenings of time spent mostly in the reference section of the library. Ask the reference librarian to direct you to the latest census information from the government, the almanac, an encyclopedia, and a number of books on the occupation(s) or skills you intend to address with your product. This material should allow you to quickly localize the size and age information.

Also check the software, dealer, VAR and other computer magazines; they often contain market research results (as do periodic mailings these publications often make to potential advertisers). These magazines regularly publish such data: *Computer & Software News, Computer Reseller News, Macintosh Today,* and *MacWeek*. Often you can get data from magazines you might advertise in; give them a call and ask what demographic or other research data they have that could help you decide on placing advertising there. Keep the advertising director on a short enough string and he will eventually come up with better and better statistics on the audience that his publications address. Typically, the more specialized the publication the better the breakdown on subscriber information.

On-line databases are also useful for both marketing data and information on business firms and educational institutions. Get help in formulating your search from a *trained* on-line search expert (at a local university or public library, or through the nearest chapter of the American Society for Information Science).

In many market segments you will find an association that provides communication between the active members of your market and collects further statistics. Many of the professional organizations maintain libraries, research librarians, and on-line information that is available to the members of the organization and to persons who are interested in that organization. They also hold trade shows and meetings that will eventually become some of your strongest marketing tools when the product is finished.

Products for home use or for the educational market may seem at first to be harder to specify, but the National Education Association maintains an extensive set of resources to assist in design of education software and the Department of Health and Human Services in Washington D.C. maintains an extensive database on the habits and needs of the average household. Both of these organizations welcome questions from interested individuals or companies.

PRICE VS. SALES

Once you have developed the size and statistics on the market it is time to develop information on the price that the market will support for your product and a curve that shows what your price vs. sales curve is likely to look like [see the section entitled "Pricing a CD-ROM" for further discussion of this topic]. A number of market research organizations will do this for you, for a price. Their price may be worth paying in the long run if you are looking for financial backing of any sort. Most banks and venture capital firms want to know explicitly what the experts think the market for your product will be. If you choose to do this part for yourself a few steps will give you a sufficiently detailed analysis for internal use:

1. Look at the products that are already on the market to determine both the list and discount prices of the products. Ask the members of a large user group to tell you how many of them have a) purchased a copy of each product and b) how many of them use each product. Ensure that you ask both questions because (unfortunately) the answers will always be different and many times very different. A single page survey handed out at a meeting of the group with a dollar or two paid to each individual who turns one back in will get you 30–40% of the surveys back. A sample of 50–100 surveys can be considered valid if your qualification questions do not eliminate too many of the users group. If you are targeting mechanical engineers and only get one survey back from a mechanical engineer, you do not have a valid sample. This information will form your competition base for your volume vs. pricing information.

2. Determine the features of the products on the market. Determine where the features to be included in your product place it in the spectrum of products. Will you have more useful features and be able to do operations with fewer keystrokes and faster? Or will you do the basics well and leave the advanced features to someone else? This will form the base for your market positioning and an evaluation of the price versus the value of your competitors products.

3. What gains in productivity do you offer your user? What special features might your product present? In other words what

BUYING AND SELLING LASERBASES

The real key to making CD-ROM successful in the marketplace is to make it very easy for a publisher to bring current materials into optical disc form and then take those materials and work with them to take advantage of the multimedia capabilites.

Marketing personnel must position their new products rather than leaving the positioning to the customer. Positioning the CD-ROM as a replacement for other storage devices is as critical a mistake as positioning the videodisc against the videocassette recorder (VCR). The distribution of large volumes of programs and/or data not subject to rapid changes is a better application and positioning for CD-ROM. The erasable CD, when available, will replace hard disk and floppy disk products, but this will not occur soon since the erasable CDs are still prototypes and will probably have slow acceptance. CD-ROMs and erasable CDs will not replace but rather complement each other. Sometimes, marketing personnel also overlook the fact that application developers comprise a major part of the hardware manufacturers' target market.

By Norman Desmarais. From *Electronic and Optical Publishing Review.*

> *Your product should never cost more than a product with more features, it should not be priced below its value to the user, it should be competitive in price with the rest of the market, and it should fit the pocket book of the users who you expect to buy it.*

is the value that your product offers the user. If you save an engineer an hour a day, you may well have a product worth a couple of thousand dollars. If you entertain a child for two hours a week, you have a $50.00 game. These are extreme examples but you can get an idea of how to form a value basis for your product.

From these three pieces of information, and the information on available income for your target market that you got from your work in the library or elsewhere, you should be able to develop a pricing strategy for your product. Like a box, these four pieces of information form the sides of your optimum pricing range. Your product should never cost more than a product with more features, it should not be priced below its value to the user, it should be competitive in price with the rest of the market, and it should fit the pocket book of the users who you expect to buy it. These four guidelines will almost always be at odds with each other and the final decision will almost always be a judgement call. The better job you do on forming your information bases the easier it will be to set the final price.

Take into account the tradeoff between high price (greater profit per unit for you) and lower unit sales volume. If you got a large enough sample from the user group in step 1 above, you may even be able to draw the price/value line for your market. Your eventual distributors and dealers will also want some input into this process. Software distributor representatives will almost always spend a few minutes talking price on a future product. Remember that distributors and dealers get a healthy discount from the retail price you just set so carefully. If you use distributors and/or dealers, you will actually get 40–60% of the eventual retail price of the software that sells. Remember this when setting your retail price, since your profit (if any) must come out of that fraction.

MEDIA DECISIONS

Once you have specified an audience in a target market, you can then look at the methods of communication that will reach the greatest number of these people without wasting money. Television is great for reaching a large number of people at one time, but you will normally waste a large amount of your budget because it is a shotgun approach, not a targeted approach. Look carefully at the trade journals, the trade shows, and the newsletters that address your specific audience. Many times you will need to split your advertising focus on a product, but look to these avenues to spend your limited advertising dollar.

Especially when your budget is tight, you should look into reviews and columnists who have a special significance in your target market. Anytime you can get a columnist to be a part of your design team or a beta tester you have just gotten a wider range of feedback than a normal tester would have and a step closer to general market acceptance. Do not ever attempt to influence what the reviewer writes about your product, only that he or she does write about your product. If you are working with Apple, get your target market's evangelist involved early in the project and keep them in the loop. Send all these people new versions of the software at least monthly and buy them lunch whenever possible. These people will help you target the publications and advertising channels to use and the reviewers who will help send your product into sales orbit. Get to know your local VAR representative at the local Apple sales office. They can get you to the VARs who are working in your area of interest and who in turn will provide you with market knowledge, leverage and experience.

For advertising purposes, once you have narrowed your choices to one or two publications, call the advertising director of the publications and ask him or her for rate cards and circulation information. These rate cards will tell you what the advertising will cost and the circulation information should be specific enough to allow you to find out if the publication axially does address your target market.

Advertising is expensive and you must do it continually to be successful. The ads must repeat on a regular basis if your product is to become well known. The circulation of a publication, times your frequency of advertising times the effectiveness of the ad will determine your level of sales. You can either advertise and sell or not advertise and pray that the reviews that you have gotten (or will soon get) will be enough to get the product launched on the market. Your research into the advertising media will allow you to take an educated guess at how often you have to place your ads, how large they should be and what they should say.

Remember to stress the features of your product and the benefits they provide to a typical user in your advertising copy. Another thing

> *Your research into the advertising media will allow you to take an educated guess at how often you have to place your ads, how large they should be and what they should say.*

to include is a way (mail or phone) to get more detailed information than is appropriate in an ad. The difference in cost for a color ad that is very well done and a black and white ad may be justified by the increase in sales that ad brings. Because magazines have a lead time of 3 months, you need to make a good guess at what your target market will do in the 3 months from ad preparation to printing, whether the first ad will be effective, and whether each month's ad copy should change. If your budget is low, work the reviewers very hard, get as many reviews as possible and pray that they are favorable.

Shows and conferences

Another route for getting your product known in your market is trade shows or conferences. Almost every association has some kind of "new products" exhibit associated with their annual meeting. Most professional associations have several of these conferences and expositions each year. You should determine which are the most important within your market and participate to the maximum level your budget allows. This is especially important for products intended for

> *If you can't afford anything else, and there are trade shows or conferences which address your market, present papers at all of them that you can get accepted for.*

use in a business or government environment, since the decision makers for this kind of software typically use the trade shows to do their comparison shopping. Trade shows take at least moderate amounts of money—typically two to five thousand dollars for the absolute minimum level of participation. To get the most sales leads for your money, try the following:

1. If the trade show or exposition or whatever it is has a conference or annual meeting associated with it, do whatever it takes to get on the agenda with a presentation. Technical societies of every type hold conferences where their largest problem is finding enough people to fill their program. Write and present a case study, survey of uses for your product in the industry of interest, or an applications report that mentions your product in a favorable manner. Offer to sit on a panel discussing issues related to the design or use of your product. Offer to recruit the other panel members, and ask someone from your weakest direct competitor. These all take prior preparation, so apply EARLY to the planning committee for the event. This technique, used alone, will let you get at least some exposure with the absolute minimum expenditure possible. You pay only for your individual travel expenses and (maybe) for a membership in the organization sponsoring the event. If you can't afford anything else, and there are trade shows or conferences which address your market, present papers at all of them that you can get accepted for.

2. Reserve your space early. Take the largest space you can afford, and pay by the reservation deadline. Talk nicely to the exhibits manager, and try to extract information about the location of a) large company booths you expect to draw a lot of traffic and b) your direct competitors. Try to get the exhibits manager to assign you a location close to a) and far from b).

3. Spend the time and money necessary to develop a GOOD demo of your product. Rehearse repeatedly. Consider coaching from a professional or hiring a consultant as a demonstrator if you do not have public speaking skills. Remember that a GOOD demo is also brief—no more than 10 minutes in its polished form. You should be able to spin it out if there is additional interest shown by your audience.

4. Staff your booth every minute that the exhibit floor is open to the public. Gather sales lead information effectively. Many shows now use embossed identification cards for attendees. Use them if they are provided. If not, a form to fill out by hand with name, address, phone number, and any particular questions or requests should be developed and on hand in copious quantities. One of these should be filled out for EVERY person you engage in conversation.

5. For every name and address gathered by the means in 4, a response should be generated within 2 weeks after the end of the

trade show. Sending a "nice to have met you" form letter and a product data sheet is the least you can do to keep your product in your potential customers' thoughts. If they had specific questions or requests, RESPOND TO THEM. The "ask a specific question and see if they answer it" technique is frequently used by professionals who are evaluating the responsiveness of potential suppliers. Don't screen yourself out because it takes an extra five minutes to jot down the response on the form letter and initial it.

DISTRIBUTION

The last thing you will need to research is distribution channels. There are basically four ways that you can distribute software for microcomputers. They differ in the amount of money each distribution scheme takes to set up, their effectiveness with different types of potential customer groups, and the level of margin that you, the software developer, can expect to receive using each. These distribution methods are: direct sales to end users, through retailers, through mail order, and through "shareware" distribution.

Direct sales is probably the most expensive, and potentially the most lucrative distribution method. This is typically used for extremely expensive (more than $5,000), highly specialized products directed at a specific, narrow market. Clinical psychiatrists in private group practice in the Midwest might be an example of a group sufficiently narrowly defined to be good candidates for this type of distribution. If you have a market used to dealing with direct sales people, such as doctors, dentists, lawyers, consultants, or the professional manager, this may be the way you should go. Start by hiring an experienced salesperson you like and trust. Take their advice about the rest.

Sales through retailers typically require software publishers to deal with distributors and with some of the major chains. This is a pain

> *Most of the publishers are looking for a marketing outlet, which they don't have now. They're looking for a distribution chain. The products have good margins, and it's an exciting technology that will help resellers sell computers.*
>
> **Fred Meyer.**
> From *Computer Dealer* **magazine.**

in the pocketbook, because you have to give them significant discounts from your established "price." There are also things like "advertising allowances," return rights, and exclusive vs. non-exclusive distribution areas to trip up the unwary. This route is NOT recommended for first-time software developers unless you have major financial resources, a good contracts lawyer, and contacts within the national distributors and the big retailing chains. If this is the route you want to go, consider selling your product to an established software company and hiring in as their Product Manager for your product.

Mail order distribution requires advertising expenditures. This distribution method is almost totally dependent on advertising to let the customers know what you have to sell and how to buy it. You also need to develop close personal relationships with your local postmaster and the UPS driver whose route you are on. Other than the actual labor of taking orders, printing invoices, packing orders and getting them to the shipper, there are no unusual expenses or real pitfalls in mail order. You should be aware of the Federal regulations regarding mail order businesses, but they are easy to follow for most software companies. Essentially, you must either ship the ordered merchandise within 30 days of receiving the order or send the customer notification of the expected shipping date and a way to cancel the order. If the customer cancels, you have 10 more days to mail a check. Take this regulation into account when you place your ads and determine your staffing budgets. Even "Acts of God" like hurricanes have not been considered sufficient excuse for non-compliance with the deadlines in the regulation. You may also be able to place your product with other firms for mail order distribution for a somewhat smaller discount than a retail distributor would require.

The "shareware" distribution method has been used less and less in the last few months, but may still be ideal for a beginning developer. HyperCard seems to have somewhat reversed that trend, and we are hoping that this spreads. Essentially, shareware works on the honor system. A developer makes his or her product widely available for potential users to try out. Those people who regularly use the product become registered users, and eligible for upgrades and technical support by sending a "shareware fee" to the developer. The amount of the fee, and the type of support it grants you access to, are included prominently in the program's internal documentation. Many shareware developers eventually upgrade their products to commercial-only, or use the shareware approach to build a reputation as a software developer so that they can get financial backing for commercial development projects.

Reprinted by permission of Doug Houseman, Anna O'Connell, and *ADPAlog*. Copyright © 1988 by Doug Houseman, Anna O'Connell, and *ADPAlog*.

Market Research: High Tech Looks Back to the Future

By Dan Woog
From *High-Tech Marketing*

[Picking up on the issues discussed in the previous overview article, we start by looking a little deeper at the role market research is playing in high-tech industries.]

That market research costs will continue to rise in the coming year is a given. But who will benefit from the accompanying rise in the amount of research itself—and the exact type of information high-tech companies will be seeking—is less certain.

"The industry is going in a direction where people don't have a choice as to whether or not to do market research," says Gary Byram, assistant vice president of marketing research for NCR in Dayton, OH. "As companies become more market-driven, rather than product- and technology-driven, they need to stay in touch, to receive better feedback. That happens in every industry, and it's happening now in high-tech."

Gwen Peterson, vice president of the computer products group at Dataquest, a San Jose, CA, market research firm, agrees. "The kind of information people are looking for is changing," she says. "It's much more niche-oriented. In the past, people were satisfied with global information, or data that assumed that all markets were the same. Now the emphasis on primary research is much greater. The data is going to have to be much more focused."

Robert G. Simko, executive director of the International Technology Group in Los Altos, CA, elaborates on the need for more focused, future-directed information. "As our industry becomes more complex, numerical comparisons with the past become irrelevant," he says. "Today's PC is yesterday's minicomputer; today's chip is yesterday's system. There's no applicability today to yesterday.

"The issue facing high-tech companies is how to position themselves in the marketplace, how to be competitive," Simko says. "It's not looking over your shoulder at the competition; it's looking ahead at the market." The research firms that can supply that future-oriented information, he implies, will be the ones that prosper in the coming year.

No longer will syndicated suppliers—Byram calls them "the IDCs and Dataquests of the world," referring to two of the larger market research houses serving the high-tech community—be able to mass-produce reports, even though they'll continue to thrive because of increasing demand for information. "We'll be pushing them because we'll do more primary research, so they'll be forced to supply more sophisticated information," the NCR executive says.

There does seem to be a growing trend toward more in-house market research, at least among the larger firms. Shari Morwood, manager, marketing information center for Hewlett-Packard, says her company will do more work in-house because of "the level of specificity. You can really define your problem when you do your own research. You have to recognize that the stuff you get from Gartner and the others like them—IBM and DEC are getting that same information too. We need to get more in touch with the marketplace. Also, we don't always agree with [the large research firms'] methodologies."

But there is a problem with in-house research, according to Simko of ITG. "A lot of companies can't differentiate between market research, market planning and product planning," he says. "They need to go outside to understand the difference."

And, adds Peterson of Dataquest, outside firms keep costs down by sharing them among many customers. They also have expertise many firms lack in-house.

Firms that decide to keep their research in-house may cut corners—in terms of both time and money—by using one of market research's latest high-tech alternatives: on-line databases.

These databases—the use of which is expected to grow considerably, especially among smaller high-tech companies—allow marketers to tap into on-line reports and directories containing a huge variety of information.

Some examples of the more popular databases: Investex, which contains analysts' reports

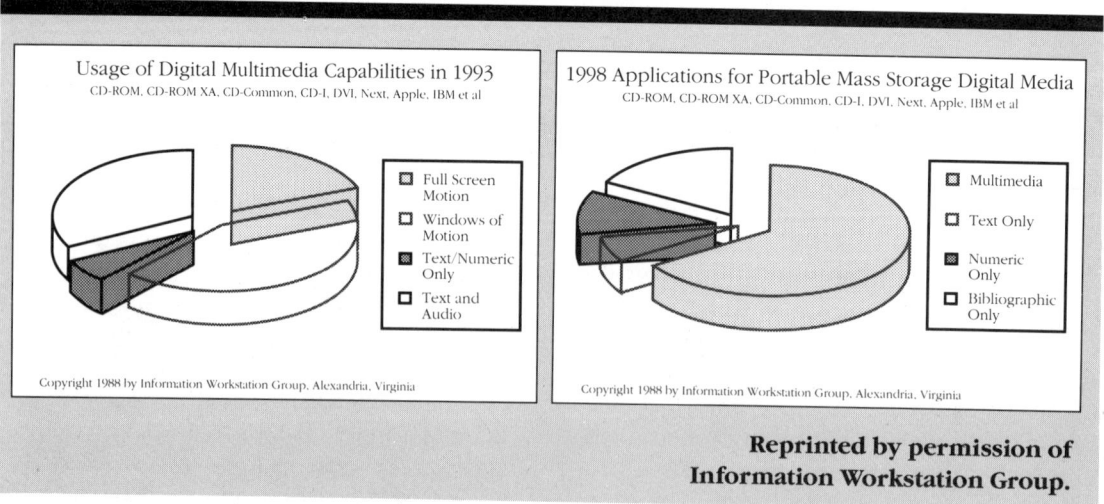

Reprinted by permission of Information Workstation Group.

on 2,500 major companies and 50 industries; Dun & Bradstreet Electronic Yellow Pages, which lists almost 9 million public and private companies, with addresses, major business activity and company size; and Standard & Poor's Register—Corporate, which provides background information on more than 45,000 public and private companies.

But whether it is done in-house or outside, research is sure to be affected by the current easing of the high-tech slump, or so the experts say.

Peterson believes that as companies' discretionary income rises, they'll spend more on market research.

"As we come out the other side of the blip, we realize the market isn't the same as when we went in. Things that were adequate three or four years ago are certainly not true today—and people are going to have to conduct market research to find out what is true."

The rosiest assessment—from a market researcher's point of view, at least—comes from Robert Simko.

FINDING A SHOE THAT FITS

When asked about the barriers in the CD-ROM industry, [Matilda] Butler responded with a story. "Two men were sent to the jungle to sell shoes. One man wrote home saying, 'No market. No one wears shoes.' The other man sent back a letter saying 'Great market! No one wears shoes!'"

From *CD-ROM Review*.

"It's already too late to have done market research for this year," he says. "As we go into the upswing, following the economic hiccup, everyone will be playing catch-up next year." And that, he believes, could lead to market research spending twice the size of the marketplace's concurrent percentage growth.

Reprinted by permission of Steve F. Tiberi.

The European CD-ROM Market

By Julie B. Schwerin

[Market research and market definition don't have to stop at the borders of the North American continent. In this article, Julie Schwerin discusses the current state of the CD-ROM industry in Western Europe and the things developers should keep in mind when contemplating expansion into European markets.]

CD-ROM today exists technologically in the context of the international standards for CD-ROM physical formats set by Philips and Sony and the international file-format standards developed by the High Sierra Group and approved by the International Standards Organization as ISO 9660. In Europe, CD-ROM exists in the context of the European Economic Community, the European computer industry, the European information industry and, ultimately, an international optical publishing industry. This article introduces some of these contexts as they relate to the market for CD-ROM in Europe and to conditions that distinguish the European market from the U.S. market.

THE EUROPEAN MARKET

Europe is a geographic entity with two major political and economic factions. *Eastern Europe* describes the Soviet Union and its satellites in the COMECON bloc, while *Western Europe* typically means every nation west of the bloc. The European Economic Community (EEC or the Common Market) is a subset of Western Europe that includes as members France, Great Britain, Ireland, West Germany, Italy, Spain, Portugal, Greece, Belgium, Denmark, The Netherlands, and Luxembourg, but does not include Austria, Norway, Sweden, Finland, or Switzerland.

Among the twelve Common Market nations there are twelve sovereign governments, twelve state-owned and operated telephone and telecommunications monopolies (called PTTs) and nine primary languages.

The central administration of the EEC is an overlying layer of government and judiciary, but one which has relatively little power today and spends most of its budget on agricultural subsidies. The individual nations within the EEC are, however, relinquishing certain aspects of their sovereignty to the central administration in an effort to regain the economic parity lost to the U.S. and Japan in the postwar years, and they are thereby reviving and extending the economic reforms intended in the original EEC formation. Trade barriers and other inhibitors to free trade between Common Market countries are scheduled for dismantling by 1992, and product standards are set for normalization by the same date. These actions will create a large economic entity comparable to the U.S. in size. Once adjustments are made, the benefits of competition and free enterprise are expected to result in significant gains in jobs and prosperity by all EEC nations.

THE EUROPEAN COMPUTER INDUSTRY

In computerization, a lower saturation level than in the U.S. or Japan makes Europe a higher growth market. Established national computer manufacturers, however, face increasingly tough competition from the multinational operations of U.S. and Japanese manufacturers. The removal of trade barriers in 1992 is a major benefit that European computer makers will have to deliberately exploit, lest the benefits instead fall to foreign makers with extensive European operations. German, French, Italian, British, and Dutch computer makers will have to become more European through mergers (least desirable to them), joint ventures, or cooperative R&D partnerships, such as the EEC's ESPRIT project for cooperatively developing next-generation architectures and semiconductors.

According to Dataquest figures, IBM dominates the $9.2 billion mainframe market with almost two-thirds of the sales, compared to the collective one-quarter of Siemens, Bull, and ICL. IBM, DEC, and Hewlett-Packard together control one-third of the $12.4 billion minicomputer market versus the one-third shared by Siemens, Bull, ICL, and Nixdorf. IBM alone sells one-third of the $9.3 billion worth of microcomputers;

JULIE B. SCHWERIN

Home: Pittsfield, Vermont
Job: President, InfoTech
Quote: *"The CD-ROM industry has a solid business base and a healthy growth curve with some exciting innovations and diversifications ahead. It is a bust only to those who had mistakenly predicted a boom."*

Compaq and Apple each have about 5 percent of the market, Olivetti has about 10 percent, and Philips is pushing hard.

European computer makers no longer can rely solely on the assured business of their national markets and governments. But because of the dominance of the U.S. computers and a European push for open standards in workstations and minicomputers, no proprietary European system standard exists for these classes of machines. Thus, European hardware and software firms have access to U.S. markets for products similar to those they sell in Europe. Bull, through its merger with Honeywell, and Olivetti, through its joint venture with AT&T, are leading the reverse thrust along with French and British software makers.

THE EUROPEAN INFORMATION INDUSTRY

The online information industry in Europe is much smaller than that in the U.S. for several reasons. The PTTs individually control access to

> *As financial markets become increasingly international and the lowering of trade barriers by 1992 creates many more multinational companies trading goods and services more freely across national frontiers, international information products will represent a truly phenomenal growth opportunity for visionary publishers.*

their national networks, among which there are varying degrees of complexity and reliability. This segmentation and lack of uniformity make it fairly difficult and impractical for a researcher in Brussels to log onto a database mounted in Milan. Statistically, it is also fairly likely that the user will be disconnected before the search is complete. Finally, for the effort to be made at all there must exist Italian information of high interest to a Belgian with a good command of the Italian language. On the positive side, however, state subsidies of databases and online host networks are common in Western European nations, and the European Commission directly and indirectly supports the online information industry through its DGXIII operations in Luxembourg.

The premier example of positive government intervention is the Minitel in France. Over the last five years, the French government has completely replaced telephone directories printed on paper with an online directory and interactive terminals installed in virtually every home and business. A universal installed base and a population conversant with keyboards and ASCII screens prompted the offering of hundreds of value-added information services for home and professional use and resulted in a public/private partnership for videotex that other nations envy—especially the U.S., which has spent hundreds of millions of dollars to create one, so far in vain.

The few "European" databases in science and medicine could be joined by many more, particularly in business and finance, in the next few years. This expansion requires the ranks of the few truly "European" publishers to be joined by the many national publishers and a sizable entrepreneurial group. But multinational databases are unlike computers, which don't care what language the bytes they manipulate represent. Information content in Europe is comprised of many languages, and translation thus remains a human effort that is necessarily expensive. As financial markets become increasingly international and the lowering of trade barriers by 1992 creates many more multinational companies trading goods and services more freely across national frontiers, international information products will represent a truly phenomenal growth opportunity for visionary publishers.

THE EUROPEAN CD-ROM INDUSTRY

Optical publishing began in the U.S. as early as 1982, when several entrepreneurial firms commercialized technology for the delivery of large databases on laser videodiscs. By 1985, these firms joined many others to support CD-ROM as the delivery medium of choice for distributed access to large databases. Today, according to figures published by InfoTech, there are 250 commercial CD-ROM titles, more than 150 in-house titles, and an installed base of more than 100,000 CD-ROM drives. The major portion of this growth, and the corresponding $150 million in revenues, has been generated by U.S. firms; less than one-third has come from firms in Europe.

In another sense, however, the optical publishing industry began in Europe, specifically in Eindhoven, The Netherlands, where the idea to extend the CD Audio player as a data-delivery peripheral known today as a CD-ROM reader began inside Philips. Although the large, primarily English-speaking U.S. market was chosen for the first big push and the hardware was much less expensive in the U.S. than in Europe, especially in the first few years, models for the European market have been available for almost as long. Because the computer platforms are the same or similar in Europe and the compact-disc standards are truly international, the only difference is in the voltage and the plugs.

Discs, readers or drives, interfaces, CPUs, monitors, operating systems, and even search and retrieval software are all interchangeable between the U.S. and Europe. This advantage transcends differences in television broadcast standards (and thus videotape and videodisc) and data interchange protocols between telecommunications networks, but cannot alleviate differences in language and content interest or usability. CD-ROM does not create international demand for the message it delivers; it only facilitates the delivery. Thus, European CD-ROM products today are more monolingual and national in scope than they are multilingual and multinational. They provide Italian tax laws, Swiss telephone directories, and British Post Code directories, and are therefore comparable to market niches in the U.S.

> *Over the last five years, the French government has completely replaced telephone directories printed on paper with an online directory and interactive terminals installed in virtually every home and business.*

TOWARD AN INTERNATIONAL CD-ROM INDUSTRY

CD-ROM, as a worldwide standard with interchangeable computer platforms and retrieval software, is at the forefront of the emerging international information industry. But expectations for the future must be realistic, within the contexts of European markets and the computer and information industries.

Many positive and exciting developments signal the acceleration of an international information industry using CD-ROM as a delivery medium, among them:

- Four of the largest CD-ROM publishers—SilverPlatter, Lotus, Disclosure, and Microsoft—have operations in both the U.S. and Europe.

- Many of the major CD-ROM retrieval software firms, including KnowledgeSet and

Dataware, are also multinational distributors.

- Boeing 757 maintenance documentation using KnowledgeSet software is being produced by Pergamon Compact Solutions for British Airways.

- Chadwyck-Healey is producing census data and maps on CD-ROM for the U.S., Europe, and Australia.

- A joint venture called EIKON has been established by Microsoft, Olivetti, and STET to produce a series of European titles.

- West Publishing has licensed Jouve, the French printer, to produce legal texts with its software.

- TriStar in the U.S. has collaborated with Oxford University Press to produce and market the *Oxford English Dictionary*.

- At least one CD-ROM drive manufacturer has a model with a switchable external 110/220-volt power supply.

- DEC, Olivetti, Apple, and Hewlett-Packard are major international computer makers with significant commitments to CD-ROM products.

In 1986, European firms participated in the High Sierra committee through the Optical Disc Forum. In 1987, more than a dozen nations were represented at Optica, the optical publishing and storage conference in Amsterdam, and the largest demonstration of CD-ROM titles in the world was held at the International Online Meeting in London. In 1988, there will be nearly 100 titles available from European publishers. In 1989, the OpticalInfo Conference (formerly called Optica) in Amsterdam will again showcase the international optical publishing and storage industry.

EUROPEAN CD-ROM MARKET CAUTIOUS

Findings of a new report from Knowledge Research, a London-based market research company, indicate that with the exception of Italy Europeans are taking a cautious approach to CD-ROM. Reasons for this caution are put down to a fear that CD-ROM will erode revenues from existing alternative publications and an unwillingness to commit to the large up-front investments needed. Hardware manufacturers in particular have shown little interest in entering the market. This may be changing though, the report says, as some "significant announcements are expected this year."

To date, the strongest commitment to CD-ROM has come from relatively small software publishers seeking to expand their markets. However, compared with US companies at a similar stage of development, their efforts look rather weak: only twenty per cent of online databases are being converted to CD-ROM in Europe compared with a forty per cent conversion rate in the US.

This discrepancy should not be taken entirely as evidence of timidity on the part of European software publishers. The US has three times the penetration of PCs as in Europe, its libraries are wealthier. On top of that, prices for CD-ROM products are generally cheaper in the US. Clearly, European vendors have a smaller and less affluent market to contend with.

The report, entitled *Market Opportunities for CD-ROM 1987–1992*, is optimistic about the future. One of the most viable applications in the future, it says, could be in the use of CD-ROM to overcome the language barriers in Europe—already several multilingual titles have been published. The report predicts that a great number of titles for a variety of industries will be launched in 1988 and that sales will increase rapidly through 1989. By 1990 the installed base of CD-ROM drives is expected to be 100,500 throughout Europe, a substantial increase from the 1987 total of 6,700. The report also predicts that Italian sales, although remaining strong, will be overtaken by Britain and Germany in the early 1990s.

Reprinted from *The Electronic Library* by permission of Learned Information, Oxford, England and Medford, New Jersey.

This is just the beginning of the international optical publishing industry. Over time, the distinctions between countries of origin will become increasingly difficult to discern and, perhaps, become increasingly meaningless. As the world becomes smaller, optical publishing of information worldwide will inevitably grow larger.

[Julie Schwerin is President of InfoTech, an international market research and development firm in Pittsfield, VT. InfoTech assists clients in quantifying and optimizing market oportunities for information products, using CD-ROM and other optical disks and information technology.]

Hiring a Public Relations Agency

By Denise M. Topolnicki
Excerpted from "Putting Your Best Foot Forward,"
***Venture* magazine**

[Companies are often reluctant to hire in-house people to perform public-relations duties, preferring instead to concentrate personnel resources on product development and sales efforts. Often, public relations is tacked onto the job description of an overworked administrative assistant, who barely has time to generate press releases, much less cultivate the relationships that might result in highly desirable free publicity. An alternative is to "rent" public-relations expertise, by entrusting this important function to an agency that specializes in the visibility programs that will get your company and your product noticed.]

There are thousands of public relations (PR) firms, so you'll have to narrow the field by asking business associates for their recommendations. Here's who to question:

- Your business consultants, including your suppliers and your advertising agency, if you have one.

- Editors and writers who cover your industry. They know the difference beween a competent professional and a pain in the neck.

- Your venture capitalists. For example, Jeanne Mitchell, director of investor relations for Dougery, Jones & Wilder, Mountain View, Calif., regularly screens PR firms for Dougery Jones's portfolio companies. When one of them needs PR, she recommends two or three agencies for the entrepreneur to interview.

- Other entrepreneurs in your field. If you spot a young company that's getting a lot of press coverage, call and ask about its PR agency.

The firms that will be recommended to you will probably be small, which generally is in your best interest. Says Mitchell: "One of the biggest problems start-ups have if they use a big agency is that they think they'll be getting the top honcho when they'll really be getting Bernie Plotzwotz who's a junior junior staffer." If your small account is important to an agency's bottom line, however, you'll more likely get attention from senior people.

Small shouldn't mean fly-by-night, however. Carefully consider the experience and qualifications of a firm's principals and staff. Also find out if they belong to the Public Relations Society of America, a professional organization whose members pledge to adhere to a code of ethics.

To pare your list of recommendations, first find out which PR firms understand your industry. There are two arguments for hiring a specialist: You will not have to spend as much time educating your PR representatives, and they will be well-connected to the editors, venture capitalists, and industry analysts you want to reach.

Consider the case of fashion designer Bill Dugan, who left Halston after a dozen years to create his own line of women's clothing. After working out of his apartment on a tiny budget for two years, Dugan found financing early this year and immediately hired a public relations company to coordinate his fall fashion shows. Nancy Dugan, Bill's wife and the firm's vice president, says, "We felt that expanded visibility would create more buyer interest. To gain that visibility, we needed someone with clout in the industry."

The Dugans hope the clout will come from Gottfried & Loving Inc., a seven-person New York agency that specializes in the fashion industry. They were especially attracted to Gottfried & Loving, whose client roster includes established designers like Donna Karan, because of its history of experience in retailing.

Of course, there's a chance that a PR firm that specializes in your industry will have to turn you away because they're already working for your competition. Even if a PR person claims that he or she has no conflicts of interest, you may worry that your trade secrets will leak out. To ease your concerns, ask your PR reps to sign

> *There are two arguments for hiring a specialist: You will not have to spend as much time educating your PR representatives, and they will be well-connected to the editors, venture capitalists, and industry analysts you want to reach.*

nondisclosure agreements, which stipulate that all information you give them is proprietary.

Surprisingly, nondisclosure agreements aren't all that common. Catherine Johnson of CJ Associates, Boston, is exceptional: She signs such agreements with all of the high-technology firms she represents. On the other hand, none of the companies Denise Burrows of Capital Relations Inc., Agoura Hills, Calif., serves demand nondisclosure contracts. But Burrows requires new employees to sign contracts stipulating that information they learn is proprietary.

A final word on trimming your list of recommendations: If you cannot afford to spend much money on long-distance phone calls or air travel, hire an agency close to home. Naturally, that rule doesn't apply if you start a biotech business in Biloxi and cannot find a local publicist who knows the difference between DNA and DOA.

Once your list is narrowed down to four or five firms, it's time for serious interviewing. Expect the finalists to pitch for your account in oral and written presentations. Here's what to watch for during the dog and pony shows:

- Evaluate the quantity and quality of the press clippings that a firm has gotten for its clients. If one firm has managed to get its clients mentioned in dozens of publications as diverse as *Working Woman* and *The Wall Street Journal*, it's doing a better job than the agency that has little to show but tiny items in trade magazines.

- Find out if your would-be account reps know the people you want to reach. If you want to make a splash on Wall Street in advance of an initial public offering, for example, you should look for PR people who count industry analysts and financial editors among their contacts.

   There are a couple of quick ways to determine if a PR firm maintains up-to-date lists of editors and writers. The firm's library should contain the latest issues of the publications in which you want to appear. You can also check magazine mastheads for the names of key editors you want to reach and ask PR people whom they intend to contact from those publications.

- See that the firm can fill all of your needs. For instance, do they have experience with focus groups, videotapes, or trade show displays?

- Determine if the agency is well run. You don't want to miss a deadline because their check to their printer bounced. Ask for supplier references and examine invoices and other standard forms to gauge the agency's professionalism.

- Ask for client references and find out if they are satisfied with the service they've received.

- Most important, figure out if you can live with their fees and billing procedures. Fees vary tremendously, depending upon a PR firm's size and reputation. While small agencies may charge $2,000 to $4,000 a month to service an entrepreneurial firm, larger, more established companies command $5,000 or more.

Many agencies charge monthly retainers, which are payable in advance. Retainers cover the time your PR rep spends preparing press releases and other materials and talking with the press. These monthly fees generally don't cover work on special projects like press conferences or telephone, photocopying, and other expenses.

Other firms charge hourly fees against an annual budget that you approve. Before you okay an hourly fee arrangement, find out how little time your PR rep will spend on your account before starting his or her clock. Some PR firms start charging after 15 minutes; others wait until an hour has elapsed. Also ask about the maximum number of hours you can be charged per day as well as how travel time is billed. To avoid nasty surprises, ask your PR reps to call you before proceeding with budget-busting work.

It's also advisable to examine a sample invoice. Beware of columns for miscellaneous expenses, which may mysteriously expand. The more detailed the invoice the better, like Denise Burrow's 10-page reports that list every call she makes on the client's behalf.

If you cannot afford to pay $24,000 or more a year for PR, you can hire a firm that's willing to publicize a new product or arrange a press tour for a set fee. A handful of agencies charge only for press coverage they manage to get you.

If you simply cannot afford the going retainer rate, find out if an agency will accept equity in your business in lieu of cold cash or in addition to a discounted retainer. Suppose the agency that you want to hire charges $3,000 a month, but you can only pay half that. You pay the balance by purchasing $1,500 worth of stock options at the insider's price for the PR firm. If you're caught in a cash crunch, other PR agencies may negotiate to collect a percentage of your profits later; 10% to 25% is typical.

You should also know that some agencies will adjust billings to your needs. For example, Harriet Blacker, president of Harriet Blacker Inc., New York, charged a retainer to promote author Stuart Jacobson's *The Art of Giving* after the book was published last winter. But now she's billing Jacobson only for the hours she spends on his other projects.

Finding a PR firm, like hiring a lawyer or any other professional, is somewhat subjective. To determine whether the chemistry between you and would-be PR reps is right, you should pose some hypothetical problems for the candidates to solve. For example, you could ask what the PR firm would do if one of your products was found to be defective. You'll find out whether they're willing to deviate from their standard sales pitch and think on their feet.

Reprinted from the August 1988 issue of *VENTURE, For Entrepreneurial Business Owners and Investors,* by special permission. Copyright © 1988 Venture Magazine, Inc., 521 Fifth Ave., New York, NY 10175-0028.

Recruiting an Ad Agency

By W. K. Schoonmaker

[From PR agencies, we turn to advertising agencies. Most companies recognize the need for coherent programs that will maximize the return for each advertising dollar and most turn to outside specialists, rather than relying on in-house efforts. How do you evaluate the advertising agencies competing for your account? This article gives some pointers.]

I've seen the agency from all sides. As an agency research/media director, I prepared the brief and then rode shotgun for the smooth talking egg-dancer in new account presentations. I've been on the client side with a huge budget to cover space, collateral, promotion, publicity, trade shows, market research and sales training...as well as a miniscule budget that barely extended beyond staff to a schedule of fractional pages. And I've been a consultant to publications, advising how to make the most of agency contacts. So there is nothing vicarious in what follows.

Of course there are pretentious, incompetent agencies. But a majority are capable...the differences among competent agencies are minute compared to the disparities between the acceptable and the unacceptable. The problems in client-agency relationships are often traceable to mismatching and the following failure to meet expectations. The anxious agency may take on an account whose goals and needs are not fully understood. More often, the client hasn't done an adequate job of presenting its requirements, reducing candidates to those that fit an appropriate profile and obliging these to make their case on their terms. So, increase the odds of an effective match of your need and their abilities by:

- Writing a job description. Be specific about what functions the agency is to perform...space, artwork, media selection, collateral, publicity, market research, trade shows, etc. Stipulate which are reserved to the company, which are to be provided by third parties.

- Asking candidates for written documentation as an element of their presentations. A portfolio of past accomplishments, audio-visuals and verbal hypes can be flashy and still devoid of content. The written presentation should oblige them to acquire facts about you, your competition, products and markets beyond what you provide. You can judge their ability to analyze data, reach conclusions and make recommendations. *If they can't put their ideas into instructive and persuasive words, why believe they can do any better for you?*

- Asking to meet the team that will serve your account. The theatrics of an agency presentation may be handled by charming seniors who you will rarely see again. The account executive need not be an expert on copy and art, but expect him to know something about your industry, the media serving it, your markets as well as marketing methods. The copywriter need not be technically competent in your product areas, but she should be conversant with technical concepts. If you like that team, your agreement should include an option to terminate should they be changed without your prior approval. If the agency will assemble teams from the bull pen on a project basis, run to the nearest exit.

- Asking which functions are performed in-house and which are subcontracted. Sometimes the agency merely farms work out. You may prefer to control such items directly, if only to minimize incompetence and/or reduce costs.

- Asking for a list of their clients. Demand not only the current roster, but also those who were represented in the past five years and are no longer with them. These can give you brickbats as well as testimonials. But don't stop there. See if the media salespeople can give you omissions. Use the phone to check; silences and evasions can be informative.

- Putting your financial department to work. Ask them to pull credit reports on the agency. They can query the publications used by the agency. And they can finally give you an opinion on the financial stability of the agency. The reason is bluntly that an agency concerned about its financial problems is less likely to be worrying about your marketing problems.

- Determine the philosophical inclination of the agency. Does it concentrate soley on high tech or is it carrying consumer accounts as well? Is it inclined to image advertising or does it focus on nuts and bolts? Do its publicity people just grind out new product/literature releases or do they try to place exclusive stories?

The problems in client-agency relationships are often traceable to mismatching and the following failure to meet expectations.

I admit to some prejudices that would act as knock-out factors when a client asks me to get involved. I'm turned off by:

- The agency that relies heavily on a Plans Board or equivalent committee to generate ideas, discuss problems and review solutions. Most of the best concepts I've seen were the result of an individual's effort.

- The agency that is guided by "the client won't like it" rule. I want to see all of their "thumbnails" and pick which ones are to be fully developed, not the imposition of someone else's judgement on what will fly.

- The agency that tries end-runs around the ad manager to top management. If management doesn't have faith in who fills the slot, then spend more to get someone who they'll trust to make the right decisions.

- The agency that fails to substantiate its bills with its time sheets, and suppliers' bills or has not cleared its billing procedure with your accounts payable or has no procedure to answer client's questions on bills.

- The agency that overemphasizes "corporate" advertising. Such campaigns are costly and results hard to prove, but it's an easy play for the "creatives." Creativity can be a cloak for the lack of product knowledge and awareness of the markets. How many of those award-winning ads paid off in sales?

- The agency that is neither demanding on the client for product/market information nor makes an effort to acquire such on its own.

- The agency that uses deadlines to force clients into settling for what has been offered. It is better to be absent than run an inept ad. If the agency isn't cured by a few cancellations at their expense, it's time to find a new agency.

Above all, remember that the courtship shouldn't be over when the account is awarded...it's just begun. So, a stringent application of these guides will reduce the candidates to those most likely to perform.

Reprinted by permission of W. K. Schoonmaker, publisher of *Mainly Marketing,* the monthly newsletter for technical management. Copyright © 1988 Schoonmaker Assoc., Coram, N.Y. All rights reserved.

The ABC's of List Sales

By Linda Hanson
From *The Desktop Publishing Journal*

[In the following article, Linda Hanson takes a double-vision look at direct-mail advertising, from the point of view of those selling lists and those buying them. She explains some of the virtues — as well as warning against potential hazards — as seen through the eyes of long-time advertising maven, David Ogilvy.]

David Ogilvy, long considered the guru of world-wide advertising, and the creator of concepts used in Dove and American Express ad campaigns, some of which are still being used over 25 years later, has this story to tell about direct mail marketing, "One day a man walked into a London ad agency and asked to see the boss. He had bought a country house and was about to open it as a hotel. Could the agency help him get customers? He had $500 to spend. Not surprisingly, the head of the agency turned him over to the office boy (who happened to be David Ogilvy). I invested his money in penny postcards and mailed them to well-heeled people living in the neighborhood. Six weeks later the hotel opened to a full house. *I had tasted blood.*"

Direct mail marketing is in essence list sales. In David Ogilvy's case, the "list" was probably from a phone book or a selected zip code area listing. The best part of using a list is the ability to select only certain criteria while omitting everything else.

WHAT IS A LIST?

A list consists of your subscribers' names and addresses as well as age, income, occupation, subscriber history and other information you feel is significant. You might also refer to this information as your demographics (your audience). Let's suppose that you are *Playboy Magazine,* and are interested in "renting" a list from a major computer magazine. You already know that the majority of your readers are male, between the ages of 28 to 48 and make a minimum of $25,000 per year, so you would only be interested in purchasing names that

> *The use of computers has been a major boon to direct mail marketing by making the selection process a simple, viable one.*

meet that criteria. If the computer magazine had done their homework they would know the sex, age, and income of most of their subscribers. By using a computer, they could isolate just the names and addresses of those who meet your criteria.

LISTS

The use of computers has been a major boon to direct mail marketing by making the selection process a simple, viable one. Prior to computers, list management was a tedious, time-consuming task relegated to secretarial staff when utilized at all. It wasn't considered a sserious form of marketing until the 1970's. During the 70's the process was refined and tested until is has become almost a science in the 80's.

PROFITABILITY

Why would you sell your customers' names to a possible competitor? Let's look at a list of 50,000 names. The average list rents for approximately $55/M according to recent advertisements in *Folio Magazine* (an East Coast Bible of the advertising industry). That's $2,750 from one sale! Subtract the 20% commission you would have to pay if you used a list agency to aid in your sale and that becomes a $2,200 net profit from one sale. Let's say that you are able to "rent" it out 10 times in one year. You've made $22,000 using information you have to collect during the normal course of operating your business effectively.

HOW MUCH DO I CHARGE?

List pricing can be tricky. Most buyers react negatively to any list costing more than $100 per thousand. Using a list size of 50,000 again, let's calculate some possiblities.

If the objective is to maximize your profit, then the pricing must be quantified. By lowering your price, you make the list more enticing and could actually increase your profitability over all. It may take more sales, but by making it a reasonable price you would attract more customers for your list and could ultimately attract even more revenue.

HOW TO PROTECT YOUR LIST FROM BEING COPIED

By adding decoy names to your list using your own address and variations of your name for each customer you sell your list to, you can track unscrupulous usage of your list. These decoy names should be distinctive and easily recognizable. If your name is John R. Williams you could use variations such as John A. Williams, or Johnny B. Williams. By changing the spelling of your last name slightly your mailman would still deliver mail to you. As long as you document the variations accurately, you can detect unauthorized usage. Do not respond to the mailer's offerings under the varied names as this could cause additional problems in trying to prove your case. You should always include in any list rental contract a condition that the names will be used once and no copy will be retained in any shape, manner or form.

Some companies will use a scramble and replace computer program to randomly change your name (such as using J. Williams or misspelling it slightly) and then the above system of detection will not work. The most effective way of detecting unauthorized usage is to seed your list with completely fictitious names. This can be accomplished by establishing a post office box in a fictitious name and using it only for detection of unauthorized list usage.

HOW DO I SELL MY LIST?

There are several ways to sell your list. You can advertize directly in local ad or marketing magazines that your list is for sale. Nationally *Folio Magazine*, published out of Stamford, CT, is a wonderful tool for advertising your list. You can also contact a listing agent and have them represent your list for a percentage of the sale. Their fee is usually about 20% and this may be a worthwhile alternative as they have contacts beyond any you could probably make advertising your list yourself. Generally the listing manager handles sales and collections, record keeping, and develops comprehensive ad campaigns which may include listing your availability along with others.

WHAT ABOUT INCREASING MY OWN SUBSCRIBER BASE?

Another side of list management is the use of outside lists to increase your own subscription or product revenues. If you do want to do a mailing run from a rented list, the first thing you must do is develop a strong idea of the audience you want to reach. If you are a regional magazine on fly-fishing, you know you need the names and addresses of people in the particular region you service. What is your audience? I would guess males, between the ages of 18 and 60. So you only want to purchase a listing of males' names. Does your publication appeal to any particular trade sector? Maybe fly tackle shops and sporting equipment shops would be interested in selling your magazine at their counter or news stand.

> *The most effective way of detecting unauthorized usage is to seed your list with completely fictitious names.*

At this point I see a need to divide your mailing into two groups—profession and subscription. I would send one type of mailing to the professional group and another to the subscribers. Now, as a mailing is an expensive proposition it's best to test the waters with a sampling before doing an extensive and expensive mailing.

LIST TESTING

Testing a list (also called sampling) refers to the taking of a small sample from a list and mailing one type of literature to those selected few Based on their response to the mailing, the next step would be to either redesign the letter or brochure if the results were negative, or mail a second testing with a broader section of the list. Results considered positive are usually in the one half of one percent response range. One percent is considered wonderful and anything above that is miraculous.

The price you ask for your subscription and the terms of payment are critical and can be tested by mailing samples. Asking full price and cash with any one will reduce the response. Offering a free premium, cash prizes, free offers, and low prices will increase reader response.

While there are no certainties in list testing there is a law of probabilities. There are too many variables to keep list testing from ever

> *Results considered positive are usually in the one half of one percent response range. One percent is considered wonderful and anything above that is miraculous.*

becoming an exact science. By using statistical mathematics, listing professionals can calculate a probability factor that may be highly accurate, but there seems to be no way to guarantee success.

DIRECT RESPONSE LISTS

There are specific lists available which include the names of people who have previously responded to a direct marketing effort. If you obtain access to such lists, you will be mailing to those people predisposed or receptive to buying or subscribing by mail.

SEASONALITY

The time of year plays an important factor in the success of your mailing. The Kleid Company in 1985 compiled and released a listing of the top months in mail, depending on who you wish to attract. This is an important step in correlating volume of mail to profitability and shows how strong the seasonal factor is in deciding when to mail literature to increase your subscriber base.

DAY OF THE WEEK

According to several experts there are certain days of the week that generate more direct mail business than others. If you are mailing to a business, Friday is the worst day to send out mailers. Because of the weekend and the natural tendency of people to do their clean-up work on Friday, businesses receive more mail on Monday and have less time to pay attention to it than any other day of the week. The highest rate of returns result when mail is received on Tuesday, Wednesday, or Thursday. Home mailings received on Friday or Saturday are most fruitful as the recipient has more time to go through the mail.

THE MOST COMMON DIRECT MAIL MISTAKES

Getting personal

Sending mail that is slick and impersonal does not move people to respond. Novices make the mistake of trying to be too clever and end up alienating the people they are trying to reach. Generally, the more a mailing resembles a personal letter the better the results. Even a letter that has the recipient's name in the body that was obviously entered by a computer pulls more than one that uses Dear Sir. A letter with the signature in different ink from the black in the words will pull better. The more personal, caring, and direct the tone, the greater the response will be.

Easy replying

Another common mistake made by novice mailers is not making it easy for addressees to respond. Sending a reply card increases responses. Even better results are obtained by making the reply card self-addressed and stamped. The very best results are obtained when the reply card has the addressee's name imprinted and all he or she needs to do is drop the card in the mail.

Calling in expert advice

The single biggest mistake that can be made by an advertiser is handling the designing of the mailing himself. Leave this to experts. It has been proven that bad ad campaigns can actually decrease sales. By handling the creation of the campaign you could be hurting your company sales! Get some good outside advice even if you handle the mailing yourself.

David Ogilvy tells of several wrong advertising campaigns in his book, *Ogilvy on Advertising*. "The wrong advertising can actually reduce the sales of a product. I am told that George Hay Brown, at one time the head of marketing research at Ford, inserted advertisements in every other copy of *Reader's Digest*. At the end of the year, the people who had not been exposed to the advertising had bought more Fords than those who had.

In another survey it was found that the consumption of a certain brand of beer was lower among people who remembered its advertising than those who did not. The brewer had spent millions of dollars on advertising which un-sold his beer."

KEEPING RECORDS

When using direct mail to increase subscription sales it is extremely important to document results in order to ascertain if your campaign is successful. You may have to change the typeface and send out your mailer again. Watch the response rates and you will know what works for you.

Keeping track of the results will help you to learn what works for you. By paying careful attention to the meaning of your results you can begin to plan carefully and project times of increased cash flow and protect yourself from the down times. You will also begin to learn which mailings increase business, the best time of year to do mailings, and how to protect yourself from wasteful mailings that are expensive and ineffective.

THE DOWN SIDE OF DIRECT MAIL

[Bill] Ford [President of Online Computer Systems, Inc.] says his company, which makes several CD-ROM software products, has had little success with direct sales because of the extremely high cost per sale. Direct mail has performed even more poorly. "We buy mailing lists, write glorious letters about the future of this technology, get lots of inquiries, and then we don't sell anything," he says, shaking his head. "We're not quitting, but we're not happy with the results."

From *Computer Dealer*.

Some of the numbers you should be tracking are:

1. Actual mail quantity.
2. Number of orders obtained.
3. Percent response.
4. Package cost per thousand.
5. List cost per thousand.
6. Total cost.
7. Total cost per thousand.
8. Gross cost per subscriber.
9. Percent credit.
10. Percent bad pay.
11. Net subscribers.
12. Net percent response.
13. Net cost per subscriber.
14. Total revenue (on net).
15. Net revenue (total revenue minus total cost).
16. Net revenue per subscriber.

> *Whichever way you decide to use lists to increase revenues, direct mail marketing is a highly profitable area of advertising and shouldn't be overlooked in your quest for a higher share of your market or some extra capital to run your business.*

Moment of truth

What do these figures mean and how do we arrive at them? We will use the following arbitrarily selected numbers as examples to help you follow the formulas below:

1. Actual mail quantity. From the postal receipt received at the post office by the mailing shop or whomever mailed them.

2. Number of orders. These numbers are generated through the order entry system in the company uses.

3. Percent response. Based on the number of orders divided by the mail quantity:
    If we mailed 150,615 and received 3,269 orders it would look like this:

    $$\frac{3{,}269}{150{,}615} = 2.17\%$$

4. Cost per thousand. This is the actual cost which includes: promotion package, merge/purge costs, letter shop costs to insert, sort and mail including postage.

5. List cost per thousands. Based on actual rental costs.

6. Total cost for this promotion. Actual costs are derived from invoices received for services plus postage.

7. Total cost per thousands. This is arrived at by taking the total cost divided by the mailing quantity:

    $$\frac{\$41{,}451}{150{,}615} = \$275.21/M$$

8. Cost per subscriber. The total cost ($41,451) divided by the number of orders (3,269) equals $12.68.

9. Percent credit. Since the offer included a bill-me option, this factor is input at order entry for billing purposes. In this case, 90.4 percent of the orders requested credit.

10. Percent bad pay. The 33.16 percent figure is developed from the billing cycle. The figure represents customers or prospects that did not pay.

11. Net subscribers. This figure represents the final number of paid subscribers:

    — 3,269 gross orders × 90.4 = 2,955 credit orders

    — 3,269 − 2,955 credit orders = 314 cash orders

    Of the 2,955 credit orders, 33.16 percent did not pay:

    — 2,955 × 33.16 percent = 980

    So, if we take 2,955 credit orders minus the 980 who did not pay and add the cash orders, we get net orders of 2,289.

    — 2,955 − 980 + 314 = 2,289

12. Net percent response.

$$\frac{2{,}289}{150{,}615} = 1.52$$

13. Net cost per subscriber.

$$\frac{\$41{,}451}{2{,}289} = \$18.11$$

14. Total revenue (on net).

$$2{,}289 \times 19.97 = \$45{,}711$$

15. Net revenue (total revenue minus total cost).

$$\$45{,}711 - \$41{,}451 = \$4{,}260$$

16. Net revenue per subscriber.

$$\frac{\$4{,}260 \text{ net revenue}}{2{,}289 \text{ net orders}} = \$1.86$$

By tracking these figures you will be able to tell how much money you actually net per subscriber. By keeping figures such as this for each mailing you will begin to develop a keen sense of when is the best and worst time to mail out for your subject matter. You will also be able to track which lists are the most effective. Whichever way you decide to use lists to increase revenues, direct mail marketing is a highly profitable area of advertising and shouldn't be overlooked in your quest for a higher share of your market or some extra capital to run your business. By starting small and keeping excellent records on your success rate you will develop a sure-fire skill to tread water in a highly competitive marketplace. By utilizing your customer list in an effort to earn money you are truly working with entrepreneurial spirit.

Reprinted by permission of Linda Hanson.

Please, Take My Card

By Echo M. Garrett and Webster E. Williams, additional reporting by Gail Ignacio
From *Venture* magazine

[Is it worth spending the money to exhibit at trade shows and conferences? The answer is a qualified "yes," according to this article. For those comtemplating where best to exhibit in 1989, we include a list of CD-ROM related conferences, organized by state.]

While the trade shows Jon Osgood attends may not be as exciting as his company's business—organizing raft and canoe trips for corporate groups—he does get a charge out of the business his attendance generates. "It costs me $500 to exhibit at a two-day show in Los Angeles," says Osgood, 40, founder of Libra Expeditions Inc., Sunland, Calif. "A typical show can generate $30,000 to $40,000 in new business."

Trade shows and conferences are well worth the time and money required to get there, according to many of the 630 respondents to *Venture*'s June survey: 44% attend trade shows three or more times a year, 17% attend twice a year, and 28% attend once a year. Only 5% said they never darken the door. Conferences are only slightly less popular: 34% frequently attend conferences, 44% sometimes attend, 19% rarely attend, and only 4% never go to conferences.

Thom Golden, founder and president of Dr. Baby Proofer Inc., Dallas, a retailer of child safety products, finds both trade shows and conferences useful. He is among the 32% of respondents who attend conferences to learn how to run their businesses better. An additional 31% consider networking the primary motivation for going to conferences, while 16% think attending increases their companies' visibility.

Golden, 40, like 19% of our respondents, depends on trade shows to increase his company's visibility. "From the name Dr. Baby Proofer, people don't understand what I do," says the entrepreneur. "One person thought I was an abortionist, and another thought I devised tests for determining fatherhood."

While 18% claim trade shows generate sales leads and 14% say they actually gained customers, the best reason for attending trade shows, say 30% of our respondents, is to check out the competition. "I go to see what's out there," says Michael J. Rosen, president and founder of Labrynth Systems Inc., Great Neck, N.Y., a software development company. But like the majority (57%) of our respondents, he has yet to exhibit his own wares. "All the big companies that pay more money are put in the middle of the floor, and then the small guys get lost," says Rosen, who attends three trade shows a year.

Osgood, among the 43% who do exhibit at trade shows, knows exactly how effective each show is for his company. He codes the brochures at his booth at each show. When potential clients call up, they are asked for the code on the brochure. If a show fails to produce enough interest, he marks it off his list.

Gerald W. Timm exhibits at trade shows to increase name recognition, like 38% of our respondents; to garner new clients, like 34%; and to introduce new products, like 22%. "The price to exhibit isn't really a factor, because there are certain shows we have to be at in my industry," says Timm, 47, founder, president, and chief executive officer of Dacomed Corp., Minneapolis, a manufacturer of diagnostic tests and therapeutic implant prostheses. On the low end, says Timm, the cost may be $3,000, but some shows may cost exhibitors as much as $50,000.

In fact more than two-thirds of those in the manufacturing business exhibit at trade shows, followed by 57% of those with high-technology companies. Seventy percent of respondents whose companies have revenues of $10 million to $50 million have had exhibits in the past 12 months. Not surprising, the least likely to exhibit (27%) are respondents whose companies have less than $500,000 in revenues.

What would make conferences and trade shows more useful to entrepreneurs? "The speaker at the last conference I attended hadn't done her homework and addressed a topic that the audience wasn't interested in," says Osgood, one of the 28% who say speakers could use some polishing.

Sid Phillips, 36, vice president of marketing for Professional Lighting & Supply Co. Inc., Greensboro, N.C., agreed with the 32% who say that the content of conference programs needs improvement. At the last conference Phillips attended, the source of his problem was a brochure that didn't accurately describe what was being offered. The cost of attending is also a sore point with 23% of our respondents. Says Phillips, "Most of the conferences reserve rooms at top-of-the-line hotels. If you want to be more economical, you're on your own." Another 19% say conference sessions were too long, and 18% would prefer different locations.

A chronic problem at trade shows, says Rosen, is the chore of simply getting registered. Timm agrees that the little annoyances are what get you down, like "the location of your booth, the electrician who doesn't come."

Meeting and greeting rates high with conference and trade show attendees. A whopping 77% of our respondents prefer to have time to meet other participants. Golden, however, was one of the 21% who hold a contrary view. "I like to have activities scheduled constantly at a conference or a show," he says. "I can spend my free time before or after the show meeting people and sight-seeing, but during it I want to get my money's worth."

Reprinted from the September 1988 issue of *VENTURE, For Entrepreneurial Business Owners and Investors,* by special permission. Copyright © 1988 Venture Magazine, Inc., 521 Fifth Ave., New York, NY 10175-0028.

CD-ROM AND RELATED CONFERENCES

State	Conference	City	Date
CA	OE LASE '89	Los Angeles	01/15/89–01/20/89
	Optical Data Storage Topical Meeting	Los Angeles	01/17/89–01/19/89
	Electronic Imaging Forum VI	San Francisco	01/30/89–01/31/89
	CD-ROM: Technology and Applications	Los Angeles	March
	Interactive Videodisc Applications and Training Seminar	Los Angeles	03/13/89–03/14/89
	Seybold Seminars '89	San Francisco	03/13/89–03/17/89
	14th Annual West Coast Computer Faire	San Francisco	03/17/89–03/19/89
	Microsoft's Fourth International Conference on CD-ROM	Anaheim	03/28/89–03/30/89
	Electronic Imaging '89 West	Pasadena	04/10/89–04/13/89
	Defense and Government Computer Graphics Conference/Spring '89	Anaheim	04/26/89
	Federal Computer Conference/Spring '89	Anaheim	04/26/89
	Optical Storage '89	San Jose	05/10/89–05/12/89
	CD-ROM Developers Seminar '89	San Jose	05/18/89
	ASIS Mid-Year	San Diego	05/21/89–05/24/89
	AIIM Conference and Exposition	San Francisco	06/05/89–06/08/89
	HyperExpo	San Francisco	06/20/89–06/22/89
	Imaging: The Multimedia Conference and Exposition	San Francisco	06/20/89–06/22/89
	Third Annual *Optical Drive and Media Manufacturing*	San Francisco	07/25/89–07/27/89
	Optical Disk Workshop	Los Angeles	September
	Data Storage '89	San Jose	09/18/89–09/20/89
	Supercomputing World Conference	San Francisco	10/17/89–10/20/89
CO	CD-ROM Application Development Seminar	Boulder	Series
DC	Annual NFAIS Conference	Washington	02/26/89–03/01/89
	FOSE Conference and Exposition	Washington	03/06/89–03/09/89
	CD-ROM Developers Seminar '89	Washington	04/12/89

State	Conference	City	Date
DC	Fed Micro Conference and Exposition	Washington	09/06/89–09/07/89
	CD-ROM EXPO	Washington	10/02/89–10/05/89
	Defense and Government Computer Graphics Conference/Fall '89	Washington	10/23/89
	Federal Computer Conference/Fall '89	Washington	10/23/89
	ASIS Annual	Washington	10/29/89–11/02/89
	Interactive Videodisc Applications and Training Seminar	Washington	11/20/89–11/21/89
FL	Optics '89: OSA Annual Meeting	Orlando	10/15/89–10/20/89
GA	Interactive Videodisc Applications and Training Seminar	Atlanta	10/02/89–10/03/89
IL	LaserActive '89: Chicago	Chicago	April
	COMDEX/Spring '89	Chicago	04/10/89–04/13/89
	Optical Disk Workshop	Chicago	May
	International Summer Consumer Electronics Show	Chicago	06/03/89–06/06/89
	CD-ROM Developers Seminar '89	Chicago	10/16/89
LA	ARMA	New Orleans	10/02/89–10/05/89
MA	Optical Disk Workshop	Boston	March
	The Technology Forum	Cambridge	04/03/89–04/05/89
	LaserActive '89: Boston	Boston	October
	Electronic Imaging '89 East	Boston	10/02/89–10/05/89
	The Seventh Annual Seybold Executive Forum	Boston	11/08/89–11/10/89
NV	International Winter Consumer Electronics Show	Las Vegas	01/07/89–01/10/89
	COMDEX/Fall '89	Las Vegas	11/13/89–11/17/89
NY	Fifth Annual Computer Graphics New York Show	New York	01/17/89–01/19/89
	Interactive Videodisc Applications and Training Seminar	New York	05/08/89–05/09/89

(continued)

CD-ROM AND RELATED CONFERENCES *continued.*

State	Conference	City	Date
NY	National Online Meeting	New York	05/09/89–05/11/89
	SLA Annual Conference	New York	06/10/89–06/15/89
	INFO '89—Information Management Exposition and Conference	New York	10/10/89–10/13/89
	Fourth Annual *Optical Storage for Large Systems*	New York	10/17/89–10/19/89
PA	NCGA '89	Philadelphia	04/16/89–04/20/89
	Groupware - The Next Wave	Allentown	05/25-89–05/28/89
TX	CD-ROM Developers Seminar '89	Dallas	11/16/89
VA	SIGCAT Meeting	Reston	Monthly
	Interactive Videodisc in Education and Training	Arlington	08/23/89–08/25/89
	Optical Information Systems (OIS) '89	Arlington	09/06/89–09/08/89
Canada	LaserActive '89: Toronto	Toronto	June
England	CD-ROM Developers Seminar '89	London	01/31/89
	Third Annual *Optical Memory Applications*	London	04/18/89–04/20/89
West Germany	CD-ROM Developers Seminar '89	Munich	02/07/89

Compiled by Online Press Inc.

PUBLISHING PERSPECTIVES

GAMBLING ON CD-ROM
By John B. Lowe

WHAT TYPES OF PRODUCTS ARE CD-ROM PUBLISHERS LOOKING FOR?
By Ron Rietdyk

CD-ROM PROPOSAL GUIDELINES
By Ed Kelly

Gambling on CD-ROM

By John B. Lowe
From the *Library Journal*

[In this article, John Lowe uses the analogy of a card game to describe the CD-ROM publishing scene and to explain why many publishers are taking a cautious, "wait and see" position rather than whole-heartedly embracing the new technology.]

The CD-ROM revolution is upon us, and, at least in the beginning, it is going to be expensive. After all, someone is going to have to pay for the learning and experimentation necessary to make this new publishing format work. Eventually, many of the existing players will of necessity fold their cards and find another game to play. There is a tacit understanding of this among the current players, as is indicated by the caution with which new products are being introduced into the marketplace.

Who, then, is going to finance the learning curve? Who will pay for creating the equipment and software upon which the industry will be based? And how will this new medium affect other trends in the information industry, such as the growing privatization of data gathering and dissemination?

Many weighty factors influence the answers to these questions. This article will note in passing the importance that standards, [1] marketing, [2] pricing strategies, [3] and the nature of information as a commodity [4] have on the success of CD-ROM technology. Also noted en passant are the difficult problems associated with making the decision on whether and how to network resources, [5] which may dramatically alter how information is actually distributed once it is electronically published.

CD-ROM represents a trump card in the publishing world. It is built on a highly successful, well-established recording technology and promises great economies of scale. However, until its place in publishing is established, each player is going to expect the others to pay for opening the game and keeping it going.

CD-ROM ECONOMICS

The CD-ROM is a publishing medium, much like paper. Making the master disc is expensive, as is the typesetting for a book; pressing copies is inexpensive, as is printing the copies of a book once the plates have been made. CD-ROM is therefore a volume-dependent medium. Over and above the cost of the original data and its organization, one disc costs about $4050, 10 cost about $430 each and 1000 cost about $14 each. Since the costs for data acquisition and preprocessing are relatively fixed regardless of the number of copies made, they too become lower and lower per copy as volume increases.

By Peter B. Schipma. From the January 1988 issue of the Journal of American Society for Information Sciences. Reprinted by permission of John Wiley & Sons, Inc.

THE PLAYERS

The "up-front" costs of the CD-ROM revolution must be borne by either the information providers (who will naturally expect to recoup their expenses over time), or the information consumers (who may be willing to take some of the risks themselves in order to save money and maintain control in the future).

In the information providers' corner we have:

1. The private sector. These institutions are responsible for most "information products:" journals and their indices, reference works, monographs, and so on. It includes both producers of hardcopy as well as vendors of online services. In some cases purveyors of hardcopy compete with their online counterparts; in other cases the electronic and hardcopy products are the left and right hands of the same entity. Most of these are for-profit institutions, and if they could be assured of making the same or more money from CD-ROM products, they would happily support such endeavors.

2. The public sector. Included here are nonprofit organizations such as ERIC, and federal, state, and local governments. Often the information produced is in the public domain, and is fair game for those who would produce CD-ROM as a value-added product. In many cases, these institutions are required by law to collect and distribute information. Therefore, if CD-ROM costs were to drop below current production costs, these institutions would gladly support the CD revolution. Note also that these institutions often support innovation (public and private) through grants and subsidies.

In the information consumers' corner, the same divisions of public and private exist, but the pie may be sliced in other ways as well:

1. Educational institutions, both public and private, are among the largest consumers of information. Indeed, much of the attention of the CD-ROM developers has been directed at educational institutions and academic libraries in particular. For example, two-tier pricing for subscriptions, in which libraries pay higher rates than others, provides additional incentive to information providers to give this group special attention. [6]

2. Public institutions, especially public libraries. Inasmuch as public libraries serve the "public at large," they represent a sizable section of the consumer market for CD-ROM products. It is unlikely, however, that they can support much of the development of CD-ROM products themselves; rather, they are likely to become users of the more popular CD-ROM products, and to widen the market for CD-ROM generally.

3. Individuals. Certainly the dream of CD-ROM providers is that the CD-ROM will become an indispensable household item,

as much or even more than the PC has. Certainly audio CD has been widely embraced, and as the information age progresses there are good reasons to think that CD-ROM may enjoy a comparable status. Corporate consumers may be included here, since the forces driving corporate consumption are similar to those of individuals.

THE GAME

What are the stakes in CD-ROM publishing? That is, what is the ante, how much can the stakes be raised, and how much can be won (both in terms of financial rewards as well as in terms of improved access and function)?

The "ante" consists not only of the cost of producing a sufficient quantity of CD-ROMs, but also in developing a hardware base: the microcomputers, CD-ROM drives, and other required goodies.

1. Development costs. These are the costs associated with acquiring the data (licensing it, keying it), developing specifications and documentation, producing any special software needed to either produce the disc or access the data on disc once mastered.

2. The cost of producing the data in a format suitable for mastering on CD-ROM. These costs are highly dependent on the type of application. Some databases may require only trivial preparation before being mastered, others may require substantial effort in the way of generating indices and formatting.

3. The cost of producing a master CD. CD-ROM technology is similar to LP record technology: plastic copies are stamped from a master disc. Production of a master disc currently costs in the range of $3000.

4. The costs of duplication. This is a fixed cost per duplicate, and declines as volume goes up.

5. Distribution costs. This is the cost to package discs, mail them, and handle special processing (returns, refunds, other administrative overhead).

REFERENCES

[1] Lowe, J. B., Lynch, C. A., and Brownrigg, E. B., "Publishing Bibliographic Data on Optical Disk: A Prototypical Application and Its Implications," *SPIE Vol. 529, Optical Mass Data Storage*, Los Angeles, January 22–24, 1985, page 231.

[2] Bishop, E. F., and Clayton, A., "An Application of Market Research Techniques to the Dissemination of Scientific and Technical Information," *The Value of Information: Collection of Papers*. 6th Mid-Year Meeting, ASIS, May 19–21, 1977, page 14.

[3] Lindquist, Mats G., *The Dynamics of Information Search Services*. Stockholm: Royal Institute for Technology Library, 1978, pages 22–23.

[4] Braunstein, Yale, "Information as a Commodity," in *Information Services: Economics, Management, and Technology*. Mason, 1981.

[5] Lynch, Clifford, *Optical Disk Database Servers*. Proceedings, ASIS Midyear Conference, May 1986.

[6] O'Connor, Mary Ann, "Education and CD-ROM," *Optical Information Systems*, July/August 1986, pages 329–331.

[7] The steps and cost involved in CD-ROM production are covered thoroughly in Section III of *CD-ROM: The New Papyrus*, cited below.

[8] Laub, Leonard, "What Is CD-ROM?" in *CD-ROM: The New Papyrus*. Microsoft Press, 1986, page 48.

> *CD-ROM represents a trump card in the publishing world. It is built on a highly successful, well-established recording technology and promises great economies of scale. However, until its place in publishing is established, each player is going to expect the others to pay for opening the game and keeping it going.*

6. The costs of the workstation. Given the performance characteristics of CD-ROM, it is likely that only a small number of users can simultaneously access a particular disc. It has even been asserted that CD-ROM should realistically be used at only one workstation at a time. The workstation may or may not require additional hardware in the form of added memory or graphics capability. Just how much CD-ROM applications can "piggyback" on the installed base of microcomputers is unclear.

7. The cost of the CD-ROM drive. The computer version of the CD player is quite similar to the audio version. The cost of this component has rapidly become a small fraction of the total cost of the system due to the effects of standardization and consumer acceptance of CD audio products.

8. The cost of software using the CD. Currently, each CD does require its own program in order to be used. Much of the cost of development will have been absorbed in the initial design phases of the publishing effort. Also, it may now be possible to use existing software to access CDs. [7]

The "betting" is represented by the cost of maintenance, updating, and distributing discs and other recurring costs; also, we should include here some more intangible trade-offs, such as market share and exposure that affect the commitment of the player to CD-ROM publishing.

1. If there is no change in the data on the CD, then more can be produced from the same master, at marginal costs, though they can be sold at the price comparable to the originals, which carried the burden of the costs of development and pre-production. Indeed, this notion is well understood though not much discussed, and is one of the major attractions to CD-ROM publishing. In contrast, the marginal costs of hardcopy publishing are quite a substantial portion of original costs. [8]

2. Hardware and software maintenance. Since the technology is so new, this is a bigger unknown than it appears on the surface; nevertheless, a great deal of experience in managing this kind of technology exists, upon which CD-ROM developers can draw.

3. The price the market will bear. There is certainly a great deal of price elasticity in the information business, which is both a

good and bad thing: it's good because there is some room to maneuver, and it's bad inasmuch as it makes it difficult to price products to start with. [*For more discussion on this point, see the section entitled "Pricing a CD-ROM."*]

PLAYING YOUR HAND: STRATEGY

CD-ROM publishing has aspects of the two "traditional" types of information service: hardcopy publication and online search and retrieval. On one hand, the user receives an entire work on CD-ROM, and on the other, they access it bit by bit, in the same fashion as an online search. Indeed, here is the crux of the matter: the unit cost of the database, distributed over the user base, may be exorbitant (especially if spread over the current very small base); on the other hand, there is no reasonable way to make a per use charge on a stand-alone CD-ROM system. Furthermore, when a database is distributed in its entirety on CD-ROM, the use (and consequently the value and sales) of printed products may fall. If the data are available through an existing online service, the online version may not be used enough to merit keeping it available via dial-up.

The users of information (or at least those who pay for the use of it) will be making the obvious calculations: If I buy the CD-ROM version of a database, how much can I save in dial-up, subscription, or purchase costs? If the cost of the CD-ROM system is comparable to the cost of existing service, it is quite likely that the user will select the CD-ROM product. Of course, other factors besides economics enter into the decision: increased functionality, "sex appeal," anxieties about reliability and shareability, and so on.

Initially, CD-ROM products will be accepted if they meet existing needs at the same or lower cost as comparable printed or dial-up products. [9] Later, however, different principles may come into play.

> *If the cost of the CD-ROM system is comparable to the cost of existing service, it is quite likely that the user will select the CD-ROM product. Of course, other factors besides economics enter into the decision: increased functionality, "sex appeal," anxieties about reliability and shareability, and so on.*

LEARNING TO SHARE

It may not be possible to deliberately decide a priori how to implement the aforementioned "different principles," and how to divide the spoils of the exploitation of CD-ROM in such a way as to ensure that everyone gets a fair share. But if it were, consider this scenario, which should appeal to those who advocate a laissez faire attitude toward information distribution, as well as those who would extend the "democratization of information" to this new medium.

Private information brokers contract with public agencies to take the results of public domain data-gathering efforts and produce a set of compatible products. These two players, now linking arms with the educational and research institutions of this country, arrange to have academia develop the tools necessary to use these products in the academic environment. The grants process and other public and private funds are used to subsidize both the initial installation of the hardware base (hardware manufacturers discounting their prices in return for volume and exposure) as well as the R&D effort required to produce workable tools for production and access. Public libraries provide a "litmus test" of new products, giving both financial backers and product developers feedback on public acceptance of new techniques and databases.

A user community (small and somewhat esoteric) springs up. In this better-defined world, information producers can introduce new products, containing costs by using the newly developed expertise and distributing the costs over a growing user base. Other institutions, public and private, also now water at this trough. Eventually, most publishing migrates to "dense media," providing wider and fuller access to information and at a lower cost than previously possible.

Too utopian? The reader may be justifiably skeptical of this vision of the future, but there is evidence that some of its elements are already coming to pass, though right now most of the players are holding their cards pretty close to their chests.

Reprinted from the July 1988 issue of the *Library Journal* by special permission. Copyright © 1988 by Reed Publishing, USA, a division of Reed Holdings Inc.

What Types of Products Are CD-ROM Publishers Looking For?

By Ron Rietdyk

["In 1989, CD-ROM products must move into the hands of the professionals," says Ron Rietdyk in this analysis of trends in CD-ROM publishing. Although the price of CD-ROM drives must come down for CD-ROM to gain widespread acceptance, Rietdyk feels the onus is also on publishers to develop the products people need.]

CD-ROM publishers look for a bestseller: a product that will stimulate sale of CD-ROM drives as Lotus 1-2-3 and dBase stimulated sales of personal computers. Bestsellers establish a large enough user base to justify the development and distribution of exciting new CD-ROM products and, consequently, open up the market for other, more specialized, products.

At the end of 1988, CD-ROM bestsellers can be defined as products with a sales volume of 1000 units or more. Because vendors generally are not open about their sales, we have to estimate from our own experiences and from various secondhand sources. On this basis, we can assume that at least ten products fit the bestseller criterion, among them *Books in Print*,

RON RIETDYK

Home: Cambridge, Massachusetts
Job: President, SilverPlatter Information, Inc.
Quote: *"Until recently CD-ROM publishers were knocking on the doors of information providers asking for their data to distribute on CD-ROM. Today the situation has reversed itself. Information providers, who are now realizing the potential, are in the queue to get CD products out to the market."*

ERIC database (combined sales through different vendors), *The Grolier Encyclopedia, PC-SIG,* and *Microsoft Bookshelf.*

TODAY'S COMMERCIAL MARKET

Currently, the CD-ROM market is not very different from the CD audio market of a few years ago. Lack of bestseller products and too few CD drives limit the growth of the market. Our experience with CD-ROM demonstrates that, once the equipment is in place and a product has been used for some time, additional products are purchased and the production of even more products is requested of vendors.

To date, libraries are the largest market for CD-ROM products. Therefore, the natural target for developers of early CD-ROM products has been bibliographic and reference databases and directories that were previously available only in print form or through online access. Ease of use of the CD-ROM products, unlimited access, and a fixed price structure justified the initial high prices of these products.

NEW MARKETS

Because most of the products developed so far are oriented toward reference and research, the potential market has been limited. Once professionals in markets such as law, medicine, and engineering are reached, the volume of CD-ROM sales will increase tremendously. But with a few exceptions, such as *Poisonindex* from Micromedex (used in emergency rooms), *One Source* from Lotus (used by investors), and *OSH-ROM* from SilverPlatter (used by occupational safety and health specialists), most available CD-ROM products have not gained the attention of these markets. Because these types of professionals need actual data that they can use immediately on the job, the next logical step for CD publishers is to produce data banks, statistical data, and full-text products.

Overseas interest in CD-ROM has increased in the last year. As a result of this interest, some U.S. companies are now shipping almost 40 percent of their CD-ROM products to foreign countries. From this foreign interest, a market in developing countries has clearly emerged [*see Julie Schwerin's article, entitled "The European CD-ROM Market," for a discussion of the market in Europe*]. These countries are bypassing the paper media and going directly to electronic resources.

NEW PRODUCTS

In 1989, CD-ROM publishers should concentrate on developing products with the following characteristics:

- Emphasis on the needs of the professional end user.

- Inclusion of pictures (preferably in color) and graphics.

- Inclusion of multiple databases on a single CD or multiple databases merged into a single file.
- Ability to run on equipment other than the PC.
- Ability to be used without restrictions in a network environment.

In 1987, CD-ROM products made the giant leap from demonstrations at conferences and exhibits to hands-on use in the library environment. In 1988, CD-ROM has gained widespread acceptance in libraries. In 1989, CD-ROM products must move into the hands of the professionals.

One important prerequisite will be lower prices for CD-ROM drives. End-user prices ought to drop below $500 in order to overcome the initial investment obstacle.

Access through networking has become a prominent issue for academic and corporate libraries. Networking will make multiple-disc databases easier to sell because the entire database set can be mounted and accessed by anyone in the network. Publishers with products that can be used in a network without complex surcharges will sell more products and, in the end, achieve a larger market share.

WHAT TRENDS AND PRODUCTS WILL EMERGE IN 1989?

Health databases with a clinical orientation will provide information to physicians so that they can make diagnostic decisions and get the latest research information on diseases. Atlases of the human body will guide doctors and students through human anatomy with pictures and outlines.

Reference databases will be linked to the actual full-text documents, either through online document delivery systems or through distribution of the most requested articles in full-text form on CD-ROM.

> *Publishers with products that can be used in a network without complex surcharges will sell more products and, in the end, achieve a larger market share.*

There will be more of a demand for multiple products covering the same topic. CD-ROM publishers will respond by offering families of products in series form. Combining related databases on one CD will provide end users with a single source of information and thus make access easier and faster. Although this idea is an attractive one for users, pricing products from multiple suppliers can cause complications and interfere with the smooth introduction of the concept.

Marketeers, telephone operators, and other people who need frequent retrieval of telephone numbers will welcome the availability of CD-ROMs that store the data now available in the white pages of a phone book. Various publishers are working on products that enable fast retrieval of name and telephone number. A couple of these products will be available in 1989.

Shortage of space continues to push libraries to look for ways to reduce the storage of out-of-date material. To help solve this problem, some publishers will develop CD-ROM versions for the backfiles of their journals. These CD products will be sold in the same way annual cumulative paper indexes are sold. Subscribers to the printed product will receive a CD at the end of the year and can then discard the printed version.

The IBM personal computer and compatibles, the most popular vehicle for CD-ROM products to date, will face serious competition from the Apple Macintosh. Because the Macintosh's more intuitive user interface will attract the professionals who are the end users, CD-ROM products must be made to work in the Mac environment in order to sell well in this market.

Although we will see more trends and products evolve as 1989 passes, what's been noted here indicates the diversity of the CD-ROM marketplace—one that will become more and more driven by user demands. Publishers who listen carefully will know what their next steps must be.

[Ron Rietdyk received his Masters degree from the Technical University of Delft. After various jobs in different software companies, he started his own information-service company, Scan Laser, in Amsterdam. In 1985, he founded the U.S. branch of SilverPlatter. Rietdyk lives in Cambridge, MA, and believes one hour of Zazen (sitting silently, doing nothing) keeps him alive in this hectic industry.]

CD-ROM Proposal Guidelines

By Ed Kelly

[We conclude this section with some nuts-and-bolts advice from the Acquisitions Manager of a leading CD-ROM publisher about what publishers look for in a proposal for a CD-ROM product. As Ed Kelly explains, it's not enough to simply come up with an idea. The people evaluating your proposal will want to know why you think the product will be successful and what you can contribute to its production.]

CD-ROM is probably the most fascinating segment of the computer industry. Current CD-ROM applications range in subject from agriculture to medicine; from the Bible to business; from science and electronics to real estate. In the future, because of the extraordinary explosion of CD-ROM technology, consumers will have a great new range of CD-ROM applications available to them—applications that combine the most refined images and the highest fidelity sound and that present diverse information for users to interact with in ways not yet imagined.

The purpose of this article is to provide a few guidelines on how you can propose your idea for a CD-ROM product to a publisher and bring it to reality.

Proposing a CD-ROM product does not require that you be extremely knowledgeable about CD-ROM technology. You need not have produced a CD-ROM project or be a computer professional. What is important is that you provide the publisher with a clear understanding of the product concept and your contribution to its success.

The world of CD-ROM publishing is open to literally everyone who has a good, marketable idea: artist, writer, academic, musician, or professional of any type. That's because, just as anyone can have an idea for a book, anyone can have an idea for a CD-ROM publication.

THE BASICS

CD-ROM publishing has evolved somewhat in its few years of existence. In the early days, a CD-ROM project consisted mainly of text, often of collections of books that had been translated from paper to electronic form. Today, however,

ED KELLEY

Home: Woodinville, Washington
Job: Acquisitions Manager, Microsoft Press CD-ROM Group
Quote: "It's easy for anyone to be overawed by the pace of computer technology, which tends at times to obscure the human role. But recent developments, especially in CD-ROM and multimedia, pave the way for a new era of human creative expression. The future of publishing and personal computers are, indeed, in the hands of creative individuals in every area of expertise."

a CD-ROM project can combine databases of screen images, text, animation, and sound.

As you make your proposal, you should have available detailed information about the databases to be included, a clear understanding of the market for the application, and the ability to discern how applications lend themselves specifically to CD-ROM technology.

THE CONCEPT

The essence of a CD-ROM project is the idea, or concept, clearly defined and expressed, which can mature into a useful CD-ROM application. Existing at first only in the proposer's mind, the concept and its presentation are what will interest a publisher in backing the project. As can be seen from current CD-ROM applications, the concept can encompass almost any subject.

You must make your idea clear to the publisher. The best way to do this is to prepare a preliminary story board to submit with your written proposal. It can be done either on paper or electronically and should clearly convey the interactions of the various elements and the way the product ideally should look and feel. The publisher needs to understand your proposed product's purpose and usefulness to your intended audience.

DATABASES

A CD-ROM application will probably include a number of databases—collections of data that can be anything from a massive assembly of government statistics requiring graphics software to display graphs and charts to an encyclopedia of literature or science incorporating images, sound, and animation.

As a result, a publisher will be looking for you to clearly delineate what databases will have to be acquired for the project. Obviously, the publisher also has to know where they can be acquired and what the acquisitions will cost.

Related to this component is the issue of timeliness. Some databases—books of poetry for instance—are pretty stable in their value. On the other hand, a database of government census statistics is volatile; it becomes more obsolete with each passing year. An important question for you to answer as proposer is, "How long will it be before any of the included databases becomes obsolete?" Perhaps the database can be updated on a regular schedule. In that case, what would you recommend as a time interval between updates?

Another factor related to databases is the condition of the material. Is the information in machine-readable form or will the text and images need to be scanned? Is the audio in digital form? Answering these questions will be helpful.

MARKETING

The main reason anyone puts effort into publishing a CD-ROM product is to make the product attractive enough to sell into a market willing to buy it. As a result, a publisher will expect you to clearly indicate the market for your CD-ROM application. Your proposal should speak in terms of who will buy it, why they will buy it, and what you think they should expect to pay.

YOUR BACKGROUND AND PARTICIPATION

CD-ROM applications are a cooperative effort. This effort includes people who complete the application's program code; others who can prepare and format the data, develop the human interface, links, and interactions; and still others who write and edit the documentation. With the levels of complexity required to produce an acceptable and successful product, the production team personnel will represent a major commitment of resources to any CD-ROM applications project.

You may want to participate at some level in the production of your CD-ROM idea, or perhaps you feel your name, associations, or past accomplishments will strengthen and legitimize the product. In that case, the publisher would be interested in your credentials—the special expertise you can bring to the project—and in the specific contribution you want to make. Take time in your proposal to tell the publisher about yourself. You should also elaborate, but concisely, on any project you have done. And if you would like to bring in a production team, the publisher needs to know the backgrounds and credentials of the team members, including descriptions of their previous projects and successes.

LICENSING TO A MARKETING ORGANIZATION

If your company is in the information business, but doesn't necessarily want to be in the marketing/distribution or CD-ROM production business, licensing can be an attractive alternative. The advantage is that the licensee does most of the work and carries most of the cost of producing the application and taking it to market, and returns a royalty stream to the information provider.

Even this option doesn't entirely relieve you of the responsibility for the application production, despite what the marketing organization may tell you. As the owner of the information, you know how it is structured and how it will be used, so your participation in the application design process is important. You must also consider how the pricing and marketing of the CD-ROM application may affect your customers who currently use the information. Although licensing to a CD-ROM marketer doesn't require as great an investment on your part, the royalty percentage that you will receive may also be much less than the profit you might make if you produced and marketed the application yourself (or it might be more, if you would have to set up new channels to market and support the application). In other words, don't consider the CD-ROM marketer option as a panacea; instead, evaluate it against your company's needs and goals to see how well it fits with your business strategy.

**By Laura Buddine and Elizabeth Young.
From *The Brady Guide to CD-ROM*.
Copyright © 1987. Used by permission of
the publisher, Brady, New York.**

CONCLUSION

It's easy for anyone to be overawed by the pace of computer technology, which tends at times to obscure the human role. But the recent developments, especially in CD-ROM and multimedia, pave the way for a new era of human expression. The future of publishing and personal computers are, indeed, in the hands of creative individuals in every area of expertise.

[Ed Kelly is Acquisitions Manager for the CD-ROM Divison of Microsoft Press, which publishes optical media for business and consumer markets. He is responsible for the acquisition of materials for multimedia products. Prior to joining Microsoft Corporation, Kelly gained experience in software, technical-book, and magazine publishing at Byte/McGraw-Hill, Addison Wesley, and Houghton Mifflin.]

PRICING A CD-ROM

$49 OR $10,000?
By Matilda Butler

HOW TO PRICE A CD-ROM PRODUCT
By David Roux

HOW TO DECIDE WHAT TO CHARGE FOR A CD-ROM
By Dennis Burke

CD-ROM DISCS AND DRIVES: A DEALER'S PERSPECTIVE
By Barry Cinnamon

SOLUTIONS FOR CD-ROM PRICING AND DATA SECURITY PROBLEMS
By Victor Shear

$49 or $10,000?

By Matilda Butler

[In this article, Matilda Butler discusses the many factors that go into pricing decisions and explains why simple economics keeps the price of CD-ROMs at their current levels.]

Some books sell for $2 while others sell for $200. What's the difference? Sometimes the price reflects a difference in the cost of production, sometimes a difference in the royalty structure. Sometimes the difference is in the cost of marketing, and sometimes in the potential size of the audience. And sometimes the price reflects the difference in the *value of the information* found in the books. For instance, bibliographic information is never priced at the same level as corporate financial information. The marketplace puts a different *value* on each of these types of information. This value is reflected in the price.

Although we are living in the information age, there continues to be confusion over the value of information. Some people think information should be free, while others consider its financial value. Publishers find that the translation of this value into dollars can be simple, or it can be complex.

For example, my company produces many electronic directories. Such directories should be the easiest products to price because they replace sets of mailing labels, information products with known prices. Most mailing labels can be purchased within the range of $40 to about $125 per 1000. Assume there are 50,000 individuals in the set. If the labels themselves were previously marketed at the low end of the range, the new CD-ROM product should sell for $2000, whereas if the labels were marketed at the high end, the CD-ROM version would translate to a $6250 price tag.

Easy to price? No. Most mailing lists are rented for one-time use. The CD-ROM can be used many times for repeated mailings. Therefore, the price should be multiplied at least by a factor of 2 and possibly by a factor of 3. This translates to a minimum of $4000 and a maximum of $18,750.

Now do we have the price? No. The CD-ROM product has considerable flexibility over both the printed directory version and the mailing-label version of this information. While the information has *value,* the new CD-ROM product has *added value.* More can be done with the electronic version than is possible with either of the two other versions. As implemented on CD-ROM, numerous target audiences can be selected to receive sample test mailings. Custom codes can be put on each label. The autodialer

MATILDA BUTLER

Home: Oklahoma City, Oklahoma
Job: President, Knowledge Access International
Quote: *"By the end of the 1990's, 'information integration' (II) will be the key concept. By then, CD-E (Compact Disc-Erasable) will join CD-ROM to provide an inexpensive optical storage solution. Local resources will be maintained using CD-E and distributed or published resources will be stored on CD-ROM. The growing number of knowledge workers will find the integration of information resources so seamless that they will easily move through their tasks, rarely aware of the differences in storage devices.*

"With the hardware technologies moving so rapidly, the challenge for software developers like Knowledge Access is to provide smart systems that help the knowledge worker intelligently manage the vast number of resources. Hardware provides the opportunity for information integration, and software brings it to fruition."

can be activated for telemarketing follow up. User defined, searchable fields with sales information can be added. In other words, the customer has been given control over the information. The price certainly needs to reflect the value-added elements of the product. Even adding a minimal amount for the added functionality, the new price range for this CD-ROM with 50,000 names and addresses becomes $5000 to $20,000.

Now have we got a price? No. Until now, all the pricing considerations have been from the perspective of the data owner. What about the potential customer? Can we achieve a price that is acceptable to the customer? Yes.

Recognize that the customer might be interested in only a fraction of the entire database on the CD-ROM. Do not ask him or her to pay the premium value for the information that we just calculated. If we do, the customer will probably decline and continue with current access from the printed directory or the mailing labels rather than move to the new CD-ROM product. In other words, price matters. You need to find a price that reflects the value of the information and the value of the added functionality, and balance that price with what the customer can pay. Our research indicates that the CD-ROM with 50,000 names and addresses should be priced between $995 and $3995. We have even had one such product, targeted to libraries, priced at $495.

RECOVERING RESEARCH AND DEVELOPMENT INVESTMENT

The cost of research and development is another factor influencing the pricing of CD-ROM products. Although CD-ROM hardware companies have been able to build on their R&D efforts to produce CD audio equipment, CD-ROM software companies have no such base. The introduction of software might be more similar to the introduction of long distance telephoning. When New York-to-San Francisco long distance service was inaugurated in January 1915, a three-minute call cost $20.70, or about $207 in today's money. Bell Laboratories had spent considerable resources on developing the service, and the expense had to be recouped. The cost of long distance calls has dropped significantly since then. A three-minute coast-to-coast call in 1988 is about 86 cents.

The cost of developing CD-ROM retrieval systems, like the cost of developing CD-ROM hardware, must be recovered. Simple systems may not be expensive, but others, with many added-value features, may have a high R&D cost.

The cost of developing the information database must be recovered if it has not already been with other print or electronic versions of the product.

IT COSTS TO MARKET

The CD-ROM industry is still in its infancy. According to Theodore Levitt's four stages in the life of a successful product, CD-ROM products are in Stage 1, Market Development. [1] Levitt describes Stage 1 as a time when "a new product is first brought to market, before there is a proved demand for it and often before it has been fully proved out technically in all respects. Sales are low and creep along slowly."

What are the costs to market these new CD-ROM products? Marketing to an uneducated market is expensive. We have to sell both the technology and the information product. With CD-ROM, this can mean selling hardware, software, and information.

Distribution channels are not yet in place. The cost of creating new ones, or of getting existing ones to carry the new products is expensive. Even direct marketing has its drawbacks because the time from lead generation to closing can be several months.

A LARGE MARKET SUPPORTS A LOW PRICE

A prerequisite of inexpensive CD-ROM products is high sales volume. In the current "chicken or egg" situation, it is impossible to believe in high volume with only about 50,000 drives in place across numerous vertical markets. Let's say that the annual revenue goal for a CD-ROM product is $500,000 in the first year, with increases of 20 percent per year thereafter. A 1987 plan to reach that goal might have been 500 units at $1000. A 1988 plan might be 1000 units at $600, and a 1989 plan might be 2400 units at $300. To reach a $100 price in 1990, we would have to sell 8640 units.

It might be that years of 10,000-unit sales will no longer be the exception when we reach the $100 price and when the number of CD-ROM drives climbs toward one million. For now, however, small market size is one of the fundamental reasons why the $100 CD-ROM disc will remain a rarity.

OTHER PRICING FACTORS

At least four other factors influence the final price: the cost of the same information in other media, production costs, product support costs, and profit.

Balancing the price of information in more than one medium

William Paisley, speaking at the Third International Conference on CD-ROM in 1988 pointed out that "there can be good reasons to price a CD-ROM product at $1000, $10,000, or even $100. One possibility is that the publisher or vendor is protecting the market of an existing print or online product by handicapping the CD-ROM price at a certain multiple of the cost of using the same information in print or online."[2] No publisher is going to cannibalize a current product revenue stream unless it is clear that the new product will open significantly larger markets.

REFERENCES

[1] Levitt, Theodore. *The Marketing Imagination.* New York: The Free Press, 1986.

[2] Paisley, William. "CD-ROM Is Not the Product, Retrieval Is Not the Promotion, $1000 Is Not the Price, the Library Is Not the (Only) Place." Paper presented at Third International Conference on CD-ROM, Seattle, WA, March 1–3, 1988.

Production costs

Assuming the information has already been converted from print to computer tape (a false assumption for most of the world's information), it must be processed, indexed, formatted for display, tested, premastered, and mastered. There must be packaging and user manuals. The more complex the file (multiple fields versus full text) and the "messier" the file (typesetting codes versus pure ASCII), the higher the costs.

CD-ROM TITLE PRICES DROPPING

The average price of a CD-ROM title dropped nearly 13% from 1987 to $1,883, excluding business/financial titles. Business/financial titles were by far the most expensive CD-ROM products this year, at $8,865 per title on average.

Statistics are from the new edition of the Information Industry *Factbook*, published by Digital Information Group (publisher of *IIB*). *Factbook* compares pricing of 233 titles available in 1988 with 90 available in 1987. Even though more titles were available in both years, not all had fixed prices so were excluded from the pricing analysis.

CD-ROM PRICE CHANGES FROM 1987 TO 1988
(by average price)

Market segments	1988	1987	Change
Business/finance	$8,865	$8,236	7.6%
Industry-specific	3,077	3,564	−13.6%
Government	3,039	3,597	−15.5%
Marketing information	2,809	2,610	7.6%
Market research	2,238	n/a	n/a
Professional information	1,829	1,753	4.3%
Health care	1,335	1,767	−24.4%
Science/technology	1,289	1,587	−18.7%
General interest	284	297	−4.5%
Average	2,752	2,615	5.2%
Excluding business/financial	1,883	2,161	−12.9%

The only other market segment that raised prices in 1988 was the professional information segment, which primarily serves legal and library markets.

Professional information publishers charged $1,829 on average for their titles, a 4.3% gain over 1987. Titles published for the health care market had the steepest price decrease, at 24% on average. Other than general interest, science/technology titles were least expensive at $1,289 per title on average.

Even though print information publishers generally raise their prices annually, it appears that CD-ROM publishers are trying to build their business by lowering prices. A combination of factors may account for the price decreases:

- The upfront cost of building a CD-ROM title is decreasing because costs are spread over more than one title.
- The cost of CD-ROM technology is declining somewhat.
- Replicators are charging less for their services.
- The potential audience is growing as the installed base of readers grows.

Prices tend to be raised in the more successful areas of CD-ROM publishing. Publishers of business/financial titles tend to generate more revenue on average than the overall market, which indicates that they're more successful than other segments of CD-ROM publishing. For example, Lotus Development generated more than $15 million in CD-ROM sales in 1987, putting average revenue per title at more than $750,000. The entire CD-ROM market last year, however, was about $60 million, according to *Factbook* estimates, putting the overall average revenue per title at about $375,000.

Excerpted from "CD-ROM Title Prices Dropping," October 6, 1988 issue of *Digital Information Group's Industry Factbook*, Digital Information Group, Stamford, Conn., by special permission.

Product support costs

"Never underestimate the cost of technical support." That's the best advice I've ever heard about CD-ROM products. Even with an easy-to-use system, calls still come in. Some relate to hardware, others to the software, and still others to the information on the disc. The costs are real and must be provided for because they relate to current and future use of the specific product and to future sales of new products. They are a cost directly spent *on the customer* rather than spent on producing *for the customer* or marketing *to the customer*.

Profit

Profit is a concept rarely mentioned in the CD-ROM industry, yet it is an important element providing companies with resources for R&D on new products, for expansion, and for market research. Without funds from profit, the CD-ROM industry will stagnate.

FUTURE PRICES

Today, all these factors have to be taken into account in order to set pricing levels. Although I wish our company could make money by offering $49 CD-ROM products, we can't. In order to be in business next year and ten years from now, we have to sell at considerably higher prices.

However, we don't want this new technology to increase the gap between the information haves and the information have-nots. We believe in a future in which prices will be lower, and we are currently exploring a number of alternative strategies that might help to lower costs sooner than we had originally estimated. But in the final analysis, the original value of the information as well as the added value that can be brought to the electronic version will dominate the pricing decisions.

[*Matilda Butler is President of Knowledge Access International, a leading publisher of business, professional, and educational databases on magnetic disk and CD-ROM. Prior to co-founding Knowledge Access, Butler was Chair of the Technology and Communication Department at Far West Laboratory.*]

> *Although I wish our company could make money by offering $49 CD-ROM products, we can't. In order to be in business next year and ten years from now, we have to sell at considerably higher prices.*

How to Price a CD-ROM Product

By David Roux

[David Roux advocates a value-based pricing strategy rather than a cost-based strategy. This strategy, he claims, is more likely to yield the reserves publishers need for customer support and ongoing research and development.]

Many CD-ROM publishers use a cost-based pricing strategy to price their products. A common mistake when using this strategy is underestimating the true costs of producing a product. Another mistake is failing to take into account the value of the product to the customer.

Four factors determine the minimum price of a CD-ROM product: cost of the information, operating costs, development expenses, and distribution costs. The sum is the cost of putting a product in a box in a store.

By evaluating only these base costs, however, a publisher may fail to account for the costs that are needed for long-term success such as second-generation development costs and post-sale service and support costs. In an emerging industry like the CD-ROM industry, the costs of service and support can be high. Training and education, in the form of seminars, documentation, and collateral materials, must be available for customers as well as sales and support staff.

In addition, many publishers completely overlook the need to redirect cash flow into continued development of new as well as existing products. A long-term development strategy that consists of regular updates and evolves as new technologies evolve is necessary if a publisher is to be successful in meeting the long-term needs of its customers.

Thus, to determine the real cost of delivering a product to a customer, publishers must consider the costs associated with satisfying customers' ongoing needs, providing for future growth and rewarding shareholders.

An alternative to cost-based pricing is value-based pricing. The key to the value-based pricing strategy is in determining the product's worth to the customer. The easiest way to make this determination is to compare your product to other products in the marketplace. How much does it cost to get the same information from another source? Then, depending on how

DAVID ROUX

Home: Winchester, Massachusetts
Job: Vice President, Information Services Group, Lotus Development Corp.
Quote: *"Technology should be invisible to users, because what customers want are solutions."*

your product stacks up against the other products, price it higher or lower.

If there is no comparable product, however, estimating a product's worth becomes more difficult. In this case, market research is needed to establish the market's perception of value as a guide to effective pricing.

By using value-based pricing, a publisher can capture the real value of his product. This will enable the publisher to adequately reinvest in future research and development. Ongoing research and development is particularly important in the CD-ROM industry, where new technologies will continue to evolve and publishers must be prepared to meet changing requirements.

[David Roux is Corporate Vice President of Lotus Development Corporation's Information Services Group. He directs the development, marketing, and distribution of the company's One Source *family of business and financial databases delivered on CD-ROM, as well as* Signal *and* QuoTrek, *the company's market quotation products. In addition, he oversees Lotus's multiple partnerships with information providers.]*

How to Decide What to Charge for a CD-ROM

By Dennis Burke

[To the factors outlined by Matilda Butler in her discussion of pricing components, Dennis Burke adds one more: PPA (read on for a definition). PPA is a necessary evil in an infant market, adding confusion and unpredictability to the market's pricing structure.]

Can you believe it? CD-ROM prices range from $29.95 to $10,000. What's the rub here? Who's making these wild decisions and why? This market has become a confusing mess, but let's try to wade through the reasoning.

What we have seen in the past two or three years is an explosion in the number of startup CD-ROM firms. Coupled with this is an explosive growth in CD-ROM titles and in indexing/search-and-retrieval software packages. Every new company has brought new philosophies and pricing structures to the market.

PHILOSOPHY

Four philosophies currently dominate CD-ROM publishing: privatization of public data, joint-venture publishing, outright purchase of databases, and internal corporate or government publishing.

The federal, state, and local governments of the United States have a wealth of databases. Unfortunately, many of these databases are not stored in magnetic form. The so-called privatization of these public databases has been concentrated on those databases already in magnetic form.

Privatization of public data has also taken place in the realm of public domain software. Public domain software is, as the name implies, software that is free to use and distribute. Several CD-ROM firms have released public domain software discs.

Second-tier and third-tier print publishers at present do not have the resources to "go it alone" and publish their own CD-ROMs. Joint-venture arrangements are an approach that many in the industry have taken with these traditional print publishers. The CD-ROM publishing rights are granted in return for a royalty on disc sales. This approach is currently very attractive and popular among CD-ROM developers.

The outright purchase of data for CD-ROM is a fairly expensive and unpopular avenue for CD-ROM developers. While a few firms have taken this approach, do not look at this as a continuing trend.

Many CD-ROM discs never make it to the general market after publication. Many discs are published internally for corporate and government clients. Usually this type of publication involves up-front payments by the client in exchange for a final published disc. The CD-ROMs are then used internally. Occasionally, these discs are released for general public use when there is a market for them and no legal or security restrictions hamper distribution.

PRICING STRUCTURE

The pricing of CD-ROM discs is influenced by five unique problems: disc preparation, license fees, disc royalties, dealer/distributor discounting, and…PPA. What is PPA? It is a well-exploited concept used by many in the industry. Though it is not talked about on the record, you can hear about it in off-the-cuff remarks. Quite simply, PPA stands for "Pulling the Price out of the Air."

The preparation of a CD-ROM includes the pricing of variables such as data capture costs, indexing/search-and-retrieval software license fees, and labor costs. Data capture costs are incurred when the database you are working with is not in magnetic form. The conversion process is very time-consuming and expensive. An average 8½-by-11-inch page of text can cost $2.00 to convert to magnetic form. If a firm must convert tens of thousands of printed pages to magnetic form, it is certainly going to charge a premium price for its CD-ROM.

> *The traditional image of a distributor is one of a middleman, a conduit between manufacturer and retailer, warehousing product and moving it into the appropriate channels. Although often maligned as a "necessary evil," distributors are essential factors in almost every manufacturing-based industry. The personal computer industry is no exception.*
>
> **Barry Schuler**
> From "Distribution: Part of the Marketing Mix," in *Marketing Computers*

Use and license fees for IS&R software vary considerably. A firm must weigh IS&R fees against what it perceives the final CD-ROM will look like. Does the database need hypertext searching? How quickly does data need to be retrieved? Can the data be indexed at the PC level, or does it have to be sent to a subcontractor

DENNIS BURKE

Home: Minneapolis, Minnesota
Job: Development Manager, ALDE Publishing
Quote: *"I feel that in the next 12 to 18 months software and hardware vendors will be forced to lower their fees and prices or they will face extinction. The market is finally moving into the retail channels with Egghead Software, Heath/Zenith, and Radio Shack. Those that are unwilling to price software and hardware for the mass market will be 'shaken out' of the industry."*

with a VAX? Can the color and sophistication of the user interface be changed? These issues all cost the CD-ROM developer money, and the expense, of course, is passed on to the end user.

Traditional print publishers over the years have been offering a 4 percent to 15 percent royalty on sales to their clients. When a CD-ROM developer approaches these traditional publishers with the idea of CD-ROM publishing, the traditional publisher expects a larger royalty. Usual CD-ROM royalty percentages fall between 10 percent and 50 percent. As these royalties go up, so do disc prices.

If a CD-ROM firm wants to sell to a large market, it must have a network of dealers and distributors. This network has become necessary because of the ever-changing market. Microcomputer sales outlets and distributors are looking for that next "big thing," and they are starting to realize that CD-ROM is it. Dealers usually want a discount of 35 percent to 50 percent off list price. Distributors usually ask for 45 percent to 65 percent off list price. These percentages may be hard to take, but for the sake of wide distribution, the CD-ROM developer is forced into it.

Taken together, all the factors outlined above should constitute an explanation of how and why a CD-ROM developer settles on a price for each disc. There is no standard template for these pricing calculations. And for all we know, many firms in and out of the CD-ROM business might be using the PPA method for their pricing structure.

CD-ROM is still an infant market, and no one can reliably predict the pricing structure of the future. One conclusion is certain, however: This market is expanding, and developers are responding with appropriate CD-ROM titles and confusing prices.

[Dennis Burke is Development Manager at ALDE Publishing. A life-time resident of Minnesota, he has a background in defense analysis and computers.]

CD-ROM Discs and Drives: A Dealer's Perspective

By Barry Cinnamon

[CD-ROM dealers have a champion in Barry Cinnamon, who voices concerns about the effects of drive prices and CD-ROM publication prices on the overall ability of the market to grow at projected rates.]

Until recently the two established parties in the CD-ROM industry—title/drive developers and customers—accounted for the vast majority of business activity. Now, a new participant is emerging: third-party CD-ROM dealers—companies that either specialize in CD-ROM products or sell CD-ROM products along with other computer or information products. This article will examine some of the CD-ROM product and pricing issues that are important from a CD-ROM dealer's perspective.

The CD-ROM industry can grow only to a certain size by selling directly to customers. If the past history of the PC hardware and software industry is any indication, third-party dealers are likely to create much of the subsequent growth in title and drive shipments. However, there are still a number of practical barriers to widespread dealer participation. These barriers, and some potential solutions, are discussed in more detail below.

First, the vast majority of potential end users have no intention of spending more than $500 for a CD-ROM drive. At the present pricing levels, this means that most of the potential market for CD-ROM—the market that all the forecasts have promised—cannot be reached. Although the prices of the drives did not have

BARRY CINNAMON

Home: Upper Montclair, New Jersey
Job: President, Bureau of Electronic Publishing
Quote: *"The market projections I have seen over the past few years simply do not take into account the amount of groundwork that is necessary for an industry to prosper.... Those of us who are part of the industry's growth phase will continue to see gradual month-to-month sales improvements."*

much effect on sales when the majority of CD-ROM titles were expensive, drive price is critical for the less expensive titles. As a result of current high drive prices, the only people who are interested in these inexpensive titles are those who already have a drive. Drive prices will have to come down into the $200 to $400 range before complete CD-ROM packages (drives and titles) become affordable to the current installed base of PC users.

Second, there are still only a handful of CD-ROM titles (fewer than 50) that appeal to a broad, horizontal spectrum of PC users. These are the titles that can be sold by a dealer and typically range in price from $50 to $500. These titles are where the action will eventually be. Now, however, there are no indications of a widespread stampede to buy CD-ROM drives to use with these horizontal market titles.

Third, the importance of selling low-price titles becomes even more significant when a dealer pursues customers who already have CD-ROM drives. In many cases, people who already have drives are desperate for other interesting titles that they can use. Titles priced in the $30 to $200 range seem to sell particularly well to these people.

Fourth, certain CD-ROM products are very price sensitive. Although this is contrary to some conventional CD-ROM wisdom, we have seen how price can have a significant effect on the sales of two very similar CD-ROM products. In particular, if the contents of a disc are well defined (as in an electronic Bible or an existing print publication), price is critical. CD-ROM discs that are somewhat of a novelty (not purchased for primary use with a drive) are also price sensitive, and prices in the $30 to $100 range are of most interest. On the other hand, if people perceive a relationship between a title's price and its value, somewhat higher prices are justified. For example, with some public domain software discs, customers assume that a $100 disc contains much more information than a $29 disc does, and they will buy the $100 disc.

Fifth, information targeted toward narrow vertical markets can continue to support high title and drive prices. The high price of the complete package (drive and title), however, and the focused nature of the application mean that these products are unlikely to develop into a significant portion of the market. Also, these titles are also generally sold directly to end users and bypass the dealer sales channel completely.

Sixth, the traditional computer dealers—both for the PC and the Mac—have been oversold on CD-ROM technology. Their stocks of drives and titles do not sell particularly well. Walk-in traffic for these products is low, and dealers generally are not trained on these products and have only a few complementary titles in stock to sell as add-ons. In a nutshell, dealers cannot sell CD-ROM drives and titles in the same way that they sell many of their other products, and it may be that conditions are still not ripe for traditional dealer involvement. There seems to be a dichotomy between the dealer's interest in selling horizontal CD-ROM products, and the fact that the successful CD-ROM products to date are directed toward narrow, vertical markets. Perhaps dealers should stock those few horizontal products that sell well and have a means by which they can quickly order the vertical market titles that appeal to their customers.

Finally, price-skimming tactics (charging high prices for early adopters of CD-ROM) might be profitable for the drive manufacturers, but they are putting some of the aggressive, low-priced title developers out of business. As a result, the mass-market title developers and the drive manufacturers are at odds with each other—the result of a very shortsighted strategy that is having a tendency to throttle market expansion.

The CD-ROM dealer concerns described above are certainly important. However, regardless of the actions taken by dealers to accelerate the growth of the market, such growth will still take time. The CD-ROM industry did not explode over the past few years, and it is unlikely to do so in the next year. Instead, the industry is more likely to continue to grow steadily. It will still take time for the benefits of the existing horizontal market titles to diffuse out to a larger audience and for sales of targeted vertical market titles to accumulate. Dealers will be in a much better position to realistically assess their potential with CD-ROM products if they keep the factors discussed above in mind.

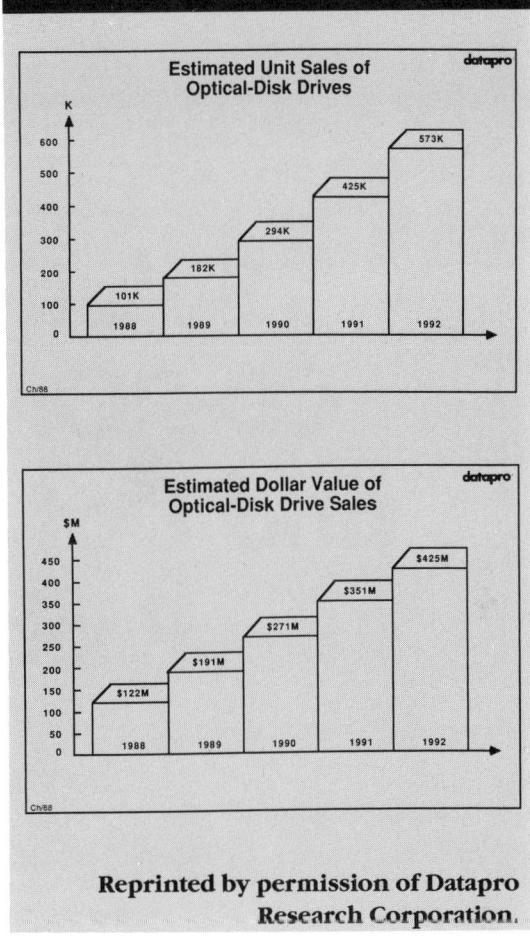

Reprinted by permission of Datapro Research Corporation.

[Barry Cinnamon is the President of the Bureau of Electronic Publishing. The Bureau is the largest independent reseller of CD-ROM products for the PC and Mac, and currently carries over 150 different drives and titles. Author of Optical Disk Document Storage and Retrieval Systems *(published in 1988 by AIIM), Mr. Cinnamon has an MBA degree in Marketing from the Wharton School and a BS degree in Engineering from MIT.]*

Solutions for CD-ROM Pricing and Data Security Problems

By Victor Shear

[Victor Shear gives us a new perspective on CD-ROM pricing, arguing that access to CD-ROM is essentially blocked for a large number of potential users who are deterred by the substantial upfront investment required. An alternative, Shear maintains, is a usage-billing system that will open up the technology to more users and thereby increase the revenues of publishers and database owners.]

The issues of maintaining a publisher's control over information assets and of creating a workable and non-self-defeating billing strategy are fundamental to the growth of the CD-ROM market. With the advent of inexpensive mass storage devices, information-on-demand products can achieve widespread success in a short period of time, as long as the basic problems of product pricing and database protection are solved. ROI (for Return On Investment) is a low cost hardware/software computer peripheral that exemplifies this information-on-demand technology and solves the fundamental CD-ROM problem of eliminating customer product-pricing resistance and of achieving effective administration of, and security for, CD-ROM published products. Personal Library Software, Inc., the owner of ROI technology, will shortly be receiving broad conceptual patent protection covering ROI products.

CD publishers need database protection that is both transparent to the user and effective security by any practical standard. Customers need flexible options including usage, usage/

subscription, and multilevel subscription billing strategies, or a combination of these features. ROI addresses these needs and offers a low-cost solution that can greatly accelerate the market penetration of CD-ROM published products and markedly improve publisher revenues, profitability, and adminstrative efficiency.

USAGE-BASED BILLING

The ROI peripheral retains a very secure audit trail of the "vital statistics" of each access to a database made by a client: the time, date, database, property within the database, block within the property, the I.D. of both the workstation and the individual user, or some combination of these items. The peripheral stores these usage identifiers until, at some later point, the information is sent by modem (or by some other means) to the publisher. The client normally transmits his or her history of database usage by loading an ROI program and pressing a function key that activates a secured, two-way telecommunications connection with the publisher. Based on the customer's history of database usage, the publisher can then calculate the appropriate fee to charge the customer. As a result of this audit trail, a database publisher can receive a revenue stream from each client that is commensurate with the amount of each customer's database usage.

For billing purposes, ROI can also distinguish between database material that is browsed and that which is copied, transmitted, or otherwise removed from a database by a user. This distinction between browsing and actual usage allows different billing rates for browsing versus "purchase" of a copy of the data.

The ROI peripheral also makes it practical for publishers to include in the same database a number of information resources owned by different organizations. Accordingly, CD-ROM publishers will be able to market an array of different databases on a disc providing comprehensive information on a topic area. The peripheral also allows the owners of properties

VICTOR SHEAR

Home: Bethesda, Maryland
Job: Chairman, Personal Library Software, Inc.
Quote: *"The market potential for electronic desktop information is enormous. But this potential will not be realized until both usage based billing and reasonable schemes for the protection of data base properties are implemented."*

provided to a database to set prices for the use of their products. Each contributing property owner can then receive a "copyright royalty" return on investment reflecting actual customer usage of its product(s). Owners contributing properties that are more important, popular, or expensive to develop than others would earn revenues commensurate with the market demands and pricing strategies for their products.

DATABASE SECURITY

When using ROI, a publisher can use one or more encryption methods to secure the database. A computer can then read the encrypted CD-ROM disc only if an appropriate decryption/usage history peripheral is employed within the user's system. An encryption algorithm can be as sophisticated as the publisher needs or wants. Sophisticated encryption techniques will prevent all but the most dedicated and high-powered computer thieves from being able to copy a CD-ROM product's contents.

> *CD-ROM publishers should no more bypass clients who are willing to pay $100–300 than, for example, the telephone company should restrict telephone availability to clients with billings of more than $2000 a year.*

A database publisher can establish a budget for each client on either an individual workstation or an organization-wide basis. MIS and other managers within an organization can also set database budgets for groups, workstations, or individuals. In addition, when it is anticipated that a CD-ROM product will be used primarily as reference resource, the publisher can limit a given access to a certain number of logically contiguous screens of information—500 or perhaps 1000 screens of information in a row. The combination of a budget for consecutive blocks of information and a budget for the percentage of a database that can be accessed provides the client with control over cost and usage.

The ROI peripheral also will allow publishers to maintain control over their CD-ROM products if clients prove to be unreliable. For example, the peripheral can automatically deactivate its decryption capabilities if the client's billing usage identifiers have not been reported within the required billing time period or if payment hasn't been received by a certain date. These features, when combined with budgets for usage amounts and for consecutive blocks of information that can be read, allow the publisher to retain control over the CD-ROM's contents, even though the client has physical possession of the CD-ROM disc itself.

MARKETING IMPLICATIONS

Publishers who adopt subscription-based pricing strategies are likely to encourage both database copying and usage of a single license throughout a group or organization. In addition, subscription-only CD-ROM products will tend to be accessed across networks or will be physically located in an organization's library. In either instance, CD publishing revenues will be reduced seriously because an entire organization can be served by a single license.

In contrast, usage-billing strategies will encourage both organizations and individuals to acquire licenses. When an organization wishes to provide access to CD-ROM databases, ROI will be transparent to network usage, it will provide its full array of database protection features, and it will retain for the client as well as the publisher a complete audit of database usage by each workstation (or end user) for billing and resource-management purposes. The peripheral will also provide an array of database-administration utilities that, among other features, allows the administrator to apportion database access and usage rights among user subclasses and to individual end users.

Usage billing will thus allow publishers to ensure maximum return on their investments. For example, if the subscription fee for a CD-ROM product is $2000 a year, users who are seriously considering such a product are likely to be individuals or companies who are confident that they will receive value from its use that significantly exceeds the CD-ROM's upfront product cost. Without usage billing, the publisher loses the difference between the subscription price and the value of this kind of client's actual usage. At the other end of the scale, lack of usage billing leaves users who might be willing to pay $100, $200, or $300 out in the cold. Usage billing provides options that allow these users to experience the benefits of CD-ROM databases while providing additional revenue and profits to CD-ROM publishers. CD-ROM publishers should no more bypass these potential clients than, for example, the telephone company should restrict telephone availability to clients with billings of more than $2000 a year.

It makes no sense to arbitrarily eliminate the bulk of the potential market from participatng in the information-on-demand revolution. But there are also very important social arguments against implementing a CD-ROM pricing system that limits the availability of CD-ROM and other optical information bases to large corporations and to the wealthy. An ROI-based, CD-ROM product strategy can allow large numbers of customers to acquire CD reference disks at low initial costs and at little or no risk because their billing can be based on usage, or a combination of usage and subscription or subscription-only strategies. This low cost and flexibility will encourage potential clients to experiment with CD-ROM products, whereas the current costly annual or one-time license fees of most CD-ROM products actually discourage widespread use.

Marketing of CD-ROM databases will be enhanced not only by enabling all interested potential clients to acquire discs easily, but also by the combination of billing and security features, which will motivate CD-ROM publishers to integrate the information properties of different owners into a single database, or, alternatively, to provide multiple databases on a single disc. This integration of synergistic information can substantially increase the usefulness and market appeal of a given database by producing more comprehensive and reliable retrieval results. Without an ROI-type technology, integration of different database properties owned by different vendors will often be impractical because providing a portion of fixed-subscription revenues to each property owner becomes arbitrary.

IN SUMMARY

A very large database is a substantial business asset of the organization that owns it. It is somewhat paradoxical for organizations to invest significant resources in the creation of large and very useful products, only to have these products be too expensive (as a result of a single-level subscription billing) for general use. The very advantage of most good databases—size and breadth of resources—often makes these products too expensive for the market they were designed to serve if one price must fit all clients.

There are numerous successful precedents for combined usage/subscription payment options, two of the most notable being the usage versus Watts payment strategies of telephone companies and hardware rental versus purchase strategies of personal computer dealers. A third precedent for usage billing and combined usage/subscription is the online database industry's primary reliance on usage billing. CD-ROM's enormous storage capacity gives it many capabilities (and some advantages) that are analogous to those of online databases. The momentum and success of the online marketplace is in sharp contrast to the overall uncertainty of the subscription-based CD-ROM publishing market. Lessons can and should be learned from the success of online databases, particularly because online is the prime competitor of CD-ROM publishing.

ROI technology enables CD-ROM to offer online's fundamental security and billing attributes while allowing CD-ROM to continue to offer its significant advantages over online. With this technology everyone wins: The publishers can experience much greater revenues, and the public will have much greater access to useful information products.

[Victor Shear is cofounder and Chairman of Personal Library Software, a leading supplier of text, document, and image database management software for both the magnetic and optical markets.]

FINANCING YOUR CD-ROM ENDEAVORS

DEBT VERSUS EQUITY FINANCING
By Daniel Remer, Paul Remer, and Robert Dunaway

EVALUATING A VENTURE CAPITAL FIRM TO MEET YOUR COMPANY'S NEEDS
By Accel Partners

Debt Versus Equity Financing

By Daniel Remer, Paul Remer, and Robert Dunaway
Excerpted from *Silicon Valley Guide to Financial Success in Software*

[In this practical yet entertaining book, the authors advise developers on how to make it in the highly competitive software industry. Just as applicable to CD-ROM developers, this excerpt explores options for raising capital to fund the development process. A word of caution: tax laws may have changed between the time the authors wrote this piece and the time you are reading it. Consult your tax attorney before deciding how to raise the money you need.]

To borrow some money or to sell some stock—that is the question. And if you need cash, it is the first question you must answer. Both borrowing and selling have advantages and potential problems. The advantage of borrowing money is that you don't have to give up ownership of part of your company; the problem with borrowing money is that you have to pay it back. The advantage of equity financing, or selling stock, is that you don't have a debt to pay back; the problem is that you end up owning less of your company. Often an entrepreneur both borrows and sells equity. Let's first take a closer look at borrowing.

BORROWING

In *Hamlet,* Polonius advises his son Laertes, "Neither a borrower nor a lender be." The implication is not that Laertes ought to sell stock, but that he ought to live within his means. Most entrepreneurs, especially those who want their companies to grow fast, can't live within their means, so sooner or later they ask themselves, "Where can I borrow some money?" There are two possible answers: from personal contacts, and from banks.

> *If you are the sort of person who has moneyed connections and wouldn't hesitate to make use of them, there are several advantages to private loans.*

Personal loans

Some people wouldn't think twice about obtaining money from family, friends, and acquaintances. Others would rather go through a bankruptcy than borrow a dime from dad. If you are the sort of person who has moneyed connections and wouldn't hesitate to make use of them, there are several advantages to private loans.

First, you probably won't have to go through a rigorous and prolonged negotiating session to get the funds. (However, we know some uncles who make hardened venture capitalists seem like fairy godmothers.) Second, you probably won't have to secure the loan using your personal or business assets, leaving these assets available for borrowing more money later from a bank that will insist on some collateral. Third, you may be able to get favorable terms, such as interest-only payments with the loan amount itself payable in ten years. Fourth, if you run into a cash-flow problem and can't make your payments for a while, your favorite cousin, the doctor, is less likely to initiate legal proceedings. Fifth, if you have a cozy relationship with your creditor, the loan could be made to you personally and paid back by you personally, thereby keeping the loan off your balance sheet and making the company seem stronger to future sources of capital.

The disadvantages of dealing with those you know and love is that if your venture fails, you may hurt them or at least hurt your relationship with them. Even if you don't hurt anyone, you may not want your Uncle Bert saying to your father every time the two of them get together, "Tom, your son's a bright boy, but I just don't know where he got his money sense from."

One final thought. If your parents or other close relatives are into estate planning, you might want to drop the hint that they can give you up to $10,000 a year tax fee. If you're going to inherit the money eventually and they don't need it, you may be able to convince them that it is much more important to you now than it will be later on, when opportunity may have slipped through your fingers.

Bank loans

Banks and other lending institutions, such as credit unions and savings and loans, are easy sources of money, provided that you have two things: collateral and cash flow. Your collateral can be anything the bank feels is worth about 150 percent of the loan; your house, car, boat, or diamonds. If your business is just beginning, it will probably not have much—if any—collateral. As far as cash flow goes, you might not have much of that either. If you have another source of income besides your new business, or if you have a well-paid spouse, that might do. You simply fill out the bank's forms and presto—cash. Well, it might not be that simple. Here are some tips.

Suppose you are working full-time for a company other than your own. Your new start-up needs some cash and you believe that one way or another you will be able to repay a bank loan. Perhaps you will stay at your job, or you have other sources of cash, or your new start-up will become profitable quickly enough to make your loan payments. You explain all this to your friendly banker who nods and smiles and says, "I'll have to run this through our loan committee"—a polite way of saying, "No dice."

We can see all the bankers among you cringing as they read this, but the simple truth is that, despite those unctuous radio commercials we hear every day, banks will generally not lend money to new businesses unless they have substantial collateral and substantial cash flow. Period. You'll do better if you tell your banker that you're going to spend the loan proceeds on a Hawaiian vacation or braces for your niece than on (heaven forbid!) a new business. If you really want the money, don't breathe a word about your start-up venture, and apply for the loan before you even think of quitting your other job. Pretend that you will be living in your current home until they come to bury you, and that the last thing you would ever do is something as crazy as try to get rich by starting your own company. When you get to the question on the loan application asking you what you are going to do with the money, type in, "Investments." There will be little or no mention of loan committees and you'll get your money if you are creditworthy.

Maybe that seems too devious for you. Perhaps your company has a few assets and you'd like to try a more straightforward approach. What sort of collateral will banks accept? Here is where your business plan and salesmanship come in. If you can convince a banker that you are smart and will succeed, he or she just might be willing to lend you money based upon your accounts receivable and fixed assets. The fixed assets might be your computers and office furniture, for example, though neither of these are usually particularly impressive to a bank.

Another asset might be any contracts you have with publishers or OEMs. It's a good idea, whenever you negotiate a contract, to try to make it "bankable"; that is, to try to include minimum payments and advances that guarantee cash flow and that enable you to use the contract as collateral. Try to have any advances against royalties recoupable at a 50-percent rate. For example, if you receive an advance of $10,000 for a program and the first quarter's royalties amount to only $5,000, a 50-percent

> *The simple truth is that, despite those unctuous radio commercials we hear every day, banks will generally not lend money to new businesses unless they have substantial collateral and substantial cash flow. Period.*

recoup rate would mean that only $2,500 of the advance could be recouped. This makes the contract bankable.

Once you have a track record of receivables (money owed to you), and you prove that you can collect them in a reasonably timely manner, some banks will lend you between 50 and 80 percent of the value of the receivables. You will still have to prove to the bank that you are profitable, and that your company will be able to pay back the loan and still be able to meet its own cash needs. Financial statements audited by your CPA will help you prove that you are serious about your business and that what you say is true.

When you present yourself to your banker, don't assume that he or she is going to be your buddy. While there are exceptions, you can probably assume that your typical loan officer is more than a little jealous of your position as an entrepreneur. You may be earning twice what he or she is earning and you have a chance of earning enough over the next couple of years so

> *If you have good people working with you and you have a track record, you might be able to raise the capital you need by signing a good chunk of your company over to the bank.*

that you'll never have to work again. So don't be surprised if your banker receives you a little coolly. Here are a few hints on how to get a loan officer to warm up to your requests for money.

Presenting yourself in the best possible light: There are a couple of simple and obvious things that you can do to make your company look as profitable as possible. Talk to your CPA about the need to accrue as much income in your current quarter as possible. For example, if you have a contract to write a program for Commodore and it provides for a non-refundable advance of $20,000, talk to your CPA about recording all $20,000 in the current quarter, even though you might not actually receive the money until next quarter. Depending on the actual terms of your contract, this may be perfectly legitimate according to GAAP rules.

Another way to increase your apparent profitability is to capitalize or depreciate as many of the things you buy as you can. Items will thus appear on your balance sheet as assets rather than on your income statement as expenses. For example, if you buy a modem, you have the choice of adding it to your balance sheet as an asset or deducting its cost from your income. There is quite a bit of latitude here, but you have to choose an amount below which you deduct items and above which you capitalize them, and you must be consistent. Your CPA will help you decide what that amount should be.

At this point you may be thinking, "If I follow this advice, I'll have to pay more taxes," and you are right! You will have to pay more taxes, at least in the short run. The more profit you show on your books, the more taxes you pay. But the more taxes you pay, the more a banker will believe in your enterprise. For this reason, one of our clients even purposely paid more taxes than he owed by overestimating the amount of accrued sales he had made. There is a fine line between presenting yourself in the best possible light and stretching things so far that you begin to smell like long-dead halibut.

It may seem silly not to be straightforward. You would think that you could explain to your bank that through careful tax planning, your tax returns show a net loss for last year even though you actually made quite a lot of money. The banks believe, however, that tax planning is a given, and that if you actually paid taxes on profits, then the profits were really there.

You will have to be the judge of how to run your business, how to pay taxes, and so forth. If you business is making plenty of money, you may not want to borrow money, sell the business, or go public, so try to minimize your tax liability by minimizing your profit. If you want to do any of these things, try to show as much profit as you legally can. And pay the taxes.

SELLING STOCK

Now that you know about borrowing, what about selling stock? The primary advantage of selling stock over borrowing money is that you aren't indebted to someone. If the business fails, your stockholders have no recourse against you unless you made misrepresentations in connection with the sale of the stock.

A potential advantage of selling stock is that your investors can be of enormous help to your business. Some will even sit on your board of directors and will help steer you clear of the sharks and keep you on target. For example, when a venture capitalist invests, he or she certainly wants your business to succeed and therefore you may find yourself with a ready source of business advice. But therein also lies a potential problem. There is a difference between accepting business advice and taking orders from your friendly investor. More about this later.

There are basically two ways of selling stock; publicly and privately. Here, we'll take a look at the kinds of investors who might be interested in buying a piece of your company.

Banks

Ironically, the larger banks, which will give you the line about running your application past the loan committee when you apply for a start-up loan, also have venture-capital investment arms that invest in ventures so speculative they would probably make your little venture seem as safe an investment as U.S. Government Savings Bonds. Unfortunately for the small operator, these venture-capital divisions, which are operated as limited partnerships with the bank acting as the limited partner, are looking for huge potential gains. If you can't prove to them, on paper at least, that an investment in you will make the bank a 700- to 1000-percent return on its money, then don't waste your time with them.

If your venture has this sort of upside potential, and if you need from $500,000 to several million dollars, do call the main branch of your bank and find out if it has a venture-capital division. Have them take you out to lunch and be prepared to be interrogated. Have your business plan ready and make sure it's bulletproof. If you have good people working with you and you have a track record, you might be able to raise the capital you need by signing a good chunk of your company over to the bank.

Venture capitalists

To some entrepreneurs, they are Santa Clauses carrying sacks of cash. Others would just as soon sleep with garlic wreaths around their necks to keep them away. The image of the venture capitalist is always controversial, often myth-shrouded; yet few people have a clear idea of what and who venture capitalists really are. We hate to dispel the myth, but venture capitalists are merely professional investors who like to risk their money and spend their time with small, emerging companies. They are neither Santas nor Draculas; more often than not, the money they invest is not even their own.

Despite their sometimes ruthless image, venture capitalists are rarely devious, almost never dishonest, and their motives are easy to understand. They simply want to invest in a company, obtaining as much stock as they can for as little money as possible. Then they want the company to get as big as it can, attracting more investors along the way. At the most auspicious moment, they want to sell the company or take it public, thus getting their investment back along with as large a return as possible.

Once you fully understand the venture capitalists' motives, you will find it easy to understand why they would like to control your board of directors, why they would like you to hire professional managers, why they would like you to keep your books in tip-top condition, and why they would want to get their investments out of your company within five years....

Limited partnerships

In our discussion of the different types of business, we mentioned the limited partnership as a means of raising money. A limited partnership consists of a general partner and one or more limited partners who contribute money for their share of the partnership.

The advantage to the general partner is that he or she receives cash without having an

> *In an equity partnership, the investors are co-owners of the business with the founders; in an R&D partnership, they are merely providing funds for the development of a product, with an expected rate of return limited by prior agreement.*

investor who can insist on offering management "help." In addition, when a normal limited partnership is formed, there are usually no restrictions on how the money contributed by the limited partner can be used. For example, the money could be used for development or marketing, for advertising or salaries. Of course, there is an implied and enforceable obligation on the part of the general partner to spend the money for the good of the partnership.

The advantage to the investor is that, unlike a general partnership, the investor only stands to lose the money he contributed; there can be no further liability. In addition, if losses are incurred, the limited partner can deduct them directly for tax purposes, which is not the case if the company is instead organized as a regular corporation with the investor as a stockholder.

In spite of these advantages, the limited partnership is not used very frequently when forming a software company, because many of the tax and liability advantages can also be obtained by incorporating the business as an S corporation. In addition, as we mentioned earlier, a corporation has other advantages, including limited liability for all the stockholders, not just the limited partners. Entrepreneurs do, however, use variations of the limited partnership to raise capital.

R&D limited partnerships: One common variation, known as the R&D limited partnership, is set up to raise money for development while at the same time providing tax incentives to investors.... This is a somewhat grey and changing area of the law and you should definitely discuss the matter with a CPA or tax lawyer....

Equity partnerships: A variation of the typical R&D limited partnership, called the equity partnership, combines the benefits of partnership operations with eventual stock ownership. Among other advantages, equity partnerships provide investors with the opportunity to risk their pre-tax investment dollars while removing the limit on upside potential returns that is normally present in typical R&D-partnership royalty agreements. The distinction between the two types of investment lies in the investors' connection to the partnership. In an equity partnership, the investors are co-owners of the business with the founders; in an R&D partnership, they are merely providing funds for the development of a product, with an expected rate of return limited by prior agreement....

What are the advantages for investors? Equity partnerships offer a combination of advantages to investors that are not offered by a traditional partnership nor available to traditional stockholders. The following list includes the most common advantages.

- The opportunity to participate in first-round equity financing with its potential for greatest return.

- Increased after-tax returns through direct pass-through of start-up-period losses.

- The ability to specially allocate tax losses between investors and the entrepreneurial group.

- Higher potential profit through absence of the "cap" present in normal royalty agreements.

After incorporation and contribution of partnership interests in return for stock, additional benefits to investors are:

- The ownership of preferred stock, which has preferential treatment regarding dividends and liquidating distributions.

- The ability to convert preferred stock to common stock.

- The potential for generating capital-gains income through merger, redemption, or sale after public offering.

- Shelter from the tax consequences of immediate pass-through of the company's income.

- Greater flexibility in estate planning than with partnership interests.

What are the advantages for entrepreneurs? Equity partnerships also provide entrepreneurs with various benefits, some not available in a traditional sale of equity and some not available in a partnership. Among them are:

- Greater incentive because the entrepreneur retains a greater share of the company.

- Complete flexibility regarding subsequent financing.

- Complete control of operations during developmental stages.

- The ability to structure ownership interests in the new corporation so that there is very limited potential for adverse tax consequences to the entrepreneurs.

- Post-incorporation shelter from general liability.

Are there any disadvantages? Although equity partnerships in many ways provide the best of both worlds, there could be several disadvantages, depending on the desires and the tax and financial objectives of the involved parties. The specific nature and risk of the venture itself and the amount of funds necessary might also influence the decision to set up an equity partnership. The less attractive features to be considered include:

- Greater difficulty in balancing control between investors and entrepreneurs (although this is usually dealt with by establishing a corporate general partner).

- Unlimited liability for a general partner.

- Delayed return on investment.

These factors, along with others, must be carefully weighed against the benefits before reaching a decision on how to structure the venture.

Reprinted by permission of Microsoft Press.

WHERE VENTURE CAPITAL IS INVESTING NOW

Company	Assets	1987-1988 investments	Special interests	Comments
Accel Partners 1 Palmer Square Princeton, NJ 08542 (609)683-4500	$120 million	$15 million in 1987, about the same in 1988	Software, telecommunications, medical products, and biotechnology; neural networks and superconductivity to a lesser extent	**Partner Arthur Paterson:** "The benefit of concentrating on specific industries is to know the people and the marketplace in depth. You have to fund the creation of companies in good times and bad; you can't jump in and out. Besides, we invest for five to ten years, so you can't make decisions on what's happening that day, or even over a few months."
Allen Patricoff Associates 545 Madison Ave. New York, NY 10022 (212)753-6300	$500 million worldwide, about half in high technology	About $25 million — half in high technology — in 1987; about the same in 1988	Telecommunications, banking, leveraged buyouts	**Partner John Baker:** "The venture business will be backing fewer startups this year. The number of new companies will not be as high. The risks have been higher than anyone anticipated. Instead, we'll be looking at more mature companies, in part because of changes in the economic environment."
Brentwood Associates 11661 San Vincente Blvd. Los Angeles, CA 90049 (213)826-6581	About $350 million	$30 million — about $18 million in high technology — in 1987; about the same in 1988	Leveraged buyouts, medical technology; also active in communications and software	**General Partner G. Bradford Jones:** "It's a mistake to target a specific market area. We're not close enough to it. We fund people, not industries. We look for good managers in a given area who see a market need."

Burr, Egan, Deleage & Company 1 Post Office Square Boston, MA 02109 (617) 482-8020	$250 million	About $30 million—80 to 90 percent in high technology—in 1987; about the same in 1988	Medical and biomedical products, semiconductors, voice and data communications, software	Partner William P. Egan: "1988 will not be bad for venture capital. One, we'll see more projects, because if companies need financing, they'll have to turn to us. Two, if public-company valuations are down, we can invest on more attractive terms. There may be a liquidity problem, but that's what our business is all about—being patient."
Institutional Venture Partners 3000 Sand Hill Rd. Menlo Park, CA 94025 (415) 854-0132	$150 million, 90 percent in high technology	$20 million—almost 90 percent in high technology—in 1987; slightly less in 1988	Semiconductors and semiconductor equipment, technical and scientific computers, computer-aided software engineering, computer-aided design and manufacturing, medical equipment, telecommunications, information management and data storage	Partner Reid Dennis: "If the market doesn't recover, there's no point in investing in private companies—they can't go public. We've been buying former venture-capital deals that are now public. We're using them as a place to park cash until we need it. But public stocks have not replaced private deals. We're still looking, still active, and still honoring our commitments. We'd sell the stocks if we found a private deal that looked attractive."
Kleiner Perkins Caufield & Byers 4 Embarcadero Center San Francisco, CA 94111 (415) 421-3110	$400 million, all in high technology	1987 investments not disclosed; should rise in 1988 with more later-stage deals	All areas of high technology, including medical products, biotechnology, computers, and software; also telecommunications in 1988	General Partner James Lolly: "It's unclear what the long-term results of the crash will be. It's only certain the market is not going to remain the way it is now. The mezzanine financing market could reappear almost overnight,

(continued)

FINANCING YOUR CD-ROM ENDEAVORS

WHERE VENTURE CAPITAL IS INVESTING NOW *continued*

Company	Assets	1987–1988 investments	Special interests	Comments
				or another investment vehicle could fill the gap. Long-term plans based on the events of October will probably have to be revised at some point."
New Enterprise Associates 1119 Saint Paul St. Baltimore, MD 21202 (301) 244-0115	$400 million	$40 million—70 to 75 percent in high technology—in 1987; about the same in 1988	Computers (including maintenance and leasing), health-care services and products (but not biotechnology), defense electronics	**General Partner Arthur Marks:** "We'll put some of the money in public companies this year because stock prices are so low. On a price/reward basis, stocks are more attractive than many new businesses."
Norwest Venture Capital Management 2800 Piper Jaffray Tower Minneapolis, MN 55402 (612) 372-8770	$250 million	About $100 million—70 percent in high technology—in 1987; $40 million in 1988	Historically, mainframe computers, peripherals, and software; medical technology; biotechnology; lasers. In 1988, materials technology, waste management, aerospace, medical technology, telecommunications, and computers	**President Daniel Haggerty:** "We're not scared off by bad economic times. Startup companies have one- to three-year incubation terms. The early stages of a company don't create revenue anyway; the return is later. So what better thing to do than put money there now and hit the market on the upswing later?"
Oak Investment Partners 257 Riverside Ave. Westport, CT 06880 (203) 226-8346	$250 million, 95 percent in high technology	About $25 million—75 percent in high technology—in 1987; about the same in 1988	Biotechnology; distributed computing, including telecommunications; very high-performance semiconductors; design automation	**Partner David Best:** "I see a lot of confusion, a lot of organizations sitting back and saying, 'I can't for the life of me see the next wave.' Deals are not coming to us as complete or as packaged as they used to; typically, it's a

			couple of engineers with a bright idea. Or, we find entrepreneurs, and we give them an office and tell them to think."
Sequoia Capital 3000 Sand Hill Rd. Menlo Park, CA 94025 (415)854-3927	$300 million, mostly in high technology	$22 million in 1987; will add later-stage financings to earlier concentrations on seed and early stage deals in 1988	Broad participation in medical and life sciences, computer software, services, computer software, and semiconductors	**Partner Michael Moritz:** "Many later-stage funds had gravitated to seed and early stage deals. There's not as much later-stage financing available, and we say there's a bit of a black hole in the market. With what's happened to the market, we're in a great position to invest in companies that can't go public or don't want to go public."
Sutter Hill 2 Palo Alto Square Palo Alto, CA 94306 (415)493-5600	Substantially more than $100 million, 90 percent in high technology	$10-$15 million—90 percent in high technology—in 1987; about the same in 1988	More in biotech, less in the computer industry; specialty semiconductors and niche-market computers	**Partner Leonard Baker Jr.:** "I don't expect any big changes from 1987. We do primarily startups, and I don't think what's happened in the stock market, or what may happen in the economy, will affect our startup investing plans at all."
T.A. Associates 45 Milk St. Boston, MA 02109 (617)338-0800	$400 million	$50-$75 million in 1987; $75 million in 1988	Software and computer services; environmental services; communications; health care, especially medical products	**Associate Brian Conway:** "It's obvious that the stock market's troubles impacted some of our liquidity plans; we had three companies postpone their initial public offerings. But strong companies are a long-term investment. They'll get their liquidity later."

(continued)

WHERE VENTURE CAPITAL IS INVESTING NOW continued

Company	Assets	1987–1988 investments	Special interests	Comments
Welsh, Carson, Anderson & Stowe 1 World Financial Center New York, NY 10281 (212)945–2000	$540 million	$120 million, mostly in later-stage financing and leveraged buyouts; 1988 plans not available	Companies with recurring income, such as technology services, including software and computer services; health-care products	**General Partner Andrew Paul:** "Spending up to $50 million in one deal, we're moving more toward being a merchant bank than a venture-capital firm. We changed because we made a lot more money in leveraged buyouts. It's much harder to make money in the pure venture-capital game."
Warburg, Pincus Ventures 466 Lexington Ave. New York, NY 10017 (212)878–0600	$1.5 billion, with a significant percentage in high technology	Not available	Neural networks, superconductivity, high-end and niche-market semiconductors, advanced materials and ceramics, special areas in telecommunications	**Managing Director and Partner Nissan Boury:** "For those of us with lots of cash, this market is very attractive across the board. As institutional sources of capital become conservative, we think there may be more investment opportunities for venture capitalists in more mature companies than there were before, both late-round private financing and public companies. But we still strongly believe in startup and seed companies."

By Frederic Paul. Reprinted by permission of Info Technology Publishing Corp., from *High Technology Business*. Copyright © 1988.

Evaluating a Venture Capital Firm to Meet Your Company's Needs

By Accel Partners

[When looking for venture capital, Accel Partners urges you to evaluate how the venture firm can enhance your decision-making process and help you steer a definite course toward success and prosperity.]

What is the best way to approach and work with a venture capital firm? What do venture firms look for in evaluating a new company? How should the entrepreneur go about evaluating that firm and any financing it offers to provide his company?

Venture firms are as different as entrepreneurs. There is thus a wide range among these firms in terms of their industry expertise, business experience and most importantly, their ability to work effectively with you.

Your process of selecting a venture firm is, therefore, much more analogous to the selection of other key managers in your company than it is to the selection of your bank for a loan. With a banker, the appropriate question is "How much money will he give me?" With a venture firm, the right question is "How much money will he make me?"

This is because your venture firm, if used effectively, will be an important element in the continuous decision making of your company. The venture capitalist can bring a broad perspective of experience to your corporate problems based on multiple other corporate situations in your industry with which he has been involved. This experience enables him to recognize patterns within your company and industry niche which may be invisible to you. For example, he must be aware of external factors beyond your control which are already influencing other market niches in your industry and which your company will either capitalize on or be limited by.

When you select a venture firm, you are likely to be embarking on a relationship that will last five to ten years or more and which can be a pivotal influence in turning your company into a major enterprise. Because of the rate at which a high growth venture company encounters new challenges, the relationship with your venture firm can be critical as decision making times can be greatly shortened.

A talented venture firm reinforces management's naturally good instincts on solving corporate problems and discerning industry directions. The less experience you have in some matters, the more you may need to rely on your venture firm's advice. The more experience you have, the more you will appreciate the quality of the advice.

The venture firm's investment makes it uniquely dedicated to your success. Venture firms only "succeed" if you succeed and this frequently depends on their ability to persuade you to do what is in your own self-interest. Therefore, the key question to ask in evaluating a venture firm is: Do you believe that you can develop a relationship with the firm such that your confidence in it will accelerate your prob-

WRITING YOUR BUSINESS PLAN

Can you write a business plan by yourself, without a consultant, using only a book on the subject for guidance? Depends. Consultants, naturally, insist you can't; authors of such books are less insistent on that point. Certainly reading a book—or several books—on the topic is a good idea, even if you plan to call in a consultant eventually. It's obviously an excellent idea if you expect to go it alone.

The problem is which book, or books, to read, since there are scores of them out there. Some titles come up again and again in conversations with experts. They (or their authors) are well known among entrepreneurs and investors and consequently are often recommended to entrepreneurs in need. Here's what we think of them.

How to Write a Winning Business Plan
by Joseph R. Mancuso
Prentice Hall, 1985, $12.95 paperback

A witty, urbane compendium from the founder and director of the Center for Entrepreneurial Management, New York, the book reads like a long conversation. As one of the U.S.'s experts on small business, Mancuso is streetwise about start-up financing. The business plan is the "steak" you're serving the venture capitalist, but what you're sellng is the "sizzle." That means you have to romance the investor. Your plan, your product, and your presentation all need sex appeal.

Faced, for example, with a hard-to-sell investment deal, Mancuso suggests you tell each potential investor that the deal is already 80% committed, and that you just need another $50,000. In other words you sell the last investment five times. Some of Mancuso's best ideas are sales-oriented, and you probably won't get them from other sources. Often wordy, the book is still an entertaining read. A great feature of this book, which is standard reading for many entrepreneurs, is the appendix: Enormous and invaluable, it includes three sample business plans (*Venture*'s is one), a source directory, and an ample index.

The Arthur Young Business Plan Guide
by Eric S. Siegel, Loren A. Schultz,
and Brian R. Ford
John Wiley & Sons, 1987, $22.95

The heart of this book is a dissection of the business plan for the hypothetical Good Foods Inc., an all-natural baby and children's food company. Annotating the plan with a crisp commentary, the authors steer clear of the cheerleading and cult-of-the-entrepreneur hooey that suffuses many entrepreneurial how-to books. The format encourages you to read the plan like an investor rather than an entrepreneur, and right there is the key to the whole business. You learn to look not only for exaggerated sales figures and low-ball assessments of the competition, but also to be on the alert for more subtle errors of omission.

lem solving and decision making to enable you to emerge as a world class competitor in your industry?

HOW VENTURE FIRMS EVALUATE YOU

This a two way process: You should be evaluating venture firms and how well they understand your market at the same time they are evaluating you. Unless you have previously known and worked with a venture firm, you should expect to have a number of intensive meetings with the firm's principals to develop a personal relationship. Remember, the venture firm is backing you and your team as individuals. A new start-up is like a marriage—both parties must get to know one another well before any long term plans can be made.

THE BUSINESS PLAN

The business plan you present to a venture capital firm will likely be the single most important written document in the early years of your firm. Investigation of this plan by the venture firm will account for much of the specific discussion you have with the venture firm. It is the vehicle around which you get to know each other.

The plan should contain the business concept, the marketing, production and technology elements, the backgrounds of the principal founders and how much money will be required. The more specific the plan, the better—

The Business Planning Guide: Creating a Plan for Success in Your Business
by David H. Bangs Jr.
Upstart Publishing Co., Fifth edition 1987, $16.95

This book by a former Bank of America lending officer—and ex-philosophy teacher—guides you step-by-step through the planning process as the partners of a Maine fish market analyze their business, plan its future growth, and apply to a local bank for a loan of $120,000. The method is Socratic, with question clusters to guide the reader through the planning process. Rather than cautioning you to avoid overemphasis on product benefits, for example, Bangs explains, "The key question is not, 'What are your products or services,' but rather, 'What are you selling?'" The message is subtle but valuable: Whatever you have on your shelves, your customers are buying intangibles like convenience and consumer values. The message need not be limited to retail businesses.

There are also sections on basic bookkeeping and accounting that will help those without formal business training. Many definitions of business concepts will enlighten the uninitiated. But Mr. Bangs, why such a skimpy index?

Business Plans That Win $$$: Lessons from the MIT Enterprise Forum
by Stanley R. Rich and David Gumpert
Harper & Row, 1985, $19.95

Getting through this book must be like making a presentation at a session of the renowned MIT Enterprise Forum: at once exhilarating, instructive, and dangerous to the ego. Present your plan, then duck under the hail of criticism and analogies. This book is the same way: valuable criticisms and suggestions, served up with a helping of glibness. For example, should entrepreneurs reach an impasse during the writing of the plan, the standoff can be resolved by "good editing" and "a sense of humor." Exactly what those qualities are we are not told.

Organization is weak. Important suggestions appear almost randomly; subheads flagging them would have helped. Repetition is a problem. For instance, the authors warn against the trend toward padding plans with "reams of Visi-Calc or other spreadsheet data" on page 40, four pages after this caveat appeared the first time. The authors should heed their own advice: edit, edit, edit.

Despite these flaws, the book is well worth obtaining. The authors have impressive credentials. Rich is a cofounder of the MIT Enterprise Forum, and Gumpert is a former small business editor of the *Harvard Business Review*. And no question about it, both men are at home in the entrepreneurial trenches.

By Warren Strugatch. From "The Practical Entrepreneur," the June 1988 issue of *VENTURE, For Enterpreneurial Business Owners & Investors,* by special permission. Copyright © 1988 Venture Magazine, Inc., 521 Fifth Ave., New York, N.Y. 10175-0028.

both for the venture capitalist now and you later on. Ironically, experience has shown that the longer the plan, the lower the likelihood of success. The concise articulation of a simple but powerful concept for an innovative solution to an emerging but important unmet customer need is a hallmark of a good business plan.

As every business has different needs and goals, one really cannot be much more specific about what should be included in a plan. However, there are some general principles that can be followed, both in developing the plan and in the subsequent dealings with the venture firm. You can keep these principles in mind and assess your own plans and discussions against them.

DEFINING YOUR CONTRIBUTIONS

It may seem self-evident to say that a new company must make a true contribution to prosper, but attention to this fundamental discipline of a free market system is often lost in the enthusiasm to start a new company in a growth market. Unfortunately, despite that growth, market share will only go to a new company if it is adding value by solving unmet customer needs.

A simple formula venture capitalists tend to use in evaluating the potential size of your company is:

Market Size × Market Growth × Your Contribution = Size

Naturally, the more experienced the venture capitalist is in your industry, the more readily he is likely to grasp the significance of your contribution to the target customers.

In defining your company's contribution, a balance must be struck between biting off too much too soon and not having adequate "value added" to justify starting the company. If the definition of "served customer needs" is too narrow, the company will tend to be vulnerable, small and potentially trapped in a limited growth path. On the other hand, too broad a definition requires resources beyond what the company will have for years.

Ideally, a company should initially serve highly specific customer needs that lie within a broader generic category of needs of the same customers or industry. The company can then execute profitably in the short-term as well as grow smoothly through a coherent product line and market expansion. To grow continuously, a company must constantly and more broadly redefine its contribution to the market. Last year's contribution must become next year's "feature" within a broader definition.

A venture firm can substantially assist an entrepreneur in defining and focusing his company's contribution by bringing a broad horizontal view of industry market needs to complement management's in-depth, vertical niche view. The business plan is the vehicle to articulate this definition.

INDEPENDENT VERIFICATION OF KEY PLAN ASSUMPTIONS

Every business plan rests on certain key assumptions. These often include the technological expertise of the founders, production techniques and marketing strategies.

The analytical role of the venture firm is to identify these key assumptions and then independently correlate them with both independent sources of information and the venture firm's own experience. Time can easily be wasted performing due diligence on irrelevancies.

You can help this process, and thus speed up decision making, by clearly stating key assumptions on which your new firm's success will be based and identifying independent sources—customers, former employers or industry experts—for verification. Of course, the more knowledgeable a venture firm is in your industry, the easier it will be for them to recognize the key assumptions and independently verify them with their own sources.

RISK IDENTIFICATION

Venture firms approach the venture business as much from the standpoint of "risk reduction" as from opportunity maximization. That is, the operating assumption is that opportunities can be realized by eliminating the risks (impediments) to their achievement.

Almost by definition, the companies in which venture firms invest will be standing in the middle of enormous opportunities. The practical problem then becomes eliminating the impediments to achieving this success.

Thus, your plan and your discussions with the venture firm must address the question of risk reduction: How much money will it take to eliminate each major risk, and what will be the milestones in measuring whether that goal is being achieved?

Obviously, risk can never be fully eliminated; however, there are definite benchmarks in technical and marketing accomplishments that represent the lowering of risk levels.

Performing an analysis with respect to risk reduction will put you on the same wavelength as your potential venture investors. You can evaluate in this process whether the venture firm really appreciated the risks particular to your industry.

Of course, each milestone of risk reduction achieved is the basis for raising additional money for the company.

COMPETITIVE ANALYSIS

The absence of good analysis and lack of an appreciation of the competition are probably the most common mistakes made by new entrepreneurs. Therefore, one way to distinguish yourself and your business plan from the many others a venture firm is reviewing is through the quality and completeness of your analysis of the competition.

If you have done such an analysis, you will be able to easily convince the venture firm that your key assumptions are realistic and reasonable. Furthermore, in the process of describing

> *The absence of good analysis and lack of an appreciation of the competition are probably the most common mistakes made by new entrepreneurs.*

the competition, you will accelerate the education of the venture firm vis-a-vis your relative position in the market. You will find that this "relative" information is very important to the venture firm in reaching a decision.

Insightful understanding of competition in your market place by the venture firm can be critical to your obtaining their backing. Usually, new technology driven markets emerge at the intersection of two or more established markets. A subtle grasp of why the traditional suppliers will be slow to cross into this emerging product market category is critical to comprehending the opportunity for a new company. Of course, when it comes to assisting in future product strategy and money raising, this competitive understanding by your venture firm is critical.

OPENNESS

Entrepreneurs often worry that venture firms will be frightened off if they know how many risks are really involved in accomplishing the business plan of a new venture. This can be a fatal mistake for the entrepreneur, because an experienced venture capitalist is not likely to make a positive decision until these questions have been answered.

Your objective, assuming you want to do business with a particular venture firm, is to get the venture capitalist comfortable with the project and management team. The venture firm must not be made to feel there are "unknowns" lurking the background yet to be discovered.

In your first meetings with a venture capitalist, it may appear that his limited knowledge about your particular industry niche makes it unnecessary or unwise to tell him all the problems that your company will face. This is a serious error to make. When a venture capitalist doesn't know what the right questions are, he won't make a positive decision. Rather, he will just keep asking questions until he feels he has asked the right ones. Since your objective is to get the venture capitalist to make a quick, positive decision, you may as well identify what all the problems are right up front.

Remember: A venture firm is in the business of working with the problems you foresee in your company's growth, so you need not be concerned that identifying these will frighten off the firm. Dealing with risks and uncertainties is a venture capitalist's business, and you need to get him quickly to the point of feeling he knows what those uncertainties are.

Most venture firms also realize that every management team will initially have significant gaps in its experience. Often the team has the

125 MORE CHANCES

The facts speak for themselves. Venture capital is hard to come by. Unless you're prepared to meet a venture capitalist's stringent criteria, your business isn't going to receive the dollars you desire.

Take heed: It's your business plan and your connections (attorney, accountant, another entrepreneur) that get you through the door. Of 16,800 business plans received by the 10 most active venture capital firms on the Venture Capital 100, only six over-the-transom plans—those that came in without a recommendation from someone known to the venture capitalist—received funding.

Given those odds, entrepreneurs better be dead certain that their companies meet basic criteria. Why waste time better spent looking for money elsewhere?

"The deal has got to make an awful lot of money," says David Gladstone, president of Allied Capital Corp., Washington. Entrepreneurs ought to remember that not even all soundly profitable companies will look awfully profitable to a venture investor. Robert D. Pavey, a general partner at Morgenthaler Ventures, Cleveland, compares two growing seed companies. In both instances the venture capitalist could invest $1 million for 50% of the companies' equity. Five years later projected sales at both companies should be $20 million.

One, a widget company, is in an industry in which companies are normally priced at 10 times earnings. Therefore, based on this company's projected $1 million annual profits, total value of the company would be $10 million. Owning 50%, the venture capitalist would make a $4 million profit on a $1 million investment in five years. This falls short of the ideal 50% compounded annual return on investment in that time span by about $2.6 million. That goal could have been achieved by owning about 80% of the company's equity, but, Pavey declares, "We're in the partnership business, not selling the entrepreneur into bondage."

In the other case, a medical company projects a net income of $2 million and a multiple of 15. Therefore, total value of the company would be $30 million. In this instance the venture capitalist, again owning 50%, would make $15 million.

Since an early stage company has little or no history, venture capitalists will analyze your sales projections and your market research. "We do valuations all the time, but at the seed stage they're a little different," says Thomas A. Penn, president of Genesis Seed Management Co., Malvern Pa. "You have to throw in subjective things: What do I really think, what do I feel."

All business and personal references and credit reports will be checked. "Life's too short to give money to people you don't trust," says Pavey.

By Frances C. Marshman. Reprinted from the June 1988 issue of VENTURE, For Entrepreneurial Business Owners and Investors by special permission. Copyright © 1988 Venture Magazine, Inc., 521 Fifth Ave., New York, NY 10175-0028.

technical expertise necessary to build the product but only limited marketing and general management experience. Actually, this can be a positive and low-cost approach to getting started.

The best way to protect against easily frightened—or worse, less-than-capable—venture capitalists is to be open about the problems. If they are frightened off, don't regret it. When a venture capitalist only wants to hear about the opportunities and not the problems, then you should be nervous.

OBJECTIVE STANDARDS

Evaluate a venture capital firm the same way you would evaluate any other key management team member. That is, look at the firm's record of experience, external contacts and accomplishments. How directly relevant to your company's challenges is this record? Has the firm done it before? If you don't feel comfortable with first hand impressions, check with other entrepreneurs with whom the firm has worked. Some specific areas about which you might inquire include:

- What companies has the firm been involved with in the past, and how does the history of those companies compare with the future you envision for your company?

- What was the firm's relationship with those companies? Was it as a passive investor, or did it make a constructive contribution?

- What do the entrepreneurs in those companies say about the firm's contribution?

- What industries is the firm investing in? Does the firm have sufficient experience in your industry to understand and contribute to your potential?

- How helpful is the firm going to be in the future financing of the company? What has it done for other companies along this line in the past? Has it stuck by its companies in difficult times?

In practice, the price will not vary much from firm to firm—after all, venture financings are a free and competitive market. No venture firm will remain in business long if its pricing is not essentially competitive and fair.

- Does it have a reputation that will attract other financial sources? Does it know how to handle investment banks and other financial sources to minimize the future dilution?

- What is the depth of resources of the firm in terms of people and money? You should get to know as many of the principals and consultants of any firm as possible since they all represent potential resources available to you in the future.

- Will the firm be helpful in establishing overseas sales and distribution for you? For technology companies, overseas sales can be key to a company's financial success.

- Will the firm be helpful in finding and attracting key managers when needed by your company? Do the firm's historical associations suggest: access to high quality technology managers in your industry, a reputation that will help attract them to an embryonic company, and experience in evaluating such managers?

The answers to these questions will be infinitely more important to the eventual value of your company than the terms or amount of your initial financing. Indeed, while every entrepreneur's first objective must be to get a good price for his company, a common mistake among first time entrepreneurs is being overly concerned with this goal.

Excessive preoccupation with achieving the "best deal" can result in a delayed project or, worse, becoming "over shopped" to the point of not being able to be financed. In practice, the price will not vary much from firm to firm—after all, venture financings are a free and competitive market. No venture firm will remain in business long if its pricing is not essentially competitive and fair.

New companies should add to their management team the highest quality people who can be found. Never compromise in favor of someone who can be added for a little less salary or equity. The higher the quality of the individuals, the more likely they are to make key contributions.

The same advice holds in evaluating and selecting a venture firm: Aim for the very best.

Reprinted by permission of Accel Partners, a Princeton, New Jersey, based venture capital firm specializing in high-tech investments.

CREATIVE COLLABORATION

BEYOND VERTICAL INTEGRATION: THE RISE OF THE VALUE-ADDING PARTNERSHIP
By Russell Johnston and Paul R. Lawrence

WORKING TOGETHER FOR CD-ROM
By Richard A. Bowers

TOWARD AN ALLIANCE BETWEEN INTERACTIVE TECHNOLOGIES AND HOLLYWOOD
By Harvey E. Harrison

Beyond Vertical Integration: The Rise of the Value-Adding Partnership

By Russell Johnston and Paul R. Lawrence

From Harvard Business Review

[Although not specific to the CD-ROM industry or even to the larger electronics industry, this article offers an interesting analysis of a concept that could play a significant role in the development of strong CD-ROM markets. According to the authors, the value-adding partnership (VAP) offers the potential for cooperation and coordination from which all partners benefit. From their descriptions of working VAPs in the pharmaceutical and textile industries, we can identify similar relationships that have already developed in the CD-ROM industry and can envision how the creation of partnerships between industries might affect the future of CD-ROM.]

For decades large, vertically integrated companies have reaped the benefits of their size, growing stronger with every competitor they eliminated or engulfed. But the elephants aren't grazing so freely anymore. Another beast has been nibbling at the herbage, and its presence is beginning to be felt.

That beast is the "value-adding partnership"—a set of independent companies that work closely together to manage the flow of

> *Today, low-cost computing and communication seem to be tipping the competitive advantage back toward partnerships of smaller companies, each of which performs one part of the value-added chain and coordinates its activities with the rest of the chain.*

goods and services along the entire value-added chain. It is an organizational form much like the putting-out system of the early industrial revolution, whereby manufacturing was done in cottages and coordinated by a merchant-manufacturer who supplied the raw materials and sold the final product. But the value-adding partnership, or VAP, is not an anachronism. It is a product of its time, and its time may well have come.

Most historians agree that the development of cheap, centralized power and efficient but costly production machinery tipped the competitive advantage toward large companies that could achieve economies of scale. Today, low-cost computing and communication seem to be tipping the competitive advantage back toward partnerships of smaller companies, each of which performs one part of the value-added chain and coordinates its activities with the rest of the chain.

VAPs are not, however, necessarily technology driven. They may emerge as the result of computerized links between companies or they may exist before the technical links have been made. In all cases, they depend largely on the attitudes and practices of the participating managers. Computers simply make it easier to communicate, share information, and respond quickly to shifts in demand. They facilitate VAPs but alone don't create them.

To better understand what a value-adding partnership is and how it works, let's look at some that are doing especially well. [1]

McKesson Corporation, the $6.67 billion distributor of drugs, health care products, and other consumer goods, is among the most successful. The business press has often cited McKesson for its innovative use of information technology to improve customer service and cut order-entry costs. But McKesson's story is much richer than most people know. Once a conventional wholesale distributor squeezed by vertically integrated chain stores, McKesson has transformed itself into the hub of a large value-adding partnership that can more than hold its own against the chains.

McKesson's evolution to a VAP was triggered by fierce competition from large drugstore chains, which were eating into the business of the independent stores McKesson serviced. McKesson realized that if the independents died, it would soon follow suit. To protect their business, McKesson's managers began to look for ways to help customers.

Their search focused on a rudimentary order-entry system at one of McKesson's warehouses. In the early stages, the system included data-collection devices, powered by car batteries, that were wheeled around customers' stores in shopping carts. The system dramatically cut the costs of processing orders by expediting the steps of checking inventory, calling in an order, manually recording the order, and eventually packing and shipping it. McKesson soon discovered that the system could also specify how to pack orders so that they coincided with the arrangement of customers' shelves. Doing so made restocking more efficient.

These successful uses of information technology spurred the search for others. McKesson managers soon realized they could use the computer to manipulate data to help customers set prices and design store layouts to maximize the profits of each particular store. They also began using it to perform accounting services, such as producing balance sheets and income statements. And they discovered that the system could be used to warn consumers of potentially harmful drug combinations by tracking prescription histories.

McKesson thus offered the independent drugstores many advantages of computerized systems that no one store could afford by itself. The drugstores were able to offer their customers better prices, a more targeted product mix, and better service, all of which helped them stand up against the chains. Still, the drugstores maintained their autonomy, so they could be responsive to the needs of the local area and form lasting ties with the community. This actually gave them an advantage over the chain stores, whose managers had to answer to headquarters and could be transferred from one location to another.

McKesson, of course, benefited from the independents' good health. The user fees covered the cost of service development plus provided a return on the investment. Since the system was introduced in 1976, sales to pharmacies have soared from $900 million to over $5 billion. And the more efficient ordering systems allowed the company to reduce its warehouses from 130 to 54, eliminate 500 clerical jobs devoted to taking telephone orders, strengthen its customer base from 20,000 customers averaging $4,000 a month in orders to 15,000 customers averaging $12,000 to $15,000 a month, and reduce the average number of shipments per customer from two per day to two per week while lowering its own and customers' inventory costs.

The close and productive link with customers wasn't good enough, however, to satisfy McKesson's imagination. The company recognized that the up-to-date information on sales had immense value to product managers of consumer goods manufacturers and proceeded to sell it to its own suppliers. Suppliers used it to make more timely shipments to McKesson in much the same way as McKesson had done with the drugstores. Computer-to-computer ordering from suppliers permitted McKesson to cut its staff of buyers from 140 to 12. Meanwhile, suppliers could schedule production more efficiently and streamline their inventories.

Another McKesson innovation was to use the computer system to help process insurance claim applications for prescription reimbursement. This strengthened the ties among insurance companies, consumers, and drugstores by speeding payments and smoothing administrative hassles. McKesson's total network

---

WHAT'S A VALUE-ADDED CHAIN?

The term *value-added chain* comes from the field of microeconomics, where it is used to describe the various steps a good or service goes through from raw material to final consumption. Economics has traditionally conceived of transactions between steps in the chain as being arm's-length relationships or hierarchies of common ownership. Value-adding partnerships are an alternative to those two types of relationships. Usually, the partnerships first develop between organizations that perform adjacent steps in the chain.

A value-added chain for packaged foods might look like this:

farmer → broker → basic processor → packaged goods producer → distributor → retailer → consumer

thus includes manufacturer, distributor, retailer, consumer, and third-party insurance supplier.

What makes McKesson so powerful—and what makes it a VAP—is the understanding that each player in the value-added chain has a stake in the others' success. McKesson managers see the entire VAP—not just one part of it—as one competitive unit. It was this awareness that allowed McKesson's managers to look for opportunities beyond their own corporate boundaries. They looked for ways the resources at one part of the value-added chain could be used in another. And their efforts to be competitive went beyond cost cutting. Many companies focus on trimming costs to increase profits, and they consider opportunities only within the unit defined by ownership. McKesson also looks for ways to add value by creating new services.

This ability to see beyond the corporate boundaries has another important advantage. It permits recognition of serious threats that lie elsewhere along the value-added chain. Because McKesson knows its own fate depends on that of its suppliers and customers, the company monitors competitive dynamics throughout the chain and tries to fix weaknesses wherever they occur. When all the partners are strong, the entire value-added chain can stand up to the toughest of competitors, integrated or not.

The McKesson partnership is so successful that others in the pharmacy distribution business have emulated it or withdrawn entirely. But most have missed the point. It is easy to make the mistake of thinking that McKesson's network is nothing more than a computer system with terminals in someone else's building. The wires and processors are not what make McKesson successful. True, the McKesson VAP grew out of the company's computer system, but information technology did not create the VAP. Rather, it was the managers who understood the relationships along the entire value-added chain and the need for each link in the chain to be as strong as possible. Information technology is not even a necessary ingredient in a VAP, as the next example demonstrates.

The textile industry of central Italy comprises many successful VAPs, which have evolved very differently from McKesson. [2] Over the past 20 years, 15,000 to 20,000 smaller companies have replaced all but one of the large, vertically integrated textile mills of the Prato area. By 1982, these companies were employing 70,000 people and exporting about $1.5 billion worth of products. The industry's disintegration may have begun partly to avoid labor legislation, but the new structure has allowed the industry to thrive for more basic reasons.

The Italian story really begins in the early 1970s, when Massimo Menichetti took over a large, integrated textile mill from his father. [3] At that time the company's future—indeed that of the whole Italian textile industry—looked bleak. Labor costs were soaring throughout Italy, and foreign competition was intensifying. Furthermore, a trend toward greater product variety meant that companies had to be able to create new designs quickly and efficiently, shifting production from one product to another without wasting time or materials. Innovation and flexibility had become critical to survival. Increasingly squeezed between rising production costs and falling market prices, Menichetti's mill had been losing money for several years.

Menichetti believed that the company had become too big and bureaucratic to adapt to the new competitive demands, so he proceeded to break the company into eight independent organizations. He arranged to sell between 30% and 50% of the stock in those companies to key employees, who would make the purchases with company profits—thus enabling them to become part owners without putting up any of their own money. The ownership transfer was to be gradual, over the course of three years. By the end of that period, the new enterprises would have to make half their sales to outside companies—to avoid a slip into complacency.

To demonstrate his resolve to play only an advisory role and keep out of operations, Menichetti also started a marketing company in New York. He stipulated that it could represent no more than 30% of the production volume of the Menichetti group.

Within three years, the dismantling of the Menichetti mill was complete and business was being conducted very differently. Since then, other integrated mills have patterned themselves after the Menichetti VAP. Small companies with cooperative relationships are now spread through the entire Prato area of central Italy.

Formerly, in each large mill, one group of managers oversaw the entire process, from assessing the market to designing fabric to supervising every detail of production. Now, small groups—sometimes a family—take total responsibility for their part in the process. Each shop has certain special skills. One may be particularly good at producing high-quality knits for dresses; another may be expert at mixing colors. Work is contracted out to whichever shop can meet the market's needs at the time. Each, therefore, has great incentive to stay in touch with fashion trends and environmental changes and to be ready to react quickly. Otherwise, it would lose business to other producers and might even go out of business.

At the center of each set of small companies is an independent master broker, or *impannatore*. In the Menichetti VAP, Massimo Menichetti himself plays this role. The *impannatore* manage the relationships among the various shops. They are facilitators and problem solvers who carry information from one place along the value-added chain to wherever it will be most useful. They get involved in all aspects of the textile business: raw materials purchases, fabric design, production contracts, transportation, and sales. They look at the weaver's samples for next year and if they think they will sell, take them to customers all over the world. If the market objects to the weaver's price, the *impannatore* may help the weaver find ways to trim costs. They also negotiate with raw materials suppliers and transportation providers.

Being close to the customer, the *impannatore* were the first to realize that market changes required increased innovation and flexibility. They took the lesson to heart and, more importantly, carried the word back to the small manufacturers. To avoid losing business because of an inability to react fast enough, the production shops have adopted the latest textile machinery, including numerically controlled

REFERENCES

[1] For other discussions of the new organizational forms, see Raymond Miles and Charles Snow, "Network Organizations: New Concepts for New Forms," *California Management Review,* Spring 1987, page 62; Robert G. Eccles, "The Quasifirm in the Construction Industry," *Journal of Economic Behavior and Organization,* December 1981, page 335; Calvin Pava, "Managing the New Information Technology: Design or Default?" in *HRM Trends and Challenges,* ed. Richard E. Walton and Paul R. Lawrence (Boston: Harvard Business School Press, 1985); and Andrea Larson, "Networks as Organizations," unpublished manuscript, 1987.

[2] This description draws heavily on Michael J. Piore and Charles F. Sabel, *The Second Industrial Divide* (New York: Basic Books, 1984) and on Gianni Lorenzoni, *Una Politica Innovative* (Milan: Etas Libri, 1979).

[3] The facts about Massimo Menichetti are excerpted from the HBS case, Massimo Menichetti (B) 686-135, revised October 1986, prepared by Ramchandran Jaikumar.

> *Sharing information is very different from sharing rewards. In a VAP, as in any other industrial or organizational structure, innovation and adaptation must be rewarded if they are to be encouraged.*

looms. Whole chains, not just individual players, adapted quickly to the market information, and all have benefited.

Realizing that their partners must also be financially sound, efficient, and marketwise if they themselves are to be competitive, the players in the Italian textile VAPs are eager to share information and cooperate. In recent years, they have developed computer systems that rush information from partner to partner. The technology enhances coordination and boosts the speed and quality of responses to the market. The computer systems enhance the VAPs, but again, do not create them.

Of course, sharing information is very different from sharing rewards. In a VAP, as in any other industrial or organizational structure, innovation and adaptation must be rewarded if they are to be encouraged. In the Prato area, the *impannatore* can ensure that the rewards are shared appropriately by influencing prices and channeling work only to cooperative members. They can, for instance, withhold work from a shop that is trying to drive out otherwise successful competitors through predatory pricing.

The Prato mammoths gave way quietly and gracefully to the extraordinarily successful VAPs. Systematic, close coordination is now the rule, not the exception. In fact, the ties exist not only vertically, with suppliers and customers, but also horizontally, with what would usually be considered direct competitors. A weaver that guesses wrong one season might well receive overflow orders from a competitor that guessed right. They both understand that next year their roles may be reversed. And they know that if they help each other through tough times, they can avoid building overcapacity that could eventually hurt them all. Computer networks have been extended to interconnect the Italian VAPs, so when one VAP cannot deliver, another can be called on right away.

After only five years, all Menichetti's productive units had over 90% utilization of their machines. Both labor and machine productivity had increased. New machines had been added, increasing capacity by 25%. Product variety was increased in each of the eight units from an average of 600 to 6,000 different yarns. Average in-process and finished-goods inventory dropped from four months to 15 days. What works for Menichetti works for the Italian textile industry as a whole. From 1970 to 1982, Prato production of textiles more than doubled, while that in the rest of Europe declined steeply.

Other VAPs are alive and well and show that Prato and McKesson are not flukes. The construction industry is a third example. It has operated like a value-adding partnership since the time of the Roman Empire. General contractors subcontract almost all the work on a construction job, soliciting bids from a selected set of subcontractors they trust and making contracts with "partners" who offer reasonable prices—not always the lowest bid.

Japanese trading companies are venerable VAPs that are even more extensive than those in the construction industry. They arrange for the buying and selling of goods at every step of the value-added chain, from mines to household consumers, across several continents. They never get involved in operations. Although some Japanese companies are now choosing to develop their own brand images and find their own way to foreign markets, trading companies remain central to Japan's economic success.

Japanese auto companies also operate as VAPs. Toyota, for example, directly produces only 20% or so of the value of its cars, while GM and Ford produce 70% and 50% respectively. Chrysler's comeback was due in part to the creation of a VAP with its suppliers, distributors, and union. It produces only around 30% of the value of the cars it sells. Many industry observers attribute Ford's recent gains on GM to Ford's aggressive moves to form partnerships with suppliers.

In the past 30 years, book publishing has evolved toward a VAP. The leading competitors have taken turns divesting various operations that were formerly vertically integrated. The printing function was one of the first to be farmed out, followed by graphics and artwork. Now the usual core function of publishing is brokerage and marketing.

The movie industry has been moving in a somewhat parallel way. Full-blown movie studios that hold exclusive long-term contracts with actors and directors, have a staff of full-time composers and scriptwriters, and own and operate fully equipped production lots are a thing of the past. Now the studios act like brokers who negotiate a set of contracts for a single film production. Old-fashioned studios have been unable to compete.

At least in theory, whenever a nonintegrated company deals with another company that performs the next phase of the value-added chain, both stand to benefit from the other's success. But usually, such companies hold each other at arm's length and struggle to keep any economic gains to themselves. In fact, organizations often try to weaken a supplier or customer to ensure their own control of profits. This is understandable, given that the widely followed competitive

> *A weaver that guesses wrong one season might well receive overflow orders from a competitor that guessed right. They both understand that next year their roles may be reversed. And they know that if they help each other through tough times, they can avoid building overcapacity that could eventually hurt them all.*

model suggests that companies will lose bargaining power—and therefore the ability to control profits—as suppliers or customers gain strength.

The relationship between companies connected only by free-market business transactions and guided by such a model of competitiveness is often guarded, if not antagonistic, and rooted in fear that the other will become a competitor or engage in some other opportunistic behavior. Naturally, such companies tend to share as little information as possible, and consequently managers often lack knowledge of the activities

> *At least in theory, whenever a nonintegrated company deals with another company that performs the next phase of the value-added chain, both stand to benefit from the other's success. But usually, such companies hold each other at arm's length and struggle to keep any economic gains to themselves*

elsewhere along the value-added chain. If a company perceives a trading partner as an adversary, it may ship shoddy materials, squeeze margins, delay payments, pirate employees, steal ideas, start price wars, or corner a critical resource—all practices that reveal a lack of concern for the supplier's or customer's well-being.

The conventional solution for ending such destructive games and for controlling resources is vertical integration. When organizations along the value chain are under one management, it is presumed that they can coordinate their activities and work toward a common purpose.

And, of course, they can often realize economies of scale.

But vertical integration has its weaknesses. In the process of exploiting their distinctive competences, many large, integrated companies emphasize one competitive dimension. In an integrated company, such focus can actually be a liability, because the strong culture that supports that focus makes it hard to perform tasks that require distinctly different orientations and values. A business that emphasizes low cost, for instance, may run its factories well, but its R&D, design, or marketing functions may have trouble innovating. In a chemical company dominated by commodity production, the culture may inhibit specialty operations. The packaging division of a large paper manufacturer that emphasizes mass production may have trouble responding to the market as an independent competitor.

Perhaps the best example of this problem is in manufacturing. Many manufacturing companies that have invested heavily in flexible manufacturing systems in recent years have trouble making the new technology achieve its potential. The culture and practices that support long production runs of standardized parts don't fit the new emphasis on wide product variety.

The problem of focus applies to horizontally integrated companies as well. A manufacturer of automobile parts is unlikely to be equally successful at making other products. Although the similarities may be many, whatever differences exist are likely to keep one or the other lines from doing as well as it could if it were the company's sole product. And in many companies, large size itself creates a certain complexity that inhibits communication, innovation, and flexibility.

In a VAP, each small operating company focuses on doing just one step of the value-added chain. Therefore, each unit can tailor all aspects of the organization to this single task. Personnel, plant and equipment, compensation schemes, career tracks, accounting systems, and management styles—all vary depending on the work to be done. The drugstores in the McKesson VAP can attend to their customers' needs and let someone else concentrate on getting the products on the shelf at the right time. In the Prato area, the small companies that produce fabric strive for low cost, coupled with flexibility; those who design the fabric emphasize innovation and creativity.

This sense of focus translates into low overhead, lean staff, and few middle managers. Decisions are made and executed quickly, so response time is short. Creative ideas are less likely to be suppressed, and more employees are exposed to the demands of the market. The fact that each company in a VAP is free to be different from the others creates a diversity that can be the seedbed of innovation. And marketing orientation becomes not an edict nor a difficult task. It follows naturally from the free flow of information throughout the value-added chain to so many of the people who actually do the work.

At the same time, value-adding partnerships have some of the advantages of vertically integrated companies. Managers in a VAP take an interest in the success of other companies in the value-added chain. Their partnership orientation means they work toward the common goal of making the whole VAP competitive. They have command of facts about the market and empathy for the other organizations they deal with. Because information is shared throughout the chain, they know a lot about the competition. And they coordinate their activities with those of their trading partners.

VAPs can also secure the benefits of economies of scale by sharing such things as purchasing services, warehouses, research and development centers, and of course information. McKesson's partners share access to the computer system. Partners in the Menichetti VAP are so congenial that they are housed under one roof; lines on the floor mark where one ends and the other begins. And that VAP has a cooperative transport system.

> *The fact that each company in a VAP is free to be different from the others creates a diversity that can be the seedbed of innovation.*

The power of the VAP is undeniable. To a great extent, VAPs have the best of both worlds: the coordination and scale associated with large companies and the flexibility, creativity, and low overhead usually found in small companies. VAPs share knowledge and insight but aren't burdened with guidelines from a distant headquarters. They don't have long forms to fill out and weekly reports to render. They can act promptly, without having to consult a thick manual of standard operating procedures. In an increasing number of industries, they are proving to be fiercely competitive against both large companies and small independents.

Indeed, the spate of failed mergers and subsequent divestitures and spin-offs, what some people call downsizing, demonstrates that conglomerates and vertically integrated corporations are not always the most competitive organizational forms. The largest organizations in the United States seem to be losing their footing. Employment at the approximately 800 companies ranked in the *Forbes* "500" on sales, profits, assets, or market value declined from more than 23 million in 1979 to 20.6 million in 1986. Average employment at the companies declined from nearly 29,000 to just over 26,000 during the same period. These numbers fell despite a significant rise in total U.S. employment, not to mention the acquisition programs many of these large companies pursued.

NEW TECHNOLOGICAL TOOLS HELP CREATE VAPS

Tools	*Implications*
Minicomputers and PCs; user friendly languages; inexpensive general-purpose software packages	Drastically improves the economics of small scale, providing wider access to information power to include the *smallest* organizations and the *lowest* organizational levels.
Data standards; bar codes	Enable rapid, inexpensive, accurate capture and use of information in electronic form, lowering transaction costs *between* organizations.
Information networking capability	Permits instantaneous sharing of information *between* organizations with shared interests—thus increasing speed and economy of coordinated response to market changes.
Computer-aided design	Improves speed and economy of response to customer needs by improving coordination *between* organizations in design functions.
Computer-aided manufacturing	Permits use of just-in-time practices *between* organizations.

Small size alone is not the answer. Many small companies that have open-market relationships with other businesses survive only at the whim of a larger competitor, customer, or supplier that could readily drive it out of business or acquire it if margins become attractive enough. Always constrained by fierce competitiveness and trading partners that know no loyalty, they have little freedom to make financial and operating decisions that are best in the long run.

The delicate issue of control raises questions about the viability of a VAP over time. Let's not forget how creative businesspeople can be. They can invent dozens of ways to take advantage of each other. What prevents them from playing destructive games with their VAP partners, who are, after all, potential competitors? What prevents hostile takeovers? In short, what is to stop a VAP from devolving into anarchy or back to a vertically integrated giant?

For a VAP to exist, its partners must adopt and adhere to a set of ground rules that generates trustworthy transactions. The sense of partnership must become an enforceable reality, despite the many uncertainties and opportunities for playing games. Advice on the best way to do this comes not only from the examples of successful VAPs but also from economists and political scientists who have experimented with the "prisoner's dilemma." The prisoner's dilemma is a game in which two "prisoners" are separated. Each has the option of either squealing on the other, thereby getting more lenient treatment for himself, or remaining silent, thereby saving both himself and his partner in crime. Of course, if one prisoner remains silent but the partner squeals, the silent person will suffer.

When the games are repeated over and over again, the strategy proving most beneficial is "tit for tat." That is, those players who cooperate on the first round and thereafter do whatever the other player did on the previous move are more successful. Those who don't catch on get eliminated. Robert Axelrod has summarized the extensive studies of the prisoner's dilemma in his 1984 book, *The Evolution of Cooperation*. His advice is particularly relevant to businesspeople in a VAP: (1) don't be the first to play games, (2) reciprocate with both cooperation and lack of it, (3) don't be too greedy, and (4) don't be too clever and try to outsmart your partner.

Studies of existing VAPs are far from conclusive, but early indications are that VAPs follow Axelrod's advice intuitively. They are thus very different from the theoretically perfect markets of economic theory, in which bidders balance supply and demand around price and caveat emptor is the guiding principle. Each company in a VAP cultivates relationships with only a few (from two to six) suppliers of critical items and customers. Having too many partners means few repeat transactions and no time for close relationships to develop. At the same time, partners avoid becoming overdependent on one relationship. A company can keep potential partners "on reserve" through occasional transactions so its welfare won't be harmed if a regular player fails to cooperate.

If partners are to help one another, VAPs must have ways of sharing information. If a partner's costs are creeping out of line, others must know so they can explore ways of helping with cost controls. Technological developments are making it easier for companies to exchange information (see the accompanying list of computer tools and their implications). But also important, successful VAPs must be able to punish partners for acts of opportunism and gaming.

In the Prato textile area, late delivery sometimes calls for withholding of new orders until the problem is rectified. And the construction industry has invented many ways to cope with changes in job specifications and raw materials costs as well as strikes and bad weather. The ultimate sanction, of course, is to terminate the partnership. In the Prato area, this could happen if, for instance, an *impannatore* failed to pass orders back to the weaver who had supplied the fabric design that was being sold.

It seems clear that, for at least some value-added chains, a value-adding partnership is a viable and advantageous means of achieving the benefits of vertical integration. By observing the characteristics of and the processes followed by successful partnerships, executives can deter-

> *To a great extent, VAPs have the best of both worlds: the coordination and scale associated with large companies and the flexibility, creativity, and low overhead usually found in small companies.*

mine whether VAPs might pay off for their organizations. Business relationships premised on the need to achieve bargaining power may be more aggressively competitive than is in their best interest. Remember that the examples cited earlier—U.S. automobiles, Italian textiles, and drug distribution—all evolved from competitive, sometimes acrimonious, relationships.

The economic logic of the VAP is compelling. And at least for now, VAPs are part of the business landscape. Others should mind their feeding grounds and watering holes, for even giants have their vulnerabilities.

Reprinted by permission of *Harvard Business Review.* "Beyond Vertical Integration: The Rise of the Value-Adding Partnership" by Russell Johnston and Paul R. Lawrence (July–August 1988). Copyright © 1988 by the President and Fellows of Harvard College; all rights reserved.

Working Together for CD-ROM

By Richard A. Bowers

[Here is another, less formal way to foster cooperation among the various players in the CD-ROM arena. As Richard Bowers explains, the Optical Publishing Association has an aggressive program to promote acceptance of optical media in the world at large and to enhance communication between industry participants.]

Success used to be a fairly straightforward proposition. A clever person came up with an idea for a product, assembled the pieces, and offered the result for a few coins of the realm. If the inventor's neighbors became customers, the product was a success. If they rode the inventor out of town on a rail, it was back to the drawing board.

Our entrepreneurial lives are considerably more complicated today. Advanced technology has made changes for the better in our lives, but it has wreaked havoc with the inventor and the entrepreneur.

Optical publishing on CD-ROM, CD-I, or any of their offspring or cousins, requires a complex technology dependent on many components and experts. No one is likely to undertake CD-ROM development alone. As a result, there are no lone wolves in the optical publishing business. The industry is a complex, tightly integrated, dynamic system. The fortunes of one player are impacted by the fortunes of many others.

Even with this tight integration, there are still problems to address and issues to be resolved. Physical interfaces for optical peripherals (such as CD-ROM readers) have become much easier to deal with over the last three years. But there are still probably too many decisions for a consumer to grapple with. The devices and their software drivers are not yet transparent. Software designs are still considered too complicated. Publishers and content owners who want to get involved in this new medium need help in understanding the opportunities and the issues in protecting their investment while they work in new ways with new distribution channels and, possibly, new customers.

And, perhaps most importantly, those in the marketplace have a long way to go in understanding the benefits of optical publishing, what to expect, how to evaluate products and applications, and how to meld a new type of information resource into their work and entertainment.

Enter the Optical Publishing Association (OPA). Introduced at Microsoft's Third International CD-ROM Conference in March 1988, and officially formed in September 1988, the OPA has set about the ambitious task of introducing CD-ROM and other optical media into the mainstream of information products, while promoting its distinct advantages for delivering information in radically new and effective ways.

OPA's program includes the following activities:

- Market development:
  - A specially designed press package to be made available to a wide range of media representatives to increase the levels of awareness and accuracy in the press about the potentials and issues of optical publishing.
  - A continuing series of articles and article ideas for various media ensuring exposure of the benefits and potentials of optical publishing.

- Public and professional information:
  - A series of pamphlets and brochures introducing the potentials and issues involved in optical publishing, including brief sketches of the process, discussion of product-development techniques, and a membership list by category of the OPA.
  - A service to members providing tips and techniques on product promotion, access to lists of suggested recipients for press releases, and a mailing service for press releases and promotional material.

- Technical forum:
  - A committee of industry advisors to provide OPA's recommendations on new standards in the optical publishing arena.
  - A task force to examine continuing issues of standardization and compatibility within the environment of MS-DOS and MS-DOS extensions.

- Information services: An OPA newsletter to provide organizational news and to serve as a communication medium among the membership.

As the industry and the OPA grow, these services and activities will change to meet the needs of members.

CD-ROM and other optical media offer important new opportunities to present and distribute information. Optical publishing must not be perceived as simply another delivery mechanism for information products as we have always known them. To be successful in presenting optical publishing, we must learn how to take advantage of the unique characteristics of the medium and to market those characteristics effectively. Few business organizations have the resources to undertake such mammoth tasks on their own. The OPA is the entrepreneur's way to combine individual resources with those of others who have common concerns and interests.

If you would like more information about the OPA and its program, contact:

Richard A. Bowers, Executive Director
Optical Publishing Association
1880 Marckenzie Drive, Suite 111
Columbus, OH 43220
(614)442–1955, FAX (614)442–6522

[*Richard A. Bowers is Director of Development at the Applied Information Technologies Research Center in Columbus, Ohio, and Executive Director of the Optical Publishing Association. Having written extensively about optical applications, Bowers created the* Optical Publishing Directory, *the first printed guide to CD-ROM titles.]*

Toward an Alliance Between Interactive Technologies and Hollywood

By Harvey E. Harrison

[According to Harvey Harrison, it's time to renew the relationship between the film and television industries and the interactive technologies, but it is the fledgling interactive industry that must come courting. Hollywood will need to be convinced that CD-ROM and interactive multi media are not just a fad—another boom that will inevitably go bust.]

I advocate an alliance between interactive technologies and Hollywood, an alliance that I will explore from creative, business, and historical perspectives. I will also look at challenges this alliance may face in the future.

For simplicity, with deliberate imprecision, I refer here to motion picture, cable, network and syndicated television, home video, and related areas simply as "Hollywood." The "interactive technologies" and "interactive entertainment technologies," as I sometimes refer to them, are even broader and vaguer than film/television; they include CD-I, DVI, interactive videotape and, surely, many things not yet identified.

THE CREATIVE ENTERPRISES OF HOLLYWOOD AND INTERACTIVE TECHNOLOGIES

I see two profound creative similarities between Hollywood (film/television) and the interactive technologies: They are collaborative, and they are lifelike. In the Good Old Days (more about this era later) approximately five years ago, production of interactive entertainment software was commonly accomplished by young people hunched in drafty garages hacking manically on

HARVEY E. HARRISON

Home: Los Angeles, California
Job: Vice President of Business Affairs, Columbia Pictures
Quote: *"The industry should be headed toward the convergence of interactive technologies and the established motion picture and television media."*

their Apples. The creative work was largely solitary and cheap. Yet emerging interactive technologies require the talents of a growing number of audio, graphics, and other technical artists. Interactive entertainment is becoming the work of a group. Film/television also are group efforts and, while far from operating perfectly, they offer an invaluable opportunity to study truly collaborative artistic media for their positive and negative lessons.

Film/television and interactive technologies are both lifelike. When Obi-wan Kenobi says, "May the Force be with you," it feels as though he is saying, "May the Force be with *you*." A good film makes you feel as if you are actually in it. Yet I dare to say that interactive entertainment technologies intrinsically are even more lifelike, for they are active or interactive while Hollywood remains forever passive. Certainly the audiovisual capabilities of interactive entertainment are still primitive in comparison to those of film/television, but the ability of interactive technologies to allow involvement in entertainment points to a lifelike quality in art never before imagined.

In their common likeness to life, what can Hollywood teach interactive technologies? As motion pictures near their one hundredth anniversary, it seems clear that what distinguishes great films and television is that which makes life most engaging: *who* is involved and *what* is going on—simply put, character and plot, the art of storytelling adapted to audiovisual media. Interactive technologies are audiovisual media, too, and the hard-learned lessons of Hollywood storytelling offer a crucial foundation for discovery of the art of interactive storytelling.

In turn, the art of interactive storytelling is absolutely crucial to the success of the interactive entertainment technologies. A story about an early filmmaker illustrates this point. When asked to predict the future of motion pictures, the filmmaker replied, "Except as a limited tool to produce parlor magicians' illusions, I see little future for it." Then D.W. Griffith appeared. So did Chaplin and Keaton. All were artists who, with works of genius, elevated a parlor-trick technology to enduring art. We are now at the beginning of the era in which the interactive entertainment technologies must find their founding storytellers. The lessons of film/television will be invaluable in this effort.

THE BUSINESSES OF HOLLYWOOD AND INTERACTIVE TECHNOLOGIES

As I said earlier, making interactive entertainment was cheap in the Good Old Days. Interactive entertainment today and in the future will not be. Some estimates of CD-I program production costs are comparable to the production costs for a half-hour, Saturday-morning animated program for network television. Marketing and distribution costs in interactive entertainment will also rise sharply, to the levels of such costs in film/television. The business of interactive entertainment is becoming one of substantial financial investment, just as in Hollywood.

On a daily, project-by-project basis, Hollywood must answer tough business questions. What creative elements justify this large investment? Which of the parties involved bears the financial risks? Which parties enjoy the rewards of success? While Hollywood makes fun of itself in works such as *Network, S.O.B.,* and *Sullivan's Travels,* the film and television industries have a vigorous system of studios, agents, unions, and related people and institutions that make the American film/television media the most successful of such businesses in the world.

Interactive entertainment will inevitably face the issues described above, and it will do so without Hollywood's history or its support systems. The "wheel" of the film/television businesses has already been invented, and it carries its products successfully to market. Interactive technologies should study this wheel with care because it might be possible to adapt it to carry products to the new interactive entertainment market.

HISTORY: THE GOOD OLD DAYS REVISITED

Let us return to the Good Old Days. In the history of interactive entertainment, a mere decade takes us back to the Good Old Days. As I see this history, Nolan Bushnell was Christopher Columbus and he named his New World *Pong.*

In those Good Old Days, a powerful alliance inexorably seemed to be emerging between Hollywood and the interactive technologies. Not long after youthful artists hacked out video games on Apples in garages, giant entertainment companies positioned themselves for prominence in interactive entertainment: Atari/Warner Brothers/Warner Software appeared, as did Sega/Paramount/Simon and Schuster Software. Just as theatrical motion pictures are moved through a sequence of exploitations from theatrical distribution to cable to home video to network television, and then to free television, it seemed Warners and Paramount wished to do the same with interactive entertainment. First the studio would release an arcade version, then perhaps a television version, and next a home cartridge or computer version.

Other overlaps between film/television and interactive technologies occurred. *Star Wars* and other successful feature films became arcade games. Successful arcade games—PacMan, Donkey Kong, Frogger, and Qbert all appeared as animated Saturday morning network television programs. The Good Old Days were good indeed: There seemed to be not merely an alliance of film/television and interactive technologies but a convergence of these media. Then, quite abruptly, the alliance fell apart, and film/television producers went on with their

> *The "wheel" of the film/television businesses has already been invented, and it carries its products successfully to market. Interactive technologies should study this wheel with care because it might be possible to adapt it to carry products to the new interactive entertainment market.*

> *Successful film/television people enjoy huge financial rewards and intoxicating creative opportunities. It may prove difficult to interest such people in the financially and creatively immature interactive technologies.*

main businesses, largely ignoring interactive technologies.

Why this happened is unclear but might be due to the fact that Hollywood is a business of trends and fashion. Hollywood saw the fad of arcade games and embraced it, but that fad proved to be a bubble that popped. About the same time, the personal computer appeared as a consumer phenomenon, and for a short while it seemed that the home computer would be as popular as the home videocassette recorder was about to become. Hollywood's relationship with interactive technologies in those Good Old Days was a boom, and a boom that went bust.

THE CHALLENGE TO REVIVE THE ALLIANCE

I urge the formation of a new alliance between Hollywood and the interactive technologies. Yet I recognize that there are imposing challenges to this alliance. The film/television technologies are unique, but they resemble other fashion industries (like clothing and toys) in that events occur at a dizzying pace. The first challenge to this alliance is the fact that film/television people are interested in next year's feature motion picture releases or the Fall network schedule; they are not, as a rule, concerned with the next decade's new entertainment media. The attention span of Hollywood is short.

Most of those active in film/television ignore interactive technologies. One major studio executive I know who is acquainted with interactive technologies said, "We'll wait until some succeed and some fail in these new areas, and we'll buy one of the winners." Similarly, a major motion picture producer I know who has to some extent investigated interactive technologies said, "Those people [in interactive technologies] can't understand verb tenses. They talk about the new media as if they are here in the present when, in reality, they're way off in the future."

Another challenge to the alliance is that rewards for success in Hollywood are high. Successful film/television people enjoy huge financial rewards and intoxicating creative opportunities. It may prove difficult to interest such people in the financially and creatively immature interactive technologies.

How, then, can we revive the alliance between the film/television and interactive technologies? The impetus must come from those working with interactive technologies; indeed, some companies and individuals within interactive technologies are already working vigorously for the alliance of these media. Here are some tactical suggestions:

- Study Hollywood, from both the creative and business perspectives.
- Establish rapport with those active in film/television.

- Design specific approaches to an alliance that address the interests of those in film/television.

I have no magic to offer, but I do offer warm encouragement. The interactive technologies are, in my experience, populated by futurists, pioneers, and visionaries. These are people equipped for the challenges described here. Happily too, I believe there is magic in what interactive technologies and Hollywood can accomplish together, and I believe that this magic will ultimately prevail.

[Harvey E. Harrison is Vice President of Business Affairs at Columbia Pictures Television, Inc./Tri-Star Television. Prior to joining Columbia, he had primary sales and business responsibility for TMS Entertainment Inc., an animation company that produced series and special television programs for clients such as CBS, Disney, Universal, and King World.]

CD-ROM INDUSTRY PROFILE

MICROSOFT THIRD INTERNATIONAL CONFERENCE ON CD-ROM: THE SURVEY

Microsoft Third International Conference on CD-ROM: The Survey

[By surveying conference attendees of the 1988 Third International Conference on CD-ROM, Microsoft obtained a profile of CD-ROM industry participants. A questionnaire was included in the program materials for the conference, held March 1–3, 1988. Of the 1200 conference attendees, 936 people completed surveys, for a response rate of 78 percent.

Percentages are based on the total count for each question. For questions with multiple parts, percentages are usually based on the total count for each part. For questions requiring a write-in response or containing the category "other," unique answers were gleaned from all 936 surveys. Depending on the diversity of responses, these questions may list percentages for the highest ranking responses in the category, or the responses may be tabulated in a separate section, where total counts for each response and percentages based on the total count for the category are given.]

SURVEY RESULTS

1. How are you involved with the CD-ROM industry?

Percent	Profession
18%	Application designer
16%	Management
16%	Marketing
16%	Software developer
10%	Consultant
8%	Press
7%	Other
6%	End user
4%	Hardware designer

Other (percentages based on total for this category)

24%	Media manufacturer
16%	Publisher
16%	Research/product development

2. How is your company involved with the CD-ROM industry?

Percent	Company focus
17%	Publisher/information provider
14%	Software developer
10%	CD-ROM title developer
9%	CD-ROM drive manufacturer
9%	Computer manufacturer
9%	Consultant/custom developer
7%	Data preparation
7%	End user
6%	Press
5%	Internal publishing
3%	Other
2%	Dealer/distributor

Other (percentages based on total for this category)

50%	Media manufacturer
18%	Investor
10%	Government

3. What were your company's sales last year?

Percent	Sales
25%	Over $1 billion
20%	Under $1 million
13%	$1 million–$10 million
12%	$10 million–$50 million
9%	$250 million–$1 billion
9%	don't know
7%	$100 million–$250 million
4%	$50 million–$100 million

4. What portion of your company's sales were CD-ROM-related?

Percent	CD-ROM sales
58%	Under $100,000
18%	Don't know
8%	$100,000–$500,000
7%	$1 million–$10 million
4%	$500,000–$1 million
3%	$10 million–$50 million
2%	None (user added)
1%	Over $50 million

5. Which publications do you regularly read?

Percent	Publication
22%	*CD-ROM Review*
14%	*Infoworld*
14%	Other (see the "Publications" section for a full listing)
10%	*CD-Data Report*
10%	*Computerworld*
9%	*CD-I News*
6%	*Information Week*
6%	*Videodisc Monitor*
4%	*Optical Memory News*
3%	*Information Today*

Other (percentages based on total for this category)

Percent	Publication
32%	Macintosh publications
15%	*PC Magazine*
13%	*PC Week*
6%	*Byte*
3%	*Wall Street Journal*

6. Which of these publications is your primary source of information about CD-ROM?

Percent	Primary source
62%	*CD-ROM Review*
15%	*CD-Data Report*
7%	*Infoworld*
5%	*CD-I News*
4%	*Optical Memory News*
3%	*Computerworld*
3%	*Videodisc Monitor*
1%	*Information Today*
1%	*Information Week*

7. Where do you think businesses will purchase CD-ROM products?

Percent	Business purchases
28%	Direct sales
27%	Computer dealers
16%	Software specialty stores
15%	Mail order
9%	Bookstores
4%	Don't know
2%	Other

Other (percentages based on total for this category)

Percent	
16%	Consultants
16%	Systems integrators

8. Where do you think consumers will purchase CD-ROM products?

Percent	Consumer purchases
20%	Computer dealers
17%	Software specialty stores
16%	Bookstores
15%	Mail order
8%	Discount stores
7%	Direct sales
7%	Record stores
7%	Video stores
3%	Don't know
1%	Other

9. Over the next two years, what applications do you think will be the consumer market's "best sellers" and at what price?

The following are the three applications receiving the most votes accompanied by their most popular price range. Percentages are based on the combined totals for the three applications. For a full listing of all applications, please see "Best Sellers" later on in this section.

Percent	Application	Price
43%	Encyclopedias	$100
29%	*Bookshelf*	$200
28%	Educational applications	$50

10. List three CD-ROM applications you are aware of and/or familiar with.

The three applications receiving the most votes follow. Percentages are based on the combined totals for the three applications. For a full listing of all applications, please see the "Existing Applications" section.

Percent	Application
60%	*Bookshelf*
29%	Grolier's *Encyclopedia*
11%	R.R. Bowker's *Books in Print*

11. Which companies do you view as leaders in the CD-ROM industry?

The five companies receiving the most votes follow. Percentages are based on the combined totals for the five applications. For a full listing of all companies, please see the "Companies" section.

Percent	Company
43%	Microsoft
19%	Philips
13%	Sony
13%	Apple
12%	Hitachi

12. Do you have a need for software authoring tools that would permit you to develop in-house CD-ROM applications (full text searching, multimedia) on a PC?

68%	Yes
32%	No

13. If you answered *yes* to question 12, which features would you like to see in these authoring tools?

Percent	Feature
15%	Hypertext/multimedia
15%	Index and search package
11%	Raster (bit-mapped) graphics
11%	Windowing environment
10%	Networking ability
10%	Photographs (grey scale)
10%	Printer output
10%	Searching multiple databases
6%	Vector graphics
2%	Other

Other (percentages based on total for this category)

18%	Full motion video
18%	Mac availability
7%	Compression/encryption

14. Would you buy these authoring tools?

Percent	Response
82%	Yes
18%	No

15. How much would you be willing to pay?

Pay flat fee:

Percent	Price
25%	Don't know
12%	$10,000
11%	$5,000
9%	$2,000
6%	$1,000
6%	$500

Pay royalty:

Percent	Royalty
18%	5% of revenue
18%	2% of revenue
15%	Don't know
12%	10% of revenue
12%	1% of revenue

Buy runtime copies (1 per client):

Percent	Price
33%	Don't know
10%	$20
10%	$5

Pay per disc charge:

Percent	Price
13%	$10
9%	$5
9%	$2–$4
9%	$2
9%	Don't know

16. Is your company currently involved in producing a CD-ROM application—or will it be in the next year or two?

Percent	
80%	Yes
20%	No

17. If your answer to question 16 is yes, please answer below:

a. Which stage of development is the application in?

Percent	Stage
45%	Application is currently in development
32%	Development will begin within next 2 years
23%	Application is completed and in distribution

b. How many titles will you have completed by the end of 1988? 1989?

1988	1989	# of titles
86%	62%	0–5
7%	17%	6–10
2%	11%	11–25
2%	4%	26–50
1%	2%	51–100
1%	2%	101–500
	1%	501–1000

c. Which markets will these address?

Percent	Market
20%	Education/training
14%	General business
13%	Consumer
11%	Other
10%	Accounting/financial
10%	Engineering information
8%	Medical information
7%	Legal information
7%	Scientific information

Other (percentages based on total for this category)

Percent	
21%	Libraries
17%	Government
9%	Publishing

d. What type of application is it?

Percent	Type
31%	Database distribution
18%	Multimedia publishing
10%	Image publishing
10%	Periodical publishing
9%	Training
8%	Software distribution
6%	Expert system
5%	Other
2%	Audio publishing

Other (percentages based on total for this category)

Percent	
16%	Technical documents/manuals
9%	Education
9%	Games
9%	Library holdings

e. How will this application be used?

Percent	Use
51%	For resale
25%	For internal company use
24%	For a specific client

f. How far away is your first release date?

Percent	Release in
38%	Less than 6 months
29%	6 months to 1 year
18%	1 to 2 years
9%	Not sure
6%	More than 2 years

g. What approximate price do you expect to charge per title?

Percent	Price
16%	Not applicable
13%	Don't know
12%	$1,000–$5,000
11%	$100–$250
10%	$50–$100
9%	Under $50
9%	$250–$500
9%	$500–$1,000
7%	$5,000–$10,000
4%	over $10,000

h. Will you offer this application on a subscription basis?

Percent	Subscription
38%	Yes
26%	No
24%	Don't know
12%	Not applicable

i. How often will you update the application?

Percent	Update frequency
29%	Quarterly
21%	Don't know
14%	Monthly
13%	Semi-annually
13%	Annually
5%	Not updated
5%	Not applicable

18. What CD-ROM applications would you like to see developed?

See the "Future Applications" section for a full listing.

19. What problems/barriers do you feel are facing the CD-ROM industry?

See the "Problems/Barriers" section for a full listing.

20. Do you feel there is a need for interleaved audio in CD-ROM?

Percent	Subscription
82%	Yes
18%	No

PUBLICATIONS

5. Which publications do you regularly read?

Publication	Response
Byte	9
CD Computer News	1
CD-ROM Librarian	4
Communication News	1
Communication Week	1
Computer Dealer	1
Computer Design	1
Computer Language	1
Computer Research News	3
Computer Science News	2
Consumer Reports	1
Database Advisor	1
Datamation	1
Datanet	1
Dr. Dobbs	1
EE Times	1
Forbes	1
German publications	1
IEEE	1
IIB	2
Interactivity Report	2
Internal information	1
Italian publications	1
Lotus	1
Macintosh publications	51
Memory Optique	4
MIS Quarterly	1
MIS Week	2
Newsnet	1
OIS	1
Optical Insights	1
PC Magazine	23
PC Week	20
PC World	2
Personal Computing	1
Photonics	1
Publishers Weekly	1
Release 1.0	1
Satsop PC Letter	1
Spectra	1
Time	1
Videocomputing	3
Wall Street Journal	5

BEST SELLERS
Over the next two years, what applications do you think will be the consumer market's "best sellers" and at what price?

Responses are listed by application followed by price. Question marks indicate that no suggested price was supplied.

   Fifteen people gave *None: There are/will be no consumer best sellers because of industry problems/shortcomings* as their response.

Application	Responses	Price
ABI Inform	1	?
Accounting	1	$3000
Adult applications	1	?
	1	$50
Artificial Intelligence	1	$100/hour
ALDE Shareware	1	$99
Almanacs	2	?
	1	$35
	1	$50
Animation/video cut and paste libraries	1	$50
Any large compendium of knowledge	1	<$300
Apple Applications for Kids	2	<$100
Appliance repair	1	$99
Application collections (word processing, spreadsheets, graphics)	1	<$500
Art collections/artwork	1	$149
	1	$100–200
Atlases	1	$59
Audio/visual discs	1	$150
Auto repair	1	$89
Bibliographic indexes	1	$200–1000
Bibliographies	1	$100
Biographies	1	<$100
Biographies of celebrities (famous speeches, songs, concerts, masterpiece performances, interviews, etc.)	1	$39.95
BOC Test Disc #2	1	$125
Books:		
General	1	$299
Great Books	2	$50
	2	$99
	1	$200
"Live" books	1	$75–100
Talking books	1	$25
Bookshelf	1	free with drive purchase

Application	Responses	Price
Bookshelf	10	$1–50
	7	$51–99
	7	$100–199
	8	$200–299
	4	$300 and over
	37 total	
Bookshelf-like applications/writer's tools	1	$99
	1	$200
Books in Print (BIP)	2	?
	1	<$100
	BIP + Ulrich's	same cost as hard copy
Business applications:		
Business information sources (BIS)	1	<$200
	1	$400
Business class applications (like Actavision)	1	$150
General	1	$100
	2	$200–299
	1	$300
	1	$500
	2	$1000 and above
CAI applications	1	?
CAP CD-ROM	1	$1500
Car navigation	1	$500
Catalogs:		
Mail order/shopping catalogs	4	?
	1	free
	1	$4
	1	$100
With direct dial capability	1	<$200
Parts catalogs	1	$1000
Product catalogs	1	?
	1	$250
Sears Catalog	1	free
CD-I applications	1	?
CD-ROM Sourcedisc	1	$90
Census data	2	$1000
Children's applications	1	?
City information (maps, telephone directories, ZIP codes, yellow pages)	1	$49
Cliff Notes	1	$100

(continued)

BEST SELLERS *continued*

Application	Responses	Price
Clip art/video libraries	1	<$500
College entrance exam trends for past years	1	$400
COM/fiche replacement	1	?
Compuserve/BBS forum	1	$49.50
Congressional Record	1	?
Consumer directories (retail, etc.)	1	$50
	1	$150
Consumer market applications	1	<$300
Consumer Reports	2	$99
Cooking	1	$50
County and state libraries	1	?
Databases	1	?
	1	$1000
Database subscriptions	1	$40/month
Small text databases	1	<$800
Datext	1	$10,000
Demos	1	$49
Desktop presentations	1	$100–400
Desktop publishing	1	$250
Dictionaries:		
Dictionaries/electronic encyclopedias	1	$195
OED	1	$200
General	2	?
	1	$59
	3	$100–199
	1	$200
	1	$300–400
	1	$500
Directories (association members,etc.)	2	$100–400
	1	$200
Directories (businesses)	1	$500–1000
Directories (U.S. and State officials, etc.)	1	$595
Dissertation Abstracts (UMI)	1	?
DVI applications	1	?
	1	<$100
Educational applications:		
Educational courses	1	$900
Educational hypertext applications	1	?
	1	$150

Application	Responses	Price
General	4	?
	15	up to $50
	8	$51–100
	6	$101–199
	3	$200–299
	1	$300–600
	37 Total	
Remedial education tools	1	$50
Encyclopedias:		
Encyclopaedia Brittanica	1	$250 per year with yearbooks included in annual re-releases
Encyclopedias and atlases	1	$150
General	2	?
	9	up to $100
	11	$101–200
	8	$201–300
	8	$301–500
	4	$501–1000
	42 Total	
Graphics encyclopedias	1	<$200
Medical	1	<$100
Multimedia	3	<$100
	1	$195
	1	$500
Subject specialty	1	$75
World Book	1	$50
Entertainment	2	?
	7	<$50
	2	<$100
Entertainment (interactive)	1	$50
ERIC	1	$650
"Everything you ever wanted to know about…"	1	?
Excel	1	?
Exercise information	1	?
Jane Fonda interactive	1	<$50
Expert system	1	$100

(continued)

BEST SELLERS *continued*

Application	Responses	Price
Financial data:		
Financial planning	1	$50–500
General	1	?
	1	$100
	2	$250
Historical financial data	1	$500
Fiscal/legal information	1	$3000
Fonts	1	$495
Games:		
Adventure games	1	$50
Games (interactive)	3	$30–50
	1	$100
General	1	?
	3	$10–25
	5	$31–50
	3	$51–100
	12 Total	
Multiple game discs	3	$25–60
	1	$100
Party games	1	$50
Spy games	1	$70
Trivial Pursuit	1	$400
Geographic applications	1	$500
Geovision/US.Atlas disc	1	$495
"Gloria" applications	1	$500
Government applications	1	?
	1	$300
	1	$1000
Graphics:		
Digitized graphics	1	?
Graphics libraries	1	$500
Grolier's Encyclopedia	1	?
	1	$125
	1	$200
Guinness Book of World Records	11	<$100
Handbooks	1	$100
Health care aids	1	$150–200
Health and occupational hazards	1	$100
High technology	1	$200–300

Application	Responses	Price
Hobbies:		
General	2	?
	1	<$50
Hobby histories (golf, football, poetry)	1	<$99
Home market applications:		
Family finance/legal advisor applications	1	$99.50
Family medical advisor applications	2	$99
General	3	$10–40
	2	$50–100
Home libraries	1	$300
Home schooling/education	1	?
Household hints	1	$99
Household repair	1	?
	1	$49
"How to" applications	1	$5–10
	1	<$50
	3	$49–99
	1	$199
H.W. Wilson discs	1	$1500
HyperCard applications	3	?
	1	$50
Hypermedia applications	1	$79.95
	2	$100
	2	$199
	1	$695
Industry information	1	$5000
Information	2	?
	1	<$100
Instructions	1	<$25
	1	$100
Interactive fiction	1	$75
Interactive video	1	$100
	1	$1000
Internal company data	1	?
Knowledgeset	1	?
Legal applications	1	<$200
	1	$500
	1	$1200
	1	$2500

(continued)

BEST SELLERS *continued*

Application	Responses	Price
Library applications:		
Library abstracts	2	?
Library automation aids	1	$100
Library card catalogs	1	?
Linguistic applications:		
General	1	<$100
	1	$300–400
Language study	1	$75
Multilingual interactive	1	?
Translation tools for teaching	1	$300
LISE	1	?
Literature	1	$100
	1	half the hardcopy cost
Lotus applications:		
Lotus master (collection of applications)	1	$49
Lotus *One Source*	1	?
Lotus related products	1	?
Map applications:		
General	2	$100–199
	1	$200
	2	$300
Map/locator	1	$395
Maps with vacation pictures	1	$89.95
Marketing applications:		
General	1	<$100
	2	<$195
Market research data	1	?
Medical applications:		
General	2	$25–50
	2	$200–300
	1	$500
Medline	1	?
	1	$1000–2000
Dr. Spock	1	<$50
Nutritional/medical reference	1	$75–100
PDR product	1	?
Physician's libraries	1	$1000
Wellness	1	$69

Application	Responses	Price
Movie applications:		
Films	1	$2.98
	2	$20–30
Histories (of Greta Garbo, etc.)	1	<$100
Movie catalogs	1	$49
Movie maps of places	1	<$100
Movie reviews	1	?
Music applications:		
General	1	$100
Music catalogs	1	$15.95
Music catalogs with illustrations	1	$20
Music lessons	1	$500
Music libraries	1	<$400
Music theory/listening	1	$500
MIDI-oriented discs for music industry	1	$35–75
Record libraries	1	$29
	1	$50
	1	<$80
Museum tours	1	<$50
OAG	1	$50
Online database replacement	1	?
PCSIG type applications	4	?
	1	<$50
	1	$99
	1	<$250
Periodical applications:		
General	2	$300
	1	$500
Magazines (interactive)	1	$20/issue
Magazines (special interest)	1	$200
Newspapers (back issues)	1	?
Reference (all back issues of *Byte* with other related periodicals on a single disc)	1	<$100
Population	1	$99
Pornographic CD-I	1	$50
POS	1	$200
Private usage (single shot)	1	$20,000
Product analysis	1	$20–30

(continued)

BEST SELLERS *continued*

Application	Responses	Price
Productivity applications	1	$300–500
Professional services	1	$1000
Public domain software	1	$30
Publication applications	1	?
Purchasing decisions	1	?
Reader's Guide to Periodical Literature	1	?
Real estate	1	$12
Recreation	1	<$100
Reference applications:		
General	2	?
	4	$25–49
	3	$50–99
	12	$100–200
	2	$250
	2	$300–400
	25 Total	
Reference libraries	1	<$1000
Reference (specialized)	1	$500
Regulatory information	1	$100
Religion:		
Bible	1	$200
Religions of the World disc (with subject index and hypertext features)	1	$200
Research applications	1	?
Restaurant guides	1	$79
Samplers	1	$29
SAT study guide	1	$1000
SBC	1	$150
Self-improvement	1	$90
Diets/menus	1	$95
Sidekick	1	$99
SilverPlatter titles	1	$500–800 each
Simulation	1	$100
	1	$149 with DVI
Small business aids	1	?
	2	$149
	1	<$1000
Sound/pictures discs	1	<$100
Specifications and standards	1	$2000

Application	Responses	Price
Sports statistics	1	?
	2	$50–100
Sports with interactive video	1	?
Spreadsheet applications	1	$300
Statistical data	1	$300
Stat Pack	1	$100
	2	$120
	1	$125
Stock market information	1	$50
"Super CD" of CD-I discs	1	$20–25
Surveys	1	?
Sweet's Catalog	1	$150
SWPM	1	$100
Tax preparation disc	1	?
Taxes with artificial intelligence	1	<$150
Technical documentation/manuals:	3	?
	1	$200
Service manuals	1	150% of hardcopy cost
Telephone directories:		
Business white pages	1	$150
General	2	$15–50
	2	$100
	5	$101–400
	3	$500 and above
	12 Total	
Yellow and white pages with phone interface		$125/year
Yellow pages	1	<$500
Toll free numbers + ZIP codes	1	$79–89
Thesaurus:		
General	1	$59
	1	$200
Thesaurus and Dictionary	1	$199
Thomas Register	1	$300
"Time Line"	1	$100–200
Training courses	1	<$100
Travel/tourism applications:		
City travel directories	1	$25–50
General	1	?
	5	$10–50

(continued)

BEST SELLERS continued

Application	Responses	Price
Surrogate travel discs	1	$50
Timetables	1	$50
Tour guides	1	$3
Travelogues	1	?
"Walkaround city"	1	$100–200
Upscale market applications	1	$10
U.S. data	1	$125
User group libraries	1	<$100
Vendor/sales data sheets	1	$500
Vertical specialty applications	5	?
Video applications	1	?
VDI	1	<$2000
Video databases	1	$200–500
Video magazines	1	$10
Video/rock mixtures	1	$20
Visual art databases	1	$300
Western Library Network (WLN)	1	$2000
WINGZ	1	?
Wordprocessing	4	$100–200
	1	$300
ZIP code/country code applications	1	$150

EXISTING APPLICATIONS

List three CD-ROM applications you are aware of and/or familiar with.

Applications are listed alphabetically, followed by the number of responses received.

Application	Responses	Application	Responses
ABI Inform	1	Datext	12
Abstracts	1	Desk reference set	1
Adonis	1	DIALOG on Disc	10
AIDS disc	2	Dictionary	2
Airline technical publications	2	Diocles	2
Apple showcase disc	2	Disclosure	6
Atlas of the U.S.	1	Discovery samples	1
Audit preparation	1	DMA data	1
Automobile parts	2	DOD applications	1
Bell & Howell automobile catalog	2	Drugindex	1
Bible	2	Dutox	2
Bibliofile	8	EDOK: European Kompars Directory	1
Bibliographic tools	4	Educational applications	5
Big Weather	1	Electronic book	1
Biotechnologies	1	Encyclopedias	7
BOC Test Disc #1	1	*Encyclopaedia Brittanica*	1
Boeing 757 Manual	4	ERIC	6
Bookshelf	232	ERM	1
Bowker BIP	43	ESL	1
Bowker BIP International	1	*Facts on File*	6
Brady Guide to CD-ROM	1	Financial applications	5
Business application	1	Font storage/retrieval applications	1
CAB	1	Geovision	16
Catalogs	2	Government applications	3
CATS	1	*Grolier's Encyclopedia*	113
CCOHS/CCINFO	4	Homebase/BusBase	1
CD-Fiche	1	Honda parts	1
CD-Word	1	HPLaseROM	7
Census	4	HydroData	1
Compact Cambridge	1	HyperCard	1
Compustat	1	InfoDisc	1
Constitution	3	InfotracII	3
COSIP	1	Intelligent Catalog	2
Databases	3		

(continued)

EXISTING APPLICATIONS *continued*

Application	Responses
Interactive video applications	1
Internal use CD-ROMs	1
ISI Science Citation Index	1
I Speak English/Intechnica	1
Knowledgeset	1
Kwikee Ad	2
Land surveys USGS	1
Lasercat (WLN)	1
LC Catalog	1
Learnbyte (German)	1
Learning Disc	1
Legal applications	4
Lexical database (HM)	1
Library applications	4
Library catalogs (LPAC)	5
LISE	2
Manuals	3
Maps	5
Marketing applications	2
Mastersearch	1
Medical applications	7
Medline	25
Metroscan Property System	1
MGH Sci/Tech Encyclopedia	5
Micromedex Poisonindex	12
Microsoft Programmer's Library	1
Moody's corporate data	1
MultiAd	4
NASA archive disc	1
National Decision Systems	1
Noah's Ark	1
Nynex Telephone Directory	2
OED	8
One Source (Lotus)	32
One Stop	1
PAIS	1
Palenque DVI	2
Parts catalogs	2
PartMaster (GM)	7
PCPlus	1
PCSIG	9
Personnet	1
Public domain software	1
Rainbow Homebase (Canada)	2
Reference materials	7
Research abstracts	1
Sabrevision	1
SBC	5
Science Helper	1
Scientific American Medicine	1
Service manuals	1
SilverPlatter discs	2
Simon's Taxes	1
Software distribution disc	2
Spreadsheets	1
Statistical applications	1
Stat Pack	7
Stock market applications	1
Tax analyst/private rulings	1
Tax discs	1
Technical documents	1
Telephone directories	6
Termdok (multilingual dict)	2
Testing applications	1
Textbooks	1
Thomas Register of American Manufacturers	1
TLODC (in-house application)	1
Training applications	1
Tristar patent disc	1
U.S. Post Office AVS+ZIP+4	1
Visual Dictionary	6
Whole Earth Review	4
Who's Who	1
Who Sells What (German)	1
WilsonDisc	1
Xearch by Xiphias	1
Your Marketing Consultant	3
ZIP codes	1
ZIP Plus	1

COMPANIES

Which companies do you view as leaders in the CD-ROM industry?

Companies are listed alphabetically, followed by the total number of responses received.

Company	Responses
3M	7
AIM	1
ALDE	1
Amdek	5
Apple	73
Archetype	2
Atari	1
Batelle	1
Bell & Howell	1
Bowker	6
Cedrom	1
Dataware	2
DEC	4
Denon	1
DIALOG	4
Disclosure	1
Discovery Systems	3
Disctronics	4
Dun & Bradstreet	1
Dupont	5
Fulcrum	3
GE (DVI)	19
Geovision	1
Government	2
Grolier	14
Hewlett Packard	3
Hitachi	68
IBM	4
Intel	1
IVID Communications	1
Knowledgeset	17
Library Corporation	1
Lotus	48
LSMI	3
Macromind	1
McGraw-Hill	2
Mead	1
Meridian Data	34
Micromedex	1
Microsoft	248
Mitsubishi	1
NEC	2
Northern Telecom	1
Online Computer Systems	3
Optical Media International	1
Pergamon	1
Philips	113
Publishers	1
Quantum Access Inc.	2
Reference Technology	21
Relational Technology	1
Rctcaco	5
Rothchild	1
SilverPlatter	12
Sony	81
Spectrum Interactive	2
STR	1
TMS	5
Toshiba	3
Tri-Star Publishers	2
Unibase Systems Inc.	1
US West Knowledge & Engineering	1
H.W. Wilson	1
Yamaha	1

FUTURE APPLICATIONS

What CD-ROM applications would you like to see developed?

CD-ROM applications are listed alphabetically, followed by the number of responses received.

Application	Responses
ABC information on flights	1
Advanced full-text retrieval	1
Advanced studies/specialized research field applications	1
Airline guide	1
Airline schedules	1
Animated tutorials for computer software	2
Apple applications	1
Applications that appeal to consumer market and are readily transferrable to CDI	1
Apple/Mac and Microsoft Windows use of WYSIWYG interface	1
Architecture database	1
Archive of computer conference procedures	1
Archive templates for historical materials	1
Archive technical publications	1
Artistic applications	1
Audio-controlled database for blind	1
Audio manipulation—powerful applications	1
Authoring tools	2
Automatic/semi-auto links of information- object in hyper-text products	1
Batch imaging	1
Bestseller, fun application, that all people would want to have	3
Bettmann Archive on disc	1
Bible (King James version)	1
Biographies of "great men and women" with documentation on their works	2
Books-in-Print type applications	1

Application	Responses
Books-in-Print expanded with book descriptions	1
Bookshelf in other languages (German)	1
Bookshelf for the Mac	1
Brainstorming utility/interface for CD-ROM data	1
Built-in telecommunications for searching remote databases as well as on disc	1
Business forms	1
Business information applications	1
Business plan developer	1
Business tools for small businesses	3
Camera, scanner, or imaging standards coupled with index, roam functions in authoring	1
Car navigation	2
Cartography	1
CASE tools	1
Catalogs	3
Catalogs—multimedia	2
CDI	2
Census data	1
Chemical abstracts	1
Children's applications	2
Children's applications—interactive	1
City maps	1
Clip art graphics	2
Collection of papers on state-of-the-art CD-ROM and computer technology	1
Collection of street software with intelligent search by application	1

602 SECTION VI: THE CD-ROM BUSINESS

Application	Responses
Company profiles for foreign countries with current data as well	1
Comprehensive collections in subject areas	1
Computer companies and products	1
Computer data sources database with index of products, company information and a "truth factor" index	1
Computer manuals	1
Computer science and reference works	2
Congressional Record	1
Consumer applications	8
Cooking	1
Cooking—recipe book	1
Databases	3
Databases (large textual type)	1
Databases/retrieval software available on an OEM/VAR basis at reasonable prices	1
Data libraries for objects	1
Demographic information	2
Demo/marketing applications	1
Developer's toolkit	1
Dictionary	2
Dictionary with fast search capability	1
Dictionaries integrated with reference and word processor and syntax checker	1
Dictionary—Japanese	1
Digital/analog interleaved system	1
Digitized graphics imbedded in applications	1
Digital olfactory output	1
Directories	3
DOS commands needed to access CD-ROM data	1
DVI	6
Earth science data	1

Application	Responses
Education	19
Education—large-scale databases for college-educated	1
Education—elementary and secondary school student/teacher resource	1
Education—educational applications for home use with text, graphics & sound	1
Education—university courses on disc	1
"Edutainment"	1
Effective indexing for converting large databases to CD-ROM	1
Electronic book	1
Electronic book reader with pictures	1
Electronics specs (IC, CSI)	1
Encyclopedia	12
Encyclopedia—Encyclopaedia Brittanica	3
Encyclopedia—DVI	1
Encyclopedia—Multi-media	3
Encyclopedia—Super	1
Encyclopedia—thematic subjects (art, aerospace, hi-fi, history)	1
End user ability to order disc configured with desired application software	1
Engineering	2
Engineering drawings	1
Engineering reference works: steel manuals, reinforced concrete manuals	1
Entertainment	7
Entry-level workstation for multimedia	1
Eraseable media	1
European financial data	1
"Everything known to man" CDI	1
Expanded print value-added products	1

(continued)

FUTURE APPLICATIONS *continued*

Application	Responses
Expert systems—interactive	1
Exploration stories	1
Export/import information	1
Family tree of world corporations	1
Financial data (i.e., CRISP databases)	4
Font library for laser printers	1
Font storage and manipulation application	1
Forms and publishing data	1
Full text/graphics on computer	1
Full text links	2
Full text products that lend themselves to many uses	1
Games	2
Games—adventures with many outcomes with sound & graphics	1
Geneology disc	1
Geodemographic information system	1
Geographic atlas with 3-D bird's eye view	1
Geographic data	3
Geographic information on foreign countries	1
Good text and image for display on high-resolution black & white monitor	1
Government data	2
Government regulations	1
Graphics compatibility with formats like SCODL	1
Graphics library with CAD software	1
Graphics/text database reference library	1
Help for information systems professionals (i.e., docs, configuration management), thereby expanding CD-ROM market definition	1
Historical/archival publications	1

Application	Responses
Home reference (i.e., Time-Life Books)	1
Horizontal applications	3
Horticultural text database	1
Hotel references	1
"How to" applications	1
HyperCard animation	1
HyperCard application to preview CDs in record stores	1
Hypertext applications	1
Hypertext access to encyclopedia-like database	1
Hypertext with graphics and efficient search engine	1
Identification system for internal use by employees	1
Image applications	1
Image database such as trademarks	1
Image retrieval capabilities	1
Indexing aids	1
Industry information	1
Industry-specific decision tools	1
Information services with a narrow target	2
Instructional applications with speech and sound usage	1
Interactive application that explains CD-ROM	1
Interactive book	3
Interactive fiction	1
Interactive information services	1
Interactive NOVA-type materials	1
Interactive presentation tools for business presentation, training	1
Interactive software	1
Interactive titles	2
Interactive video	1
Interactive video editing	3
Interactive voice tools for search software user interface	1

Application	Responses
Interface between CD-ROM-stored information and dynamic network-based information	1
Interface database with current events	1
Interface systems (word processor, spreadsheet)	1
International information application	1
Inventions database	1
Jane's Military Books	1
Jukebox	1
Language applications	3
Language—foreign language education pack	1
Larger compression scheme	1
Law enforcement (fingerprints, etc.)	1
Legal applications	1
Legal form books	1
Legal—retrieval of case law, statutes, legal forms, attorney general opinions	1
Learning products based upon existing database products	1
Lexicon	2
Library end user expert systems—interactive systems linking text and databases	1
Library CD-PAC	1
Library of Congress	2
Library of literary works/classics	2
Literature resources	4
Lotus—European versions	1
Macintosh applications	1
Mainframe access to display on IBM 3250 type terminals	1
Many databases accessed with one interface	1
Maps	1
Map/locator tied to ZIP codes, cities, with map generation	1
Maps/street	1

Application	Responses
Market research data	3
Mathematics helper	1
Mead Data Central publish some/all of Lexis/Nexis in CD-ROM series with jukebox player	1
Medtext	1
Microfiche to CD-ROM scanner	1
Modular seach engine and indexing components	1
MS-DOS Extensions to run on network	1
MS-DOS dictionary	1
MS-DOS reference library	1
Microsoft peripheral support of Apple and Apple extensions	1
Multimedia with AI	1
Multimedia consumer applications	2
Multimedia textbooks	1
Multimedia presentation tools	1
Multiuser LAN application with SQL retrieval to minimize network traffic	1
Music encyclopedia	1
Music—printable sheet music library	1
National Geographic with pictures, sound, and animation	1
Naval vessel repairs on disc	1
Navigation system	1
Networking interfaces	2
News (text) database of general items compiled annually	1
Non-text retrieval tools	1
Numeric/text databases	1
Office and factory automation related products	1
Online help for major CD-ROM applications	1
Out of print books	1
Patents	1
PC Software resource	3
Periodical applications	6
(back issues)	2

(continued)

FUTURE APPLICATIONS *continued*

Application	Responses
Current journal information	1
Complete computer periodical index	1
Computer periodicals	2
Historical newspapers	1
Scientific American, New York Times, Wall Street Journal, Sports Illustrated, Science Journal	5
Personal book storage	1
Point of sale	2
Population	1
Professional discs for undergraduate education/corporate use	1
Programmers reference library	1
Publishing applications	2
Raw data	1
Reader's Guide to Periodical Literature	1
Real estate	1
Reference	7
General reference works	2
Top 10 home reference works on disc	1
Replace COM	1
Research publications	1
Research tools database with expert front end	1
Retrieval software (intelligent)	3
Scholar's workstation	1
Scientific information	1
Searching chemical graphics	1
SGML tagging program for ASCII text	1
Shakespeare's works with analytical tools	1
Single product to do authoring and hypersearch	1

Application	Responses
Small business taxes with forms	1
Software tools distribution	3
Software that provides seamless link between CD-ROM and online database	1
Sophisticated financial planning tool	1
Sounds catalog	1
Source code library	1
Source to develop company applications (i.e., manuals, software, company databases) for 2000 discs	1
Special libraries that are subject-based	1
Statistical data	2
Statistical data with atlas	1
Stat Pack (updated version)	1
Stat Pack type applications	1
Support for remote dialing access	1
Survey data	1
Tax reference	1
Technical publishing for Fortune 100	1
Technical reference guides	7
Technology primers	1
Telephone and address book with audio	5
Text with illustrations and photos	1
Thesaurus	1
Training applications	8
Management simulation training	1
Travel/tourism	1
Travel guide: countries, culture, Maps and how to get around	1
World Traveller (business class)	1

Application	Responses	Application	Responses
Universal event calendar	1	Word processing	2
UNIX file system	1	WORM drives	2
Visicalc on disc	1	X-ray image database	1
Walking tour/history of world art	1		

PROBLEMS/BARRIERS

What problems/barriers do you feel are facing the CD-ROM industry?

Problems are listed alphabetically, followed by the number of responses received.

Problem	Responses	Problem	Responses
Ability of industry to maximize on converging media potential in products	1	Consumer doesn't need CD-ROM technology now	5
Administrative systems	1	Consumer resistance	1
Application of standards across a wide range of needs	1	Copyright/royalty issues	1
		Cost flux	1
Applications need to reflect user needs	1	Cost of mastering/replication	2
		Creating significant value-added services	2
Audio standards	3	Credibility of industry (due to changes in technology, etc.)	4
Authoring tools insufficiency	5		
Band width problem	1	Cross-disc use of copyrighted materials	3
Better understanding of the opportunity	1		
		Customers feel cheated by hardware costs	1
Can't be read in bed!	1		
CD-I/DVI/Multimedia compatibility issues	15	Data prep and development cost issues	7
CMI	1	Data security issues	1
Competition for limited capital	4	Data transfer rate	1
Confusion of competing technologies	3	Development of good interactive software	2
Compatible workstations	2	Development tools are weak	2
Computer friendliness/ease of use	6	Disc access time issue (indexing issues)	10
Confusion over toy vs. tool	1	Distribution (of information, methods, etc.)	2
Connectivity	1		
Conservative tendency in higher education	1	Distribution not sufficient	7
		Drivers for CD-ROM players	1
Consolidation/merging of industry needed	1	Exploring ability	1
		Focus on hardware technology, not on content/delivery	1
Consumer awareness/education	29		

(continued)

PROBLEMS/BARRIERS *continued*

Problem	Responses
Focus on old data	1
Full motion video	1
Future—overemphasis on the future	2
Getting people to move away from paper; willingness to change	2
Growth rate too slow	1
Hardware availability/ease of installation	15
High production costs	8
Human acceptance of technology and challenge	1
IBM PS/2 non-use of 5 ¼" drive	1
IBM endorsement	1
Inadequate AI to help users search efficiently	1
Incompatible drives/software	4
Incompatible with EROM	1
Information overload	1
Insufficient understanding by CD technologists of publishing business	1
Information update issue	1
Installed base of drives too small	39
Integration of CD-ROM for general PC user	1
Integration into mainstream PC market	1
Interim technology concept	2
Joining with online services to provide historical and time-sensitive data	1
Lack of quality applications/horizontal titles	47
Lack of commitment from major industry players	4
Lack of common user interface	17
Lack of communication among developers	1
Lack of creativity and imagination	10

Problem	Responses
Lack of distribution of extensions	4
Lack of emphasis on finding unmet needs that CD-ROM can fulfill	1
Lack of European products	1
Lack of graphics standards	1
Lack of innovative software	1
Lack of leadership	3
Lack of magazine (6–10 disc player)	2
Lack of momentum	6
Lack of PCs in home	1
Lack of public awareness	4
Lack of standards for indexing/retrieval	8
Lack of standardization in hardware/installation interface	1
Lack of standards generally	46
Lack of support by hardware vendors	1
Lack of video	1
Licensing	1
Low storage capacity of CD-ROM	2
Market definitions	13
Mastering ease	2
Mastering expense	2
MS-DOS/OS2 issues	2
MS-DOS extensions/device driver sourcing	1
MS-DOS machines lack of good graphics	1
More compact drive needed	1
Motion and video	1
Multimedia hardware platform	1
Multiple use applications	1
Need for metering software	1
Networking	4
New applications such as DVI	1
Noise	1

Problem	Responses
None	3
Non-graphics PCs	1
Obsolescence	1
Overemphasis by MS on MS-DOS-based CD-ROM solutions	1
Overemphasis on standards	2
Overinvolvement of computer-related companies	1
Overpricing for short term gain	1
Price	26
Applications	15
Drive	40
Publishing industry inertia and conservatism	4
Requiring programmers to be involved in applications production	1
Sales volume	2
Screen quality on PCs	1
Slow development; could exceed life of technology	4
Standard for caddy/Support for drive distributors	1
Terminology	1
Time	1
Transmission/communication of image	1

For questions regarding the survey results, contact:

Beth Preslar
Microsoft Corporation
16011 NE 36th Place
Box 97017
Redmond, WA 98073-9717

FUTURE BUSINESS

THE POTENTIAL OF HYPERMEDIA
By David Traub

PERSEVERENCE: MARKETING A NEW TECHNOLOGY
By Minoru Arakawa

COPING WITH THE COMING SHAKEOUT IN THE CD-ROM BUSINESS
By Ashok Mathur

CD-ROM: THE FINAL COUNTDOWN
By Lou CasaBianca

WHERE WE'RE HEADED
By Other Industry Leaders

The Potential of Hypermedia

By David Traub

[The future for David Traub is a hypermedia renaissance. Although early hypermedia technologies floundered, he anticipates a kind of technological cross-pollination that will result in multi-format product development. He offers an exciting vision of global markets and international joint ventures.]

Those associated with computers, publishing, media, and education know the promise of merging their respective technologies and methodologies. They understand that the future is bright, but that it will take time for multimedia computing to be integrated into the fabric of our daily lives. Leaps of attitude and commitment must be made before tomorrow becomes today.

Imagine the following: your OS/2-based PS/3 playing host to Letterman reruns, courtesy of AT&T fiber optics; a Macintosh-based, feature-film editing suite that simultaneously allows visual cut-and-paste among shots, sequence, and soundtrack; a tri-lingual word processor with a built-in writer's-block utility that speaks insightful phrases of encouragement. Imagine...a toaster oven with an RS-232 interface.

This imagining represents idealized products consisting of components and methodologies that exist today. The word processor might incorporate CD-ROM delivery. A large enough fiber optic highway is now in place to deliver interactive television. Nearly 100 percent of the recording studios in the United States now use a MIDI-capable Macintosh that can also drive multiple videotape recorders for editing feature films and video.

In other words, there is a significant, *inevitable* convergence of television and computer technologies that we can now view within a single conceptual framework. We can call this convergence *hypermedia*.

I have written this article to define and tie together the various faces of hypermedia in a single extended context that enables us to explore the breadth of today's developments. Given this context, we can explore the potential of hypermedia and determine how we can participate in it, to greet its arrival most expeditiously.

THE FIVE FACES OF HYPERMEDIA

Although the concept of hypermedia is now more than 20 years old, it has recently become synonymous with other terms, such as *multimedia, interactive multimedia, interactive A/V,* and *the new media*. The term *hypermedia* is used to describe production methodologies. For example, some use it to describe the simultaneous consideration of such media areas as video, film, 3-D graphics, and audio within a single production mix. Others use hypermedia to describe workstations, and yet others embrace the concept of "hypermedia distribution."

Above all, hypermedia is a "physics of convergence." It describes the marriage of data types, of equipment, and of markets, and it might describe the computer workstation of the 1990s *(see sidebar).*

In all, there are five distinct hypermedia trends to explore: interactive delivery, mixed-media production, trans-format content migration, international repurposing, and interactive grammar.

INTERACTIVE DELIVERY

"...By the way, it might be best if you also pump out a CD version of that proposal on the Silent Lake thing. And don't forget to include the video clips that were shown on the news...."

The term *hypermedia* was first coined by Ted Nelson in the sixties to denote the multimedia extension of his concept of *hypertext,* defined as the nonsequential reading and writing of text. In this sense, hypermedia "extends the functionality of hypertext to include mixed media components such as two and three-

THE HYPERMEDIA COMPUTER

An appropriate microcomputer platform for hypermedia delivery is approaching. It will comprise a majority of the following 12 features. Although these features now exist, only recently are they all beginning to converge at a realistic price point on what might be considered a personal workstation. The following features will eventually enable the mythic "computer in every home," anticipated for arrival sometime in the middle 1990s:

- Multi-operating system (MS-DOS software under UNIX desktop).
- Multi-standard (composite monitors integrating RGB and NTSC signals).
- Multi-format (optical peripheral capable of playing both digital and analog formats).
- Multimedia (capable of processing a mix of data, graphics, animation, video, sound, and other data types).
- Multitasking (parallel, simultaneous operations under desktop).
- Mass memory (sufficient external optical and magnetic storage to enable casual facility with "storage-expansive" files, such as sound and video; sufficient RAM to manipulate "high-overhead" packages, such as animation and 3-D computer graphics).
- Microprocessor speed (sufficient to maintain attention span).
- Icon-based graphic desktop (enabling real-time, intuitive use).
- Hypertext/expert systems management systems (enabling non-sequential, user-defined database applications).
- High-quality sound (bridging the gap to CD-quality audio).
- High-quality data highway (for multimedia telecommunications).
- High-quality desktop publishing output (to share the wealth).

dimensional graphics, paint graphics, video, spreadsheets, sound, and animation drawn from computer memory, audio tape, videotape, videodisc or other optical or magnetic storage." [1]

The introduction of compact disc formats such as CD-ROM and CD-I as multimedia storage media has sparked renewed hope for the immediate future of hypermedia. With storage vast enough to enable interactive access to a rich mixture of data, graphics, sound, and, increasingly, video, evangelists are again heralding the path to the future as they did with the videodisc, and as they will when phone companies win legislation permitting them to own cable, videotext, and other content entities that exploit their digital, fiber-optic highway and ISDN video switches.

Early hypermedia technologies have had their difficulties. These problems primarily have been due to marketing issues, such as price point, and to competing standards, which confused buyers. The technologies themselves— videodisc, for example—work quite well.

There will be increasingly numerous hypermedia-capable players and configurations, such as CD-ROM and Philips' Omniplayer, which will play multiple formats including CD-ROM and CD-DA, or CD-DA, CD-ROM XA, CD-I, and CD-V (videodisc). These interactive delivery media fall into two distinct groups: "hosted," which are single-user or multi-user systems requiring networked linkage to off-site transmission, and "stand-alone," which operate autonomously *(see sidebar on pages 616 and 617).*

Any delivery medium that integrates multimedia data types and permits non-sequential reading or reading and writing might be considered hypermedia. Applications will increasingly incorporate the advantages of mass memory and intelligent interface.

MIXED MEDIA-PRODUCTION

"As the screen jumped back to life, the desktop revealed a window containing the first frame of each of the last nine film sequences I had chosen. As I selected each of these images, the chosen sequence would cycle through at 30 frames per second. A pair of speakers on the shelf above simultaneously played the appropriate music and dialog as reflected in a second window below."

Production has become a hypermedia consideration for several reasons:

- The phenomenon of digitization.
- The evolution of small-format optical storage.
- The movement to enable feature-film length, full-motion video to be stored on a digital compact disc.
- The decreasing cost of high-end production technology.
- The integration of workstations into single-host microcomputer systems.
- The movement of these technologies to the desktop.
- The movement to empower non-technical personnel in production, creative, and management areas to produce desktop presentations.

These factors again reflect the convergent nature of the faces of hypermedia. Digitization has enabled audio, video, desktop-publishing, and other disciplines to be produced on a single workstation. CD-ROM and other optical formats allow the marriage of mixed-media data types on a single disc. Long-playing CD-based digital video will mean feature films delivered on CD-ROM and the development of skills required to produce and master them. Decreasing equipment costs and the movement to micro-based desktop workstations have led to the current phenomena of in-house desktop publishing, desktop presentations, desktop video and, increasingly, desktop optical—CD-ROM's and other optical media produced in house.

INTERACTIVE DELIVERY MEDIA

"Stand-alone" hypermedia	
Information managers (software only)	HyperCard (Apple Computer)
	Guide I and II (OWL International)
	Xanadu (AutoDesk)
	HyperDoc (GECI)
	Microanalytics (Gofer)
	Seaside (Askam)
	Dayflo (Dayflo)
	Houdini (MaxThink)
	Info-XL (Valor)
	Agenda (Lotus)
	Memory-Mate (Broderbund)
	Ise (Persoft)
	GRID (Digital Image Systems)
	Others (Hypertext now proliferates)
Analog optical delivery	Videodisc (1970s)
	Interactive Videotape (Hasbro, 1989)
Digital optical delivery	CD + G (CD-DA plus graphics, 1988)
	CD-ROM, Mode 1 (1983)
	CD-ROM, Mode 2 (Multimedia, 1987)
	CD-ROM XA (Extended Architecture, CD-I Audio/Graphics, 1988)
	CD-I (Interactive, 1989)
	CD-IX (CD-I + 2 floppy disks/expansion slots, 1989)
	CD-X (CD-I + all-digital, full-motion, full-frame video, 1990s)
	DVI (Digital Video Interactive, GE, 1989)
	CD-ROM Video (paperback movies, MIT/Apple, 1990s)
	CD-PROM (programmable ROM, 1988)
	CD-TRON (OS-9/CD-I-like O.S., Japan only, 1990s)
	CD-WO (write-once; WORM, CD-ROM, CD-DA, 1988)

"Stand-alone" hypermedia	CD-RAM/erasable (Tandy, 1990)
	CD-ROM/erasable hybrids (1990s)
	CD-ROM/WORM configurations (Online Computer Systems, 1988)
Analog/digital hybrid delivery	LV-ROM (Laserdisc-ROM, BBC, 1987)
	CD-V (Compact Disc Video, Philips, 1988)
	CD-Extended Play (Laserdisc and digital sound, DATE)
	CVD (Compact Video Disc, SOCS Management, 1988)
	CD-IV (CD-I + analog video, Philips, 1990s)
	Omni/Combi-Players (CD-DA, CD-I, CD-ROM XA, CD-V, Laserdisc in one box, 1989)
	CDVI (Compact Disc Video Interactive, CDI&PLCDV, Philips, 1990)
	CD-Assist (software for CD-ROM/Laserdisc Coop, 1988)
	OMDR (Optical Memory Disc [Field] Recorder, 1988)
	DRAW (Direct Read And Write [Field] Recorder, 1987)
	"Hosted" hypermedia (networked groupware)
Networked delivery (single-user or multi-user)	Interactive television (ACTV, 1988)
	Interactive distance learning (i.e., Encyclopaedia Britannica, Inc., 1988)
	Computer-supported cooperative workstations (i.e., Douglas Engelbart's "Augment" Program, 1960s)
	Videotext (i.e., Trintex Prodigy, 1988)
	Fiber optic home (i.e., Pacific Bell's "Project Victoria," 1987)
	UNIX-based networked "hyperwebs" (i.e., Brown University's "Intermedia" Project, 1980s)
	Networked CD-ROM or other optical peripherals

Copyright © 1988 by HyperMedia Publishing.
Note: The above advanced announcement dates are speculative.

Workstations will increasingly have the extended capabilities shown in Figure 6-1.

These mixed-media scenarios now demand cross-discipline skills, understanding, and language from producers, engineers, programmers, and other communications executives. The same scenerios are forging a need for rapid development of familiarity with diverse communications technologies and media types that were previously ignored as noncompetitive or irrelevant. They are also paving the way for icon-based, hypertext front-ends that will drive an entire mixed-media production suite from a single host computer. These applications will be intuitive enough to allow non-engineering producers to manage entire projects.

The potential of these integrated workstations is the continued movement to desktop-based production and publishing productivity.

TRANS-FORMAT CONTENT MIGRATION

"...You might as well also get him the CD-ROM version. He can take it with him to school."

A revolutionary hypermedia trend that will become increasingly manifest is the leveraging of a single item across a multitude of previously unrelated formats. For example, imagine the film *Who Framed Roger Rabbit* additionally

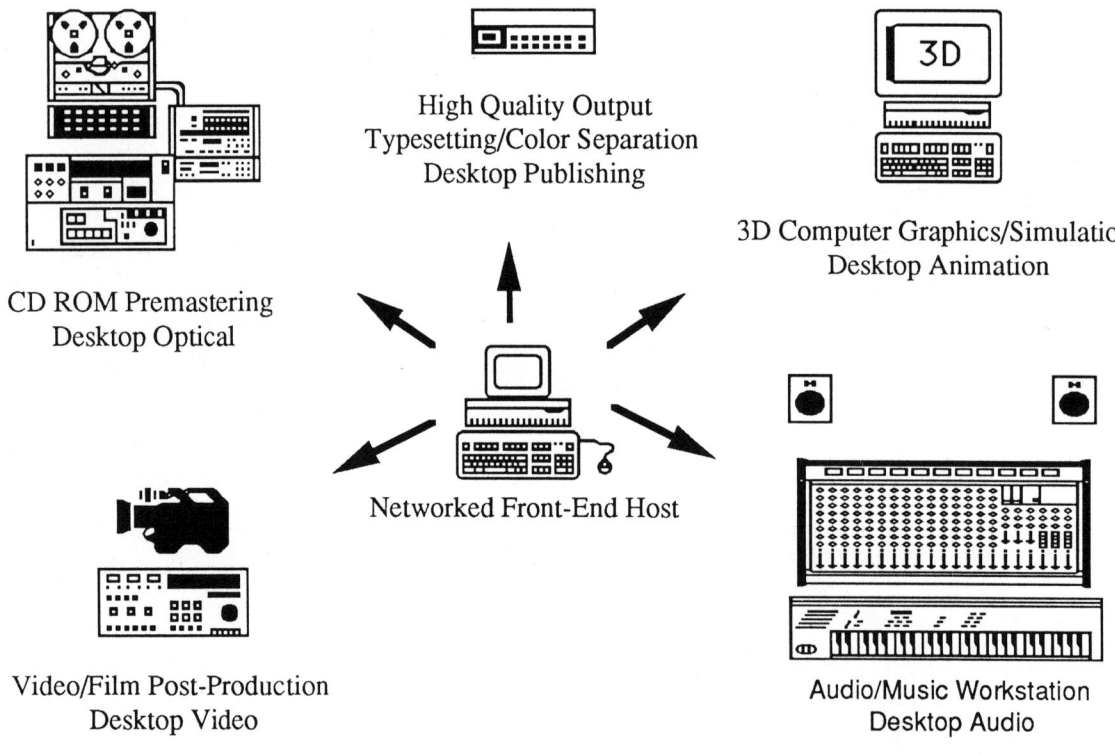

Note: Acknowledgment to Hypermedia Publishing for use of Icons/Configurations Copyright. © 1988 Hypermedia Publishing (Icons/Configurations)

Figure 6-1: Hypermedia Workstation

merchandised as a home video, a soundtrack, a HyperCard-driven laserdisc game, an education/entertainment-oriented multimedia CD-ROM, and as an R-rated CD-I fantasy. The producers would plan for the production of each of these incarnations from scripting and storyboard through post-production, filming sufficient shooting ratios and branching possibilities to enable all the necessary visuals. Yet this early-stage planning would eliminate unnecessary duplication and bring in all versions well under what each would have cost to produce separately.

This multi-format planning (see Figure 6-2) will have several results:

- Increased efficiency in development, production, and promotion.

- Multiple profit streams derived of each media type.

- Reinforced drawing power as a title sold through each market.

- Recasting of existing single-media libraries into other formats.

Multi-format design and management is yet another example of the convergent nature of hypermedia. As optical-oriented mass markets mature, the large entertainment companies will begin hunting for individual talent or companies capable of managing the trans-format content migration of appropriate existing and new properties. [2] Imagine "Fantasia" or "The Hobbit" on a CD-ROM near you.

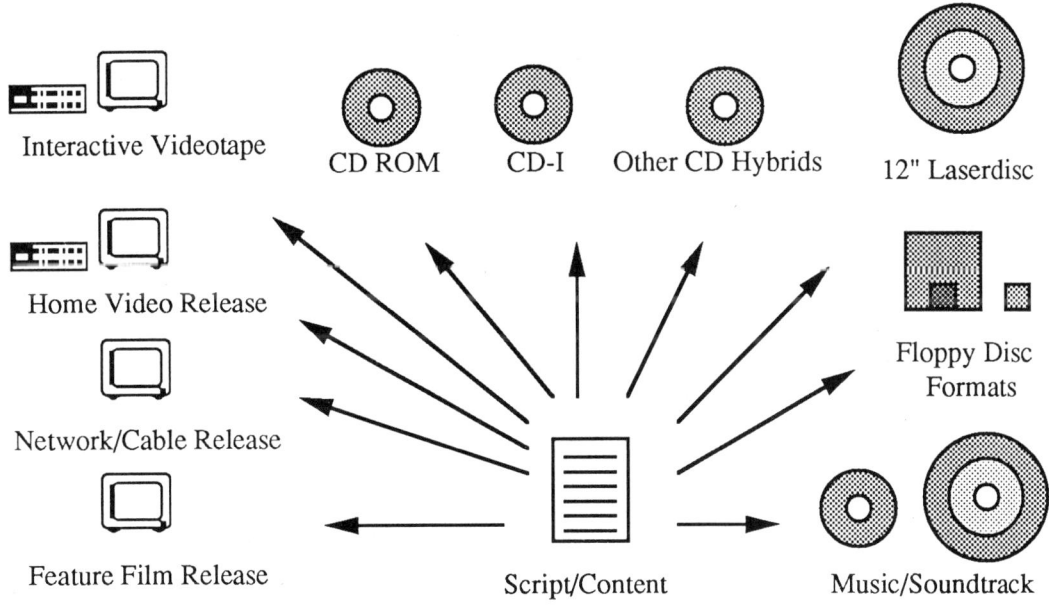

Note: Acknowledgment to Lou CasaBianca for use of migration model. Copyright © 1987 Lou CasaBianca, Hypermedia Publishing.

Figure 6-2: Trans-Format Content Migration

DAVID C. TRAUB

Home: Berkeley, California
Job: Associate Producer, Hypermedia Publishing
Quote: *"The future of education? CD-ROM/erasable hybrids. The future of entertainment? Call my agent."*

INTERNATIONAL PACKAGING FOR GLOBAL MARKETS

"Wild. Hey, Jackie, check out Sesame Street in Chinese...."

With the introduction of CD-ROM, a number of CD-based English/German, Arabic/French, and other multilingual products were developed for European and Middle-Eastern markets. This signified two important phenomena: the acceptance of the CD-ROM file format as a single world standard, and the introduction of a mass-storage optical medium capable of delivering multiple-language versions of a single product on disc. Optical memory and unified standards mean the hypermedia "convergence" of once separate global markets into a single sales equation.

This convergence also signifies that, in the future:

- Producers will have access to extended global markets.

- They will be able to sell projects on the basis of this greater access.

- They will have to learn more of the foreign cultures for which they are developing, particularly in terms of interface.

- We will see a profusion of trans-cultural programming tools and utilities that will enable translation and product localization.

- We will see an increasing number of trans-cultural products in the United States that exhibit perspectives that are less American, or even anti-American, in bias.

- We will thus develop new perceptions about ourselves.

- Strong ethnocentric programming will be developed in response to increasing media stress upon cultural identities.

- There will be more international joint ventures and buyouts.

- These new trans-cultural relationships will support translations, promotions, advertising, and the development of extended global distribution.

- A greater homogeneity of newly introduced delivery standards, such as HDTV, will appear as users begin to demand similar trans-cultural programming.

- Increased movement toward the global acceptance of unified standards will happen earlier in the development cycle.

- Accelerated growth will occur in significant industry bodies charged with this lobbying responsibility.

The integrative nature of single-standard, optically based products will deliver an international market to hypermedia developers, particularly as CD-ROM's become able to deliver feature-length movies in multiple-language renditions.

INTERACTIVE GRAMMAR

"And in Los Angeles, the.... For more on local news, press 2, for more on entertainment, press...request which...request either current work, history or.... Peter Gabriel began his political career...would you like more information on other political entertainers...."

The greatest impact of hypermedia will be in the software it delivers. A recent feature article in *Newsweek* magazine stated that "...[hypermedia] is the ultimate research tool for a generation raised on television and stereo."[3] The article was describing several new computer-based educational and entertainment applications that present a strong mix of television-oriented features, such as video, sound, and photography.

Newsweek was lauding the same novel, mixed-media "grammar" described by Ted Nelson. A grammar that today is also sometimes referred to as interactive multimedia or the new media. As with these other terms, *Hypermedia* was Nelson's attempt to describe the nonlinear, individualized means by which people would eventually travel through and synthesize computer-based knowledge, data, and media.

The interrogative, mixed-media grammar that hypermedia implies will be the means by which many of tomorrow's education, productivity, and other information-oriented problems will be eased. For example, hypermedia software will enable teaching computers to:

- Tune into the user's individual reading, viewing and thinking style.
- Present dramatic, simulation-oriented scenarios that engage the user in actual conflict with important historic characters.
- Use the likeness of the user's favorite idols as information "seek-and-synthesis" agents or as guides.

REFERENCES

[1] Por, George, "Hypermedia and Education," *Computer Currents* (August 1987): 74.

[2] Note: Initially, very few dramatic productions like feature films will be amenable to the type of interactive delivery capable in multimedia CD formats. This situation will change, however, as the use of computer animation increases and, particularly, as both audience and producer develop a better idea of what interactivity can really mean as an entertainment experience.

[3] "Here Comes Hypermedia," *Newsweek*, (October 3, 1988): 44.

- Provide multiple paths to a lesson's conclusion, with appropriate feedback for those who fail in their first attempt.
- Provide rote and repetition-based aspects of learning, enabling the teacher to take greater responsibility for more important aids to learning, such as reinforcement, facilitation, and "cheerleading."
- Provide lessons that extend beyond the classic realm of the three "Rs" to include other vital issues, such as mental health and employment.

As computer speed, processing, storage and multimedia handling abilities improve, we will witness the appearance of new dimensions and classes of hypermedia software products. They will work to eliminate the "interrogative shadow" between user and content, the distance between an application's fully extended capabilities and the user's intuitive ability to access those capabilities.

The VisiCalcs of the 90s will be those products that thoroughly eliminate the distance between the user's intended goal and the actual results. These will be products that exploit the laws of some as-yet unwritten *user-sensual*

> *We have a mythology that heralds the hope of conquering illiteracy, expanding productivity, and exploring the greatest potential of all—the human potential.*

interactive grammar—a mode of interface characterized by complete sensitivity to the individual user's mode of perception, associative style, and branching inclinations.

WHAT'S IN A NAME?

Hypermedia is the sum of all the above parts. Hypermedia will also become process control in the home, distance learning at work, and banking while you sleep.

Perhaps it is a term that is inescapably vague, a term for which too many definitions have evolved, in part perhaps because of the generality of its effervescent root words, *hyper* and *media*.

The word itself doesn't matter. Certainly the buyers won't care. They'll be sold "compact disc movies," or "Sing with Sting," or "Talk with Letterman," or "Choose the News." They might even like to try "Let's Cook from the Couch."

HYPERMEDIA AS A MYTHOLOGY

Hypermedia might best be considered a modern "mythology." We have entrepreneur heros, corporate values, and predictive milestones. We have computers from NeXT linked by Shiva modems to computers from Apple. We even have "evangelists," and we have "inevitability."

We have a mythology that heralds the hope of conquering illiteracy, expanding productivity, and exploring the greatest potential of all—the human potential. We have an optimistic and hopeful mythology that heralds a supreme aesthetic principle: integration.

That the future we await is within grasp is well known. Whether its promise is reflected in our quarterly statements in the early, mid, or late 1990s will be a direct result of when we:

- Thoroughly embrace the principal of integration at the core of all R&D design and marketing activities.

- Offer pervasive, workstation-amenable products and solutions, especially those that integrate products from multiple vendors.

- Explore the potential of the new interactive grammar as a serious science.

- Encourage industry leaders and government to jointly sponsor significant high-profile, public-interest projects that portray the value of hypermedia solutions.

- Employ high-profile, popular figures to promote these projects as part of our evolving turn-of-the-century culture.

- Join more strongly to work together for industry-wide standards, particularly those that allow for the integrative use of multiple existing formats.

Only then, as industries and disciplines merge, as the worlds of our most popular forms of communications combine transparently into user-friendly solutions, and as society accepts this convergence as part of daily life, can we begin to realize the true potential of hypermedia.

Only then can we realize the vision of an icon of toast in 16 million colors slowly fading to black...

[David Traub is Associate Producer of Hypermedia Publishing and Producer of The Hypermedia Guide. *He is a contributing editor for* Hypermedia Magazine *and has written and lectured extensively on hypermedia and new technologies. Traub is also a video and multimedia producer.*]

Perseverence: Marketing a New Technology

By Minoru Arakawa

[What can the infant CD-ROM industry learn from the world's most successful home video-game publisher? In this article, Minoru Arakawa discusses business strategies that have contributed to Nintendo's success and that could well serve as models for the CD-ROM companies of the future.]

As recently as 12 to 18 months ago, industry "experts" thought that home video-game technology was a fad that had come and gone. We at Nintendo think there is ample proof that they were wrong. But it takes true perseverance and vision to ensure that the soothsayers' prophecies don't become self-fulfilling.

Knowing this is, we believe, important for those who are attempting to establish the usefulness and potential of CD-ROM technology and the product categories related to CD-ROM. We are particularly concerned because we believe CD-ROM could play a significant role in the evolution of our own category of products.

VIDEO-GAME HISTORY

The history of the home video-game industry offers a good illustration of the value of perseverance and innovation in an area "fated" by the experts for extinction. In 1979, sales took off with the popularity of Pong, the first video game. Consumers were buying nothing more than a monochromatic, dedicated game system with a small memory capacity. The graphics were primitive. But the overwhelmingly positive consumer reaction was amazing.

Even though video games then advanced from one game in one color to many games in several colors, many, if not most of the games were poorly designed. And, as is the case with such novelties, the phenomenon proved to be short-lived and wore out.

At first, people played these games and were excited because video games represented a new technology. But the games had low "play value," and as people became "video-game savvy" playing the then-popular Atari at home and other games in arcades, they also grew restless. Why? Because the home video games didn't keep up with the arcade games in the quality of the graphics and the quality of the game play. People were bored. They wanted a new technology that would extend the play value of the home games.

About that time, Nintendo introduced its advanced technology to the marketplace. Accompanying the hardware technology was an important concept: Much like the recording business, the home video-game industry is a software-driven category. And that's why having the best, most creative software is important.

There is no doubt that the software has become much more sophisticated than in the days of Pong. It now has a greatly expanded memory capacity that permits the development of a totally new standard of game play. Hot titles, such as *Super Mario Bros., The Legend of Zelda,* and *Mike Tyson's Punch Out!* have proven that they not only produce million-plus sales of their own, but that they also drive total hardware sales.

BUSINESS STRATEGY

Coupled with the hardware and software technology, Nintendo has relied on an approach that dictates a strong, conservative, business-like approach to competing in the home video-game category.

We manage our business on the basis of a belief that video games are really part of a burgeoning category that encompasses aspects of the toy business, the feature film business, the computer software business, and the recording industry. Specifically, video games represent a hybrid category we refer to as the "Home Entertainment Systems" industry.

Why is this industry no longer in the "novelty" category it occupied earlier in the decade? We believe the current generation of home video leaders have built an industry with longevity in mind, longevity manifested in two

MINORU ARAKAWA

Home: Redmond, Washington
Job: President, Nintendo of America, Inc.
Quote: *"While the video-game industry's advanced technology is meeting the needs of consumers today, we also believe that CD-ROM offers the potential to meet those needs tomorrow."*

key ways: the use of new hardware and software technology, and openness to the next step in the evolution of that technology; and management of the business from a Home Entertainment Systems perspective.

In the U.S., that management perspective means that we at Nintendo are also looking at ways to expand our basic system so that it has a use for every member of the family. We are developing new software and peripheral products that will appeal to segments of the population that have not normally been closely associated with home video games. Expanding the uses of home video games will become more important as the household penetration levels go up.

Games such as *Anticipation, The Wheel of Fortune,* and *Jeopardy,* and items such as the *Power Pad, Dance Aerobics,* and a series of Sesame Street games have, and will continue to strengthen the appeal to larger audiences of different interests and age levels.

This expanded demographic appeal is evident in the number of women who are purchasers or users of the Nintendo Entertainment

> *Our maxim holds that working for the benefit of retailers and consumers is the best way to serve our own interests as well.*

System. Women now (in 1988) constitute 34 percent of our purchasers and 21 percent of our primary users. Both figures represent a substantial increase over last year.

In addition, by keeping one skill level ahead of traditional game players and by broadening the range of skills necessary for video-game success, we hope to build higher penetration levels in the U.S. than were achievable with the technology of 1983. And CD-ROM has the potential to let our industry explore those limits further.

MUTUAL INTERESTS

As the market leader—with a market share of more than 75 percent of the Home Entertainment Systems market—we work hard to manage growth for the best benefit of our category, and for the benefit of retailers. Our maxim holds that working for the benefit of retailers and consumers is the best way to serve our own interests as well.

Part of this interest means being careful about helping retailers monitor not only how quickly their stock turns, but how manageable their inventory is and what product mix works best in each store environment. As in traditional entertainment-oriented businesses such as feature films and record albums, we support and assist retailers with day-to-day sales-rate tracking.

We advocate a conservative approach to inventory management, partly because our products are dependent on evolving technology. We don't want retailers to be caught with old technology that won't sell. Retailer sophistication is cultivated as the technology matures.

Sensitivity to retailer perceptions and to consumer concerns has allowed for sales that are as stunning as those of the early 1980s. But it is the conservative management we espouse that ensures that growth doesn't come at the sacrifice of a well-balanced, steady industry.

AN EYE ON TOMORROW

What all this shows is the importance of letting the business control the product rather than letting the product control the business, all the while focusing on consumer-driven uses for the technology.

Yet no technology is permanent. While the industry's advanced technology is meeting the needs of consumers today, we also believe that CD-ROM offers the potential to meet those needs tomorrow. It is the next step in the evolution. We look forward to that upcoming epoch in the history of home video games.

[Minoru Arakawa is President of Nintendo of America Inc., the U.S. subsidiary of Japan's leading manufacturer of electronic games, Nintendo Company Ltd. His responsibilities include managing the consumer home video, commercial, and coin-op divisions of the company. Prior to joining Nintendo, Arakawa was an executive with Marc-narod, a Canadian construction firm based in Vancouver, British Columbia.]

Coping with the Coming Shakeout in the CD-ROM Business

By Ashok Mathur

[For a variety of reasons, says Ashok Mathur, CD-ROM markets have been slow to evolve. The result is an oversupply of services, and the potential for shakeout. The author predicts that such a shakeout will affect different segments of the industry differently, and explains why.]

It has been several years now since CD-ROM was introduced. The technology was introduced with much fanfare, and from the outset it appeared that the medium would be extremely successful because of some very compelling reasons:

1. A number of prestigious organizations contributed support to the technology by participating in the process through which physical and logical standards were set. The physical standards were set by Sony and Philips, two organizations that are known and respected throughout the world for their technological and marketing prowess. Later, an ad hoc proposal known as the *High Sierra Proposal* was suggested by a consortium of organizations that included Digital Equipment Corporation, Apple Computer, Microsoft Corporation, 3M Corporation, Sony, Philips, TMS, and Reference Technology. The *High Sierra Proposal,* with relatively minor modifications, was later adopted as the ISO Standard.

2. Low-cost drives and discs became available. CD ROM is a derivative of the compact disc, a very successful product in the consumer market. Prices of CD players

ASHOK MATHUR

Home: Stillwater, Oklahoma
Job: Vice President, TMS, Inc.
Quote: *"A number of organizations have entered the CD-ROM industry and many of these new entrants offer tools and services that have no distinctive features. I would not be a bit surprised if there are at least as many riches-to-rags stories as there are rags-to-riches stories in the industry."*

came down sharply, and this price drop set the stage for low-cost CD-ROM drives. Furthermore, a very large manufacturing capacity for compact discs was created by several organizations throughout the world. This, in turn, assured the market of the availability of low-cost discs.

3. CD-ROM is a low-cost publishing medium. This technology makes it possible to replicate more than 500 megabytes of information at a marginal cost of less than $10. To the publisher or printer, this is the equivalent of reproducing a page at a minimal cost—less than a small fraction of a penny. This cost of reproducing information was—and still is—the lowest known to man.

Because of this combination of factors, it appeared self-evident that large markets had been created for disc mastering and replication services, systems integration and software, and CD-ROM drives. This optimistic view was reinforced by the rosy projections of a number of self-appointed industry pundits (otherwise known as consultants) who suddenly appeared out of the woodwork and rushed onto the scene. The prospect of large and growing markets attracted a number of vendors from each market segment to the CD-ROM business. These vendors, who had a primarily technological orientation, became the driving force in the marketplace.

For a variety of reasons, however, the markets have been relatively slow to evolve. Among the factors that have led to this slow evolution of the market are the following:

1. The cost of data capture is very high. It costs at least $2 per kilobyte to key in data with a reasonable level of accuracy, and optical character recognition is still too limited to be a viable alternative in many circumstances. Two dollars per kilobyte translates into $1 million for every 500 megabytes. This cost is the single greatest barrier to entry. It is surprising that most forecasters do not consider this simple fact when making projections.

2. A number of large and successful publishing organizations wanted to be sure that CD-ROM publishing would not hurt their traditional publishing enterprises. The publishing business has, over the years, been very profitable, and one cannot really find fault with organizations that have chosen to adopt this somewhat safe and conservative strategic posture.

3. The installed base of CD-ROM drives is growing slowly. This installed base is being expanded primarily through some vertical market applications; no horizontal market applications have sold in very large numbers. Many people have correctly identified this situation as a "chicken or

egg" problem. People will be reluctant to buy a CD-ROM drive unless there is a "useful" application, but such applications will not be vigorously created for general use unless there is a large installed base of drives.

The fact that a large number of vendors did enter a market that has grown at a slower rate than expected has resulted in an oversupply of goods and services. Competition is more intense than might be expected. Let us examine the implications for some of the segments of our industry and see what the forthcoming scenario might be.

> *Once the shakeout among the suppliers of goods and services is complete, a healthy and vibrant new industry is likely to remain and endure.*

SYSTEMS INTEGRATORS AND SOFTWARE PROVIDERS

LINK Resources Corporation of New York has forecasted that the market for systems integrators and software providers for 1988 is likely to be less than $30 million and that, in 1989, the market is likely to grow to about $50 million. This implies that the average revenue per vendor is likely to be about $600,000 in 1988 and about $1 million in 1989. What is very likely is that a few of the more sucessful vendors will acquire a significant share of the market, while a large number will struggle to survive. It is extremely difficult, if not impossible, to run a software development and services organization on a revenue base as low as $600,000 per year. Clearly, a shakeout is imminent for the systems integrators and software providers.

What factors are likely to distinguish the organizations that will grow and thrive from the organizations that will languish and die? Here are some of the contributing factors:

1. Successful organizations are likely to have a continuing record of creativity and innovation. This is the factor that will permit them to differentiate their products from those of the competition. Product differentiation will create unique selling attributes.

2. Successful organizations are likely to be stable. Organizations in which there is a high rate of turnover of key employees are not likely to be successful in producing innovative solutions on an ongoing basis.

3. Successful organizations are likely to have a growing client base. If a large proportion of the revenue comes from a small number of customers, the situation is inherently unhealthy. The organization in such a situation is likely to be dependent on a few customers. This, in turn, places the organization in a weak position because, in the final analysis, power is the obverse of dependence.

4. Successful organizations will be willing to cater to the special needs of their customers. Large and powerful industrial buyers are likely to demand products that are differentiated, and organizations that cannot cater to special needs will find it difficult to build a large and loyal customer base.

MASTERING AND REPLICATION SERVICES

The situation for organizations that offer mastering and replication services is much less optimistic. Capacity is far in excess of demand. The products are largely undifferentiated by virtue of the fact that so much effort and agreement went into the standardization of the CD-ROM disc. Fixed costs are also very high. These factors have led to an extremely competitive situation. The prices at which mastering and replication services are offered are less than half of the LINK Resources Corporation forecast for 1988. Revenues for 1988 for the entire mastering and replication segment of the CD-ROM industry is likely to be less than $6 million. This, by any standard, is a bleak situation. To make matters worse, the margins for CD audio discs have also dropped dramatically. One mastering and replication house has already reorganized under bankruptcy laws, and there would be little surprise if others follow suit. The survivors are likely to provide quality service and have economies of scale.

DRIVE MANUFACTURERS

The CD-ROM drive, despite being highly standardized, can be differentiated. The better drives will be more robust and reliable and will allow quicker seeks. The innovative manufacturer will also find other ways to differentiate the product—for example, allowing several disc surfaces to be read simultaneously. CD-ROM drives are therefore not likely to become as much of a commodity item as are CD-ROM discs, and innovative and reliable manufacturers will probably do reasonably well.

Thus, the outlook for each segment of the industry is different. The prospects for systems integrators and drive manufacturers can be good if the firms pursue sound strategies, while the outlook in the mastering and replication segment is daunting. But whatever the outlook for vendors, the fact remains that CD-ROM is a compact, inexpensive, and promising publishing medium. A number of publishers have already exploited these advantages to create successful CD-ROM publishing strategies. The use of the medium will continue to grow at a healthy rate. Once the shakeout among the suppliers of goods and services is complete, a healthy and vibrant new industry is likely to remain and endure.

The author is indebted to Mr. Steven Sieck of LINK Resources Corp. and to Ms. Jana Stone of TMS, Inc. for their assistance in preparing this paper.

[Ashok Mathur is the Vice President of TMS, Inc., which builds tools for the information industry. TMS, Inc. is one of the pioneers of the CD-ROM industry. Prior to joining TMS, Mathur worked with ITC Ltd., the Indian subsidiary of BAT Industries.]

CD-ROM: The Final Countdown

By Lou CasaBianca

[In this article, Lou CasaBianca identifies three steps that are critical to the successful launching of the CD-ROM industry and describes an integrated multimedia methodology that, he feels, will facilitate the development of a viable optical publishing community.]

Who are the market leaders in the rollout and pursuit of the promise of CD-ROM? What key factors will influence its successful maturation, and when will this infant technology reach critical mass? Where are the programs that establish the unequivocal value of this hybrid medium? Why does there seem to be so much indecision about the application of CD-ROM discs? How will potential optical publishers and producers attain CD-ROM literacy? Will CD-ROM survive in what is rapidly becoming a crowded and confused technological marketplace? Do our expectations match the realities of the technology? After years of anticipation, is CD-ROM in the final countdown?

EDUCATING THE MARKET

The factors that will determine success or failure are the technology, services, and resources that can be brought to publishers for application of CD-ROM in education, government, business, and entertainment. The key first step is the education of potential new optical publishers by the CD-ROM industry. The launch of CD-Audio was engineered by the CD Association, which was composed of members from competing companies who joined together to help make CD-Audio among the most successful consumer electronics products ever. CD-ROM premastering systems groups, drive manufacturers, replicators, and software producers must consciously choose to work individually and together to create a positive commercial environment [*see the section entitled "Creative Collaboration" for information about the Optical Publishing Association*]. The hardware and software manufacturers and the mastering facilities need to provide the entry-level evangelism necessary to convince publishers and producers that there is and will continue to be a CD-ROM market.

LOU CASABIANCA

Home: San Francisco, California
Job: Editor/Publisher, *HyperMedia Guide*
Quote: *"The progression from desktop publishing to desktop optical will bring about the platinum CD-ROM."*

Sectors of government and industry that use microfiche for mass storage have already recognized the benefits of switching to CD-ROM. The real challenge is for companies that can take advantage of the storage and multimedia capabilities to understand how to produce and apply CD-ROMs in their day-to-day training, sales, and marketing activities.

Let's take a look at the future: user-definable human interfaces; integrated multimedia workstations; optical mass storage; parallel co-processing and multitasking; local and wide area networking; laptop computers; large, full-color, flat-screen, typeset-resolution monitors; voice-activated interactive applications. Let's see if we can predict the "off-the-shelf technology" and developments that should become available within the next two years.

GETTING A FOOTHOLD

The second step in the countdown to CD-ROM will be the use of CD-ROM in marketing and training. The multimedia CD-ROM drive can become a gateway to a company's, university's, or government bureau's database. The database materials will include sales presentations, training programs, corporate-image programs, inventories, competitive specifications, and more.

Regardless of the application, CD-ROM producers will have to begin to rely on broadcast television production values. Sound, color, and motion are critical elements to achieving this qualitative production level. Sterile, silent, black-and-white presentations should be considered part of the "pre-Industrial Age" of CD-ROM and an anathema in the multimedia optical realm. Consistent high-quality screen designs and menus, matched with good writing, graphic design, and creative imagination will become the critical front end to the CD-ROM success scenario.

Technical issues will become more and more transparent as expert system-based design and production tools filter into the marketplace. While there is no absolute approach to producing a CD-ROM disc, it is clear that certain organic elements must be developed and prepared for the premastering and final replication of the disc.

MOVING INTO THE MAIN STREAM

The third step necessary for CD-ROM to become viable is the integration of what I have been calling *desktop optical*. As CD-ROMs begin to populate higher education and business environments, many desktop print publishers will need to make the transition into desktop optical. Although the technical level of complexity increases, publishers should be able to enhance knowledge based on the use of the personal computer and transfer that knowledge to the optical production process. Self-indexing software, predesigned and debugged code, powerful search and retrieval engines, optically based stock art and sound, and intelligent authoring tools will be available for the next generation of CD-ROM producers. Part of the success of CD-ROM publishers will be based on their understanding of when *not* to use CD-ROM. Its cost and benefit features will be appropriate only some of the time. In fact, in many cases floppy disk, videodisc, or both types of presentations may be more effective in terms of cost and design.

The platinum CD-ROM

Can you think of an existing CD-ROM program that is so powerful, so important, so well executed that you would go out and buy a $1000 CD-ROM drive just to be able to access this program? This kind of disc programming is critical to the dissemination of CD-ROM. What are some of the elements that will contribute to making a disc essential? What about interactive design and programming questions? How do we generate enhanced functionality and develop entertainment value?

As I've said, the production values established by broadcast television have become the criteria applied subconsciously by virtually everyone judging the quality of sound and images projected on a screen. However inappropriate this evaluation may seem, it is reality. Digital sound, exciting color, and appropriate motion must be built into CD-ROM programming if it is to have any chance of being used repeatedly. The digital audio and music capabilities of multimedia CD-ROM may well spawn new CD-ROM "record" labels. Existing and new CD audio music tracks will be supplemented with lyrics, sheet music, spoken-word and photographic visuals, discographies, and so forth.

Future vision: Education 1992

It is 1992. A teacher is preparing a learning disc on astronomy. Instead of analyzing and reading textbooks and charts, the student will take an optical guided tour of the solar system. The teacher sits in front of two monitors, one is a computer CD-ROM display, the other is a video monitor displaying a hypermedia program. On the video screen, in an animated sequence,

> *Part of the success of CD-ROM publishers will be based on their understanding of when* not *to use CD-ROM. Its cost and benefit features will be appropriate only some of the time.*

Galileo introduces the subject and invites the viewer into his study. At the same time, the other screen displays color video showing the orbits of the planets as they track through cobalt-blue space on a field of distant stars. On the first screen, Galileo discusses how humanity's knowledge of the solar system and of space has expanded as much in the last century as in all of history up until that point. Galileo's theories are in his notebooks and files on the screens in front of the teacher.

Using a mouse to move the on-screen image of a tiny planet, the teacher opens a file folder marked *observations*. In an instant, the orbiting planets are replaced by the image of an astronomer talking about the planet he discovered. The animated file contains many similar interviews with astronomers, astrophysicists, and scientists, along with animated maps and articles about the universe. With the mouse, the teacher can browse through the text, films, videos, and animated sequences, using associative thought processes as a guide through the information—in the end creating a vision of the forces and factors driving the solar system. This journey consists of guided simulations of a tour through our solar system. There is no single plot or right answer. Instead, these tools present a new process for thinking, learning, and creating.

Hypermedia workstations will bring vast new capabilities to students and teachers. Hypermedia is not the future; hypermedia is here and now. After ten years the personal computer has enabled the powerful convergence of text, audio, video, and graphics that is showing up on college campuses and in industry applications. With the computer screen serving as the gateway to hypermedia, researchers are developing new tools that will transform education, government, business, and entertainment.

Thousands of color photographs, thousands of pages of text, and hours of sound can be stored on CD-ROM, CD-I, and videodiscs. Self-indexing, hypertext-based software will provide database organization and browsing capability to allow us to move seamlessly from subject to subject. Multimedia integrated databased authoring systems (MIDAS) use the computer as a command center controlling optical, audio, and video devices. In the short term, hypertext will prove useful for managing information, with the help of such products as Guide and HyperCard. It will become an essential part of the infrastructure of CD-ROM for learning and business tasks. People will begin to view hypertext as representing digital books of information linked within themselves and with other digital media. Many CD-ROM enthusiasts believe that hypermedia has arrived just in time to save us all from drowning in our data.

We can expect hypermedia tools to become an important industry supporting the growth of multimedia publishing. CD-ROM works best in an integrated multimedia environment, combined with hard-copy (printed) instructional materials, writeable floppy disks, and videotape or videodisc—all vital media for teaching and marketing. In some cases, the most effective design approach might be a combination of sound and stills on CD-ROM and motion sequences on videodisc. CD-ROM should be designed to work in a complementary fashion with other media, surrounding the presenter or teacher with the ultimate support system and providing the student or user with multiple-

CD-ROM: NICKELODEON FOR MODERN TIMES

Today's Mac equipped with a CD-ROM player is at the same stage in its evolution as the early nickelodeon. In 1905, people never imagined that this amazing little novelty was the beginning of a gigantic, influential industry. But it certainly had entertainment value.

That is more than can be said about CD-ROM. Today, the CD-ROM player is an exotic peripheral. Expensive. And there is precious little to play on it. But that's how mass media seem to start. Look at how the motion picture industry evolved when early movie makers turned their attention to the mass market. They did the simplest, quickest thing to get going. They set up their rudimentary gear in front of a theatrical stage and proceeded to film a live play.

By today's standards, the result was a yawn. But then, in the first phase of the motion picture business, the results were tantalizing. The early movie makers allowed a crude system of distribution to be set up: the nickelodeon. They trained the first group of people in the technique of film. And they set up a business that generated cash.

In essence, the first movies were made with a shovel. Take big scoops of this play and put them on that film. The results were just about ready-made—and cheap to produce.

But it didn't matter to the audiences. They were captivated and wanted more. The same applies to the CD-ROM business today. The first products—things like Microsoft's *Bookshelf* and Grolier's *Electronic Encyclopedia*—are shovel products. These are books straight off the shelf and into CD-ROM. Clever, effective and simple. It's just enough to tantalize, enough to build the infrastructure of an industry.

This same scenario has been played out with every new medium. Radio stole from Victrolas until somebody figured out the advantages of radio. Television stole from radio until people figured out the unique benefits of TV.

And as it was with movies, some guys standing on the sidelines, in a mixture of boredom and inspiration, will try something different.

choice options for reading, listening, watching, and interacting.

Hypervision

My own "hypervision" of the future is focused beyond this two-year window into the early 1990s. In order to secure the promise of hypermedia, in a very real sense we must return to square one—the human factor. We need to rethink and understand what it means to be a teacher, a writer, a publisher, a producer, or a knowledge worker. Hypermedia production also involves business planning, project management, marketing, publishing, space planning, and more. Hypermedia producers need to have the means to distribute products in multiple formats.

The information-management media-production workstation industry must transcend its preoccupation with "black boxes." Hardware wars, while ultimately helping to establish dominant formats or systems, are excessive and create graveyards of abandoned technology. The time has come to expand our perception of the production and publishing process. There is no reason why the same personal computer you use for letters and spreadsheets can't be used for CD-ROM premastering. Developing an offline indexing and edit decision list with time-code addresses for cuts, dissolves, fades, and special effects can decrease the cost of online premastering production and increase the quality of life for the producer.

In the hypermedia production scenario, the personal computer screen becomes a window into all of the different creative, technical, and business worlds involved in the production process. Computers can be used to produce and manage proposals, scripts, and storyboards. They are an invaluable asset in the development of client proposals, including work processing, budgets, project schedules, and graphics.

Desktop media and integrated workstations have reached power levels and economic price points that allow them to serve as offline systems with quality now reaching levels

---

Movie makers tried writing their own stories. They tried shooting from different camera positions. They experimented with fades, dissolves and special effects. The results were unique and wonderful. Movies began to make money, and there started to be a lot of movies.

Now CD-ROM is about to enter its second phase. That's when you'll see some interesting stuff for CD-ROM—exclusive to CD-ROM. Hypermedia is the catch-word for the aggregate of techniques, some known, some yet barely imagined, that will constitute the cuts, dissolves, zooms, fades and special effects of CD-ROM.

One of the neatest examples using hypermedia is *The Electric Cadaver*, now in production at Stanford Medical School. Poke that on-screen man in the eye and the program zooms in, revealing secrets only doctors know.

Then there's the *Timetable of Science and Innovation* from my company, Xiphias. We've written almost 6,000 stories for CD, not for books. Each has a full set of key words that link it to other stories. Each word on the screen is hot. Click on the word, and you automatically search for other stories with the same word.

Key words are not limited to the text of the story. The term "barbed wire" would normally yield the key words of "barbed," "wire," "steel," "cows" and, maybe, "agriculture." Xiphias added "war" and "politics" because the combatants of World War I found uses for the stuff that had nothing to do with cows.

That kind of interaction gives an inkling of the capabilities of this medium. We don't know where the future leads. But we can dream. Imagine novels written this way. The events of *Red Storm Rising* or *Gone with the Wind* from the points of view of eight different characters.

Imagine never having to struggle to figure out where the action is taking place on the cruddy little map placed inside the front cover. Where, if you forget who a particular character is, the answer is a button away. Where you might even become a participant in the story yourself—with unpredictable results.

This is important stuff. Stay tuned.

By Peter Black. From *MacWEEK*, August 23, 1988 issue. Copyright © 1988 by Ziff Communications Company.

> *In order to secure the promise of hypermedia, in a very real sense we must return to square one — the human factor. We need to rethink and understand what it means to be a teacher, a writer, a publisher, a producer, or a knowledge worker.*

comparable to that of an online production environment.

Currently, there are a number of powerful desktop publishing, digital audio, digital video, and 3-D graphics workstations built around the Macintosh, the IBM PC, and other computers. So where do we go from here? There's a need for better telecommunications software, to ease delivery of documents and multimedia files from one personal computer to another. With telephones, FAX machines, and copiers getting smaller, less expensive, and more portable, the definition of "document" is up for redefinition. What is really needed is an integrated media workstation with production software specifically designed to help producers run the business of CD-ROM and hypermedia production.

The full potential of hypermedia information management and media production will not be realized until all of these activities are successfully integrated into one system. The intriguing fact about the hypermedia revolution is that it can be accomplished with existing technology. The missing ingredient is the establishment of universal standards allowing for open architecture between machines and operating systems, between different software packages, and between different media types.

The driving force behind this merger of media is the increasing trend toward digitization of information. Now we can cut and paste knowledge with ease. We've already seen the world of sound becoming digital with CDs and digital audio tape (DAT). We're beginning to see the world of pictures — of animation and movies — become digitized as well, with laserdisc movies and with text and images on compact discs.

In much the same way, the technological innovation that's creating laserdiscs, personal computers, and CD-ROM as tools for writers, moviemakers, and animators is going to create a richer world. Not only will we be able to merge the properties of television, magazines, and movies into a single medium: For the first time we'll have the added dimension of interactivity in that medium.

The result will be a new era of socializing, as your friends gather in your home to watch a full-screen video with all the wonderful media forms you've put together from your library and from what you've captured. In the future, people will have "hyperparties," with multimedia devices recording and playing back the party as a realtime program. And as the MIT media lab predicts, feature films will become "paperback movies" that are distributed to homes over the ISDN network or on low-cost CD-ROMs.

The skills used to make movies are most likely going to be the same skills that will dominate the new age of hypermedia. When you merge publishing, television, and movies, the moviemaker has the definite advantage because it's precisely his or her skills that are going to bring about the convergence of multimedia. That's the type of talent and expertise we will need to create the innovative CD-ROMs and CD-Is of the future.

THE PROBLEM: MULTIMEDIA MADNESS

As dramatically as the information management and media production environment has changed in the last ten years, the common wisdom about information and media has remained relatively constant. Educational, corporate, and governmental facilities are inundated with advice about the need to "modernize," along with all that it implies about information management and media production: buying new equipment, learning new approaches to using it, and developing new ways to manage hypertext and multimedia services.

Meanwhile, we are being confronted with shortened product life cycles, an increasingly confusing competitive environment, an intensifying technological revolution, and changing requirements for professional skills—factors that make the old rules increasingly difficult to use in information management and media production. I believe that an important part of the solution to this complex problem lies in creating a new methodology for setting up databases and producing multimedia. To create this methodology requires accessing expert knowledge designed to help you improve performance by increasing technical, creative, and management productivity.

THE SOLUTION: HYPERMEDIA METHODOLOGY

To this end, I have proposed the development of a HyperMedia Methodology (see Figure 6-3). This methodology is built around one central idea: that there is a "DNA" underlying the way we communicate, and that expert systems and open systems architecture applications will allow us to create a universal model for hypermedia design and authoring. The development of database models, visual maps, and expert-generated templates create geodesic thinking that will in turn be used to better understand and author hypermedia designs and programs. Generic database designs and the use of iconic visual languages that incorporate shape, form, and color will allow a picture or image to communicate concepts or processes that would otherwise take pages of text and multiple columns of numbers to communicate.

My hypermedia methodology is designed to provide a "wholistic" approach to multimedia design and production. The ability to leverage text and audio across multiple media formats is

> *The intriguing fact about the hypermedia revolution is that it can be accomplished with existing technology. The missing ingredient is the establishment of universal standards allowing for open architecture between machines and operating systems, between different software packages, and between different media types.*

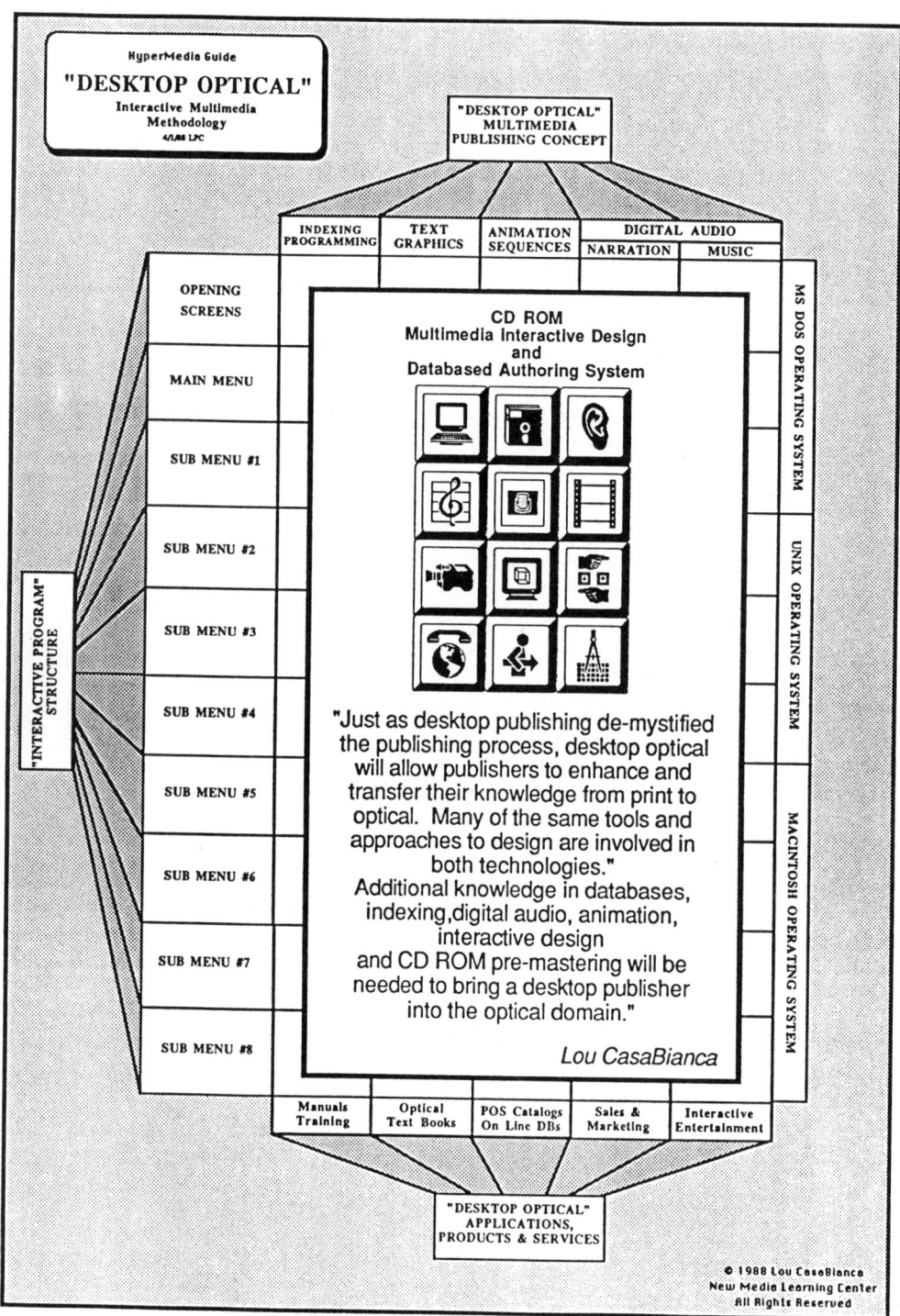

Figure 6-3. Desktop Optical: an interactive multimedia methodology.

a good example of the type of creative and economic efficiencies that can be derived from an integrated authoring approach. Until recently, there has been little need to address hypermedia on personal computers, largely because of the limited amount of information most computers could manage "online" at any one time. But if CD-ROM and readable, writeable, and re-recordable optical discs become standard on computers, they will place on our desktops more information than the largest mainframe computers managed ten years ago.

The hardware that holds and manipulates the information is only one side of the hypermedia equation, however. The other side of the equation—and unquestionably the more critical part—is the software that lets us navigate in a hypermedia environment. By navigate, I mean the ability to work with linked multimedia information in a natural, intuitive, and interactive way. Such navigation does not mean putting information delivery and multimedia into the hands of computer professionals, but giving everyone sufficient power to bring information to life. Programs like HyperCard and Guide will eventually help put CD-ROM and hypermedia into the hands of nearly every personal computer user.

My own experience is a case in point. During my professional career I have been developing in my mind's eye a dream application to help manage time and information, write and storyboard scripts, and manage multiple projects. Even though I have had a strong idea of what the program should do, I didn't have the time to master computer programming to make the program do what I needed. Most programs didn't offer the flexibility I required. But working in the HyperCard and ACIUS 4th Dimension environment I have finally been able to turn this dream into a practical program. Thus was born the hypermedia methodology.

This story is being repeated by many designers, for many applications, and it will become a standard part of computing in the years ahead. This, I believe, is a major strength of hypertext and hypermedia: It dissolves the barrier between a person's information-handling ideals and program design goals and the realization of those ideals and goals. The expertise embodied in hypertext applications will be the expertise of business people, professional people, artists, and educators. All who work with information and information media will be able to pour their knowledge into hyperwells for others to drink from.

In a world of technological overkill, hypermedia represents one of the most important hopes for greater access to knowledge, as well as for the ability to project and share our own thoughts, emotions, and creations with others. CD-ROM is an essential part of the hypermedia landscape. Wouldn't it be great if all the possibilities could come together and become realities just by our visualizing the future in strong enough and clear enough terms, and then in unison counting down...3-2-1-CD-ROM!

[Lou CasaBianca is Publisher and Editor of Hypermedia Magazine *and* The Hpermedia Guide, *the multimedia version of* Hypermedia Magazine. *He is also President of The New Media Group, an interactive design, production, and consulting group. CasaBianca's background in the music, audio, video, television, graphic, and computer industries has prepared him to take advantage of today's converging technologies.]*

Where We're Headed

By Other Industry Leaders

[Not all the influential people in the CD-ROM industry had time to write an article for this Yearbook. But many of the people we were able to contact, or who contacted us, were willing to say something for the record about the direction in which they think the industry is headed.]

ALLEN ADKINS

Home: Portola Valley, California
Job: Founder and President, Optical Media International
Quote: *"It's been a great three years since we started our CD-ROM business and we're succeeding very well. The CD-ROM publishing industry is really starting to come alive. We are looking forward to seeing the CD being the ideal data and multi-media publishing medium for decades to come."*

MARK ARPS

Home: St. Paul, Minnesota
Job: Sales Marketing Manager, 3M
Quote: *"The CD-ROM industry is entering a pivotal year in 1989. The media, drives, and retrieval software have all improved significantly in the past year. This, along with one-day turnaround on discs and the demonstrated ability to do weekly updates, has removed barriers that previously prevented development of CD-ROM products. We anticipate a significant increase in titles pressed industry-wide in 1989."*

MARTIN BROOKS

Home: New York, New York
Job: Executive Editor, Bowker Electronic Publishing
Quote: *"The industry has made tremendous strides in the last year. Not only are there many more titles at lower prices, but we're starting to see projects that incorporate graphics, sound, and many diverse databases. Perhaps more importantly, we're also starting to see user interfaces that are powerful, yet intuitive. We're finally breaking away from looking at CD-ROM as a distribution medium, and incorporating powerful tools to manipulate data to make people's lives easier and more productive. It's important in the next year that we don't let extensions to the CD-ROM standards erode consumer confidence by causing confusion."*

MARC CANTER

Home: Chicago, Illinois
Job: President, MacroMind, Inc.
Quote: *"Optical storage is the perfect device for distributing multimedia. But until there are more drives available, CD-ROM is a Catch-22."*

WILLIAM H. FORD, JR.

Home: Germantown, Maryland
Job: President, Online Computer Systems, Inc.
Quote: *"We at Online believe the current CD-ROM electronic-publishing activities represent the first wave of placing information in the hands of the end-user. The challenge facing information providers/publishers is in packaging products with sufficent value-add to make the electronic version 'vastly more valuable' than the hard copy or online service.*

"Illustrations, maps, images, and sound offer new opportunities in the delivery of information. Optical publishing is in its infancy and we as the pioneers must seek the best ways to apply this powerful communications medium."

DIANA GAGNON

Home: Manhattan, New York
Job: Research Associate, MIT Media Laboratory
Quote: *"With the movement toward multimedia databases, we must focus on the development of more sophisticated human interfaces that better integrate our growing understanding of users, cognition and artificial intelligence."*

JOHN C. GALE

Home: Alexandria, Virginia
Job: President, Information Workstation Group
Quote: *"The CD-ROM industry is growing at an increasing rate. It will be a billion dollar industry in 1991."*

CAROLYN KUHN

Home: Austin, Texas
Job: President, Software Mart, Inc.
Quote: *"We have in hand the tools and machinery for a new information transportation system. How well we use compact disc to enhance knowledge and motivate learning is a measure of our creative vision, convictions, and persistence."*

SUSAN LAMMERS

Home: Seattle, Washington
Job: Director, CD-ROM Division, Microsoft Corp.
Quote: *"What is the value of information? It supports thought. How do we think? We think interactively, non-linearly, in color, in black and white, verbally, graphically, and aloud. Interactive multimedia technologies bring us closer to presenting information in a form that more closely resembles the richness and complexity of thought. This is revolutionary. This is powerful. And this will increase greatly the value of information."*

KEN LEESE

Home: Ottawa, Canada
Job: President, Fulcrum Technologies Inc.
Quote: *"We've already seen the market go from tire-kickers to buyers. The next step will see system designers incorporating CD-ROM as a component of their overall information architecture."*

PARKE LIGHTBOWN

Home: San Ramone, California
Job: Vice President, UTLAS International
Quote: *"I feel there will be slow, steady growth in the number of CD-ROM products available and in the sales of those products. I feel libraries will continue to be the major users of CD-ROM for the next several years."*

THOMAS M. LOPEZ

Home: Seattle, Washington
Job: Chairman, Mammoth MicroProductions, Inc.
Quote: *"I believe that the real promise of CD-ROM lies in its emerging potential to deliver Digital Multi-Media Interactive (DMMI) applications for business and the home. Natural images, animation, digital audio, and motion video will bring high emotional appeal to inform, educate, and entertain the end-user. Computers will become friendlier and easier to use with DMMI.*

There are several impediments to the advent of DMMI applications on CD-ROM: low-cost hardware platforms (they are coming); reasonable authoring tools (Mammoth and others are working on them now); and the particular combination of necessary creative and technical skills. This last factor will be the most important in determining the overall success of the medium.

DMMI is a new medium, just as motion pictures and television were once new media. And as there were opportunities for film and TV pioneers, there are now opportunities for DMMI pioneers — latter-day D. W. Griffiths and William S. Paleys.

An exciting future is before us."

THEODOR HOLM NELSON

Home: Sausalito, California
Job: Designer/Distinguished Fellow, AutoDesk, Inc.
Quote: *"I consider CD-ROM to be a retrograde step away from the universal access we truly need."*

IAN RITCHIE

Home: Edinburgh, Scotland
Job: Managing Director, Office Workstations, Ltd.
Quote: *"The greatest challenge in the application of CD-ROM is to find simple and pleasant ways for readers to explore material on computer screens."*

BOB OGDON

Home: Evergreen, Colorado
Job: President, Ogdon Micro Design
Quote: *"As people become aware of the powerful impact of multimedia, new vertical, commercial, and consumer markets will emerge. And while consumers will be the slowest to accept this new medium, they will eventually be the largest portion of the market."*

MARTHA STEFFAN

Home: San Jose, California
Job: CD-ROM Evangelist, Apple Computer, Inc.
Quote: *"I believe that the consumer market for CD-ROM titles will be viable within twelve to eighteen months."*

SECTION VII

DIRECTORY LISTINGS

CD-ROM TITLES

DISC DRIVES

RETRIEVAL SYSTEMS

DATA PREPARATION HOUSES

MASTERING/ REPLICATION FACILITIES

CD-ROM RESOURCES

CD-ROM AND RELATED CONFERENCES

DIRECTORY OF CD-ROM TITLES

ALPHABETICAL LISTING OF CD-ROM TITLES

CD-ROM TITLES BY SUBJECT

ALPHABETICAL LISTING OF CD-ROM TITLES

Title	Publisher	Description	Audience
6-Bit Sample Library	Optical Media International 495 Alberto Way Los Gatos, CA 95032 (408)395–4332	5,000 sound effects including percussion.	
The $99.00 Disc	ALDE Publishing 4830 West 77th Street P.O. Box 35326 Minneapolis, MN 55435 (612)835–5240	Over 5,000 public domain programs.	Horizontal markets.
1982 Census of Agriculture	Slater Hall Information Products 1522 K Street N.W. Suite 522 Washington, DC 20005 (202)682–1350	The complete Census Bureau County file: acreage, operating expenses, production, sales, crops, livestock, and more, with 3,360 data items for each county and state, and U.S. totals for each item.	Libraries, agribusiness companies, market researchers.
A-V ONLINE	SilverPlatter Information, Inc. 37 Walnut Street Wellesley Hills, MA 02181 (617)239–0306	Complete database of audiovisual materials from the NICEM.	School districts, media centers, libraries.
ABI/INFORM Ondisc	UMI (University Microfilms International) 300 North Zeeb Road Ann Arbor, MI 48106 (800)521–3044	Abstracting and indexing to 800 business and management periodicals.	Libraries and corporate libraries.
Academic Index on InfoTrac II	Information Access Company 362 Lakeside Drive Foster City, CA 94404 (800)227–8431	Indexing to 390 of the most widely-read scholarly and general-interest periodicals PLUS 6 months indexing of the *New York Times*.	College and university libraries.
Access Pennsylvania High School Library Catalog, 3rd Edition	Pennsylvania State Library Pennsylvania Department of Education School Library Media Services 333 Market Street Harrisburg, PA 17126-0333 (717)787–6704	Full MARC records of 400 school, public, and academic libraries.	Libraries.
ADA ROM	ALDE Publishing 4830 West 77th Street P.O. Box 35326 Minneapolis, MN 55435 (612)835–5240	ADA source codes, templates, utilities, and programs.	Government contractors, programmers.

*Please contact publisher for prices.

Retrieval System	Computer Compatibility	Minimum Memory	Initial Release Date	Update Frequency	Price
					$995.00/Disc
None	PC/XT/AT	640K	03/88	Annually	$99.00/Disc
SEARCHER Slater Hall	PC/XT/AT	512K	11/86		$1,200.00/Disc
			09/86	Annually	$795.00/Disc
UMI RESEARCH UMI (University Microfilms International)	PC/XT/AT with hard disk	640K	01/88	Bimonthly	$4,950.00/Year
Proprietary Information Access Company		640K	01/88	Monthly	$4,000.00/Year
Le Pac Brodart Automation	PC/XT/AT	640K	09/15/88	Yearly	*
None	PC/XT/AT	640K	07/88	Annually	$99.00/Disc

(continued)

ALPHABETICAL LISTING OF CD-ROM TITLES *continued*

Title	Publisher	Description	Audience
AdBuilder Electronic	Multi-Ad Services, Inc. 1720 West Detweiler Drive Peoria, IL 61615-1530 (800)447–1950	High quality PostScript illustrations and Ad Layouts for newspaper advertising systems.	Newspapers, advertisers, publishing, graphics.
AfterCare Instructions	Micromedex, Inc. 660 Bannock Street Suite 300 Denver, CO 80204-4506 (800)525-9083	AfterCare Instructions is a simple-to-use system that provides easily understood instructions for health care professionals to give to patients discharged from an emergency department or clinic setting, and referenced protocols for the medical evaluation and treatment of individuals exposed to chemical agents are provided. Protocols for initial response to incidents (fires, spills, leaks) from hazardous materials are also included. Agents are indexed by chemical names, synonyms, and commonly associated numbers (CAS, RTECS/NIOSH, UN, NA ENT, USAF, etc.).	Physicians, nurses, healthcare professionals.
Agri/Stats I	Hopkins Technology 421 Hazel Lane Hopkins, MN 55343-7117 (612)931–9376	Contains U.S. agricultural statistics including Crop Estimates, Grain Stocks, County Estimates—Crops and Livestock, Hog and Pig Estimates, Cattle Inventory, Cattle on Feed, and Meat Animals. These files date back as far as 1939.	Agriculture producers, traders, financial university.
AGRICOLA and CRIS Databases 1983-present	OCLC 6565 Frantz Road Dublin, OH 43017-0702 (800)848–5878		Libraries, educational organizations.
AGRICOLA Retrospective Files 1979-1982	OCLC 6565 Frantz Road Dublin, OH 43017-0702 (800)848–5878		Libraries, educational organizations.
AGRICOLA/CRIS	SilverPlatter Information, Inc. 37 Walnut Street Wellesley Hills, MA 02181 (617)239–0306	AGRICOLA contains citations of publications relating to all aspects of agriculture as compiled by the National Agricultural Library. CRIS contains nearly 30,000 descriptions of current publicly supported agricultural and forestry research projects.	Library reference market.

*Please contact publisher for prices.

Retrieval System	Computer Compatibility	Minimum Memory	Initial Release Date	Update Frequency	Price
PictureBase Retriever Symmetry Corporation	Macintosh SE/II/Plus, EPS-compatible software, and PostScript printer	1 MB	11/88		*
Proprietary Micromedex, Inc.	PC/XT/AT with DOS version 3.1 or higher	512K	05/88	Quarterly	*
QuAcc Hopkins Technology	PC with MS-DOS version 3.1 or higher and MS-DOS CD-ROM Extensions	200K	10/88	Annually	$49.00/Disc
Search CD450 OCLC	PC/XT/AT or Macintosh	512K		Quarterly	$795.00/Year
Search CD450 OCLC	PC/XT/AT or Macintosh	512K			$350.00/Set
SilverPlatter Information Retrieval System SilverPlatter Information, Inc.	PC with DOS version 2.1 or higher	640K	01/87	Quarterly	$950.00/Year

(continued)

ALPHABETICAL LISTING OF CD-ROM TITLES continued

Title	Publisher	Description	Audience
Agriculture Library	OCLC 6565 Frantz Road Dublin, OH 43017-0702 (800)848–5878	Over 300,000 bibliographic records on agriculture-related subjects. Topics include farm economics and management, field crops, forestry policy, animal breeds and breeding, wildlife management, soil conservation, horticulture, parks and public reservations, dairying and dairy products, and rural sociology.	Libraries, educational organizations.
AIDS Supplement	Digital Diagnostics, Inc. 601 University Avenue Suite 255 Sacramento, CA 95825 (916)921–6629	Over 40,000 citations from the last 8 years, with cross references to 47 separate medical subject heading terms.	Health professionals.
Applied Science & Technology Index	H.W. Wilson Company 950 University Avenue Bronx, NY 10452 (800)367–6770	Index of 339 English-language periodicals in applied science and technology. Retrospective from 10-83.	Libraries.
Art Index	H.W. Wilson Company 950 University Avenue Bronx, NY 10452 (800)367–6770	Index of articles from 227 domestic and foreign periodicals, yearbooks, etc. Retrospective from 9-84.	Libraries.
ArtRoom	Image Club Graphics Inc. 2915 19th Street East Suite 206 Calgary, AB T2E 7A2 CANADA (403)250–1969	Contains over 1000 high-resolution Encapsulated PostScript clip art and images, the complete library of over 100 PostScript typefaces, and over 50 pages of useful publishing templates.	Desktop publishers.
Automated Parts Catalog	ADP 1950 Hassell Road Hoffman Estates, IL 60195-2308 (312)397–1700	General Motors automotive parts catalog for 1976-1989.	GM dealers.
AVS+ (Address Verification System Plus)	Information Update Inc. 1190 Saratoga Avenue Suite 210 San Jose, CA 95129-3456 (408)236–3297	A database of every deliverable address in the United States.	Postal services, direct mailers, banks, insurance companies.
BIB-BASE/CD-ROM	Small Library Computing		

*Please contact publisher for prices.

Retrieval System	Computer Compatibility	Minimum Memory	Initial Release Date	Update Frequency	Price
Search CD450 OCLC	PC/XT/AT or Macintosh	512K		Annually	$350.00/Year
Proprietary Digital Diagnostics, Inc.	PC/XT/AT	640K	03/88	Quarterly	$350.00/Year
WILSONDISC H.W. Wilson Company	PC/XT/AT	640K	04/87	Quarterly	$1,495.00/Year
WILSONDISC H.W. Wilson Company	PC/XT/AT	640K	06/87	Quarterly	$1,495.00/Year
	Macintosh Plus/SE/II				$999.00/Disc
Proprietary ADP	ADP Proprietary Hardware	640K	01/89	As available from General Motors	*
Proprietary Information Update Inc.	PC/XT/AT with 12 MB hard disk and MS-DOS	512K	07/87	Quarterly	$3,950.00/Year
					*

(continued)

ALPHABETICAL LISTING OF CD-ROM TITLES *continued*

Title	Publisher	Description	Audience
Die Bibel	Deutsche Bibelgesellschaft Balingerstrasse 31 7000 Stuttgart 80 WEST GERMANY 0711/71810	The Luther bible.	
The Bible Library	Ellis Enterprises Inc. 225 N.W. 13th Street Oklahoma City, OK 73103 (405)235–7660	A comprehensive, powerful, and fun Bible study tool, including 9 versions of the Bible, 2 Bible language dictionaries, 3 word studies, 6 dictionaries and references, 2 commentaries, 1 book of hymn stories, 6 books of sermon outlines and illustrations.	Ministers and laymen, religious organizations and bookstores, theology students.
BIBLIOFILE Catalog Maintenance	Library Corporation P.O. Box 40035 Washington DC 20016 (800)624–0559	Based on the BIBLIOFILE Catalog Production system, allows you to maintain your own database/MARC file.	Libraries.
BIBLIOFILE Catalog Production	Library Corporation P.O. Box 40035 Washington, DC 20016 (800)624–0559	Catalog card and label production in MARC II format.	Libraries.
BiblioMed	Digital Diagnostics, Inc. 601 University Avenue Suite 255 Sacramento, CA 95825 (916)921–6629	Excerpts from the National Library of Medicine's MEDLINE database: 500 journals for 3 years.	Health professionals.
Biography Index	H.W. Wilson Company 950 University Avenue Bronx, NY 10452 (800)367–6770	Index of biographic materials. Retrospective from 7-84.	Libraries.
Biological & Agricultural Index	H.W. Wilson Company 950 University Avenue Bronx, NY 10452 (800)367–6770	Covering 202 key periodicals in the life sciences, this database offers balanced coverage of biological and agricultural disciplines, among them biochemistry, botany, cytology, forestry, genetics, horticulture, microbiology, soil science, and zoology. Retrospective from 7-83.	Libraries.
Blue Sail on CD-ROM	ALDE Publishing 4830 West 77th Street P.O. Box 35326 Minneapolis, MN 55435 (612)835–5240	1,000 floppy public domain library.	Horizontal markets.

*Please contact publisher for prices.

Retrieval System	Computer Compatibility	Minimum Memory	Initial Release Date	Update Frequency	Price
COBRA Bertlemann	PC/XT/AT with MS-DOS version 2.0 or higher	512K	03/87		*
MARCON AIRS, Inc.	PC/XT/AT	640K	07/88	Annually	$595.00/Disc
BIBLIOFILE Library Corporation	PC/XT/AT	640K	01/86		*
BIBLIOFILE Library Corporation	PC/XT/AT or PS/2 Model 30	512K	12/84		$1,750.00/Start package
Proprietary Digital Diagnostics, Inc.	PC/XT/AT	640K	10/87	Quarterly	$950.00/Year
WILSONDISC H.W. Wilson Company	PC/XT/AT	640K	06/87	Quarterly	$1,095.00/Year
WILSONDISC H.W. Wilson Company	PC/XT/AT	640K	03/88	Quarterly	$1,495.00/Year
Proprietary Menu Blue Sail Software	PC/XT/AT	640K	04/88	Annually	$149.00/Disc

(continued)

ALPHABETICAL LISTING OF CD-ROM TITLES *continued*

Title	*Publisher*	*Description*	*Audience*
BMUG PD ROM	BMUG (Berkeley Mac User's Group) 1442A Walnut #62 Berkeley, CA 94709 (415)549–BMUG	Over 300 MB of publicly distributable information. Also included on the disc are digests of electronic messages from USEnet, Delphi, InfoMac, and Arts & Farces, and many color Mac II pictures and large digitized sounds.	Macintosh users.
Book Review Digest	H.W. Wilson Company 950 University Avenue Bronx, NY 10452 (800)367–6770	Providing excerpts from and citations to reviews of current adult and juvenile fiction and non-fiction, BRD covers nearly 6,000 English-language books each year, with concise critical evaluations culled from more than 80 selected American, British, and Canadian periodicals. Retrospective from 3-83.	Libraries.
Books In Print Plus	Bowker Electronic Publishing 245 West 17th Street New York, NY 10011 (800)323–3288	Access the entire *Books In Print* database of over 800,000 titles (over 1,000,000 bindings). Search and browse 22 search categories including nearly 65,000 LC subject headings and 6,500 Sears and LC headings for children's titles. Includes name, address, and phone number for all publishers and ability to print, save, and electronically order titles from major distributors.	Libraries, bookstores, publishers.
Books In Print with Book Reviews Plus	Bowker Electronic Publishing 245 West 17th Street New York, NY 10011 (800)323–3288	Includes all features of *Books In Print Plus* with the addition of over 70,000 full-text book reviews from *Booklist, Choice, Library Journal, Publishers Weekly, School Library Journal, Research and Reference Book News,* and *SciTech Book News.*	Libraries, bookstores, publishers.
Books Out-of-Print Plus	Bowker Electronic Publishing 245 West 17th Street New York, NY 10011 (800)323–3288	Search and Browse 400,000 titles declared out-of-print or out-of-stock indefinitely from 1979 to the present using up to 18 different search categories. Includes ability to print, save, and edit five different display formats.	Libraries, bookstores, publishers.
British Library/Bibliotheque Nationale Pilot Disc	British Library 2 Sheraton Street London W1V 4BH ENGLAND 01/323-7073	Subsets of national bibliographies from the British Library and the Bibliothèque Nationale.	Libraries.

Retrieval System	Computer Compatibility	Minimum Memory	Initial Release Date	Update Frequency	Price
HyperCard Apple	Mac SE with System Release 5.0				$100.00/Disc
WILSONDISC H.W. Wilson Company	PC/XT/AT	640K	03/88	Quarterly	$1,095.00/Year
CD-ROM Search and Retrieval Software Online Computer Systems, Inc.	PC/XT/AT or PS/2	640K	10/86	Quarterly	$995.00/Year
CD-ROM Search and Retrieval Software Online Computer Systems, Inc.	PC/XT/AT or PS/2	640K	10/87	Quarterly	$1,395.00/Year
CD-ROM Search and Retrieval Software Online Computer Systems, Inc.	PC/XT/AT or PS/2	640K	10/87	Quarterly	$395.00/Year
OCSI Software Online Computer Systems Inc.	PC/XT/AT	512K	10/88		Free

(continued)

ALPHABETICAL LISTING OF CD-ROM TITLES *continued*

Title	*Publisher*	*Description*	*Audience*
Busi/Stats	Hopkins Technology 421 Hazel Lane Hopkins, MN 55343-7117 (612)931–9376	Profiles of businesses from federal databases.	Planners, corporate, academic.
Business Indicators	Slater Hall Information Products 1522 K Street N.W. Suite 522 Washington, DC 20005 (202)682–1350	The complete National Income and Product Accounts (1929-present), 1,900 economic series from the "Blue Pages" of the Survey of Current Business (annually from 1961, monthly from 1981), and income and employment by industry for all states and regions (1969-present).	Libraries, business economists, federal agencies.
Business Periodicals Index	H.W. Wilson Company 950 University Avenue Bronx, NY 10452 (800)367–6770	Index of 296 leading business magazines. Retrospective from 6-82.	Libraries.
C CD-ROM	ALDE Publishing 4830 West 77th Street P.O. Box 35326 Minneapolis, MN 55435 (612)835–5240	C source codes, templates and utilities.	C programmers.
CANCER-CD	SilverPlatter Information, Inc. 37 Walnut Street Wellesley Hills, MA 02181 (617)239–0306	References, abstracts and commentaries of the world's literature in cancer and related subjects. Coverage from 1983 to present.	Library reference market.
CancerLIT	Online Research Systems Inc. 2901 Broadway Suite 154 New York, NY 10025 (212)408–3311	NTIS CancerLIT database.	Cancer researchers, clinicians.
CAP CD-ROM	Computer Aided Planning Inc. 169-C Monroe N.W. Grand Rapids, MI 49503 (616)454–0000	Electronic catalogs and CAD libraries for the contract office furniture industry.	Office furniture manufacturers and dealers, architectural and design firms, facilities managers.

Retrieval System	Computer Compatibility	Minimum Memory	Initial Release Date	Update Frequency	Price
QuAcc Hopkins Technology	PC with MS-DOS version 3.1 or higher and MS-DOS CD-ROM Extensions	200K	02/89	Annually	$59.00/Disc
SEARCHER Slater Hall	PC/XT/AT with hard disk	512K	01/88	Monthly	$2,200.00/Year
WILSONDISC H.W. Wilson Company	PC/XT/AT	640K		Quarterly	$1,495.00/Year
None	PC/XT/AT	640K	09/88	Annually	$99.00/Disc
SilverPlatter Information Retrieval System SilverPlatter Information, Inc.	PC with DOS version 2.1 or higher	640K	10/87	Quarterly	$1,750.00/Year
CD-Plus Online Research Systems, Inc.	PC/XT/AT with MS-DOS CD-ROM Extensions	640K	01/89	Monthly	$1,995.00/Year
CAP Computer Aided Planning Inc.	PC/XT/AT/Compaq with 10 MB hard drive	640K	09/87	Monthly	$1,500.00/Year

(continued)

ALPHABETICAL LISTING OF CD-ROM TITLES continued

Title	Publisher	Description	Audience
CCINFOdisc: Series A1 and A2: Chemical Information	Canadian Centre for Occupational Health & Safety 250 Main Street East Hamilton, ON L8N 1H6 CANADA (416)572–2981	Chemical safety information in French and English, as created by CCOHS or supplied by contributors. Series A1 includes: TRADE NAMES Data Base, CHEMINFO Data Base, Regulatory Information on Pesticide Products (RIPP) Data Base, and Videotex Information Packages. Series A2 includes: CHEMINFO Data Base, Registry of Toxic Effects of Chemical Substances (RTECS) Data Base, Transportation of Dangerous Goods (TDG) Data Base, CCOHS publications, New Jersey Department of Health Hazardous Substance Fact Sheets, and Videotex Information Packages.	Labor, employers, governments, professionals, health and safety committees.
CCINFOdisc: Series B Occupational Health and Safety Information	Canadian Centre for Occupational Health & Safety 250 Main Street East Hamilton, ON L8N 1H6 CANADA (416)572–2981	Entries on all aspects of occupational health and safety, in French and English as created by CCOHS or supplied by contributors. Series B includes: CANADIAN STUDIES Data Base, RESOURCE ORGANIZATIONS Data Base, RESOURCE PEOPLE Data Base, CANADIANA Data Base, ESSENTIALS Data Base, CASE LAW Data Base, STANDARDS AND DIRECTORIES Data Base, NOISE LEVELS Data Base, CISILO Data Base, NIOSHTIC Data Base, and Videotex Information Packages.	Labor, employers, governments, professionals, health and safety committees.
CD NOCS	Dai Nippon Ichigaya-kagacho Shinjuka-ku Tokyo 162 JAPAN 03/266–2111	Nippon Online Communications System.	
CD Town Page	Dai Nippon Ichigaya-kagacho Shinjuka-ku Tokyo 162 JAPAN 03/266–2111	Tokyo business phone numbers.	
CD WORD: Multilingual Dictionary	Dai Nippon Ichigaya-kagacho Shinjuku-ku Tokyo 162 JAPAN 03/266–2111		

*Please contact publisher for prices.

Retrieval System	Computer Compatibility	Minimum Memory	Initial Release Date	Update Frequency	Price
FindIt Reteaco, Inc.	PC/XT/AT with DOS version 3.0 or higher and MS-DOS CD-ROM Extensions version 2.0	512K	08/87	Quarterly	$114.00/Year
FindIt Reteaco, Inc.	PC/XT/AT with DOS version 3.0 or higher and MS-DOS CD-ROM Extensions version 2.0	512K	08/87	Quarterly	$114.00/Disc

(continued)

ALPHABETICAL LISTING OF CD-ROM TITLES *continued*

Title	*Publisher*	*Description*	*Audience*
CD/Banking	Lotus Development Corporation One Cambridge Center Cambridge, MA 02142 (800)554–5501	Complete coverage of all federally insured institutions: Call report information on 13,500 federally insured commercial banks, thrift financial report information on 3,100 savings & loans, and Y-9 data for 6,000 bank holding companies.	Banks, investment houses, consulting firms, insurance companies, Fortune 1000 companies.
CD-CATSS	Utlas International 2150 Shattuck Avenue Suite 402 Berkeley, CA 94704 (415)841–9442	4 discs with approximately 2 million bibliographic records from 1984-present.	Libraries.
CD/Corp Tech	Lotus Development Corporation One Cambridge Center Cambridge, MA 02142 (800)554–5501	Summary data on 25,000 high technology companies with detailed product data on each.	Banks, investment houses, consulting firms, insurance companies, Fortune 100 companies.
CD/Corporate	Lotus Development Corporation One Cambridge Center Cambridge, MA 02142 (800)554–5501	CD/Corporate allows you to access the important financial, strategic, or competitive information you need from one compact disc. CD/Corporate combines industry-standard databases with report-generating software so you can quickly prepare custom reports that are incisive and in-depth.	Banks, investment houses, consulting firms, insurance companies, Fortune 1000 companies.
CD-FICHE	USA Information Systems, Inc. 3303 Duke Street Alexandria, VA 22314 (800)USA–8830	The Federal Supply Catalog—over 12 million part numbers purchased by the government on a regular basis, on 4 discs.	Government procurement centers and contractors.
CD/International	Lotus Development Corporation One Cambridge Center Cambridge, MA 02142 (800)554–5501	Financial information on 4,500 of the world's leading industrial corporations, banks, insurance companies, and financial service firms. Current financial data including income statements, balance sheets, and funds flow statements, over 250 financial variables per company, company-specific accounting practices, critical footnotes to financial statements, and native currency or U.S. dollar report options.	Banks, investment houses, consulting firms, insurance companies, Fortune 1000 companies.
CD/Investment	Lotus Development Corporation One Cambridge Center Cambridge, MA 02142 (800)554–5501	Comprehensive financials on companies, stocks, and financial issues, from seven leading industry-standard databases.	Banks, investment houses, consulting firms, insurance companies, Fortune 1000 companies.

Retrieval System	Computer Compatibility	Minimum Memory	Initial Release Date	Update Frequency	Price
Lotus One Source Lotus Development Corporation	PC/XT/AT	640K		Quarterly	$16,000.00/Year
CD-CATSS Utlas International	PC/XT/AT	640K	10/88	Quarterly	$1,800.00/Year
Lotus One Source Lotus Development Corporation	PC/XT/AT	640K		Quarterly	$7,500.00/Year
Lotus One Source Lotus Development Corporation	PC/XT/AT	640K		Monthly	$17,500.00/Year
Proprietary USA Information Systems, Inc.	PC/XT/AT or PS/2 with MS-DOS version 3.1 or higher	640K	04/87	Quarterly	$3,250.00/Year
Lotus One Source Lotus Development Corporation	PC/XT/AT	640K		Monthly	$1,950.00/Year
Lotus One Source Lotus Development Corporation	PC/XT/AT	640K		Weekly	$11,000.00/Year

(continued)

ALPHABETICAL LISTING OF CD-ROM TITLES *continued*

Title	Publisher	Description	Audience
CDMARC Bibliographic	Library of Congress Cataloging Distribution Service Washington, DC 20541 (202)287–6100	Entire Library of Congress bibliographic file containing books, serials, maps, visual materials, and music.	Libraries.
CDMARC Names	Library of Congress Cataloging Distribution Service Washington, DC 20541 (202)287–6100	Personal and corporate name authority file of the Library of Congress, on 3 discs.	Libraries.
CDMARC Subjects	Library of Congress Cataloging Distribution Service Washington, DC 20541 (202)287–6100	Subject Authority file from the Library of Congress.	Libraries.
CD/Newsline	Lotus Development Corporation One Cambridge Center Cambridge, MA 02142 (800)554–5501	Dow Jones News/Retrieval Service.	Banks, investment houses, consulting firms, insurance companies, Fortune 1000 companies.
CD/Private+	Lotus Development Corporation One Cambridge Center Cambridge, MA 02142 (800)554–5501	Provides profiles on 110,000 private firms and more detailed information on the leading 6,000 private firms and 10,000 public companies.	Banks, investment houses, consulting forms, insurance companies, Fortune 1000 companies.
CD-ROM Sampler	Discovery Systems 7001 Discovery Boulevard Dublin, OH 43017 (614)761–2000	The CD-ROM Sampler is an innovative, multimedia CD-ROM disc developed to demonstrate the wide range of applications addressable by CD-ROM technology in the MS-DOS environment. Featuring software products submitted by over 50 software publishers, the Sampler includes a variety of hands-on PC demo applications as well as an integrated natural image and graphics-based tutorial on CD-ROM complete with audio narration and music.	

*Please contact publisher for prices.

Retrieval System	Computer Compatibility	Minimum Memory	Initial Release Date	Update Frequency	Price
Online	PC/XT/AT with DOS version 3.1 or higher and hard disk	640K			*
Online	PC/XT/AT with DOS version 3.1 or higher and hard disk	640K	03/89	Quarterly	*
Online	PC/XT/AT with DOS version 3.1 or higher and hard disk	640K	06/88	Quarterly	$300.00/Year
Lotus One Source Lotus Development Corporation	PC/XT/AT	640K		Quarterly	$2,000.00/Year
Lotus One Source Lotus Development Corporation	PC/XT/AT	640K		Quarterly	$6,500.00/Year
	PC/XT/AT with DOS version 3.1 or higher	640K	10/87	Annually	$10.00/Disc

(continued)

ALPHABETICAL LISTING OF CD-ROM TITLES continued

Title	Publisher	Description	Audience
CD-ROM SourceDisc	Diversified Data Resources Inc. 6609 Rosecroft Place Falls Church, VA 22043 (703)237–0682	Information on over 300 commercially available CD-ROM titles and a glossary and acronym list of CD-ROM-related terms. Also included are *CD-ROM: The New Papyrus* and *CD-ROM: Optical Publishing* from Microsoft Press, and an electronic brochure on DV-I from General Electric.	Anyone who owns a CD-ROM.
CD-ROM: The Conference Disc	PDO 1402 Foulk Road Suite 200 Wilmington, DE 19803 (302)479–2500	Cooperative effort of attendees of the Microsoft Second International Conference on CD-ROM.	
CDX (Corporate Data Exchange)	LaFountain Research Corporation 15 Park Row Suite 700 New York, NY 10038 (212)766–3777	Central repository of financial information sponsored by corporate clients.	Brokerage firms, large corporations and institutions.
Census Test Disk 2	U.S. Bureau of the Census Customer Services Washington, DC 20233 (301)763–4100	Contains data from the Census of Agriculture, 1982: Final County File; and the Census of Retail Trade, 1982: ZIP Code File. Data is arranged in dBASE III input format. Paper copy of technical documentation is included. Both files are included on a single disc.	
CHEM-BANK	SilverPlatter Information, Inc. 37 Walnut Street Wellesley Hills, MA 02181 (617)239–0306	A collection of databanks of potentially hazardous chemicals, containing three complete major databanks: RTECS, OHMTADS, and CHRIS.	Library reference market.
Chrysler Parts Catalog	Bell and Howell 5700 Lombardo Center Suite 220 Seven Hills, OH 44351 (216)642–9060	Electronic parts catalog.	Automotive dealers.
CIS Congressional Masterfile, 1789-1969	Congressional Information Service, Inc. 4520 East-West Highway Suite 800 Bethesda, MD 20814-3389 (800)638–8380	Includes the CIS U.S. Congressional Committee Hearings Index (1833-1969), CIS Unpublished U.S. Senate Committee Hearings (1823-1964), CIS U.S. Serial Set Index (1789-1969), and the CIS U.S. Congressional Committee Prints Index (1830-1969). Also available in any combination of the above.	

*Please contact publisher for prices.

Retrieval System	Computer Compatibility	Minimum Memory	Initial Release Date	Update Frequency	Price
Norton Demo Proprietary LASERTEX Knowledge Based Systems Windows Personal Librarian Personal Library Software	PC/XT/AT with DOS version 3.1 or higher	640K	11/88	Annually	$89.95/Disc
					$20.00/Disc
None		None	10/88	Quarterly	*
	PC/XT/AT		06/88		$125.00/Disc
SilverPlatter Information Retrieval System SilverPlatter Information, Inc.	PC with DOS version 2.1 or higher	640K	05/87	Quarterly	$1,350.00/Year
Proprietary Bell and Howell	IDB 2000 Image Retrieval System		02/88	Monthly	*
Proprietary Congressional Information Service, Inc.	PC or PS/2	640K	11/88		*

(continued)

ALPHABETICAL LISTING OF CD-ROM TITLES *continued*

Title	Publisher	Description	Audience
Climatedata — Central/Eastern States	US WEST Optical Publishing 90 Madison Street Suite 200 Denver, CO 80206 (800)222–0920	Daily climate data from the National Climatic Data Center for Central and Eastern states.	Engineers, scientists, colleges, universities, meteorologists.
Climatedata — Hourly Precipitation	US WEST Optical Publishing 90 Madison Street Suite 200 Denver, CO 80206 (800)222–0920	NCDC hourly precipitation measurements.	Engineers, scientists, colleges, universities, meteorologists.
Climatedata — Western States	US WEST Optical Publishing 90 Madison Street Suite 200 Denver, CO 80206 (800)222–0920	Daily climate data from the National Climatic Data Center for the Western United States.	Engineers, scientists, colleges, universities, meteorologists.
ClubMac	Quantum Access, Inc. 1700 West Loop South Suite 1460 Houston, TX 77027 (713)622–3211	450 MB of public domain shareware and clip art.	Macintosh users.
Compact Cambridge Aquatic Sciences and Fisheries Abstracts	Cambridge Scientific Abstracts 7200 Wisconsin Avenue Suite 601 Bethesda, MD 20816 (301)961–6700	Abstracts covering biological and ecological aspects of marine, freshwater and brackish environments, marine technology and engineering, oceanography, and pollution of aquatic environments.	Universities, oceanographic researchers.
Compact Cambridge CancerLit (Cancer Literature)	Cambridge Scientific Abstracts 7200 Wisconsin Avenue Suite 601 Bethesda, MD 20816 (301)961–6700	Citations and abstracts taken by the National Cancer Institute from over 3,000 biomedical journals, including papers, reports, and doctoral theses.	Hospitals, universities, researchers.
Compact Cambridge Drugs Database	Cambridge Scientific Abstracts 7200 Wisconsin Avenue Suite 601 Bethesda, MD 20816 (301)961–6700	Database from the American Society of Hospital Pharmacists including drug indication uses, side effects, toxicity, dosages, interaction, and chemical stability	Hospitals, pharmaceutical companies.
Compact Cambridge Life Sciences Collection	Cambridge Scientific Abstracts 7200 Wisconsin Avenue Suite 601 Bethesda, MD 20816 (301)961–6700	A comprehensive life sciences database with abstracts including indepth coverage of AIDS research, bacteriology, immunology, toxicology, virology, microbiology, biochemistry, biotechnology, and ecology.	Universities, medical schools, hospitals, researchers.

*Please contact publisher for prices.

Retrieval System	Computer Compatibility	Minimum Memory	Initial Release Date	Update Frequency	Price
Proprietary US WEST Optical Publishing	PC/XT/AT with DOS version 2.0 or higher	512K	05/88	Annually	$295.00/Year
Proprietary US WEST Optical Publishing	PC/XT/AT with DOS version 2.0 or higher	512K	12/88	Annually	$295.00/Year
Proprietary US WEST Optical Publishing	PC/XT/AT with DOS version 2.0 or higher	512K	05/88	Annually	$295.00/Year
HyperCard Apple	Macintosh		07/88	Quarterly	$350.00/Year
Compact Cambridge Cambridge Scientific Abstracts	PC/XT/AT	512K	06/86	Biannually	$1,250.00/Year
Compact Cambridge Cambridge Scientific Abstracts	PC/XT/AT	512K	09/88	Quarterly	$995.00/Year
Compact Cambridge Cambridge Scientific Abstracts	PC/XT/AT	512K	10/88	Monthly	$1,950.00/Year
Compact Cambridge Cambridge Scientific Abstracts	PC/XT/AT	512K	06/86	Biannually	$1,250.00/Year

(continued)

ALPHABETICAL LISTING OF CD-ROM TITLES *continued*

Title	*Publisher*	*Description*	*Audience*
Compact Cambridge MEDLINE	Cambridge Scientific Abstracts 7200 Wisconsin Avenue Suite 601 Bethesda, MD 20816 (301)961–6700	The complete MEDLINE database and abstracts including all journals and all languages.	Universities, medical schools, hospitals and pharmaceutical companies.
Compact Cambridge PDQ (Physicians' Data Query)	Cambridge Scientific Abstracts 7200 Wisconsin Avenue Suite 601 Bethesda, MD 20816 (301)961–6700	The National Cancer Institute's database consisting of cancer treatment information, ongoing treatment protocols (information on over 1000 treatment protocols and a limited number of standard treatment regimens), and a directory of over 12,000 physicians and surgeons and 1400 organizations that provide cancer care.	Universities, hospitals, researchers.
Compact Disclosure	Disclosure Incorporated 5161 River Road Bethesda, MD 20816 (800)843–7747	Financial and textual data extracted from documents filed with the SEC on over 12,000 public companies. Over 250 variables are searchable.	Investment bankers, brokers, and advisors; university and public libraries; accountants, lawyers, management consultants, commercial banks.
Compact Library: AIDS	Medical Publishing Group 1440 Main Street Waltham, MA 02254 (617)893–3800	Comprehensive library of AIDS information including the AIDS Knowledge Base, MEDLINE citations dealing with AIDS, and the complete text of AIDS articles from 7 leading journals.	Health care professionals.
Compact Med-Base	Online Research Systems Inc. 2901 Broadway Suite 154 New York, NY 10025 (212)408–3311	NTIS Medline database.	Medical libraries, hospital departments.
Company Accounts Register of the Belgian National Bank	Bureau Marcel van Dijk 250 Avenue Louise Suite 14 1050 Bruxelles BELGIUM 02/648–6697	Company accounts of 123,000 Belgian corporations.	
COMPREHENSIVE MEDLINE/ EBSCO CD-ROM	EBSCO Electronic Information P.O. Box 13787 Torrance, CA 90503 (800)888–EBSCO	The complete MEDLINE file from 1986-present, including Index Medicus, International Nursing Index, and Index to Dental Literature.	Medical and hospital libraries, health professionals.

*Please contact publisher for prices.

Retrieval System	Computer Compatibility	Minimum Memory	Initial Release Date	Update Frequency	Price
Compact Cambridge Cambridge Scientific Abstracts	PC/XT/AT	512K	06/86	Quarterly	$1,250.00/Year
Compact Cambridge Cambridge Scientific Abstracts	PC/XT/AT	512K	08/88	Monthly	$950.00/Year
	PC/XT/AT or PS/2 with hard disk drive	640K		Bimonthly	$3,700.00/Year
Proprietary Medical Publishing Group	PC/XT/AT with MS-DOS CD-ROM Extensions version 2.0 and DOS version 3.1 or higher	640K	10/88	Quarterly	$875.00/Year
CD-Plus Online Research Systems, Inc.	PC/XT/AT with MS-DOS CD-ROM Extensions	640K	05/88	Monthly	$3,495.00/Year
Proprietary Bureau Marcel van Dijk	PC/XT/AT with hard disk OR Macintosh SE/II/Plus	640K	08/87	Quarterly	$2,500.00/Year
EBSCO-CD EBSCO Electronic Information	PC/XT/AT with MS-DOS version 3.1 or higher and 10 MB hard disk	640K	10/88	Quarterly	$1,000.00/Year

(continued)

ALPHABETICAL LISTING OF CD-ROM TITLES *continued*

Title	Publisher	Description	Audience
COMPU-INFO	SilverPlatter Information, Inc. 37 Walnut Street Wellesley Hills, MA 02181 (617)239-0306	A database of 12,000 computer product listings. It contains information about mainframes, minicomputers, microcomputers, operating systems, communications, display terminals, teleprinters, and other peripherals.	Library reference market.
Compustat PC Plus	Standard and Poor Compustat Services 7400 South Alton Court Englewood, CO 90112 (303)740-4510	A detailed database of 7,187 public companies.	
Computer Library	Computer Library/ Ziff Communications 1 Park Avenue New York, NY 10016 (212)503-4400	12 months worth of full-text articles and abstracts from over 120 computer publications.	Infocenter managers, MIS managers, PC coordinators, computer product marketers and developers.
Computer Library	OCLC 6565 Frantz Road Dublin, OH 43017-0702 (800)848-5878	Over 250,000 records that cover the subject from the earliest days of computer development to the microchip revolution that's made the supercomputers of today possible. Government, academic, and private industry resources are all utilized to provide you with the most comprehensive body of information available on the computer industry.	Libraries, educational organizations.
Comstock Desktop Photography	Comstock Inc. 30 Irving Place New York, NY 10003 (212)353-8686	449 black and white photographs in TIFF files in High Sierra and Mac HFS format.	Art directors, graphic designers, corporate communications departments, schools, hospitals.
Connecticut Real Estate Transaction Database	Knowledge Access International, Inc. 2685 Marine Way Suite 1305 Mountain View, CA 94043 (415)969-0606	Real estate transfer records from 1987 for the state of Connecticut.	Bankers, real estate agencies, city planners, real estate aftermarket companies.
The Constitution Papers	Optical Media International Reflective Arts International 495 Alberto Way Los Gatos, CA 95032 (408)395-4332	Contains the U.S. Constitution Papers and an audio file "Heartland/An American Anthem."	

*Please contact publisher for prices.

Retrieval System	Computer Compatibility	Minimum Memory	Initial Release Date	Update Frequency	Price
SilverPlatter Information Retrieval System SilverPlatter Information, Inc.	PC with DOS version 2.1 or higher	640K	12/87	Semiannually	$1,250.00/Year
					$12,000.00
BlueFish Lotus Development Corporation	PC/XT/AT/COMPAQ with MS-DOS version 3.1 or higher	512K	09/20/88	Monthly	$695.00/Year
Search CD450 OCLC	PC/XT/AT or Macintosh	512K		Annually	$350.00
None	PC/XT/AT/ Macintosh	200K	08/89		$500.00/Disc
KAware2 Knowledge Access International, Inc.	PC/XT/AT	640K	10/88	Annually	$1,500.00/State
Electronic Text Corporation					$29.95

(continued)

ALPHABETICAL LISTING OF CD-ROM TITLES *continued*

Title	Publisher	Description	Audience
Construction Activity Locater	Knowledge Access International, Inc./ CD Productions 2685 Marine Way Suite 1305 Mountain View, CA 94043 (415)969–0606	Tracks 430,014 building permits and valuations for 17,000 cities with 38 variables for each city. Includes monthly building permits reported to Bureau of Census on form C-404 since January, 1987; and state, county, and Consolidated Metropolitan Statistical Area totals.	Utility companies, construction firms, real estate firms, development planners, state and city governments, construction after-market companies.
Construction Criteria Base	National Institute of Building Sciences 1015 15th Street N.W. Suite 700 Washington, DC 20005 (202)347–5710	NAVFAC, Corps of Engineers, NASA, and VA guide specifications, Corps of Engineers Civil Works Specifications and Reserve Centers, NAVFAC Design Manuals, Federal and Military Specifications.	Architects, engineers.
Consu/Stats I	Hopkins Technology 421 Hazel Lane Hopkins, MN 55343-7117 (612)931–9376	Contains the complete public use source data files on 1984 Surveys of Consumer Expenditures including detailed interview and diary data. These huge databases cover hundreds of characteristics of consumer units, family members, income and expenditures. The data also includes major appliance inventories and purchases, trips and vacations, vehicle purchases and vehicle disposals.	Marketers, university, library, financial.
CORE MEDLINE/EBSCO CD-ROM	EBSCO Electronic Information P.O. Box 13787 Torrance, CA 90503 (800)888–EBSCO	A subset of the MEDLINE file for the past 2 years plus current year: Over 560 journals indexed; over 330,000 citations on one disc.	Medical and hospital libraries, health care professionals.
Corporate & Industry Research Reports (CIRR)	SilverPlatter Information, Inc. 37 Walnut Street Wellesley Hills, MA 02181 (617)239–0306	A cumulative index with abstracts to over 70,000 corporate and industry reports written by securities and investment banking firms from 1979 to present.	Library reference market.
County, metro area statistics	Slater Hall Information Products 1522 K Street N.W. Suite 522 Washington, DC 20005 (202)682–1350	Population, housing, health, education, business, agriculture, crime statistics, and more; with over 1,000 data items for each county, state, and metro area.	Libraries, corporations, state and local governments.

*Please contact publisher for prices.

Retrieval System	Computer Compatibility	Minimum Memory	Initial Release Date	Update Frequency	Price
KAware2 Knowledge Access International, Inc.	PC/XT/AT	640K	12/88	Annually	$4,100.00/Disc
FastFind Unibase	PC/XT/AT with MS- or PC-DOS version 3.0 or higher and a 20 MB hard disk, EGA Color Monitor	512K	10/87	Quarterly	$970.00/Year
QuAcc Hopkins Technology	PC with MS-DOS version 3.1 or higher and MS-DOS CD-ROM Extensions	200K	07/88		$49.00/Disc
EBSCO-CD EBSCO Electronic Information	PC/XT/AT with MS-DOS version 3.1 or higher and 10 MB hard disk	640K	01/88	Quarterly	$1,400.00/Year
SilverPlatter Information Retrieval System SilverPlatter Information, Inc.	PC with DOS version 2.1 or higher	640K	03/88	Quarterly	$1,250.00/Year
SEARCHER Slater Hall	PC/XT/AT	512K	12/87	Yearly	$1,200.00/Disc

(continued)

ALPHABETICAL LISTING OF CD-ROM TITLES *continued*

Title	Publisher	Description	Audience
Crime/Stats	Hopkins Technology 421 Hazel Lane Hopkins, MN 55343-7117 (612)931–9376	Crime and jail statistics produced by federal agencies.	Government, social studies, universities.
Cumulative Book Index	H.W. Wilson Company 950 University Avenue Bronx, NY 10452 (800)367–6770	Bibliographic information on the approximately 50,000 English-language books published internationally. Retrospective from 1-82.	Libraries.
DarkRoom	Image Club Graphics Inc. 2915 19th Street East Suite 206 Calgary, AB T2E 7A2 CANADA (403)250–1969	A stock photo library of more than 500 professional ready-to-use photos, categorized according to Sports, Lifestyle, Business, and Travel. Comes complete with a full-color reference catalog.	
Decision Series: California Decisions	ROM Publishers Inc. 1033 'O' Street Mezzanine Level Lincoln, NE 68508 (402)476–2965	California case law.	Attorneys, corporate legal divisions.
Decision Series: Federal Decisions	ROM Publishers Inc. 1033 'O' Street Mezzanine Level Lincoln, NE 68508 (402)476–2965	Federal Court of Appeals case law.	Attorneys, corporate legal divisions.
Decision Series: Federal Supplemental Decisions	ROM Publishers Inc. 1033 'O' Street Mezzanine Level Lincoln, NE 68508 (402)476–2965	Federal District Court case law.	Attorneys, corporate legal divisions.
Decision Series: Northwest Regional Decisions	ROM Publishers Inc. 1033 'O' Street Mezzanine Level Lincoln, NE 68508 (402)476–2965	Case law from a 7 state region including North Dakota, South Dakota, Nebraska, Iowa, Wisconsin, Michigan, and Minnesota.	Attorneys, corporate legal divisions.
DeLorme's World Atlas	DeLorme Mapping Systems P.O. Box 298 Freeport, ME 04032 (207)865–4171	Worldwide vector-based atlas.	

*Please contact publisher for prices.

Retrieval System	Computer Compatibility	Minimum Memory	Initial Release Date	Update Frequency	Price
QuAcc Hopkins Technology	PC with MS-DOS version 3.1 or higher and MS-DOS CD-ROM Extensions	200K	05/89	Every 2 years	$49.00/Disc
WILSONDISC H.W. Wilson Company	PC/XT/AT	640K	06/87	Quarterly	$1,295.00/Year
	Macintosh SE/II/Plus	1 MB			$499.00/Disc
Reference Technology, Inc.	PC/XT/AT with hard disk	640K	01/89	Quarterly	$2,695.00/Year
Reference Technology, Inc.	PC/XT/AT with hard disk	640K	03/89	Quarterly	$5,400.00/Year
Reference Technology, Inc.	PC/XT/AT with hard disk	640K	03/89	Quarterly	$5,780.00/Year
Reference Technology, Inc.	PC/XT/AT with hard disk	640K	09/88	Quarterly	$2,690.00/Year

*

(continued)

ALPHABETICAL LISTING OF CD-ROM TITLES *continued*

Title	Publisher	Description	Audience
DIALOG OnDisc AGRIBUSINESS U.S.A.	Dialog Information Services, Inc./Pioneer Hi-Bred International 3460 Hillview Avenue Palo Alto, CA 94304 (800)334-2564	Provides indexing for more than 200 agribusiness trade journals and more than 100 USDA reports. Important data from international sources such as the United Nations Food and Agriculture Organization and the European Economic Community are also included. Records contain either the complete text or full tables (for statistical publications) or controlled-vocabulary indexing and informative abstracts. Covers 1985-present.	Libraries.
DIALOG OnDisc Canadian Business and Current Affairs	Dialog Information Services Inc./Micromedia Ltd. 3460 Hillview Avenue Palo Alto, CA 94394 (800)334-2564	More than 220,000 articles per year from 200 business periodicals, 300 popular magazines, and 10 newspapers, including the Globe & Mail, Toronto Star, and Montreal Gazette. Coverage extends from 1981 through the current year. Covers 1981-present.	Libraries.
DIALOG OnDisc ERIC	Dialog Information Services Inc. 3460 Hillview Avenue Palo Alto, CA 94304 (800)334-2564	Provides immediate access to abstracts of articles published in over 700 educational journals, and thousands of research reports, evaluation studies, curriculum guides, and lesson plans collected by the U.S. Department of Education. Covers 1980-present.	Libraries.
DIALOG OnDisc MEDLINE	Dialog Information Services, Inc. 3460 Hillview Avenue Palo Alto, CA 94304 (800)334-2564	Includes references and abstracts from approximately 3,200 journals published in over 70 countries. 300,000 records are added each year, 70% of which represent publications written in the English language. Covers 1987-present.	Libraries.
DIALOG OnDisc NTIS	Dialog Information Services Inc. 3460 Hillview Avenue Palo Alto, CA 94304 (800)334-2564	U.S. government-sponsored research, development, and engineering reports and analyses prepared by federal agencies, their contractors, and grantees. It contains abstracts of unclassified, publicly available reports, software packages, and data files from 300 government agencies and some state and local government agencies. Covers 1984-present.	Libraries.

*Please contact publisher for prices.

Retrieval System	Computer Compatibility	Minimum Memory	Initial Release Date	Update Frequency	Price
	PC or PS/2 with PC- or MS-DOS version 3.1 or higher and 1 MB hard disk	512K		Quarterly	$2,000.00/Year
	PC or PS/2 with PC- or MS-DOS version 3.1 or higher and 1 MB hard disk	512K		Quarterly	$1,450.00/Year
	PC or PS/2 Model 30 with PC- or MS-DOS version 2.0 or higher and 1 MB hard disk	512K		Quarterly	$950.00/Year
	PC or PS/2 with PC- or MS-DOS version 2.0 or higher and 1 MB hard disk	512K		Quarterly	$1,250.00/Year
	PC or PS/2 with PC- or MS-DOS version 2.0 or higher and 1 MB hard disk	512K		Quarterly	$2,700.00/Year

(continued)

ALPHABETICAL LISTING OF CD-ROM TITLES *continued*

Title	*Publisher*	*Description*	*Audience*
Digit Art	Image Club Graphics Inc. 2915 19th Street N.E. Suite 206 Calgary, AB T2E 7A2 CANADA (403)250–1969	Ten volumes of clip art from elements to illustrations in Encapsulated PostScript format—over 1000 high-resolution images.	Desktop publishers.
Directory of Library and Information Professionals	Knowledge Access International, Inc. 2685 Marine Way Suite 1305 Mountain View, CA 94043 (415)969–0606	Biographical data on approximately 45,000 individuals in the information community.	Librarians, library vendors, researchers.
Disclosure/Spectrum Ownership Database	Disclosure Incorporated 5161 River Road Bethesda, MD 20816 (800)843–7747	Financial and textual data extracted from documents filed with the SEC on over 12,000 public companies. Over 250 variables are searchable. Also included: detailed stock ownership information for companies extracted from documents filed with the SEC by Corporate insiders, five percent owners and institutional owners.	Investment bankers, brokers, and advisors; university and public libraries; accountants, lawyers, management consultants, commercial banks.
Discon	Utlas International 8300 College Boulevard Overland Park, KS 66210 (800)33–UTLAS	6 million brief bibliographic records from the Library of Congress card catalog, up to 1984, on 4 discs.	Libraries.
Dissertation Abstracts Ondisc: Archival Edition	UMI (University Microfilms International) 300 North Zeeb Road Ann Arbor, MI 48106 (800)521–3044	Bibliographic citations for dissertations and masters theses published from 1861 through June 1984.	Academic and corporate libraries, researchers.
Dissertation Abstracts Ondisc: Current Edition	UMI (University Microfilms International) 300 North Zeeb Road Ann Arbor, MI 48106 (800)521–3044	Bibliographic citations and 350-word abstracts for 100,000 doctoral dissertations and masters theses.	Academic and corporate libraries, researchers.
DOSING & THERAPEUTIC TOOLS	Micromedex, Inc. 660 Bannock Street Suite 300 Denver, CO 80204-4506 (800)525–9083	Dosing and Therapeutic Tools is a database that contains Nomograms and Drug Dosing, EKG Rhythm Strips, Diagnostic and Therapeutic Pearls, Different Diagnostic Lists, and Calculators. This database helps clinicians make calculations or decisions regarding specific patient problems.	Physicians, healthcare professionals.

*Please contact publisher for prices.

Retrieval System	Computer Compatibility	Minimum Memory	Initial Release Date	Update Frequency	Price
	Macintosh Plus/SE/II, PC/XT/AT				*
KAware2 Knowledge Access International, Inc.	PC/XT/AT with MS-DOS version 3.1 or higher	640K	05/88	Every 2 years	$495.00
	PC/XT/AT or PS/2 with hard disk drive	640K		Bimonthly	$2,000.00/Year
CD-CATSS Utlas International	PC/XT/AT	640K	06/86		$680.00/Month
UMI RESEARCH UMI (University Microfilms International)	PC/XT/AT with hard disk	640K	09/87		$5,495.00/System
UMI RESEARCH UMI (University Microfilms International)	PC/XT/AT with hard disk	640K	04/87	Semiannually	$1,695.00/Year
Proprietary Micromedex, Inc.	PC/XT/AT with DOS version 3.1 or higher	512K	08/87	Quarterly	*

(continued)

ALPHABETICAL LISTING OF CD-ROM TITLES continued

Title	Publisher	Description	Audience
Drug Information Source	American Society of Hospital Pharmacists 4630 Montgomery Avenue Bethesda, MD 20814 (301)657–3000	Current issues of AHFS Drug Information and the Handbook on Injectable Drugs, plus over 15 years of International Pharmaceutical Abstracts (IPA) relating to drugs covered in those compilations.	Pharmacists, pharmaceutical companies, medical libraries.
DRUGDEX System	Micromedex, Inc. 660 Bannock Street Suite 300 Denver, CO 80204-4506 (800)525–9083	The DRUGDEX System is an up-to-date, unbiased, and referenced drug information system. This system includes both Drug Evaluation Monographs and Drug Consults on investigational, foreign, FDA approved, and OTC preparations. This system is indexed by U.S. and foreign brand/trade names, generic names, and disease states.	Physicians, pharmacists, health care professionals.
Earth Science Data Directory (ESDD)	OCLC 6565 Frantz Road Dublin, OH 43017-0702 (800)848–5878	A central repository of information about earth science and natural resource databases, both machine-readable and eye-readable, produced by government agencies, academic institutions, and the private sector.	Libraries, educational organizations.
Econ/Stats I	Hopkins Technology 421 Hazel Lane Hopkins, MN 55343-7117 (612)931–9376	Contains the following databases: Consumer Price Index, Producer Price Index, Export-Import Price Index, Industrial Production Index, Money Stock, Selected Interest Rates, Industry Employment Hours & Earnings and Capacity Utilization.	Financial, corporate, university, high school.
Education Index	H.W. Wilson Company 950 University Avenue Bronx, NY 10452 (800)367–6770	Indexing of 345 English-language periodicals, yearbooks and monographs covering all areas of importance to educators. Retrospective from 12-83.	Libraries.
Education Library	OCLC 6565 Frantz Road Dublin, OH 43017-0702 (800)848–5878	Over 450,000 bibliographic records for materials pertaining to education.	Libraries, educational organizations.
EDUCORP's CD-ROM	EDUCORP 531 Stevens Avenue Suite B Solana Beach, CA 92075 (619)259–0255	310 MB of public domain and shareware software.	Software users.

*Please contact publisher for prices.

Retrieval System	Computer Compatibility	Minimum Memory	Initial Release Date	Update Frequency	Price
Compact Cambridge Cambridge Information Group	PC/XT/AT Compaq	640K	12/88	Semiannually	$1,950.00/Year
Proprietary Micromedex, Inc.	PC/XT/AT with DOS version 3.1 or higher	512K	07/85	Quarterly	*
Search CD450 OCLC	PC/XT/AT or Macintosh	512K		Quarterly	$350.00/Year
QuAcc Hopkins Technology	PC with MS-DOS version 3.1 or higher and MS-DOS CD-ROM Extensions	200K	06/88	Annually	$49.00/Disc
WILSONDISC H.W. Wilson Company	PC/XT/AT	640K	04/87	Quarterly	$1,295.00/Year
Search CD450 OCLC	PC/XT/AT or Macintosh	512K		Annually	$350.00/Year
Macintosh HFS Apple	Macintosh SE/II/Plus		09/26/88	Triannually	$199.00/Disc

(continued)

ALPHABETICAL LISTING OF CD-ROM TITLES *continued*

Title	Publisher	Description	Audience
ei:Intellifile	éclat intelligent systems inc. 14470 Doolittle Drive San Leandro, CA 94577 (415)483–2030	A furniture catalog which actually designs your office space for you! Furniture from Herman Miller, Steelcase, Harter Contract, Harper's, CoryHiebert, Westinghouse, Hayworth, and others. Also included are demos of Versacad, ei:Microspec, and other programs.	Designers, furniture dealers, facilities managers, architects.
Eidetic	Eidetic Knowledge Systems 50 Valley Stream Parkway Malvern, PA 19355 (215)889–9780	Neuro- and renalpathology images and associated case data.	Medical professionals, students.
EINECS plus-CD	SilverPlatter Information, Inc. 37 Walnut Street Wellesley Hills, MA 02181 (617)239–0306	Lists pertinent information about more than 100,000 chemicals that were available in Europe between 1971 and 1981, before European notification requirements for chemicals went into effect.	Library reference market.
The Electronic Map Cabinet	Highlighted Data, Inc. Washington-Dallas International Airport P.O. Box 17229 Washington, DC 20041 (703)241–1180	U.S. geographics.	
Electronic Sweet's	McGraw-Hill Book Company 11 West 19th Street New York, NY 10011 (212)512–2000	Manufacturing product catalog.	
The Electronic Whole Earth Catalog	Broderbund Software 17 Paul Drive San Rafael, CA 94903-2101 (800)527–6263	Provides access to tools and ideas on a vast array of subjects, from psychological self-care, building your own home, managing and operating a small business, beekeeping and grassland preservation to desktop publishing, mysticism, ultralight aircraft, blacksmithing and city restoration.	

*Please contact publisher for prices.

Retrieval System	Computer Compatibility	Minimum Memory	Initial Release Date	Update Frequency	Price
Microspec éclat intelligent systems, inc.		512K	09/87	Quarterly	First copy free
Proprietary Eidetic Knowledge Systems	Sun Microsystems		01/89		$600.00
SilverPlatter Information Retrieval System SilverPlatter Information, Inc.	PC with DOS version 2.1 or higher	640K	12/88		$1,400.00/Disc
Proprietary Highlighted Data, Inc.	Mac SE, Plus, or II with 1 MB	1 MB	09/88		$199.95/Disc
					$115.00/Disc
HyperCard Apple	Apple Macintosh	1 MB	01/89		$149.95/Disc

(continued)

ALPHABETICAL LISTING OF CD-ROM TITLES *continued*

Title	Publisher	Description	Audience
EMERGINDEX System	Micromedex, Inc. 660 Bannock Street Suite 300 Denver, CO 80204-4506 (800)525–9083	The EMERGINDEX System is a referenced clinical information system that presents pertinent data for the practice of acute care medicine. It is designed to help those who deal with acute medical/surgical disease and traumatic injuries to more quickly and efficiently diagnose and treat the multitude of problems encountered daily. The system includes Clinical Reviews, Clinical Abstracts, and Pre-Hospital Care Protocols. The database is indexed by a 40,000 key word medical thesaurus.	Physicians, health care professionals.
Encyclopedia of Polymer Science & Engineering	John Wiley & Sons, Inc. 605 Third Avenue New York, NY 10158 (212)850–6000	19 volumes of articles reflecting the vast changes which have occurred in polymer science in recent years.	
Energy Library	OCLC 6565 Frantz Road Dublin, OH 43017-0702 (800)848–5878	Over 290,000 records on hundreds of energy-related topics.	Libraries, educational organizations.
Energy/Stats	Hopkins Technology 421 Hazel Lane Hopkins, MN 55343-7117 (612)931–9376	Federal statistics on energy sources and uses.	Corporate, academic.
Enflex Info	ERM Computer Services Inc. 855 Springdale Drive Exton, PA 19341 (800)544–3118	A database of federal and state environmental regulations including federal waste, air, water, DOT, and OSHA information.	Industrial companies, manufacturers; anyone who must comply with EPA regulations.
Enhanced BIBLIOFILE	Library Corporation P.O. Box 40035 Washington DC 20016 (800)624–0559	A central processing special package based on a custom profile of the library.	Libraries.
Environment Library	OCLC 6565 Frantz Road Dublin, OH 43017-0702 (800)848–5878	Over 400,000 records that touch upon every facet of this complex and fascinating subject.	Libraries, educational organizations.
ERIC	SilverPlatter Information, Inc. 37 Walnut Street Wellesley Hills, MA 02181 (617)239–0306	Bibliographic database sponsored by the U.S. Department of Education, consisting of the RIE file and the CIJE file. Current disc covers 1983-present.	Library reference market.

*Please contact publisher for prices.

Retrieval System	Computer Compatibility	Minimum Memory	Initial Release Date	Update Frequency	Price
Proprietary Micromedex, Inc.	PC/XT/AT with DOS version 3.1 or higher	512K	07/85	Quarterly	*
FindIt Reteaco, Inc.	PC/XT/AT	640K			$3,200.00/Disc
Search CD450 OCLC	PC/XT/AT or Macintosh	512K		Annually	$350.00
QuAcc Hopkins Technology	PC with MS-DOS version 3.1 or higher and MS-DOS CD-ROM Extensions	200K	04/89	Every 2 years	$59.00/Disc
MARCON AIRS Inc.	PC/XT/AT	550K	02/12/87	Bimonthly	*
BIBLIOFILE Library Corporation					*
Search CD450 OCLC	PC/XT/AT or Macintosh	512K		Annually	$350.00
SilverPlatter Information Retrieval System SilverPlatter Information, Inc.	PC with DOS version 2.1 or higher	640K	06/86	Quarterly	$650.00/Year

(continued)

ALPHABETICAL LISTING OF CD-ROM TITLES *continued*

Title	Publisher	Description	Audience
ERIC-Current Files	OCLC 6565 Frantz Road Dublin, OH 43017-0702 (800)848–5878	Citations to education data compiled from 1982 to the present, consisting of CIJE and RIE.	Libraries, educational organizations.
ERIC-Retrospective Files	OCLC 6565 Frantz Road Dublin, OH 43017-0702 (800)848–5878	RIE 1967-1981 and CIJE 1969-1982.	Libraries, educational organizations.
Essay and General Literature Index	H.W. Wilson Company 950 University Avenue Bronx, NY 10452 (800)367–6770	Emphasizing the humanities and social sciences, this database offers access to a wide variety of information in English-language essay collections and anthologies, including criticisms of literary works, drama, and film; bibliographies; and books by and about authors from all periods of history and of all nationalities. Retrospective from 1-85.	Libraries.
EtakMap National Transportation Network	ETAK, Inc. 1455 Adams Drive Menlo Park, CA 94025 (415)328–3825	A national street network database with metro areas digitized from USGS 1/24,000 quad maps, including all Census Bureau DIME address and political attribute information.	
Facts on File News Digest CD-ROM	Facts on File, Inc. 460 Park Avenue South New York, NY 10016 (800)322–8755	8 years of news compiled from major sources. Also included are 500 maps relating to current affairs.	Libraries, high schools, universities.
The Federal Procurement Disc	ALDE Publishing 4830 West 77th Street P.O. Box 35326 Minneapolis, MN 55435 (612)835–5240	Title 41/48, GSA Supply Catalog, and 75 MB of public domain software.	Government and government contractors.
Film Literature Index	H.W. Wilson Company 950 University Avenue Bronx, NY 10452 (800)367–6770	Covers more than 200 international periodicals providing significant information on contemporary cinema and television.	Libraries.

*Please contact publisher for prices.

Retrieval System	Computer Compatibility	Minimum Memory	Initial Release Date	Update Frequency	Price
Search CD450 OCLC	PC/XT/AT or Macintosh	512K		Quarterly	$425.00/Year
Search CD450 OCLC	PC/XT/AT or Macintosh	512K			$900.00/Set
WILSONDISC H.W. Wilson Company	PC/XT/AT	640K	03/88	Annually	$695.00/Year
ETAK Geocoder ETAK	386 PC SCO XENIX	4MB			*
Media-Mixer Software Mart Inc.	PC/XT/AT/ Macintosh	640K	10/88	Annually	$695.00/Disc
RESEARCH TMS, Inc.	PC/XT/AT	640K	11/86	Annually	$495.00/Disc
WILSONDISC H.W. Wilson Company	PC/XT/AT	640K		Quarterly	$695.00/Year

(continued)

ALPHABETICAL LISTING OF CD-ROM TITLES *continued*

Title	*Publisher*	*Description*	*Audience*
First National Item Bank & Test Development System	TESCOR, Inc. 12020 Sunrise Valley Drive Suite 260 Reston, VA 22091 (703)476–8000	A desktop test publishing system that uses a database of nationally-validated test questions to allow educators to create professional-quality, curriculum-based tests. The database, or item bank, contains over 60,000 test questions, linked to 6,500 instructional objectives, in over thirty K-12 subject areas. High-resolution graphics for test items are included on the CD-ROM disc and are inserted automatically, eliminating the need for cutting and pasting. (There are over 5,000 items with graphics.) Selected items may be edited and original items added to tests before downloading to the laser printer. Users may modify tests and re-format test-page layout from the keyboard.	Educators.
Food/Stats	Hopkins Technology 421 Hazel Lane Hopkins, MN 55343-7117 (612)931–9376	Food nutritive values.	Consumers.
FORM41: Airline Carrier Filings	Data Base Products, Inc. 12770 Coit Road #1111 Dallas, TX 75251-1314 (800)345–2876	Detailed financial data (income statements, balance sheets, and other financial information) derived from carrier filings with the Department of Transportation on the 'B' and 'P' schedules of DOT Form 41. The FORM41 data is principally quarterly, semi-annual, and annual in frequency, with some monthly data, and includes the standard ratios of interest to airlines. Depth of historical detail varies by line item.	Airlines, airports, transportation consultants, state and federal transportation agencies, transportation-related industries, aircraft manufacturers, investment/securities firms.
Gale Experiment Data Set	Department of Atmospheric Sciences Mail Stop AK-40 University of Washington Seattle, WA 98195 (206)545–0910	Surface and upper-air meteorological data collected during the Genesis of Atlantic Lows Experiment.	Universities, government, research and library communities.
Gale GlobalAccess: Associations	Knowledge Access International, Inc. 2685 Marine Way Suite 1305 Mountain View, CA 94043 (415)969–0606	Provides fast and easy access to nearly 100,000 descriptive entries covering more than 80,000 associations from Gale's Encyclopedia of Associations and other related Gale databases.	Bankers, real estate agencies, city planners, real estate aftermarket companies.

*Please contact publisher for prices.

Retrieval System	Computer Compatibility	Minimum Memory	Initial Release Date	Update Frequency	Price
		640K	06/87	Semiannually	$300.00/Month
QuAcc Hopkins Technology	PC with MS-DOS version 3.1 or higher and MS-DOS CD-ROM Extensions	200K	11/88	Every 2 years	$49.00/Disc
Proprietary Data Base Products, Inc.	PC/XT/AT/COM-PAQ or other very compatible with 10 MB hard disk, using MS- or PC-DOS version 3.1 or higher.	640K	02/89	Quarterly	$10,000.00/Year
CLASIX Full-text Manager Reference Technology Inc.	PC/XT/AT/ Microvax II	512K	07/87		$50.00/Disc
KAware2 Knowledge Access International, Inc.	PC/XT/AT with MS-DOS version 3.1 or higher	640K	12/88	Biannually	$2,295.00/Entire state

(continued)

ALPHABETICAL LISTING OF CD-ROM TITLES *continued*

Title	Publisher	Description	Audience
General Periodicals Index (Academic Library Edition) on InfoTrac	Information Access Company 362 Lakeside Drive Foster City, CA 94404 (800)227–8431	An index to approximately 1100 general interest and scholarly publications. Subject areas covered include social sciences, general sciences, humanities, business, management, economics and current affairs. Selected titles include abstracts.	University and college libraries.
General Periodicals Index (Public Library Edition) on InfoTrac	Information Access Company 362 Lakeside Drive Foster City, CA 94404 (800)227–8431	Includes indexing of approximately 1100 popular magazines and journals. Covers current events, consumer information, arts and entertainment, business, management and economics. Selected titles include abstracts.	Public libraries.
General Science Index	H.W. Wilson Company 950 University Avenue Bronx, NY 10452 (800)367–6770	Guide to current information in 108 English-language science periodicals. Retrospective from 5-84.	Libraries.
GEOdisc State Atlas Series	Geovision, Inc. 270 Scientific Drive Suite 1 Norcross, GA 30092 (404)448–8224	Geographic database of detailed vector graphic information for individual states showing all major roads and highways, railroads, water features, political boundaries, and proper place names. Also included are minor and secondary roads, seasonal water features, and power lines.	Utility companies, oil and gas site explorers, politicians, surveyors, federal, state, and local government, consulting engineers, hazardous waste managers, transportation managers.
GEOdisc U.S. Atlas	Geovision, Inc. 270 Scientific Drive Suite 1 Norcross, GA 30092 (404)448–8224	Geographic database of detailed vector graphic information showing all major roads and highways, railroads, water features, political boundaries, and over 1 million proper place names. Also included are minor and secondary roads, seasonal water features, and power lines.	Utility companies, oil and gas site surveyors, politicians, transportation, natural resource managers, hazardous waste, education, government.
GeoIndex	OCLC 6565 Frantz Road Dublin, OH 43017-0702 (800)848–5878	Citations to more than 15,000 published geologic maps of the United States and its territories.	Libraries, educational organizations.
Geological Information Disc	U.S. Geological Survey 804 National Center Reston, VA 22092 (703)648–4000	Geological information.	

*Please contact publisher for prices.

Retrieval System	Computer Compatibility	Minimum Memory	Initial Release Date	Update Frequency	Price
Proprietary Information Access Company		640K	01/85	Monthly	$7,500.00/Year
Proprietary Information Access Company			03/88	Monthly	$7,500.00/Year
WILSONDISC H.W. Wilson Company	PC/XT/AT	640K	04/87	Quarterly	$1,295.00/Year
Windows/On the World or PC CAD interface Geovision, Inc.	PC/AT or PS/2 with hard disk drive and mouse	640K	07/88	Every 24 months	$1,995.00/Disc
Windows/On the World or PC CAD interface Geovision, Inc.	PC/AT or PS/2 with hard disk drive and mouse	640K	01/88	Every 24 months	$495.00/Disc
Search CD450 OCLC	PC/XT/AT or Macintosh	512K		Quarterly	$350.00/Year
					$35.00/Disc

(continued)

ALPHABETICAL LISTING OF CD-ROM TITLES *continued*

Title	Publisher	Description	Audience
GM Parts Catalog	Bell and Howell 5700 Lombardo Center Suite 220 Seven Hills, OH 44351 (216)642–9060	Electronic parts catalog.	Automotive dealers.
Government Documents Catalog Subscription (GDCS) CD-ROM	Auto-Graphics, Inc. 3201 Temple Avenue Pomona, CA 91768 (800)325–7961	All GPO records since 1976.	Libraries.
Government Publications Index on InfoTrac	Information Access Company 362 Lakeside Drive Foster City, CA 94404 (800)227–8431	An index to the Monthly Catalog of the Government Printing Office. Includes indexing to public documents generated by legislative and executive branches of the U.S. government. Coverage begins with 1976.	Public, academic, and law libraries.
GPO on SilverPlatter	SilverPlatter Information, Inc. 37 Walnut Street Wellesley Hills, MA 02181 (617)239–0306	Contains citations from 1976-present for government publications, such as books, reports, studies, serials, maps, and more from the Monthly Catalog published by the Government Printing Office.	Library reference market.
Graphics Lab	ALDE Publishing 4830 West 77th Street P.O. Box 35326 Minneapolis, MN 55435 (612)835–5240	Contains .GIF, .PIC, and .MAC graphics files.	Desktop publishers.
Haystack	Ziff-Davis Technical Information Company 80 Blanchard Road Burlington, MA 01803 (617)273–5500	Logistics information of parts purchased by the government and their technical characteristics.	Military, defense contractors.
Health Index on InfoTrac	Information Access Company 362 Lakeside Drive Foster City, CA 94404 (800)227–8431	Indexing to consumer health literature and health-related articles from newspapers and popular business and academic journals.	Public, academic, special librarians.
Health Planning and Administration	Online Research Systems Inc. 2901 Broadway Suite 154 New York, NY 10025 (212)408–3311	Information relating to health care delivery.	Hospitals.

*Please contact publisher for prices.

Retrieval System	Computer Compatibility	Minimum Memory	Initial Release Date	Update Frequency	Price
Proprietary Bell and Howell	IDB 2000 Image Retrieval System		02/88	Monthly	*
Impact Auto-Graphics Inc.	PC/XT/AT	512K	11/87	Monthly or Bimonthly	*
Proprietary Information Access Company		640K	01/86	Monthly	$2,500.00/ System per Year
SilverPlatter Information Retrieval System SilverPlatter Information, Inc.	PC with DOS version 2.1 or higher	640K	05/88	Bimonthly	$950.00/Disc
None	PC/XT/AT	640K	09/88		$99.00/Disc
Proprietary Ziff-Davis Technical Information Company	PC/XT with 5 MB free on hard disk and MS-DOS version 3.0 or higher	640K		Quarterly	*
Proprietary Information Access Company		640K	10/88	Monthly	$2,000.00/ System per Year
CD-Plus Online Research Systems, Inc.	PC/XT/AT with MS-DOS CD-ROM Extensions	640K	01/89	Monthly	$1,995.00/Year

(continued)

ALPHABETICAL LISTING OF CD-ROM TITLES *continued*

Title	*Publisher*	*Description*	*Audience*
Health/Stats	Hopkins Technology 421 Hazel Lane Hopkins, MN 55343-7117 (612)931–9376	Health studies and statistics.	Libraries, universities, corporate.
Honda/Acura Parts Catalog	Bell and Howell 5700 Lombardo Center Suite 220 Seven Hills, OH 44351 (216)642–9060	Electronic parts catalog.	Automotive dealers.
HotType	Image Club Graphics Inc. 2915 19th Street N.E. Suite 206 Calgary, AB T2E 7A2 CANADA (403)250–1969	A complete library of over 100 PostScript typefaces.	Desktop publishers.
HP LaserROM	Hewlett-Packard Company 3000 Hanover Street Palo Alto, CA 94304 (415)857–1501	Online manual system for HP 3000 users.	HP 3000 users.
Humanities Index	H.W. Wilson Company 950 University Avenue Bronx, NY 10452 (212)588–8400	Index of articles in 347 periodicals covering art, archaeology, etc. Retrospective from 2-84.	Libraries.
Hydrodata Canada	US WEST Optical Publishing 90 Madison Street Suite 200 Denver, CO 80206 (800)222–0920	Daily and peak streamflow discharges for Canada.	Engineers, scientists, colleges, universities.
Hydrodata — Central States USGS Daily Values	US WEST Optical Publishing 90 Madison Street Suite 200 Denver, CO 80206 (800)222–0920	USGS daily streamflow measurements for the Central states.	Engineers, scientists, colleges, universities.
Hydrodata — Eastern States USGS Daily Values	US WEST Optical Publishing 90 Madison Street Suite 200 Denver, CO 80206 (800)222–0920	USGS daily streamflow measurements for Eastern states.	Engineers, scientists, colleges, universities.

*Please contact publisher for prices.

Retrieval System	Computer Compatibility	Minimum Memory	Initial Release Date	Update Frequency	Price
QuAcc Hopkins Technology	PC with MS-DOS version 3.1 or higher and MS-DOS CD-ROM Extensions	200K	01/89	Every 2 years	$49.00/Disc
Proprietary Bell and Howell	IDB 2000 Image Retrieval System		02/88	Monthly	*
	Macintosh Plus/SE/II				$149.00/Set
LaserRETRIEVE Hewlett-Packard Company	Vectra or PC/AT with 5 MB hard disk, mouse, and DOS version 3.1 or higher	640K	02/88	Monthly	$3,420.00/Year
WILSONDISC H.W. Wilson Company	PC/XT/AT	640K		Quarterly	$1,295.00/Year
Proprietary US WEST Optical Publishing	PC/XT/AT with DOS version 2.0 or higher	512K	11/88	Annually	$295.00/Year
Proprietary US WEST Optical Publishing	PC/XT/AT with DOS version 2.0 or higher	512K	08/87	Annually	$295.00/Year
Proprietary US WEST Optical Publishing	PC/XT/AT with DOS version 2.0 or higher	512K	08/87	Annually	$295.00/Year

(continued)

ALPHABETICAL LISTING OF CD-ROM TITLES *continued*

Title	*Publisher*	*Description*	*Audience*
Hydrodata — USGS Peak Values	US WEST Optical Publishing 90 Madison Street Suite 200 Denver, CO 80206 (800)222–0920	USGS peak streamflow measurements for streams nationwide.	Engineers, scientists, colleges, universities.
Hydrodata USGS Quality of Water — Central States	US WEST Optical Publishing 90 Madison Street Suite 200 Denver, CO 80206 (800)222–0920	Water Quality data compiled by the USGS for the past 80 years for the Central United States.	Engineers, scientists, colleges, universities.
Hydrodata USGS Quality of Water — Eastern States	US WEST Optical Publishing 90 Madison Street Suite 200 Denver, CO 80206 (800)222–0920	Water Quality data compiled by the USGS for the past 80 years for the Eastern States.	Engineers, scientists, colleges, universities.
Hydrodata USGS Quality of Water — Western States	US WEST Optical Publishing 90 Madison Street Suite 200 Denver, CO 80206 (800)222–0920	Water Quality data compiled by the USGS for the past 80 years for the Western United States.	Engineers, scientists, colleges, universities.
Hydrodata — Western States USGS Daily Values	US WEST Optical Publishing 90 Madison Street Suite 200 Denver, CO 80206 (800)222–0920	USGS daily streamflow measurements for Western states.	Engineers, scientists, colleges, universities.
IDENTIDEX System	Micromedex, Inc. 660 Bannock Street Suite 300 Denver, CO 80204-4506 (800)525–9083	The IDENTIDEX System is a unique comprehensive tablet and capsule identification system that provides identification of pharmaceuticals primarily by the manufacturer's imprint code with secondary characteristics, such as color and shape, as descriptors. Descriptions of manufacturers' logos assist in differentiating among similar logos. Manufacturers' telephone numbers are also included. The IDENTIDEX System contains vast identification information on U.S. prescription and OTC drugs, both trademarked and generic. Many foreign drugs, street drugs, and timely street slang terminology are also included.	Physicians, pharmacists, health care professionals, law enforcement agencies.

*Please contact publisher for prices.

Retrieval System	Computer Compatibility	Minimum Memory	Initial Release Date	Update Frequency	Price
Proprietary US WEST Optical Publishing	PC/XT/AT with DOS version 2.0 or higher	640K	09/88	Annually	$295.00/Year
Proprietary US WEST Optical Publishing	PC/XT/AT with DOS version 2.0 or higher	512K	12/88	Annually	$295.00/Year
Proprietary US WEST Optical Publishing	PC/XT/AT with DOS version 2.0 or higher	512K	12/88	Annually	$295.00/Year
Proprietary US WEST Optical Publishing	PC/XT/AT with DOS version 2.0 or higher	512K	01/15/89	Annually	$295.00/Year
Proprietary US WEST Optical Publishing	PC/XT/AT with DOS version 2.0 or higher	512K		Annually	$295.00/Year
Proprietary Micromedex, Inc.	PC/XT/AT with DOS version 3.1 or higher	512K	07/85	Quarterly	*

(continued)

ALPHABETICAL LISTING OF CD-ROM TITLES *continued*

Title	Publisher	Description	Audience
Index to Legal Periodicals	H.W. Wilson Company 950 University Avenue Bronx, NY 10452 (800)367–6770	Index of articles from approximately 500 legal journals, yearbooks, etc. Retrospective from 8-81.	
Index to U.S. Government Periodicals (IGP)	H.W. Wilson Company 950 University Avenue Bronx, NY 10452 (800)367–6770	Produced by Infordata International, Inc., this database offers access to information in 185 periodicals issued by more than 100 U.S. government agencies, including information on agriculture, industry, defense policy, energy, and more. Retrospective from 1-80.	Libraries.
Ingram — Books In Print Plus	Bowker Electronic Publishing 245 West 17th Street New York, NY 10011 (800)323–3288	Includes all features of *Books In Print Plus* with the addition of weekly (diskette-based) updates of 70,000 Ingram inventoried titles.	Bookstores, Libraries.
The Intelligent Catalog	Library Corporation P.O. Box 40035 Washington, DC 20016 (800)624–0559	Library's own holdings.	Libraries.
International Books-in-Print	Saur Verlag KG Postfach 711009 Possenbacherstrasse 2B 8000 München WEST GERMANY (8979)10480	Covers 162,500 English language titles published outside the U.S. and the U.K.	
INTERNATIONAL: International Airline Passenger Traffic	Data Base Products, Inc. 12770 Coit Road #1111 Dallas, TX 75251-1314 (800)345–2876	International onboard traffic, traffic flow, and origin and destination information derived from carrier filings with the Department of Transportation and with the Immigration and Naturalization Service of the Department of Justice. INTERNATIONAL includes both monthly and quarterly data, and is available as an annual subscription with quarterly updates for the most recent information. Subscription to this database is limited to those eligible for access as determined by the U.S. Department of Transportation.	Airlines, airports, transportation consultants, state and federal transportation agencies, transportation-related industries (hotels, car rental agencies), aircraft manufacturers, investment/securities firms.
Iowa Locater, 3rd Edition	Iowa State Library Networking Department East 12th and Grand Des Moines, IA 50319 (515)281–4118	Holdings of 400 Iowa libraries.	Libraries.

*Please contact publisher for prices.

Retrieval System	Computer Compatibility	Minimum Memory	Initial Release Date	Update Frequency	Price
		640K	04/87	Quarterly	$1,495.00/Year
WILSONDISC H.W. Wilson Company	PC/XT/AT	640K	03/88	Annually	$995.00/Year
CD-ROM Search and Retrieval Software Online Computer Systems, Inc.	PC/XT/AT or PS/2	640K	10/15/88	Quarterly (CD-ROM)/Weekly (Floppy diskettes)	$1,200.00/Year
Proprietary Library Corporation	Proprietary system		01/87	Monthly	$2,770.00/Workstation
Dataware 7000	PC with MS-DOS		07/87	Quarterly	*
Proprietary Data Base Products, Inc.	PC/XT/AT/COMPAQ or other very compatible computer with a 10 MB hard disk, using MS- or PC-DOS version 3.1 or higher.	640K	12/30/87	Quarterly	$10,000.00/Year
Locater Iowa State Library	PC/XT/AT with 2 CD-ROM drives.	640K	09/15/88	Quarterly	$50.00/Quarter

(continued)

ALPHABETICAL LISTING OF CD-ROM TITLES *continued*

Title	Publisher	Description	Audience
ITINERARIES	Data Base Products, Inc. 12770 Coit Road #1111 Dallas, TX 75251-1314 (800)345–2876	Detailed passenger itinerary data extracted from the Department of Transportation's quarterly survey of airline passenger traffic. ITINERARIES contains the equivalent of the DOT's Table 12 with such additional information as fares included. Each release contains two full years of data plus as many quarters of the release year as are currently available—up to three full years of data.	Airlines, airports, transportation consultants, state and federal transportation agencies, transportation-related industries (hotels, car rental agencies), aircraft manufacturers, investment/securities firms.
The Kansas Library Catalog	Kansas State Library Statehouse 3rd Floor Topeka, KS 66612-1593 (913)296–3296	Union catalog of approximately 2 million bibliographic titles and 5 million holding statements for 450 libraries in Kansas. Covers 1974–March 1988 on 2 discs.	Kansas libraries.
King James Bible	Quantum Access, Inc. 1700 West Loop South Suite 1460 Houston, TX 77027 (713)622–3211	The King James bible.	
Kirk-Othmer Encyclopedia of Chemical Technology	John Wiley & Sons, Inc. 605 Third Avenue New York, NY 10158 (212)850–6000	All 1200 articles from the 25-volume set, plus supplements, indexing, abstracts, and 6000 tables.	
Kojien: Japanese Dictionary	Dai Nippon Ichigaya-kagacho Shinjuku-ku Tokyo 162 JAPAN 03/266–2111	Japanese dictionary for word processors.	
Kwikee INHOUSE Pal	Multi-Ad Services Inc. 1720 West Detweiler Drive Peoria, IL 61615 (800)447–1950	Vector art, potpourri collection.	
Kwikee INHOUSE Complete '88	Multi-Ad Services, Inc. 1720 West Detweiler Drive Peoria, IL 61615-1530 (800)447–1950	Over 1400 quality PostScript illustrations for desktop presentations and publishing applications.	Newspapers, advertising, graphics, publishers.
Kwikee INHOUSE Pal "Potpourri" Collection	Multi-Ad Services, Inc. 1720 West Detweiler Drive Peoria, IL 61615-1530 (800)447–1950	300 quality PostScript illustrations for desktop presentations and publishing applications.	Newspapers, advertising, graphics, publishers.

*Please contact publisher for prices.

Retrieval System	Computer Compatibility	Minimum Memory	Initial Release Date	Update Frequency	Price
Proprietary Data Base Products, Inc.	PC/XT/AT/COMPAQ and other compatibles with a 10 MB hard disk, using MS- or PC-DOS version 3.1 or higher.	640K	07/89	Quarterly	$10,000.00/Year
Le Pac Brodart Automation	PC/XT/AT	640K	08/88	Annually	*
Quantum Leap Quantum Access, Inc.	PC/XT/AT	512K	06/87		$99.00/Disc
FindIt Reteaco, Inc.	PC/XT/AT	640K			$895.00/Disc
					*
					$149.95/Disc
PictureBase Retriever Symmetry Corporation	Macintosh SE/II/Plus, PostScript printer	1 MB	10/88		$995.00/Disc
PictureBase Retriever Symmetry Corporation	PC/XT/AT or Macintosh SE/II/Plus, EPS-compatible software, and PostScript printer	512K or 1 MB	05/88		$149.95/Disc

(continued)

ALPHABETICAL LISTING OF CD-ROM TITLES *continued*

Title	*Publisher*	*Description*	*Audience*
LaserCat	Western Library Network Mail Stop AJ-11W Olympia, WA 98504-0111 (206)459-6518	A portion of the Western Library Network database containing information about approximately 2.4 million titles and 11 million library call numbers.	Libraries.
LAsernet Database	State Library of Louisiana P.O. Box 131 Baton Rouge, LA 70821 (504)342-4923	Union catalog containing over one million MARC records and holding codes for over 100 Louisiana public and academic libraries, linked to an automated statewide interlibrary loan referral system.	Louisiana libraries.
LaserQuest	General Research Corporation, Library Systems 5383 Hollister Avenue Santa Barbara, CA 93111 (800)235-6788	LaserQuest, a CD-ROM cataloging system for libraries, contains the GRC Resource Database of 6 million MARC records from the Library of Congress and the National Library of Canada, including more than 2 million contributed records. LaserQuest provides foreign and English titles as well as music, serials, A/V, maps, and mauscripts. More than 1.9 million records are pre-1968. The cumulated bimonthly supplement adds about 150,000 new and newly cataloged old materials.	Public, academic, and special libraries.
LAW MARC	Utlas International 8300 College Boulevard Overland Park, KS 66210 (800)33-UTLAS	The entire Library of Congress file of law-related bibliographic records.	Libraries.
Le Pac: Government Documents Option	Brodart Automation, a division of Brodart Company 500 Arch Street Williamsport, PA 17705 (800)233-8467	U.S. Government Printing Office Monthly Catalog: 230,000 depository and non-depository titles.	Libraries.
LegalTrac on InfoTrac	Information Access Company 362 Lakeside Drive Foster City, CA 94404 (800)227-8431	Provides indexing of over 800 legal publications, including all major law reviews, bar association journals, specialty publications, and seven legal newspapers, with coverage from 1980 to the present.	Law school libraries.
Library Literature	H.W. Wilson Company 950 University Avenue Bronx, NY 10452 (800)367-6770	Indexes library periodicals, state journals, monographs, and films from around the world. Retrospective from 12-84.	Libraries.

*Please contact publisher for prices.

Retrieval System	Computer Compatibility	Minimum Memory	Initial Release Date	Update Frequency	Price
Proprietary Western Library Network	Requires 2 Hitachi or Sony drives (uses Meridian Data low level driver)	512K	02/87	Quarterly	$1,300.00/Year
Spectrum 1000 Library Systems and Services, Inc. (LSSI)	PC/XT or PS/2 with 20 MB hard disk and DOS version 3.1 or higher	640K	01/89	Biannually	*
LaserQuest General Research Corporation, Library Systems	PC/XT/AT or PS/2 Model 30	512K	07/86	Bimonthly	*
CD-CATSS Utlas Internatioanl	PC/XT/AT	640K	06/88		$750.00/Disc
Le Pac Brodart Automation	PC/XT/AT	512K	11/86	Bimonthly	$2,900.00/Year
Proprietary Information Access Company		640K	08/85	Monthly	$5,000.00/ System per Year
WILSONDISC H.W. Wilson Company	PC/XT/AT	640K	04/87	Quarterly	$1,095.00/Year

(continued)

ALPHABETICAL LISTING OF CD-ROM TITLES *continued*

Title	Publisher	Description	Audience
LILACS	PAHO (Pan American World Health Organization) 525 23rd Street N.W. Washington, DC 20037 (202)861–3366	Bibliographic citations provided by regional medical centers throughout Latin America.	Distributed to health-related or public institutions in Latin America.
LISA	SilverPlatter Information, Inc. 37 Walnut Street Wellesley Hills, MA 02181 (617)239–0306	Abstracts of the world's literature in librarianship, information science, and related disciplines as compiled by Library Association Publishing, Ltd. Covers the complete database from 1969 with records from 1967 and 1968.	Library reference market.
LISE	LaserMedia		
LZ Services	Lasertrak Corporation 6235-B Lookout Road Boulder, CO 80301 (303)530–2711	Aeronautical navigation and flight planning information.	Pilots, corporate aircraft operators, commercial airlines.
Macintosh Showcase	Discovery Systems 7001 Discovery Boulevard Dublin, OH 43017 (614)761–2000	With several multimedia Hypercard stacks, the Macintosh Showcase CD-ROM disc is a full-featured demonstration of CD-ROM technology in the Apple Macintosh environment. Complete with a multimedia interview with Bill Atkinson, the author of Hypercard, and a tutorial on CD-ROM technology, the Macintosh Showcase offers many items of interest to a prospect evaluating Apple systems.	
Magazine Index/PLUS on InfoTrac	Information Access Company 362 Lakeside Drive Foster City, CA 94404 (800)227–8431	Index to 400 popular periodicals PLUS 2 months indexing of the *New York Times*.	Public and academic libraries.
MaineCat	Maine State Library Statehouse Station #64 Augusta, ME 04333 (207)289–5600	Statewide database of approximately 1 million titles representing approximately 2 million volumes, on 2 discs.	Libraries.
Marcive/GPO CAT PAC	Marcive, Inc. P.O. Box 47508 San Antonio, TX 78265 (800)531–7678	U.S. government printing office data since 1976.	Libraries.

*Please contact publisher for prices.

Retrieval System	Computer Compatibility	Minimum Memory	Initial Release Date	Update Frequency	Price
ISIS UNESCO	PC/XT/AT with DOS version 2.x/3.x and a 2.5 MB hard disk	640K	07/88	Biannually	*
SilverPlatter Information Retrieval System SilverPlatter Information, Inc.	PC with DOS version 2.1 or higher	640K	02/87	Semiannually	$995.00/Unit
					*
Proprietary Lasertrak Corporation	Proprietary system	2 MB	07/87	Every 28 days	$250.00/Year
HyperSEARCH Discover Systems	Macintosh SE/II/Plus	1 MB	03/88	Annually	$10.00/Disc
Proprietary Information Access Company		640K	08/87	Monthly	$4,000.00/System per Year
Impact Auto-Graphics	PC/XT/AT with DOS version 3.1 or higher and 2 drives	640K	11/88	Biannually	*
Marcive/PAC Marcive, Inc.	PC/XT/AT with DOS version 3.0 or higher and 20 MB hard disk	640K	09/88	Bimonthly	$995.00/Year

(continued)

ALPHABETICAL LISTING OF CD-ROM TITLES *continued*

Title	Publisher	Description	Audience
MARTINDALE: The Extra Pharmacopoeia	Micromedex, Inc. 660 Bannock Street Suite 300 Denver, CO 80204-4506 (800)525–9083	The CD-ROM version of the well-respected textbook published by the British Pharmaceutical Society, Martindale: The Extra Pharmacopoeia, is an extensive resource of information on drug products available in the United Kingdom. It includes information regarding chemical forms, therapeutic uses, adverse effects, and world-wide trade names. This version of the database also offers the ability to search by old English terms or their modern English synonyms. The database can be searched by international trade name, generic name, chemical name, and disease state.	Physicians, pharmacists, health care professionals.
Massachusetts Real Estate Transaction Database	Knowledge Access International, Inc. 2685 Marine Way Suite 1305 Mountain View, CA 94043 (415)969–0606	Real estate transfer records from 1982-1987 for the state of Massachusetts.	Bankers, real estate agencies, city planners, real estate aftermarket companies.
Master Search Bible: Comparative Bible Research	Tri Star Publishing 475 Virginia Drive Fort Washington, PA 19034 (800)872–2828	A powerful new tool incorporating on a single compact disc a comprehensive biblical reference library of classical and contemporary works. It combines three of today's most popular Bible versions with an impressive array of selected reference volumes.	Bible colleges, pastors, laymen.
Material Safety Data System	National Safety Data Corporation 259 West Road Salem, CT 06415 (203)859–1162	35,000 Material Safety Data Sheets used for determining the hazards of chemicals.	Safety and health professionals.
MathSci Disc	SilverPlatter Information, Inc. 37 Walnut Street Wellesley Hills, MA 02181 (617)239–0306	The Mathematical Reviews from 1985 through 1988 and more than 50,000 entries from Current Mathematical Publications. Covers the literature of mathematics and related fields such as statistics, computer science, and engineering.	Library reference market.
MAXX: Maximum Access to Diagnosis and Therapy	Little, Brown and Company 34 Beacon Street Boston, MA 02108 (617)227–0730		Health care professionals.

*Please contact publisher for prices.

Retrieval System	Computer Compatibility	Minimum Memory	Initial Release Date	Update Frequency	Price
Proprietary Micromedex, Inc.	PC/XT/AT with DOS version 3.1 or higher	512K	05/87	Annually	*
KAware2 Knowledge Access International, Inc.	PC/XT/AT	640K	10/88	Annually	$4,800.00/State
Proprietary Tri Star Publishing	PC/XT/AT	640K	08/10/88		$549.00/Disc
Quantum Leap Quantum Access	PC/XT/AT	640K	11/87		$750.00
SilverPlatter Information Retrieval System SilverPlatter Information, Inc.	PC with DOS version 2.1 or higher	640K	01/89	Semiannually	$3,510.00/Year

*

(continued)

ALPHABETICAL LISTING OF CD-ROM TITLES continued

Title	Publisher	Description	Audience
MCAT (Missouri Union Catalog)	Missouri State Library P.O. Box 387 Jefferson City, MO 65102 (314)751-3033	Union catalog of library holdings in Missouri. Some 230 Missouri libraries are participating in the project, including every public library, most academic libraries, and many special and school libraries. Intended to improve and enhance resource sharing among Missouri libraries.	Libraries.
McGraw-Hill CD-ROM Science & Technical Reference Set	McGraw-Hill Book Company 11 West 19th Street New York, NY 10011 (212)512-2000	Science & Technology Encyclopedia, Dictionary of Scientific Terms.	
McGraw-Hill Science and Technical Reference Set	McGraw-Hill Book Company 11 West 19th Street New York, NY 10011 (212)512-2000	Science and Technology Encyclopedia, Dictionary of Scientific Terms.	
MEDLINE on SilverPlatter	SilverPlatter Information, Inc. 37 Walnut Street Wellesley Hills, MA 02181 (617)239-0306	The entire MEDLINE database of the National Library of Medicine from 1983 to present, containing bibliographic citations and abstracts for biomedical literature, and includes all foreign languages, all data elements, and is fully indexed.	Library reference market.
MEDLINE: BRS/Colleague Disc	BRS Information Technologies 1200 Route 7 Latham, NY 12110 (800)468-0908	English language citations and abstracts from the National Library of Medicine's MEDLINE database.	Universities, researchers, medical professionals, pharmaceutical companies, medical students.
MEDLINE Knowledge Server	Aries Systems Corporation 79 Boxford Street North Andover, MA 01845-3219 (508)689-9334	5 years of the more important journals from the National Library of Medicine's database. Also full, unabridged MEDLINE discs.	Medical libraries and educators, physicians.
MEGA-ROM	Quantum Leap Technologies, Inc. 314 Romano Avenue Coral Gables, FL 33134 (305)447-0745	300 megabytes of Macintosh public domain software.	
Menu: Software Catalogue	The Menu P.O. Box MENU Pittsburg, PA 15241		

*Please contact publisher for prices.

712 SECTION VII: DIRECTORY LISTINGS

Retrieval System	Computer Compatibility	Minimum Memory	Initial Release Date	Update Frequency	Price
Le Pac Brodart Automation	PC/XT/AT	640K	09/30/88	Quarterly	*
					$300.00/Disc
CLASIX Full-text Manager Reference Technology Inc.	PC/XT/AT	640K	04/87		$300.00
SilverPlatter Information Retrieval System Silver Platter Information, Inc.	PC with DOS version 2.1 or higher	640K	06/87	Quarterly	$950.00/Year
BRS/Search BRS Information Technologies	PC/XT/AT	640K	07/87	Quarterly	$995.00/Year
Knowledge Finder and *Knowledge Server* for networks Aries Systems Corporation	Macintosh Plus, SE, II	1 MB	01/88	Quarterly	*
	Macintosh		09/88		$30.00/disc
					*

(continued)

ALPHABETICAL LISTING OF CD-ROM TITLES *continued*

Title	Publisher	Description	Audience
Merriam Webster's Ninth New Collegiate Dictionary	Highlighted Data, Inc. Washington-Dallas International Airport P.O. Box 17229 Washington, DC 20041 (703)241–1180	The full-text, illustrations, and recorded pronunciation of every word in Webster's Ninth New Collegiate Dictionary.	Educators, students.
MetroScan: El Dorado County	Digital Diagnostics, Inc. 601 University Avenue Suite 255 Sacramento, CA 95825 (916)921–6629	Descriptions of all land parcels in El Dorado county.	Real estate industry: appraisers, title companies, realtors, developers.
MetroScan: Placer County	Digital Diagnostics, Inc. 601 University Avenue Suite 255 Sacramento, CA 95825 (916)921–6629	Descriptions of all land parcels in Placer County.	Real estate industry: appraisers, title companies, realtors, developers.
MetroScan: Sacramento County	Digital Diagnostics, Inc. 601 University Avenue Suite 255 Sacramento, CA 95825 (916)921–6629	Descriptions of all land parcels in Sacramento county.	Real estate industry: appraisers, title companies, realtors, developers.
MetroScan: Yolo County	Digital Diagnostics, Inc. 601 University Avenue Suite 255 Sacramento, CA 95825 (916)921–6629	Descriptions of all land parcels in Yolo county.	Real estate industry: appraisers, title companies, realtors, developers.
Microsoft Bookshelf	Microsoft Corporation 16011 N.E. 36th Way P.O. Box 97017 Redmond, WA 98073-9717 (206)882–8080	A tool for writers, Bookshelf contains ten major reference works including the *American Heritage Dictionary, Bartlett's Familiar Quotations, The World Almanac,* and the U.S. ZIP Code Directory. Access these reference works through your word processor, without ever leaving your document, a simple copy and paste inserts information directly into your document.	Anyone who uses a word processor for reports, letters, speeches or articles.
Microsoft Small Business Consultant	Microsoft Corporation 16011 N.E. 36th Way P.O. Box 97017 Redmond, WA 98073-9717 (206)882–8080	220 publications from the Small Business Administration, U.S. Government agencies, and the accounting firm of Deloitte Haskins + Sells. Information on starting and operating a small business; from creating a business plan and obtaining financing and credit, to acquiring a patent and handling personnel issues.	Small business owners or middle management of large corporations.

*Please contact publisher for prices.

Retrieval System	Computer Compatibility	Minimum Memory	Initial Release Date	Update Frequency	Price
Proprietary Highlighted Data, Inc.	Mac SE/II/Plus	1 MB	01/88		$199.95/Disc
Proprietary Digital Diagnostics, Inc.	PC/XT/AT	640K	10/87	Monthly	$350.00/Year
Proprietary Digital Diagnostics, Inc.	PC/XT/AT	640K	10/87	Monthly	$350.00/Year
Proprietary Digital Diagnostics, Inc.	PC/XT/AT	640K	10/87	Monthly	$600.00/Year
Proprietary Digital Diagnostics, Inc.	PC/XT/AT	640K	10/87	Monthly	$300.00/Year
Proprietary Microsoft Corporation	PC/XT/AT with MS-DOS version 3.1, 3.2, or 3.3 and MS-DOS CD-ROM Extensions.	640K	08/87		$295.00/Disc
Proprietary Microsoft Corporation	PC/XT/AT or compatible with DOS version 3.1, 3.2, or 3.3 and MS-DOS CD-ROM Extensions	640K	10/88		$125.00/Disc

(continued)

ALPHABETICAL LISTING OF CD-ROM TITLES *continued*

Title	Publisher	Description	Audience
Microsoft Stat Pack	Microsoft Corporation 16011 N.E. 36th Way P.O. Box 97017 Redmond, WA 98073-9717 (206)882–8080	Easy access to government statistics including the U.S. Statistical Abstracts, Area Wage Surveys, and Land and Agricultural Statistics. Works with a word processor and contains spreadsheet files for Microsoft Excel and Lotus 123 to allow manipulation of the available data.	Researchers, writers, students, libraries.
Million Dollar Directory	Dun's Marketing Service 3 Sylvan Way Parsippany, NJ 07054-3896 (201)455–0900	Business demographics and individual company listings.	
MLA International Bibliography	H.W. Wilson Company 950 University Avenue Bronx, NY 10452 (800)367–6770	Published by the Modern Language Association of America, this database covers current scholarship in the modern languages, literature, and folklore, providing bibliographic data on some 3,000 journals and series, monographs, and book collections, yielding more than 40,000 new records annually. Retrospective from 1-81.	Libraries.
Multilingual Dictionary Database	Sansyusya Publishing Company Ltd. 1-5-34 Taito-ku Tokyo 110 JAPAN	Chinese, Dutch, English, French, German, Italian, Japanese, Spanish.	
Multilingual Dictionary of Science & Technology	Sansyusya Publishing Co. Ltd. 1-5-34 Taito-ku Tokyo 110 JAPAN	English, German, Japanese.	
NATASHA: National Archive on Sexuality, Health & Adolescence	Knowledge Access International, Inc. 2685 Marine Way Suite 1305 Mountain View, CA 94043 (415)969–0606	109 data sets and 39,815 uniquely identified variables from 82 major studies relevant to the national problem of teenage pregnancy. Information on adolescent sexuality, health, marriage, education, and employment; more general information on family planning, infant health, and attitudes toward sexual issues; and information on social demographics are all included in this product at national, regional, and individual levels.	

*Please contact publisher for prices.

Retrieval System	Computer Compatibility	Minimum Memory	Initial Release Date	Update Frequency	Price
Proprietary Microsoft Corporation	PC/XT/AT with MS-DOS version 3.1, 3.2, or 3.3 and MS-DOS CD-ROM Extensions	640K	10/88		$149.00/Disc
Conquest Donnelly Marketing	PC/XT/AT	640K	12/88	Annually	*
WILSONDISC H.W. Wilson Company	PC/XT/AT	640K	10/87	Quarterly	$1,495.00/Year
					*
					*
KAware2 Knowledge Access International, Inc.	PC with MS-DOS version 3.1 or higher				$495.00

(continued)

ALPHABETICAL LISTING OF CD-ROM TITLES *continued*

Title	Publisher	Description	Audience
The National Directory	Xiphias 13464 Washington Boulevard Marina Del Rey, CA 90292 (213)821-0074	Every telephone number and address for businesses, corporations, government agencies, and other key institutions in North America. Applications include Auto Dialing and Auto Label Printing. Based on best-selling directory published by General Information.	Tele-marketing agencies.
National Meteorological Center Grid Point Data Set	Department of Atmospheric Sciences Mail Stop AK-40 University of Washington Seattle, WA 98195 (206)545-0910		Research, educational, and library communities.
National Newspaper Index on InfoTrac	Information Access Company 362 Lakeside Drive Foster City, CA 94404 (800)227-8431	Index to the *New York Times, Wall Street Journal, Christian Science Monitor, Washington Post,* and *Los Angeles Times.* Coverage includes past 3 years plus the current year.	Public and academic libraries.
The New Electronic Encyclopedia	Grolier Electronic Publishing Inc. Sherman Turnpike Danbury, CT 06816 (800)356-5590	The full-text version of the 20-volume *Academic American Encyclopedia,* which includes 30,000 articles and 9 million words.	
The NewsBank Electronic Index	Newsbank, Inc. 58 Pine Street New Canaan, CT 06840-5408 (800)223-4739	A powerful, comprehensive, fully contained reference resource. Virtually every newsworthy issue that has affected the U.S. over the past half decade can be researched on the NewsBank Electronic Index. Includes NEWSBANK 1982-present, BUSINESS NEWSBANK 1985-present, NAMES IN THE NEWS 1982-present, and REVIEW OF THE ARTS 1982-present.	School libraries.
Newspaper Abstracts Ondisc	UMI (University Microfilms International) 300 North Zeeb Road Ann Arbor, MI 48106 (800)521-3044	Indexes and abstracts from eight major newspapers.	Libraries.
NTIS	SilverPlatter Information, Inc. 37 Walnut Street Wellesley Hills, MA 02181 (617)239-0306	Bibliographic citations and abstracts to government sponsored research and development reports produces by the National Technical Information Service. Coverage from 1983-present.	Library reference market.

*Please contact publisher for prices.

Retrieval System	Computer Compatibility	Minimum Memory	Initial Release Date	Update Frequency	Price
Xearch Xiphias	Macintosh SE/II/Plus	1 MB	01/89	Annually	$150.00/Disc
CLASIX Reference Technology Inc.	PC/XT/AT/Microvex II	512K	01/87		$50.00/Disc
Proprietary Information Access Company		640K	09/88	Monthly	$4,000.00/System per Year
Proprietary Online Computer Systems, Inc.	PC/XT/AT	512K	01/86	Annually	$395.00/Product
Proprietary Newsbank, Inc.	PC/XT/AT	256K	06/85	Monthly	*
UMI RESEARCH UMI (University Microfilms International)	PC/XT/AT with hard disk	640K	01/88	Bimonthly	*
SilverPlatter Information Retrieval System SilverPlatter Information, Inc.	PC with DOS version 2.1 or higher	640K	08/87	Quarterly	$2,500.00/Year

(continued)

ALPHABETICAL LISTING OF CD-ROM TITLES continued

Title	Publisher	Description	Audience
NTIS (1983-present)	OCLC 6565 Frantz Road Dublin, OH 43017-0702 (800)848–5878	Citations to reports from the Department of Energy, Department of Defense, and NASA, covering a wide variety of topics in engineering, mathematics, physical, biological, and social sciences and business.	Libraries, educational organizations.
The Nurse Library	Ellis Enterprises Inc. 225 N.W. Thirteenth Street Oklahoma City, OK 73103 (405)235–7660		Nurses, hospitals.
NYNEX Fast Track	NYNEX Information Resources Company 195 Market Street 5th Floor Lynn, MA 01901 (617)581–4674	NYNEX white pages directories. Over 10 million names, addresses, phone numbers, and ZIP codes. Used mainly by companies with high-volume listing verification and identification needs.	Financial institutions and retail companies (credit and collection departments), government agencies, publishing companies (circulation department).
O & D PLUS: Airline Passenger Statistics	Data Base Products, Inc. 12770 Coit Road #1111 Dallas, TX 75251-1314 (800)345–2876	A current and ongoing subscription database, consisting of comprehensive domestic origin and destination information from the Department of Transportation's quarterly survey of airline passenger traffic. Each release contains two full years of historical data plus as many quarters of the current release year as are presently available—in other words, up to three full years of data. O & D PLUS contains all the data from the standard published tables (1 through 10), including true O & D, online local and online connecting O & D, as well as much information not included in the standard tables: fares, yield, airport-pair detail, reported coupons, etc.	Airlines, airports, transportation consultants, state and federal transportation agencies, transportation-related industries (hotels, car rental agencies), aircraft manufacturers, investment/securities firms.
O & D PLUS HISTORICAL	Data Base Products, Inc. 12770 Coit Road #1111 Dallas, TX 75251-1314 (800)345–2876	An historical archive consisting of seven full years (1979-1985) of comprehensive domestic origin and destination information from the Department of Transportation's quarterly survey of airline passenger traffic. O & D PLUS HISTORICAL contains all the quarterly data from the standard published tables (1 through 10), including true O & D, online local and online connecting O & D, as well as much information not included in the standard tables: fares, yield, airport-pair detail, reported coupons, etc.	Airlines, airports, transportation consultants, state and federal transportation agencies, transportation-related industries (hotels, car rental agencies), aircraft manufacturers, investment/securities firms.

*Please contact publisher for prices.

Retrieval System	Computer Compatibility	Minimum Memory	Initial Release Date	Update Frequency	Price
Search CD450 OCLC	PC/XT/AT or Macintosh	512K		Quarterly	$2,395.00
	PC/XT/AT	512K	02/89	Yearly	$700.00/Year
Proprietary NYNEX Information Resources Company	PC/XT/AT with hard disk	512K	11/87	Monthly	$10,000.00/Year
Proprietary Data Base Products, Inc.	PC/XT/AT/COMPAQ and other very compatibles with a 10 MB hard disk, using MS- or PC-DOS version 3.1 or higher.	640K	03/87	Quarterly	$7,000.00/Year
Proprietary Data Base Products, Inc.	PC/XT/AT/COMPAQ and other compatibles with a 10 MB hard disk, using MS- or PC-DOS version 3.1 or higher.	640K	03/88	Disc will be updated in 1990.	$7,000.00

(continued)

ALPHABETICAL LISTING OF CD-ROM TITLES continued

Title	Publisher	Description	Audience
OHS MSDS ON DISC	Occupational Health Services, Inc. 450 Seventh Avenue Suite 2407 New York, NY 10123 (800)445–6737	Thousands of Material Safety Data Sheets.	Emergency response units, corporations, universities, federal, state, and local governments.
ONBOARD: Airline Passenger Traffic Statistics	Data Base Products, Inc. 12770 Coit Road #1111 Dallas, TX 75251-1314 (800)345–2876	Comprehensive domestic onboard traffic and service segment data derived from carrier filings with the Department of Transportation under Economic Regulation 586 and from the traffic schedules of Form 41. ONBOARD includes monthly quarterly, and annual data. Each release contains two full years of data plus as many months/quarters of the release year as are currently available. Some historical data begins with 1972.	Airlines, airports, transportation consultants, state and federal transportation agencies, transportation-related industries (hotels, car rental agencies), aircraft manufacturers, investment/securities firms.
Oncodisc	J.B. Lippincott Company East Washington Square Philadelphia, PA 19105 (215)238–4200	2 database from the National Cancer Institute: PDQ: Physicians Data Query and CancerLit. Also included is "Principles and Practices of Oncology" from Lippincott. Other Lippincott books will be added in future updates.	Hospitals, medical libraries, oncologists, cancer professionals.
One Source	Lotus Development Corporation One Cambridge Center Cambridge, MA 02142 (617)577–8500	Daily stock price history, value line, Ford investor services, Disclosure II.	
Online Hotline News	ALDE Publishing 4830 West 77th Street P.O. Box 35326 Minneapolis, MN 55435 (612)835–5240	A news service about online systems.	OnLine HotLine subscribers.
Optext	VLS, Inc. 310 South Reynolds Road Toledo, OH 43623 (419)536–5820	The Code of Federal Regulations and the Federal Register.	Libraries, law libraries, heavily regulated industries.

*Please contact publisher for prices.

Retrieval System	Computer Compatibility	Minimum Memory	Initial Release Date	Update Frequency	Price
RESEARCH TMS, Inc.	PC/XT/AT with DOS version 3.1 or higher	Negligible	05/87	Quarterly	$5,000.00/ First year
Proprietary Data Base Products, Inc.	PC/XT/AT/COM-PAQ with MS- or PC-DOS version 3.1 or higher and a 10 MB hard disk.	640K	08/15/88	Quarterly	$7,000.00/Year
SearchLITE I.S. Grupe	PC/XT/AT	640K	07/88	Bimonthly	$1,950.00/Year
Proprietary Lotus Development Corporation	PC/XT/AT or PS/2	640K			$11,000.00/Year
FastFind Creative Index	PC/XT/AT	640K	10/88	Annually	$199.95/Disc
Optext RESEARCH TMS, Inc.	PC/XT/AT or PS/2 with 10 MB hard disk	512K		Quarterly	$1,390.00/Year

(continued)

ALPHABETICAL LISTING OF CD-ROM TITLES *continued*

Title	*Publisher*	*Description*	*Audience*
The Original Oxford English Dictionary on Compact Disc	Tri Star Publishing 475 Virginia Drive Fort Washington, PA 19034 (800)872–2828	The original 12-volume *Oxford English Dictionary* on one compact disc.	Educational community, lexicographers, etymologists, writers, authors.
OSH-ROM	SilverPlatter Information, Inc. 37 Walnut Street Wellesley Hills, MA 02181 (617)239–0306	A database of occupational health and safety information, containing three complete bibliographic databases: NIOSHTIC, HSELINE, and CISDOC, collectively containing over 240,000 citations taken from over 500 journals and 100,000 monographs and technical reports.	
PAIS on CD-ROM	Public Affairs Information Service, Inc. 521 West 43rd Street New York, NY 10036-4396 (212)736–6629	The combined records of the PAIS BULLETIN and the PAIS FOREIGN LANGUAGE INDEX.	Libraries.
Parts-Master	National Standards Association Inc. 1200 Quince Orchard Boulevard Gaithersburg, MD 20878 (800)638–8094	Information on over 12 million parts and products procured and/or stocked by the U.S. government.	
PC-Blue: MS-DOS Public Domain Library	ALDE Publishing 4830 West 77th Street P.O. Box 35326 Minneapolis, MN 55435 (612)835–5240	PC-Blue public domain library.	Horizontal markets.
The PC-SIG Library on CD-ROM	PC-SIG Inc. 1030-D East Duane Avenue Sunnyvale, CA 94086 (408)730–9291	1000 discs of shareware software.	Educators, users groups, corporate and personal users.
Periodical Abstracts Ondisc	UMI (University Microfilms International) 300 North Zeeb Road Ann Arbor, MI 48106 (800)521–3044	Abstracting and indexing to 300 current general reference periodicals.	Libraries.
PEST-BANK	SilverPlatter Information, Inc. 37 Walnut Street Wellesley Hills, MA 02181 (617)239–0306	A database on pesticides and their use in agriculture, based on the National Pesticide Information Retrieval System.	Library reference market.

*Please contact publisher for prices.

Retrieval System	Computer Compatibility	Minimum Memory	Initial Release Date	Update Frequency	Price
Proprietary Tri Star Publishing	PC/XT/AT	640K	12/87		$950.00/Disc
SilverPlatter Information Retrieval System	PC with DOS version 2.1 or higher.	640K		Quarterly	$900.00/Year
CD-ROM Search and Retrieval Software Online Computer Systems Inc.	PC/XT/AT or PS/2 with DOS version 3.1 or higher. Hard disk recommended.	640K	10/87	Quarterly	$1,795.00/Year
	PC/XT/AT with DOS version 3.1 or higher	640K	11/86	Monthly	$6,650.00/Year
None	PC/XT/AT	640K	07/88	Annually	$199.00/Disc
	PC/XT/AT with DOS version 3.1 or higher	256K	05/86	Biannually	$295.00/Disc
UMI RESEARCH UMI (University Microfilms International)	PC/XT/AT with hard disk	640K	06/88	Bimonthly	$1,175.00/Year
SilverPlatter Information Retrieval System SilverPlatter Information, Inc.	PC with DOS version 2.1 or higher	640K	11/88	Quarterly	$2,850.00/Year

(continued)

ALPHABETICAL LISTING OF CD-ROM TITLES *continued*

Title	Publisher	Description	Audience
Peterson's College Database	SilverPlatter Information, Inc. 37 Walnut Street Wellesley Hills, MA 02181 (617)239–0306	Full-text database containing over 3,200 profiles of all accredited, degree-granting colleges in the U.S. and Canada. Each profile includes information about student enrollment, ethnic/geographic mix, SAT/ACT score ranges and admissions, expenses, financial aid, special programs, housing and campus life, athletics, and majors.	Library reference market.
Peterson's Gradline	SilverPlatter Information, Inc. 37 Walnut Street Wellesley Hills, MA 02181 (617)239–0306	Full-text database containing over 26,000 profiles of graduate and professional programs in 300 academic disciplines, offered by more than 1,400 colleges and universities in the U.S. and Canada. Includes names and addresses of institutions, faculty and their research specialties, degree levels and specific concentrations, research facilities, financial aid, and more.	Library reference market.
PHINet-American Federal Tax Reports	Prentice Hall Information Network 1 Gulf & Western Plaza 18th Floor New York, NY 10023 (212)373–8600	Tax-related court decisions from the federal court system, with PH Headnotes.	Tax professionals: accountants, law firms, corporate tax departments, U.S. government.
PHINet-Private Letter Rulings	Prentice Hall Information Network 1 Gulf & Western Plaza 18th Floor New York, NY 10023 (212)373–8600	IRS Private Letter Rulings, with PH Headnotes.	Tax professionals: accountants, law firms, corporate tax departments, U.S. government.
PHINet-Revenue Rulings and Procedures	Prentice Hall Information Network 1 Gulf & Western Plaza 18th Floor New York, NY 10023 (212)373–8600	IRS Revenue Rulings and Procedures, with PH Headnotes.	Tax professionals: accountants, law firms, corporate tax departments, U.S. government.
PHINet-Tax Court Reported and Memorandum Decisions	Prentice Hall Information Network 1 Gulf & Western Plaza 18th Floor New York, NY 10023 (212)373–8600	Tax court memorandum and reported decisions, with PH Headnotes.	Tax professionals: accountants, law firms, corporate tax departments, U.S. government.

*Please contact publisher for prices.

Retrieval System	Computer Compatibility	Minimum Memory	Initial Release Date	Update Frequency	Price
SilverPlatter Information Retrieval System SilverPlatter Information, Inc.	PC with DOS version 2.1 or higher	640K	04/88	Annually	$595.00/Year
SilverPlatter Information Retrieval System SilverPlatter Information, Inc.	PC with DOS version 2.1 or higher	640K	02/89	Annually	$695.00/Year
Fulltext Manager/ Docufind Reference Technology/Emanuel Data Systems	PC/XT/AT with 2 MB free space on hard disk. 286 recommended.	640K	01/88	Semiannually (CD-ROM)/Daily (Online)	$2,500.00/Disc
Fulltext Manager/ Docufind Reference Technology/Emanuel Data Systems	PC/XT/AT with 2 MB free space on hard disk. 286 recommended.	640K	01/87	Semiannually (CD-ROM)/Daily (Online)	$2,500.00/Disc
Fulltext Manager/ Docufind Reference Technology/Emanuel Data Systems	PC/XT/AT with 2 MB free space on hard disk. 286 recommended.	640K	12/86	Semiannually (CD-ROM)/ Daily(Online)	$2,500.00/Disc
Fulltext Manager/ Docufind Reference Technology/Emanuel Data Systems	PC/XT/AT with 2 MB free space on hard disk. 286 recommended.	640K	01/87	Semiannually (CD-ROM)/Daily (Online)	$2,500.00/Disc

(continued)

ALPHABETICAL LISTING OF CD-ROM TITLES *continued*

Title	*Publisher*	*Description*	*Audience*
Phonedisc	Digital Directory Assistance Inc. 5161 River Road Building 6 Bethesda, MD 20816 (301)657-8548	All 10 million telephone listings in New York, Vermont, New England, New Hampshire, Maine, Connecticut, Massachusetts, and Rhode Island, indexed by name, address, and phone number.	Fortune 500 companies, law enforcement, credit collection.
The Physician Library	Ellis Enterprises Inc. 225 N.W. Thirteenth Street Oklahoma City, OK 73103 (405)235-7660		Physicians, public, hospitals.
Physicians' Desk Reference on CD-ROM	Medical Economics Company P.O. Box 551 Oradell, NJ 07649 (800)526-4870	Contains official FDA-approved prescribing information on 1800 prescription drugs, and 1100 non-prescription drugs and ophthalmology products, plus the contents of PDR's 900-page Drug Interactions and Side Effects Index.	Libraries, physicians, hospitals, pharmacies.
Place-Name Index	Buckmaster Publishing Route 3 Box 56 Mineral, VA 23117 (703)894-5777	Over 1 million place names from Geological Survey topographic maps.	Libraries, geologists, researchers, historians.
Plus^{37}	Phillips Electronic Instruments Inc. 85 McKee Drive Mahwah, NJ 07430 (201)529-3800	Diffraction parameters in 1987 JCPDS PDF-2 database.	
POISINDEX System	Micromedex, Inc. 660 Bannock Street Suite 300 Denver, CO 80204-4506 (800)525-9083	The POISINDEX System is a detailed toxicology database designed to identify and provide ingredient information for over one-half million domestic and foreign commercial, industrial, pharmaceutical, zoologic, and botanic substances. The POISINDEX System also provides detailed symptomatology and management/treatment protocols in the event of a toxicology problem due to ingestion, dermal absorption, eye exposure, or inhalation of any of the substances listed. The POISINDEX database may be searched by brand or trade name, manufacturer's name, generic or chemical name, street or slang terminology, or botanic and common name.	Physicians, pharmacists, health care professionals.

*Please contact publisher for prices.

Retrieval System	Computer Compatibility	Minimum Memory	Initial Release Date	Update Frequency	Price
Phonedisc Digital Directory Assistance Inc.	PC/XT/AT with MS-DOS version 3.0 or higher	512K	05/88	Monthly	$10,000.00/Year
	PC/XT/AT	512K	02/89	Yearly	$1,000.00/Year
Proprietary Medical Economics Company	PC/XT/AT with DOS version 3.1 or higher	640K	06/88	Triannually	$595.00/Year
Textware Unibase	PC/XT/AT		03/88	Annually	$295.00/Year
					$5,000.00/Disc
Proprietary Micromedex, Inc.	PC/XT/AT with DOS version 3.1 or higher	512K	07/85	Quarterly	*

(continued)

ALPHABETICAL LISTING OF CD-ROM TITLES *continued*

Title	*Publisher*	*Description*	*Audience*
POPLINE	SilverPlatter Information, Inc. 37 Walnut Street Wellesley Hills, MA 02181 (617)239–0306	The world's largest bibliographic population database, containing more than 150,000 citations on population, family planning and related health care, law and policy issues.	Library reference market.
Population Statistics on CD-ROM	Slater Hall Information Products 1522 K Street N.W. Suite 522 Washington, DC 20005 (202)682–1350	Full range of population and housing characteristics from the 1980 census for the U.S. All states, metro areas, counties, places of 10,000 or more, and congressional districts.	Libraries, state and local government agencies, market researchers.
Powder Diffraction File	International Centre for Diffraction Data 1601 Park Lane Swarthmore, PA 19801 (215)328–9400	A file of approximately 59,000 X-ray diffraction patterns of inorganic/organic materials, crystallographic and physical data.	University, academic, and industrial users, for the identification of unknown materials.
Pravda 1987 on CD-ROM	ALDE Publishing 4830 West 77th Street P.O. Box 35326 Minneapolis, MN 55435 (612)835–5240	Translation of the Pravda newspaper, '86-'87.	Libraries, schools, intelligence community.
ProArt Professional Art Library: the "Business" Collection	Multi-Ad Services, Inc. 1720 West Detweiler Drive Peoria, IL 61615-1530 (800)447–1950	100 quality PostScript illustrations for Desktop Presentations and Publishing applications.	Publishing, graphics.
ProArt Professional Art Library: the "Holidays" Collection	Multi-Ad Services, Inc. 1720 West Detweiler Drive Peoria, IL 61615-1530 (800)447–1950	100 quality PostScript illustrations for Desktop Presentations and Publishing applications.	Publishing, graphics.
ProArt Professional Art Library: the "Sports" Collection	Multi-Ad Services, Inc. 1720 West Detweiler Drive Peoria, IL 61615-1530 (800)447–1950	100 quality PostScript illustrations for Desktop Presentations and Publishing applications.	Publishing, graphics.

*Please contact publisher for prices.

Retrieval System	Computer Compatibility	Minimum Memory	Initial Release Date	Update Frequency	Price
SilverPlatter Information Retrieval System SilverPlatter Information, Inc.	PC with DOS version 2.1 or higher	640K	11/88	Semiannually	$750.00/Year
SEARCHER Slater Hall	PC/XT/AT	512K	07/88		$1,200.00/Disc
PC-PDF Reference Technology, Inc.	PC/XT/AT or PS/2 with MS-DOS version 3.2 or higher and 400K of hard disk space	640K	09/87	Annually	*
FastFind Creative Index	PC/XT/AT	640K		Annually	$249.00/Disc
PictureBase Retriever Symmetry Corporation	PC/XT/AT or Macintosh SE/II/Plus, EPS-compatible software, and PostScript printer	512K or 1 MB	01/89		$139.95/Disc
PictureBase Retriever Symmetry Corporation	PC/XT/AT or Macintosh SE/II/Plus, EPS-compatible software, and PostScript printer	512K or 1 MB	01/89		$139.95/Disc
PictureBase Retriever Symmetry Corporation	PC/XT/AT or Macintosh SE/II/Plus, EPS-compatible software, and PostScript printer	512K or 1 MB	01/89		$139.95/Disc

(continued)

ALPHABETICAL LISTING OF CD-ROM TITLES *continued*

Title	Publisher	Description	Audience
Programmer's Library	Microsoft Corporation 16011 N.E. 36th Way Box 97017 Redmond, WA 98073-9717 (206)882–8080	A tool for programmers containing 48 Microsoft technical manuals and reference books, plus more than 1200 sample programs not available anywhere else. The material can be copied directly into the programmer's editor, without interrupting concentration.	Language programmers (particularly C and MASM), technical professionals and writers.
PsycLIT	SilverPlatter Information, Inc. 37 Walnut Street Wellesley Hills, MA 02181 (617)239–0306	Journal citations with abstracts in psychology and behavioral sciences from the PsychINFO department of the American Psychological Association. Coverage from 1984-present.	Library reference market.
Public Domain Software on File CD-ROM	Facts on File, Inc. 460 Park Avenue South New York, NY 10016 (800)322–8755	A collection of 200 debugged public domain software programs for the Apple II.	Libraries, high schools, universities.
Publishers International Directory	Saur Verlag KG Postfach 711009 Possenbacherstrasse 2B 8000 München WEST GERMANY (8979)10480	Covers over 190,000 publishers throughout the world.	
Readers' Guide Abstracts	H.W. Wilson Company 950 University Avenue Bronx, NY 10452 (800)367–6770	Indexing and abstracting for more than 180 periodicals from September 1984 to present. Indexing retrospective from 1-83. Abstracting retrospective from 9-84.	Libraries.
Readers' Guide to Periodical Literature	H.W. Wilson Company 950 University Avenue Bronx, NY 10452 (800)367–6770	Index of general interest popular magazines covering news, current events, fashion, etc. Retrospective from 1-83.	Libraries.
Registry of Mass Spectral Data	John Wiley & Sons, Inc. 605 Third Avenue New York, NY 10158 (212)850–6000	Over 123,000 spectra plus all of the additional data provided on the mainframe version.	
Resors	PCI Inc. 50 West Wilmont Street Richmond Hill, ON L4B 1M5 CANADA (416)764–0614	Bibliography of authors who have written on the subject of remote sensing.	Libraries, universities, government offices, mining companies, fisheries.

*Please contact publisher for prices.

Retrieval System	Computer Compatibility	Minimum Memory	Initial Release Date	Update Frequency	Price
Proprietary Microsoft Corporation	PC/XT/AT or compatible	640K	09/13/88		$395.00/Disc
SilverPlatter Information Retrieval System SilverPlatter Information, Inc.	PC with DOS version 2.1 or higher	640K	06/86	Quarterly	$3,995.00/Year
Proprietary Facts on File Publications Inc.	Apple II series	64K	06/88		$195.00/Disc
	PC with MS-DOS.		07/87	Quarterly	*
WILSONDISC H.W. Wilson Company	PC/XT/AT	640K	10/87	Quarterly	$1,995.00/Year
WILSONDISC H.W. Wilson Company	PC/XT/AT	640K	04/87	Quarterly	$1,095.00/Year
PBM/STIRS	PC/XT/AT	640K			$2,895.00/Disc
FindIt Reteaco, Inc.	PC/XT/AT	640K	09/86	Biannually	$500.00/Disc

(continued)

ALPHABETICAL LISTING OF CD-ROM TITLES continued

Title	Publisher	Description	Audience
Resource/One	UMI (University Microfilms International) 300 North Zeeb Road Ann Arbor, MI 48106 (800)521–3044	Indexing and abstracting for 130 current general reference periodicals and *The New York Times Current Events Edition*.	Small libraries.
Science Citation Index	Institute for Scientific Information 3501 Market Street Philadelphia, PA 19104 (215)386–0100	Citation Index to scientific and technical literature spanning over 100 disciplines with the value added feature of related records.	Scientists, researchers, librarians, information managers, students, educators.
Science Helper (K-8)	PC-SIG Inc. 1030-D East Duane Avenue Sunnyvale, CA 94086 (408)730–9291	Nearly 1000 science and mathematic lesson plans for teachers of Kindergarten through 8th grade-level students.	Educators.
Selected Water Resources Abstracts (SWRA)	OCLC 6565 Frantz Road Dublin, OH 43017-0702 (800)848–5878	200,000 abstracts (1967-present) on two discs, including abstracts of current and earlier pertinent monographs, journal articles, reports, and other publication formats.	Libraries, educational organizations.
Serials	Utlas International 8300 College Boulevard Overland Park, KS 66210 (800)33–UTLAS	460,000 MARC serials.	Libraries.
THE SERIALS DIRECTORY/ EBSCO CD-ROM	EBSCO Publishing P.O. Box 1493 Birmingham, AL 35201 (800)826–3024	Detailed bibliographic and ordering information on over 114,000 serials, annuals, and irregular series published worldwide. Includes indepth abstract/index coverage as well as UD, LC, DD, NLM classifications and CODEN.	Library and Information Science Specialists.
Social Sciences Index	H.W. Wilson Company 950 University Avenue Bronx, NY 10452 (800)367–6770	Index of articles in 353 English-language periodicals covering the social sciences. Retrospective from 4-83.	Libraries.
sociofile	SilverPlatter Information, Inc. 37 Walnut Street Wellesley Hills, MA 02181 (617)239–0306	Index to and abstracts of the world's journals in sociology as compiled by Sociological Abstracts. Contains abstracts of journal articles published in Sociological Abstracts since 1974 and the enhanced bibliographic citations for dissertations in sociology and related disciplines that have been added to the database since 1986.	Library reference market.

*Please contact publisher for prices.

Retrieval System	Computer Compatibility	Minimum Memory	Initial Release Date	Update Frequency	Price
UMI RESEARCH UMI (University Microfilms International)	PC/XT/AT with hard disk	640K	06/88	Bimonthly	$795.00/Year
Proprietary Institute for Scientific Information	PC/XT/AT or PS/2 with DOS version 3.1 or higher	640K	05/88	Quarterly	*
	PC/XT/AT with DOS version 3.1 or higher	256K	06/87		$195.00/Disc
Search CD450 OCLC	PC/XT/AT or Macintosh	512K		Quarterly	$750.00/Year
CD-CATSS Utlas International	PC/XT/AT	640K	06/88		$1,250.00/Disc
EBSCO-CD EBSCO Electronic Information	PC/XT/AT with MS-DOS version 3.1 or higher and 10 MB hard disk	640K	07/88	Quarterly	$495.00/Year
WILSONDISC H.W. Wilson Company	PC/XT/AT	640K	04/87	Quarterly	$1,295.00/Year
SilverPlatter Information Retrieval System SilverPlatter Information, Inc.	PC with DOS version 2.1 or higher	640K	04/87	Semiannually	$1,950.00/Year

(continued)

ALPHABETICAL LISTING OF CD-ROM TITLES *continued*

Title	Publisher	Description	Audience
Software Library Dataplate	Reference Technology Inc. 5700 Flatiron Parkway Boulder, CO 80301 (303)449–4157	Public domain software programs.	
SOFTWARE-CD	SilverPlatter Information, Inc. 37 Walnut Street Wellesley Hills, MA 02181 (617)239–0306	Over 10,000 listings of software packages for the business, professional, and technical communities.	Library reference market.
Space Science Sampler Volume 1: Voyager 2 Images of Uranus, Its Rings and Satellites	University of Colorado LASP Campus Box 392 Boulder, CO 80309 (303)492–6867	800 images of Uranus from NASA's Voyager spacecraft.	Educators, libraries, universities, scientists, amateur astronomers.
Space Science Sampler Volume 2	University of Colorado LASP Campus Box 392 Boulder, CO 80309 (303)492–6867	A collection of NASA scientific data on the Earth and our solar system.	Educators, libraries, universities, scientists, amateur astronomers.
Sports Discus	SilverPlatter Information, Inc. 37 Walnut Street Wellesley Hills, MA 02181 (617)239–0306	The international sports database corresponding to the printed publication *Sport Bibliography*. The database covers areas such as exercise physiology, medicine, biomechanics, coaching, counseling, psychology, and sports medicine. The database dates from 1972 and is based on more than 2,000 international sources.	
STANDARD & POOR'S CORPORATIONS	Dialog Information Services Inc./Standard & Poor's 3460 Hillview Avenue Palo Alto, CA 94304 (800)334–2564	Consists of data from S & P's Corporate Descriptions, S & P's Register (Biographical and Corporate), and S & P's Compustat Services.	Libraries.
SuperCAT Library of Congress MARC: English	Gaylord Information Systems P.O. Box 4901 Syracuse, NY 13221-4901 (315)457–5070	The Library of Congress MARC records in English.	Libraries.
SuperCAT Library of Congress MARC: Foreign Languages	Gaylord Information Systems P.O. Box 4901 Syracuse, NY 13221-4901 (315)457–5070	Library of Congress MARC records in all foreign languages.	Libraries.

*Please contact publisher for prices.

Retrieval System	Computer Compatibility	Minimum Memory	Initial Release Date	Update Frequency	Price
					$195.00
SilverPlatter Information Retrieval System SilverPlatter Information, Inc.	PC or compatible, MS- or PC-DOS 2.1 or higher.	640K	04/88	Semiannually	$1,250.00/Year
Proprietary NASA Jet Propulsion Laboratory	PC/XT/AT with VGA or EGA extended memory monitors	640K	12/88		$25.00/Disc
Proprietary NASA Jet Propulsion Laboratory	PC/XT/AT with VGA or EGA extended memory monitors	640K	12/88		$25.00/Disc
SilverPlatter Information Retrieval System SilverPlatter Information, Inc.	PC with DOS version 2.1 or higher	640K	01/15/89	Semiannually	$1,250.00/Year
	PC or PS/2 with PC- or MS-DOS version 3.1 or higher and 1 MB hard disk	512K		Bimonthly	$4,250.00
SuperCAT Gaylord Information Systems	PC/XT or PS/2 Model 30	640K	09/15/88	Quarterly	$850.00/Year
SuperCAT Gaylord Information Systems	PC/XT or PS/2 Model 30	640K	09/15/88	Quarterly	$500.00/Year

(continued)

ALPHABETICAL LISTING OF CD-ROM TITLES *continued*

Title	Publisher	Description	Audience
Supermap 1.0 1981 Australian Census	Chadwyck-Healy Ltd. Cambridge Place Cambridge CB2 1NR ENGLAND 0223 311479	Data from the 1981 Australian census.	
Supermap 1.1 1980 U.S. Census County Level	Chadwyck-Healy Ltd. Cambridge Place Cambridge CB2 1NR ENGLAND 0223 311479	Contains the two main summary tape files from the 1980 U.S. census.	
Surface Hourly Data from 1987	Department of Atmospheric Science Mail Stop AK-40 University of Washington Seattle, WA 98195 (206)545–0910	Hourly weather data collected from weather stations all across North America over a 1 year period.	Research, educational, and library communities.
Tax/Stats	Hopkins Technology 421 Hazel Lane Hopkins, MN 55343-7117 (612)931–9376	Federal income tax data provided by the IRS.	Consumer, corporate.
The Telerate Expert	Telerate Systems, Inc. One World Trade Center 104th Floor New York, NY 10048 (212)938–5400	Training in money market, foreign exchange, mortgage-backed securities, Euro markets, corporate finance, and technical analysis. Offers basic knowledge and advanced trading skills.	Banks, investment counselors, universities, brokerage houses, back office staff, programmers. From novice to senior level executives.
The Texas Attorney General Documents	Quantum Access Inc. 1700 West Loop South Suite 1460 Houston, TX 77027 (713)622–3211	Attorney General opinions, open records, and decisions from 1973-1988.	Administrative lawyers.
Texas Education Encyclopedia	Quantum Access Inc. 1700 West Loop South Suite 1460 Houston, TX 77027 (713)622–3211	State and federal documents related to education in Texas.	Texas school districts and universities.
Time Table of Science and Innovation	Xiphias 13464 Washington Boulevard Marina Del Rey, CA 90292 (213)821–0074	Multi-media presentation of over 5700 key events in the history of science. Implemented under HyperCard.	Early innovators, K-12 and higher education.

*Please contact publisher for prices.

Retrieval System	Computer Compatibility	Minimum Memory	Initial Release Date	Update Frequency	Price
	PC/XT/AT	512K min.	04/87		*
	PC/XT/AT	512K	10/87		$990.00
CLASIX Full-text Manager Reference Technology Inc.		512K	01/89		$100.00
QuAcc Hopkins Technology	PC with MS-DOS version 3.1 or higher and MS-DOS CD-ROM Extensions	200K	03/89	Annually	$49.00
Key disk Expert Financial Systems, Dublin	PC/XT/AT	540K	01/88	Quarterly	$850.00/Month
Quantum Leap Quantum Access Inc.	PC/XT/AT	512K		Sporadically	$600.00/Disc
Quantum Leap Quantum Access Inc.	PC/XT/AT	512K	09/86	Quarterly	$2,000.00/Year
Xearch Xiphias	Macintosh SE/II/Plus and Atari ST	1 MB	07/88	Annually	$150.00/Disc

(continued)

ALPHABETICAL LISTING OF CD-ROM TITLES *continued*

Title	*Publisher*	*Description*	*Audience*
TLRN-CD2	Innovative Technology Inc. 7927 Jones Branch Drive McLean, VA 22102 (703)734–3000	Federal Supply Catalog.	Procurement, provisioning, and cataloging.
TOM	Information Access Company 362 Lakeside Drive Foster City, CA 94404 (800)227–8431	An index designed exclusively for secondary school libraries. Contains indexing to 100 popular general interest magazines. Full-text of cited articles is available on microfilm. Coverage begins January 1980.	Secondary school libraries.
TOMES System	Micromedex, Inc. 660 Bannock Street Suite 300 Denver, CO 80204-4506 (800)525–9083	The TOMES System is an industrial chemical database with in-depth coverage of clinical effects, range of toxicity, workplace standards, kinetics, and physiochemical parameters. Detailed, comprehensive, and referenced protocols for the medical evaluation and treatment of individuals exposed to chemical agents are provided. Protocols for initial response to incidents (fires, spills, leaks) from hazardous materials are also included. Agents are indexed by chemical names, synonyms, and commonly associated numbers (CAS, RTECS/NIOSH, UN, NA ENT, USAF, etc.)	Physicians, occupational healthcare professionals.
Ulrich's Plus	Bowker Electronic Publishing 245 West 17th Street New York, NY 10011 (800)323–3288	Search and Browse Bowker's complete *Ulrich's* and *Irregular Serials and Annuals* database—comprising more than 92,000 regularly-issued periodicals plus 46,000 irregular serials. Search by 22 categories including first year of publication, price, publisher, circulation, ZIP code, title, subject, and keyword.	Libraries, bookstores, publishers.
The Universe of Sounds Volumes 1-2	Optical Media International 495 Alberto Way Los Gatos, CA 95032 (408)395–4332	Music samples and sound effects.	
U.S. Government Printing Office Monthly Catalog (GPO)	H.W. Wilson Company 950 University Avenue Bronx, NY 10452 (800)367–6770	The online counterpart to the printed Monthly Catalog of U.S. Government Publications, this database provides access to bibliographic data on publications generated by Federal Government agencies, including reports, studies, fact sheets, conference proceedings, and more. Retrospective from 7-76.	Libraries.

*Please contact publisher for prices.

Retrieval System	Computer Compatibility	Minimum Memory	Initial Release Date	Update Frequency	Price
B-Tree Faircom	PC/XT/AT	512K	11/87	Quarterly	*
Proprietary Information Access Company				Monthly	*
Proprietary Micromedex, Inc.	PC/XT/AT with DOS version 3.1 or higher	512K	08/87	Quarterly	*
CD-ROM Search and Retrieval Software Online Computer Systems, Inc.	PC/XT/AT or PS/2	640K	12/86	Quarterly	$395.00/Year
	System requires the CDS3 disc drive-$1995.				$795.00/Disc
WILSONDISC H.W. Wilson Company	PC/XT/AT	640K	03/88	Annually	$995.00/Year

(continued)

ALPHABETICAL LISTING OF CD-ROM TITLES *continued*

Title	*Publisher*	*Description*	*Audience*
USGS Library Catalog	OCLC 6565 Frantz Road Dublin, OH 43017-0702 (800)848–5878	The acquisitions of four of the U.S. Geological Survey Libraries since 1975, currently consisting of approximately 125,000 records. It is a comprehensive core collection of materials pertaining to all areas of earth science.	Libraries, educational organizations.
Variety's Video Directory Plus	Bowker Electronic Publishing 245 West 17th Street New York, NY 10011 (800)323–3288	Includes bibliographic data for virtually every cassette in active distribution (currently 36,000). Most citations include annotations and many will include full-text reviews.	Retail video stores, video publishers, collectors.
Verzeichnis Lieferbarer Büecher: German Books-in-Print	Buchhandler Vereinigung GmbH Grosser Hirschgraben 17-21 Postfach 10042 6000 Frankfurt am Main 1 WEST GERMANY	1.2 million titles of german books in print.	Libraries, researchers, students.
The Virginia Disc One	Virginia Polytechnic Institute Department of Computers Blacksburg, VA 24061 (703)961–5593	28 databases of historical bibliographic records, and much more.	Libraries, extension agents.
The Visual Dictionary	Facts on File, Inc. 460 Park Avenue South New York, NY 10016 (800)322–8755	A collection of pictures, text, and sound in French, Spanish, and English.	Language teachers.
Voyagers to the Outer Planets: Volume 1	University of Colorado LASP Campus Box 392 Boulder, CO 80309 (303)492–6867	The first of a multiple disk set of data from NASA's Voyager spacecraft. This disk has images of Uranus.	Educators, libraries, universities, scientists, amateur astronomers.
Water Resources Abstracts (SWRA File)	National Information Services Corporation (NISC) 335 Paint Branch Drive College Park, MD 20742 (301)454–8039	210,000 citations of water resource data compiled by WRSIC/USGS. Abstracts about water resources from 1967-present. The entire database is on one disc.	Libraries, professional users, foreign governments.
WILSONDISC Demonstration Disc	H.W. Wilson Company 950 University Avenue Bronx, NY 10452 (800)367–6770	The specially-priced WILSONDISC Demonstration Disc contains six months of data from 16 Wilson databases, and allows all of the CD-ROM search capabilities available with WILSONDISC.	Libraries.

*Please contact publisher for prices.

Retrieval System	Computer Compatibility	Minimum Memory	Initial Release Date	Update Frequency	Price
Search CD450 OCLC	PC/XT/AT or Macintosh	512K		Quarterly	$350.00/Year
CD-ROM Search and Retrieval Software Online Computer Systems, Inc.	PC/XT/AT or PS/2	640K	11/88	Quarterly	$295.00/Year
CD-ROM Search and Retrieval Software Online Computer Systems, Inc.	PC/XT/AT	512K			*
Several different retrieval systems on disc	PC/XT/AT		10/88		*
Media-Mixer Software Mart Inc.	PC/Macintosh/Apple				*
Proprietary NASA Jet Propulsion Laboratory	PC/XT/AT with VGA or EGA extended memory monitors	640K	02/89		$25.00/Disc
ROMWare ElmSoft, Inc.	PC/XT/AT	512K	08/88	Biannually	$575.00/Year
WILSONDISC H.W. Wilson Company	PC/XT/AT	640K	01/87		$99.00/Disc

(continued)

ALPHABETICAL LISTING OF CD-ROM TITLES continued

Title	Publisher	Description	Audience
WISCAT	Wisconsin Reference and Loan Library 2109 South Stoughton Road Madison, WI 53716 (608)221-6161	3.25 million bibliographic records from 365 Wisconsin libraries. A total of 14.5 million holdings.	Wisconsin libraries.
A World of Language on CD	CALI, Inc. 526 East Quail Road Orem, UT 84057 (801)226-6886	A series of educational programs including VERSATEXT, Culturgrams, Focused on Listening, American English Pronunciation, VIP, and Multilingual Gameshow.	Educators, ESL.
WorldWeather Disc	Department of Atmospheric Sciences Mail Stop AK-40 University of Washington Seattle, WA 98195 (206)545-0910	Climatogical data from over 4000 weather stations around the world. Detailed summaries of several thousand U.S. locations.	Educational community, reference libraries, researchers, television stations.
Yellow Page Demo	Compact Discoveries 1050 South Federal Highway Delray Beach, FL 33444 (407)243-1453		
Your Marketing Consultant: Advanced Consumer	Knowledge Access International, Inc. 2685 Marine Way Suite 1305 Mountain View, CA 94043 (415)969-0606	Demographic marketing data on 3,137 counties, 316 metropolitan areas, and 423 other U.S. geographical units, as well as a complete set of on-screen state maps which can be displayed at three levels of magnification.	Site locaters, market researchers, media buyers, sales managers, educators.
Your Marketing Consultant: Business to Business	Knowledge Access International, Inc. 2685 Marine Way Suite 1305 Mountain View, CA 94043 (415)969-0606	Demographic marketing data on 3,137 counties, 316 metropolitan areas, and 423 other U.S. geographical units as well as a complete set of on-screen state maps which can be displayed at three levels of magnification.	Site locaters, market researchers, media buyers, sales managers.

*Please contact publisher for prices.

Retrieval System	Computer Compatibility	Minimum Memory	Initial Release Date	Update Frequency	Price
Le Pac Brodart Automation	PC/XT/AT	640K	01/89	Annually	$60.00/Year
Proprietary CALI, Inc.	PC/XT/AT with DOS version 3.1 or higher	512K	01/89		$295.00/Disc
File Manager Reference Technology Inc.	PC/XT/AT/ Microvax II	512K	11/88	Biannually	$295.00/Disc
					*
KAware2 Knowledge Access International	PC/XT/AT with MS-DOS version 3.1 or higher	640K	09/87	Annually	$950.00/Year
KAware2 Knowledge Access International, Inc.	PC/XT/AT with MS-DOS version 3.1 or higher	640K	09/87	Annually	$950.00/Year

CD-ROM TITLES BY SUBJECT

Subject	Title	Publisher	Description
AGRICULTURE	Agri/Stats I	Hopkins Technology 421 Hazel Lane Hopkins, MN 55343-7117 (612)931–9376	Contains U.S. agricultural statistics including Crop Estimates, Grain Stocks, County Estimates —Crops and Livestock, Hog and Pig Estimates, Cattle Inventory, Cattle on Feed, and Meat Animals. These files date back as far as 1939.
	AGRICOLA/CRIS	SilverPlatter Information, Inc. 37 Walnut Street Wellesley Hills, MA 02181 (617)239–0306	AGRICOLA contains citations of publications relating to all aspects of agriculture as compiled by the National Agricultural Library. CRIS contains nearly 30,000 descriptions of current publicly supported agricultural and forestry research projects.
	AGRICOLA and CRIS Databases 1983-present	OCLC 6565 Frantz Road Dublin, OH 43017-0702 (800)848–5878	
	AGRICOLA Retrospective Files 1979-1982	OCLC 6565 Frantz Road Dublin, OH 43017-0702 (800)848–5878	
	Agriculture Library	OCLC 6565 Frantz Road Dublin, OH 43017-0702 (800)848–5878	Over 300,000 bibliographic records on agriculture-related subjects. Topics include farm economics and management, field crops, forestry policy, animal breeds and breeding, wildlife management, soil conservation, horticulture, parks and public reservations, dairying and dairy products, and rural sociology.
	Biological & Agricultural Index	H.W. Wilson Company 950 University Avenue Bronx, NY 10452 (800)367–6770	Covering 202 key periodicals in the life sciences, this database offers balanced coverage of biological and agricultural disciplines, among them biochemistry, botany, cytology, forestry, genetics, horticulture, microbiology, soil science, and zoology. Retrospective from 7-83.

Audience	Retrieval System	Computer Compatibility	Minimum Memory	Initial Release Date	Update Freq./Price
Agriculture producers, traders, financial university.	QuAcc Hopkins Technology	PC with MS-DOS version 3.1 or higher and MS-DOS CD-ROM Extensions	200K	10/88	Annually $49.00/Disc
Library reference market.	SilverPlatter Information Retrieval System SilverPlatter Information, Inc.	PC with DOS version 2.1 or higher	640K	01/87	Quarterly $950.00/Year
Libraries, educational organizations.	Search CD450 OCLC	PC/XT/AT or Macintosh	512K		Quarterly $795.00/Year
Libraries, educational organizations.	Search CD450 OCLC	PC/XT/AT or Macintosh	512K		$350.00/Set
Libraries, educational organizations.	Search CD450 OCLC	PC/XT/AT or Macintosh	512K		Annually $350.00/Year
Libraries.	WILSONDISC H.W. Wilson Company	PC/XT/AT	640K	03/88	Quarterly $1,495.00/Year

(continued)

CD-ROM TITLES BY SUBJECT *continued*

Subject	Title	Publisher	Description
AGRICULTURE *continued*	*DIALOG OnDisc AGRIBUSINESS U.S.A.*	Dialog Information Services, Inc./Pioneer Hi-Bred International 3460 Hillview Avenue Palo Alto, CA 94304 (800)334–2564	Provides indexing for more than 200 agribusiness trade journals and more than 100 USDA reports. Important data from international sources such as the United Nations Food and Agriculture Organization and the European Economic Community are also included. Records contain either the complete text or full tables (for statistical publications) or controlled-vocabulary indexing and informative abstracts. Covers 1985-present.
AIRLINES	*FORM41: Airline Carrier Filings*	Data Base Products, Inc. 12770 Coit Road #1111 Dallas, TX 75251-1314 (800)345–2876	Detailed financial data (income statements, balance sheets, and other financial information) derived from carrier filings with the Department of Transportation on the 'B' and 'P' schedules of DOT Form 41. The FORM41 data is principally quarterly, semi-annual, and annual in frequency, with some monthly data, and includes the standard ratios of interest to airlines. Depth of historical detail varies by line item.
	INTERNATIONAL: International Airline Passenger Traffic	Data Base Products, Inc. 12770 Coit Road #1111 Dallas, TX 75251-1314 (800)345–2876	International onboard traffic, traffic flow, and origin and destination information derived from carrier filings with the Department of Transportation and with the Immigration and Naturalization Service of the Department of Justice. INTERNATIONAL includes both monthly and quarterly data, and is available as an annual subscription with quarterly updates for the most recent information. Subscription to this database is limited to those eligible for access as determined by the U.S. Department of Transportation.
	ITINERARIES	Data Base Products, Inc. 12770 Coit Road #1111 Dallas, TX 75251-1314 (800)345–2876	Detailed passenger itinerary data extracted from the Department of Transportation's quarterly survey of airline passenger traffic. ITINERARIES contains the equivalent of the DOT's Table 12 with such additional information as fares included. Each release contains two full years of data plus as many quarters of the release year as are currently available—up to three full years of data.
	LZ Services	Lasertrak Corporation 6235-B Lookout Road Boulder, CO 80301 (303)530–2711	Aeronautical navigation and flight planning information.

Audience	Retrieval System	Computer Compatibility	Minimum Memory	Initial Release Date	Update Freq./Price
Libraries.		PC or PS/2 with PC- or MS-DOS version 3.1 or higher and 1 MB hard disk	512K		Quarterly $2,000.00/Year
Airlines, airports, transportation consultants, state and federal transportation agencies, transportation-related industries, aircraft manufacturers, investment/securities firms.	Proprietary Data Base Products, Inc.	PC/XT/AT/COMPAQ or other very compatible with 10 MB hard disk, using MS- or PC-DOS version 3.1 or higher.	640K	02/89	Quarterly $10,000.00/Year
Airlines, airports, transportation consultants, state and federal transportation agencies, transportation-related industries (hotels, car rental agencies), aircraft manufacturers, investment/securities firms.	Proprietary Data Base Products, Inc.	PC/XT/AT/COMPAQ or other very compatible computer with a 10 MB hard disk, using MS- or PC-DOS version 3.1 or higher.	640K	12/30/87	Quarterly $10,000.00/Year
Airlines, airports, transportation consultants, state and federal transportation agencies, transportation-related industries (hotels, car rental agencies), aircraft manufacturers, investment/securities firms.	Proprietary Data Base Products, Inc.	PC/XT/AT/COMPAQ and other very compatibles with a 10 MB hard disk, using MS- or PC-DOS version 3.1 or higher.	640K	07/89	Quarterly $10,000.00/Year
Pilots, corporate aircraft operators, commercial airlines.	Proprietary Lasertrak Corporation	Proprietary system	2 MB	07/87	Every 28 days $250.00/Year

(continued)

CD-ROM TITLES BY SUBJECT *continued*

Subject	Title	Publisher	Description
AIRLINES *continued*	O & D PLUS HISTORICAL	Data Base Products, Inc. 12770 Coit Road #1111 Dallas, TX 75251-1314 (800)345–2876	An historical archive consisting of seven full years (1979-1985) of comprehensive domestic origin and destination information from the Department of Transportation's quarterly survey of airline passenger traffic. O & D PLUS HISTORICAL contains all the quarterly data from the standard published tables (1 through 10), including true O & D, online local and online connecting O & D, as well as much information not included in the standard tables: fares, yield, airport-pair detail, reported coupons, etc.
	O & D PLUS: Airline Passenger Statistics	Data Base Products, Inc. 12770 Coit Road #1111 Dallas, TX 75251-1314 (800)345–2876	A current and ongoing subscription database, consisting of comprehensive domestic origin and destination information from the Department of Transportation's quarterly survey of airline passenger traffic. Each release contains two full years of historical data plus as many quarters of the current release year as are presently available—in other words, up to three full years of data. O & D PLUS contains all the data from the standard published tables (1 through 10), including true O & D, online local and online connecting O & D, as well as much information not included in the standard tables: fares, yield, airport-pair detail, reported coupons, etc.
	ONBOARD: Airline Passenger Traffic Statistics	Data Base Products, Inc. 12770 Coit Road #1111 Dallas, TX 75251-1314 (800)345–2876	Comprehensive domestic onboard traffic and service segment data derived from carrier filings with the Department of Transportation under Economic Regulation 586 and from the traffic schedules of Form 41. ONBOARD includes monthly, quarterly, and annual data. Each release contains two full years of data plus as many months/quarters of the release year as are currently available. Some historical data begins with 1972.
ART	AdBuilder Electronic	Multi-Ad Services, Inc. 1720 West Detweiler Drive Peoria, IL 61615-1530 (800)447–1950	High quality PostScript illustrations and ad layouts for newspaper advertising systems.

*Please contact publisher for prices.

Audience	Retrieval System	Computer Compatibility	Minimum Memory	Initial Release Date	Update Freq./Price
Airlines, airports, transportation consultants, state and federal transportation agencies, transportation-related industries (hotels, car rental agencies), aircraft manufacturers, investment/securities firms.	*Proprietary* Data Base Products, Inc.	PC/XT/AT/COMPAQ and other very compatibles with a 10 MB hard disk, using MS- or PC-DOS version 3.1 or higher.	640K	03/88	Disc will be updated in 1990. $7,000.00
Airlines, airports, transportation consultants, state and federal transportation agencies, transportation-related industries (hotels, car rental agencies), aircraft manufacturers, investment/securities firms.	*Proprietary* Data Base Products, Inc.	PC/XT/AT/COMPAQ and other very compatibles with a 10 MB hard disk, using MS- or PC-DOS version 3.1 or higher.	640K	03/87	Quarterly $7,000.00/Year
Airlines, airports, transportation consultants, state and federal transportation agencies, transportation-related industries (hotels, car rental agencies), aircraft manufacturers, investment/securities firms.	*Proprietary* Data Base Products, Inc.	PC/XT/AT/COMPAQ or other very compatible computer with a 10 MB hard disk, using MS- or PC-DOS version 3.1 or higher.	640K	08/15/88	Quarterly $7,000.00/Year
Newspapers, advertisers, publishing, graphics.	*PictureBase Retriever* Symmetry Corporation	Macintosh SE/II/Plus, EPS-compatible software, and PostScript printer	1 MB	11/88	*

(continued)

CD-ROM TITLES BY SUBJECT *continued*

Subject	Title	Publisher	Description
ART *continued*	ArtRoom	Image Club Graphics Inc. 2915 19th Street East Suite 206 Calgary, AB T2E 7A2 CANADA (403)250–1969	Contains over 1000 high-resolution Encapsulated PostScript clip art and images, the complete library of over 100 PostScript typefaces, and over 50 pages of useful publishing templates.
	Comstock Desktop Photography	Comstock Inc. 30 Irving Place New York, NY 10003 (212)353–8686	449 black and white photographs in TIFF files in High Sierra and Mac HFS format.
	DarkRoom	Image Club Graphics Inc. 2915 19th Street East Suite 206 Calgary, AB T2E 7A2 CANADA (403)250–1969	A stock photo library of more than 500 professional ready-to-use photos, categorized according to Sports, Lifestyle, Business, and Travel. Comes complete with a full-color reference catalog.
	Digit Art	Image Club Graphics Inc. 2915 19th Street N.E. Suite 206 Calgary, AB T2E 7A2 CANADA (403)250–1969	Ten volumes of clip art from elements to illustrations in Encapsulated PostScript format—over 1000 high-resolution images.
	Graphics Lab	ALDE Publishing 4830 West 77th Street P.O. Box 35326 Minneapolis, MN 55435 (612)835–5240	Contains .GIF, .PIC, and .MAC graphics files.
	HotType	Image Club Graphics Inc. 2915 19th Street N.E. Suite 206 Calgary, AB T2E 7A2 CANADA (403)250–1969	A complete library of over 100 PostScript typefaces.
	Kwikee INHOUSE Complete '88	Multi-Ad Services, Inc. 1720 West Detweiler Drive Peoria, IL 61615-1530 (800)447–1950	Over 1400 quality PostScript illustrations for Desktop Presentations and Publishing applications.
	Kwikee INHOUSE Pal "Potpourri" Collection	Multi-Ad Services, Inc. 1720 West Detweiler Drive Peoria, IL 61615-1530 (800)447–1950	300 quality PostScript illustrations for Desktop Presentations and Publishing applications.

*Please contact publisher for prices.

Audience	Retrieval System	Computer Compatibility	Minimum Memory	Initial Release Date	Update Freq./Price
Desktop publishers.		Macintosh Plus/SE/II			$999.00/Disc
Art directors, graphic designers, corporate communications departments, schools, hospitals.	None	PC/XT/AT/Macintosh	200K	08/89	$500.00/Disc
		Macintosh Plus/SE/II	1 MB		$499.00/Disc
Desktop publishers.		Macintosh Plus/SE/II, PC/XT/AT			*
Desktop publishers.	None	PC/XT/AT	640K	09/88	$99.00/Disc
Desktop publishers.		Macintosh Plus/SE/II			$149.00/Set
Newspapers, advertising, graphics, publishers.	*PictureBase Retriever* Symmetry Corporation	Macintosh SE/II/Plus, PostScript printer	1 MB	10/88	$995.00/Disc
Newspapers, advertising, graphics, publishers.	*PictureBase Retriever* Symmetry Corporation	PC/XT/AT or Macintosh SE/II/Plus, EPS-compatible software, and PostScript printer	512K or 1 MB	05/88	$149.95/Disc

(continued)

CD-ROM TITLES BY SUBJECT *continued*

Subject	Title	Publisher	Description
ART *continued*	ProArt Professional Art Library: the "Business" Collection	Multi-Ad Services, Inc. 1720 West Detweiler Drive Peoria, IL 61615-1530 (800)447–1950	100 quality PostScript illustrations for Desktop Presentations and Publishing applications.
	ProArt Professional Art Library: the "Sports" Collection	Multi-Ad Services, Inc. 1720 West Detweiler Drive Peoria, IL 61615-1530 (800)447–1950	100 quality PostScript illustrations for Desktop Presentations and Publishing applications.
	ProArt Professional Art Library: the "Holidays" Collection	Multi-Ad Services, Inc. 1720 West Detweiler Drive Peoria, IL 61615-1530 (800)447–1950	100 quality PostScript illustrations for Desktop Presentations and Publishing applications.
AUDIO	16-Bit Sample Library	Optical Media International 495 Alberto Way Los Gatos, CA 95032 (408)395–4332	5,000 sound effects including percussion.
	The Universe of Sounds Volumes 1-2	Optical Media International 495 Alberto Way Los Gatos, CA 95032 (408)395–4332	Music samples and sound effects.
AUTOMOTIVE	Automated Parts Catalog	ADP 1950 Hassell Road Hoffman Estates, IL 60195-2308 (312)397–1700	General Motors automotive parts catalog for 1976-1989.
	Chrysler Parts Catalog	Bell and Howell 5700 Lombardo Center Suite 220 Seven Hills, OH 44351 (216)642–9060	Electronic parts catalog.
	GM Parts Catalog	Bell and Howell 5700 Lombardo Center Suite 220 Seven Hills, OH 44351 (216)642–9060	Electronic parts catalog.
	Honda/Acura Parts Catalog	Bell and Howell 5700 Lombardo Center Suite 220 Seven Hills, OH 44351 (216)642–9060	Electronic parts catalog.

*Please contact publisher for prices.

Audience	Retrieval System	Computer Compatibility	Minimum Memory	Initial Release Date	Update Freq./Price
Publishing, graphics.	*PictureBase Retriever* Symmetry Corporation	PC/XT/AT or Macintosh SE/II/Plus, EPS-compatible software, and PostScript printer	512K or 1 MB	01/89	$139.95/Disc
Publishing, graphics.	*PictureBase Retriever* Symmetry Corporation	PC/XT/AT or Macintosh SE/II/Plus, EPS-compatible software, and PostScript printer	512K or 1 MB	01/89	$139.95/Disc
Publishing, graphics.	*PictureBase Retriever* Symmetry Corporation	PC/XT/AT or Macintosh SE/II/Plus, EPS-compatible software, and PostScript printer	512K or 1 MB	01/89	$139.95/Disc
					$995.00/Disc
		System requires the CDS3 disc drive-$1995.			$795.00/Disc
GM dealers.	*Proprietary* ADP	ADP Proprietary Hardware	640K	01/89	As available from General Motors *
Automotive dealers.	*Proprietary* Bell and Howell	IDB 2000 Image Retrieval System		02/88	Monthly *
Automotive dealers.	*Proprietary* Bell and Howell	IDB 2000 Image Retrieval System		02/88	Monthly *
Automotive dealers.	*Proprietary* Bell and Howell	IDB 2000 Image Retrieval System		02/88	Monthly /System

(continued)

CD-ROM TITLES BY SUBJECT *continued*

Subject	Title	Publisher	Description
BUSINESS	*Busi/Stats*	Hopkins Technology 421 Hazel Lane Hopkins, MN 55343-7117 (612)931–9376	Profiles of businesses from federal databases.
	Business Indicators	Slater Hall Information Products 1522 K Street N.W. Suite 522 Washington, DC 20005 (202)682–1350	The complete National Income and Product Accounts (1929-present), 1,900 economic series from the "Blue Pages" of the Survey of Current Business (annually from 1961, monthly from 1981), and income and employment by industry for all states and regions (1969-present).
	Compustat PC Plus	Standard & Poor's Compustat Services 7400 South Alton Court Englewood, CO 90112 (303)740–4510	A detailed database of 7,187 public companies.
	DIALOG OnDisc Canadian Business and Current Affairs	Dialog Information Services Inc./Micromedia Ltd. 3460 Hillview Avenue Palo Alto, CA 94394 (800)334-2564	More than 220,000 articles per year from 200 business periodicals, 300 popular magazines, and 10 newspapers, including the Globe & Mail, Toronto Star, and Montreal Gazette. Coverage extends from 1981 through the current year. Covers 1981-present.
	Microsoft Small Business Consultant	Microsoft Corporation 16011 N.E. 36th Way P.O. Box 97017 Redmond, WA 98073-9717 (206)882–8080	220 publications from the Small Business Administration, U.S. Government agencies, and the accounting firm of Deloitte Haskins + Sells. Information on starting and operating a small business; from creating a business plan and obtaining financing and credit, to acquiring a patent and handling personnel issues.
	STANDARD & POOR'S CORPORATIONS	Dialog Information Services Inc./Standard & Poor's 3460 Hillview Avenue Palo Alto, CA 94394 (800)334-2564	Consists of data from S & P's Corporate Descriptions, S & P's Register (Biographical and Corporate), and S & P's Compustat Services.
CHEMICALS	*CHEM-BANK*	SilverPlatter Information, Inc. 37 Walnut Street Wellesley Hills, MA 02181 (617)239–0306	A collection of databanks of potentially hazardous chemicals, containing three complete major databanks: RTECS, OHMTADS, and CHRIS.

Audience	Retrieval System	Computer Compatibility	Minimum Memory	Initial Release Date	Update Freq./Price
Planners, corporate, academic.	QuAcc Hopkins Technology	PC with MS-DOS version 3.1 or higher and MS-DOS CD-ROM Extensions	200K	02/89	Annually $59.00/Disc
Libraries, business economists, federal agencies.	SEARCHER Slater Hall	PC/XT/AT with hard disk	512K	01/88	Monthly $2,200.00/Year
					$12,000.00
Libraries.		PC or PS/2 with PC- or MS-DOS version 3.1 or higher and 1 MB hard disk	512K		Quarterly $1,450.00/Year
Small business owners or middle management of large corporations.	Proprietary Microsoft Corporation	PC/XT/AT or compatible with DOS version 3.1, 3.2, or 3.3 and MS-DOS CD-ROM Extensions	640K	10/88	$125.00/Disc
Libraries.		PC or PS/2 with PC- or MS-DOS version 3.1 or higher and 1 MB hard disk	512K		Bimonthly $4,250.00
Library reference market.	SilverPlatter Information Retrieval System SilverPlatter Information, Inc.	PC with DOS version 2.1 or higher	640K	05/87	Quarterly $1,350.00/Year

(continued)

CD-ROM TITLES BY SUBJECT *continued*

Subject	Title	Publisher	Description
CHEMICALS *continued*	*EINECS plus-CD*	SilverPlatter Information, Inc. 37 Walnut Street Wellesley Hills, MA 02181 (617)239–0306	Lists pertinent information about more than 100,000 chemicals that were available in Europe between 1971 and 1981, before European notification requirements for chemicals went into effect.
COMMUNICATIONS AND DIRECTORIES	*AVS+ (Address Verification System Plus)*	Information Update Inc. 1190 Saratoga Avenue Suite 210 San Jose, CA 95129-3456 (408)236–3297	A database of every deliverable address in the United States.
	CD NOCS	Dai Nippon Ichigaya-kagacho Shinjuka-ku Tokyo 162 JAPAN 03/266–2111	Nippon Online Communications System.
	Directory of Library and Information Professionals	Knowledge Access International, Inc. 2685 Marine Way Suite 1305 Mountain View, CA 94043 (415)969–0606	Biographical data on approximately 45,000 individuals in the information community.
COMPUTERS	*ADA ROM*	ALDE Publishing 4830 West 77th Street P.O. Box 35326 Minneapolis, MN 55435 (612)835–5240	ADA source codes, templates, utilities, and programs.
	C CD-ROM	ALDE Publishing 4830 West 77th Street P.O. Box 35326 Minneapolis, MN 55435 (612)835–5240	C source codes, templates and utilities.
	COMPU-INFO	SilverPlatter Information, Inc. 37 Walnut Street Wellesley Hills, MA 02181 (617)239–0306	A database of 12,000 computer product listings. It contains information about mainframes, minicomputers, microcomputers, operating systems, communications, display terminals, teleprinters, and other peripherals.

*Please contact publisher for prices.

Audience	Retrieval System	Computer Compatibility	Minimum Memory	Initial Release Date	Update Freq./Price
Library reference market.	SilverPlatter Information Retrieval System SilverPlatter Information, Inc.	PC with DOS version 2.1 or higher	640K	12/88	$1,400.00/Disc
Postal services, direct mailers, banks, insurance companies.	Proprietary Information Update Inc.	PC/XT/AT with 12 MB hard disk and MS-DOS	512K	07/87	Quarterly $3,950.00/Year
Librarians, library vendors, researchers.	KAware2 Knowledge Access International, Inc.	PC/XT/AT with MS-DOS version 3.1 or higher	640K	05/88	Every 2 years $495.00
Government contractors, programmers.	None	PC/XT/AT	640K	07/88	Annually $99.00/Disc
C programmers.	None	PC/XT/AT	640K	09/88	Annually $99.00/Disc
Library reference market.	SilverPlatter Information Retrieval System SilverPlatter Information, Inc.	PC with DOS version 2.1 or higher	640K	12/87	Semiannually $1,250.00/Year

(continued)

CD-ROM TITLES BY SUBJECT *continued*

Subject	Title	Publisher	Description
COMPUTERS *continued*	*Computer Library*	OCLC 6565 Frantz Road Dublin, OH 43017-0702 (800)848–5878	Over 250,000 records that cover the subject from the earliest days of computer development to the microchip revolution that's made the supercomputers of today possible. Government, academic, and private industry resources are all utilized to provide you with the most comprehensive body of information available on the computer industry.
	HP LaserROM	Hewlett-Packard Company 3000 Hanover Street Palo Alto, CA 94304 (415)857–1501	Online manual system for HP 3000 users.
CONSTRUCTION	*Construction Activity Locater*	Knowledge Access International, Inc./CD Productions 2685 Marine Way Suite 1305 Mountain View, CA 94043 (415)969–0606	Tracks 430,014 building permits and valuations for 17,000 cities with 38 variables for each city. Includes monthly building permits reported to Bureau of Census on form C-404 since January, 1987; and state, county, and Consolidated Metropolitan Statistical Area totals.
CRIME	*Crime/Stats*	Hopkins Technology 421 Hazel Lane Hopkins, MN 55343-7117 (612)931–9376	Crime and jail statistics produced by federal agencies.
DEMO	*CD-ROM Sampler*	Discovery Systems 7001 Discovery Boulevard Dublin, OH 43017 (614)761–2000	The CD-ROM Sampler is an innovative, multimedia CD-ROM disc developed to demonstrate the wide range of applications addressable by CD-ROM technology in the MS-DOS environment. Featuring software products submitted by over 50 software publishers, the Sampler includes a variety of hands-on PC demo applications as well as an integrated natural image and graphics-based tutorial on CD-ROM complete with audio narration and music.
	Macintosh Showcase	Discovery Systems 7001 Discovery Boulevard Dublin, OH 43017 (614)761–2000	With several multimedia HyperCard stacks, the Macintosh Showcase CD-ROM disc is a full-featured demonstration of CD-ROM technology in the Apple Macintosh environment. Complete with a multimedia interview with Bill Atkinson, the author of HyperCard, and a tutorial on CD-ROM technology, the Macintosh Showcase offers many items of interest to a prospect evaluating Apple systems.

Audience	Retrieval System	Computer Compatibility	Minimum Memory	Initial Release Date	Update Freq./Price
Libraries, educational organizations.	*Search CD450* OCLC	PC/XT/AT or Macintosh	512K		Annually $350.00
HP 3000 users.	*LaserRETRIEVE* Hewlett-Packard Company	Vectra or PC/AT with 5 MB hard disk, Mouse, and DOS version 3.1 or higher	640K	02/88	Monthly $3,420.00/Year
Utility companies, construction firms, real estate firms, development planners, state and city governments, construction after-market companies.	*KAware2* Knowledge Access International, Inc.	PC/XT/AT	640K	12/88	Annually $4,100.00/Disc
Government, social studies, universities.	*QuAcc* Hopkins Technology	PC with MS-DOS version 3.1 or higher and MS-DOS CD-ROM Extensions	200K	05/89	Every 2 years $49.00/Disc
		PC/XT/AT with DOS version 3.1 or higher	640K		$10.00/Disc
	HyperCard Apple	Macintosh SE/II/Plus	1 MB		$10.00/Disc

(continued)

CD-ROM TITLES BY SUBJECT *continued*

Subject	Title	Publisher	Description
DEMO *continued*	*WILSONDISC Demonstration Disc*	H.W. Wilson Company 950 University Avenue Bronx, NY 10452 (800)367–6770	The specially-priced WILSONDISC Demonstration Disc contains six months of data from 16 Wilson databases, and allows all of the CD-ROM search capabilities available with WILSONDISC.
EARTH SCIENCES	*Climatedata — Central/Eastern States*	US WEST Optical Publishing 90 Madison Street Suite 200 Denver, CO 80206 (800)222–0920	Daily climate data from the National Climatic Data Center for Central and Eastern states.
	Climatedata — Hourly Precipitation	US WEST Optical Publishing 90 Madison Street Suite 200 Denver, CO 80206 (800)222–0920	NCDC hourly precipitation measurements.
	Climatedata — Western States	US WEST Optical Publishing 90 Madison Street Suite 200 Denver, CO 80206 (800)222–0920	Daily climate data from the National Climatic Data Center for the Western United States.
	Compact Cambridge Aquatic Sciences and Fisheries Abstracts	Cambridge Scientific Abstracts 7200 Wisconsin Avenue Suite 601 Bethesda, MD 20816 (301)961–6700	Abstracts covering biological and ecological aspects of marine, freshwater and brackish environments, marine technology and engineering, oceanography, and pollution of aquatic environments.
	Earth Science Data Directory (ESDD)	OCLC 6565 Frantz Road Dublin, OH 43017-0702 (800)848–5878	A central repository of information about earth science and natural resource databases, both machine-readable and eye-readable, produced by government agencies, academic institutions, and the private sector.
	Environment Library	OCLC 6565 Frantz Road Dublin, OH 43017-0702 (800)848–5878	Over 400,000 records that touch upon every facet of this complex and fascinating subject.
	Gale Experiment Data Set	Department of Atmospheric Sciences Mail Stop AK-40 University of Washington Seattle, WA 98195 (206)545–0910	Surface and upper-air meteorological data collected during the Genesis of Atlantic Lows Experiment.

Audience	Retrieval System	Computer Compatibility	Minimum Memory	Initial Release Date	Update Freq./Price
Libraries.	WILSONDISC H.W. Wilson Company	PC/XT/AT	640K	01/87	$99.00/Disc
Engineers, scientists, colleges, universities, meteorologists.	Proprietary US WEST Optical Publishing	PC/XT/AT with DOS version 2.0 or higher	512K	05/88	Annually $295.00/Year
Engineers, scientists, colleges, universities, meteorologists.	Proprietary US WEST Optical Publishing	PC/XT/AT with DOS version 2.0 or higher	512K	12/88	Annually $295.00/Year
Engineers, scientists, colleges, universities, meteorologists.	Proprietary US WEST Optical Publishing	PC/XT/AT with DOS version 2.0 or higher	512K	05/88	Annually $295.00/Year
Universities, oceanographic researchers.	Compact Cambridge Cambridge Scientific Abstracts	PC/XT/AT	512K	06/86	Biannually $1,250.00/Year
Libraries, educational organizations.	Search CD450 OCLC	PC/XT/AT or Macintosh	512K		Quarterly $350.00/Year
Libraries, educational organizations.	Search CD450 OCLC	PC/XT/AT or Macintosh	512K		Annually $350.00
Universities, government, research and library communities.	CLASIX Full-Text Manager Reference Technology Inc.	PC/XT/AT/Microvax II	512K	07/87	$50.00/Disc

(continued)

CD-ROM TITLES BY SUBJECT *continued*

Subject	Title	Publisher	Description
EARTH SCIENCES *continued*	GeoIndex	OCLC 6565 Frantz Road Dublin, OH 43017-0702 (800)848–5878	Citations to more than 15,000 published geologic maps of the United States and its territories.
	Geological Information Disc	U.S. Geological Survey 804 National Center Reston, VA 22092 (703)648–4000	Geological information.
	Hydrodata — Central States USGS Daily Values	US WEST Optical Publishing 90 Madison Street Suite 200 Denver, CO 80206 (800)222–0920	USGS daily streamflow measurements for the Central states.
	Hydrodata — Eastern States USGS Daily Values	US WEST Optical Publishing 90 Madison Street Suite 200 Denver, CO 80206 (800)222–0920	USGS daily streamflow measurements for Eastern states.
	Hydrodata — USGS Peak Values	US WEST Optical Publishing 90 Madison Street Suite 200 Denver, CO 80206 (800)222–0920	USGS peak streamflow measurements for streams nationwide.
	Hydrodata — Western States USGS Daily Values	US WEST Optical Publishing 90 Madison Street Suite 200 Denver, CO 80206 (800)222–0920	USGS daily streamflow measurements for Western states.
	Hydrodata Canada	US WEST Optical Publishing 90 Madison Street Suite 200 Denver, CO 80206 (800)222–0920	Daily and peak streamflow discharges for Canada.
	Hydrodata USGS Quality of Water — Central States	US WEST Optical Publishing 90 Madison Street Suite 200 Denver, CO 80206 (800)222–0920	Water Quality data compiled by the USGS for the past 80 years for the Central United States.

Audience	Retrieval System	Computer Compatibility	Minimum Memory	Initial Release Date	Update Freq./Price
Libraries, educational organizations.	Search CD450 OCLC	PC/XT/AT or Macintosh	512K		Quarterly $350.00/Year
					$35.00/Disc
Engineers, scientists, colleges, universities.	Proprietary US WEST Optical Publishing	PC/XT/AT with DOS version 2.0 or higher	512K	08/87	Annually $295.00/Year
Engineers, scientists, colleges, universities.	Proprietary US WEST Optical Publishing	PC/XT/AT with DOS version 2.0 or higher	512K	08/87	Annually $295.00/Year
Engineers, scientists, colleges, universities.	Proprietary US WEST Optical Publishing	PC/XT/AT with DOS version 2.0 or higher	640K	09/88	Annually $295.00/Year
Engineers, scientists, colleges, universities.	Proprietary US WEST Optical Publishing	PC/XT/AT with DOS version 2.0 or higher	512K		Annually $295.00/Year
Engineers, scientists, colleges, universities.	Proprietary US WEST Optical Publishing	PC/XT/AT with DOS version 2.0 or higher	512K	11/88	Annually $295.00/Year
Engineers, scientists, colleges, universities.	Proprietary US WEST Optical Publishing	PC/XT/AT with DOS version 2.0 or higher	512K	12/88	Annually $295.00/Year

(continued)

CD-ROM TITLES BY SUBJECT *continued*

Subject	Title	Publisher	Description
EARTH SCIENCES *continued*	*Hydrodata USGS Quality of Water — Eastern States*	US WEST Optical Publishing 90 Madison Street Suite 200 Denver, CO 80206 (800)222–0920	Water Quality data compiled by the USGS for the past 80 years for the Eastern States.
	Hydrodata USGS Quality of Water — Western States	US WEST Optical Publishing 90 Madison Street Suite 200 Denver, CO 80206 (800)222–0920	Water Quality data compiled by the USGS for the past 80 years for the Western United States.
	National Meteorological Center Grid Point Data Set	Department of Atmospheric Sciences Mail Stop AK-40 University of Washington Seattle, WA 98195 (206)545–0910	
	Selected Water Resources Abstracts (SWRA)	OCLC 6565 Frantz Road Dublin, OH 43017-0702 (800)848–5878	200,000 abstracts (1967-present) on two discs, including abstracts of current and earlier pertinent monographs, journal articles, reports, and other publication formats.
	Surface Hourly Data from 1987	Department of Atmospheric Sciences Mail Stop AK-40 University of Washington Seattle, WA 98195 (206)545–0910	Hourly weather data collected from weather stations all across North America over a 1 year period.
	USGS Library Catalog	OCLC 6565 Frantz Road Dublin, OH 43017-0702 (800)848–5878	The acquisitions of four of the U.S. Geological Survey Libraries since 1975, currently consisting of approximately 125,000 records. It is a comprehensive core collection of materials pertaining to all areas of earth science.
	Water Resources Abstracts (SWRA File)	National Information Services Corporation (NISC) 335 Paint Branch Drive College Park, MD 20742 (301)454–8039	210,000 citations of water resource data compiled by WRSIC/USGS. Abstracts about water resources from 1967-present. The entire database is on one disc.
	WorldWeather Disc	Department of Atmospheric Sciences Mail Stop AK-40 University of Washington Seattle, WA 98195 (206)545–0910	Climatogical data from over 4000 weather stations around the world. Detailed summaries of several thousand U.S. locations.

Audience	Retrieval System	Computer Compatibility	Minimum Memory	Initial Release Date	Update Freq./Price
Engineers, scientists, colleges, universities.	Proprietary US WEST Optical Publishing	PC/XT/AT with DOS version 2.0 or higher	512K	12/88	Annually $295.00/Year
Engineers, scientists, colleges, universities.	Proprietary US WEST Optical Publishing	PC/XT/AT with DOS version 2.0 or higher	512K	01/15/89	Annually $295.00/Year
Research, educational, and library communities.	CLASIX Reference Technology Inc.	PC/XT/AT/Microvex II	512K	01/87	$50.00/Disc
Libraries, educational organizations.	Search CD450 OCLC	PC/XT/AT or Macintosh	512K		Quarterly $750.00/Year
Research, educational, and library communities.	CLASIX Full-Text Manager Reference Technology Inc.		512K	01/89	$100.00
Libraries, educational organizations.	Search CD450 OCLC	PC/XT/AT or Macintosh	512K		Quarterly $350.00/Year
Libraries, professional users, foreign governments.	ROMWare ElmSoft, Inc.	PC/XT/AT	512K	08/88	Biannually $575.00/Year
Educational community, reference libraries, researchers, television stations.	File Manager Reference Technology Inc.	PC/XT/AT/Microvax II	512K	11/88	Biannually $295.00/Disc

(continued)

CD-ROM TITLES BY SUBJECT *continued*

Subject	Title	Publisher	Description
EDUCATION	*A World of Language on CD*	CALI, Inc. 526 East Quail Road Orem, UT 84057 (801)226–6886	A series of educational programs including VERSATEXT, Culturgrams, Focused on Listening, American English Pronunciation, VIP, and Multilingual Gameshow.
	A-V ONLINE	SilverPlatter Information, Inc. 37 Walnut Street Wellesley Hills, MA 02181 (617)239–0306	Complete database of audiovisual materials from the NICEM.
	DIALOG OnDisc ERIC	Dialog Information Services Inc. 3460 Hillview Avenue Palo Alto, CA 94304 (800)334–2564	Provides immediate access to abstracts of articles published in over 700 educational journals, and thousands of research reports, evaluation studies, curriculum guides, and lesson plans collected by the U.S. Department of Education. Covers 1980-present.
	Education Index	H.W. Wilson Company 950 University Avenue Bronx, NY 10452 (800)367–6770	Indexing of 345 English-language periodicals, yearbooks and monographs covering all areas of importance to educators. Retrospective from 12-83.
	Education Library	OCLC 6565 Frantz Road Dublin, OH 43017-0702 (800)848–5878	Over 450,000 bibliographic records for materials pertaining to education.
	ERIC	SilverPlatter Information, Inc. 37 Walnut Street Wellesley Hills, MA 02181 (617)239–0306	Bibliographic database sponsored by the U.S. Department of Education, consisting of the RIE file and the CIJE file. Current disc covers 1983-present.
	ERIC-Current Files	OCLC 6565 Frantz Road Dublin, OH 43017-0702 (800)848–5878	Citations to education data compiled from 1982 to the present, consisting of CIJE and RIE.
	ERIC-Retrospective Files	OCLC 6565 Frantz Road Dublin, OH 43017-0702 (800)848–5878	RIE 1967-1981 and CIJE 1969-1982.

Audience	Retrieval System	Computer Compatibility	Minimum Memory	Initial Release Date	Update Freq./Price
Educators, ESL.	*Proprietary* CALI, Inc.	PC/XT/AT with DOS version 3.1 or higher	512K	01/89	$295.00/Disc
School districts, media centers, libraries.				09/86	Annually $795.00/Disc
Libraries.		PC or PS/2 Model 30 with PC- or MS-DOS version 2.0 or higher and 1 MB hard disk	512K		Quarterly $950.00/Year
Libraries.	*WILSONDISC* H.W. Wilson Company	PC/XT/AT	640K	04/87	Quarterly $1,295.00/Year
Libraries, educational organizations.	*Search CD450* OCLC	PC/XT/AT or Macintosh	512K		Annually $350.00/Year
Library reference market.	*SilverPlatter Information Retrieval System* SilverPlatter Information, Inc.	PC with DOS version 2.1 or higher	640K	06/86	Quarterly $650.00/Year
Libraries, educational organizations.	*Search CD450* OCLC	PC/XT/AT or Macintosh	512K		Quarterly $425.00/Year
Libraries, educational organizations.	*Search CD450* OCLC	PC/XT/AT or Macintosh	512K		$900.00/Set

(continued)

CD-ROM TITLES BY SUBJECT *continued*

Subject	Title	Publisher	Description
EDUCATION *continued*	*First National Item Bank & Test Development System*	TESCOR, Inc. 12020 Sunrise Valley Drive Suite 260 Reston, VA 22091 (703)476–8000	A desktop test publishing system that uses a database of nationally-validated test questions to allow educators to create professional-quality, curriculum-based tests. The database, or item bank, contains over 60,000 test questions, linked to 6,500 instructional objectives, in over thirty K-12 subject areas. High-resolution graphics for test items are included on the CD-ROM disc and are inserted automatically, eliminating the need for cutting and pasting. (There are over 5,000 items with graphics.) Selected items may be edited and original items added to tests before downloading to the laser printer. Users may modify tests and re-format test-page layout from the keyboard.
	Peterson's College Database	SilverPlatter Information, Inc. 37 Walnut Street Wellesley Hills, MA 02181 (617)239–0306	Full-text database containing over 3,200 profiles of all accredited, degree-granting colleges in the U.S. and Canada. Each profile includes information about student enrollment, ethnic/geographic mix, SAT/ACT score ranges and admissions, expenses, financial aid, special programs, housing and campus life, athletics, and majors.
	Peterson's Gradline	SilverPlatter Information, Inc. 37 Walnut Street Wellesley Hills, MA 02181 (617)239–0306	Full-text database containing over 26,000 profiles of graduate and professional programs in 300 academic disciplines, offered by more than 1,400 colleges and universities in the U.S. and Canada. Includes names and addresses of institutions, faculty and their research specialties, degree levels and specific concentrations, research facilities, financial aid, and more.
	Science Helper (K-8)	PC-SIG Inc. 1030-D East Duane Avenue Sunnyvale, CA 94086 (408)730–9291	Nearly 1000 science and mathematic lesson plans for teachers of Kindergarten through 8th grade-level students.

Audience	Retrieval System	Computer Compatibility	Minimum Memory	Initial Release Date	Update Freq./Price
Educators.			640K	06/87	Semiannually $300.00/Month
Library reference market.	*SilverPlatter Information Retrieval System* SilverPlatter Information, Inc.	PC with DOS version 2.1 or higher	640K	02/89	Annually $695.00/Year
Library reference market.	*SilverPlatter Information Retrieval System* SilverPlatter Information, Inc.	PC with DOS version 2.1 or higher	640K	04/88	Annually $595.00/Year
Educators.		PC/XT/AT with DOS version 3.1 or higher	256K	06/87	$195.00/Disc

(continued)

CD-ROM TITLES BY SUBJECT *continued*

Subject	Title	Publisher	Description
EDUCATION *continued*	Texas Education Encyclopedia	Quantum Access Inc. 1700 West Loop South Suite 1460 Houston, TX 77027 (713)622–3211	State and federal documents related to education in Texas.
ENERGY	Energy Library	OCLC 6565 Frantz Road Dublin, OH 43017-0702 (800)848–5878	Over 290,000 records on hundreds of energy-related topics.
	Energy/Stats	Hopkins Technology 421 Hazel Lane Hopkins, MN 55343-7117 (612)931–9376	Federal statistics on energy sources and uses.
ENTERTAINMENT	Film Literature Index	H.W. Wilson Company 950 University Avenue Bronx, NY 10452 (800)367–6770	Covers more than 200 international periodicals providing significant information on contemporary cinema and television.
	Variety's Video Directory Plus	Bowker Electronic Publishing 245 West 17th Street New York, NY 10011 (800)323–3288	Includes bibliographic data for virtually every cassette in active distribution (currently 36,000). Most citations include annotations and many will include full-text reviews.
FINANCIAL	Business Periodicals Index	H.W. Wilson Company 950 University Avenue Bronx, NY 10452 (800)367–6770	Index of 296 leading business magazines. Retrospective from 6-82.
	CD/Banking	Lotus Development Corporation One Cambridge Center Cambridge, MA 02142 (800)554–5501	Complete coverage of all federally insured institutions: Call report information on 13,500 federally insured commercial banks, thrift financial report information on 3,100 savings and loans, and Y-9 data for 6,000 bank holding companies.
	CD/Corp Tech	Lotus Development Corporation One Cambridge Center Cambridge, MA 02142 (800)554–5501	Summary data on 25,000 high technology companies with detailed product data on each.

Audience	Retrieval System	Computer Compatibility	Minimum Memory	Initial Release Date	Update Freq./Price
Texas school districts and universities.	Quantum Leap Quantum Access Inc.	PC/XT/AT	512K	09/86	Quarterly $2,000.00/Year
Libraries, educational organizations.	Search CD450 OCLC	PC/XT/AT or Macintosh	512K		Annually $350.00
Corporate, academic.	QuAcc Hopkins Technology	PC with MS-DOS version 3.1 or higher and MS-DOS CD-ROM Extensions	200K	04/89	Every 2 years $59.00/Disc
Libraries.	WILSONDISC H.W. Wilson Company	PC/XT/AT	640K		Quarterly $695.00/Year
Retail video stores, video publishers, collectors.	CD-ROM Search and Retrieval Software Online Computer Systems, Inc.	PC/XT/AT or PS/2	640K	11/88	Quarterly $295.00/Year
Libraries.	WILSONDISC H.W. Wilson Company	PC/XT/AT	640K		Quarterly $1,495.00/Year
Banks, investment houses, consulting firms, insurance companies, Fortune 1000 companies.	Lotus One Source Lotus Development Corporation	PC/XT/AT	640K		Quarterly $16,000.00/Year
Banks, investment houses, consulting firms, insurance companies, Fortune 1000 companies.	Lotus One Source Lotus Development Corporation	PC/XT/AT	640K		Quarterly $7,500.00/Year

(continued)

CD-ROM TITLES BY SUBJECT *continued*

Subject	Title	Publisher	Description
FINANCIAL *continued*	*CD/Corporate*	Lotus Development Corporation One Cambridge Center Cambridge, MA 02142 (800)554–5501	CD/Corporate allows you to access the important financial, strategic, or competitive information you need from one compact disc. CD/Corporate combines industry-standard databases with report-generating software so you can quickly prepare custom reports that are incisive and in-depth.
	CD/International	Lotus Development Corporation One Cambridge Center Cambridge, MA 02142 (800)554–5501	Financial information on 4,500 of the world's leading industrial corporations, banks, insurance companies, and financial service firms. Current financial data including income statements, balance sheets, and funds flow statements, over 250 financial variables per company, company-specific accounting practices, critical footnotes to financial statements, and native currency or U.S. dollar report options.
	CD/Investment	Lotus Development Corporation One Cambridge Center Cambridge, MA 02142 (800)554–5501	Comprehensive financials on companies, stocks, and financial issues, from seven leading industry-standard databases.
	CD/Newsline	Lotus Development Corporation One Cambridge Center Cambridge, MA 02142 (800)554–5501	Dow Jones News/Retrieval Service.
	CD/Private+	Lotus Development Corporation One Cambridge Center Cambridge, MA 02142 (800)554–5501	Provides profiles on 110,000 private firms and more detailed information on the leading 6,000 private firms and 10,000 public companies.
	CDX (Corporate Data Exchange)	LaFountain Research Corporation 15 Park Row Suite 700 New York, NY 10038 (212)766–3777	Central repository of financial information sponsored by corporate clients.
	Compact Disclosure	Disclosure Incorporated 5161 River Road Bethesda, MD 20816 (800)843–7747	Financial and textual data extracted from documents filed with the SEC on over 12,000 public companies. Over 250 variables are searchable.

*Please contact publisher for prices.

Audience	Retrieval System	Computer Compatibility	Minimum Memory	Initial Release Date	Update Freq./Price
Banks, investment houses, consulting firms, insurance companies, Fortune 1000 companies.	*Lotus One Source* Lotus Development Corporation	PC/XT/AT	640K		Monthly $17,500.00/Year
Banks, investment houses, consulting firms, insurance companies, Fortune 1000 companies.	*Lotus One Source* Lotus Development Corporation	PC/XT/AT	640K		Monthly $1,950.00/Year
Banks, investment houses, consulting firms, insurance companies, Fortune 1000 companies.	*Lotus One Source* Lotus Development Corporation	PC/XT/AT	640K		Weekly $11,000.00/Year
Banks, investment houses, consulting firms, insurance companies, Fortune 1000 companies.	*Lotus One Source* Lotus Development Corporation	PC/XT/AT	640K		Quarterly $2,000.00/Year
Banks, investment houses, consulting forms, insurance companies, Fortune 1000 companies.	*Lotus One Source* Lotus Development Corporation	PC/XT/AT	640K		Quarterly $6,500.00/Year
Brokerage firms, large corporations and institutions.	None	None	10/88		Quarterly •
Investment bankers, brokers, and advisors; university and public libraries; accountants, lawyers, management consultants, commercial banks.		PC/XT/AT or PS/2 with hard disk drive	640K		Bimonthly $3,700.00/Year

(continued)

CD-ROM TITLES BY SUBJECT *continued*

Subject	Title	Publisher	Description
FINANCIAL *continued*	*Company Accounts Register of the Belgian National Bank*	Bureau Marcel van Dijk 250 Avenue Louise Suite 14 1050 Bruxelles BELGIUM 02/648–6697	Company accounts of 123,000 Belgian corporations.
	Corporate & Industry Research Reports (CIRR)	SilverPlatter Information, Inc. 37 Walnut Street Wellesley Hills, MA 02181 (617)239–0306	A cumulative index with abstracts to over 70,000 corporate and industry reports written by securities and investment banking firms from 1979 to present.
	Disclosure/Spectrum Ownership Database	Disclosure Incorporated 5161 River Road Bethesda, MD 20816 (800)843–7747	Financial and textual data extracted from documents filed with the SEC on over 12,000 public companies. Over 250 variables are searchable. Also included: detailed stock ownership information for companies extracted from documents filed with the SEC by Corporate insiders, five percent owners and institutional owners.
	Econ/Stats I	Hopkins Technology 421 Hazel Lane Hopkins, MN 55343-7117 (612)931–9376	Contains the following databases: Consumer Price Index, Producer Price Index, Export-Import Price Index, Industrial Production Index, Money Stock, Selected Interest Rates, Industry Employment Hours & Earnings and Capacity Utilization.
	Million Dollar Directory	Dun's Marketing Service 3 Sylvan Way Parsippany, NJ 07054-3896 (201)455–0900	Business demographics and individual company listings.
	One Source	Lotus Development Corporation One Cambridge Center Cambridge, MA 02142 (617)577–8500	Daily stock price history, value line, Ford investor services, Disclosure II.

*Please contact publisher for prices.

Audience	Retrieval System	Computer Compatibility	Minimum Memory	Initial Release Date	Update Freq./Price
	Proprietary Bureau Marcel van Dijk	PC/XT/AT with hard disk OR Macintosh SE/II/Plus	640K	08/87	Quarterly $2,500.00/Year
Library reference market.	*SilverPlatter Information Retrieval System* SilverPlatter Information, Inc.	PC with DOS version 2.1 or higher	640K	03/88	Quarterly $1,250.00/Year
Investment bankers, brokers, and advisors; university and public libraries; accountants, lawyers, management consultants, commercial banks.		PC/XT/AT or PS/2 with hard disk drive	640K		Bimonthly $2,000.00/Year
Financial, corporate, university, high school.	*QuAcc* Hopkins Technology	PC with MS-DOS version 3.1 or higher and MS-DOS CD-ROM Extensions	200K	06/88	Annually $49.00/Disc
	Conquest Donnelly Marketing	PC/XT/AT	640K	12/88	Annually *
	Proprietary Lotus Development Corporation	PC/XT/AT or PS/2	640K		$11,000.00/Year

(continued)

CD-ROM TITLES BY SUBJECT *continued*

Subject	Title	Publisher	Description
FINANCIAL *continued*	*The Telerate Expert*	Telerate Systems, Inc. One World Trade Center 104th Floor New York, NY 10048 (212)938–5400	Training in money market, foreign exchange, mortgage-backed securities, Euro markets, corporate finance, and technical analysis. Offers basic knowledge and advanced trading skills.
FOOD	*Food/Stats*	Hopkins Technology 421 Hazel Lane Hopkins, MN 55343-7117 (612)931–9376	Food nutritive values.
FURNITURE	*CAP CD-ROM*	Computer Aided Planning Inc. 169-C Monroe N.W. Grand Rapids, MI 49503 (616)454–0000	Electronic catalogs and CAD libraries for the contract office furniture industry.
	ei:Intellifile	éclat intelligent systems inc. 14470 Doolittle Drive San Leandro, CA 94577 (415)483–2030	A furniture catalog which actually designs your office space for you! Furniture from Herman Miller, Steelcase, Harter Contract, Harper's, CoryHiebert, Westinghouse, Hayworth, and others. Also included are demos of Versacad, ei:Microspec, and other programs.
GOVERNMENT	*CD-FICHE*	USA Information Systems, Inc. 3303 Duke Street Alexandria, VA 22314 (800)USA–8830	The Federal Supply Catalog—over 12 million part numbers purchased by the government on a regular basis, on 4 discs.
	CIS Congressional Masterfile, 1789-1969	Congressional Information Service, Inc. 4520 East-West Highway Suite 800 Bethesda, MD 20814-3389 (800)638–8380	Includes the CIS U.S. Congressional Committee Hearings Index (1833-1969), CIS Unpublished U.S. Senate Committee Hearings (1823-1964), CIS U.S. Serial Set Index (1789-1969), and the CIS U.S. Congressional Committee Prints Index (1830-1969). Also available in any combination of the above.
	Construction Criteria Base	National Institute of Building Sciences 1015 15th Street N.W. Suite 700 Washington, DC 20005 (202)347–5710	NAVFAC, Corps of Engineers, NASA, and VA guide specifications, Corps of Engineers Civil Works Specifications and Reserve Centers, NAVFAC Design Manuals, Federal and Military Specifications.

*Please contact publisher for prices.

Audience	Retrieval System	Computer Compatibility	Minimum Memory	Initial Release Date	Update Freq./Price
Banks, investment counselors, universities, brokerage houses, back office staff, programmers. From novice to senior level executives.	Key disk Expert Financial Systems, Dublin	PC/XT/AT	540K	01/88	Quarterly $850.00/Month
Consumers.	QuAcc Hopkins Technology	PC with MS-DOS version 3.1 or higher and MS-DOS CD-ROM Extensions	200K	11/88	Every 2 years $49.00/Disc
Office furniture manufacturers and dealers, architectural and design firms, facilities managers.	CAP Computer Aided Planning Inc.	PC/XT/AT/Compaq with 10 MB hard drive	640K	09/87	Monthly $1,500.00/Year
Designers, furniture dealers, facilities managers, architects.	Microspec éclat intelligent systems, inc.		512K	09/87	Quarterly First copy free
Government procurement centers and contractors.	Proprietary USA Information Systems, Inc.	PC/XT/AT or PS/2 with MS-DOS version 3.1 or higher	640K	04/87	Quarterly $3,250.00/Year
	Proprietary Congressional Information Service, Inc.	PC or PS/2	640K	11/88	*
Architects, engineers.	FastFind Unibase	PC/XT/AT with MS- or PC-DOS version 3.0 or higher and a 20 MB hard disk, EGA Color Monitor	512K	10/87	Quarterly $970.00/Year

(continued)

CD-ROM TITLES BY SUBJECT *continued*

Subject	Title	Publisher	Description
GOVERNMENT *continued*	*DIALOG OnDisc NTIS*	Dialog Information Services Inc. 3460 Hillview Avenue Palo Alto, CA 94304 (800)334–2564	U.S. Government-sponsored research, development, and engineering reports and analyses prepared by federal agencies, their contractors, and grantees. It contains abstracts of unclassified, publicly available reports, software packages, and data files from 300 Government agencies and some state and local government agencies. Covers 1984-present.
	Enflex Info	ERM Computer Services Inc. 855 Springdale Drive Exton, PA 19341 (800)544–3118	A database of federal and state environmental regulations including federal waste, air, water, DOT, and OSHA information.
	The Federal Procurement Disc	ALDE Publishing 4830 West 77th Street P.O. Box 35326 Minneapolis, MN 55435 (612)835–5240	Title 41/48, GSA Supply Catalog, and 75 MB of public domain software.
	Government Documents Catalog Subscription (GDCS) CD-ROM	Auto-Graphics, Inc. 3201 Temple Avenue Pomona, CA 91768 (800)325–7961	All GPO records since 1976.
	Government Publications Index on InfoTrac	Information Access Company 362 Lakeside Drive Foster City, CA 94404 (800)227–8431	An index to the Monthly Catalog of the Government Printing Office. Includes indexing to public documents generated by legislative and executive branches of the U.S. government. Coverage begins with 1976.
	GPO on SilverPlatter	SilverPlatter Information, Inc. 37 Walnut Street Wellesley Hills, MA 02181 (617)239–0306	Contains citations from 1976-present for government publications, such as books, reports, studies, serials, maps, and more from the Monthly Catalog published by the Government Printing Office.
	Index to U.S. Government Periodicals (IGP)	H.W. Wilson Company 950 University Avenue Bronx, NY 10452 (800)367–6770	Produced by Infordata International, Inc., this database offers access to information in 185 periodicals issued by more than 100 U.S. government agencies, including information on agriculture, industry, defense policy, energy, and more. Retrospective from 1-80.

*Please contact publisher for prices.

Audience	Retrieval System	Computer Compatibility	Minimum Memory	Initial Release Date	Update Freq./Price
Libraries.		PC or PS/2 with PC- or MS-DOS version 2.0 or higher and 1 MB hard disk	512K		Quarterly $2,700.00/Year
Industrial companies, manufacturers; anyone who must comply with EPA regulations.	MARCON AIRS Inc.	PC/XT/AT	550K	02/12/87	Bimonthly *
Government and government contractors.	RESEARCH TMS, Inc.	PC/XT/AT	640K	11/86	Annually $495.00/Disc
Libraries.	Impact Auto-Graphics Inc.	PC/XT/AT	512K	11/87	Monthly or Bimonthly *
Public, academic, and law libraries.	Proprietary Information Access Company		640K	01/86	Monthly $2,500.00/ System per Year
Library reference market.	SilverPlatter Information Retrieval System SilverPlatter Information, Inc.	PC with DOS version 2.1 or higher	640K	05/88	Bimonthly $950.00/Disc
Libraries.	WILSONDISC H.W. Wilson Company	PC/XT/AT	640K	03/88	Annually $995.00/Year

(continued)

CD-ROM TITLES BY SUBJECT *continued*

Subject	Title	Publisher	Description
GOVERNMENT *continued*	*Le Pac: Government Documents Option*	Brodart Automation, a division of Brodart Company 500 Arch Street Williamsport, PA 17705 (800)233–8467	U.S. Government Printing Office Monthly Catalog: 230,000 depository and non-depository titles.
	Marcive/GPO CAT PAC	Marcive, Inc. P.O. Box 47508 San Antonio, TX 78265 (800)531–7678	U.S. government printing office data since 1976.
	Microsoft Stat Pack	Microsoft Corporation 16011 N.E. 36th Way P.O. Box 97017 Redmond, WA 98073-9717 (206)882–8080	Easy access to government statistics including the U.S. Statistical Abstracts, Area Wage Surveys, and Land and Agricultural Statistics. Works with a word processor and contains spreadsheet files for Microsoft Excel and Lotus 123 to allow manipulation of the available data.
	Optext	VLS, Inc. 310 South Reynolds Road Toledo, OH 43623 (419)536–5820	The Code of Federal Regulations and the Federal Register.
	PAIS on CD-ROM	Public Affairs Information Service, Inc. 521 West 43rd Street New York, NY 10036-4396 (212)736–6629	The combined records of the PAIS BULLETIN and the PAIS FOREIGN LANGUAGE INDEX.
	Parts-Master	National Standards Association Inc. 1200 Quince Orchard Boulevard Gaithersburg, MD 20878 (800)638–8094	Information on over 12 million parts and products procured and/or stocked by the U.S. government.
	TLRN-CD2	Innovative Technology Inc. 7927 Jones Branch Drive McLean, VA 22102 (703)734–3000	Federal Supply Catalog.

*Please contact publisher for prices.

Audience	Retrieval System	Computer Compatibility	Minimum Memory	Initial Release Date	Update Freq./Price
Libraries.	*Le Pac* Brodart Automation	PC/XT/AT	512K	11/86	Bimonthly $2,900.00/Year
Libraries.	*Marcive/PAC* Marcive, Inc.	PC/XT/AT with DOS version 3.0 or higher and 20 MB hard disk	640K	09/88	Bimonthly $995.00/Year
Researchers, writers, students, libraries.	*Proprietary* Microsoft Corporation	PC/XT/AT or compatible with DOS version 3.1, 3.2, or 3.3 and MS-DOS CD-ROM Extensions	640K	10/88	$149.00/Disc
Libraries, law libraries, heavily regulated industries.	*Optext RESEARCH* TMS, Inc.	PC/XT/AT or PS/2 with 10 MB hard disk	512K		Quarterly $1,390.00/Year
Libraries.	*CD-ROM Search and Retrieval Software* Online Computer Systems Inc.	PC/XT/AT or PS/2 with DOS version 3.1 or higher. Hard disk recommended.	640K	10/87	Quarterly $1,795.00/Year
		PC/XT/AT with DOS version 3.1 or higher	640K	11/86	Monthly $6,650.00/Year
Procurement, provisioning, and cataloging.	*B-Tree* Faircom	PC/XT/AT	512K	11/87	Quarterly *

(continued)

CD-ROM TITLES BY SUBJECT *continued*

Subject	Title	Publisher	Description
GOVERNMENT *continued*	*U.S. Government Printing Office Monthly Catalog (GPO)*	H.W. Wilson Company 950 University Avenue Bronx, NY 10452 (800)367–6770	The online counterpart to the printed Monthly Catalog of U.S. Government Publications, this database provides access to bibliographic data on publications generated by Federal Government agencies, including reports, studies, fact sheets, conference proceedings, and more. Retrospective from 7-76.
HEALTH AND SAFETY	*CCINFOdisc: Series A1 and A2: Chemical Information*	Canadian Centre for Occupational Health & Safety 250 Main Street East Hamilton, ON L8N 1H6 CANADA (416)572–2981	Chemical safety information in French and English, as created by CCOHS or supplied by contributors. Series A1 includes: TRADE NAMES Data Base, CHEMINFO Data Base, Regulatory Information on Pesticide Products (RIPP) Data Base, and Videotex Information Packages. Series A2 includes: CHEMINFO Data Base, Registry of Toxic Effects of Chemical Substances (RTECS) Data Base, Transportation of Dangerous Goods (TDG) Data Base, CCOHS publications, New Jersey Department of Health Hazardous Substance Fact Sheets, and Videotex Information Packages.
	CCINFOdisc: Series B Occupational Health and Safety Information	Canadian Centre for Occupational Health & Safety 250 Main Street East Hamilton, ON L8N 1H6 CANADA (416)572–2981	Entries on all aspects of occupational health and safety, in French and English as created by CCOHS or supplied by contributors. Series B includes: CANADIAN STUDIES Data Base, RESOURCE ORGANIZATIONS Data Base, RESOURCE PEOPLE Data Base, CANADIANA Data Base, ESSENTIALS Data Base, CASE LAW Data Base, STANDARDS AND DIRECTORIES Data Base, NOISE LEVELS Data Base, CISILO Data Base, NIOSHTIC Data Base, and Videotex Information Packages.
	Health Index on InfoTrac	Information Access Company 362 Lakeside Drive Foster City, CA 94404 (800)227–8431	Indexing to consumer health literature and health-related articles from newspapers and popular business and academic journals.
	Health/Stats	Hopkins Technology 421 Hazel Lane Hopkins, MN 55343-7117 (612)931–9376	Health studies and statistics.
	Material Safety Data System	National Safety Data Corporation 259 West Road Salem, CT 06415 (203)859–1162	35,000 Material Safety Data Sheets used for determining the hazards of chemicals.

Audience	Retrieval System	Computer Compatibility	Minimum Memory	Initial Release Date	Update Freq./Price
Libraries.	WILSONDISC H.W. Wilson Company	PC/XT/AT	640K	03/88	Annually $995.00/Year
Labor, employers, governments, professionals, health and safety committee.	FindIt Reteaco, Inc.	PC/XT/AT with DOS version 3.0 or higher and MS-DOS CD-ROM Extensions version 2.0	512K	08/87	Quarterly $114.00/Year
Labor, employers, governments, professionals, health and safety committees.	FindIt Reteaco, Inc.	PC/XT/AT with DOS version 3.0 or higher and MS-DOS CD-ROM Extensions version 2.0	512K	08/87	Quarterly $114.00/Disc
Public, academic, special librarians.	Proprietary Information Access Company		640K	10/88	Monthly $2,000.00/System per Year
Libraries, universities, corporate.	QuAcc Hopkins Technology	PC with MS-DOS version 3.1 or higher and MS-DOS CD-ROM Extensions	200K	01/89	Every 2 years $49.00/Disc
Safety and health professionals.	Quantum Leap Quantum Access	PC/XT/AT	640K	11/87	$750.00

(continued)

CD-ROM TITLES BY SUBJECT *continued*

Subject	Title	Publisher	Description
HEALTH AND SAFETY *continued*	OHS MSDS ON DISC	Occupational Health Services, Inc. 450 Seventh Avenue Suite 2407 New York, NY 10123 (800)445–6737	Thousands of Material Safety Data Sheets.
INDUSTRIAL	CD-ROM: The Conference Disc	PDO 1402 Foulk Road Suite 200 Wilmington, DE 19803 (302)479–2500	Cooperative effort of attendees of the Microsoft Second International Conference on CD-ROM.
	Electronic Sweet's	McGraw-Hill Book Company 11 West 19th Street New York, NY 10011 (212)512–2000	Manufacturing product catalog.
	Kwikee Inhouse Pal	Multi-Ad Services Inc. 1720 West Detweiler Drive Peoria, IL 61615 (800)447–1950	Vector art, potpourri collection.
LANGUAGE & LITERATURE	Computer Library	Computer Library/Ziff Communications 1 Park Avenue New York, NY 10016 (212)503–4400	12 months worth of full-text articles and abstracts from over 120 computer publications.
	The Constitution Papers	Optical Media International Reflective Arts International 495 Alberto Way Los Gatos, CA 95032 (408)395–4332	Contains the U.S. Constitution Papers and an audio file "Heartland/An American Anthem."
	Dissertation Abstracts Ondisc: Archival Edition	UMI (University Microfilms International) 300 North Zeeb Road Ann Arbor, MI 48106 (800)521–3044	Bibliographic citations for dissertations and masters theses published from 1861 through June 1984.
	Dissertation Abstracts Ondisc: Current Edition	UMI (University Microfilms International) 300 North Zeeb Road Ann Arbor, MI 48106 (800)521–3044	Bibliographic citations and 350-word abstracts for 100,000 doctoral dissertations and masters theses.

Audience	Retrieval System	Computer Compatibility	Minimum Memory	Initial Release Date	Update Freq./Price
Emergency response units, corporations, universities, federal, state, and local governments.	RESEARCH TMS, Inc.	PC/XT/AT with DOS version 3.1 or higher	Negligible	05/87	Quarterly $5,000.00/First year
					$20.00/Disc
					$115.00/Disc
					$149.95/Disc
Infocenter managers, MIS managers, PC coordinators, computer product marketers and developers.	BlueFish Lotus Development Corporation	PC/XT/AT with .5 MB free hard disk space and MS-DOS version 3.1 or higher	512K	09/20/88	Monthly $695.00/Year
	Electronic Text Corporation				$29.95
Academic and corporate libraries, researchers.	UMI RESEARCH UMI (University Microfilms International)	PC/XT/AT with hard disk	640K	09/87	$5,495.00/System
Academic and corporate libraries, researchers.	UMI RESEARCH UMI (University Microfilms International)	PC/XT/AT with hard disk	640K	04/87	Semiannually $1,695.00/Year

(continued)

CD-ROM TITLES BY SUBJECT *continued*

Subject	Title	Publisher	Description
LANGUAGE AND LITERATURE *continued*	*Essay and General Literature Index*	H.W. Wilson Company 950 University Avenue Bronx, NY 10452 (800)367–6770	Emphasizing the humanities and social sciences, this database offers access to a wide variety of information in English-language essay collections and anthologies, including criticisms of literary works, drama, and film; bibliographies; and books by and about authors from all periods of history and of all nationalities. Retrospective from 1-85.
	LISA	SilverPlatter Information, Inc. 37 Walnut Street Wellesley Hills, MA 02181 (617)239–0306	Abstracts of the world's literature in librarianship, information science, and related disciplines as compiled by Library Association Publishing, Ltd. Covers the complete database from 1969 with records from 1967 and 1968.
	MLA International Bibliography	H.W. Wilson Company 950 University Avenue Bronx, NY 10452 (800)367–6770	Published by the Modern Language Association of America, this database covers current scholarship in the modern languages, literature, and folklore, providing bibliographic data on some 3,000 journals and series, monographs, and book collections, yielding more than 40,000 new records annually. Retrospective from 1-81.
	National Newspaper Index on InfoTrac	Information Access Company 362 Lakeside Drive Foster City, CA 94404 (800)227–8431	Index to the *New York Times, Wall Street Journal, Christian Science Monitor, Washington Post,* and *Los Angeles Times.* Coverage includes past 3 years plus the current year.
	OCLC Compact Disc Cataloging System	Online Computer Library Center 6565 Frantz Road Dublin, OH 43017-0702 (614)764–6000	
	Pravda 1987 on CD-ROM	ALDE Publishing 4830 West 77th Street P.O. Box 35326 Minneapolis, MN 55435 (612)835–5240	Translation of the Pravda newspaper, '86-'87.
	Readers' Guide Abstracts	H.W. Wilson Company 950 University Avenue Bronx, NY 10452 (800)367–6770	Indexing and abstracting for more than 180 periodicals from September 1984 to present. Indexing retrospective from 1-83. Abstracting retrospective from 9-84.

*Please contact publisher for prices.

Audience	Retrieval System	Computer Compatibility	Minimum Memory	Initial Release Date	Update Freq./Price
Libraries.	WILSONDISC H.W. Wilson Company	PC/XT/AT	640K	03/88	Annually $695.00/Year
Library reference market.	SilverPlatter Information Retrieval System SilverPlatter Information, Inc.	PC with DOS version 2.1 or higher	640K	02/87	Semiannually $995.00/Unit
Libraries.	WILSONDISC H.W. Wilson Company	PC/XT/AT	640K	10/87	Quarterly $1,495.00/Year
Public and academic libraries.	Proprietary Information Access Company		640K	09/88	Monthly $4,000.00/ System per Year
					Monthly or quarterly *
Libraries, schools, intelligence community.	FastFind Creative Index	PC/XT/AT	640K		Annually $249.00/Disc
Libraries.	WILSONDISC H.W. Wilson Company	PC/XT/AT	640K	10/87	Quarterly $1,995.00/Year

(continued)

CD-ROM TITLES BY SUBJECT *continued*

Subject	Title	Publisher	Description
LANGUAGE AND LITERATURE *continued*	*Readers' Guide to Periodical Literature*	H.W. Wilson Company 950 University Avenue Bronx, NY 10452 (800)367–6770	Index of general interest popular magazines covering news, current events, fashion, etc. Retrospective from 1-83.
	The Visual Dictionary	Facts on File, Inc. 460 Park Avenue South New York, NY 10016 (800)322–8755	A collection of pictures, text, and sound in French, Spanish, and English.
LEGAL	*LAW MARC*	Utlas International 8300 College Boulevard Overland Park, KS 66210 (800)33–UTLAS	The entire Library of Congress file of law-related bibliographic records.
	Decision Series: California Decisions	ROM Publishers Inc. 1033 'O' Street Mezzanine Level Lincoln, NE 68508 (402)476–2965	California case law.
	Decision Series: Federal Decisions	ROM Publishers Inc. 1033 'O' Street Mezzanine Level Lincoln, NE 68508 (402)476–2965	Federal Court of Appeals case law.
	Decision Series: Federal Supplemental Decisions	ROM Publishers Inc. 1033 'O' Street Mezzanine Level Lincoln, NE 68508 (402)476–2965	Federal District Court case law.
	Decision Series: Northwest Regional Decisions	ROM Publishers Inc. 1033 'O' Street Mezzanine Level Lincoln, NE 68508 (402)476–2965	Case law from a 7 state region including North Dakota, South Dakota, Nebraska, Iowa, Wisconsin, Michigan, and Minnesota.
	Index to Legal Periodicals	H.W. Wilson Company 950 University Avenue Bronx, NY 10452 (800)367–6770	Index of articles from approximately 500 legal journals, yearbooks, etc. Retrospective from 8-81.
	LegalTrac on InfoTrac	Information Access Company 362 Lakeside Drive Foster City, CA 94404 (800)227–8431	Provides indexing of over 800 legal publications, including all major law reviews, bar association journals, specialty publications, and seven legal newspapers, with coverage from 1980 to the present.

*Please contact publisher for prices.

Audience	Retrieval System	Computer Compatibility	Minimum Memory	Initial Release Date	Update Freq./Price
Libraries.	WILSONDISC H.W. Wilson Company	PC/XT/AT	640K	04/87	Quarterly $1,095.00/Year
Language teachers.	Media-Mixer Software Mart Inc.	PC/Macintosh/Apple			*
Libraries.	CD-CATSS Utlas Internatioanl	PC/XT/AT	640K	06/88	$750.00/Disc
Attorneys, corporate legal divisions.	Reference Technology, Inc.	PC/XT/AT with hard disk	640K	01/89	Quarterly $2,695.00/Year
Attorneys, corporate legal divisions.	Reference Technology, Inc.	PC/XT/AT with hard disk	640K	03/89	Quarterly $5,400.00/Year
Attorneys, corporate legal divisions.	Reference Technology, Inc.	PC/XT/AT with hard disk	640K	03/89	Quarterly $5,780.00/Year
Attorneys, corporate legal divisions.	Reference Technology, Inc.	PC/XT/AT with hard disk	640K	09/88	Quarterly $2,690.00/Year
			640K	04/87	Quarterly $1,495.00/Year
Law school libraries.	Proprietary Information Access Company		640K	08/85	Monthly $5,000.00/ System per Year

(continued)

CD-ROM TITLES BY SUBJECT *continued*

Subject	Title	Publisher	Description
LEGAL *continued*	*The Texas Attorney General Documents*	Quantum Access Inc. 1700 West Loop South Suite 1460 Houston, TX 77027 (713)622–3211	Attorney General opinions, open records, and decisions from 1973-1988.
LIBRARIES	*Access Pennsylvania High School Library Catalog, 3rd Edition*	Pennsylvania State Library Pennsylvania Department of Education School Library Media Services 333 Market Street Harrisburg, PA 17126-0333 (717)787–6704	Full MARC records of 400 school, public, and academic libraries.
	BIBLIOFILE Catalog Production	Library Corporation P.O. Box 40035 Washington, DC 20016 (800)624–0559	Catalog card and label production in MARC II format.
	BIBLIOFILE Catalog Maintenance	Library Corporation P.O. Box 40035 Washington DC 20016 (800)624–0559	Based on the BIBLIOFILE Catalog Production system, allows you to maintain your own database/MARC file.
	British Library/ Bibliotheque Nationale Pilot Disc	British Library 2 Sheraton Street London W1V 4BH ENGLAND 01/323-7073	Subsets of national bibliographies from the British Library and the Bibliotheque Nationale.
	CDMARC Bibliographic	Library of Congress Cataloging Distribution Service Washington, DC 20541 (202)287–6100	Entire Library of Congress bibliographic file containing books, serials, maps, visual materials, and music.
	CD-CATSS	Utlas International 2150 Shattuck Avenue Suite 402 Berkeley, CA 94704 (415)841–9442	4 discs with approximately 2 million bibliographic records from 1984-present.
	CDMARC Names	Library of Congress Cataloging Distribution Service Washington, DC 20541 (202)287–6100	Personal and corporate name authority file of the Library of Congress, on 3 discs.

*Please contact publisher for prices.

Audience	Retrieval System	Computer Compatibility	Minimum Memory	Initial Release Date	Update Freq./Price
Administrative lawyers.	Quantum Leap Quantum Access Inc.	PC/XT/AT	512K		Sporadically $600.00/Disc
Libraries.	Le Pac Brodart Automation	PC/XT/AT	640K	09/15/88	Annually *
Libraries.	BIBLIOFILE Library Corporation	PC/XT/AT or PS/2 Model 30	512K	12/84	* $1,750.00/ Startup package
Libraries.	BIBLIOFILE Library Corporation	PC/XT/AT	640K	01/86	*
Libraries.	OCSI Software Online Computer Systems Inc.	PC/XT/AT	512K	10/88	Free
Libraries.	Online	PC/XT/AT with DOS version 3.1 or higher and hard disk	640K		*
Libraries.	CD-CATSS Utlas International	PC/XT/AT	640K	10/88	Quarterly $1,800.00/Year
Libraries.	Online	PC/XT/AT with DOS version 3.1 or higher and hard disk	640K	03/89	Quarterly *

(continued)

CD-ROM TITLES BY SUBJECT *continued*

Subject	Title	Publisher	Description
LIBRARIES *continued*	CDMARC Subjects	Library of Congress Cataloging Distribution Service Washington, DC 20541 (202)287–6100	Subject Authority file from the Library of Congress.
	Enhanced BIBLIOFILE	Library Corporation P.O. Box 40035 Washington DC 20016 (800)624–0559	A central processing special package based on a custom profile of the library.
	The Intelligent Catalog	Library Corporation P.O. Box 40035 Washington, DC 20016 (800)624–0559	Library's own holdings.
	Iowa Locater, 3rd Edition	Iowa State Library Networking Department East 12th and Grand Des Moines, IA 50319 (515)281–4118	Holdings of 400 Iowa libraries.
	The Kansas Library Catalog	Kansas State Library Statehouse 3rd Floor Topeka, KS 66612-1593 (913)296–3296	Union catalog of approximately 2 million bibliographic titles and 5 million holding statements for 450 libraries in Kansas. Covers 1974—March 1988 on 2 discs.
	LaserCat	Western Library Network Mail Stop AJ-11W Olympia, WA 98504-0111 (206)459–6518	A portion of the Western Library Network database containing information about approximately 2.4 million titles and 11 million library call numbers.
	LAsernet Database	State Library of Louisiana P.O. Box 131 Baton Rouge, LA 70821 (504)342–4923	Union catalog containing over one million MARC records and holding codes for over 100 Louisiana public and academic libraries, linked to an automated statewide interlibrary loan referral system.
	LaserQuest	General Research Corporation, Library Systems 5383 Hollister Avenue Santa Barbara, CA 93111 (800)235–6788	LaserQuest, a CD-ROM cataloging system for libraries, contains the GRC Resource Database of 6 million MARC records from the Library of Congress and the National Library of Canada, including more than 2 million contributed records. LaserQuest provides foreign and English titles as well as music, serials, A/V, maps, and mauscripts. More than 1.9 million records are pre-1968. The cumulated bimonthly supplement adds about 150,000 new and newly cataloged old materials.

*Please contact publisher for prices.

Audience	Retrieval System	Computer Compatibility	Minimum Memory	Initial Release Date	Update Freq./Price
Libraries.	Online	PC/XT/AT with DOS version 3.1 or higher and hard disk	640K	06/88	Quarterly $300.00/Year
Libraries.	*BIBLIOFILE* Library Corporation				*
Libraries.	*Proprietary* Library Corporation	Proprietary system		01/87	Monthly $2,770.00/ Workstation
Libraries.	*Locater* Iowa State Library	PC/XT/AT with 2 CD-ROM drives.	640K	09/15/88	Quarterly $50.00/Quarter
Kansas libraries.	*Le Pac* Brodart Automation	PC/XT/AT	640K	08/88	Annually *
Libraries.	*Proprietary* Western Library Network	Requires 2 Hitachi or Sony drives (uses Meridian Data low level driver)	512K	02/87	Quarterly $1,300.00/Year
Louisiana libraries.	*Spectrum 1000* Library Systems and Services, Inc. (LSSI)	PC/XT or PS/2 with 20 MB hard disk and DOS version 3.1 or higher	640K	01/89	Biannually *
Public, academic, and special libraries.	*LaserQuest* General Research Corporation, Library Systems	PC/XT/AT or PS/2 Model 30	512K	07/86	Bimonthly *

(continued)

CD-ROM TITLES BY SUBJECT *continued*

Subject	Title	Publisher	Description
LIBRARIES *continued*	*Library Literature*	H.W. Wilson Company 950 University Avenue Bronx, NY 10452 (800)367–6770	Indexes library periodicals, state journals, monographs, and films from around the world. Retrospective from 12-84.
	MaineCat	Maine State Library Statehouse Station #64 Augusta, ME 04333 (207)289–5600	Statewide database of approximately 1 million titles representing approximately 2 million volumes, on 2 discs.
	MCAT (Missouri Union Catalog)	Missouri State Library P.O. Box 387 Jefferson City, MO 65102 (314)751–3033	Unioon catalog of library holdings in Missouri. Some 230 Missouri libraries are participating in the project, including every public library, most academic libraries, and many special and school libraries. Intended to improve and enhance resource sharing among Missouri libraries.
	SuperCAT Library of Congress MARC: English	Gaylord Information Systems P.O. Box 4901 Syracuse, NY 13221-4901 (315)457–5070	The Library of Congress MARC records in English.
	SuperCAT Library of Congress MARC: Foreign Languages	Gaylord Information Systems P.O. Box 4901 Syracuse, NY 13221-4901 (315)457–5070	Library of Congress MARC records in all foreign languages.
	WISCAT	Wisconsin Reference and Loan Library 2109 South Stoughton Road Madison, WI 53716 (608)221–6161	3.25 million bibliographic records from 365 Wisconsin libraries. A total of 14.5 million holdings.
LIBRARIES & PUBLIC SERVICE	*Discon*	Utlas International 8300 College Boulevard Overland Park, KS 66210 (800)33–UTLAS	6 million brief bibliographic records from the Library of Congress card catalog, up to 1984, on 4 discs.
MAPS & CENSUS	*1982 Census of Agriculture*	Slater Hall Information Products 1522 K Street N.W. Suite 522 Washington, DC 20005 (202)682–1350	The complete Census Bureau County file: acreage, operating expenses, production, sales, crops, livestock, and more, with 3,360 data items for each county and state, and U.S. totals for each item.

*Please contact publisher for prices.

Audience	Retrieval System	Computer Compatibility	Minimum Memory	Initial Release Date	Update Freq./Price
Libraries.	WILSONDISC H.W. Wilson Company	PC/XT/AT	640K	04/87	Quarterly $1,095.00/Year
Libraries.	Impact Auto-Graphics	PC/XT/AT with DOS version 3.1 or higher and 2 drives	640K	11/88	Biannually *
Libraries.	Le Pac Brodart Automation	PC/XT/AT	640K	09/30/88	Quarterly *
Libraries.	SuperCAT Gaylord Information Systems	PC/XT or PS/2 Model 30	640K	09/15/88	Quarterly $850.00/Year
Libraries.	SuperCAT Gaylord Information Systems	PC/XT or PS/2 Model 30	640K	09/15/88	Quarterly $500.00/Year
Wisconsin libraries.	Le Pac Brodart Automation	PC/XT/AT	640K	01/89	Annually $60.00/Year
Libraries.	CD-CATSS Utlas International	PC/XT/AT	640K	06/86	$680.00/Month
Libraries, agribusiness companies, market researchers.	SEARCHER Slater Hall	PC/XT/AT	512K	11/86	$1,200.00/Disc

(continued)

CD-ROM TITLES BY SUBJECT *continued*

Subject	Title	Publisher	Description
MAPS AND CENSUS *continued*	*Census Test Disk 2*	U.S. Bureau of the Census Customer Services Washington, DC 20233 (301)763–4100	Contains data from the Census of Agriculture, 1982: Final County File; and the Census of Retail Trade, 1982: ZIP Code File. Data is arranged in dBASE III input format. Paper copy of technical documentation is included. Both files are included on a single disc.
	Consu/Stats I	Hopkins Technology 421 Hazel Lane Hopkins, MN 55343-7117 (612)931–9376	Contains the complete public use source data files on 1984 Surveys of Consumer Expenditures including detailed interview and diary data. These huge databases cover hundreds of characteristics of consumer units, family members, income and expenditures. The data also includes major appliance inventories and purchases, trips and vacations, vehicle purchases and vehicle disposals.
	County, metro area statistics	Slater Hall Information Products 1522 K Street N.W. Suite 522 Washington, DC 20005 (202)682–1350	Population, housing, health, education, business, agriculture, crime statistics, and more; with over 1,000 data items for each county, state, and metro area.
	DeLorme's World Atlas	DeLorme Mapping Systems P.O. Box 298 Freeport, ME 04032 (207)865–4171	Worldwide vector-based atlas.
	The Electronic Map Cabinet	Highlighted Data, Inc. Washington-Dallas International Airport P.O. Box 17229 Washington, DC 20041 (703)241–1180	U.S. geographics.
	EtakMap National Transportation Network	ETAK, Inc. 1455 Adams Drive Menlo Park, CA 94025 (415)328–3825	A national street network database with metro areas digitized from USGS 1/24,000 quad maps, including all Census Bureau DIME address and political attribute information.

*Please contact publisher for prices.

Audience	Retrieval System	Computer Compatibility	Minimum Memory	Initial Release Date	Update Freq./Price
		PC/XT/AT		06/88	$125.00/Disc
Marketers, university, library, financial.	QuAcc Hopkins Technology	PC with MS-DOS version 3.1 or higher and MS-DOS CD-ROM Extensions	200K	07/88	$49.00/Disc
Libraries, corporations, state and local governments.	SEARCHER Slater Hall	PC/XT/AT	512K	12/87	Annually $1,200.00/Disc
					*
	Proprietary Highlighted Data, Inc.	Mac SE, Plus, or II with 1 MB	1 MB	09/88	$199.95/Disc
	ETAK Geocoder ETAK	386 PC SCO XENIX	4MB		*

(continued)

CD-ROM TITLES BY SUBJECT *continued*

Subject	Title	Publisher	Description
MAPS AND CENSUS *continued*	*GEOdisc State Atlas Series*	Geovision, Inc. 270 Scientific Drive Suite 1 Norcross, GA 30092 (404)448–8224	Geographic database of detailed vector graphic information for individual states showing all major roads and highways, railroads, water features, political boundaries, and proper place names. Also included are minor and secondary roads, seasonal water features, and power lines.
	GEOdisc U.S. Atlas	Geovision, Inc. 270 Scientific Drive Suite 1 Norcross, GA 30092 (404)448–8224	Geographic database of detailed vector graphic information showing all major roads and highways, railroads, water features, political boundaries, and over 1 million proper place names. Also included are minor and secondary roads, seasonal water features, and power lines.
	MetroScan: El Dorado County	Digital Diagnostics, Inc. 601 University Avenue Suite 255 Sacramento, CA 95825 (916)921–6629	Descriptions of all land parcels in El Dorado county.
	MetroScan: Placer County	Digital Diagnostics, Inc. 601 University Avenue Suite 255 Sacramento, CA 95825 (916)921–6629	Descriptions of all land parcels in Placer County.
	MetroScan: Sacramento County	Digital Diagnostics, Inc. 601 University Avenue Suite 255 Sacramento, CA 95825 (916)921–6629	Descriptions of all land parcels in Sacramento county.
	MetroScan: Yolo County	Digital Diagnostics, Inc. 601 University Avenue Suite 255 Sacramento, CA 95825 (916)921–6629	Descriptions of all land parcels in Yolo county.
	Place-Name Index	Buckmaster Publishing Route 3 Box 56 Mineral, VA 23117 (703)894–5777	Over 1 million place names from Geological Survey topographic maps.

Audience	Retrieval System	Computer Compatibility	Minimum Memory	Initial Release Date	Update Freq./Price
Utility companies, oil and gas site explorers, politicians, surveyors, federal, state, and local government, consulting engineers, hazardous waste managers, transportation managers.	*Windows/On the World or PC CAD interface* Geovision, Inc.	PC/AT or PS/2 with hard disk drive and mouse	640K	07/88	Every 24 months $1,995.00/Disc
Utility companies, oil and gas site surveyors, politicians, transportation, natural resource managers, hazardous waste, education, government.	*Windows/On the World or PC CAD interface* Geovision, Inc.	PC/AT or PS/2 with hard disk drive and mouse	640K	01/88	Every 24 months $495.00/Disc
Real estate industry: appraisers, title companies, realtors, developers.	*Proprietary* Digital Diagnostics, Inc.	PC/XT/AT	640K	10/87	Monthly $350.00/Year
Real estate industry: appraisers, title companies, realtors, developers.	*Proprietary* Digital Diagnostics, Inc.	PC/XT/AT	640K	10/87	Monthly $350.00/Year
Real estate industry: appraisers, title companies, realtors, developers.	*Proprietary* Digital Diagnostics, Inc.	PC/XT/AT	640K	10/87	Monthly $600.00/Year
Real estate industry: appraisers, title companies, realtors, developers.	*Proprietary* Digital Diagnostics, Inc.	PC/XT/AT	640K	10/87	Monthly $300.00/Year
Libraries, geologists, researchers, historians.	*Textware* Unibase	PC/XT/AT		03/88	Annually $295.00/Year

(continued)

CD-ROM TITLES BY SUBJECT *continued*

Subject	Title	Publisher	Description
MAPS AND CENSUS *continued*	*POPLINE*	SilverPlatter Information, Inc. 37 Walnut Street Wellesley Hills, MA 02181 (617)239–0306	The world's largest bibliographic population database, containing more than 150,000 citations on population, family planning and related health care, law and policy issues.
	Population Statistics on CD-ROM	Slater Hall Information Products 1522 K Street N.W. Suite 522 Washington, DC 20005 (202)682–1350	Full range of population and housing characteristics from the 1980 census for the U.S. All states, metro areas, counties, places of 10,000 or more, and congressional districts.
	Supermap 1.0 1981 Australian Census	Chadwyck-Healy Ltd. Cambridge Place Cambridge CB2 1NR ENGLAND 0223 311479	Data from the 1981 Australian census.
	Supermap 1.1 1980 U.S. Census County Level	Chadwyck-Healy Ltd. Cambridge Place Cambridge CB2 1NR ENGLAND 0223 311479	Contains the two main summary tape files from the 1980 U.S. census.
	Swedish Census Data	National Land Survey of Sweden 80112 Havle SWEDEN 026/100340	Maps depicting all areas of Sweden on several different scales, including census data.
MARKETING AND SALES	*CD Town Page*	Dai Nippon Ichigaya-kagacho Shinjuka-ku Tokyo 162 JAPAN 03/266–2111	Tokyo business phone numbers.
	Your Marketing Consultant: Advanced Consumer	Knowledge Access International, Inc. 2685 Marine Way Suite 1305 Mountain View, CA 94043 (415)969–0606	Demographic marketing data on 3,137 counties, 316 metropolitan areas, and 423 other U.S. geographical units, as well as a complete set of on-screen state maps which can be displayed at three levels of magnification.

*Please contact publisher for prices.

Audience	Retrieval System	Computer Compatibility	Minimum Memory	Initial Release Date	Update Freq./Price
Library reference market.	*SilverPlatter Information Retrieval System* SilverPlatter Information, Inc.	PC with DOS version 2.1 or higher	640K	11/88	Semiannually $750.00/Year
Libraries, state and local government agencies, market researchers.	*SEARCHER* Slater Hall	PC/XT/AT	512K	07/88	$1,200.00/Disc
		PC/XT/AT	512K min.	04/87	*
		PC/XT/AT	512K min.	10/87	$990.00
	CENTEK TOPO	PC/AT		09/87	*
					*
Site locaters, market researchers, media buyers, sales managers, educators.	*KAware2* Knowledge Access International	PC	640K	09/87	Annually $950.00/Year

(continued)

CD-ROM TITLES BY SUBJECT *continued*

Subject	Title	Publisher	Description
MARKETING AND SALES *continued*	*Your Marketing Consultant: Business to Business*	Knowledge Access International, Inc. 2685 Marine Way Suite 1305 Mountain View, CA 94043 (415)969–0606	Demographic marketing data on 3,137 counties, 316 metropolitan areas, and 423 other U.S. geographical units as well as a complete set of on-screen state maps which can be displayed at three levels of magnification.
MATHEMATICS	*MathSci Disc*	SilverPlatter Information, Inc. 37 Walnut Street Wellesley Hills, MA 02181 (617)239–0306	The Mathematical Reviews from 1985 through 1988 and more than 50,000 entries from Current Mathematical Publications. Covers the literature of mathematics and related fields such as statistics, computer science, and engineering.
MEDICAL	*AfterCare Instructions*	Micromedex, Inc. 660 Bannock Street Suite 300 Denver, CO 80204-4506 (800)525–9083	AfterCare Instructions is a simple-to-use system that provides easily understood instructions for health care professionals to give to patients discharged from an emergency department or clinic setting, and referenced protocols for the medical evaluation and treatment of individuals exposed to chemical agents are provided. Protocols for initial response to incidents (fires, spills, leaks) from hazardous materials are also included. Agents are indexed by chemical names, synonyms, and commonly associated numbers (CAS, RTECS/NIOSH, UN, NA ENT, USAF, etc.).
	AIDS Supplement	Digital Diagnostics, Inc. 601 University Avenue Suite 255 Sacramento, CA 95825 (916)921–6629	Over 40,000 citations from the last 8 years, with cross references to 47 separate medical subject heading terms.
	BiblioMed	Digital Diagnostics, Inc. 601 University Avenue Suite 255 Sacramento, CA 95825 (916)921–6629	Excerpts from the National Library of Medicine's MEDLINE database: 500 journals for 3 years.
	CANCER-CD	SilverPlatter Information, Inc. 37 Walnut Street Wellesley Hills, MA 02181 (617)239–0306	References, abstracts and commentaries of the world's literature in cancer and related subjects. Coverage from 1983 to present.

*Please contact publisher for prices.

Audience	Retrieval System	Computer Compatibility	Minimum Memory	Initial Release Date	Update Freq./Price
Site locaters, market researchers, media buyers, sales managers.	KAware2 Knowledge Access International, Inc.	PC/XT/AT with MS-DOS version 3.1 or higher	640K	09/87	Annually $950.00/Year
Library reference market.	SilverPlatter Information Retrieval System SilverPlatter Information, Inc.	PC with DOS version 2.1 or higher	640K	01/89	Semiannually $3,510.00/Year
Physicians, nurses, healthcare professionals.	Proprietary Micromedex, Inc.	PC/XT/AT with DOS version 3.1 or higher	512K	05/88	Quarterly *
Health professionals.	Proprietary Digital Diagnostics, Inc	PC/XT/AT	640K	03/88	Quarterly $350.00/Year
Health professionals.	Proprietary Digital Diagnostics, Inc.	PC/XT/AT	640K	10/87	Quarterly $950.00/Year
Library reference market.	SilverPlatter Information Retrieval System SilverPlatter Information, Inc.	PC with DOS version 2.1 or higher	640K	10/87	Quarterly $1,750.00/Year

(continued)

CD-ROM TITLES BY SUBJECT *continued*

Subject	Title	Publisher	Description
MEDICAL *continued*	*CancerLIT*	Online Research Systems Inc. 2901 Broadway Suite 154 New York, NY 10025 (212)408-3311	NTIS CancerLIT database.
	Compact Cambridge MEDLINE	Cambridge Scientific Abstracts 7200 Wisconsin Avenue Suite 601 Bethesda, MD 20816 (301)961-6700	The complete MEDLINE database and abstracts including all journals and all languages.
	Compact Cambridge CancerLit (Cancer Literature)	Cambridge Scientific Abstracts 7200 Wisconsin Avenue Suite 601 Bethesda, MD 20816 (301)961-6700	Citations and abstracts taken by the National Cancer Institute from over 3,000 biomedical journals, including papers, reports, and doctoral theses.
	Compact Cambridge Drugs Database	Cambridge Scientific Abstracts 7200 Wisconsin Avenue Suite 601 Bethesda, MD 20816 (301)961-6700	Database from the American Society of Hospital Pharmacists including drug indication uses, side effects, toxicity, dosages, interaction, and chemical stability
	Compact Cambridge PDQ (Physicians' Data Query)	Cambridge Scientific Abstracts 7200 Wisconsin Avenue Suite 601 Bethesda, MD 20816 (301)961-6700	The National Cancer Institute's database consisting of cancer treatment information, ongoing treatment protocols (information on over 1000 treatment protocols and a limited number of standard treatment regimens), and a directory of over 12,000 physicians and surgeons and 1400 organizations that provide cancer care.
	Compact Library: AIDS	Medical Publishing Group 1440 Main Street Waltham, MA 02254 (617)893-3800	Comprehensive library of AIDS information including the AIDS Knowledge Base, MEDLINE citations dealing with AIDS, and the complete text of AIDS articles from 7 leading journals.
	Compact Med-Base	Online Research Systems Inc. 2901 Broadway Suite 154 New York, NY 10025 (212)408-3311	NTIS Medline database.

Audience	Retrieval System	Computer Compatibility	Minimum Memory	Initial Release Date	Update Freq./Price
Cancer researchers, clinicians.	CD-Plus Online Research Systems, Inc.	PC/XT/AT with MS-DOS CD-ROM Extensions	640K	01/89	Monthly $1,995.00/Year
Universities, medical schools, hospitals and pharmaceutical companies.	Compact Cambridge Cambridge Scientific Abstracts	PC/XT/AT	512K	06/86	Quarterly $1,250.00/Year
Hospitals, universities, researchers.	Compact Cambridge Cambridge Scientific Abstracts	PC/XT/AT	512K	09/88	Quarterly $995.00/Year
Hospitals, pharmaceutical companies.	Compact Cambridge Cambridge Scientific Abstracts	PC/XT/AT	512K	10/88	Monthly $1,950.00/Year
Universities, hospitals, researchers.	Compact Cambridge Cambridge Scientific Abstracts	PC/XT/AT	512K	08/88	Monthly $950.00/Year
Health care professionals.	Proprietary Medical Publishing Group	PC/XT/AT with MS-DOS CD-ROM Extensions version 2.0 and DOS version 3.1 or higher	640K	10/88	Quarterly $875.00/Year
Medical libraries, hospital departments.	CD-Plus Online Research Systems, Inc.	PC/XT/AT with MS-DOS CD-ROM Extensions	640K	05/88	Monthly $3,495.00/Year

(continued)

CD-ROM TITLES BY SUBJECT *continued*

Subject	Title	Publisher	Description
MEDICAL *continued*	COMPREHENSIVE MEDLINE/EBSCO CD-ROM	EBSCO Electronic Information P.O. Box 13787 Torrance, CA 90503 (800)888–EBSCO	The complete MEDLINE file from 1986-present, including Index Medicus, International Nursing Index, and Index to Dental Literature.
	CORE MEDLINE/ EBSCO CD-ROM	EBSCO Electronic Information P.O. Box 13787 Torrance, CA 90503 (800)888–EBSCO	A subset of the MEDLINE file for the past 2 years plus current year: Over 560 journals indexed; over 330,000 citations on one disc.
	DIALOG OnDisc MEDLINE	Dialog Information Services, Inc. 3460 Hillview Avenue Palo Alto, CA 94304 (800)334–2564	Includes references and abstracts from approximately 3,200 journals published in over 70 countries. 300,000 records are added each year, 70% of which represent publications written in the English language. Covers 1987-present.
	DOSING & THERAPEUTIC TOOLS	Micromedex, Inc. 660 Bannock Street Suite 300 Denver, CO 80204-4506 (800)525–9083	Dosing and Therapeutic Tools is a database that contains Nomograms and Drug Dosing, EKG Rhythm Strips, Diagnostic and Therapeutic Pearls, Different Diagnostic Lists, and Calculators. This database helps clinicians make calculations or decisions regarding specific patient problems.
	Drug Information Source	American Society of Hospital Pharmacists 4630 Montgomery Avenue Bethesda, MD 20814 (301)657–3000	Current issues of AHFS Drug Information and the Handbook on Injectable Drugs, plus over 15 years of International Pharmaceutical Abstracts (IPA) relating to drugs covered in those compilations.
	DRUGDEX System	Micromedex, Inc. 660 Bannock Street Suite 300 Denver, CO 80204-4506 (800)525–9083	The DRUGDEX System is an up-to-date, unbiased, and referenced drug information system. This system includes both Drug Evaluation Monographs and Drug Consults on investigational, foreign, FDA approved, and OTC preparations. This system is indexed by U.S. and foreign brand/trade names, generic names, and disease states.
	Eidetic	Eidetic Knowledge Systems 50 Valley Stream Parkway Malvern, PA 19355 (215)889–9780	Neuro- and renalpathology images and associated case data.

*Please contact publisher for prices.

Audience	Retrieval System	Computer Compatibility	Minimum Memory	Initial Release Date	Update Freq./Price
Medical and hospital libraries, health care professionals.	*EBSCO-CD* EBSCO Electronic Information	PC/XT/AT with MS-DOS version 3.1 or higher and 10 MB hard disk	640K	10/88	Quarterly $1,000.00/Year
Medical and hospital libraries, health care professionals.	*EBSCO-CD* EBSCO Electronic Information	PC/XT/AT with MS-DOS version 3.1 or higher and 10 MB hard disk	640K	01/88	Quarterly $1,400.00/Year
Libraries.		PC or PS/2 with PC- or MS-DOS version 2.0 or higher and 1 MB hard disk	512K		Quarterly $1,250.00/Year
Physicians, health care professionals.	*Proprietary* Micromedex, Inc.	PC/XT/AT with DOS version 3.1 or higher	512K	08/87	Quarterly *
Pharmacists, pharmaceutical companies, medical libraries.	*Compact Cambridge* Cambridge Information Group	PC/XT/AT/COMPAQ	640K	12/88	Semiannually $1,950.00/Year
Physicians, pharmacists, health care professionals.	*Proprietary* Micromedex, Inc.	PC/XT/AT with DOS version 3.1 or higher	512K	07/85	Quarterly *
Medical researchers, scientists.	*Proprietary* Eidetic Knowledge Systems	Sun Microsystems		01/89	$600.00

(continued)

CD-ROM TITLES BY SUBJECT *continued*

Subject	Title	Publisher	Description
MEDICAL *continued*	*EMERGINDEX System*	Micromedex, Inc. 660 Bannock Street Suite 300 Denver, CO 80204-4506 (800)525-9083	The EMERGINDEX System is a referenced clinical information system that presents pertinent data for the practice of acute care medicine. It is designed to help those who deal with acute medical/surgical disease and traumatic injuries to more quickly and efficiently diagnose and treat the multitude of problems encountered daily. The system includes Clinical Reviews, Clinical Abstracts, and Pre-Hospital Care Protocols. The database is indexed by a 40,000 key word medical thesaurus.
	Health Planning and Administration	Online Research Systems Inc. 2901 Broadway Suite 154 New York, NY 10025 (212)408-3311	Information relating to health care delivery.
	IDENTIDEX System	Micromedex, Inc. 660 Bannock Street Suite 300 Denver, CO 80204-4506 (800)525-9083	The IDENTIDEX System is a unique comprehensive tablet and capsule identification system that provides identification of pharmaceuticals primarily by the manufacturer's imprint code with secondary characteristics, such as color and shape, as descriptors. Descriptions of manufacturers' logos assist in differentiating among similar logos. Manufacturers' telephone numbers are also included. The IDENTIDEX System contains vast identification information on U.S. prescription and OTC drugs, both trademarked and generic. Many foreign drugs, street drugs, and timely street slang terminology are also included.
	LILACS	PAHO (Pan American World Health Organization) 525 23rd Street N.W. Washington, DC 20037 (202)861-3366	Bibliographic citations provided by regional medical centers throughout Latin America.

*Please contact publisher for prices.

Audience	Retrieval System	Computer Compatibility	Minimum Memory	Initial Release Date	Update Freq./Price
Physicians, health care professionals.	Proprietary Micromedex, Inc.	PC/XT/AT with DOS version 3.1 or higher	512K	07/85	Quarterly •
Hospitals.	CD-Plus Online Research Systems, Inc.	PC/XT/AT with MS-DOS CD-ROM Extensions	640K	01/89	Monthly $1,995.00/Year
Physicians, pharmacists, health care professionals, law enforcement agencies.	Proprietary Micromedex, Inc.	PC/XT/AT with DOS version 3.1 or higher	512K	07/85	Quarterly •
Distributed to health-related or public institutions in Latin America.	ISIS UNESCO	PC/XT/AT with DOS version 2.x/3.x and a 2.5 MB hard disk	640K	07/88	Biannually •

(continued)

CD-ROM TITLES BY SUBJECT *continued*

Subject	Title	Publisher	Description
MEDICAL *continued*	*MARTINDALE: The Extra Pharmacopoeia*	Micromedex, Inc. 660 Bannock Street Suite 300 Denver, CO 80204-4506 (800)525-9083	The CD-ROM version of the well-respected textbook published by the British Pharmaceutical Society, Martindale: The Extra Pharmacopoeia, is and extensive resource of information on drug products available in the United Kingdom. It includes information regarding chemical forms, therapeutic uses, adverse effects, and world-wide trade names. This version of the database also offers the ability to search by old English terms or their modern English synonyms. The database can be searched by international trade name, generic name, chemical name, and disease state.
	MAXX: Maximum Access to Diagnosis and Therapy	Little, Brown and Company 34 Beacon Street Boston, MA 02108 (617)227-0730	
	MEDLINE on SilverPlatter	SilverPlatter Information, Inc. 37 Walnut Street Wellesley Hills, MA 02181 (617)239-0306	The entire MEDLINE database of the National Library of Medicine from 1983 to present, containing bibliographic citations and abstracts for biomedical literature, and includes all foreign languages, all data elements, and is fully indexed.
	MEDLINE Knowledge Server	Aries Systems Corporation 79 Boxford Street North Andover, MA 01845-3219 (508)689-9334	5 years of the more important journals from the National Library of Medicine's database. Also full, unabridged MEDLINE discs.
	MEDLINE: BRS/ Colleague Disc	BRS Information Technologies 1200 Route 7 Latham, NY 12110 (800)468-0908	English language citations and abstracts from the National Library of Medicine's MEDLINE database.
	NATASHA: National Archive on Sexuality, Health & Adolescence	Knowledge Access International, Inc. 2685 Marine Way Suite 1305 Mountain View, CA 94043 (415)969-0606	109 data sets and 39,815 uniquely identified variables from 82 major studies relevant to the national problem of teenage pregnancy. Information on adolescent sexuality, health, marriage, education, and employment; more general information on family planning, infant health, and attitudes toward sexual issues; and information on social demographics are all included in this product at national, regional, and individual levels.

*Please contact publisher for prices.

Audience	Retrieval System	Computer Compatibility	Minimum Memory	Initial Release Date	Update Freq./Price
Physicians, pharmacists, health care professionals.	Proprietary Micromedex, Inc.	PC/XT/AT with DOS version 3.1 or higher	512K	05/87	Annually •
Health care professionals.					•
Library reference market.	SilverPlatter Information Retrieval System Silver Platter Information, Inc.	PC with DOS version 2.1 or higher	640K	06/87	Quarterly $950.00/Year
Medical libraries and educators, physicians.	Knowledge Finder and Knowledge Server for networks Aries Systems Corporation	Macintosh Plus/SE/II	1 MB	01/88	Quarterly •
Universities, researchers, medical professionals, pharmaceutical companies, medical students.	BRS/Search BRS Information Technologies	PC/XT/AT	640K	07/87	Quarterly $995.00/Year
	KAware2 Knowledge Access International, Inc.	PC with MS-DOS version 3.1 or higher			$495.00

(continued)

CD-ROM TITLES BY SUBJECT continued

Subject	Title	Publisher	Description
MEDICAL continued	The Nurse Library	Ellis Enterprises Inc. 225 N.W. Thirteenth Street Oklahoma City, OK 73103 (405)235–7660	
	Oncodisc	J.B. Lippincott Company East Washington Square Philadelphia, PA 19105 (215)238–4200	2 database from the National Cancer Institute: PDQ: Physicians Data Query and CancerLit. Also included is "Principles and Practices of Oncology" from Lippincott. Other Lippincott books will be added in future updates.
	OSH-ROM	SilverPlatter Information, Inc. 37 Walnut Street Wellesley Hills, MA 02181 (617)239–0306	A database of occupational health and safety information, containing three complete bibliographic databases: NIOSHTIC, HSELINE, and CISDOC, collectively containing over 240,000 citations taken from over 500 journals and 100,000 monographs and technical reports.
	The Physician Library	Ellis Enterprises Inc. 225 N.W. Thirteenth Street Oklahoma City, OK 73103 (405)235–7660	
	Physicians' Desk Reference on CD-ROM	Medical Economics Company P.O. Box 551 Oradell, NJ 07649 (800)526–4870	Contains official FDA-approved prescribing information on 1800 prescription drugs, and 1100 non-prescription drugs and ophthalmology products, plus the contents of PDR's 900-page Drug Interactions and Side Effects Index.
	POISINDEX System	Micromedex, Inc. 660 Bannock Street Suite 300 Denver, CO 80204-4506 (800)525–9083	The POISINDEX System is a detailed toxicology database designed to identify and provide ingredient information for over one-half million domestic and foreign commercial, industrial, pharmaceutical, zoologic, and botanic substances. The POISINDEX System also provides detailed symptomatology and management/treatment protocols in the event of a toxicology problem due to ingestion, dermal absorption, eye exposure, or inhalation of any of the substances listed. The POISINDEX database may be searched by brand or trade name, manufacturer's name, generic or chemical name, street or slang terminology, or botanic and common name.

*Please contact publisher for prices.

Audience	Retrieval System	Computer Compatibility	Minimum Memory	Initial Release Date	Update Freq./Price
Nurses, hospitals.		PC/XT/AT	512K	02/89	Annually $700.00/Year
Hospitals, medical libraries, oncologists, cancer professionals.	*SearchLITE* I.S. Grupe	PC/XT/AT	640K	07/88	Bimonthly $1,950.00/Year
					Quarterly $900.00/Year
Physicians, public, hospitals.		PC/XT/AT	512K	02/89	Annually $1,000.00/Year
Libraries, physicians, hospitals, pharmacies.	*Proprietary* Medical Economics Company	PC/XT/AT with DOS version 3.1 or higher	640K	06/88	Triannually $595.00/Year
Physicians, pharmacists, health care professionals.	*Proprietary* Micromedex, Inc.	PC/XT/AT with DOS version 3.1 or higher	512K	07/85	Quarterly *

(continued)

CD-ROM TITLES BY SUBJECT *continued*

Subject	Title	Publisher	Description
MEDICAL *continued*	*TOMES System*	Micromedex, Inc. 660 Bannock Street Suite 300 Denver, CO 80204-4506 (800)525–9083	The TOMES System is an industrial chemical database with in-depth coverage of clinical effects, range of toxicity, workplace standards, kinetics, and physiochemical parameters. Detailed, comprehensive, and referenced protocols for the medical evaluation and treatment of individuals exposed to chemical agents are provided. Protocols for initial response to incidents (fires, spills, leaks) from hazardous materials are also included. Agents are indexed by chemical names, synonyms, and commonly associated numbers (CAS, RTECS/NIOSH, UN, NA ENT, USAF, etc.)
ONLINE	*Online Hotline News*	ALDE Publishing 4830 West 77th Street P.O. Box 35326 Minneapolis, MN 55435 (612)835–5240	A news service about online systems.
PESTICIDES	*PEST-BANK*	SilverPlatter Information, Inc. 37 Walnut Street Wellesley Hills, MA 02181 (617)239–0306	A database on pesticides and their use in agriculture, based on the National Pesticide Information Retrieval System.
PSYCHOLOGY	*PsycLIT*	SilverPlatter Information, Inc. 37 Walnut Street Wellesley Hills, MA 02181 (617)239–0306	Journal citations with abstracts in psychology and behavioral sciences from the PsychINFO department of the American Psychological Association. Coverage from 1984-present.
REAL ESTATE	*Connecticut Real Estate Transaction Database*	Knowledge Access International, Inc. 2685 Marine Way Suite 1305 Mountain View, CA 94043 (415)969–0606	Real estate transfer records from 1987 for the state of Connecticut.
	Massachusetts Real Estate Transaction Database	Knowledge Access International, Inc. 2685 Marine Way Suite 1305 Mountain View, CA 94043 (415)969–0606	Real estate transfer records from 1982-1987 for the state of Massachusetts.
REFERENCE	*ABI/INFORM Ondisc*	UMI (University Microfilms International) 300 North Zeeb Road Ann Arbor, MI 48106 (800)521–3044	Abstracting and indexing to 800 business and management periodicals.

*Please contact publisher for prices.

Audience	Retrieval System	Computer Compatibility	Minimum Memory	Initial Release Date	Update Freq./Price
Physicians, occupational healthcare professionals.	*Proprietary* Micromedex, Inc.	PC/XT/AT with DOS version 3.1 or higher	512K	08/87	Quarterly *
OnLine HotLine subscribers.	*FastFind* Creative Index	PC/XT/AT	640K	10/88	Annually $199.95/Disc
Library reference market.	*SilverPlatter Information Retrieval System* SilverPlatter Information, Inc.	PC with DOS version 2.1 or higher	640K	11/88	Quarterly $2,850.00/Year
Library reference market.	*SilverPlatter Information Retrieval System* SilverPlatter Information, Inc.	PC with DOS version 2.1 or higher	640K	06/86	Quarterly $3,995.00/Year
Bankers, real estate agencies, city planners, real estate aftermarket companies.	*KAware2* Knowledge Access International, Inc.	PC/XT/AT	640K	10/88	Annually $1,500.00/State
Bankers, real estate agencies, city planners, real estate aftermarket companies.	*KAware2* Knowledge Access International, Inc.	PC/XT/AT	640K	10/88	Annually $4,800.00/State
Libraries and corporate libraries.	*UMI RESEARCH* UMI (University Microfilms International)	PC/XT/AT with hard disk	640K	01/88	Bimonthly $4,950.00/Year

(continued)

CD-ROM TITLES BY SUBJECT *continued*

Subject	Title	Publisher	Description
REFERENCE *continued*	*Academic Index on InfoTrac II*	Information Access Company 362 Lakeside Drive Foster City, CA 94404 (800)227–8431	Indexing to 390 of the most widely-read scholarly and general-interest periodicals PLUS 6 months indexing of the *New York Times*.
	Art Index	H.W. Wilson Company 950 University Avenue Bronx, NY 10452 (800)367–6770	Index of articles from 227 domestic and foreign periodicals, yearbooks, etc. Retrospective from 9-84.
	Biography Index	H.W. Wilson Company 950 University Avenue Bronx, NY 10452 (800)367–6770	Index of biographic materials. Retrospective from 7-84.
	Books In Print Plus	Bowker Electronic Publishing 245 West 17th Street New York, NY 10011 (800)323–3288	Access the entire *Books In Print* database of over 800,000 titles (over 1,000,000 bindings). Search and browse 22 search categories including nearly 65,000 LC subject headings and 6,500 Sears and LC headings for children's titles. Includes name, address, and phone number for all publishers and ability to print, save, and electronically order titles from major distributors.
	Books In Print with Book Reviews Plus	Bowker Electronic Publishing 245 West 17th Street New York, NY 10011 (800)323–3288	Includes all features of *Books In Print Plus* with the addition of over 70,000 full-text book reviews from *Booklist, Choice, Library Journal, Publishers Weekly, School Library Journal, Research and Reference Book News* and *SciTech Book News*.
	Book Review Digest	H.W. Wilson Company 950 University Avenue Bronx, NY 10452 (800)367–6770	Providing excerpts from and citations to reviews of current adult and juvenile fiction and non-fiction, BRD covers nearly 6,000 English-language books each year, with concise critical evaluations culled from more than 80 selected American, British, and Canadian periodicals. Retrospective from 3-83.
	CD WORD: Multilingual Dictionary	Dai Nippon Ichigaya-kagacho Shinjuku-ku Tokyo 162 JAPAN 03/266–2111	

*Please contact publisher for prices.

Audience	Retrieval System	Computer Compatibility	Minimum Memory	Initial Release Date	Update Freq./Price
College and university libraries.	Proprietary Information Access Company		640K	01/88	Monthly $4,000.00/Year
Libraries.	WILSONDISC H.W. Wilson Company	PC/XT/AT	640K	06/87	Quarterly $1,495.00/Year
Libraries.	WILSONDISC H.W. Wilson Company	PC/XT/AT	640K	06/87	Quarterly $1,095.00/Year
Libraries, bookstores, publishers.	CD-ROM Search and Retrieval Software Online Computer Systems, Inc.	PC/XT/AT or PS/2	640K	10/86	Quarterly $995.00/Year
Libraries, bookstores, publishers.	CD-ROM Search and Retrieval Software Online Computer Systems, Inc.	PC/XT/AT or PS/2	640K	10/87	Quarterly $1,395.00/Year
Libraries.	WILSONDISC H.W. Wilson Company	PC/XT/AT	640K	03/88	Quarterly $1,095.00/Year

(continued)

CD-ROM TITLES BY SUBJECT *continued*

Subject	Title	Publisher	Description
REFERENCE *continued*	*CD-ROM SourceDisc*	Diversified Data Resources Inc. 6609 Rosecroft Place Falls Church, VA 22043 (703)237–0682	Information on over 300 commercially available CD-ROM titles and a glossary and acronym list of CD-ROM-related terms. Also included are CD-ROM: The New Papyrus and CD-ROM: Optical Publishing from Microsoft Press, and an electronic brochure on DV-I from General Electric.
	Cumulative Book Index	H.W. Wilson Company 950 University Avenue Bronx, NY 10452 (800)367–6770	Bibliographic information on the approximately 50,000 English-language books published internationally. Retrospective from 1-82.
	Facts on File News Digest CD-ROM	Facts on File, Inc. 460 Park Avenue South New York, NY 10016 (800)322–8755	8 years of news compiled from major sources. Also included are 500 maps relating to current affairs.
	Gale GlobalAccess: Associations	Knowledge Access International, Inc. 2685 Marine Way Suite 1305 Mountain View, CA 94043 (415)969–0606	Provides fast and easy access to nearly 100,000 descriptive entries covering more than 80,000 associations from Gale's Encyclopedia of Associations and other related Gale databases.
	General Periodicals Index (Academic Library Edition) on InfoTrac	Information Access Company 362 Lakeside Drive Foster City, CA 94404 (800)227–8431	An index to approximately 1100 general interest and scholarly publications. Subject areas covered include social sciences, general sciences, humanities, business, management, economics and current affairs. Selected titles include abstracts.
	General Periodicals Index (Public Library Edition) on InfoTrac	Information Access Company 362 Lakeside Drive Foster City, CA 94404 (800)227–8431	Includes indexing of approximately 1100 popular magazines and journals. Covers current events, consumer information, arts and entertainment, business, management and economics. Selected titles include abstracts.
	Humanities Index	H.W. Wilson Company 950 University Avenue Bronx, NY 10452 (212)588–8400	Index of articles in 347 periodicals covering art, archaeology, etc. Retrospective from 2-84.

Audience	Retrieval System	Computer Compatibility	Minimum Memory	Initial Release Date	Update Freq./Price
Anyone who owns a CD-ROM.	*Norton Demo 2* Proprietary *LASERTEX* Knowledge Based Systems *Windows Personal Librarian* Personal Library Software	PC/XT/AT with DOS version 3.1 or higher	640K	11/88	Annually $89.95/Disc
Libraries.	*WILSONDISC* H.W. Wilson Company	PC/XT/AT	640K	06/87	Quarterly $1,295.00/Year
Libraries, high schools, universities.	*Media-Mixer* Software Mart Inc.	PC/XT/AT/Macintosh	640K	10/88	Annually $695.00/Disc
Bankers, real estate agencies, city planners, real estate aftermarket companies.	*KAware2* Knowledge Access International, Inc.	PC/XT/AT with MS-DOS version 3.1 or higher	640K	12/88	Biannually $2,295.00/State
University and college libraries.	*Proprietary* Information Access Company		640K	01/85	Monthly $7,500.00/Year
Public libraries.	*Proprietary* Information Access Company			03/88	Monthly $7,500.00/Year
Libraries.	*WILSONDISC* H.W. Wilson Company	PC/XT/AT	640K		Quarterly $1,295.00/Year

(continued)

CD-ROM TITLES BY SUBJECT *continued*

Subject	Title	Publisher	Description
REFERENCE *continued*	*Ingram-Books in Print PLUS*	Bowker Electronic Publishing 245 West 17th Street New York, NY 10011 (800)323–3288	Includes all features of *Books In Print Plus* with the addition of weekly (diskette-based) updates of 70,000 Ingram inventoried titles.
	International Books-in-Print	Saur Verlag KG Postfach 711009 Possenbacherstrasse 2B 8000 München WEST GERMANY (8979)10480	Covers 162,500 English language titles published outside the U.S. and the U.K.
	Kojien: Japanese Dictionary	Dai Nippon Ichigaya-kagacho Shinjuku-ku Tokyo 162 JAPAN 03/266–2111	Japanese dictionary for word processors.
	Magazine Index/PLUS on InfoTrac	Information Access Company 362 Lakeside Drive Foster City, CA 94404 (800)227–8431	Index to 400 popular periodicals PLUS 2 months indexing of the *New York Times*.
	McGraw-Hill Science and Technical Reference Set	McGraw-Hill Book Company 11 West 19th Street New York, NY 10011 (212)512–2000	Science and Technology Encyclopedia, Dictionary of Scientific Terms.
	Merriam Webster's Ninth New Collegiate Dictionary	Highlighted Data, Inc. Washington-Dallas International Airport P.O. Box 17229 Washington, DC 20041 (703)241–1180	The full-text, illustrations, and recorded pronunciation of every word in *Webster's Ninth New Collegiate Dictionary*.
	Microsoft Bookshelf	Microsoft Corporation 16011 N.E. 36th Way P.O. Box 97017 Redmond, WA 98073-9717 (206)882–8080	A tool for writers, Bookshelf contains ten major reference works including the *American Heritage Dictionary, Bartlett's Familiar Quotations, The World Almanac,* and the U.S. Zip Code Directory. Access these reference works through your word processor, without ever leaving your document, a simple copy and paste inserts information directly into your document.

*Please contact publisher for prices.

Audience	Retrieval System	Computer Compatibility	Minimum Memory	Initial Release Date	Update Freq./Price
Bookstores.	CD-ROM Search and Retrieval Software Online Computer Systems, Inc.	PC/XT/AT or PS/2	640K	10/15/88	Quarterly (CD-ROM)/ Weekly (Floppy diskettes) $1,200.00/Year
	Dataware 7000	PC with MS-DOS		07/87	Quarterly *
					*
Public and academic libraries.	Proprietary Information Access Company		640K	08/87	Monthly $4,000.00/ System per Year
	CLASIX Full-Text Manager Reference Technology Inc.	PC/XT/AT	640K	04/87	$300.00
Educators, students.	Proprietary Highlighted Data, Inc.	Mac SE/II/Plus	1 MB	01/88	$199.95/Disc
Anyone who uses a word processor for reports, letters, speeches or articles.	Proprietary Microsoft Corporation	PC/XT/AT or compatible with MS-DOS version 3.1, 3.2, or 3.3 and MS-DOS CD-ROM extensions.	640K	08/87	$295.00/Disc

(continued)

CD-ROM TITLES BY SUBJECT *continued*

Subject	Title	Publisher	Description
REFERENCE *continued*	*Multilingual Dictionary Database*	Sansyusya Publishing Company Ltd. 1-5-34 Taito-ku Tokyo 110 JAPAN	Chinese, Dutch, English, French, German, Italian, Japanese, Spanish.
	Multilingual Dictionary of Science & Technology	Sansyusya Publishing Company Ltd. 1-5-34 Taito-ku Tokyo 110 JAPAN	English, German, Japanese.
	The New Electronic Encyclopedia	Grolier Electronic Publishing Inc. Sherman Turnpike Danbury, CT 06816 (800)356–5590	The full-text version of the 20-volume *Academic American Encyclopedia*, which includes 30,000 articles and 9 million words.
	The NewsBank Electronic Index	Newsbank, Inc. 58 Pine Street New Canaan, CT 06840-5408 (800)223–4739	A powerful, comprehensive, fully contained reference resource. Virtually every newsworthy issue that has affected the U.S. over the past half decade can be researched on the NewsBank Electronic Index. Includes NEWSBANK 1982-present, BUSINESS NEWSBANK 1985-present, NAMES IN THE NEWS 1982-present, and REVIEW OF THE ARTS 1982-present.
	Newspaper Abstracts Ondisc	UMI (University Microfilms International) 300 North Zeeb Road Ann Arbor, MI 48106 (800)521–3044	Indexes and abstracts from eight major newspapers.
	Periodical Abstracts Ondisc	UMI (University Microfilms International) 300 North Zeeb Road Ann Arbor, MI 48106 (800)521–3044	Abstracting and indexing to 300 current general reference periodicals.
	Programmer's Library	Microsoft Corporation 16011 N.E. 36th Way Box 97017 Redmond, WA 98073-9717 (206)882–8080	A tool for programmers containing 48 Microsoft technical manuals and reference books, plus more than 1200 sample programs not available anywhere else. The material can be copied directly into the programmer's editor, without interrupting concentration.

*Please contact publisher for prices.

Audience	Retrieval System	Computer Compatibility	Minimum Memory	Initial Release Date	Update Freq./Price
					*
					*
	Proprietary Online Computer Systems, Inc.	PC/XT/AT	512K	01/86	Annually $395.00/Product
School libraries.	*Proprietary* Newsbank, Inc.	PC/XT/AT	256K	06/85	Monthly *
Libraries.	*UMI RESEARCH* UMI (University Microfilms International)	PC/XT/AT with hard disk	640K	01/88	Bimonthly *
Libraries.	*UMI RESEARCH* UMI (University Microfilms International)	PC/XT/AT with hard disk	640K	06/88	Bimonthly $1,175.00/Year
Language programmers (particularly C and MASM), technical professionals and writers.	*Proprietary* Microsoft Corporation	PC/XT/AT or compatible	640K	09/13/88	$395.00/Disc

(continued)

CD-ROM TITLES BY SUBJECT *continued*

Subject	Title	Publisher	Description
REFERENCE *continued*	Publishers International Directory	Saur Verlag KG Postfach 711009 Possenbacherstrasse 2B 8000 München WEST GERMANY (8979)10480	Covers over 190,000 publishers throughout the world.
	Resource/One	UMI (University Microfilms International) 300 North Zeeb Road Ann Arbor, MI 48106 (800)521–3044	Indexing and abstracting for 130 current general reference periodicals and the *New York Times Current Events Edition*.
	Social Sciences Index	H.W. Wilson Company 950 University Avenue Bronx, NY 10452 (800)367–6770	Index of articles in 353 English-language periodicals covering the social sciences. Retrospective from 4-83.
	The Electronic Whole Earth Catalog	Broderbund Software 17 Paul Drive San Rafael, CA 94903-2101 (800)527–6263	Provides access to tools and ideas on a vast array of subjects, from psychological self-care, building your own home, managing and operating a small business, beekeeping and grassland preservation to desktop publishing, mysticism, ultralight aircraft, blacksmithing and city restoration.
	The Original Oxford English Dictionary on Compact Disc	Tri Star Publishing 475 Virginia Drive Fort Washington, PA 19034 (800)872–2828	The original 12-volume *Oxford English Dictionary* on one compact disc.
	TOM	Information Access Company 362 Lakeside Drive Foster City, CA 94404 (800)227–8431	An index designed exclusively for secondary school libraries. Contains indexing to 100 popular general interest magazines. Full-text of cited articles is available on microfilm. Coverage begins January 1980.
	Ulrich's Plus	Bowker Electronic Publishing 245 West 17th Street New York, NY 10011 (800)323–3288	Search and Browse Bowker's complete *Ulrich's* and *Irregular Serials and Annuals* database—comprising more than 92,000 regularly-issued periodicals plus 46,000 irregular serials. Search by 22 categories including first year of publication, price, publisher, circulation, zip code, title, subject, and keyword.

*Please contact publisher for prices.

Audience	Retrieval System	Computer Compatibility	Minimum Memory	Initial Release Date	Update Freq./Price
		PC with MS-DOS.		07/87	Quarterly *
Small libraries.	UMI RESEARCH UMI (University Microfilms International)	PC/XT/AT with hard disk	640K	06/88	Bimonthly $795.00/Year
Libraries.	WILSONDISC H.W. Wilson Company	PC/XT/AT	640K	04/87	Quarterly $1,295.00/Year
	HyperCard Apple	Apple Macintosh	1 MB	01/89	$149.95/Disc
Educational community, lexicographers, etymologists, writers, authors.	Proprietary Tri Star Publishing	PC/XT/AT	640K	12/87	$950.00/Disc
Secondary school libraries.	Proprietary Information Access Company				Monthly *
Libraries, bookstores, publishers.	CD-ROM Search and Retrieval Software Online Computer Systems, Inc.	PC/XT/AT or PS/2	640K	12/86	Quarterly $395.00/Year

(continued)

CD-ROM TITLES BY SUBJECT *continued*

Subject	Title	Publisher	Description
REFERENCE *continued*	*Verzeichnis Lieferbarer Büecher: German Books-in-Print*	Buchhandler Vereinigung GmbH Grosser Hirschgraben 17-21 Postfach 10042 6000 Frankfurt am Main 1 WEST GERMANY	1.2 million titles of german books in print.
	Books Out-of-Print Plus	Bowker Electronic Publishing 245 West 17th Street New York, NY 10011 (800)323–3288	Search and Browse 400,000 titles declared out-of-print or out-of-stock indefinitely from 1979 to the present using up to 18 different search categories. Includes ability to print, save and edit five different display formats.
RELIGION	*The Bible Library*	Ellis Enterprises Inc. 225 N.W. 13th Street Oklahoma City, OK 73103 (405)235–7660	A comprehensive, powerful, and fun Bible study tool, including 9 versions of the Bible, 2 Bible language dictionaries, 3 word studies, 6 dictionaries and references, 2 commentaries, 1 book of hymn stories, 6 books of sermon outlines and illustrations.
	Die Bibel	Deutsche Bibelgesellschaft Balingerstrasse 31 7000 Stuttgart 80 WEST GERMANY 0711/71810	The Luther bible.
	King James Bible	Quantum Access, Inc. 1700 West Loop South Suite 1460 Houston, TX 77027 (713)622–3211	The King James bible.
	Master Search Bible: Comparative Bible Research	Tri Star Publishing 475 Virginia Drive Fort Washington, PA 19034 (800)872–2828	A powerful new tool incorporating on a single compact disc a comprehensive biblical reference library of classical and contemporary works. It combines three of today's most popular Bible versions with an impressive array of selected reference volumes.
REMOTE SENSING	*Resors*	PCI Inc. 50 West Wilmont Street Richmond Hill, ON L4B 1M5 CANADA (416)764–0614	Bibliography of authors who have written on the subject of remote sensing.

*Please contact publisher for prices.

Audience	Retrieval System	Computer Compatibility	Minimum Memory	Initial Release Date	Update Freq./Price
Libraries, researchers, students.	CD-ROM Search and Retrieval Software Online Computer Systems, Inc.	PC/XT/AT	512K		•
Libraries, bookstores, publishers.	CD-ROM Search and Retrieval Software Online Computer Systems, Inc.	PC/XT/AT or PS/2	640K	10/87	Quarterly $395.00/Year
Ministers and laymen, religious organizations and bookstores, theology students.	MARCON AIRS, Inc.	PC/XT/AT	640K	07/88	Annually $595.00/Disc
	COBRA Bertlemann	PC/XT/AT with MS-DOS version 2.0 or higher	512K	03/87	•
	Quantum Leap Quantum Access, Inc.	PC/XT/AT	512K	06/87	$99.00/Disc
Bible colleges, pastors, laymen.	Proprietary Tri Star Publishing	PC/XT/AT	640K	08/10/88	$549.00/Disc
Libraries, universities, government offices, mining companies, fisheries.	FindIt Reteaco, Inc.	PC/XT/AT	640K	09/86	Biannually $500.00/Disc

(continued)

CD-ROM TITLES BY SUBJECT *continued*

Subject	Title	Publisher	Description
SCIENCE AND TECHNOLOGY	*Applied Science & Technology Index*	H.W. Wilson Company 950 University Avenue Bronx, NY 10452 (800)367–6770	Index of 339 English-language periodicals in applied science and technology. Retrospective from 10-83.
	Compact Cambridge Life Sciences Collection	Cambridge Scientific Abstracts 7200 Wisconsin Avenue Suite 601 Bethesda, MD 20816 (301)961–6700	A comprehensive life sciences database with abstracts including indepth coverage of AIDS research, bacteriology, immunology, toxicology, virology, microbiology, biochemistry, biotechnology, and ecology.
	Encyclopedia of Polymer Science & Engineering	John Wiley & Sons, Inc. 605 Third Avenue New York, NY 10158 (212)850–6000	19-volumes of articles reflecting the vast changes which have occurred in polymer science in recent years.
	General Science Index	H.W. Wilson Company 950 University Avenue Bronx, NY 10452 (800)367–6770	Guide to current information in 108 English-language science periodicals. Retrospective from 5-84.
	Haystack	Ziff-Davis Technical Information Company 80 Blanchard Road Burlington, MA 01803 (617)273–5500	Logistics information of parts purchased by the government and their technical characteristics.
	Kirk-Othmer Encyclopedia of Chemical Technology	John Wiley & Sons, Inc. 605 Third Avenue New York, NY 10158 (212)850–6000	All 1200 articles from the 25-volume set, plus supplements, indexing, abstracts, and 6000 tables.
	McGraw-Hill CD-ROM Science & Technical Reference Set	McGraw-Hill Book Company 11 West 19th Street New York, NY 10011 (212)512–2000	Science & Technology Encyclopedia, Dictionary of Scientific Terms.
	NTIS (1983-present)	OCLC 6565 Frantz Road Dublin, OH 43017-0702 (800)848–5878	Citations to reports from the Department of Energy, Department of Defense, and NASA, covering a wide variety of topics in engineering, mathematics, physical, biological, and social sciences and business.
	NTIS	SilverPlatter Information, Inc. 37 Walnut Street Wellesley Hills, MA 02181 (617)239–0306	Bibliographic citations and abstracts to government sponsored research and development reports produces by the National Technical Information Service. Coverage from 1983-present.

*Please contact publisher for prices.

Audience	Retrieval System	Computer Compatibility	Minimum Memory	Initial Release Date	Update Freq./Price
Libraries.	*WILSONDISC* H.W. Wilson Company	PC/XT/AT	640K	04/87	Quarterly $1,495.00/Year
Universities, medical schools, hospitals, researchers.	*Compact Cambridge* Cambridge Scientific Abstracts	PC/XT/AT	512K	06/86	Biannually $1,250.00/Year
	FindIt Reteaco, Inc.	PC/XT/AT	640K		$3,200.00/Disc
Libraries.	*WILSONDISC* H.W. Wilson Company	PC/XT/AT	640K	04/87	Quarterly $1,295.00/Year
Military, defense contractors.	*Proprietary* Ziff-Davis Technical Information Company	PC/XT with 5 MB free on hard disk and MS-DOS version 3.0 or higher	640K		Quarterly *
	FindIt Reteaco, Inc.	PC/XT/AT	640K		$895.00/Disc
					$300.00/Disc
Libraries, educational organizations.	*Search CD450* OCLC	PC/XT/AT or Macintosh	512K		Quarterly $2,395.00
Library reference market.	*SilverPlatter Information Retrieval System* SilverPlatter Information, Inc.	PC with DOS version 2.1 or higher	640K	08/87	Quarterly $2,500.00/Year

(continued)

CD-ROM TITLES BY SUBJECT *continued*

Subject	Title	Publisher	Description
SCIENCE AND TECHNOLOGY *continued*	Plus³⁷	Phillips Electronic Instruments Inc. 85 McKee Drive Mahwah, NJ 07430 (201)529-3800	Diffraction parameters in 1987 JCPDS PDF-2 database.
	Powder Diffraction File	International Centre for Diffraction Data 1601 Park Lane Swarthmore, PA 19801 (215)328-9400	A file of approximately 59,000 X-ray diffraction patterns of inorganic/organic materials, crystallographic and physical data.
	Registry of Mass Spectral Data	John Wiley & Sons, Inc. 605 Third Avenue New York, NY 10158 (212)850-6000	Over 123,000 spectra plus all of the additional data provided on the mainframe version.
	Science Citation Index	Institute for Scientific Information 3501 Market Street Philadelphia, PA 19104 (215)386-0100	Citation Index to scientific and technical literature spanning over 100 disciplines with the value added feature of related records.
	Time Table of Science and Innovation	Xiphias 13464 Washington Boulevard Marina Del Rey, CA 90292 (213)821-0074	Multi-media presentation of over 5700 key events in the history of science. Implemented under HyperCard.
SERIALS	*Serials*	Utlas International 8300 College Boulevard Overland Park, KS 66210 (800)33-UTLAS	460,000 MARC serials.
	THE SERIALS DIRECTORY/EBSCO CD-ROM	EBSCO Publishing P.O. Box 1493 Birmingham, AL 35201 (800)826-3024	Detailed bibliographic and ordering information on over 114,000 serials, annuals, and irregular series published worldwide. Includes indepth abstract/index coverage as well as UD, LC, DD, NLM classifications and CODEN.
SOCIOLOGY	*sociofile*	SilverPlatter Information, Inc. 37 Walnut Street Wellesley Hills, MA 02181 (617)239-0306	Index to and abstracts of the world's journals in sociology as compiled by Sociological Abstracts. Contains abstracts of journal articles published in Sociological Abstracts since 1974 and the enhanced bibliographic citations for dissertations in sociology and related disciplines that have been added to the database since 1986.

*Please contact publisher for prices.

Audience	Retrieval System	Computer Compatibility	Minimum Memory	Initial Release Date	Update Freq./Price
					$5,000.00/Disc
University, academic, and industrial users, for the identification of unknown materials.	*PC-PDF* Reference Technology, Inc.	PC/XT/AT or PS/2 with MS-DOS version 3.2 or higher and 400K of hard disk space	640K	09/87	Annually *
	PBM/STIRS	PC/XT/AT	640K		$2,895.00/Disc
Scientists, researchers, librarians, information managers, students, educators.	*Proprietary* Institute for Scientific Information	PC/XT/AT or PS/2 with DOS version 3.1 or higher	640K	05/88	Quarterly *
Early innovators, K-12 and higher education.	*Xearch* Xiphias	Macintosh SE/II/Plus and Atari ST	1 MB	07/88	Annually $150.00/Disc
Libraries.	*CD-CATSS* Utlas International	PC/XT/AT	640K	06/88	$1,250.00/Disc
Library and information science specialists.	*EBSCO-CD* EBSCO Electronic Information	PC/XT/AT with MS-DOS version 3.1 or higher and 10 MB hard disk	640K	07/88	Quarterly $495.00/Year
Library reference market.	*SilverPlatter Information Retrieval System* SilverPlatter Information, Inc.	PC with DOS version 2.1 or higher	640K	04/87	Semiannually $1,950.00/Year

(continued)

CD-ROM TITLES BY SUBJECT *continued*

Subject	Title	Publisher	Description
SOFTWARE	The $99.00 Disc	ALDE Publishing 4830 West 77th Street P.O. Box 35326 Minneapolis, MN 55435 (612)835–5240	Over 5,000 public domain programs.
	Blue Sail on CD-ROM	ALDE Publishing 4830 West 77th Street P.O. Box 35326 Minneapolis, MN 55435 (612)835–5240	1,000 floppy public domain library.
	BMUG PD ROM	BMUG (Berkeley Mac User's Group) 1442A Walnut #62 Berkeley, CA 94709 (415)549–BMUG	Over 300 MB of publicly distributable information. Also included on the disc are digests of electronic messages from USEnet, Delphi, InfoMac, and Arts & Farces, and many color Mac II pictures and large digitized sounds.
	ClubMac	Quantum Access, Inc. 1700 West Loop South Suite 1460 Houston, TX 77027 (713)622–3211	450 MB of public domain shareware and clip art.
	EDUCORP's CD-ROM	EDUCORP 531 Stevens Avenue Suite B Solana Beach, CA 92075 (619)259–0255	310 MB of public domain and shareware software.
	MEGA-ROM	Quantum Leap Technologies, Inc. 314 Romano Avenue Coral Gables, FL 33134 (305)447–0745	300 megabytes of Macintosh public domain software.
	Menu: Software Catalogue	The Menu P.O. Box MENU Pittsburg, PA 15241	
	PC-Blue: MS-DOS Public Domain Library	ALDE Publishing 4830 West 77th Street P.O. Box 35326 Minneapolis, MN 55435 (612)835–5240	PC-Blue public domain library.

*Please contact publisher for prices.

Audience	Retrieval System	Computer Compatibility	Minimum Memory	Initial Release Date	Update Freq./Price
Horizontal markets.	None	PC/XT/AT	640K	03/88	Annually $99.00/Disc
Horizontal markets.	Proprietary Menu Blue Sail Software	PC/XT/AT	640K	04/88	Annually $149.00/Disc
Macintosh users.	HyperCard Apple	Mac SE with System Release 5.0			$100.00/Disc
Macintosh users.	HyperCard Apple	Macintosh		07/88	Quarterly $350.00/Year
Software users.	Macintosh HFS Apple	Macintosh SE/II/Plus		09/26/88	Triannually $199.00/Disc
		Macintosh		09/88	$30.00/disc
					*
Horizontal markets.	None	PC/XT/AT	640K	07/88	Annually $199.00/Disc

(continued)

CD-ROM TITLES BY SUBJECT *continued*

Subject	Title	Publisher	Description
SOFTWARE *continued*	*The PC-SIG Library on CD-ROM*	PC-SIG Inc. 1030-D East Duane Ave. Sunnyvale, CA 94086 (408)730–9291	1000 discs of shareware software.
	Public Domain Software on File CD-ROM	Facts on File, Inc. 460 Park Avenue South New York, NY 10016 (800)322–8755	A collection of 200 debugged public domain software programs for the Apple II.
	Software Library Dataplate	Reference Technology Inc. 5700 Flatiron Parkway Boulder, CO 80301 (303)449–4157	Software programs.
	SOFTWARE-CD	SilverPlatter Information, Inc. 37 Walnut Street Wellesley Hills, MA 02181 (617)239–0306	Over 10,000 listings of software packages for the business, professional, and technical communities.
SPACE	*Space Science Sampler Volume 1: Voyager 2 Images of Uranus, Its Rings and Satellites*	University of Colorado LASP Campus Box 392 Boulder, CO 80309 (303)492–6867	800 images of Uranus from NASA's Voyager spacecraft.
	Space Science Sampler Volume 2	University of Colorado LASP Campus Box 392 Boulder, CO 80309 (303)492–6867	A collection of NASA scientific data on the Earth and our solar system.
	Voyagers to the Outer Planets: Volume 1	University of Colorado LASP Campus Box 392 Boulder, CO 80309 (303)492–6867	The first of a multiple disk set of data from NASA's Voyager spacecraft. This disk has images of Uranus.
SPORTS	*Sports Discus*	SilverPlatter Information, Inc. 37 Walnut Street Wellesley Hills, MA 02181 (617)239–0306	The international sports database corresponding to the printed publication *Sport Bibliography*. The database covers areas such as exercise physiology, medicine, biomechanics, coaching, counseling, psychology, and sports medicine. The database dates from 1972 and is based on more than 2,000 international sources.

Audience	Retrieval System	Computer Compatibility	Minimum Memory	Initial Release Date	Update Freq./Price
Educators, users groups, corporate and personal users.		PC/XT/AT with DOS version 3.1 or higher	256K	05/86	Biannually $295.00/Disc
Libraries, high schools, universities.	*Proprietary* Facts on File Publications Inc.	Apple II series	64K	06/88	$195.00/Disc
					$195.00
Library reference market.	*SilverPlatter Information Retrieval System* SilverPlatter Information, Inc.	PC or compatible, MS- or PC-DOS 2.1 or higher.	640K	04/88	Semiannually $1,250.00/Year
Educators, libraries, universities, scientists, amateur astronomers.	*Proprietary* NASA Jet Propulsion Laboratory	PC/XT/AT with VGA or EGA extended memory monitors	640K	12/88	$25.00/Disc
Educators, libraries, universities, scientists, amateur astronomers.	*Proprietary* NASA Jet Propulsion Laboratory	PC/XT/AT with VGA or EGA extended memory monitors	640K	12/88	$25.00/Disc
Educators, libraries, universities, scientists, amateur astronomers.	*Proprietary* NASA Jet Propulsion Laboratory	PC/XT/AT with VGA or EGA extended memory monitors	640K	02/89	$25.00/Disc
	SilverPlatter Information Retrieval System Silver Platter Information, Inc.	PC with DOS version 2.1 or higher	640K	01/15/89	Semiannually $1,250.00/Year

(continued)

CD-ROM TITLES BY SUBJECT *continued*

Subject	Title	Publisher	Description
TAXES	*PHINet-American Federal Tax Reports*	Prentice Hall Information Network 1 Gulf & Western Plaza 18th Floor New York, NY 10023 (212)373–8600	Tax-related court decisions from the federal court system, with PH Headnotes.
	PHINet-Private Letter Rulings	Prentice Hall Information Network 1 Gulf & Western Plaza 18th Floor New York, NY 10023 (212)373–8600	IRS Private Letter Rulings, with PH Headnotes.
	PHINet-Revenue Rulings and Procedures	Prentice Hall Information Network 1 Gulf & Western Plaza 18th Floor New York, NY 10023 (212)373–8600	IRS Revenue Rulings and Procedures, with PH Headnotes.
	PHINet-Tax Court Reported and Memorandum Decisions	Prentice Hall Information Network 1 Gulf & Western Plaza 18th Floor New York, NY 10023 (212)373–8600	Tax court memorandum and reported decisions, with PH Headnotes.
	Tax/Stats	Hopkins Technology 421 Hazel Lane Hopkins, MN 55343-7117 (612)931–9376	Federal income tax data provided by the IRS.
TELEPHONE	*The National Directory*	Xiphias 13464 Washington Boulevard Marina Del Rey, CA 90292 (213)821–0074	Every telephone number and address for businesses, corporations, government agencies, and other key institutions in North America. Applications include Auto Dialing and Auto Label Printing. Based on best-selling directory published by General Information.

Audience	Retrieval System	Computer Compatibility	Minimum Memory	Initial Release Date	Update Freq./Price
Tax professionals: accountants, law firms, corporate tax departments, U.S. government.	*Fulltext Manager/ Docufind* Reference Technology/ Emanuel Data Systems	PC/XT/AT with 2 MB free space on hard disk. 286 recommended.	640K	01/88	Semiannually (CD-ROM)/ Daily (Online) $2,500.00/Disc
Tax professionals: accountants, law firms, corporate tax departments, U.S. government.	*Fulltext Manager/ Docufind* Reference Technology/ Emanuel Data Systems	PC/XT/AT with 2 MB free space on hard disk. 286 recommended.	640K	01/87	Semiannually (CD-ROM)/ Daily (Online) $2,500.00/Disc
Tax professionals: accountants, law firms, corporate tax departments, U.S. government.	*Fulltext Manager/ Docufind* Reference Technology/ Emanuel Data Systems	PC/XT/AT with 2 MB free space on hard disk. 286 recommended.	640K	12/86	Semiannually (CD-ROM)/ Daily(Online) $2,500.00/Disc
Tax professionals: accountants, law firms, corporate tax departments, U.S. government.	*Fulltext Manager/ Docufind* Reference Technology/ Emanuel Data Systems	PC/XT/AT with 2 MB free space on hard disk. 286 recommended.	640K	01/87	Semiannually (CD-ROM)/ Daily (Online $2,500.00/Disc
Consumer, corporate.	*QuAcc* Hopkins Technology	PC with MS-DOS version 3.1 or higher and MS DOS CD-ROM Extensions	200K	03/89	Annually $49.00
Tele-marketing agencies.	*Xearch* Xiphias	Macintosh SE/II/Plus	1 MB	01/89	Annually $150.00/Disc

(continued)

CD-ROM TITLES BY SUBJECT *continued*

Subject	Title	Publisher	Description
TELEPHONE *continued*	*NYNEX Fast Track*	NYNEX Information Resources Company 195 Market Street 5th Floor Lynn, MA 01901 (617)581–4674	NYNEX white pages directories. Over 10 million names, addresses, phone numbers, and zip codes. Used mainly by companies with high–volume listing verification and identification needs.
	Phonedisc	Digital Directory Assistance Inc. 5161 River Road Building 6 Bethesda, MD 20816 (301)657–8548	All 10 million telephone listings in New York, Vermont, New England, New Hampshire, Maine, Connecticut, Massachusetts, and Rhode Island, indexed by name, address, and phone number.
	Yellow Page Demo	Compact Discoveries 1050 South Federal Highway Delray Beach, FL 33444 (407)243–1453	
VIRGINIA	*The Virginia Disc One*	Virginia Polytechnic Institute Department of Computers Blacksburg, VA 24061 (703)961–5593	28 databases of historical bibliographic records, and much more.

*Please contact publisher for prices.

Audience	Retrieval System	Computer Compatibility	Minimum Memory	Initial Release Date	Update Freq./Price
Financial institutions and retail companies (credit and collection departments), government agencies, publishing companies (circulation department).	Proprietary NYNEX Information Resources Company	PC/XT/AT with hard disk	512K	11/87	Monthly $10,000.00/Year
Fortune 500 companies, law enforcement, credit collection.	Phonedisc Digital Directory Assistance Inc.	PC/XT/AT with MS-DOS version 3.0 or higher	512K	05/88	Monthly $10,000.00/Year
					*
Libraries, extension agents.	Several different retrieval systems on disc	PC/XT/AT		10/88	*

Compiled by Online Press Inc.

DIRECTORY OF CD-ROM DRIVES

CD-ROM DRIVES BY MANUFACTURER

CD-ROM DRIVES BY MANUFACTURER

Manufacturer	Drive Name	Caddy	Configuration	Interface	Price
Amdek Corporation 1901 Zanker Road San Jose, CA 95112 (408)436-8570	LASERDEK 1000		Stand alone, front loading		$995.00
Apple Computer, Inc. 20525 Mariani Avenue Cupertino, CA 95014 (408)996-1010	AppleCD SC	Sony	Stand alone, front loading	SCSI	$1,500.00
Atari Corporation 1196 Borregas Avenue Sunnyvale, CA 94088 (408)745-2000	CDAR500		Stand alone, front loading	SCSI	$599.00
Denon America 222 New Road Parsippany, NJ 077054 (201)575-7810	DRD-250	Sony	Half height, internal	SCSI	OEM
	DRD-251	Sony	Half height, front loading, internal	SCSI	OEM
	DRD-253		Stand alone, front loading		OEM
	DRD-550	Sony	Front loading, external	SCSI	OEM
Digital Equipment Corporation 2 Mount Royal Avenue Marlboro, MA 01752 (800)258-1710	RRD50-AA		Stand alone, top loading		$1,000.00
	RRD50-EA		Stand alone, top loading		$1,200.00
	RRD50-QA		Stand alone, top loading		$1,200.00
Hitachi Sales Corporation of America 401 West Artesia Boulevard Compton, CA 90220 (800)262-1502	CDR-1502S		Stand alone, front loading		$899.00
	CDR-1503S		External, front loading		$995.00
	CDR-1553S		Stand alone, front loading	SCSI, Digital Audio	$1,199.00
	CDR-2500		Front loading, internal		$899.00
	CDR-3500		Half height, internal	SCSI	$869.00

Manufacturer	Drive Name	Caddy	Configuration	Interface	Price
JVC 41 Slater Drive Elmwood Park, NJ 07404 (201)794-3900	XR-R100	JVC	Stand alone, front loading	SCSI	OEM
	XR-R1001	JVC	Half height, internal	SCSI	OEM
Laser Magnetic Storage International 4425 ArrowsWest Drive Colorado Springs, CO 80907 (303)593-4269	CM121	Philips	Stand alone, front loading		OEM
	CM131	Philips	Stand alone, front loading	SCSI	OEM
	CM132	Philips	Stand alone, front loading	SCSI, Dual drives	OEM
	CM201	Philips	Half height, internal		OEM
	CM210	Philips	Half height, internal	SCSI	OEM
Laser Optical Technology 10 Victor Square Suite 600 Scotts Valley, CA 95066 (408)426-7171	LD CD-ROM Drive		Stand alone, front loading	SCSI, Audio	$1,595
NEC Home Electronics 1255 Michael Drive Wood Dale, IL 60191-1094 (312)860-9500	CDR-77	NEC	Stand alone, front loading	SCSI	$999
	CDR-80	NEC	Half height, internal	SCSI	$899
Panasonic 1 Panasonic Way Secaucus, NJ 07094 (201)392-4602	SQ-D1	Panasonic	Half height, internal		$999
	SQ-D101	Panasonic	Stand alone, front loading	SCSI	$1,149
Reference Technology 5700 Flatiron Parkway Boulder, CO 80301 (303)449-4157	CLASIX 500		Stand alone, front loading		$990

(continued)

CD-ROM DRIVES BY MANUFACTURER *continued*

Manufacturer	Drive Name	Caddy	Configuration	Interface	Price
Sanyo 51 Joseph Street Moonachie, NJ 07074 (201)440-9300	ROM 300 ROM 2500		Stand alone, front loading Half height, internal	SCSI SCSI	OEM OEM
Sony 655 River Oaks Parkway San Jose, CA 95134 (408)432-0190	CDU-510 CDU-6100 CDU-6101 CDU-6110 CDU-6111	Sony Sony Sony Sony Sony	Half height, internal Stand alone, front loading Stand alone, front loading Stand alone, front loading Stand alone, front loading	 SCSI SCSI, Audio	OEM OEM OEM OEM OEM
Toshiba 9740 Irvine Boulevard Irvine, CA 92680 (714)583-3117	XM-2000A XM-2000B XM-2100A	Sony Sony 	Stand alone, front loading Full height, internal Stand alone, front loading	SCSI, Audio SCSI, Audio SCSI, Audio	OEM OEM OEM

Compiled by Online Press Inc.

DIRECTORY OF RETRIEVAL SYSTEMS

RETRIEVAL SYSTEMS

System	Company
Bibliofile	**Library Corporation** P.O. Box 40035 Washington, DC 20016 (800)624-0559
BlueFish	**Lotus Development Corporation** 55 Cambridge Parkway Cambridge, MA 02142
BRS/Search	**BRS Information Technologies** 1200 Route 7 Latham, NY 12110 (800)468-0908
CAIRS	**Info/DOC** P.O. Box 17109 Dulles international Airport Washington, DC 20041 (703)979-5363
CD Answer	**Dataware Inc.** 2 Greenwich Plaza Suite 100 Greenwich, CT 06830 (203)622-3908
CD-GUIDE	**OWL International** 2800 156th Avenue S.E. Bellevue, WA 98007 (206)747-3203
Compact Cambridge	**Cambridge Scientific Abstracts** 7200 Wisconsin Avenue Suite 601 Bethesda, MD 20816 (301)961-6700
Compact Disclosure	**Disclosure** 5161 River Road Bethesda, MD 20816 (800)638-8076
Customized Software Development	**Bresler Associates** 4276 22nd Street San Francisco, CA 94114 (415)282-5448
Customized Software Development	**Del Mar Group** 722 Genevieve Suite M Solana Beach, CA 92075 (619)250-0444
Customized Software Development	**Online Computer Systems Inc.** 202512 Century Boulevard Germantown, MD 20874 (301)428-3700
Delve	**Group L Corporation** 481 Carlisle Drive Herndon, VA 22070 (703)471-0030
Dialog	**IS/R Systems** 850 Bear Tavern Road Suite 207 West Trenton, NJ 08628 (609)883-6286
Dialog OnDisc	**Dialog Information** 3460 Hillview Avenue Palo Alto, CA 94304 (800)3-DIALOG
DLS/Search	**Digital Library Systems** 5161 River Road Building 6 Bethesda, MD 20816 (301)657-2997
Docufind	**Emanuel Data Systems** 1865 Palmer Avenue Larchmont, NY 10538 (914)834-5722
Dragnet	**Access Softek** 3204 Adeline Street Berkeley, CA 94703 (415)654-0116
FIND: Filed Indexed Documents	**Acctex Information Systems** 131 Steuart Street Suite 600 San Francisco, CA 94105 (415)543-4290
Findit	**Reteaco, Inc.** 716 Gordon Baker Road Willowdale, ON M2H 3B4 CANADA (416)497-0579
FreeForm	**Micro Dynamics, Ltd.** 8555 16th Street Suite 802 Silver Spring, MD 20910 (301)589-6300

System	Company	System	Company
Ful/Text	**Fulcrum Technologies, Inc.** 331 Cooper Street Ottawa, ON K2P 0G5 CANADA (613)238–1761	Le Pac	**Brodart Automation,** a division of Brodart Company 500 Arch Street Williamsport, PA 17705 (800)233–8467
FYI 300 Plus	**FYI Inc.** 4202 Spicewood Springs Road Suite 101 Austin, TX 78755 (512)346–0134	MARCON	**AIRS Inc.** 335 Paint Branch Drive College Park, MD 20742 (301)454–3832
GIS Retrieval Information System	**AXSES** Boutilier Point Halifax, NS B0J 1G0 CANADA (902)826–2440 FAX: (826)429–6521	Media Mixer	**Software Mart, Inc.** 4131 Spicewood Springs Road Suite I-3 Austin, TX 78759-8608 (512)346–7887 FAX: (512)346–1393
HP LaserRETRIEVE	**Hewlett Packard/Meridian Data** 4450 Capitola Road Suite 101 Capitola, CA 95010 (408)476–5858	MediaBase	**Crowninshield Software** 1105 Commonwealth Avenue Boston, MA 02215 (617)787–8830
HyperSearch	**Discovery Systems** 7001 Discovery Boulevard Dublin, OH 43017 (614)761–2000	Meta-Morf	**Thunderstone (EPI Inc.)** P.O. Box 83 Chesterland, OH 44143 (216)449–6104
Impact	**Auto-Graphics Inc.** 3201 Temple Avenue Pomona, CA 91768 (800)235–7961	MicroBasis	**Information Dimensions, Inc.** 505 West King Avenue Columbus, OH 43201-2693 (614)424–6314
KAware2	**Knowledge Access International, Inc.** 2685 Marine Way Suite 1305 Mountain View, CA 94043 (415)969–0606	OPTI-Search	**Amtec** 3700 Industry Avenue Lakewood, CA 90714-6050 (213)595–4756
Knowledge Finder	**Aries Systems Corporation** 79 Boxford Street North Andover, MA 01845-3219 (508)689–9334	Personal Librarian	**Personal Library Software** 15215 Shady Grove Road Suite 204 Rockville, MD 20850 (301)926–1402
KRS	**KnowledgeSet Corporation** P.O. Box 51125 Pacific Grove, CA 93950 (408)375–2638	Phonedisc	**Digital Directory Assistance Inc.** 5161 River Road Building 6 Bethesda, MD 20816 (301)657–8548

(continued)

RETRIEVAL SYSTEMS *continued*

System	Company
QA Gateway	**Quantum Access, Inc.** 1700 West Loop South Suite 1460 Houston, TX 77027 (713)622–3211
Research	**TMS, Inc.** 110 West 3rd Street P.O. Box 1358 Stillwater, OK 74076 (405)377–0880
Search CD450	**OCLC, Inc.** 6565 Frantz Road Dublin, OH 43017 (614)764–6063
SearchExpress	**Executive Technologies Inc.** 2120 16th Avenue South Birmingham, AL 35205 (205)933–5494
SilverPlatter Search and Retrieval Software	**SilverPlatter Information, Inc.** 37 Walnut Street Wellesley Hills, MA 02181 (617)239–0306
Silversmith	**Taunton Engineering Inc.** 505 Middlesex Turnpike Billerica, MA 01821 (617)663–3667
SONAR	**Virginia Systems** 5509 West Bay Court Midlothian, VA 23113 (804)739–3200
Status	**CP International** 521 Fifth Avenue New York, NY 10175 (212)949–8051 FAX: (212)883–8912

System	Company
TextWare	**Unibase Systems, Inc.** 333 Main Street Suite 300 Park City, UT 84060 (801)649–4440
VAX/VTX	**Digital Equipment Corporation** 2 Mount Royal Avenue UPO 1-3 Marlboro, MA 01752 (617)480–4816
What?	**Highlighted Data** P.O. Box 17229 Washington, DC 20041 (703)241–1180
Where?	**Highlighted Data** P.O. Box 17229 Washington, DC 20041 (703)241–1180
WILSONDISC	**H.W. Wilson Company** 950 University Avenue Bronx, NY 10452 (212)588–8400
Window Book Technology	**Box Company** 63 Howard Street Cambridge, MA 02139 (617)576–0892
Zyindex	**Zylab Corporation** 233 East Erie Street Chicago, IL 60611 (312)642–2201

Compiled by Online Press Inc.

DIRECTORY OF DATA PREPARATION HOUSES

ALPHABETICAL LISTING OF DATA PREPARATION HOUSES

DATA PREPARATION HOUSES BY STATE

Alphabetical Listing of Data Preparation Houses

3M Corporation
420 South Bernardo Avenue
Mountain View, CA 94043
(415)969–5200

AIRS Inc.
335 Paint Branch Drive
College Park, MD 20742
(301)454–3832

American Helix Technology Corporation
1857 Colonial Village Lane
Lancaster, PA 17601
(800)535–6575
FAX: (717)392–7897

AXSES
Boutilier Point
Halifax, NS B0J 1G0
CANADA
(902)826–2440
FAX: (826)429–6521

Denon America
1380 Monticello Road
Madison, GA 30650
(404)342–3425

Denon America
222 New Road
Parsippany, NJ 07054
(201)575–7810
FAX: (201)575–2532

Digital Audio Disc Corporation
1800 North Fruitridge Avenue
Terre Haute, IN 47804-1788
(812)462–8160
FAX: (812)466–9125

Discovery Systems
7001 Discovery Boulevard
Dublin, OH 43017
(614)761–4159

Disctronics Inc.
1120 Cosby Way
Anaheim, CA 92806
(714)630–6700
FAX: (714)630–1025

Disctronics Inc.
4905 Mooresmill Road
Huntsville, AL 35881
(205)859–9042
FAX: (205)859–9932

Disctronics Inc.
9 Dehavilland Road
Braeside, Vic 3197
AUSTRALIA
03/587–2633
FAX: 03/587–2901

Lasertrak Corporation
6235-B Lookout Drive
Boulder, CO 80301
(303)530–2711

Magnetic Press, Inc.
503 Broadway
New York, NY 10012
(212)219–2831
FAX: (212)334–4729

Memory Technology Inc.
2800 Summit Avenue
Plano, TX 75074
(214)881–8800

Meridian Data, Inc.
4450 Capitola Road
Suite 101
Capitola, CA 95010
(408)476–5858

Nimbus Records Inc.
P.O. Box 7305
Charlottesville, VA 22906
(804)985–1100

Nimbus Records, Ltd.
Wyastone Leys
Monmouth NP5 3SR
WALES
0600/890 682

Online Computer Systems
20251 Century Boulevard
Germantown, MD 20874
(800)922–9204

Online Press Inc.
14320 N.E. 21st Street
Suite 18
Bellevue, WA 98007
(206)641–3434

Optical Media International
485 Alberto Way
Los Gatos, CA 95032
(408)395–4332

OWL International
2800 156th Avenue S.E.
Bellevue, WA 98007
(206)747–3203

Philips and DuPont Optical
Kings Mountain
Highway 29
Grover, NC 28073
(800)433–3475
FAX: (302)479–2512

Reference Technology Inc.
5700 Flatiron Parkway
Boulder, CO 80301
(303)449–4157

Reteaco, Inc.
716 Gordon Baker Road
Willowdale, ON M2II 3B4
CANADA
(416)497–0579

SANYO Laser Products, Inc.
1767 Sheridan Street
Richmond, IN 47374
(317)935–7574
FAX: (317)935–7570

ScanText Inc.
1525 132nd N.E.
Bellevue, WA 98005
(206)451–3350

Shape Optimedia
Route 109 & Eagle Drive
Sanford, ME 04073
(207)324–1124
FAX: (207)490–1707

Software Mart
4131 Spicewood Springs Road
Suite I-3
Austin, TX 78759–8608
(512)346–7887
FAX: (512)346–1393

Tiger Media
10810 Paramount Boulevard
Suite 201
Downey, CA 90241
(213)862–5591

TMS, Inc.
110 West 3rd Street
Stillwater, OK 74076
(405)377–0880

Compiled by Online Press Inc.

Data Preparation Houses by State

State	Company
AL	**Disctronics Inc.** 4905 Mooresmill Road Huntsville, AL 35881 (205)859–9042 FAX: (205)859–9932
 CA	**3M Corporation** 420 South Bernardo Avenue Mountain View, CA 94043 (415)969–5200 **Disctronics Inc.** 1120 Cosby Way Anaheim, CA 92806 (714)630–6700 FAX: (714)630–1025 **Meridian Data, Inc.** 4450 Capitola Road Suite 101 Capitola, CA 95010 (408)476–5858 **Optical Media International** 485 Alberto Way Los Gatos, CA 95032 (408)395–4332 **Tiger Media** 10810 Paramount Boulevard Suite 201 Downey, CA 90241 (213)862–5591
CO	**Lasertrak Corporation** 6235-B Lookout Drive Boulder, CO 80301 (303)530–2711 **Reference Technology Inc.** 5700 Flatiron Parkway Boulder, CO 80301 (303)449–4157

State	Company
GA	**Denon America** 1380 Monticello Road Madison, GA 30650 (404)342–3425
IN	**Digital Audio Disc Corporation** 1800 North Fruitridge Avenue Terre Haute, IN 47804-1788 (812)462–8160 FAX: (812)466–9125 **SANYO Laser Products, Inc.** 1767 Sheridan Street Richmond, IN 47374 (317)935–7574 FAX: (317)935–7570
 ME	**Shape Optimedia** Route 109 & Eagle Drive Sanford, ME 04073 (207)324–1124 FAX: (207)490–1707
 MD	**AIRS Inc.** 335 Paint Branch Drive College Park, MD 20742 (301)454–3832 **Online Computer Systems** 20251 Century Boulevard Germantown, MD 20874 (800)922–9204
 NJ	**Denon America** 222 New Road Parsippany, NJ 07054 (201)575–7810 FAX: (201)575–2532
 NY	**Magnetic Press, Inc.** 503 Broadway New York, NY 10012 (212)219–2831 FAX: (212)334–4729

| *State* | *Company* | *State* | *Company* |

Philips and DuPont Optical
Kings Mountain
Highway 29
Grover, NC 28073
(800)433–3475
FAX: (302)479–2512

Online Press Inc.
14320 N.E. 21st Street
Suite 18
Bellevue, WA 98007
(206)641–3434

Discovery Systems
7001 Discovery Boulevard
Dublin, OH 43017
(614)761–4159

OWL International
2800 156th Avenue S.E.
Bellevue, WA 98007
(206)747–3203

TMS, Inc.
110 West 3rd Street
Stillwater, OK 74076
(405)377–0880

ScanText Inc.
1525 132nd N.E.
Bellevue, WA 98005
(206)451–3350

American Helix Technology Corporation
1857 Colonial Village Lane
Lancaster, PA 17601
(800)535–6575
FAX: (717)392–7897

Disctronics Inc.
9 Dehavilland Road
Braeside, Vic 3197
AUSTRALIA
03/587–2633
FAX: 03/587–2901

Memory Technology Inc.
2800 Summit Avenue
Plano, TX 75074
(214)881–8800

AXSES
Boutilier Point
Halifax, NS B0J 1G0
CANADA
(902)826–2440
FAX: (826)429–6521

Software Mart
4131 Spicewood Springs Road
Suite I-3
Austin, TX 78759–8608
(512)346–7887
FAX: (512)346–1393

Reteaco, Inc.
716 Gordon Baker Road
Willowdale, ON M2H 3B4
CANADA
(416)497–0579

Nimbus Records Inc.
P.O. Box 7305
Charlottesville, VA 22906
(804)985–1100

Nimbus Records, Ltd.
Wyastone Leys
Monmouth NP5 3SR
WALES
0600/890 682

Compiled by Online Press Inc.

DIRECTORY OF MASTERING/ REPLICATION FACILITIES

ALPHABETICAL LISTING OF MASTERING/REPLICATION FACILITIES

MASTERING/REPLICATION FACILITIES BY COUNTRY

ALPHABETICAL LISTING OF MASTERING/REPLICATION FACILITIES

Company	Mastering Fee	Per Disc Fee	Jewel Boxes	Artwork	Turn-around Time	Notes
3M 3M Center Optical Recording Department Building 223-5S-01 St. Paul, MN 55144 USA (612)733–1110 FAX: (612)733–0158	$1,600	$2.00	Yes	2-color	1–15 days	Mastering and per-disc fees depend on turnaround time and quantity. Also available are a wide variety of packaging/distribution options including disc serialization, 4-color prints, custom packaging, and direct distribution.
American Helix Technology Corporation 1857 Colonial Village Lane Lancaster, PA 17601 USA (800)525–6575 FAX: (717)392–7897	*					
Capitol Industries/EMI 3 Capitol Way Jacksonville, IL 62650 USA (217)245–9631	*					
CD Mastering AB Box 9173 20039 Malmo SWEDEN Country Code: 46 040/946 570 FAX: 040/949 660	*		Yes	1-color	2–3 weeks	
DADC 1800 North Fruitridge Avenue Terre Haute, IN 47804 USA (812)466–6821 FAX: (812)466–9128			Yes	2-color	3 days	Mastering fees range from $1,500–3,500.
Dai Nippon Printing Company Ltd. 1–1 Ichigaya-kagacho 1-chome Shinjuku-ku, Tokyo 162 JAPAN Country Code: 81 03/266–2111 FAX: 03/235–2594	*					

*Contact company for prices.

Company	Mastering Fee	Per Disc Fee	Jewel Boxes	Artwork	Turn-around Time	Notes
Denon America 1380 Monticello Road Madison, GA 30650 USA (404)342–3425	$1,500	$2.20	Yes	2-color		Mastering fee includes pre-mastering. Prices include insertion of customer-provided booklet, shrinkwrap, bulk packaging, and drop shipment.
Denon America 222 New Road Parsippany, NJ 07054 USA (201)575–7810 FAX: (201)575–2532	$1,500	$2.20	Yes	2-color		Mastering fee includes pre-mastering. Prices include insertion of customer-provided booklet, shrinkwrap, bulk packaging, and drop shipment.
Digipress 10 Rue de Paris 78100 St. Germain en Laye FRANCE	*					
Discovery Systems 7001 Discovery Boulevard Dublin, OH 43017 USA (614)761–2000 FAX: (614)761–4258	$1,500	$2.00	Yes	2-color	5 days	No advance notice required. Mastering done in as little as 1 day for extra charge.
Disctronics Inc. 1120 Cosby Way Anaheim, CA 92806 USA (714)630–6700 FAX: (714)630–1025	$800	$2.00				
Disctronics Inc. 24 Queen Anne's Gate London SW1H 9AD ENGLAND Country Code: 44 1/222–6878 FAX: 1/222–4407	*					

*Contact company for prices

(continued)

ALPHABETICAL LISTING OF MASTERING/REPLICATION FACILITIES *continued*

Company	Mastering Fee	Per Disc Fee	Jewel Boxes	Artwork	Turn-around Time	Notes
Disctronics Inc. 4905 Mooresmill Road Huntsville, AL 35881 USA (205)859–9042 FAX: (205)859–9932	$800	$2.00		2-color	10	As fast as 1 day turnaround time available. Extra charge for jewel box cases, booklets, shrink wrap.
Disctronics Inc. 9 Dehavilland Road Braeside, Vic 3197 AUSTRALIA Country Code: 61 03/587–2633 FAX: 03/587–2901	*					
ICM Ltd. Muehlebachstrassae 27 8800 Thalwil SWITZERLAND Country Code: 41 01/720–7942	*					
JVC Disc America Inc. 2 JVC Road Tuscaloosa, AL 35405 USA (205)556–7111	*					
Memory Technology Inc. 2800 Summit Avenue Plano, TX 75074 USA (214)881–8800	*					
Moulage Plastique de l'Ouest RC Mayenne 61B2 53700 Averton FRANCE Country Code: 33 043/032 735 FAX: 043/037 933	*					
Nimbus Records Inc. P.O. Box 7305 Charlottesville, VA 22906 USA (804)985–1100	$1,000	$2.25	Yes	2-color	72 hours	

*Contact company for prices.

Company	Mastering Fee	Per Disc Fee	Jewel Boxes	Artwork	Turn-around Time	Notes
Nimbus Records, Ltd. Wyastone Leys Monmouth NP5 3SR WALES Country Code: 222 0600/890682	$1,000	$2.25	Yes	2-color	72 hours	
Philips and DuPont Optical Customer Pressing Department Klussreide 26 3012 Langenhagen 1 WEST GERMANY Country Code: 49 0511/730–6331 FAX: 0511/731 802	*					
Philips and DuPont Optical Kings Mountain Highway 29 Grover, NC 28073 USA (800)433–3475 FAX: (302)479–2512	$1,500	$2.50	Yes	3-color	5 days	The mastering fee given is approximate, depending on the volume, contract, and customer. Includes 50 discs at no extra charge, the use of a CD Publisher for 1 day, and the Philips quality guarantee—if any sector of any disc is bad, you will receive a free master.
Sanyo Electric Company Optical Disk Products Department Ohmori Ampachi-cho Ampachi-gun, Gifu-ken 503-01 JAPAN Country Code: 81 058/464–4971 FAX: 058/464–4976	*					
Sanyo Laser Products 1767 Sheridan Street Richmond, IN 47374 USA (317)935–7574 FAX: (317)935–7570	$2,000	$5.00	Yes	2-color	7 days	Per-disc fee depends on quantity.

*Contact company for prices.

(continued)

ALPHABETICAL LISTING OF MASTERING/REPLICATION FACILITIES *continued*

Company	Mastering Fee	Per Disc Fee	Jewel Boxes	Artwork	Turn-around Time	Notes
Shape Optimedia Route 109 & Eagle Drive Sanford, ME 04073 USA (207)324–1124 FAX: (207)490–1707	$1,500	$2.50	Yes	2-color	5 days	Mastering fee is approximate.
Sonopress GmbH Carl-Bertelsmann-Strassae 161 4830 Gütersloh 1 WEST GERMANY Country Code: 49 05241/805 415 FAX: 05241/78521	$6,490	$8.90	Yes	1-color	8 days	Prices are in DM. Shorter turn-around on special request.
Toolex Alpha Esplanaden 1 P.O. Box 176 17225 Sundbyberg SWEDEN Country Code: 46 046/828–9030	*					

*Contact company for prices.

Compiled by Online Press Inc.

MASTERING/REPLICATION FACILITIES BY COUNTRY

Country/ (Code)	Company	Mastering Fee	Per Disc Fee	Jewel Boxes	Artwork	Turn- around Time	Notes
AUSTRALIA (61)	Disctronics Inc. 9 Dehavilland Road Braeside, Vic 3197 03/587–2633 FAX: 03/587–2901	*					
ENGLAND (44)	Disctronics Inc. 24 Queen Anne's Gate London SW1H 9AD 1/222–6878 FAX: 1/222–4407	*					
FRANCE (33)	Digipress 10 Rue de Paris 78100 St. Germain en Laye	*					
	Moulage Plastique de l'Ouest RC Mayenne 61B2 53700 Averton 043/032 735 FAX: 043/037 933	*					
JAPAN (81)	Dai Nippon Printing Company Ltd. 1–1 Ichigaya-kagacho 1-chome Shinjuku-ku, Tokyo 16? 03/266–2111 FAX: 03/235–2594	*					
	Sanyo Electric Company Optical Disk Products Department Ohmori Ampachi-cho Ampachi-gun, Gifu-ken 503-01 058/464–4971 FAX: 058/464–4976	*					

*Contact company for prices.

(continued)

MASTERING/REPLICATION FACILITIES BY COUNTRY *continued.*

Country / (Code)	Company	Mastering Fee	Per Disc Fee	Jewel Boxes	Artwork	Turn-around Time	Notes
SWEDEN (46)	CD Mastering AB Box 9173 20039 Malmo 040/946 570 FAX: 040/949 660	*		Yes	1-color	2–3 weeks	
	Toolex Alpha Esplanaden 1 P.O. Box 176 17225 Sundbyberg 046/828–9030	*					
SWITZERLAND (41)	ICM Ltd. Muehlebachstrassae 27 8800 Thalwil 01/720–7942	*					
USA	3M 3M Center Optical Recording Department Building 223-5S-01 St. Paul, MN 55144 (612)733–1110 FAX: (612)733–0158	$1,600	$2.00	Yes	2-color	1–15 days	Mastering and per-disc fees depend on turnaround time and quantity. Also available are a wide variety of packaging/distribution options including disc serialization, 4-color prints, custom packaging and direct distribution.
	American Helix Tech- nology Corporation 1857 Colonial Village Lane Lancaster, PA 17601 (800)525–6575 FAX: (717)392–7897	*					
	Capitol Industries/EMI 3 Capitol Way Jacksonville, IL 62650 (217)245–9631	*					

*Contact company for prices.

Country / (Code)	Company	Mastering Fee	Per Disc Fee	Jewel Boxes	Artwork	Turn-around Time	Notes
USA	DADC 1800 North Fruitridge Avenue Terre Haute, IN 47804 (812)466–6821 FAX: (812)466–9128			Yes	2-color	3 days	Mastering fees range from $1,500–3,500.
	Denon America 1380 Monticello Road Madison, GA 30650 (404)342–3425	$1,500	$2.20	Yes	2-color		Mastering fee includes pre-mastering. Prices include insertion of customer-provided booklet, shrinkwrap, bulk packaging, and drop shipment.
	Denon America 222 New Road Parsippany, NJ 07054 (201)575–7810 FAX: (201)575–2532	$1,500	$2.20	Yes	2-color		Mastering fee includes pre-mastering. Prices include insertion of customer-provided booklet, shrinkwrap, bulk packaging, and drop shipment.
	Discovery Systems 7001 Discovery Boulevard Dublin, OH 43017 (614)761–2000 FAX: (614)761–4258	$1,500	$2.00	Yes	2-color	5 days	No advance notice required. Mastering done in as little as 1 day for extra charge.
	Disctronics Inc. 4905 Mooresmill Road Huntsville, AL 35881 (205)859–9042 FAX: (205)859–9932	$800	$2.00		2-color	10	As fast as 1 day turnaround time available. Extra charge for jewel box cases, booklets, shrink wrap.
	Disctronics Inc. 1120 Cosby Way Anaheim, CA 92806 (714)630–6700 FAX: (714)630–1025	$800	$2.00				
	JVC Disc America Inc. 2 JVC Road Tuscaloosa, AL 35405 (205)556–7111	*					

*Contact company for prices.

(continued)

MASTERING/REPLICATION FACILITIES BY COUNTRY *continued.*

Country / (Code)	Company	Mastering Fee	Per Disc Fee	Jewel Boxes	Artwork	Turn- around Time	Notes
USA	Memory Technology Inc. 2800 Summit Avenue Plano, TX 75074 (214)881–8800	*					
	Nimbus Records Inc. P.O. Box 7305 Charlottesville, VA 22906 (804)985–1100	$1,000	$2.25	Yes	2-color	72 hours	
	Philips and DuPont Optical Kings Mountain Highway 29 Grover, NC 28073 (800)433–3475 FAX: (302)479–2512	$1,500	$2.50	Yes	3-color	5 days	The mastering fee given is approximate, depending on the volume, contract, and customer. Includes 50 discs at no extra charge, the use of a CD Publisher for 1 day, and the Philips quality guarantee—if any sector of any disc is bad, you will receive a free master.
	Sanyo Laser Products 1767 Sheridan Street Richmond, IN 47374 (317)935–7574 FAX: (317)935–7570	$2,000	$5.00	Yes	2-color	7 days	Per-disc fee depends on quantity. They also do premastering.
	Shape Optimedia Route 109 & Eagle Drive Sanford, ME 04073 (207)324–1124 FAX: (207)490–1707	$1,500	$2.50	Yes	2-color	5 days	Mastering fee is approximate.
WALES (222)	Nimbus Records, Ltd. Wyastone Leys Monmouth NP5 3SR 0600/890682	$1,000	$2.25	Yes	2-color	72 hours	

*Contact company for prices.

Country/ (Code)	Company	Mastering Fee	Per Disc Fee	Jewel Boxes	Artwork	Turn-around Time	Notes
WEST GERMANY (49)	Philips and DuPont Optical Customer Pressing Department Klussreide 26 3012 Langenhagen 1 0511/730–6331 FAX: 0511/731 802	*					
	Sonopress GmbH Carl-Bertelsmann-Strassae 161 4830 Gütersloh 1 05241/805 415 FAX: 05241/78521	$6,490	$8.90	Yes	1-color	8 days	Prices are in DM. Shorter turn-around on special request.

*Contact company for prices.

Compiled by Online Press Inc.

DIRECTORY OF CD-ROM RESOURCES

ALPHABETICAL LISTING OF CD-ROM RESOURCES

ALPHABETICAL LISTING OF CD-ROM RESOURCES

Title/Author	Publisher	Description	Price Per Issue	Price Per Year	Freq. of Pub.	Year of Pub.
1988 Information Industry Factbook Maureen Fleming, Melanie Rosenbaum, Jeff Silverstein, Chris Elwell, and Lee Fleming	Digital Information Group 51 Bank Street Stamford, CT 06901 (203)348-2751		$145.00		Annually	1987
1989 Information Management Sourcebook	Association for Information and Image Management 1100 Wayne Avenue Suite 1100 Silver Spring, MD 20910 (301)587-8202		$79.00			1989
	Ing. Alfredo Bronsoiler Sistemas Logicos Ejercito Nacional No. 373-801 D.F. 11520 MEXICO 203-1080	Introducing CD-ROM technology in Mexico. Representing American product lines in the Mexican market.				
Access Faxon	The Faxon Press 15 Southwest Park Westwood, MA 02090 (800)443-2966		$13.95	$24.00	Semi-annually	1988
The Brady Guide to CD-ROM Laura Buddine & Elizabeth Young	Brady Books 1 Gulf + Western Plaza New York, NY 10023 (212)373-8142 FAX: (212)373-8292		$21.95			1988

Title	Publisher/Address	Notes	Price	Subscription	Frequency	Year
Bureau of Electronic Publishing Product Guide	Bureau of Electronic Publishing P.O. Box 43131 Upper Montclair, NJ 07043 (201)746-3031	Catalog is free to Bureau customers.	$4.95	$15.00	Quarterly	1988
CALICO Journal	CALICO 3078 JKHB Brigham Young University Provo, UT 84602 (801)378-7079 FAX: (801)378-6533	Subscription includes membership in CALICO organization.	$7.50	$30.00	Quarterly	1983
CD Computing News	Worldwide Videotex P.O. Box 138 Babson Park Boston, MA 02157 (617)449-1603			$150.00	Monthly	1987
CD Data Report	Langley Publications, Inc. 1350 Beverly Road Suite 115-324 McLean, VA 22101 (703)241-2131 FAX: (703)532-5447	Archives available: 5 years for $900.	$25.00	$275.00	Monthly	1984
CD Publisher News	Meridian Data, Inc. 4450 Capitola Road Suite 101 Capitola, CA 95010 (408)476-5858 FAX: (408)476-8908		Free	Free	Quarterly	1986
CD-I and Interactive Videodisc Technology Steve Lambert and Jane Sallis	Howard W. Sams and Co., A Division of MacMillan Inc. 4300 West 62nd Street Indianapolis, IN 45268 (317)298-5400	A valuable guide to the market, tools, and techniques used to create interactive videodisc and CD-I applications.	$24.95			1987

(continued)

ALPHABETICAL LISTING OF CD-ROM RESOURCES *continued*

Title/Author	Publisher	Description	Price Per Issue	Price Per Year	Freq. of Pub.	Year of Pub.
CD-ROM 2: Optical Publishing Edited by Suzanne Ropiequet, with John Einberger and Bill Zoellick	Microsoft Press 16011 N.E. 36th Way Box 97017 Redmond, WA 98073-9717 (206)882-8080 FAX: (206)883-8101	A comprehensive overview of the entire optical publishing process as well as a practical handbook for product development. Topics include evaluating and defining the storage and retrieval method; collecting and preparing text, images, and sound; converting data formats; premastering and mastering; and protecting and copyrighting data.	$22.95			1987
CD-ROM Applications and Markets Edited by Judith Paris Roth	Meckler Corporation 11 Ferry Lane West Westport, CT 06880 (203)226-6967 FAX: (203)454-5840	An easy-to-understand guide to the application of CD-ROM in a variety of settings: information service, government and law, science and health care, and education and the humanities. The book includes a chapter on marketing the technology to various sectors as well as a brief addendum that explains the technology for those who are curious about how CD-ROM works.	$34.50			1988
CD-ROM Databases	Worldwide Videotex P.O. Box 138 Babson Park Boston, MA 02157 (617)449-1603			$150.00	Monthly	1987
CD-ROM Industry Review and Outlook, 1987-1992 Stephen Sieck	LINK Resources Corporation 79 Fifth Avenue New York, NY 10003 (212)627-1500 FAX: (212)620-3099	This updated summary of CD-ROM industry statistics, trends, and market opportunities reviews the most significant developments in the industry over the past year, and discusses its evolution in 1988 and beyond. Each major segment of CD-ROM activity—disc and drive manufacturers, data preparation/premastering services and systems vendors, software vendors, and CD-ROM publishers and information providers will be analyzed in terms of the major players, key issues, and LINK's predictions of future trends and developments.	$2,495			1988

CD-ROM Librarian Editor: Nancy Melin Nelson	Meckler Corporation 11 Ferry Lane West Westport, CT 06880 (203)226-6967 FAX: (203)454-5840	Provides information on developments in optical storage within libraries and information centers. Each issue includes the latest news, editorial comment and articles about CD-ROM hardware/software developments and applications for the library community. The major feature of the CD-ROM Librarian is its product reviews, offering readers an authoritative source of what is available.	$65.00	10 issues per year	1986
CD-ROM Markets	International Resource Development Inc. 21 Locust Avenue #1C P.O. Box 1718 New Canaan, CT 06840 (203)866-7800 FAX: (203)966-3040	A timely analysis of the markets for CD-ROM, including an account of the technology's evolution and the major applications perceived at this time.	$1,850		1986
CD-ROM Review	IDG Communications/ Peterborough 80 Elm Street Peterborough, NH 03458 (603)924-9471		$3.95	$14.97 Quarterly	1986
CD-ROM Software: Textual Retrieval and Networking Issues Edwin B. Brownrigg, Clifford A. Lynch, and John C. Gale	Information Workstation Group 501 Queen Street Alexandria, VA 22314 (703)548-4320 FAX: (703)548-4585	Introduces the transportable media technologies, discusses implications for the marketplace, addresses CD-ROM compatibility and usability, provides a set of 20 cross-reference tables and 120 pages of profiles of the CD-ROM textual retrieval systems and their developers, reviews textual database concepts, user interfaces, data sharing concepts, networking technology, licensing issues for networks, security and copyright issues, and standards. (280 pages)	$1,990		1988
CD-ROM Sourcebook	Diversified Data Resources Inc. 6609 Rosecroft Place Falls Church, VA 22043 (703)237-0682 FAX: (703)532-5547	13 sections including search and retrieval software programs, consultants, data preparation, titles, conferences, mastering and replication facilities, CD-ROM company information, industry data, authoring/premastering system, distributors, drives, systems, and publications.	$525.00	Annually	

(continued)

ALPHABETICAL LISTING OF CD-ROM RESOURCES *continued*

Title/Author	Publisher	Description	Price Per Issue	Price Per Year	Freq. of Pub.	Year of Pub.
CD-ROM Sourcedisc	Diversified Data Resources Inc. 6609 Rosecroft Place Falls Church, VA 22043 (703)237–0682 FAX: (703)532–5547	Includes information on over 300 commercially available titles and demonstrations of over 75 of these titles. A glossary of CD-ROM related terms, technical information from CD Data Report, full text versions of CD-ROM: The New Papyrus and CD-ROM 2: Optical Publishing from Microsoft Press are also included.	$89.95		Yearly	1988
CD-ROM Standards: The Book Julie B. Schwerin with Parke Lightbown, Connie Bailey and Howard Kaikow	Learned Information Ltd. Woodside Hinksey Hill Oxford OX1 5AU ENGLAND 0865/730 275 FAX: 0865/736 534	Contains hard facts and cogent descriptions of the standards, their impact on the information market, and their implementation in the computer and information industries. Included is the expedited procedure to an official international standard.	$75.00			1986
CD-ROM: The New Papyrus Edited by Steve Lambert & Suzanne Ropiequet	Microsoft Press 16011 N.E. 36th Way Box 97017 Redmond, WA 98073-9717 (206)882–8080 FAX: (206)883–8101	A compendium of 45 articles by industry experts on every facet of CD-ROM technology. Includes sections covering the basic hardware, system software, and retrieval software; data preparation and multimedia possibilities; authoring systems and project management; CD-ROM publishing; and CD-ROM applications. Foreword by Bill Gates.	$21.95			1986
CD-ROMs In Print 1988-1989 Edited by Jean-Paul Emard	Meckler Corporation 11 Ferry Lane West Westport, CT 06880 (203)226–6967 FAX: (203)454–5840	A comprehensive, international listing of CD-ROM products, providers, and distributors.	$37.50		Annually	1988
Computer Dealer Tom Farre, Editor	Gordon Publications, Inc. P.O. Box 1952 Dover, NJ 07801 (201)361–9060 FAX: (201)361-6264	Free to qualified subscribers (computer dealers).	Free	Free	Monthly	1977

Computer Lib/Dream Machines Ted Nelson	Microsoft Press 16011 N.E. 36th Way Box 97017 Redmond, WA 98073–3717 (206)882–8080 FAX: (206)883–8101	$18.95		1987	An updated reissue of the 1974 book that inspired thousands in the computer industry. The book is an irreverent, off-the-wall compendium of Nelson's visionary wisdom on the important computer issues of today: design of easy-to use computer systems, artificial intelligence, and nonlinear information-storage methods dubbed hypertext. With new commentaries, insights, and reconsiderations. Introduction by Stewart Brand.
Digital Multimedia: CD-ROM XA, CD-I, DV-I, et al.	Information Workstation Group 501 Queen Street Alexandria, VA 22314 (703)548–4320 FAX: (703)548–4585	$990.00		1988	The various digital multimedia technologies are introduced, early applications are profiled, market activities are forecast (180 pages).
Electronic and Optical Publishing Review Editor, Julie B. Schwerin	Learned Information Ltd. Woodside Hinksey Hill Oxford OX1 5AU ENGLAND 0865/730 275 FAX: 0865/736 534	$90.00	Quarterly	1981	This journal focuses on the accessing of information in electronic form with in-depth views of the significant trends and timely issues within the online and videotex industries. EOPR also covers the emerging fields of desktop publishing and optical disc technology.
Electronic Services Update	LINK Resources Corporation 79 Fifth Avenue New York, NY 10003 (212)627–1500 FAX: (212)620–3099	$425.00	Monthly	1988	Electronic Services Update encompasses a panoply of interactive communication, information, processing, and other services. Recognizing that convergence in electronic services is a fact, LINK brings all its areas of coverage together in Electronic Services Update.
Essential Guide to CD-ROM Edited by Judith Paris Roth	Meckler Corporation 11 Ferry Lane West Westport, CT 06880 (203)226–6967 FAX: (203)454–5840	$29.95		1986	An important information resource guide to the basic principles of CD-ROM technology, CD-ROM operating systems and application software and hardware, and current and future applications.

(continued)

ALPHABETICAL LISTING OF CD-ROM RESOURCES *continued*

Title/Author	Publisher	Description	Price Per Issue	Price Per Year	Freq. of Pub.	Year of Pub.
The Factbook Data Disk Maureen Fleming	Digital Information Group 51 Bank Street Stamford, CT 06901 (203)348–2751	Contains 5 data sets, including Four Year Financials of DIG Index Companies, Private Company Revenue, Addresses of DIG Index Companies, CD-ROM Price Database, and Five Year Online Subscriber Statistics.	$200.00		Annually	1988
HyperAge Magazine	Hyperage Communications, Inc. 108 East Fremont Avenue Sunnyvale, CA 94087 (408)730–5829	Covers Hypermedia, HyperCard, Optical Media, and more.	$3.95	$19.95	Bimonthly	1988
HyperLink	Publishers Guild, Inc. P.O. Box 7723 66 Club Road Suite 110 Eugene, OR 97401 (800)544–0339	Also available with a companion disk for $14.95/issue or $67.95/year.	$4.95	$25.00	Bimonthly	1988
Information Media and Technology	Cimtech Hatfield Polytechnic P.O. Box 109 College Lane Hatfield, Herts AL10 9AB ENGLAND				Bimonthly	
Inhouse Seminars	Information Workstation Group 501 Queen Street Alexandria, VA 22314 (703)548–4320 FAX: (703)548–4585	Inhouse seminars are provided at client sites. These are one day seminars for small groups. Seminars available include *How, If and When To Implement CD-ROM*, *Marketing CD-ROM Based Products*, *Implementing Document Storage and Retrieval: CD-ROM vs WORM* and *Digital Multimedia on CD-ROM, CD-ROM XA, CD-I and DV-I*. Seminar costs for a group of up to twenty employees range from $1600 to $1800 plus travel expense. Client-specific agenda and schedule arrangements can be made by contacting the Information Workstation Group.				1985

876 SECTION VII: DIRECTORY LISTINGS

Interactive Multimedia Edited by Sueann Ambron & Kristina Hooper	Microsoft Press 16011 N.E. 36th Way Box 97017 Redmond, WA 98073-9717 (206)882–8080 FAX: (206)883–8101	A forward-thinking collection of 21 articles by leading researchers on the opportunities for educational multimedia technology, including hypertext, CD-ROM, CD-I, and interactive television. Foreword by John Sculley.	$24.95 1988
Laserdisk Professional	Pemberton Press Inc. 11 Tannery Lane Weston, CT 06883 FAX: (203)222–0122	The Laserdisk Professional is a bimonthly publication designed to assist librarians and information professionals in the selection, evaluation, purchase, and operation of CD-ROMs and other laserdisks.	$14.00 $86.00 Bimonthly 1988
The Legality of Optical Storage Robert Williams	Cohasset Associates Inc. 3806 Lake Point Tower 505 North Lake Shore Drive Chicago, IL 60611 (312)527–1550 FAX: (312)449–8712		$230.00 Updated as necessary 1987
Lesco's New Tech Sourcebook: A Directory to Finding Answers in Today's Technology-Oriented World Matthew Lesco	Harper & Rowe Publishers, Inc. 10 East 53rd Street New York, NY 10022 (800)242–7737		1986
The Librarian's CD-ROM Handbook Norman Desmarais	Meckler Corporation 11 Ferry Lane West Westport, CT 06880 (203)226–6967 FAX: (203)454–5840	Selecting and implementing CD-ROM based information systems offers many new and challenging opportunities for librarians and information managers. This book demystifies the experience by discussing the various steps from the selection process right through implementation and evaluation.	$35.00 1988
Library Applications of Optical Disc and CD-ROM Technology Nancy Melin Nelson	Meckler Corporation 11 Ferry Lane West Westport, CT 06880 (203)226–6967 FAX: (203)454–5840	This volume is a guide to the various systems available for potential and actual use in libraries and information centers. The systems included are primarily those designed as databases, cataloging support systems, and public access catalogs.	$29.95 1987

(continued)

ALPHABETICAL LISTING OF CD-ROM RESOURCES *continued*

Title/Author	Publisher	Description	Price Per Issue	Price Per Year	Freq. of Pub.	Year of Pub.
Library Hi Tech Bibliography	Pieran Press, Inc. P.O. Box 1808 Ann Arbor, MI 48106 (313)434-5530	Critically annotated bibliographies on information technology topics.		$45.00	Annually	1986
Library Hi Tech Journal	Pieran Press, Inc. P.O. Box 1808 Ann Arbor, MI 48106 (313)434-5530	Covers state-of-the-art and threshold technologies that affect information delivery.	$17.50	$55.00	Quarterly	1983
Library Hi Tech News	Pieran Press, Inc. P.O. Box 1808 Ann Arbor, MI 48106 (313)434-5530	Contains timely articles, conference reports, and information on new products. Two bibliographies included in each issue, 1 monitoring approximately 220 information industry publications. Also included are reviews of software for MS-DOS, Macintosh, and UNIX environments.		$85.00	Monthly	1984
LISA Online Users Manual	Learned Information Ltd. Woodside Hinksey Hill Oxford OX1 5AU ENGLAND 0865/730 275 FAX: 0865/736 534	This updated manual enables effective and economic searching of the Library and Information Science Abstracts (LISA) database, giving details of the file, indexing policy, journal coverage, and a thesaurus of over 6,000 controlled index terms.	$45.00		Irregular	1983
MACazine	Icon Concepts Inc. 8008 Shoal Creek Boulevard Austin, TX 78758 (512)467-4550 FAX: (512)467-4503		$2.95	$23.00	Monthly	1984

Macintosh Hypermedia Michael Fraase	Scott, Foresman and Co. 1900 East Lake Avenue Glenview, IL 60025 (312)729-3000 FAX: (312)635-4150	Targeted at intermediate to advanced Macintosh users, this book will serve as a tutorial and reference covering both hardware and software tools. Offering a wide variety of information not available elsewhere, it will focus on CD-ROM and provide information about current Mac hypermedia implementations, uses and applications, social implications of hypermedia and offer a look at the future of hypermedia. Appendices include a mini source book.	$24.95		1989
MacUser	Ziff-Davis Publishing Company 950 Tower Lane Eighteenth Floor Foster City, CA 94404 (800)525-0643 FAX: (415)378-5675		$3.95	$19.97	Monthly
MacWEEK	Coastal Associates Publishing, L.P. One Park Avenue New York, NY 10016 (609)428-5000 FAX: (415)243-0513		$2.50	$75.00	Weekly 1987
MACWORLD	PCW Communications, Inc. 501 Second Street San Francisco, CA 94107 (800)525-0643		$3.95	$19.95	Monthly 1984
Marketing	T.J. Lowenhaupt, Inc. Box 1027 Jackson Heights New York, NY 11372 (718)639-4222	The best way to sell a compact disc is to give the prospect a sample of the product and demonstrate how it's used. T.J. Lowenhaupt, Inc. combines product samples, demonstrations, and tutorials on floppy diskettes. It surrounds these with creative advertising. The electronic brochure thus created is a selling tool like none before it.			

(continued)

ALPHABETICAL LISTING OF CD-ROM RESOURCES *continued*

Title/Author	Publisher	Description	Price Per Issue	Price Per Year	Freq. of Pub.	Year of Pub.
Micrographics and Optical Storage Equipment Review 1987 Edited by William Saffady	Meckler Corporation 11 Ferry Lane West Westport, CT 06880 (203)226-6967 FAX: (203)454-5840	In-depth reviews and tutorials on new equipment for library applications.	$175.00		Annually	1986
Microsoft Systems Journal	Microsoft Corporation 666 Third Avenue New York, NY 10017 (800)669-1002	A publication devoted to the concerns of the professional software developer. Articles explore issues in OS/2, DOS, Microsoft Windows, CD-ROM, programming languages (particularly C), and the 286 and 386 chips.	$10.00	$50.00	Bimonthly	1986
Network News	Meridian Data, Inc. 4450 Capitola Road Suite 101 Capitola, CA 95010 (408)476-5858 FAX: (408)476-8908		Free	Free	Quarterly	1988
Online Libraries and Microcomputers	Information Intelligence Inc. P.O. Box 31098 Phoenix, AZ 85046 (800)228-9982	Aimed at North American libraries and information centers, this newsletter deals primarily with online and microcomputer applications and library automation. Discounts available for students and non-institutional subscriptions.	$5.00	$50.00	Monthly	1983
Online Newsletter	Information Intelligence Inc. P.O. Box 31098 Phoenix, AZ 85046 (800)228-9982	Is international in scope covering all aspects of online developments throughout the world. Discounts available for students and non-institutional subscriptions.	$5.00	$50.00	Monthly	1980
Online Review	Learned Information Ltd. Woodside Hinksey Hill Oxford OX1 5AU ENGLAND 0865/730 275 FAX: 0865/736 534	Online Review is an international journal respected worldwide for its high quality and wide-ranging topical coverage. Edited by experts in the field, the reader is kept informed on the use and management of online systems, the training and education of online users, the creation and marketing of databases, and new developments in search aids.		$89.00	Bimonthly	1977

Online	Online Inc. 11 Tannery Lane Weston, CT 06883 (203)227-8466		$14.00	Bimonthly 1977
Optical Data Storage Outlook	Freeman Associates, Inc. 311 East Carrillo Street Santa Barbara, CA 93101 (805)963-3853 FAX: (805)962-1541	A comprehensive 450-page report covering CD-ROM, WORM, optical jukeboxes, erasable drives, and related subjects.	$1,750	Annually 1987
Optical Disk Document Storage and Retrieval Systems	International Resource Development Inc. 21 Locust Avenue #1C P.O. Box 1718 New Canaan, CT 06840 (203)866-7800	A study projecting the impact of optical disk technology on document storage and retrieval markets. Optical disk and competing technologies are compared, key issues are discussed, suppliers are profiled, and ten-year market forecasts are provided.	$2,100	As the market requires
Optical Disks for Data and Document Storage William Saffady	Meckler Corporation 11 Ferry Lane West Westport, CT 06880 (203)226-6967 FAX: (203)454-5840	A major report on optical disk technology, product development and applications, this book concentrates on the products and services introduced during the last few years, analyzing the features and capabilities of available systems, and comparing them with conventional magnetic storage and micrographics technologies.	$29.95	1986
Optical Disks vs Micrographics As Document Storage & Retrieval Technologies William Saffady	Meckler Corporation 11 Ferry Lane West Westport, CT 06880 (203)226-6967 FAX: (203)454-5840	Provides a detailed comparison of micrographics and optical disks as document storage and retrieval technologies. The book emphasizes the competitive relationship between micrographics and optical disks and analyzes factors which may promote or limit the utility of one or the other technology in specific situations.	$27.50	1988

(continued)

ALPHABETICAL LISTING OF CD-ROM RESOURCES *continued*

Title/Author	Publisher	Description	Price Per Issue	Price Per Year	Freq. of Pub.	Year of Pub.
Optical Information Systems '88 Conference Proceedings Edited by Judith Paris Roth	Meckler Corporation 11 Ferry Lane West Westport, CT 06880 (203)226–6967 FAX: (203)454–5840	Optical Information Systems '88 is an internationally respected educational forum for the dissemination of information on all applications of optical storage, CD-ROM, and interactive videodisc technologies, covering both hardware and software. Summaries of papers presented at the conference provide those interested in optical information systems applications with access to the latest industry developments. The 1989 conference will take place in Arlington, Virginia, September 6-8.	$30.00		Annually	1988
Optical Information Systems 1988 Buyer's Guide and Consultant Directory Norman Desmarais	Meckler Corporation 11 Ferry Lane West Westport, CT 06880 (203)226–6967 FAX: (203)454–5840	A comprehensive listing of OIS products currently on the market. It incorporates interactive videodiscs, optical disks and CD-ROMs, and, in addition to the hundreds of products and services included, provides details of the companies who produce them.	$24.95		Annually	1988
Optical Information Systems Update Editors: Mary Ann O'Connor, Judith Paris Roth, William Saffady	Meckler Corporation 11 Ferry Lane West Westport, CT 06880 (203)226–6967 FAX: (203)454–5840	A newsletter which updates events and developments in the fast developing fields of optical storage, CD-ROM and CD-I, and interactive videodisc.		$227.00	18 issues per year	1982
Optical Information Systems Editor: Judith Paris Roth	Meckler Corporation 11 Ferry Lane West Westport, CT 06880 (203)226–6967 FAX: (203)454–5840	A journal offering articles on the development and use of interactive videodisc, digital optical disk, CD-ROM, laser cards, and other media. Book reviews are also included.		$95.00	Bimonthly	1981
Optical Memory and Systems Information Service	Rothchild Consultants 256 Laguna Honda Boulevard San Francisco, CA 94116-1496 (415)681–3700 FAX: (415)681–3732	All Rothchild publications plus consultation services.				

Title	Publisher	Description	Price	Frequency	Year
Optical Memory News David Herzberg, Editor	Rothchild Consultants 256 Laguna Honda Boulevard San Francisco, CA 94116-1496 (415)681-3700 FAX: (415)681-3732	The publication of record for the optical storage industry. Readers include marketing decision-makers, technologists, end users, and system integrators. We focus on trade and technical news, as well as industry announcements, trade show coverage, and new product listings.	$395.00	Monthly	1980
Optical Memory Report: The Comprehensive Annual Sourcebook of the Optical Memory Industry Worldwide	Rothchild Consultants 256 Laguna Honda Boulevard San Francisco, CA 94116-1496 (415)681-3700 FAX: (415)681-3732	Provides complete company profiles, product listings and specifications for components, systems, and systems integrators currently involved in manufacturing or installing optical storage systems.	$1,995	Annually	1986
Optical Publishing Directory, 3rd Edition Richard A. Bowers, Editor	Learned Information, Inc. 143 Old Marlton Pike Medford, NJ 08055-8707 (609)654-6266 FAX: (609)654-4309	Features detailed profiles of nearly 200 published CD-ROM and other optical products.	$45.00	Irregular	1988
Optical Storage for Banking Applications	Rothchild Consultants 256 Laguna Honda Boulevard San Francisco, CA 94116-1496 (415)681-3700 FAX: (415)681-3732	Introductory price. Final price will be $1495.	$995.00		1988
Optical Storage for Insurance Applications	Rothchild Consultants 256 Laguna Honda Boulevard San Francisco, CA 94116-1496 (415)681-3700 FAX: (415)681-3732	Introductory price. Final price will be $1495.	$995.00		1988

(continued)

ALPHABETICAL LISTING OF CD-ROM RESOURCES *continued*

Title/Author	Publisher	Description	Price Per Issue	Price Per Year	Freq. of Pub.	Year of Pub.
Optical Storage for Pharmaceutical Applications	Rothchild Consultants 256 Laguna Honda Boulevard San Francisco, CA 94116-1496 (415)681-3700 FAX: (415)681-3732	Introductory price. Final price will be $1495.	$995.00			1988
Optical Storage of Engineering and Manufacturing Documents Dr. Gerry Walter	Rothchild Consultants 256 Laguna Honda Boulevard San Francisco, CA 94116-1496 (415)681-3700 FAX: (415)681-3732	The reference guide to components, technologies, and integration issues affecting the automation of engineering and manufacturing documents. A detailed index and market projections are included.	$1,495			1988
Optical Storage of Office and Transaction Documents Dr. Gerry Walter	Rothchild Consultants 256 Laguna Honda Boulevard San Francisco, CA 94116-1496 (415)681-3700 FAX: (415)681-3732	The reference guide to imaging technologies, storage components, and applications issues surrounding the automation of office and transaction documents.	$1,495			1988
Optical Storage Technology 1988: A State of the Art Review William Saffady	Meckler Corporation 11 Ferry Lane West Westport, CT 06880 (203)226-6967 FAX: (203)454-5840	For information management professionals and others responsible for planning and implementing economical, high-capacity systems for data and document storage, this review of recent advances in optical disk technology and applications will be of interest and value. It includes detaeied analyses of read-only and read/write technology.	$39.50		Annually	1988
Optical Storage Technology Tutorial Workbook	Rothchild Consultants 256 Laguna Honda Boulevard San Francisco, CA 94116-1496 (415)681-3700 FAX: (415)681-3732		$125.00		Quarterly	1987

Optical Storage Technology: A Bibliography William Saffady	Meckler Corporation 11 Ferry Lane West Westport, CT 06880 (203)226–6967 FAX: (203)454–5840	Provides an extensive compilation of citations to published literature dealing with all facets of optical storage technology. This book is also available on a set of four disks that conform to Pro-Cite.	$45.00	1989
Publishing with CD-ROM Patti Myers	Meckler Corporation 11 Ferry Lane West Westport, CT 06880 (203)226–6967 FAX: (203)454–5840	A guide to compact disk optical storage technologies for providers of publishing services. A definition of optical storage and its various forms introduces the subject, and is followed by a description of the different ways CD-ROMs can be used and what materials have been published and distributed on CD-ROMs to date. The book continues with a detailed examination of the publishing of a CD-ROM, and concludes with a survey of the future of CD-ROM and its implications for the providers of publishing and information services.	$22.95	1987
SIGCAT (Special Interest Group on CD-ROM Applications & Technology) E.J. (Jerry) McFaul	U.S. Geological Survey Reston, VA 22092 (703)648–7126	One of the fundamental reasons behind the establishment of SIGCAT was to share ideas and relate experiences about the use of CD-ROM in the Federal sector.	Free	Monthly
State of the CD-ROM Industry: Applications, Player, and Products Volume I	Information Workstation Group 501 Queen Street Alexandria, VA 22314 (703)548–4320 FAX: (703)548–4585	Volumes I and II together: $1990 per year. Volume I provides an introduction to the transportable digital data media industry, a comparative overview of information distribution technologies, a technology forecast, a presentation of the support industries, a discussion of market implications, a review of the relevant vertical markets and forecasts of market activities. (180 pages)	$1,350	Annually 1987
State of the CD-ROM Industry: Applications, Player, and Products Volume II	Information Workstation Group 501 Queen Street Alexandria, VA 22314 (703)548–4320 FAX: (703)548–4585	Volumes I and II together: $1990 per year. Volume II provides 360 pages of company profiles which are updated each quarter.	$750.00	Quarterly 1987

(continued)

ALPHABETICAL LISTING OF CD-ROM RESOURCES *continued*

Title/Author	Publisher	Description	Price Per Issue	Price Per Year	Freq. of Pub.	Year of Pub.
Videodiscs, Compact Discs and Digital Optical Discs Tony Hendley	Cimtech The Hatfield Polytechnic P.O. Box 109 College Lane Hatfield, Herts AL10 9AB ENGLAND	Optical information storage systems and their applications are clearly and concisely outlined in this publication designed for the users and suppliers of information systems. Three separate sections cover the major areas in the video/audio/information storage and retrieval systems: videodiscs, compact discs, and digital optical disks.	$48.00			1985

DIRECTORY OF CD-ROM AND RELATED CONFERENCES

ALPHABETICAL LISTING OF CONFERENCES

CONFERENCES BY DATE

ALPHABETICAL LISTING OF CONFERENCES

Conference	Sponsor/Description	Date/Location	Cost to Attend	Cost to Exhibit
14th Annual West Coast Computer Faire	Sponsored by The Interface Group, Inc.	03/17/89–03/19/89 Brook Falls San Francisco, CA	$15.00	$700.00
Annual NFAIS Conference	Sponsored by National Federation of Abstracting and Information Services (NFAIS). The Impact of Media Diversification: Production, Marketing, and Legal Issues.	02/26/89–03/01/89 Capitol Hilton Washington, DC	Free	Free
ARMA	Sponsored by ARMA International (Association of Records, Managers, and Administrators).	10/02/89–10/05/89 River Gate Convention Center New Orleans, LA	$490.00	$1,400.00
ASIS Annual	Sponsored by American Society for Information Science.	10/29/89–11/02/89 Omni Shoreham Hotel Washington, DC	$300.00	Free
ASIS Mid-Year	Sponsored by American Society for Information Science.	05/21/89–05/24/89 Town and Country Hotel San Diego, CA	Free	Free
CD-ROM Application Development Seminar	Sponsored by Reference Technology Inc. An intensive 2-day seminar for people considering or already involved in CD-ROM development.	03/02/89–03/03/89 05/15/89–05/16/89 Reference Technology Inc. Boulder, CO	$650.00	Free
CD-ROM Developers Seminar '89	Sponsored by Meridian Data, Inc. and Philips and DuPont Optical Company. Designed for corporate, institutional, and government CD-ROM developers, the session will outline a step-by-step approach to creating a CD-ROM product. The seminar will address key technical issues such as data conversion, data preparation, retrieval software, delivery systems, mastering, ISO file format, Microsoft CD-ROM Extensions, and multimedia considerations. Business issues such as costs, implementation analysis, and management backing will also be covered.	01/31/89 London Hilton Park Lane London, ENGLAND 02/07/89 Park Hilton Munich WEST GERMANY	$250.00	Free

Registration Contact	Program Contact	Exhibit Contact	Address	1988 Attendees	1988 Exhibitors
Registration Department (617)449–6600	Jim Collins (617)449–6600	Bill Mahan (617)449–6600	300 1st Avenue Needham, MA 02194		
Lynn Friedman (215)563–2406	Martha Cornog (215)563–2406	N/A	1429 Walnut Street 5th Floor Philadelphia, PA 19102	200	N/A
ARMA (800)422–2762	ARMA (800)422–2762	Alex Metzger (703)683–8500	4200 Somerset Drive Suite 215 Prairie Village, KS 66208	4000	300
ASIS (202)462–1000	Mark Robbins (202)462–1000	Mark Robbins (202)462–1000	1424 16th Street N.W. Suite 404 Washington DC 20036		
ASIS (202)462–1000	Mark Robbins (202)462–1000	N/A	1424 16th Street N.W. Suite 404 Washington DC 20036	460	N/A
Mike Befeler (303)449–4157	Mike Befeler (303)449–4157	N/A	5700 Flatiron Parkway Boulder, CO 80303	15	N/A
Monica Meyer (408)476–5858	Mark Sheldon (408)476–5858	N/A	4450 Capitola Road Suite 101 Capitola, CA 95010	200	9

(continued)

ALPHABETICAL LISTING OF CONFERENCES *continued*

Conference	Sponsor/Description	Date/Location	Cost to Attend	Cost to Exhibit
CD-ROM Developers Seminar '89	Sponsored by Meridian Data, Inc. and Philips and DuPont Optical Company. Designed for corporate, institutional, and government CD-ROM developers, the session will outline a step-by-step approach to creating a CD-ROM product. The seminar will address key technical issues such as data conversion, data preparation, retrieval software, delivery systems, mastering, ISO file format, Microsoft CD-ROM Extensions, and multimedia considerations. Business issues such as costs, implementation analysis, and management backing will also be covered.	04/12/89 Hyatt Crystal City Washington, DC 05/18/89 Fairmont Hotel San Jose, CA 10/16/89 Chicago Westin Chicago, IL 11/16/89 InfoMart Dallas, TX	$150.00	Free
CD-ROM: Technology and Applications	Sponsored by Database Technology. CD-ROM application development.	March Los Angeles, CA	$395.00	N/A
COMDEX/Fall '89	Sponsored by The Interface Group, Inc.	11/13/89–11/17/89 9 Las Vegas Hotels Las Vegas, NV	Free	Free
COMDEX/Spring '89	Sponsored by The Interface Group, Inc.	04/10/89–04/13/89 McCormick Place Chicago, IL	Free	Free
Defense and Government Computer Graphics Conference/Fall '89	Sponsored by World Computer Graphics Network.	10/23/89 Convention Center Washington, DC	Free	Free
Defense and Government Computer Graphics Conference/Spring '89	Sponsored by World Computer Graphics Network.	04/26/89 Anaheim Convention Center Anaheim, CA	Free	Free

Registration Contact	Program Contact	Exhibit Contact	Address	1988 Attendees	1988 Exhibitors
Monica Meyer (408)476–5858	Mark Sheldon (408)476–5858	N/A	4450 Capitola Road Suite 101 Capitola, CA 95010	200	9
Dr. Ash Pahwa (714)733–3378	Dr. Ash Pahwa (714)733–3378	N/A	18 Chenile Irvine, CA 92714		
Registration Department (617)449–6600	Jim Collins (617)449–6600	Bill Mahan (617)449–6600	300 1st Avenue Needham, MA 02194	95,000	1,600
Registration Department (617)449–6600	Jim Collins (617)449–6600	Bill Mahan (617)449–6600	300 1st Avenue Needham, MA 02194	80,000	800
National Council for Education on Information Strategies (800)343–6944	DruAnne Miller (301)961–6575	Mary Dickinson (301)961–8990	National Council P.O. Box 41045 7315 Wisconsin Avenue Suite 901-West Bethesda, MD 20814	13,500	400
National Council for Education on Information Strategies (800)343–6944	DruAnne Miller (301)961–6575	Mary Dickinson (301)961–8990	National Council P.O. Box 41045 7315 Wisconsin Avenue Suite 901-West Bethesda, MD 20814	13,500	400

(continued)

ALPHABETICAL LISTING OF CONFERENCES *continued*

Conference	Sponsor/Description	Date/Location	Cost to Attend	Cost to Exhibit
Electronic Imaging Forum VI	Sponsored by Shearson Lehman Hutton Inc. Fifth annual conference on the imaging industry. Emphasis is placed on product applications and marketing challenges.	01/30/89–01/31/89 Fairmont Hotel San Francisco, CA	$235.00	$135.00
Fed Micro Conference and Exposition	Sponsored by National Trade Productions, Inc. Organized in 1986 by the federal government's largest and most influential microcomputer organizations, this show provides government users and managers the opportunity to evaluate the latest hardware, software, and peripherals.	09/06/89–09/07/89 Convention Center Washington, DC	Free	$1,400.00
Federal Computer Conference/Fall '89	Sponsored by National Council for Education on Information Strategies.	10/23/89 Convention Center Washington, DC	Free	Free
Federal Computer Conference/Spring '89	Sponsored by National Council for Education on Information Strategies.	04/26/89 Anaheim Convention Center Anaheim, CA	Free	Free
FOSE Conference and Exposition	Sponsored by National Trade Productions, Inc. The federal government's information systems showcase, providing exhibitors with the opportunity to present their latest hardware, software, peripherals, and services.	03/06/89–03/09/89 Convention Center Washington, DC	$15.00	$2,100.00
Fourth Annual *Optical Storage for Large Systems*	Sponsored by Rothchild Consultants. End users and vendors will share their experiences of incorporating optical storage into large system architectures, providing conference attendees with a solid background in the integration issues essential for the implementation of optical storage in a large system.	10/17/89–10/19/89 The New York Hilton New York, NY	$995.00	

Registration Contact	Program Contact	Exhibit Contact	Address	1988 Attendees	1988 Exhibitors
Thomas T. McGrane (212)298–6008	Richard D. Schwarz (212)298–4950	Rena Mintern (212)640–9104	American Express Tower World Financial Center New York, NY 10285-1400	250	30
Natioanl Trade Productions, Inc. (800)638–8510	Linda Carter (800)638–8510	Sam Smith (800)638–8510	313 South Patrick Street Alexandria, VA 22314	7,000+	190
National Council (800)343–6944	DruAnne Miller (301)961–6575	Mary Dickinson (301)961–8990	P.O. Box 41045 7315 Wisconsin Avenue Suite 901-West Bethesda, MD 20814	13,500	400
National Council (800)343–6944	DruAnne Miller (301)961–6575	Mary Dickinson (301)961–8990	P.O. Box 41045 7315 Wisconsin Avenue Suite 901-West Bethesda, MD 20814	13,500	400
National Trade Productions, Inc. (800)638–8510	Linda Carter (800)638–8510	Sam Smith (800)638–8510	313 South Patrick Street Alexandria, VA 22314	41,409	395
Gail Rothchild (415)681–3700	Gail Rothchild (415)681–3700	Gail Rothchild (415)681–3700	256 Laguna Honda Boulevard San Francisco, CA 94116-1496	150	

(continued)

ALPHABETICAL LISTING OF CONFERENCES *continued*

Conference	Sponsor/Description	Date/Location	Cost to Attend	Cost to Exhibit
Groupware - The Next Wave	Sponsored by the Electronic Networking Association. The Electronic Networking Association is similar to what the Academy of Motion Picture Arts and Sciences was in the early 1900s, developing the new medium of computer-mediated communications, as the Academy developed the new medium of motion pictures. ENA is still a fledgling organization for the 'silent screen' era of computer communications.	05/25/89–05/28/89 Muhlenberg College Allentown, PA	$300.00	$50.00
Imaging: The Multimedia Conference and Exposition	Sponsored by American Expositions, Inc. The HyperExpo and Imaging: The Multimedia Expo together represent the computer movements of the 1990s. Over 10,000 attendees are expected.	06/20/89–06/22/89 Civic Auditorium San Francisco, CA	$40.00	$1,200.00
INFO '89 — Information Management Exposition and Conference	Sponsored by Cahners Exposition Group.	10/10/89–10/13/89 Javits Convention Center New York, NY	$495.00	$2,500.00
Interactive Videodisc Applications and Training Seminar	Sponsored by 3M and IBM. Developing a business case for using IVD as a training vehicle.	03/13/89–03/14/89 Los Angeles, CA 05/08/89–05/09/89 New York, NY 10/02/89–10/03/89 Atlanta, GA 11/20/89–11/21/89 Washington, DC	$395.00	N/A
Interactive Videodisc in Education and Training	Sponsored by Society for Applied Learning Technology.	08/23/89–08/25/89 Crystal Gateway Marriott Arlington, VA	$450.00	$1,375.00

Registration Contact	Program Contact	Exhibit Contact	Address	1988 Attendees	1988 Exhibitors
Nan Hanahue (215)821–7777	Ed Yarrish (215)821–7777	Ed Yarrish (215)821–7777	2744 Washington Street Allentown, PA 18104-4225	200	25
American Expositions, Inc. (212)226–4141	American Expositions, Inc. (212)226–4141	American Expositions, Inc. (212)226–4141	110 Greene Street Suite 703 New York, NY 10012	2,000	63
Kathleen Warren (203)964–0000	Kathleen Warren (203)964–0000	Frank Fazio (203)964–0000	999 Summer Street Stamford, CT 06905	45,000	300
Dr. Michael DeBloois (800)533-3907	Dr. Michael DeBloois (800)533-3907	Dr. Michael DeBloois (800)533-3907	MIKEN Communication 1436 East 3400 North Logan, UT 84321		
SALT (703)347–0055	SALT (703)347–0055	Ellen Fox (703)347–0055	50 Culpeper Street Warrenton, VA 22186	400	50

(continued)

ALPHABETICAL LISTING OF CONFERENCES continued

Conference	Sponsor/Description	Date/Location	Cost to Attend	Cost to Exhibit
International Summer Consumer Electronics Show	Sponsored by Electronic Industries Association/Consumer Electronic Group.	06/03/89–06/06/89 McCormick Place Chicago, IL	$25.00	$1,400.00
Microsoft Fourth International Conference on CD-ROM	Sponsored by Microsoft Corporation.	03/28/89–03/30/89 Anaheim Hilton & Towers Anaheim, CA	$950.00	$2,700.00
National Online Meeting	Sponsored by Learned Information, Inc.	05/09/89–05/11/89 Sheraton Centre New York, NY	$300.00	$950.00
Optical Disk Workshop	Sponsored by the Optical Disk Institute.	March Boston, MA Chicago, IL Los Angeles, CA	$545.00	N/A
The Seventh Annual Seybold Executive Forum	Sponsored by Patricia Seybold's Office Computing Group. Document Architecture.	11/08/89–11/10/89 Westin Hotel Boston, MA	$1,095.00	Free
Seybold Seminars '89	Sponsored by Seybold Seminars. Geared for professional publishers.	03/13/89–03/17/89 Hyatt Embarcadero San Francisco, CA	Free	Free
Supercomputing World Conference	Sponsored by Meeting Brokers International. The first exposition and conference to focus on the practical application of supercomputing power or the broadening spectrum of industrial, scientific, and academic needs.	10/17/89–10/20/89 Civic Auditorium San Francisco, CA		
The Technology Forum	Sponsored by Patricia Seybold's Office Computing Group. Emerging Technologies: Object Orientation and Compound Document Architecture.	04/03/89–04/05/89 Cambridge Marriott Cambridge, MA	$895.00	Free

Registration Contact	Program Contact	Exhibit Contact	Address	1988 Attendees	1988 Exhibitors
CES (202)457–8700	CES (202)457–8700	Phyllis Rosenthal (202)457–8700	1722 Eye Street N.W. Suite 200 Washington, DC 20006	98,651	1,400
Sherrie Eastman (206)882–8080	Tom Corddry (206)882–8080	Sherrie Eastman (206)882–8080	16011 N.E. 36th Way Box 97017 Redmond, WA 98073-9717	1,978	58
Dawn Wilson (609)654–6266	Dawn Wilson (609)654–6266	Carol Nixon (609)654–6266	143 Old Marlton Pike Medford, NJ 08055-8707	4,000	140
Optical Disk Institute (617)964–3925	Optical Disk Institute (617)964–3925	N/A	567 Walnut Street Newtonville, MA 02160		
Deborah Hay (617)742–5200		N/A	148 State Street Suite 612 Boston, MA 02109	300	N/A
Jill Zigoures (213)457–5850	Craig Cline (213)457–5850	Lena Lillsunde (213)457–5850	6922 Wildlife Road Malibu, CA 90265	1,200	90
MG Expositions (800)223–7126	Meeting Brokers International (203)786–5132	MG Expositions (800)223–7126	5 Science Park New Haven, CT 06511	N/A	N/A
Deborah Hay (617)742–5200		N/A	148 State Street Suite 612 Boston, MA 02109		

Compiled by Online Press Inc.

CONFERENCES BY DATE

Conference	Sponsor/Description	Date/Location	Cost to Attend	Cost to Exhibit
Electronic Imaging Forum VI	Sponsored by Shearson Lehman Hutton Inc. Fifth annual conference on the imaging industry. Emphasis is placed on product applications and marketing challenges.	01/30/89–01/31/89 Fairmont Hotel San Francisco, CA	$235.00	$135.00
CD-ROM Developers Seminar '89	Sponsored by Meridian Data, Inc. and Philips and DuPont Optical Company. Designed for corporate, institutional, and government CD-ROM developers, the session will outline a step-by-step approach to creating a CD-ROM product. The seminar will address key technical issues such as data conversion, data preparation, retrieval software, delivery systems, mastering, ISO file format, Microsoft CD-ROM Extensions, and multimedia considerations. Business issues such as costs, implementation analysis, and management backing will also be covered.	01/31/89 London Hilton Park Lane London, ENGLAND	$250.00	Free
CD-ROM Developers Seminar '89	Sponsored by Meridian Data, Inc. and Philips and DuPont Optical Company. Designed for corporate, institutional, and government CD-ROM developers, the session will outline a step-by-step approach to creating a CD-ROM product. The seminar will address key technical issues such as data conversion, data preparation, retrieval software, delivery systems, mastering, ISO file format, Microsoft CD-ROM Extensions, and multimedia considerations. Business issues such as costs, implementation analysis, and management backing will also be covered.	02/07/89 Park Hilton Munich WEST GERMANY	$250.00	Free

Registration Contact	Program Contact	Exhibit Contact	Address	1988 Attendees	1988 Exhibitors
Thomas T. McGrane (212)298–6008	Richard D. Schwarz (212)298–4950	Rena Mintern (212)640–9104	American Express Tower World Financial Center New York, NY 10285-1400	250	30
Monica Meyer (408)476–5858	Mark Sheldon (408)476–5858	N/A	4450 Capitola Road Suite 101 Capitola, CA 95010	200	9
Monica Meyer (408)476–5858	Mark Sheldon (408)476–5858	N/A	4450 Capitola Road Suite 101 Capitola, CA 95010	200	9

(continued)

CONFERENCES BY DATE *continued*

Conference	Sponsor/Description	Date/Location	Cost to Attend	Cost to Exhibit
Annual NFAIS Conference	Sponsored by National Federation of Abstracting and Information Services (NFAIS). The Impact of Media Diversification: Production, Marketing, and Legal Issues.	02/26/89–03/01/89 Capitol Hilton Washington, DC	Free	Free
CD-ROM: Technology and Applications	Sponsored by Database Technology. CD-ROM application development.	March Los Angeles, CA	$395.00	N/A
Optical Disk Workshop	Sponsored by Optical Disk Institute.	March Boston, MA	$545.00	N/A
CD-ROM Application Development Seminar	Sponsored by Reference Technology Inc. An intensive 2-day seminar for people considering or already involved in CD-ROM development.	03/02/89–03/03/89 Reference Technology Inc. Boulder, CO	$650.00	Free
FOSE Conference and Exposition	Sponsored by National Trade Productions, Inc. The federal government's information systems showcase, providing exhibitors with the opportunity to present their latest hardware, software, peripherals, and services.	03/06/89–03/09/89 Convention Center Washington, DC	$15.00	$2,100.00
Interactive Videodisc Applications and Training Seminar	Sponsored by 3M and IBM. Developing a business case for using IVD as a training vehicle.	03/13/89–03/14/89 Los Angeles, CA	$395.00	N/A
Seybold Seminars '89	Sponsored by Seybold Seminars. Geared for professional publishers.	03/13/89–03/17/89 Hyatt Embarcadero San Francisco, CA	Free	Free
14th Annual West Coast Computer Faire	Sponsored by The Interface Group, Inc.	03/17/89–03/19/89 Brook Falls San Francisco, CA	$15.00	$700.00

Registration Contact	Program Contact	Exhibit Contact	Address	1988 Attendees	1988 Exhibitors
Lynn Friedman (215)563–2406	Martha Cornog (215)563–2406	N/A	1429 Walnut Street 5th Floor Philadelphia, PA 19102	200	N/A
Dr. Ash Pahwa (714)733–3378	Dr. Ash Pahwa (714)733–3378	N/A	18 Chenile Irvine, CA 92714		
Optical Disk Institute (617)964–3925	Optical Disk Institute (617)964–3925	N/A	567 Walnut Street Newtonville, MA 02160		
Mike Befeler (303)449–4157	Mike Befeler (303)449–4157	N/A N/A	5700 Flatiron Parkway Boulder, CO 80303	15	N/A
National Trade Productions, Inc. (800)638–8510	Linda Carter (800)638–8510	Sam Smith (800)638–8510	313 South Patrick Street Alexandria, VA 22314	41,409	395
Dr. Michael DeBloois (800)533–3907	Dr. Michael DeBloois (800)533–3907	Dr. Michael DeBloois (800)533–3907	MIKEN Communication 1436 East 3400 North Logan, UT 84321		
Jill Zigoures (213)457–5850	Craig Cline (213)457–5850	Lena Lillsunde (213)457–5850	6922 Wildlife Road Malibu, CA 90265	1,200	90
Registration Department (617)449–6600	Jim Collins (617)449–6600	Bill Mahan (617)449–6600	300 1st Avenue Needham, MA 02194		

(continued)

CONFERENCES BY DATE *continued*

Conference	Sponsor/Description	Date/Location	Cost to Attend	Cost to Exhibit
Microsoft Fourth International Conference on CD-ROM	Sponsored by Microsoft Corporation.	03/28/89–03/30/89 Anaheim Hilton & Towers Anaheim, CA	$950.00	$2,700.00
The Technology Forum	Sponsored by Patricia Seybold's Office Computing Group. Emerging Technologies: Object Orientation and Compound Document Architecture.	04/03/89–04/05/89 Cambridge Marriott Cambridge, MA	$895.00	Free
COMDEX/Spring '89	Sponsored by The Interface Group, Inc.	04/10/89–04/13/89 McCormick Place Chicago, IL	Free	Free
CD-ROM Developers Seminar '89	Sponsored by Meridian Data, Inc. and Philips and DuPont Optical Company. Designed for corporate, institutional, and government CD-ROM developers, the session will outline a step-by-step approach to creating a CD-ROM product. The seminar will address key technical issues such as data conversion, data preparation, retrieval software, delivery systems, mastering, ISO file format, Microsoft CD-ROM Extensions, and multimedia considerations. Business issues such as costs, implementation analysis, and management backing will also be covered.	04/12/89 Hyatt Crystal City Washington, DC	$150.00	Free
Defense and Government Computer Graphics Conference/Spring '89	Sponsored by World Computer Graphics Network.	04/26/89 Anaheim Convention Center Anaheim, CA	Free	Free

Registration Contact	Program Contact	Exhibit Contact	Address	1988 Attendees	1988 Exhibitors
Sherrie Eastman (206)882–8080	Tom Corddry (206)882–8080	Sherrie Eastman (206)882–8080	16011 N.E. 36th Way Box 97017 Redmond, WA 98073-9717	1,978	58
Deborah Hay (617)742–5200		N/A	148 State Street Suite 612 Boston, MA 02109		
Registration Department (617)449–6600	Jim Collins (617)449–6600	Bill Mahan (617)449–6600	300 1st Avenue Needham, MA 02194	80,000	800
Monica Meyer (408)476–5858	Mark Sheldon (408)476–5858	N/A	4450 Capitola Road Suite 101 Capitola, CA 95010	200	9
National Council for Education on Information Strategies (800)343–6944	DruAnne Miller (301)961–6575	Mary Dickinson (301)961–8990	National Council P.O. Box 41045 7315 Wisconsin Avenue Suite 901-West Bethesda, MD 20814	13,500	400

(continued)

CONFERENCES BY DATE *continued*

Conference	Sponsor/Description	Date/Location	Cost to Attend	Cost to Exhibit
Federal Computer Conference/Spring '89	Sponsored by National Council for Education on Information Strategies.	04/26/89 Anaheim Convention Center Anaheim, CA	Free	Free
Optical Disk Workshop	Sponsored by Optical Disk Institute.	May Chicago, IL	$545.00	N/A
Interactive Videodisc Applications and Training Seminar	Sponsored by 3M and IBM. Developing a business case for using IVD as a training vehicle.	05/08/89–05/09/89 New York, NY	$395.00	N/A
National Online Meeting	Sponsored by Learned Information, Inc.	05/09/89–05/11/89 Sheraton Centre New York, NY	$300.00	$950.00
CD-ROM Application Development Seminar	Sponsored by Reference Technology Inc. An intensive 2-day seminar for people considering or already involved in CD-ROM development.	05/15/89–05/16/89 Reference Technology Inc. Boulder, CO	$650.00	Free
CD-ROM Developers Seminar '89	Sponsored by Meridian Data, Inc. and Philips and DuPont Optical Company. Designed for corporate, institutional, and government CD-ROM developers, the session will outline a step-by-step approach to creating a CD-ROM product. The seminar will address key technical issues such as data conversion, data preparation, retrieval software, delivery systems, mastering, ISO file format, Microsoft CD-ROM Extensions, and multimedia considerations. Business issues such as costs, implementation analysis, and management backing will also be covered.	05/18/89 Fairmont Hotel San Jose, CA	$150.00	Free

Registration Contact	Program Contact	Exhibit Contact	Address	1988 Attendees	1988 Exhibitors
National Council (800)343–6944	DruAnne Miller (301)961–6575	Mary Dickinson (301)961–8990	National Council P.O. Box 41045 7315 Wisconsin Avenue Suite 901-West Bethesda, MD 20814	13,500	400
Optical Disk Institute (617)964–3925	Optical Disk Institute (617)964–3925	N/A	567 Walnut Street Newtonville, MA 02160		
Dr. Michael DeBloois (800)533–3907	Dr. Michael DeBloois (800)533–3907	Dr. Michael DeBloois (800)533–3907	MIKEN Communication 1436 East 3400 North Logan, UT 84321		
Dawn Wilson (609)654–6266	Dawn Wilson (609)654–6266	Carol Nixon (609)654–6266	143 Old Marlton Pike Medford, NJ 08055-8707	4,000	140
Mike Befeler (303)449–4157	Mike Befeler (303)449–4157	N/A	5700 Flatiron Parkway Boulder, CO 80303	15	N/A
Monica Meyer (408)476–5858	Mark Sheldon (408)476–5858	N/A	4450 Capitola Road Suite 101 Capitola, CA 95010	200	9

(continued)

CONFERENCES BY DATE *continued*

Conference	Sponsor/Description	Date/Location	Cost to Attend	Cost to Exhibit
ASIS Mid-Year	Sponsored by American Society for Information Science.	05/21/89–05/24/89 Town and Country Hotel San Diego, CA	Free	Free
Groupware - The Next Wave	Sponsored by the Electronic Networking Association. The Electronic Networking Association is similar to what the Academy of Motion Picture Arts and Sciences was in the early 1900s, developing the new medium of computer-mediated communications, as the Academy developed the new medium of motion pictures. ENA is still a fledgling organization for the 'silent screen' era of computer communications.	05/25/89–05/28/89 Muhlenberg College Allentown, PA	$300.00	$50.00
International Summer Consumer Electronics Show	Sponsored by Electronic Industries Association/Consumer Electronic Group.	06/03/89–06/06/89 McCormick Place Chicago, IL	$25.00	$1,400.00
Imaging: The Multimedia Conference and Exposition	Sponsored by American Expositions, Inc. The HyperExpo and Imaging: The Multimedia Expo together represent the computer movements of the 1990s. Over 10,000 attendees are expected.	06/20/89–06/22/89 Civic Auditorium San Francisco, CA	$40.00	$1,200.00
Interactive Videodisc in Education and Training	Sponsored by Society for Applied Learning Technology	08/23/89–08/25/89 Crystal Gateway Marriott Arlington, VA	$450.00	$1,375.00
Optical Disk Workshop	Sponsored by Optical Disk Institute.	September Los Angeles, CA	$545.00	N/A
Fed Micro Conference and Exposition	Sponsored by National Trade Productions, Inc. Organized in 1986 by the federal government's largest and most influential microcomputer organizations, this show provides government users and managers the opportunity to evaluate the latest hardware, software, and peripherals.	09/06/89–09/07/89 Convention Center Washington, DC	Free	$1,400.00

Registration Contact	Program Contact	Exhibit Contact	Address	1988 Attendees	1988 Exhibitors
ASIS (202)462–1000	Mark Robbins (202)462–1000	N/A	1424 16th Street N.W. Suite 404 Washington DC 20036	460	N/A
Nan Hanahue (215)821–7777	Ed Yarrish (215)821–7777	Ed Yarrish (215)821–7777	2744 Washington Street Allentown, PA 18104-4225	200	25
CES (202)457–8700	CES (202)457–8700	Phyllis Rosenthal (202)457–8700	1722 Eye Street N.W. Suite 200 Washington, DC 20006	98,651	1,400
American Expositions, Inc. (212)226–4141	American Expositions, Inc. (212)226–4141	American Expositions, Inc. (212)226–4141	110 Greene Street Suite 703 New York, NY 10012	2,000	63
SALT (703)347–0055	SALT (703)347–0055	Ellen Fox (703)347–0055	50 Culpeper Street Warrenton, VA 22186	400	50
Optical Disk Institute (617)964–3925	Optical Disk Institute (617)964–3925	N/A	567 Walnut Street Newtonville, MA 02160		
National Trade Productions, Inc. (800)638–8510	Linda Carter (800)638–8510	Sam Smith (800)638–8510	313 South Patrick Street Alexandria, VA 22314	7,000+	190

(continued)

CONFERENCES BY DATE *continued*

Conference	Sponsor/Description	Date/Location	Cost to Attend	Cost to Exhibit
Interactive Videodisc Applications and Training Seminar	Sponsored by 3M and IBM. Developing a business case for using IVD as a training vehicle.	10/02/89–10/03/89 Atlanta, GA	$395.00	N/A
ARMA	Sponsored by ARMA International (Association of Records, Managers, and Administrators).	10/02/89–10/05/89 River Gate Convention Center New Orleans, LA	$490.00	$1,400.00
INFO '89—Information Management Exposition and Conference	Sponsored by Cahners Exposition Group.	10/10/89–10/13/89 Javits Convention Center New York, NY	$495.00	$2,500.00
CD-ROM Developers Seminar '89	Sponsored by Meridian Data, Inc. and Philips and DuPont Optical Company. Designed for corporate, institutional, and government CD-ROM developers, the session will outline a step-by-step approach to creating a CD-ROM product. The seminar will address key technical issues such as data conversion, data preparation, retrieval software, delivery systems, mastering, ISO file format, Microsoft CD-ROM Extensions, and multimedia considerations. Business issues such as costs, implementation analysis, and management backing will also be covered.	10/16/89 Chicago Westin Chicago, IL	$150.00	Free
Fourth Annual *Optical Storage for Large Systems*	Sponsored by Rothchild Consultants. End users and vendors will share their experiences of incorporating optical storage into large system architectures, providing conference attendees with a solid background in the integration issues essential for the implementation of optical storage in a large system.	10/17/89–10/19/89 The New York Hilton New York, NY	$995.00	
Supercomputing World Conference	Sponsored by Meeting Brokers International. The first exposition and conference to focus on the practical application of supercomputing power or the broadening spectrum of industrial, scientific, and academic needs.	10/17/89–10/20/89 Civic Auditorium San Francisco, CA		

Registration Contact	Program Contact	Exhibit Contact	Address	1988 Attendees	1988 Exhibitors
Dr. Michael DeBloois (800)533–3907	Dr. Michael DeBloois (800)533–3907	Dr. Michael DeBloois (800)533–3907	MIKEN Communication 1436 East 3400 North Logan, UT 84321		
ARMA (800)422–2762	ARMA (800)422–2762	Alex Metzger (703)683–8500	4200 Somerset Drive Suite 215 Prairie Village, KS 66208	4,000	300
Kathleen Warren (203)964–0000	Kathleen Warren (203)964–0000	Frank Fazio (203)964–0000	999 Summer Street Stamford, CT 06905	45,000	300
Monica Meyer (408)476–5858	Mark Sheldon (408)476–5858	N/A	4450 Capitola Road Suite 101 Capitola, CA 95010	200	9
Gail Rothchild (415)681–3700	Gail Rothchild (415)681–3700	Gail Rothchild (415)681–3700	256 Laguna Honda Boulevard San Francisco, CA 94116-1496	150	
MG Expositions (800)223–7126	Meeting Brokers International (203)786–5132	MG Expositions (800)223–7126	5 Science Park New Haven, CT 06511	N/A	N/A

(continued)

CONFERENCES BY DATE *continued*

Conference	*Sponsor/Description*	*Date/Location*	*Cost to Attend*	*Cost to Exhibit*
Defense and Government Computer Graphics Conference/Fall '89	Sponsored by World Computer Graphics Network.	10/23/89 Convention Center Washington, DC	Free	Free
Federal Computer Conference/Fall '89	Sponsored by National Council for Education on Information Strategies.	10/23/89 Convention Center Washington, DC	Free	Free
ASIS Annual	Sponsored by American Society for Information Science.	10/29/89–11/02/89 Omni Shoreham Hotel Washington, DC	$300.00	Free
The Seventh Annual Seybold Executive Forum	Sponsored by Patricia Seybold's Office Computing Group. Document Architecture.	11/08/89–11/10/89 Westin Hotel Boston, MA	$1,095.00	Free
COMDEX/Fall '89	Sponsored by The Interface Group, Inc.	11/13/89–11/17/89 9 Las Vegas Hotels Las Vegas, NV	Free	Free
CD-ROM Developers Seminar '89	Sponsored by Meridian Data, Inc. and Philips and DuPont Optical Company. Designed for corporate, institutional, and government CD-ROM developers, the session will outline a step-by-step approach to creating a CD-ROM product. The seminar will address key technical issues such as data conversion, data preparation, retrieval software, delivery systems, mastering, ISO file format, Microsoft CD-ROM Extensions, and multimedia considerations. Business issues such as costs, implementation analysis, and management backing will also be covered.	11/16/89 InfoMart Dallas, TX	$150.00	Free
Interactive Videodisc Applications and Training Seminar	Sponsored by 3M and IBM. Developing a business case for using IVD as a training vehicle.	11/20/89–11/21/89 Washington, DC	$395.00	N/A

Registration Contact	Program Contact	Exhibit Contact	Address	1988 Attendees	1988 Exhibitors
National Council for Education on Information Strategies (800)343–6944	DruAnne Miller (301)961–6575	Mary Dickinson (301)961–8990	National Council P.O. Box 41045 7315 Wisconsin Avenue Suite 901-West Bethesda, MD 20814	13,500	400
National Council (800)343–6944	DruAnne Miller (301)961–6575	Mary Dickinson (301)961–8990	National Council P.O. Box 41045 7315 Wisconsin Avenue Suite 901-West Bethesda, MD 20814	13,500	400
ASIS (202)462–1000	Mark Robbins (202)462–1000	Mark Robbins (202)462–1000	1424 16th Street N.W. Suite 404 Washington DC 20036		
Deborah Hay (617)742–5200		N/A	148 State Street Suite 612 Boston, MA 02109	300	N/A
Registration Department (617)449–6600	Jim Collins (617)449–6600	Bill Mahan (617)449–6600	300 1st Avenue Needham, MA 02194	95,000	1,600
Monica Meyer (408)476–5858	Mark Sheldon (408)476–5858	N/A	4450 Capitola Road Suite 101 Capitola, CA 95010	200	9
Dr. Michael DeBloois (800)533–3907	Dr. Michael DeBloois (800)533–3907	Dr. Michael DeBloois (800)533–3907	MIKEN Communication 1436 East 3400 North Logan, UT 84321		

Compiled by Online Press Inc.

SOURCES

Section I: CD-ROM YESTERDAY, TODAY, AND TOMORROW

In the Beginning

And Then There Was Light
By Dan Gutman
Reprinted by permission of *Computer Dealer* Magazine, December 1987. P.O. Box 1952, Dover, NJ 07801.
Computer Dealer Magazine
Gordon Publications
P.O. Box 1952
Dover, NJ 07801

A Laser Primer
By Bill Hanshumaker
Reprinted by permission of The Oregon Museum of Science and Industry from the August 1988 issue of *OMSI Magazine*.
OMSI Magazine
The Oregon Museum of Science and Industry
4015 S.W. Canyon
Portland, OR 97221

The Industry Emerges

Data on a Silver Platter
By David M. Roth and Kevin Strehlo
Reprinted from the August 1987 issue of *VENTURE, For Entrepreneurial Business Owners and Investors* by special permission. Copyright © 1987, Venture Magazine, Inc., 521 Fifth Ave., New York, NY 10175-0028.
Venture Magazine, Inc.
521 Fifth Avenue
New York, NY 10175-0028

Disk Memory Comparison
Reprinted from the November/December 1986 issue of *CIPS Review* (excerpted from "Cheaper by the Gigabyte—an Overview of Optical Storage") by special permission of the Canadian Information Processing Society.
CIPS
243 College Street
Fifth Floor
Toronto, ON M5T 2YI
CANADA

Solutions in Search of Problems
By William Paisley and Matilda Butler
From *Microcomputers for Information Management*.
Reprinted by permission of Ablex Publishing Corporation.
Ablex Publishing Corporation
355 Chestnut Street
Norwood, NJ 07648

Section II: THE OPTICAL MEDIA FAMILY

CD-ROM and CD-ROM XA

MS-DOS CD-ROM Extensions: A Standard PC Access Method
By Tony Rizzo
Reprinted from the *Microsoft Systems Journal* by special permission. Copyright © Microsoft Corporation.
Microsoft Systems Journal
666 Third Avenue
New York, NY 10017

A Paradigm for Standards
By Greg Riker
Reprinted from the Summer 1988 issue of *Hypermedia Guide* (excerpted from "A Paradigm for Standards") by special permission. Copyright © 1988 by Mix Publications, Inc.
Mix Magazine, Inc.
6400 Hollis Street
Suite 12
Emeryville, CA 94608

"XA" Expands CD-ROM Horizons
By Fred Meyer
From *CD Publisher News*. Copyright © 1988, Meridian Data, Inc.
Meridian Data, Inc.
4450 Capitola Road
Suite 101
Capitola, CA 95010

CD-I

High-Definition Television and Interactive Multimedia
By Tom Brown
Reprinted from the September 11, 1988 issue of the *Seattle Times* (excerpted from "High Definition Television: High-Powered Debate Rages," by Tom Brown) by special permission.
Seattle Times
P.O. Box 70
Seattle, WA 98111

Writable Discs

Compact Disc Recording Technologies: The State of the Art
By Ken C. Pohlmann
Reprinted by permission of the *Laserdisk Professional,* 11 Tannery Lane, Weston, CT 06883.
Laserdisk Professional
Pemberton Press, Inc.
11 Tannery Lane
Weston, CT 06883

Tandy Announces Re-writable CD Technology
By Abigail Shaw
Reprinted by permission of Rothchild Consultants.
Rothchild Consultants
256 Laguna Honda Boulevard
San Francisco, CA 94116–1496

Perspective
By Abigail Shaw
Reprinted by permission of the *Laserdisk Professional,* 11 Tannery Lane, Weston, CT 06883.
Laserdisk Professional
Pemberton Press, Inc.
11 Tannery Lane
Weston, CT 06883

Section III: WHO'S DOING WHAT IN CD-ROM?

Library Applications

A Step Ahead: CD-PAC at the Tacoma Public Library
By Tom Watson
Reprinted from the June 1988 issue of *Wilson Library Bulletin* by special permission of the H.W. Wilson Company.
Wilson Library Bulletin
950 University Avenue
The Bronx, NY 10452

Benefits of CD-ROM
By Chung I. Park
Reprinted from Vol. 6, No. 5 of *The COINT Reports* (excerpted from "CD-ROM: Revolution Maker, With an Annotated Current Bibliography," reported by Chung I. Park) by permission of *Info Digest.* Copyright © 1986 by *The COINT Reports.*
Info Digest
P.O. Box 165
Morton Grove, IL 60053

What's New, What's Needed
By Nancy Crane and Tamara Durfee
From *Wilson Library Bulletin.* Reprinted by permission of H.W. Wilson Company.
Wilson Library Bulletin
950 University Avenue
The Bronx, NY 10452

The Library Market
By Ron J. Rietdyk
Reprinted from the January 1988 issue of *Journal of the American Society for Information Science* (excerpted from "Creation and Distribution of CD-ROM Databases" by Ron Rietdyk) by special permission. Copyright © 1988 by *Journal of the American Society for Information Science.* Reprinted by permission of John Wiley and Sons, Inc.
Journal of ASIS
John Wiley and Sons, Inc.
605 3rd Avenue
New York, NY 10158–0012

Education and Training Applications

Finally, the Revolution in Teaching
By Steven Frankel
Reprinted from the November 23, 1986 issue of the *Washington Post.* Reprinted by permission of Steven Frankel.
The Washington Post
1150 15th Street N.W.
Washington, DC 20071

Quote by Russell Lipton
Reprinted from the October 26, 1987 issue of *Computerworld* (excerpted from "CD ROM Search for Tomorrow") by special permission. Copyright © 1987 by CW Publishing Inc., Framingham, MA 01701.
CW Publishing Inc.
375 Cochituate Road
Box 9171
Framingham, MA 01701

Quote by James Burke
Reprinted from the September/October 1987 issue of *CD-ROM Review* (excerpted from "Connecting with Burke") by special permission. Copyright © 1987 by IDG Communications.
IDG Communications
80 Elm Street
Peterborough, NH 03458

Mac Brings Ancient Philosopher Up to Date
By Frank Clancy
Reprinted from *MacWEEK,* August 23, 1988. Copyright © 1988 by Ziff Communications Company.
Ziff-Davis Publishing Company
One Park Avenue
New York, NY 10016

Teaching Languages with CD-ROM
By Verl Woodbury
Reprinted from the September 1988 issue of the *CALICO Journal* (excerpted from "CD-ROM: Potential and Practicalities" by Verl Woodbury) by special permission of Verl Woodbury and the CALICO Journal.
CALICO Journal
Brigham Young University
Provo, UT 84602

Technology Tackles the Training Dilemma
By Randy Ross
Reprinted with permission from *High Technology Business* magazine, September 1988. Copyright © Infotechnology Publishing Corporation.
Infotechnology Publishing Corporation
Suite 704
270 Lafayette Street
New York, NY 10012

Research and Reference Applications

Archiving the Archives
Reprinted from the August 24, 1987 issue of *Computerworld* by special permission. Copyright © 1987 by CW Publishing Inc., Framingham, MA 01701.
CW Publishing Inc.
375 Cochituate Road
Box 9171
Framingham, MA 01701

Quote from *The Wall Street Journal*
Reprinted from the April 27, 1988 issue of *The Wall Street Journal* (excerpted from "U.S. Computer Spending") by special permission of *The Wall Street Journal*. Copyright © 1988 by Dow Jones and Company, Inc. All rights reserved.
Dow Jones and Company Inc.
U.S. Highway No. 1
South Brunswick, NJ 08512

O.E.D., in a Gigabyte Task, to Transfer to Compact Disks
By Francis X. Clines
From *The New York Times,* October 17, 1987. Copyright © 1987 by The New York Times Company. Reprinted by permission.
The New York Times
229 West 43rd Street
New York, NY 10036

Stacking Up Candidates at ABC
By Steven Levy
Reprinted by permission of *Macworld,* from the September 1988 issue, published at 501 Second Street, San Francisco, CA 94107.
Macworld
501 Second Street
San Francisco, CA 94107

CD-ROM: Newspaper Applications
By Chung I. Park
Reprinted from Vol. 6, No. 5 of *The COINT Reports* (excerpted from "CD-ROM: Revolution Maker, With an Annotated Current Bibliography," reported by Chung I. Park) by permission of *Info Digest.* Copyright © 1986 by *The COINT Reports.*
Info Digest
P.O. Box 165
Morton Grove, IL 60053

Medical and Legal Applications

Testing the New Technology: MEDLINE on CD-ROM in an Academic Health Sciences Library
By Beryl Glitz
Reprinted from *Special Libraries,* Vol. 79, No. 1 (Winter 1988) pages 28–33. Copyright © 1988 by Special Libraries Association.
Special Libraries
1700 18th Street N.W.
Washington, DC 20009

A Physician's Perspective
By Nicholas E. Davis
From "The National Library of Medicine and the American Medical Information System: A Physician's Perspective," in the October 1986 issue of the *Bulletin of the Medical Library Association.* Reprinted by permission of the Medical Library Association. Copyright © by the Medical Library Association.
Medical Library Association, Inc.
Suite 3208
919 North Michigan Avenue
Chicago, IL 60611

Impact of Electronic Publishing
By Brian Aveny and Sheila Conneen
From "The Atomization of Information" in the January 1986 issue of the *Bulletin of the Medical Library Association*. Reprinted by permission of the Medical Library Association. Copyright © by the Medical Library Association.
Medical Library Association, Inc.
Suite 3208
919 North Michigan Avenue
Chicago, IL 60611

From Variables to Videodiscs: Interactive Video in the Clinical Setting
By Mary Anne Sweeney and Claire Gulino
Reprinted by permission of J.B. Lippincott Company, publishers of the journal *Computers in Nursing*, No. 6(4).
J.B. Lippincott Company
East Washington Square
Philadelphia, PA 19106

Integrating Computers into Law Firms
By Nora Leven
Reprinted from the January 1988 issue of *Puget Sound Computer User*, pp. 34–35 by special permission of MSP Publications, 12 S Street, Suite 400, Minneapolis, MN 55402. All rights reserved.
Computer User
MSP Publications
12 S Street
Suite 400
Minneapolis, MN 55402

Legal Applications
By Chung I. Park
Reprinted from Vol. 6, No. 5 of *The COINT Reports* (excerpted from "CD-ROM: Revolution Maker, With an Annotated Current Bibliography," reported by Chung I. Park) by permission of *Info Digest*. Copyright © 1986 by *The COINT Reports*.
Info Digest
P.O. Box 165
Morton Grove, IL 60053

In-House Applications

May I Have This Dance?
By Barbara Sehr
Reprinted from the August 24, 1987 issue of *Computerworld* by special permission. Copyright © 1987 by CW Publishing, Inc.
CW Publishing Inc.
375 Cochituate Road
Box 9171
Framingham, MA 01701

Quote by Lou Hoffman
Reprinted from the May 1988 issue of *CD Publisher News* (excerpted from "'Networked' CD-ROM Drives Catapult CD-ROM Industry to Next Plateau") by special permission. Copyright © 1988 Meridian Data, Inc.
Meridian Data, Inc.
4450 Capitola Road
Suite 101
Capitola, CA 95010

CD-ROM Makes It Big in the Automotive Industry Worldwide
Reprinted from the June 1988 issue of *Electronic Library* (excerpted from "CD-ROM Makes It Big in the Automotive Industry Worldwide") by permission of Learned Information, Oxford, England and Medford, New Jersey.
Learned Information Ltd.
Woodside
Hinksey Hill
Oxford OX1 5AU
ENGLAND

CD-ROM as Prodigy
By Roger Hilde
Reprinted from the July/August 1987 issue of *CD-ROM Review* (excerpted from "The Problems and Promise of a Child Prodigy") by special permission. Copyright © 1987 by IDG Communications.
IDG Communications
80 Elm Street
Peterborough, NH 03458

Boeing, Boeing
By Roger Strukhoff
Reprinted from the May 1988 issue of *CD-ROM Review* (excerpted from "Boeing, Boeing") by special permission. Copyright © 1988 by IDG Communications.
IDG Communications
80 Elm Street
Peterborough, NH 03458

Home Education and Entertainment Applications

The Media Lab
by Stewart Brand
Reprinted with permission of Viking Penguin Inc., publishers of *The Media Lab: Inventing the Future at MIT* by Stewart Brand. Introduction reprinted by permission of Mix Publications, Inc.
Viking Penguin Inc.
40 West 23rd Street
New York, NY 10010

Section IV: THE MAKING OF A CD-ROM

Developing a CD-ROM Product

Changing the Publishing Model with Optical Media
By Richard A. Bowers
Reprinted from the March 1987 issue of *Electronic and Optical Publishing Review,* Vol.7, No. 1, by permission of Learned Information, Oxford, England and Medford, New Jersey.
Learned Information Ltd.
Woodside
Hinksey Hill
Oxford 0X1 5AU
ENGLAND

Five Goals for CD-ROM Publishers
By Carl Binder
Reprinted from the Spring 1988 issue of *Optical Insights* (excerpted from "The Emerging Industry") by special permission of Dr. Carl Binder, *Optical Insights,* and the Boston Computer Society.
Optical Insights
The Boston Computer Society
One Center Plaza
Boston, MA 02108

Consultants: How to Find and to Hire
By Peter H. Lewis
Reprinted from the June 17, 1986 issue of *The New York Times* by special permission. Copyright © 1986 The New York Times Company.
The New York Times
229 West 43rd Street
New York, NY 10036

Multimedia Perspectives

Interactive Systems and the Design of Virtuality
By Theodor H. Nelson
Reprinted from *Replacing the Printed Word: A Complete Literacy System* (excerpted from "Interactive Systems and the Design of Virtuality") by special permission. Copyright © by Theodor H. Nelson.
Theodor H. Nelson
Autodesk, Inc.
2320 Marinship Way
Sausalito, CA 94965

Hypertext Perspectives

The Challenge of Hypertext
By Steven Jong
Reprinted by permission of the Society for Technical Communications, *Proceedings: 35th ITCC (1988),* from ATA–30 and ATA–32. Copyright © 1988.
ITCC Proceedings
The Society for Technical Communication
815 15th Street N.W.
Washington, DC 20005

Retrieval-System Perspectives

Design Considerations for CD-ROM Retrieval Software
By Edward M. Cichocki and Susan M. Ziemer
Reprinted from the January 1988 issue of *Journal of the American Society for Information Science.* Copyright © 1988 by John Wiley and Sons, Inc. Reprinted by permission of John Wiley and Sons, Inc.
John Wiley and Sons, Inc.
605 3rd Avenue
New York, NY 10158–0012

Evaluating Text Storage and Retrieval Software
By Paul Nieuwenhuysen
Reprinted from the June 1988 issue of *The Electronic Library* (excerpted from "Criteria for the Evaluation of Text Storage and Retrieval Software") by special permission. Copyright © 1988 by *The Electronic Library.*
Learned Information Ltd.
Woodside
Hinksey Hill
Oxford 0X1 5AU
ENGLAND

Preparing Text

Character Analysis
By Ben Templin
Reprinted from *MacUser,* September 1988. Copyright © 1988 Ziff Communications Company.
Ziff-Davis Publishing Company
1 Park Avenue
New York, NY 10016

OCR History
By Tom Stanton
Reprinted from the July 9, 1985 issue of *PC Magazine* (excerpted from "Peripheral Vision: A Guide to Optical Character Readers") by special permission. Copyright © 1985 Ziff Communications Company.
Ziff-Davis Publishing Company
1 Park Avenue
New York, NY 10016

OCR Future
By Scott Beamer
Reprinted by permission from the *BMUG Newsletter,* Fall 1988.
BMUG, Inc.
1442A Walnut Street #62
Berkeley, CA 94707

Preparing Graphics and Images

Envisioning Information
By Edward Tufte
Adapted by special permission from *The 1988 Personal Computing Forum,* published by EDventure Holdings Inc. Copyright © 1988 by EDventure Holdings Inc. Copyright © 1988 by Edward Tufte.

Photos Go Electronic
By Robert Chapman Wood
Reprinted from the February 1988 issue of *High Technology Business* by special permission. Copyright © Infotechnology Publishing Corporation.
Infotechnology Publishing Corporation
270 Lafayette Street
Suite 704
New York, NY 10012

Image Publishing
Reprinted from *CD-ROM and OROM Products, Applications, and Markets* by special permission. Copyright © by Rothchild Consultants.
Rothchild Consultants
256 Laguna Honda Boulevard
San Francisco, CA 94116-1496

Jazzing It All Up

Technology Ahead of Its Time
By Peter Black
Reprinted from the August 9, 1988 issue of *MacWEEK,* the MAC SOAPBOX column, by special permission. Copyright © 1988 by Ziff Communications Company.
Ziff-Davis Publishing Company
1 Park Avenue
New York, NY 10016

Essays in Animation
Created with VideoWorks II by MacroMind
Reprinted with special permission of MacroMind, Inc.
MacroMind Inc.
1028 West Wolfram
Chicago, IL 60657

An Animated Topic
By Dan Cody
From *SKY* magazine, January 1987. Reprinted by permission of Bernie Ward, Lake Worth, Florida.

Premastering/Mastering Perspectives

Detecting and Correcting Errors on CD-ROM
By Linda Helgerson
Reprinted from the April 1985 issue of *CD Data Report* by special permission of Langley Publications. Copyright © 1985 by *CD Data Report*/Langley Publications.
Langley Publications
1350 Beverley Road
Suite 115–324
McLean, VA 22101

Converting the Data for CD-ROM
By Linda Helgerson
Reprinted from the March 1985 issue of *CD Data Report* by special permission of Langley Publications. Copyright © 1985 by *CD Data Report*/Langley Publications.
Langley Publications
1350 Beverley Road
Suite 115–324
McLean, VA 22101

The PDO Show
By Roger Strukhoff
Reprinted from the September/October 1987 issue of *CD-ROM Review* by special permission. Copyright © 1987 by IDG Communications.
IDG Communications
80 Elm Street
Peterborough, NH 03458

Section V: CD-ROM AND THE LAW

Protecting Intellectual Property Rights

Who Owns Creativity? Property Rights in the Information Age
By Anne W. Branscomb
Reprinted from the May/June 1988 issue of *Technology Review* (excerpted from "Who Owns Creativity? Property Rights in the Information Age" by Anne W. Branscomb) by special permission.
Association of Alumni and Alumnae of M.I.T.
M.I.T. W-59
Cambridge, MA 02139

Let Me Scan Just This One Picture...
By Jim Seymour
Reprinted from the January 12, 1988 issue of *PC Magazine* by special permission. Copyright © 1988 by Ziff Communications Company.
Ziff-Davis Publishing Company
1 Park Avenue
New York, NY 10016

Downloading from CD-ROM
By Brian Kahin
Reprinted from the Spring 1988 issue of *Optical Insights* by special permission. Copyright © 1988 by Brian Kahin.
Optical Insights
The Boston Computer Society
One Center Plaza
Boston, MA 02108

One of CD-ROM's Deadly Sins
Reprinted from the July 1988 issue of *The Laserdisk Professional* (excerpted from "The Seven Deadly Sins of CD-ROM") by special permission.
The Laserdisk Professional
Pemberton Press
11 Tannery Lane
Weston, CT 06883

End User Licenses: Why and What
By Hank Jones
Reprinted by permission of and © 1988, 1989 Henry W. Jones III, Esq., Atlanta, GA, USA. All rights reserved.
Henry W. Jones III, Esq.
Corporate/Technology Group
Morris, Manning and Martin
3333 Peachtree Street
Suite 1600 East
Atlanta, GA 30326

A Look at Two "Creative" Answers to Electro-Copying
By Nicholas A. Veliotes
Reprinted from *Publishers Weekly* by special permission.
Publishers Weekly
P.O. Box 1979
Marion, OH 43302

Lawsuits Over Law Research
By Stephen Labaton
Reprinted from the April 20, 1988 issue of *The New York Times* by special permission. Copyright © 1988 by the New York Times Company.
The New York Times
229 West 43rd Street
New York, NY 10036

Liability Issues

What, Me Warranty?
By Henry W. Jones III
Reprinted by permission of and © 1988, 1989 Henry W. Jones III, Esq., Atlanta, GA, USA. All rights reserved.
Henry W. Jones III, Esq.
Corporate/Technology Group
Morris, Manning and Martin
3333 Peachtree Street
Suite 1600 East
Atlanta, GA 30326

Liability Insurance and Malpractice
By Joseph J. Mika and Bruce A. Shuman
Reprinted from the February 1988 issue of *American Libraries,* "Legal Issues Affecting Libraries and Librarians" by special permission. Copyright © Joseph J. Mika and Bruce A. Shuman.

Section VI: THE CD-ROM BUSINESS

Market Perspectives

The Business of Software
By Doug Houseman and Anna O'Connell
Reprinted from the January 1988 issue of *The APDAlog Newsletter and Catalog of the Apple Programmer's and Developer's Association* by special permission of the authors and the ADPAlog. Copyright © 1988 Doug Houseman, Anna O'Connell, and The ADPAlog Newsletter and Catalog.
APDAlog
290 S.W. 43rd Street
Renton, WA 98055

Buying and Selling Laserbases
Reprinted from the December 1986 issue of *Electronic and Optical Publishing Review* (excerpted from "Buying and Selling Laserbases") by special permission.
Learned Information Ltd.
Woodside
Hinksey Hill
Oxford OX1 5AU
ENGLAND

Market Research: High Tech Looks Back to the Future
By Dan Woog
Reprinted from the October/November 1987 issue of *High-Tech Marketing* by special permission.
Technical Marketing Corporation
1460 Post Road East
Westport, CT 06880

Usage charts
Reprinted by permission of Information Workstation Group.
Information Workstation Group
501 Queen Street
Alexandria, VA 22314

Finding a Shoe That Fits
Reprinted from the July/August 1987 issue of *CD-ROM Review* by special permission. Copyright © 1987 by IDG Communications.
IDG Communications
80 Elm Street
Peterborough, NH 03458

European CD-ROM Market Cautious
Reprinted from *Electronic Library* by special permission.
Learned Information Ltd.
Woodside
Hinksey Hill
Oxford OX1 5AU
ENGLAND

Hiring a Public Relations Agency
By Denise M. Topolnicki
Reprinted from the August 1988 issue of *VENTURE, for Entrepreneurial Business Owners and Investors,* (excerpted from "Putting Your Best Foot Forward") by special permission. Copyright © 1988, Venture Magazine, Inc., 521 Fifth Ave., New York, NY 10175–0028.
Venture Magazine, Inc.
521 Fifth Avenue
New York, NY 10175–0028

Recruiting an Ad Agency
By W. K. Schoonmaker
Reprinted by permission of W.K. Schoonmaker, publisher of *Mainly Marketing,* the monthly newsletter for technical managements. Copyright © 1988 Schoonmaker Assoc., Coram, NY. All rights reserved.
Schoonmaker Associates
Drawer M
Coram, NY 11727

The ABCs of List Sales
By Linda Hanson
Reprinted from the June 1988 issue of *Desktop Publishing Journal* by special permission. Copyright © 1988 Linda Hanson.
Linda Hanson
4029-C Rucker Avenue
#821
Everett, WA 98201

The Downside of Direct Mail
Reprinted from the December 1987 issue of *Computer Dealer* Magazine by special permission.
Computer Dealer Magazine
Gordon Publications
P.O. Box 1952
Dover, NJ 07801

Please Take My Card
By Echo M. Garrett and Webster E. Williams
Reprinted from the September 1988 issue of *VENTURE, For Entrepreneurial Business Owners and Investors* by special permission. Copyright © 1988, Venture Magazine, Inc., 521 Fifth Ave., New York, NY 10175–0028.
Venture Magazine, Inc.
521 Fifth Avenue
New York, NY 10175–0028

Publishing Perspectives

Gambling on CD-ROM
By John B. Lowe
Reprinted from the July 1988 issue of the *Library Journal* by special permission. Copyright © 1988 by Reed Publishing, USA, a division of Reed Holdings Inc.
Library Journal
249 West 17th Street
New York, NY 10011

CD-ROM Economics
By Peter B. Schipma
From the January 1988 issue of the *Journal of American Society for Information Sciences.* Copyright © John Wiley and Sons. Reprinted by permission of John Wiley and Sons, Inc.
John Wiley and Sons, Inc.
605 Third Avenue
New York, NY 10158

Licensing to a Marketing Organization
Reprinted from *The Brady Guide to CD-ROM* (excerpted from "Licensing to a Marketing Organization") by Laura Buddine and Elizabeth Young. Used by permission of the publisher, Brady, New York. Copyright © 1987.

Pricing a CD-ROM

CD-ROM Title Prices Dropping
Reprinted from the October 6, 1988 issue of Digital Information Group's *Information Industry Bulletin* (excerpted from "CD ROM Title Prices Dropping") by special permission.

Optical disc drive sales charts
Reprinted by permission of Datapro.
Future Computing/Datapro
8111 LBJ Freeway
Dallas, TX 75251

Financing Your CD-ROM Endeavors

Debt Versus Equity Financing
By Daniel Remer, Paul Remer, and Robert Dunaway
Reprinted from *The Silicon Valley Guide to Financial Success in Software.* Copyright © 1984 by Microsoft Press.
Microsoft Press
16011 N.E. 36th Way
Box 97017
Redmond, WA 98073–9717

Where Venture Capital Is Investing Now
By Frederic Paul
Reprinted from the March 1988 issue of *High Technology Business* (excerpted from "Where Venture Capital Is Investing Now") by special permission of Infotechnology Publishing Corporation.
Infotechnology Publishing Corporation
270 Lafayette Street
Suite 704
New York, NY 10012

Evaluating a Venture Capital Firm to Meet Your Company's Needs
By Accel Partners
Reprinted from *Advice to First Time Entrepreneurs: Evaluating a Venture Capital Firm to Meet Your Company's Needs* by special permission. Copyright © Accel Partners.
Accel Partners
One Palmer Square
Princeton, NJ 08543

Writing Your Business Plan
By Warren Strugatch
Reprinted from the June 1988 issue of *VENTURE, For Entrepreneurial Business Owners and Investors* by special permission. From "Business Plan II The Sequel: Writing It." Copyright © 1987 Venture Magazine, Inc., 521 Fifth Ave., New York, NY 10175-0028
Venture Magazine, Inc.
521 Fifth Avenue
New York, NY 10175-0028

125 More Chances
By Frances C. Marshman
Reprinted from the June 1988 issue of *VENTURE, For Entrepreneurial Business Owners and Investors* by special permission. Copyright © 1988, Venture Magazine, Inc., 521 Fifth Ave., New York, NY 10175-0028
Venture Magazine, Inc.
521 Fifth Avenue
New York, NY 10175-0028

Creative Collaboration

Beyond Vertical Integration: The Rise of the Value-Adding Parnership
By Russell Johnston and Paul R. Lawrence
Reprinted by permission of *Harvard Business Review*. "Beyond Vertical Integration: The Rise of the Value-Adding Partnership" by Russell Johnston and Paul R. Lawrence (July/August 1988). Copyright © 1988 by the President and Fellows of Harvard College; all rights reserved.

The Future

CD-ROM: Nickelodeon for Modern Times
By Peter Black
Reprinted from *MacWEEK,* August 23, 1988 issue. Copyright © 1988 Ziff Communications Company.
Ziff-Davis Publishing Company
1 Park Avenue
New York, NY 10016

Section VII: DIRECTORY LISTINGS

The listings of CD-ROM titles, disc drives, retrieval systems, data preparation houses, mastering/replication facilities, CD-ROM resources, and CD-ROM-related conferences were compiled by Online Press Inc. from brochures and advertisements in the industry literature. All information was verified through telephone interviews and follow-up letters and was current when the manuscript for this book was submitted.

Many of the product names in this book, especially those derived from private sources of information, are protected by trademarks or service marks that cover names, contents, search procedures, or other aspects of the product, or such trademarks or service marks have been applied for. We acknowledge these protections whenever they may apply to the material listed in this book. We advise readers of the book to check with the supplier before using the material or names of any product we may have listed.

TRADEMARKS

Many of the product names in this book, especially those derived from private sources of information, are protected by trademarks or service marks that cover their names, contents, search procedures, or other aspects of the product, or such trademarks or service marks have been applied for. We acknowledge these protections whenever they may apply to the material listed in this book. We advise readers of the book to check with the supplier before using the material or names of any product we may have listed.

ABI/Inform® is a registered trademark of University Microfilms, Inc.
AGRIBUSINESS U.S.A.℠ is a service mark of Pioneer Hi-Bred.
AIS® is a registered trademark of Acctex Information Systems.
Amdek® and LASERDRIVE-1® are registered trademarks of Amdek Corporation.
Apple®, LaserWriter®, Mac®, Macintosh II®, Macintosh Plus®, and Macintosh SE® are registered trademarks, Apple Programmer's and Developer's Association (APDA)™, AppleCD SC™, Apple IIGS™, HyperCard®, HyperTalk™, and QuickDraw™ are trademarks, and Scribe™ is a licensed trademark of Apple Computer, Inc.
ArtRoom™ and DarkRoom™ are trademarks of Image Club Graphics Inc.
The Bible Library™, The Nurse Library™, and The Physician Library™ are trademarks of Ellis Enterprises Inc.
BMUG PD ROM™ is a trademark of BMUG (Berkeley Mac User's Group).
Books In Print Plus™, Books In Print with Book Reviews Plus™, Books Out Of Print Plus™, Ulrich's Plus™, and The Complete Home Video Directory Plus™ are trademarks of Bowker Electronic Publishing.
CD Publisher™ is a trademark of Meridian Data.
CD-FICHE™ is a trademark of USA Information Systems, Inc.
CDR-3500™ is a trademark of Hitachi.
CDU 510™ is a trademark of Sony.
CIS Congressional Masterfile™ is a trademark of Congressional Information Service, Inc.
CM201™ is a trademark of LMSI.
Commodore™ and Commodore Amiga™ are trademarks of Commodore Electronics Limited.
Compact Disclosure® and Disclosure® are registered trademarks of Disclosure Incorporated.
COMPAQ® is a registered trademark of COMPAQ Computer Corporation.
CompuServe® is a registered trademark of CompuServe Information Service.
Compustat® is a registered trademark of Standard and Poor's.
Computer Database™ and Magazine Index™ are trademarks of Information Access Company.
Dayflo™ is a trademark of Dayflo.
dBase® is a registered trademark and FullPaint™ is a trademark of Ashton-Tate.
DEC® and VAX® are registered trademarks and VMS™ is a trademark of Digital Equipment Corporation.
DIALOG® is a registered trademark and DIALOG OnDisc™ is a trademark of Dialog Information Services.
Docufind® is a registered trademark of Emanuel Data Systems.
Donkey Kong®, The Legend of Zelda®, and Mike Tyson's Punch Out!!® are registered trademarks and Anticipation™, Dance Aerobic™, Power Pad™, and Super Mario Brothers™ are trademarks of Nintendo.

DRUGDEX®, EMERGINDEX®, and POISINDEX® are registered trademarks and IDENTIDEX™ and TOMES™ are trademarks of Micromedex, Inc.
EBSCO CD-ROM® is a trademark of EBSCO.
Facts On File® is a registered trademark and MEDIA-MIXER™ and Public Domain Software on File™ are trademarks of Facts On File, Inc.
GEOdisc™ is a trademark of Geovision, Inc.
GRID™ is a trademark of Digital Image Systems.
Guide I™ and Guide II™ are trademarks of OWL International.
Houdini™ is a trademark of MaxThink.
HP® is a registered trademark and HP LaserRETRIEVE™ is a trademark of Hewlett-Packard, Inc.
HyperDoc™ is a trademark of GECI.
IBM®, IBM PC®, IBM PC/AT®, and PS/2® are registered trademarks and Coursewriter™, IBM PC/XT™, InfoWindow™, Netview™ and Selectric™ are trademarks of International Business Machines Corporation.
Info-XL™ is a trademark of Valor.
Intel® is a registered trademark of Intel Corporation.
Ise™ is a trademark of Persoft.
Jeopardy™ is a trademark of Jeopardy Products Inc.
KAware™ and KAware2™ are trademarks of Knowledge Access International.
Knowledge Finder™ and Knowledge Server™ are trademarks of Aries Systems Corporation.
Knowledge Retrieval System®, KnowledgeSet®, and KRS® are registered trademarks of KnowledgeSet Corporation.
Kwikee® is a registered trademark of Multi-Ad Services, Inc.
Le Pac® is a registered trademark of Brodart Automation.
LEXIS® and NEXIS® are registered trademarks of Mead Data Central, Inc.
Lotus®, 1-2-3®, and One Source® are registered trademarks and CD/Banking™, CD/Corp Tech™, CD/Corporate™, CD/International™, CD/Investment™, CD/Newsline™, CD/Private+™, and Symphony™ are trademarks of Lotus Development Corporation.
MacroMind® is a registered trademark and VideoWorks II™ is a trademark of MacroMind Inc.
Master Search™ is a trademark of Tri Star Publishing.
MediaBase™ is a trademark of Crowninshield Software, Inc.
Medline® is a registered trademark of U.S. National Library of Medicine.
Memory-Mate™ is a trademark of Broderbund.
Microanalytics™ is a trademark of Gofer.
Microsoft®, the Microsoft logo, Microsoft Press®, MS®, and MS-DOS® are registered trademarks of Microsoft Corporation.
Motorola® is a registered trademark of Motorola, Inc.
Netware™ is a trademark of Novell.
NewsBank® is a registered trademark of Newsbank, Inc.
NeXT™ is a trademark of NeXT, Inc.
PacMan™ is a trademark of Namco Ltd.
PageMaker® is a registered trademark of Aldus Corporation.
Personal Librarian™ is a trademark of Personal Library Software, Inc.
Physicians' Desk Reference® is a registered trademark of Medical Economics Company.
Post-It™ is a trademark of 3M.
PostScript® is a registered trademark of Adobe Systems Inc.

Q-bert™ is a trademark of Mylstar Electronics Inc.
RESEARCH™ is a trademark of TMS, Inc.
Sargon III™ is a trademark of Spinnaker.
Science Citation Index® is a registered trademark of the Institute for Scientific Information.
Seaside™ is a trademark of Askam.
SilverPlatter® is a registered trademark and MathSci™, MultiPlatter™, and OSH-ROM™ are trademarks of SilverPlatter Information, Inc.
THE SOURCE℠ is a service mark of Source Telecomputing Corporation.
Sun™ is a trademark of Sun Microsystems, Inc.
Supermap™ is a trademark of Space-Time Research Pty Ltd.

Tandy® is a registered trademark of Radio Shack, a division of Tandy Corporation.
Text-Scan™ is a trademark of Symphony Systems, Inc.
UNIX™ is a trademark of AT&T Bell Laboratories.
VisiCalc® is a registered trademark of Software Arts, Inc.
The Wheel of Fortune™ is a trademark of Califon Products Inc.
WordPerfect® is a registered trademark of WordPerfect Corporation.
WordStar® is a registered trademark of MicroPro International Corporation.
Xanadu™ is a trademark of AutoDesc.
XM 3100-B™ is a trademark of Toshiba.
YMC Your Marketing Consultant™ is a trademark of Market Statistics.

INDEX

Numbers
3M Corporation 190, 413
68000 family 63

A
AAP markup 339, 340
ABC News 171–72
Abt, Clark 23
ACTV 144
Adaptive Delta Pulse Code Modulation
 (ADPCM) 53, 54, 60, 392–401
ADONIS 443
ADPCM (Adaptive Delta Pulse Code
 Modulation) 53, 54, 60, 392–401
advanced television research project 227
advertising 467
 agencies 484–86
 direct-mail 487–93
AHUG 255
Aiken, Calvin 367
Allen Communications Inc. 190
American Bar Association (ABA) 197, 198
American Interactive Media (AIM) 11, 63
American Library Directory 108
America's Best-Read City 103
AMI (Association for Multi-Image) 377
analog/digital hybrid delivery 617
analog optical delivery 616
animation 378–81, 382–85, 386–90
 regenerative 382–85
Apple 575
 Macintosh 383
Apple Programmer's and Developer's
 Association (APDA) 255
application
 design 246
 development process 242, 243, 246
applications
 education 119–46
 in-house 203–18
 legal 175–201
 library 95–117
 medical 175–215
 reference 147–73
 research 147–73
 training 119–46

Applied Learning Inc. 143
Arakawa, Minoru 625
Arps, Mark 641
Arthur Anderson and Company 205, 209
artificial intelligence (AI) 127, 215
ASCII
 character set 315
 codes 323
 files 217, 292
 form 338
 labels 362
 text 208, 251, 329
Association for Multi-Image (AMI) 377
audio
 Level A 60
 Level B 53, 60, 395
 Level C 54, 60, 395
audio discs 630
audiovisual content 268
A-V (audio-visual) 376
authoring 292
authoring systems 22, 275
 menu-driven 190
Automotive Parts Retrieval System 214
automotive titles 143

B
bandwidth 392–97
Bangasser, Thomas F. 7
banks 541
Bastiaens, Gaston 60
B. Dalton 18
Befeler, Michael 18, 201
Benge, Bruce 366
Berkeley Macintosh User's Group (BMUG) 255
betamax 433, 436
Bible 161–62
BiblioFile Catalog Production System 98
Bierman, Jim 134–39
bit
 dropping 367
 duplicating 367
black boxes 636
Boeing 218, 478
Boolean 130
 combinations 314

Boolean *(continued)*
   logic 300
   search techniques 130
Borland International 125
Boston Computer Society 255
Bowers, Richard A. 236
Bowman, Chris 261
Brewer, Bryan 400
Brinkley, David 171
British Air 757, 218
Brooks, Martin 642
Brown, Dr. Peter 291
browsing 283
B-tree indexes 309, 310
Buddine, Laura 267
buffering 383
bump forming media 91
Burke, Dennis 526
Bush, George 23
Bush, Vannevar 284
Bushnell, Noland 575
business
   future 611–46
   plans 551–52
   titles 166
Butler, Matilda 518

C

Calera 335
CALICO (Computer Assisted Language Learning and Instruction Consortium) 136–37
CALL (Computer Assisted Language Learning) 137
CALS (Computer Aided Logistics System) 339
Cantor, Marc 642
CAPS (Computer Animation Production System) 388
Casabianca, Lou 632
CAV (Constant Angular Velocity) 10, 11, 92, 303
CBT (Computer-Based Training) 140
CD Association 631
CD-Audio (Compact Disc-Audio) 7, 11, 15, 51, 59, 62, 83, 85, 304, 391–401, 631
CD-G (Compact Disc-Graphic) 83
CD-I (Compact Disc-Interactive) 10, 11, 16, 21, 24, 51, 52, 54, 59–61, 62–65, 83, 125–27, 140, 265, 268, 269, 275, 615
   display resolution 354
   interactivity 51, 59–61, 62–65, 125–27, 140

CD-ROM (Compact Disc-Read Only Memory) 1
   bestsellers 507
   computer products based on 21
   conferences 496–98, 887–911
   digital audio on 51, 59, 362
   disc development 243
   discs 527–29
   drives 527–29
      directory 843–45
   economics 504
   extensions 6, 35, 43–50, 52
   marketplace 509
   players 634
   pricing 515–33
   proposal guidelines 511–14
   publications 21
   publishers 507
   publishing 511
   resources 869–86
   sales 520
   shakeout 627–30
   titles 524
      alphabetical directory 649–745
      subject directory 746–841
CD-ROM Developer's Seminar 217
CD-ROM Industry Profile 579–609
CD-ROM XA (CD-ROM eXtended Architecture) 10, 21, 24, 51, 53–55, 60, 61, 265, 275, 391–401, 615
CD-RTOS (Compact Disc-Real Time Operating System) 61
CD-THOR (Compact Disc-Tandy High-intensity Optical Recording) 88, 89, 90
CD-3 83
CD-V (Compact Disc-Video) 83, 615
CD-WO (Compact Disc-Write Once) 84, 85
Census Bureau test disc 115
channels 393–97
character analysis 329–36
Chrysler 214
Cinnamon, Barry 528
Clark, Ruth 142
CLV (Constant Linear Velocity) 10, 84, 92, 303
Commodore Amiga 269
compression 10, 247, 249, 366–70, 375
   ratios 366
computer adaptive tests 123
Computer Aided Logistics System (CALS) 339
computer-based training (CBT) 140
conferences 467, 494–98, 509, 887–911

constant angular velocity (CAV) 10, 303
constant linear velocity (CLV) 10, 303
consultants 248, 249
copyright 426–34
    Act 435
    laws 64
    notices 439
    protection 439
Corporation for Public Broadcasting (CPB) 222
cost-based pricing strategies 522
costs
    production 520
    product support 521
Cox, Joyce K. 324
creative collaboration 557
cross interleaving 408–9
cross referencing 248, 249, 261, 285, 326
Culbertson, Jim 290
Cummins Engine Company 217

D

data
    access
        full-text retrieval 305, 312
        multiple-key 305, 308
        single-key 305, 306
    capture 246
    compression 312
    content 29
    conversion 247
    encryption 248
    enhancements 247
    format 261
    indexing 248
    integrity 249
    integrity loop 407
    objects 362
    preparation 243
    preparation houses 325–28
        alphabetical directory 851–53
        state directory 854–55
    storage formats 393
databases 245, 261, 262, 512, 518, 524
    design 245
    online 464
    protection 530
    relational 305
    security 531
databased authoring system 638
Dataquest 475

DataTimes 173
Datext 23
David Sarnoff Research Center 70
Daynes, Rod 222
dealers, third-party 527
debit cards 443
decompression 366–70
decryption methods 531
Del Mar Group, The 17, 18
delivery-system definition 244
design 238, 239
    considerations for retrieval software 303–12
    issues 239
    optical product 238
    teams 269
desktop optical 632, 638
development process 537
device drivers 43–50
    character 44, 45
digital 7
    audio tape 89
    image storage 356–63
    optical delivery 616, 617
Digital Research Corporation 19
digitization 615
Dillon, Mark 276
direct mail
    advertising 487–93
    downside of 491
    marketing 488
    mistakes 490
    response 490
directories 647–911
disctronics 413
disk memory comparison 16
Disney 386–90
distribution costs 469, 503
Diversified Data Resources 17
document type definition (DTD) 339, 340
documentation 64, 105, 180
Dreiss, Jack 210
drive manufacturers 630, 632, 638
drives, directory 843–45
DTD (Document Type Definition) 339, 340
DVI (Digital Video Interactive) 10, 21, 24, 69–71, 72–79, 91, 140–46, 265, 268, 269, 375
    beta sites 75–77
    pilot applications 74–75
dye-polymer 88

E

Eaker, Dean Ross 390
ECC (Error Correction Code) 406–12
EDC (Error Detection Code) 406–12
education 121, 289
   in 1992 633
   technology 123
   titles 130–31
Education Systems Corporation (ESC) 32
Einberger, John 246
electrocopying 442, 443
electroforming 414, 415
electromagnetic spectrum 6
electronic publishing 182
encryption methods 531
end user
   agreements 429
   licenses 438
energy 6
Engine Control Module 32
Englebart, Douglas 224
entrepreneurs 537, 543, 553
erasable CD technologies 83
error 405
   and ommissions insurance 453
   burst 407
   correction 405–9
   detection 405–9
   random bit 406–7
   rate 406
error correction code (ECC) 406–12
error detection code (EDC) 406–12
Europe
   Eastern 474–79
   Western 474–79

F

Faraday effect 86
FAT (File Allocation Table) 44
FAX 336
federal government, records of 149
Fenton, Jay 383
file allocation table (FAT) 44
FileMaker 278
film
   editors 277
   script 276
financing 535–56
Fisher, Robert B. 210
fonts, proportional 334

Forbes 500, 567
Ford Motor Company 16, 18, 214
Ford, William H., Jr. 643
Fortune 500 companies 211
frame-buffer display systems 382–83
frames 391
framing 286
frequency 6
front-end systems 167, 325, 327
Frost and Sullivan 79
Fuller, Buckminster 274
FullPaint 137
full-text retrieval systems 305, 312

G

Gaffner, Haines B. 24
Gagnon, Diana 643
Gale, John C. 643
General Electric 69, 142
General Motors 31, 214, 225
global markets 620
Gotti, John 343
government 153
   Defense Department 153
   Energy Department 153
   Health and Human Services Department 153
   National Aeronautics and Space
      Administration 153
   titles 152, 153
   Treasury Department 153
Groliers Encyclopedia 19, 26
graphics 261
   bit-mapped 283
Great Oxford Dictionary (GOD) 155
Green Book 53, 62, 391
Guide 291
Gutenberg 5

H

Hagedorn, Nancy 108
Hall, Bob 162
halogen light system 389
Hambourger, David 197
Hamlet 537
Hanna Barbera 388–90
Harrison, Harvey E. 574
Harvard Square 23
HDTV (High Definition Television) 61
health titles 192
Hegarty, Kevin 98

Helgerson, Linda 17, 35
Hewitt, Steve 161
Hewlett-Packard 16, 18
High Sierra Group 216, 474
High Sierra Proposal 627
High Sierra Standard 6
histograms 359, 360
Hitachi 214
Hollywood 573–77
Holmes, Lyndon 301
holograms 225, 228
Home Entertainment System 626
hot links 32
HP Tag 339
hyperactivities 287
HyperCard 134–39, 171, 172, 252, 254, 262, 270–74, 278, 287, 374
hyperediting 287
hyperillustrating 286
hypermedia 613–23, 635, 636
    computers 614
    five faces of 614–17
    mythology 637, 638
    stand-alone 616, 617
    systems 32, 33, 299
    workstations 618
hyperspace 286
HyperTalk 271
hypertext 281–95, 614
    access 299
    perspectives 281–95
    problems 293–95
hypervision 635
hyperwriting 285

I

IBM 142, 143, 227, 374
    personal computer image display program (IBMDISP) 363
IDTV/EDTV 61
Iles, Douglas 213
images 377
    archives of 22
    compressed 75, 248
    compression of 359, 366
    decompression of 366, 367
    intelligent 186
    management of 365–69
        application-size requirements 368
    processing 356–69

images *(continued)*
    resolution of 365
    still 73
    storage of 356–63
Impannatore 563–69
Independent Computer Consultant Association 248
index 313
    displaying the 313
    files 249
indexing
    full-text 245
    image/sound 249
    key-field 248
    methods 248
    preparing text for 323
    search and retrieval packages 524
information
    consumers 502
    envisioning 343
    delivery 236
    density 345
    design 345
    managers 616
    micro-macro structure of 349
    nature of 5
    providers 502
    quick reference 284
    resolution 345
    the utility value of 5
Infoware 373
initialization events 48
institutions
    educational 502
    public 503
integrated systems 29
integration 30
Intel 69, 70, 71
intellectual property rights 423–47
intelligent images 186
intelligent scaling 367
interactive 140, 275–79
    computer systems 278
    delivery 614
    grammar 621
    instructions 190
    mechanisms 267
    technologies 573–77
    video 185, 191

interfaces 253, 254, 255, 267, 289, 290, 399, 430
   designing for CD-ROM 252
interleaved
   audio 53, 54, 60, 391–401
   graphics 54, 60, 391–401
   text 60, 391–401
   tools for 396–97
Internal Revenue Service (IRS) 149, 152
International Online Meeting 479
International Standards Organization (ISO) 7, 216
investments 539
investors 542
ISO 8879 339
ISO 9960 7, 35, 43, 52, 216, 474

J

Japanese
   auto companies 565
   trading companies 564
Jennings, Peter 171
Jet Propulsion Laboratory 356–63
Jones, Henry W., III 439
jukeboxes 107

K

Kauffman, Draper 17
Kay, Alan 228
Kelly, Ed 512
Kenobi, Obi-wan 57–75
kernals 415
Kernan, John 129
Kerr effect 86
Kester, Harold 18, 30
Kildall, Gary 19
Knowledge Research 478
KnowledgeSet Corporation 19, 218
Konvalinka, John 210
Krasny, Stuart 141
Kuhn, Carolyn 644

L

Laertes 537
Lammers, Susan 644
LAN (Local Area Network) 32, 33
Langschied, Linda 106
language titles 138–39
laser
   beam 86
   technology 6

laserbase 465
Leese, Ken 645
legal titles 175
LEGO blocks 228
Levitt, Theodore 519
LEXIS 164
liabilities 440, 449–57
   insurance 455
librarians' attitudes 109
libraries
   outside of U.S. 108
   titles 100–1
   types of 108
Library Corporation 23, 98
licensing 513
Lightbown, Parke 645
limit cycling 362
limited partnerships 541–42
LINK Resources Corporation 21, 36, 165 629, 630
linkages 301
linking 286
links 283, 295
Lippman, Andy 228
list sales 487–93
literature titles 138, 139
loans
   bank 538
   personal 538
local area networks (LANs) 32, 33
Loecus Informatics Inc. 16
logical formatting 243, 250
Lotus Development Corporation 17, 451
Luskin, Bernard 63

M

MacinTEXT 332–36
Macintosh operating system 374, 383
Magna 173, 174
magneto-optical
   erasable discs 10
   recording 85
   systems 87
mail order 469
mailing
   labels 517
   lists 517
malpractice 455, 456
management information services (MIS) 532
manuals 105, 180

market
  development 519, 571
  research 471
marketing
  CD-ROM databases 533
  markup 337–40
  organizations 513
Mars 358
Martin, Mike 357
Massey, Jack 645
mastering 22, 243, 250, 261, 403–19, 630
  facilities 417–19
  and replication facilities 857–67
    alphabetical directory 858–62
    directory by country 863–67
Mathur, Ashok 628
McClare, Robert 92
McKesson Corporation 560
McLuhan, Marshall 227
McManus, Timothy J. 258
medical titles 193–95
Mead Data Central Inc. 444–47
Media Lab 224–29
Memex 284
Menichetti, Massimo 562–65
menu-driven authoring systems 190
Meridian Data Inc. 15
Merrill Lynch 145
Meyer, Fred 15, 18, 216
Meyer, Rick 164
Michaels, Richard 143
microfiche 114, 117, 164
microfilm 260
microform 114
Microsoft Corporation 6, 17, 38, 51, 126
  First International CD-ROM Conference 9, 62
  Second International CD-ROM Conference 69, 72
  Third International CD-ROM Conference 571, 579
MIDI interface 275
MIDAS (Multimedia Integrated Databased Authoring System) 634
Miller, Rockley 144
Minitel 476
Minsky, Marvin 228
Miranda 361, 363
MIS (Management Information Services) 153, 206, 207, 208, 532
  managers 205

Mischo, Lane 98
MIT 225, 226, 229
MIT Press 227
mixed media 615
modes 393–97
  inverted file 309
  multiple-key 308
  single-key 306
Morris, Sandra K. 73
MS-DOS CD-ROM Extensions 6, 35, 43–50, 52
multi-image 375–77
multimedia 7, 132, 376, 399, 636
  CD-ROMs 184, 265–69, 270–74, 275–79
  methodologies 631
  perspectives 263–79
  producers 375
  tools for presentations 271
Multimedia Integrated Databased Authoring System (MIDAS) 634
Multimedia Interactive Design 638
Murray, John III 145

N

NAS 20
NASA (National Aeronautic and Space Administration) 356
National Archives Optical Digital Image Project 149
National Computer Graphics Association 390
National Decision Systems (NDS) 30
National Space Science Data Center 357
natural-language-style expression 301
Negroponte, Nicholas 224, 225, 226, 227
Nelson, Theodor Holm 284, 645
Neptune 359
network
  access 129
  environments 107
  servers 22
networked delivery 617
New Media 266, 269
Newsreel Access Systems Inc. 17
NEXIS 164
Nintendo 624–26
node map 277
notting 286

O

OCR (Optical Character Recognition) 323, 329–36

OCR *(continued)*
  history 330, 331
  packages for the Macintosh 332–34
OED (Oxford English Dictionary) 154–56
OEMs (Original Equipment Manufacturers) 539
Ogden, Bob 646
Ogilvy, David 491
omni-font approach 333
OPA (Optical Publishing Association) 570–72
OpticaInfo 479
optical character recognition (OCR) 323, 329–36
Optical Data Inc. (ODI) 91
optical disk drive sales 529
Optical Publishing Association (OPA) 570–72
original equipment manufacturers (OEMs) 539
OS Corporation 17
OWL International Inc. 16, 18, 214
Oxford English Dictionary (OED) 154–56
Oxford University Press 154–56, 478

P

Paisley, William 519
Palentir 335
Palmer, David 99
Papert, Seymour 228
parameters
  camera-state 361
  image-format 361
PARC-based interfaces 276
parsers 340
  SGML 340
partnerships
  equity 542
  limited 541–42
  R & D 542
Perseus Project 137
Petrone, Emiel 11
Philips 11, 21, 35, 51, 59, 84, 126, 627
photo-polymerization 414
PICS 362
piracy of data 112
Playground 384–85
Pollard, Jonathan 17
Polonius 537
polymer/dye 91
Pong 575
postproduction phase 188
PPA (Pulling the Price out of the Air) 524–26
Pre-Industrial Age 632
premastering 250, 261, 403–19

preproduction phase 187
pricing decisions 515–33
private sector 502
production phase 188
program
  design 247
  development 247
program segment prefixes 45
projects
  budgets 260
  management issues 250
proximal storage 305
PTTs 475
public
  relations 480–83
  sector 502
  television 221, 222
Public Access Catalogue 319
publication prices 527
Public Broadcasting Service (PBS) 221
Public Relations Society of America 481
publishers 236, 237, 539
  CD-ROM 238
  print 526
Publishers Data Services Corporation 19
publishing
  electronic 22
  microcomputer-based 22
Publish Pac 332–36

Q

quality assurance (QA) 257–59
quality control (QC) 257–59
quanta 7
Quantum 20
QuickDraw 384

R

radiation 6
Raskin, Jef 294
raster
  drawings 261
  images 349
RCA Laboratories 72
Read It! 331–36
ReadStar II Plus 334–36
real-time animation 356
recorders 92
Red Book 391
Reed-Solomon Code 408, 409

Reeves, Thomas 142
reference titles 157–60
rendering 383
replication 22, 261, 407–16, 630
    facilities 417–19, 857–67
research and development (R & D) 518
resources
    CD-ROM, directory 869–86
retrieval
    packages 240
    performance 249
    probabilistic 301
    software 239, 245, 248, 303–12, 313–19
    system design 303–12
    system perspectives 297–319
    systems 306–11
        directory 847–49
    technologies 299–302
        navigational 299–302
        targeted 299–302
Rietdyk, Ron 508
risk reduction 553
Ritchie, Ian 646
Robbins, Richard 198
Rochester, Nat 226
ROI (Return On Investment) 530
Ropiequet, Suzanne 394
Roux, David 523
Rutherford, Rachel 255

S

safety titles 192
Saturn 358
scaling, intelligent 367
scanners 323, 330
Schwerin, Julie 475
science titles 124–25
scripting 253, 275–79
SCSI interfaces 35
search
    profiles 318
    terms 314
    wildcards 314
search and retrieval
    methods 29
    software packages 524
searching 300
    key-word 300
    navigational 301
    target 300

security 318
Selby, Binx 18
Service Bay Diagnostic System (SBDS) 214
SGML 337–40
shareware 470
Shear, Victor 531
Sickert, Julie 286
Sieck, Steven Kurt 22
SIGCAT 38
Simpson, John A. 155
SK & A Research 141
software, retrieval 239, 248
Sony 11, 19, 21, 35, 51, 59, 84, 126, 142, 348, 627
sprites, animation 383
Stackmaster 255
stacks, HyperCard 254, 262, 284
standardization 106
standards 52, 265
Star Wars 575
Stauffer, Richard A. 70
Steffan, Martha 646
stimulated emission 6
stock 540
    preferred 543
    selling 540
Stone, Linda 253
storyboard 273
Strukhoff, Roger 10
Sugiyama, Takashi 53
Sunstrand 218

T

Tacoma Public Library 97
tags 248, 325, 327, 339
talking books 11
Tandy Electronics Manufacturing 83, 92
targeted retrieval 302
technology titles 124, 125
Ten Minute Rule 312
testing 178–83
    alpha 259
    beta 259, 467
    procedures 257
    product 257–59
    rules 334
text
    data preparation 323–28
    inversion 248
TextScan 332–36
The New Papyrus 163

thermo-optical techniques 91
titles 649–841
    automotive 143
    business 166
    census 168, 169
    education 130, 131
    entertainment 219–29
    financial 206–8
    government 152, 153
    health 192
    home education 219–29
    language and literature 138, 139
    legal 200
    library 100, 101
    maps 168, 169
    medical 193–95
    reference 157–60
    safety 192
    science and technology 124–25
    tax 209
tools
    drafting 271
    new 568
    prototyping 273
    revision 273
    sketching 271
trade secrets 440
trade shows 468, 494–95
trademarks 426–34
training 140–46, 289
trans-format content migration 618, 619
Traub, David C. 620
trends 509
truncation 314
Tufte, Edward 343
Tullach, Sara 156
typesetting
    codes 261
    commands 326
    Magna 327

U

UCLA Biomedical Library 177
UMI Experiment 443
universal time corrected (UTC) 361
Uranus 358
usage-billing 532, 533
US Copyright Office 430
US Department of Defense 153, 339
US Department of Energy 153
US Department of Health and Human Services 153
US Geological Survey 357, 362
US Geological Survey National Earthquake Information Center 115, 217
US Department of Health and Human Services 153
user interface 132, 238, 430
user-requirements definition 244
UTC (Universal Time Corrected) 361

V

value
    added 237
    added chain 561, 565
    adding partnerships (VAPs) 559–69
    of information 517
    pricing strategy based on 522
VAPs (Value-Adding Partnerships) 559–69
vector CRTs 382
venture
    arrangements 525
    capital 544–56
    capitalists 541–56
    firms 544–49, 551
    investments 544–48, 554
Venus 359
vertical integration 559–69
VICAR 362
video 10
    game experts 624
    game history 624, 625
    interactive 140, 191
    motion 73
videodiscs 185, 186, 189
Vonderhaar, Mark 116

W

War of 1812 345
warranties 440
Washington Post 173
wavelength 6, 86
West Publishing Company 444–47, 478
WGBH 221, 222
"wholistic" approach 639
Williams, Joe 271
windowing environment 290
Woodsmall, William 99
WORM (Write Once Read Many) 84, 358
write-once technology 83

X
Xanadu 284
Xerox 335

Y
Yellow Book 216

Z
Zemke, Ron 146
Zimmerman, Paula S. 74

The manuscript for this book was prepared and submitted to Microsoft Press in electronic form. Text files were processed and formatted using Microsoft Word.

Cover design by Tim Girvin Design
Interior text design by Darcie S. Furlan
Production art by Becky Geisler-Johnson
Principal typography by Jean Trenary

Text composition by Microsoft Press in Garamond Light with display in Helvetica Black, using the Magna composition system and the Linotronic 300 laser imagesetter.

THE MICROSOFT PRESS
CD ROM LIBRARY

INTERACTIVE MULTIMEDIA

Visions of Multimedia for Developers, Educators, & Information Providers
Edited by Sueann Ambron and Kristina Hooper; Foreword by John Sculley

Apple® Computer Corporation brought together researchers and developers to produce this informative collection of 21 articles as a source of ideas and inspiration for software and hardware developers, educators, publishers, and information providers. INTERACTIVE MULTIMEDIA is filled with examples and pilot projects that define the new meaning of multimedia and provide imaginative ways of teaching, thinking, and solving problems with multimedia technology.

352 pages   ISBN 1-55615-124-1 $24.95

CD ROM:
The New Papyrus

The Current and Future State of the Art
Edited by Steve Lambert and Suzanne Ropiequet

"This 619-page compendium, with contributions from more than 30 optical-memory specialists, promises to become the bible of CD ROM."

Macworld

This is an excellent resource for anyone desiring in-depth information on CD ROM. The 44 articles by leading CD ROM authorities range from the technical aspects of how data is stored and retrieved to the commercial aspects of CD ROM technology. Introductory information for those new to CD ROM technology, technical information for specialists, and several resource appendixes provide a comprehensive, essential guide to this information technology.

640 pages   ISBN 0-914845-74-8 $21.95

CD ROM 2:
Optical Publishing

Edited by Suzanne Ropiequet, with John Einberger and Bill Zoellick

"Recommended reading for any information professional." *Online*

The second volume in the CD ROM series focuses on optical publishing with CD ROM. Topics include licensing and copyrighting; organizing and indexing data; collecting and preparing text, images, and sound; and designing software and integrating systems. Case studies track the evolution of two products from initial idea to final product. A glossary and resource section provide additional information.

368 pages   ISBN 1-55615-000-8 $22.95

ORDERING INFORMATION

Microsoft Press books are available wherever fine books are sold, or credit card orders can be placed by calling 1-800-638-3030 (in Maryland call collect 824-7300).

Call the number above to place an order for more copies of
THE CD ROM YEARBOOK 1989–1990.
ISBN 1-55615-179-9 $79.95

DATE DUE